A HISTORY OF
RUSSIAN WOMEN'S WRITING
1820–1992

For Ian
and for Barbara

A History of
Russian Women's Writing
1820–1992

CATRIONA KELLY

CLARENDON PRESS · OXFORD
1994

Oxford University Press, Walton Street, Oxford OX2 6DP
Oxford New York Toronto
Delhi Bombay Calcutta Madras Karachi
Kuala Lumpur Singapore Hong Kong Tokyo
Nairobi Dar es Salaam Cape Town
Melbourne Auckland Madrid
and associated companies in
Berlin Ibadan

Oxford is a trade mark of Oxford University Press

Published in the United States
by Oxford University Press Inc., New York

British Library Cataloguing in Publication Data
Data available

Library of Congress Cataloging in Publication Data
Kelly, Catriona.
A history of Russian women's writing, 1820–1992 / Catriona Kelly.
Includes bibliographical references and index.
1. Russian literature—Women authors—History and criticism.
I. Title.
PG2997.K45 1994
891.709'9287—dc20 93-26238
ISBN 0-19-815872-6

Typeset by Latimer Trend and Company Ltd., Plymouth
Printed in Great Britain
on acid-free paper by
Biddles Ltd.,
Guildford and King's Lynn

Acknowledgements

WHILST writing this book, I have benefited enormously from the generosity both of institutions, and of individuals. The British Academy funded the later parts of the project through a Post-Doctoral Fellowship and through grants for travel to Russia and Finland; my College, Christ Church, Oxford, provided a room and research facilities, and also financial support for preliminary work on the book. The University of Oxford's Inter-Faculty Committee for Slavonic and East European Studies organized exchange visits on my behalf to Moscow and to Lithuania; amongst those involved in the organization, I should particularly like to thank Judy Pallot. Help with bibliography and other research materials was given by the staff of the Taylor Institution Slavonic Annexe and of the Bodleian Library, Oxford, amongst whom I would especially mention David Howells, Richard Ramage, David Thomas, and Carole Menzies; and also by the staffs of the British Library and the Library of the School of Slavonic and East European Studies, University of London. Like many other researchers, I was able to profit by the extraordinary efficiency and helpfulness of the librarians at the Slavonic Library at the University of Helsinki; I should also like to thank the Slavonic Librarian, Jarmo Syonsyrjä, who kindly gave me permission to quote materials from the Vera Bulich archive that is held there. Despite economic and political crisis, the staffs of the Tartu University Library, the Saltykov-Shchedrin State Public Library, Leningrad/St Petersburg, and the Lenin Library, Moscow, gave me invaluable aid on my various visits; during the first stages of my research, much bibliographical help was generously given by the late Anatoly Alekseev, of Pushkin House, Leningrad/St Petersburg. The many individuals who helped me by sending offprints of their work, or information about work in progress, or by offering bibliographical guidance and intellectual support of diverse kinds, included Joe Andrew, Peter Barta, Birgit Beumers, Eva Buchwald, Philippa Bunting, Pamela Davidson, Martin Dewhirst, Maura Dooley, Peter Doyle, Barbara Engel, Beate Fieseler, Mikhail Leonovich Gasparov, Sheelagh Graham, Hannes Heino, Katherine Hodgson, Marina Liborakina, Zara Grigorievna Mints, Dimitri Obolensky, Larisa Petina, Riitta Pittman, Boris Vladimirovich Plyukhanov, Terence Ranger, Arja Rosenholm, Charlotte Rosenthal, Stephanie Sandler, Biljana Scott, David Shepherd, Irina Shevelenko, Steve Smith, Bill Swainson, Roman Davydovich Timenchik, Neill Walker, and Mary Zirin. I am also grateful to Richard Rutherford for information about Ovid; to Martin Conway for suggestions as to reading on Fascist Germany and Italy; and to Christopher Robinson for guidance on material relating to French women's writing and to the study of homosexuality in France. A considerable contribution to my work was also made by the many audiences who attended the talks at which I presented various passages of this book in preliminary form, including the Neo-Formalist Circle, the BASEES Twentieth-Century Group, the Modern Languages Seminars at the Universities of Keele and Strathclyde, the Russian Seminar at SSEES, the *Popular Culture in Question* conference at the University of Essex, the *Gender Restructuring* conference in Helsinki, and the 'Revolution of the Word' series at the South Bank Centre, London. The Seminar on Women in Eastern Europe and the Soviet Union at Birmingham has been a constant source of intellectual stimulus and companionship. Michael Nicholson, of University College, Oxford, was kind enough to relieve me of a term's teaching at a stage when I needed some months clear to finish the manuscript. I owe a debt of gratitude for their hospitality and friendship, as well as help with professional matters, to Marina Boroditskaya and Grigory Kruzhkov, Sergei Kaledin and Olga Lauer, Veronika and Svetlana Pankratova, Nataliya Lebedeva, Nataliya Pushkareva, Boris and Tatyana Uspensky in Moscow; to Lyubov Kiseleva and Mariya Plyukhanova in Tartu; and to Kseniya Kumpan, Albin Konechny, Ekaterina Golynkina and Aleksandr Zhuravlev in Leningrad/St Petersburg, as well as to my family and friends in Oxford and London. Janet Garton's editorial guidance was of great benefit in the early stages of writing; in the later stages, my editor at Oxford University Press, Andrew Lockett, has given much advice and encouragement; the technical aspects of the book have been ably dealt with by Mary Worthington. I am more grateful than I can say to Joe Andrew, Linda Edmondson, Wendy Rosslyn, Stephanie Sandler, Gerry Smith, and Nigel Thompson, who read the book manuscript in whole or in part, and made most valuable comments and suggestions.

My largest debts are to those named in the dedication of this book, both of whom not only read the manuscript in its entirety, but helped bring it into existence in the first place. Barbara Heldt did more than anyone else to inspire the writing of this history in the first place, and her advice and friendship have been indispensable to its completion. I will not say that Ian Thompson has been 'supportive', since the word to me suggests the action of an elastic stocking, not of a human being; but, though his own intellectual interests are remote from Russian culture, he has contributed immeasurably to this book, and it could not have been written without him.

Contents

PART IV

Abbreviations

Anthology	Catriona Kelly (ed.), *An Anthology of Russian Women's Writing, 1777–1992* (Oxford, 1994)
Dacha	V. V. Uchenova (ed.), *Dacha na Petergofskoi doroge: proza russkikh pisatel'nits pervoi poloviny XIX veka* (Moscow, 1986)
ECWR	Katharina M. Wilson (ed.), *Encyclopedia of Continental Women's Writing* (2 vols.; New York, 1990)
EP	*Essays in Poetics*
ES	*Entsiklopedicheskii slovar' izdaniya Brokgauza i Efrona*, ed. I. Andreevsky (80 vols. and 4 supp. vols.; St Petersburg, 1890–1907)
ISS	*Irish Slavonic Studies*
IV	*Istoricheskii vestnik*
KN	*Krasnaya nov'*
LG	*Literaturnaya gazeta*
MB	*Mir bozhii*
MERSL	*The Modern Encyclopedia of Russian and Soviet Literature*, ed. Harry B. Weber (Gulf Breeze, Florida, 1977–)
NM	*Novyi mir*
NS	*Novyi entsiklopedicheskii slovar' izdaniya Brokgauza i Efrona*, ed. K. K. Arsen'ev (29 vols.; St Petersburg, 1911–16) (edn. never completed)
OSP	*Oxford Slavonic Papers*
OZ	*Otechestvennye zapiski*
PN	*Poslednie novosti*
RB	*Russkoe bogatstvo*
RM	*Russkaya mysl'*
RV	*Russkii vestnik*
S	*Sovremennik*
SEEJ	*Slavic and East European Journal*
SEER	*Slavonic and East European Review*
SM	*Sovremennyi mir* (the continuation of *Mir bozhii*)
SOZ	*Sovremennye zapiski*
SP	*Stikhotvoreniya i poemy*
SR	*Slavic Review*
SV	*Severnyi vestnik*

Svidanie	V. V. Uchenova (ed.), *Svidanie: proza russkikh pisatel'nits 1860–1880-kh godov 19-go veka* (Moscow, 1987)
SZ	*Severnye zapiski*
Tol'ko chas	V. V. Uchenova (ed.), *Tol'ko chas: proza russkikh pisatel'nits kontsa XIX–nachala XX veka* (Moscow, 1988)
VE	*Vestnik Evropy*
ZR	*Zolotoe runo*

Note: Polnoe sobranie sochinenii and *Sobranie sochinenii* are regularly abbreviated on second and subsequent citations to *PSS* and *SS*.

Note on Transliteration and Conventions

THE transliteration of Cyrillic follows the British Standard system as adapted for *Oxford Slavonic Papers*; however, the soft sign -ь is omitted in the transcription of proper names throughout the main text, though rendered as ' in the Notes and Bibliography; the vowel modifier -й is transcribed as i in the case of proper names ending in -ei or -ai (Nikolai, Andrei; contrast Dmitry, Dostoevsky). All Cyrillic quotations are given in the new (post-1917) orthography.

All dates before October 1917 are given according to the Julian Calendar; thereafter, the Gregorian is used. The dates of works by women authors are given either according to the date of composition, where evidence is available, or according to the first publication of the work in question. In cases where no direct evidence of the date of a text's composition is available, and where it would be misleading to refer to the date of first publication (as in the case of posthumous publications of material suppressed during the Stalin years), a conjectural date of composition has been given, in the form '(*c.*1934)'.

All citations are keyed to the notes, except in cases of second and subsequent citations to a work already cited, which are then made in-text.

Unless otherwise stated in the Notes, all translations are my own.

INTRODUCTION:
'Not Written by a Lady'

UNLIKE women's writing in Japan, France, the British Isles, or Germany, Russian women's writing is a phenomenon of relatively recent origin. Women writers only began to appear just over two hundred years ago, well into the post-Petrine period; the hagiographers and chroniclers of medieval Russia had no female counterparts. In her book *Women in Old Russia* the medieval historian Nataliya Pushkareva attempted to find traces of women's writing in the medieval era, but was able to establish only one certain case (a Russian princess, married to an Italian, who produced a medical treatise in Greek), although she also argued that the *Rostov Chronicle* might have been partly authored by a woman belonging to the royal house of the city, and cited a reference in the *Trinity Chronicle* to moral tracts written by a third lady.[1] There is, equally, little evidence that a specifically female readership was recognized, let alone accommodated, by pre-Petrine written culture (*pis'mennost'*), whose emphasis on writing as an ecclesiastical and political instrument was inhibiting to women both as writers and as readers.

Even the incursion into Russian culture, from the mid-seventeenth century, of the concept 'literature' (*literatura*), a Western word acknowledging that writing might accord pleasure as well as enlightenment to its readers, did not immediately foster women's involvement in literature. As late as the mid-eighteenth century, the Russian redactions of French, Provençal and Italian romances adjusted their models so as to decrease the importance of female characters, which probably signifies that there was still only an insignificant proportion of woman readers.[2] But the reign of Catherine II (who was, famously, herself an author) marked a

---

[1] N. L. Pushkareva, *Zhenshchiny drevnei Rusi* (Moscow, 1989), 34, 39–41.
[2] An excellent close reading of one such redaction is available in D. L. L. Howells, 'The Origins of *Frantsel' Ventsian* and *Parizh i Vena*', OSP 19 (1986), 35.

turning-point, as broadening educational opportunity for girls, increasing emphasis on reading as an acceptable, indeed requisite, private pursuit, and growing acquaintance with Western literature, including books written by women, fostered an atmosphere congenial to women who wished to take up the pen. By the late 1770s, a number of women writers had made their mark; towards the end of the century, the efforts of such women were paid an indirect compliment, as Russians began to invent ancestresses for them, one notorious instance being the attribution (on entirely apocryphal grounds) of fictional works to Peter the Great's half-sister the Regent Sophia, Russia's first woman ruler.[3] The number of Russian woman writers grew steadily in the early nineteenth century. By 1820, the starting-point of this book's main narrative, women's writing was already a force to be reckoned with. The rise of Romanticism during the next decade at first had slightly dampening effects, at any rate on the poetry of women, but these were to prove of brief duration; and over the next 170 years Russian women's writing, though always, of course, profoundly affected by the larger processes of Russian literary history, continued developing its own strong and diverse traditions.

However recent its origins, Russian women's writing is now firmly established, and its individual character widely recognized. In fact, that is part of the problem. Or to rephrase: the problem is the peculiar nature of the establishment and recognition of women's writing. Everyone knows exactly what is signified by 'women's creativity' (*zhenskoe tvorchestvo*), or 'women's prose and poetry' (*zhenskaya proza/poeziya*), and few think that there is anything to admire in it. All the terms that I have just mentioned have, to a Russian ear, a belittling if not derogatory flavour; 'women's prose and poetry', for which the alternative and still more openly contemptuous expression is 'lady's [*damskaya*] prose and poetry', are assumed to show the positive merits of observation and decoration, but to have the more than compensatory demerits of sentimentality, banality, and lack of intellectual power. By implication, if not by direct statement, 'women's creativity' is the counter-image of 'masculine' and 'manly' (*muzhskoe*) writing: the huge, passionate, sprawling 'baggy monsters' of prose on the one hand, the intellectual depths of the 'philosophical lyric' on the other. (That the 'philosophical lyric' is in fact a tradition which is remarkably ill-developed in Russian poetry, seldom, if ever, reaching the heights of intellectual complexity found in, say, Hölderlin, is a factor left out of the equation.) And the most important Russian received idea of all is that women's writing is

---

[3] On the myth of Sophia as author see Lindsey Hughes, *Sophia, Regent of Russia* (London, 1990), 175.

simply not very interesting. Indeed, how could it be, when it deals with women's limited experience, rather than with men's enormous experience of the social and political issues which have been central to the dominant discourse of Russian literature, critical realism, and reflects women's small woes, rather than the tragically coloured priestly mysticism which has shaped so much Russian poetry?

Such dismissive views of women's writing recur again and again in Russian history, their recurrence being partly explained by the extreme reverence with which educated Russians regard the philosophical and aesthetic views of the past. In order for the Anglo-American outsider to grasp the Russian situation, she or he has to imagine a situation where, say, Wordsworth, Byron, or Leigh Hunt's opinions on women might be perceived, not as perspectives constructed in a well-defined political and historical context, but as the expression of indisputable revealed truths; where the views of the 1820s might in all seriousness be cited in order to justify the aesthetic theories and critical judgements of the 1990s. Yet the conservatism of Russian culture at this level should not blind us to the ways in which understanding of 'women's writing' has wavered. If assumptions of women's inferiority have been persistent, they have not by any means been ubiquitous; if the presumption that women are different from men has been universal, that difference has been understood in very various ways. The last two centuries have seen some startling reversals and upheavals in thinking about women, to which the following list can do only partial justice. Women are different from men, we learn, because they feel, rather than think; because they describe, rather than imagine; because they imagine, rather than analyse; because they have an innate comprehension of the metaphysical; because they have no comprehension of the metaphysical; because they are deficient in intellectual, political, and social education; because they are better educated than men; because nature has intended them for reproductive, rather than productive, capacities; because society expects them to do nothing but produce babies.

My narrative will trace such waverings and reversals in the understanding of 'women's writing' as well as underlining instances of persistence and homogeneity; I shall place emphasis on the contradictions and shifts within patriarchal ideology, both at a synchronic and at a diachronic level. A great deal of recent work on national identity has stressed the importance of the 'invention' or 'imagination' of tradition. Such terminology, with its underlying models of constant renewal by means of appropriation of the past, can with value be borrowed by chroniclers of the history of women's writing too. They allow us to understand how the fortunes of women's writing ebb and flow according to nationalist expediency, and to comprehend the dynamism of gender ideologies in their own right.[4] One striking example can be mentioned here. Much recent Russian women's writing is based on a mystique of motherhood as an essentially 'feminine' activity. So far from being an age-old part of literary culture, this perception is, as we shall see, a recent arrival: it can be traced back to the formation of Socialist Realist ideology during the mid-1930s.

This emphasis on changes and contradictions in gender ideologies and structures leads me to argue that Russian women's writing has been at its liveliest and most diverse during periods of political debate and social upheaval; so far as Russian women's writing goes, consensus has generally, I feel, been anything other than benign. My assertion that historical development is necessarily unpredictable also leads me to argue that the history of women's writing should not be interpreted as a steady and inevitable progress towards greater and greater achievement. Unlike some recent feminist writers, I do not think that literary history can avoid the evaluative process altogether, but an evaluative process that sees the lives of all past generations as no more than dress rehearsals for the present would be intolerably crude. Is Tatyana Tolstaya a 'better writer' than Mariya Zhukova because she was born a century and a half later? I don't think so. I have also set my face against evaluation at the level of women's individual biographies. Women's cultural history, indeed women's history in any sense, is ill served by attempts to give women from earlier generations marks out of ten for 'conformity' or 'non-conformity', or by celebration of the achievements of 'exceptional women' without any consideration of how such women managed to construct their stirring opposition to patriarchal attitudes from within the intolerance of the society in which they lived. Historical narrative cannot concern itself with the provision of role-models for the present; studies of women writers should not make themselves the equivalent of the many nineteenth- and early twentieth-century books on *Famous Women of the Past*, volumes whose intellectual content is approximately that of the

---

[4] 'The imagination of tradition' is a phrase coined by Terence Ranger (see 'The Invention of Tradition Revisited: The African Case', in T. O. Ranger and O. Vaughan (eds.), *Legimation and the State in Twentieth-Century Africa* (London, 1993)), in preference to the earlier coinage 'invention of tradition' made famous by Ranger and Eric Hobsbawm (eds.), *The Invention of Tradition* (Cambridge, 1986). A study which I found very helpful in suggesting an application of such material to the dynamics of literary history is Elaine Showalter's history of American women's writing, *Sister's Choice* (Oxford, 1991). A recent, and notorious, example of how the formation of a 'national literature' affects the representation of women's writing is Seamus Deane's *The Field Day Anthology of Irish Writing* (3 vols.; Derry, 1991), in which women are not only proportionally under-represented, most particularly in the recent selections, but are in many cases also damned with patronizing praise in the introductions.

albums containing hand-tinted photographs of Edwardian beauties that were popular at the same time.

Emphasis on the slippery nature of Russian cultural history does not of course mean that one should overstate the permissiveness of its traditions. Like other European literary cultures, Russian culture has worked to efface and suppress the work of women writers.[5] When all is said and done, only two writers, the poets Akhmatova and Tsvetaeva, at the moment enjoy an assured reputation in their own country and outside it. That is not to say that every forgotten woman writer is 'as good' as Akhmatova or Tsvetaeva, but it is to argue for the importance—aesthetic as well as historical—of recovering the past. Russian literary scholarship of the past decades, whether Western or Soviet, has combined total amnesia with regard to the actual historical processes of women's writing with a breathtaking readiness to generalize about these processes. References to women writers in the nineteenth century, whether made by Soviet or Western scholars, have frequently been misleading or frankly erroneous. The substantial achievements of pre-Revolutionary woman writers have, for example, either been erased—in such statements as 'not a single [pre-Revolutionary] authoress attained prominence'—or travestied by undue emphasis on such supposedly 'representative' works as *The Keys of Happiness*, a lurid best-selling novel written by Anastasiya Verbitskaya, which is in fact approximately as 'typical' of women's writing before 1917 as the novels of Judith Krantz are 'typical' of American women's writing today.[6] The circulation of such misinformation is to the benefit neither of scholarship, nor of literary culture in general.

Because of such forgetfulness and reduction, a certain inclusiveness is requisite in any history of Russian women's writing. But on the other hand, no one-volume history can fill the role of an encyclopedia, and it would be fatal were pluralism to descend to the level of annotated bibliography. And whilst it might, arguably, be profitable to produce a studiedly 'neutral', wide-ranging selection of women authors according to movements and affiliations, a sort of women's equivalent to D. S. Mirsky's famous *History of Russian Literature*, this book does not aim

[5] In her introduction to *Jane Austen and the War of Ideas* (2nd edn.; Oxford, 1987), Marilyn Butler has recently taken issue with feminist representations of English literary culture as hostile to women's writing, suggesting that women writers do not in practice feel constrained by the strictures of critics. However, in the Russian context, evidence from such sources as women's private diaries, memoirs, and letters suggests that, on the contrary, the notion of literary reputation has played a major part in women writers' anxieties about the act of authorship.

[6] The first view comes from Ronald Hingley, *Russian Writers and Soviet Society* (London, 1979), 171—and this in a generally excellent short overview of Soviet women's writing; the second is discussed in Adele Barker, 'Are Women Writing "Women's Writing" in the Soviet Union Today? Tolstaya and Grekova', *Studies in Comparative Communism*, 21/3–4 (1988), 357–64.

at 'breadth' in that traditional humanist sense either.[7] A process of selection has been inevitable here: it is essential that the rationale behind this process should be declared at once, and its aesthetic and ideological constraints laid bare immediately.

The use of 'experience' as a criterion to denigrate women's writing in Russia makes me suspicious, in turn, of those Anglo-American critical writings which also place 'experience' at the centre of their critical practice. In the introduction to a recent volume of essays, Janet Wolff has argued that 'the point is that *what* women write is closely related to their experience'.[8] Later in the volume, in an essay dealing with the modernist era in France and England, Wolff puts this *sententia* into practice: she links women's exclusion from the public sphere of daily life in cities with their marginalization in literature. There was no female equivalent of the *flâneur* in life, she writes, so women were excluded from the tradition of modernist urban writing which takes the *flâneur* as centre.[9]

There is a degree of over-simplification here, as a concrete example from the Russian tradition will illustrate. Turn-of-the-century women writers in Russia worked within an urban tradition of literary expression similar to that in Western Europe. But their writing was by no means always constrained by real-life factors. Imaginative escape was possible. A woman writer might imagine herself a *flâneur*, and invade his accustomed location, producing poetry identical to that of men; or else she might cast herself in the role of *demi-mondaine*, the *flâneur*'s female equivalent. A specific instance of a Russian woman writer who adopted the latter strategy was Akhmatova. The readers of her early poetry imagined that the poet was herself having an affair with Blok. In terms of the facts of Akhmatova's biography, this assumption was absurd, but in *literary* terms, it was perfectly understandable. If one reads of Blok's most famous poems, such as 'The Strange Woman' or 'In the Restaurant', and then, following that, reads the best-known poems in Akhmatova's *Evening* collection, such as 'The music in the [pleasure] garden rang out', the effect is striking. The silent, mysterious *demi-mondaine* heroines of Blok have found a voice.[10]

The facile equation between writing and experience which one finds

---

[7] D. S. Mirsky's posthumous *History of Russian Literature* (London, 1949), is actually a compilation of his *Contemporary Russian Literature 1881–1925* (London, 1926), and his *History of Russian Literature from its Earliest Times to the Death of Dostoevsky* (London, 1927). The importance of the history is made clear, and its character incisively discussed, in G. S. Smith's introduction to Mirsky, *Uncollected Writings on Russian Literature* (Berkeley, Calif., 1989), 35–6.

[8] Janet Wolff, *Feminine Sentences* (Oxford, 1991), 3.

[9] Ibid. 38–40.

[10] On Blok and Akhmatova, see also Ch. 8 on Akhmatova below.

in some Anglo-American feminist criticism has already been very adequately critiqued by Toril Moi.[11] But a simple-minded adoption of the physically defined categories associated with 'French feminism' (i.e. the theorists Luce Irigaray and Hélène Cixous) would be equally problematic. It would replicate the essentialism inherent in much current Russian thinking on gender, with its conceptualization of the male/female, masculine/feminine as an immutable binary opposition, given, not made. (The Russian preference for Jungian psychoanalytic theory over Freudian analysis can be, at least in part, traced to the fact that the Jungian polarization of masculine and feminine as static—albeit infinitely combinable—categories is conceptually more congenial than the Freudian view that such categories are constructed by experience.)[12]

So what of Moi's own response: to 'float the signifier', to argue for complete fluidity in thinking about gender? Whatever its attractiveness in utopian terms, which is considerable, it is unclear how Moi's resolutely anti-positivist aesthetic could be harnessed to the project of writing a history. As Roger Chartier recently put it, 'historians are happier with constraints than freedoms'.[13] When one is writing a piece of history, rather than utopian theory, there are dangers in placing too great an emphasis on the separateness of literature, its infinite multivalency. There would be little use to be got from a historical narrative of women's writing in Russia which took no account of constraints, of the hegemony of literary institutions and discourses, the parameters of variability as well as of variability itself. However fluid we may wish the boundaries of gender to be, philosophically speaking, we must recognize how rigid, historically speaking, they have often *seemed* to those defining them and defined by them.

As a generalization, we can state that, rather than reflecting experience, literature (itself, of course, a historically determined category) *refracts* experience: a formulation which allows us to give due attention

---

[11] Toril Moi, *Sexual/Textual Politics* (London, 1985).

[12] Freud's writings were better known during the 1920s than at any other period of Russian history—enjoying a considerable vogue amongst such left Bolsheviks as Trotsky. Even at this stage his ideas on psychological development as a dynamic process were not always properly understood, however. Voloshinov/Bakhtin's *Freidizm* (Moscow, 1928) is a reasoned, but slightly simplistic, critique which concentrates on the inadequate consideration given by Freud to a broader social context; a generally balanced short assessment by V. Gilyarovsky in the 13th edn. of the Granat Encyclopaedia (published *c.*1925) mentions the existence of theories on 'various complexes' in a single sentence. A famous representative of Russian hostility to Freud, based on the belief that he reduced the human personality to sexual feelings, was Anna Akhmatova, as repeatedly recorded in Chukovskaya's memoirs. Freud has been one of the various authors unbanned since *glasnost*, but recent issues of *Voprosy filosofii* would suggest that his popularity continues to be inferior to that of Jung.

[13] Chartier came out with this aphorism in a presentation at a conference entitled *Popular Culture in Question* held at the University of Essex, 6 Apr. 1991.

to the textual fabric, and to the specific context which has constructed it, externally and internally. Russian women's writing is the product of a society where literary, political, economic, and cultural institutions have been dominated by men, albeit to varying degrees and with varying effects at different stages. Russian society, like other European societies, is stratified according to class as well as gender; and women writers have overwhelmingly been drawn from the social élite: that is, they have belonged to a small social group whose socio-economic privileges ensure the leisure and material support without which writing would not be possible. But this does not mean that Russian women's writing has invariably conformed to a set pattern of 'élite women's literature' in ways which would be easily catalogued by the cruder kind of 'vulgar sociologist' Stalinist critic. Various complex and contradictory processes have been at work. First, it is arguable, as we shall see, that the emergence of women's writing in Russia was linked with a *decline* in women's real political and economic powers. There is a familiar paradox here between social marginalization and symbolic centrality.[14] Secondly, Russian literature has often shaped itself in despite of history: poetry in particular has been the vehicle of a powerful counter-realist tradition, inclined to deny the importance of historical and social factors. Thirdly, the boundaries of textual fictionality and non-fictionality depend as much on relations between texts as on relations with the outside world. Types of narrative patterning, such as the text-within-a-text, have, certainly, often been used by anti-realist texts as markers of contingency. But conversely, critical realism, for all its emphasis on 'facts' and 'experience', is also text-dependent. The 'truth' to which it pretends must also be achieved through textual strategies of various kinds: by exclusion of certain types of narrative marker, such as the closed ending, say, or by citation of certain formulae (such as those used to represent the human psychology) which are generally accepted as valid. And both 'realism' and 'counter-realism', different strands of the post-Romantic tradition, have legitimated themselves by reference to non-literary discourses, both positively, by conformity with aesthetic and ethical principles of the day, and negatively, since the notion of 'literature' depends on constructs of what is *not* literature, and most especially, on

---

[14] One important recent treatment of the social marginalization/symbolic centrality paradox is Peter Stallybrass and Allon White's *The Politics and Poetics of Transgression* (London, 1987). A concrete historical instance is examined by Caroline Walker Bynum in *Jesus as Mother: Studies in the Spirituality of the High Middle Ages* (Berkeley, Calif., 1982), which links women's loss of actual power in the medieval church with a rise in their spiritual authority. The conjunction between loss of political power for women and the rise of a writing tradition in Russia is further discussed in Part I of the present book.

constructs of the oral tradition, or the 'popular'—to use a not quite identical, but overlapping term.[15]

I use the term 'discourse' here to suggest the socially engaged nature of literary language. If we understand Russian literary activity during the nineteenth and twentieth centuries as a 'quarrel of discourses', then we can discuss all sorts of narrative modes—parody, irony, metafiction, as well as straight realism—inclusively, whilst recognizing the hierarchies in which these modes will be arranged at any given historical moment. The idea of a 'quarrel of discourses' facilitates observation of how assumptions about women's behaviour or experience are transmitted from text to text, where they often play a greater role than the facts of such behaviour, experienced from day to day. To take one example: an important and persistent idea, that of women's intellectual passivity, has been far more dominant in Russian written culture than has the *actuality* of men's contact with women's intellectual control (say, in schoolboy–schoolteacher relations).[16] The transmission by diverse Russian texts (philosophical, literary, discursive) of this idea has in turn made it very difficult for women authors to represent the figure of a self-conscious or a controlling woman author.

The central interest in this history is to identify texts which do execute the task of representing female creativity, and other such difficult tasks. Although this critical preference is very obviously a modernist one, and my emphasis on the text as representation of varying forms of literary identity, of a fictional self, gives my work obvious affinities with that of such Formalist critics as Yury Tynyanov, I differ from these predecessors in placing less emphasis on 'evolution', in the sense of historical development through competition.[17] A recurrent pattern in Russian culture (as in American and European culture generally) has been to welcome each new woman writer avidly. She becomes the standard against which all previous writers are measured and found wanting, until—on the discovery of another new writer—she is herself added to the pile of those found wanting. This pattern of forgetfulness means that the Formalist theory that writers consciously work to 'surpass' their predecessors is scarcely applicable to the relations between Russian women writers. If the theory has validity at all, it is only to the lives of a small number of women poets working between 1905 and 1935, who

---

[15] A discussion of Russian literature's relation to the popular tradition will be found in my *Petrushka: The Russian Carnival Puppet Theatre* (Cambridge, 1990), esp. ch. 4.

[16] This example is given because the teaching profession, like the medical profession, has during the years of Soviet rule become almost completely feminized at its lower levels.

[17] Yury Tynyanov's theories of literary evolution are extensively developed in *Arkhaisty i novatory* (Leningrad, 1929).

lived at a period when interest in women's writing reached exceptional levels.[18]

My interest in texts by women writers as representations of feminine identity has led me to emphasize women's representations of women, since this is where the most significant problems and conflicts of Russian women's writing have made themselves felt. (This is not to say that I take no interest in women writers' representation of men, but I am primarily interested in these where they differ from men's representations of themselves.) I also place an emphasis on women writers who, unconsciously as well as self-consciously, write *as women* and *as writers*: that is to say, who use a feminine authorial persona to explore the problems of representation. (The gender of first-person authorial discourse in Russian is evident through the gender marking, not only of adjectives, but also of certain verbal forms; unless an author is to speak of herself as 'we', or select impersonal forms, both of which strategies are more characteristic of academic language than of imaginative writing, she has, therefore, either to speak as a woman or a man.)

Some of the writers whom I analyse were certainly 'feminists' in the sense that they were actively involved in the Russian movement for women's liberation, but by no means all of them were. I am less concerned here with 'radical writing' in the traditional sense of work associated with the socialist or proto-socialist movement, than I am with writing that is radical in the context of Russian culture's traditional association of women with passivity. To give this radicalism its proper due does not, however, mean denying the importance of other literary pleasures: the excitements of linear narrative, say, or the delights of inconsequential detail. Indeed as we shall see, much Russian women's writing has been so puritanical in orientation that the inclusion of such detail might in itself be a gesture no less radical than that of drawing attention to the text as artefact. It has been male authors, for the most part, who have meticulously recorded the 'feminine' domain of the everyday and the domestic. This, for example, is Tolstoy's vignette of a mother and child, from *Anna Karenina*:

When Anna walked into the room, Dolly was sitting in the small drawing-room with her fair-haired pudgy little boy, who was beginning to look like his father,

---

[18] My questioning of the formalist 'Oedipal' model of conflict of course ignores the issue of women writers' possible relation to their *male* predecessors. In many cases it would be possible to argue that this conformed to the Tynyanovian pattern. But female predecessors have either been ignored altogether, or drawn in as allies. Even between 1905 and 1935, the contestatory theory of evolution appears to be supported less by evidence from literature as such, than by evidence from women's criticism: see Catriona Kelly, 'Missing Links: Russian Women Writers as Critics of Women Writers', in Faith Wigzell (ed.), *Russian Writers on Russian Writers* (forthcoming).

and hearing him read aloud in French. As he read, the boy twisted a button hanging by its last thread from his cardigan, trying to pull it away. His mother broke the thread and put the button in her pocket.

'Stop fiddling, Grisha,' she said and took up her work again, It was a blanket which she had been knitting for some time. It was something she always did at times of trial, and now she knitted nervously, finger stuck out as she counted the stitches.[19]

By contrast, here is Tsvetaeva's blistering assault on the trivial from her narrative poem *The Ratcatcher*:

> A button—let it be known—
> A button is not a joke!
>
> A button holds order, real things
> Together. Buttoned up—sober.
> A button! The shame of Adam!
> Underthings of fashion, freedom—
>
> Death. You are the philistine's Taras Bulba
> Quiff, his Buddha's navel . . .[20]

In the Anglo-American tradition, the settled domestic world of Austen or Gaskell is perhaps the most familiar kind of 'feminine writing'; in the Russian tradition, by contrast, *realia* (*byt*) are spurned, ordinarily being seen as a muddied clog that weighs down flight into the world of ideas. Many Russian women writers have not even allowed *realia* the powerful, if disgusting, charm with which they are invested by, for example, Gogol or Goncharov.[21] They may provoke magnificent bursts of anger, as they do in Tsvetaeva; they are rarely 'just there', as they are in Tolstoy, to be savoured by the reader.

It would be absurd to suggest that the inclusion of what some Russian critics, noses fastidiously wrinkled, term 'the ethnographical' might be an absolute criterion of aesthetic merit. But writing which is explicit about everyday detail, or for that matter about 'the physiological', issues gynaecological and sexual, has rarely been produced by Russian women. And so the presence or absence of such textual material, where relevant, has been recorded and glossed.

What has been said so far provides grounds for including the abnormal and marginal, material which stands out, the dynamic rather than the

---

[19] L. Tolstoy, *Anna Karenina*, pt. 1, ch. 19: *Polnoe sobranie sochinenii: yubileinoe izdanie* (90 vols.; Moscow-Leningrad, 1928–64), xviii. 71.

[20] M. Tsvetaeva, *Krysolov, SP* (see ch. 11 n. 9), iv. 190.

[21] Gogol's story 'The Old-World Landowners' and Goncharov's novel *Oblomov* are both good examples of *realia* ambivalently treated.

static. A history should, however, also be concerned, so far as possible, with norms and conventions. And so I have included analysis of some material—such as Socialist Realist prose and poetry—which is of historical importance, no matter how uncongenial it seems, and which also helps to explain why certain texts which are ideally suited to a Western feminist reading have enjoyed relatively little recognition in the Russian tradition itself. Here I note a difference between this book and Barbara Heldt's indispensable pioneering study of Russian women's writing, *Terrible Perfection*.[22] As Heldt has illustrated, some texts produced during the nineteenth and early twentieth centuries still seem extraordinarily modern; they speak across the past, as it were. However, there are some which, to the scanning eye of a late twentieth-century feminist critic, seem lost in the past beyond retrieval. Most feminists would agree with Toril Moi's observation that 'sometimes a woman imitating male discourse *is* just a woman speaking like a man'.[23] But there is much room for debate on *which* woman, and in *which* circumstances. And discussion is still further complicated by the existence of a third category, which is much larger than the first two, of texts whose dialectical relation to their culture is immediately apparent, texts which absorb and reject the norms of their historical context in unpredictable ways, constantly adjusting and reconfiguring them. These texts need to be read into; they require meditation and hard work if they are to be understood and appreciated.

Allowing this third category could call the very existence of the class of 'texts lost beyond retrieval' into question (after all, why should one do the work with one text, and not another?). And not everyone will agree with the choices that I have made; many will wonder why I have made more efforts with, say, Vera Bulich than with Mariya Petrovykh or Lidiya Alekseeva, with Olga Shapir than with Anastasiya Verbitskaya, with Sofya Soboleva and Nadezhda Khvoshchinskaya than with Evgeniya Tur. But the selection here is intended as representative in a historical sense, rather than aesthetically definitive; I hope that any perceived defects in my judgements may have a positive effect of an indirect kind, by stimulating serious consideration of those whom I have neglected or maligned. I have also been careful to call readers' attention in the notes

[22] Barbara Heldt, *Terrible Perfection: Women and Russian Literature* (Bloomington, Ind., 1987). The advantage of Heldt's anti-contextual approach to women's writing is, however, that it facilitates the comparison of women's writing across cultures—a possibility which gets lost in such a rigidly historically and geographically centred study as mine.

[23] Moi, *Sexual/Textual Politics*, 143. Margaret Thatcher is the example Moi gives. Most British feminists would probably agree; but it would be possible to argue that Thatcher did allude to her femininity on some occasions as a power strategy.

to work by other feminist critics which offers different interpretations from those which I myself have made.

What has been said so far, of course, ignores the important question of reader-text relations in the Russian cultural tradition itself. A 'sociology of the Russian reader' has not been attempted. It would swell the book to impossible proportions, and in any case, the primary sources on which such a sociology might be based are scanty at best, and secondary sources more or less non-existent. Where possible, however, I have briefly noted any evidence that exists on reception, and I have taken care to cite critical judgements of the day—though I have to say that I would not myself regard literary critics as readers in the ordinary sense of the word.

To move, now, from the principles of selection to those of structure. There are four parts, arranged chronologically. In the first, from 1820–80, I give a brief résumé of material produced by women before 1820, that is, of poetry before Romanticism, and the prose of 'sensibility'. I then move on to discuss the poetry cycles, and the 'society tales' which succeeded them, with some reference to early discussions of 'the woman question' as background. My argument here bears some relation to the central theme of Barbara Heldt's *Terrible Perfection*, but, rather than seeing *all* women's prose writing as unbearably constrained by men's representations of women, I argue that these representations played a significant role only in the post-1840 fiction of political engagement, and that even here women's fiction did display some independence from men's. I also place more emphasis than Heldt on the constraints which were experienced by women poets in the wake of Romanticism's new emphasis on the centrality of 'the genius' (a figure always assumed by Russian Romantics to be a man). The second section runs from 1881–1917, and in it I discuss the growth in diversity of women's writing at a time when the campaign for women's rights was gaining in complexity, when sensitivity to issues affecting the construction of women's autonomy (such as sexuality or self-expression) was becoming more acute, when the Russian intelligentsia was displaying increasing atomization, with many of its members acquiring aesthetic and religious preoccupations that ran contrary to the intelligentsia's old rational and secular concerns, and when Russian society in a broader sense was modernizing fast. I argue that this era saw women prose writers develop a multi-faceted and powerful critical-realist tradition, but that it also saw an increase in the power and dynamism of a contradictory, anti-realist, tradition. The third and fourth parts deal with the literary history of the post-Revolutionary period. Part III shows how women's writing developed during the Soviet drive to cultural, political, and economic centralization. Between 1918 and 1930, the central genre was a prose narrative enshrining the tenets of official doctrines on women's liberation, and on the 'class struggle', and opposing the Soviet 'new woman' to 'backward' bourgeois and peasant women. In the 1930s such prose narratives, by now refashioned according to the dictates of Socialist Realism, started to celebrate the liberation which women had supposedly been granted under Soviet rule; women appear as shock workers and model wives and mothers at one and the same time. If the Stalin period after 1935 saw Soviet views of women's family roles become more and more traditional, 'traditional' values, albeit in a very different form, were also central to the work of many of the women writers who maintained non-Soviet or anti-Soviet cultural positions, and whose work was either published outside Russia (if they lived in the West), or written without hope of publication (if they lived in Russia). Part IV covers the era of de-Stalinization, from the aftermath of the leader's death in 1953 up to the beginning of the post-Soviet period. It illustrates that cultural liberalization has permitted the resurgence of a women's critical realist tradition very like that practised before the Revolution, and has also given a new impetus to imaginative writing that would, in the Stalin years, have been branded 'decadent' or 'formalist'. But at the same time, recent decades have also witnessed something of a decline in women's institutional representation, with the abandonment of the tokenist policies of the Stalin years, and also an increase (for middle-class women) in material hardship. Women writers can still not expect the status and prestige accorded to the most successful of their male colleagues. The chapter ends with some brief observations on the state of affairs in the new post-Soviet Russia, and with some necessarily hesitant predictions for the future.

Each survey chapter is followed by three case-studies of individual authors. (In the case of the final part, there are case-studies of *four* authors, and the survey chapter is a little shorter than its three predecessors, since the secondary literature of recent years has been relatively rich in general overviews). These monographic chapters provide some biographical information, but they are not intended as 'lives-and-works' in miniature: they are, rather, intended to develop themes and problems from the main narrative, whilst also facilitating some rather more sophisticated critical readings than have been possible in the main text, given its necessarily hectic pace. These short chapters are not intended to be definitive statements on their subjects, but, rather, to give some sense of how I see a context-sensitive feminist criticism developing.

The surveys all begin with some brief general observations on historical background; but my policy has generally been to integrate 'context' into the main narrative. This avoids making too hard-and-fast a distinction between 'texts' and 'contexts', 'events' and 'reactions to events', and also, I hope, makes it easier to accommodate different degrees of familiarity with Russian and Soviet history in different readers. For non-specialist readers, however, I should at the outset briefly outline one or two differences between Russian culture and the culture of other Western countries. First, the fact that Russia has never been a parliamentary democracy in the Western style has led to some quite fundamental discrepancies between the movement for women's liberation there and in the West. The campaign for suffrage has always played an infinitely less important role in Russia than it has in other European countries and their colonial dependencies, or in America; as a result, there has been a persistent and painful split between pressure for women's political and economic rights, and pressure for freedom of expression. Secondly, the underground nature of oppositional politics has made debates about the function of writing more significant than they have been in the West; divisions between 'committed' and 'non-committed' writing have been sharper, and also more acrimonious. In the literary sphere, as in so many other areas of Russian life, diversity is little tolerated. Thirdly, the fact that literature is (as I pointed out earlier) a concept which is relatively new in Russian life has on occasion engendered a measure of strait-laced severity, a high-minded seriousness that denies the right to written life of anything ordinary or trivial. This is a written culture of five-course banquets; there is as little place in the Russian literary tradition for a well-crafted piece of entertainment as there is in the British eating tradition for a really good café or a restaurant serving regional specialities located next door to a launderette.

In generalizing literary histories, one can scarcely avoid a tone of magisterial pedestrianism, unless one becomes so self-consciously wayward as to deprive one's commentary of any efficacy whatever. The danger in a pioneering project of this kind is that comments meant to stimulate debate could in fact inhibit debate; what were meant as contingent choices and fluent standpoints could seem, to the reader, more authoritarian than was in fact my intention. To obviate that danger, I shall directly state that this book is not meant as the manifesto for an alternative canon of Russian literature, a list of set books for all time, but as an introduction to, and a stimulus to further work in, a fascinatingly diverse area that has until very recently been served only by studies of the two most famous women poets, and by occasional essays on scattered topics. I hope that a summary of general tendencies in Russian women's writing, produced at a stage when critical work is just beginning, will serve as an intermediate aid to those in need of it, standing alongside the new *Bio-Bibliographical Guide to Russian Women Writers*, and other general guides to the field; I trust also that this one-volume history of Russian literature, written from a new perspective, may counterbalance the many extant histories of Russian literature in which women have at best taken walk-on parts, and at worst figured as 'noises off'.[24]

[24] Marina Ledkovsky, Charlotte Rosenthal, and Mary Zirin (eds.), *A Bio-Bibliographical Guide to Russian Women Writers* (2 vols.; Westport, Conn., 1994). My reference to the lack of research on Russian women's writing to date is not meant to belittle the very high quality of existing studies of Tsvetaeva and Akhmatova, which will be given their due in the body of this survey. Nor is it supposed to play down the tremendous energy with which work is going on in different areas, most particularly in the USA. An indispensable current bibliographical aid on the latter is the *Women East–West* newsletter, ed. Mary Zirin, and published every two months.

PART I

I

The 'Feminine Pen' and the Imagination of National Tradition: Russian Women's Writing, 1820–1880

Russia has Sapphos now, and De La Suzes ...
(Urusova, *Heroides*)

O Corinne worthy of Plutarch,
A woman's heart, the spirit of a man ...
(Vyazemsky, 'My Library')

THE earliest era of Russian women's writing is also the most difficult to analyse, although the political and social background is in some ways more straightforward than at later dates. As I noted in my Introduction, the first half of the eighteenth century saw the publication of occasional imaginative texts by women writers; from about 1780, a consistent, though still by no means extensive, tradition of women's writing began to emerge, its appearance more or less coinciding with Catherine II's codification and consolidation of the mechanisms and class base of autocracy. Though coming under pressure in the years after the French Revolution, these mechanisms were not to be substantially altered until Alexander II's massive programme of reforms, beginning in the 1860s, laid the foundation for a limited devolution of political administration to regional level, if not for a centralized majority government, and provided the impetus for the evolution of a civil society.

Like the political framework of the country, the social composition of Russian society can be summarized quite easily. Though access to education and to cultural institutions gradually broadened during the period, and those who had not been born into the upper classes (*dvoryanstvo*) played an ever larger role in the economic and cultural development of the country, the Emancipation of the Serfs in 1861 represented the first serious threat to the division of society into a numerically insignificant, but culturally overwhelming, élite, and a numerically overwhelming, but culturally insignificant, popular mass. One should of course not overstate the élite's homogeneity; a rich aristocratic diplomat in St Petersburg and a poor country squire in his provincial wilderness were members of the *dvoryanstvo*, officially speaking, but they had little else in common. As we shall see, such divisions within the élite played some part in the early history of women's writing too, since it was above all the daughters of the country gentry, not of aristocrats, who were to be attracted by the campaign for women's rights on the one hand, the opportunity to express themselves in print on the other. However, it is an inalienable fact that every woman writer who put pen to paper in this early period did come from the élite, and that the peculiarities of that élite's privileged position were germane to the origins and development of women's writing in its initial years.[1]

In terms of its essential structures, then, Russia changed more slowly in the century before 1861, and in some ways even in the 120 years between 1760 and 1880, than it did in the four decades thereafter, when an immense and rapid process of modernization was to overtake the country. But this relatively stable and coherent background had a not entirely straightforward relation to women's history and to women's writing.

The difficulties of discussing this relation stem partly from the need to make generalizations from material which is widely dispersed and inchoate. Not until the 1840s, when what was later termed the 'woman question' began to be discussed, under French influence, by Russian radicals, did anything resembling a corpus of gender theory come into being. The attempt to analyse beliefs before that demands the collation and careful interpretation of cursory comments, remarks made in passing, and buried assumptions. This collation and interpretation have so far not been carried out systematically, and what follows can only be the

---

[1] This account of historical developments is necessarily compressed; for general background to the period, see particularly Isabel de Madariaga, *Russia in the Age of Catherine the Great* (London, 1981); B. A. Rybakov (ed.), *Ocherki russkoi kul'tury vosemnadtsatogo veka* (2 vols.; Moscow, 1985–7); R. Bartlett (ed.), *Russia and the World of the Eighteenth Century: Proceedings of the Third International Conference Organised by the Study Group on Eighteenth-Century Russia* (Columbus, Ohio, 1988); Hugh Seton-Watson, *The Russian Empire 1801–1917* (Oxford, 1967); J. N. Westwood, *Endurance and Endeavour: Russian History 1812–1980* (4th edn.; Oxford, 1992); Franco Venturi, *Roots of Revolution: A History of the Populist and Socialist Movements in Nineteenth-Century Russia*, trans. F. Haskell (London, 1960); V. R. Leikina-Svirskaya, *Intelligentsiya v Rossii vtoroi poloviny XIX-go veka* (Moscow, 1971). On general culture, see especially Yu. M. Lotman and B. A. Uspensky, *The Semiotics of Russian Culture*, ed. Ann Shukman (Ann Arbor, Mich., 1984); Yu. M. Lotman, *Aleksandr Sergeevich Pushkin: biografiya pisatelya* (Leningrad, 1982).

hesitant beginning of what is sure to be a vast work of recovering the past. But still more pressing than the problems of finding evidence are the problems of attempting to discuss the interactive and reactive dynamics, the complementary or antagonistic relations, between women's writing and the general processes of Russian culture.

To date, the early history of women's writing in Russia has generally been explained in terms either of a progressive, or of an explosive, hypothesis. The progressive hypothesis goes like this.[2] The late eighteenth and nineteenth centuries, it is argued, saw a slow but steady progress towards the liberation of women from discrimination at law, in society and in the family; not surprisingly, this was accompanied by a slow but steady improvement in the calibre of women's writing, which began timidly and feebly, but which, from about 1830, began to grow in strength and confidence. This argument has drawbacks on two levels, the first of which is the way in which it posits the relation between literature and the socio-economic background. Some socio-economic factors certainly had a direct effect on women's writing. Beginning in the reign of Catherine II, upper-class girls were routinely given an education, and so brought within reach of literary culture; also under Catherine, the enrichment of the aristocracy, resulting from its share in the exploitation of the country's huge mineral wealth, gave women as well as men the leisure necessary to the appreciation of literature, and the practice of composition. If these were the pre-conditions of women's writing, the most important immediate stimulus for its growth, as we shall see, was

---

[2] Progressivist views on women and culture are expressed, for example, in Anon. 'Emantsipatsiya zhenshchin', *ES* xl. 706–8; P. Mikhnuev, 'Zhenskii vopros', *NS*, vol. xvii, cols. 772–84; Richard Stites, *The Women's Liberation Movement in Russia: Feminism, Nihilism and Bolshevism 1860–1930* (Princeton, NJ, 1978), is one important modern source to expound a progressivist ethos. An excellent introduction to the complexity of the women's emancipation movement in Western Europe, suggesting many comparative possibilities for Russia, is Jane Rendall, *The Origins of Modern Feminism: Women in Britain, France and the United States* (Chicago, 1985). The account of women's history that follows is, again, necessarily superficial; for further material, the reader is recommended to consult the following sources: (general bibliography) Barbara Engel, 'Engendering Russia's History: Women in Post-Emancipation Russia and the Soviet Union', *SR* 51/2 (1992), 309–21; Beate Fieseler, '"Ein Huhn ist kein Vogel—ein Weib ist kein Mensch": Russischer Frauen (1860–1930) im Spiegel historischer Forschung', in Beate Fieseler and Birgit Schulze (eds.), *Frauengeschichte: gesucht, gefunden? Auskünfte zum Stand der historischen Frauenforschung* (Cologne, 1991), 214–35; Bonnie S. Anderson and Judith P. Zinsser, *A History of Their Own: Women in Europe from Prehistory to the Present Day* (2 vols.; London, 1990): see esp. vol. ii (on women's liberation, gender theory); Stites, *Women's Liberation*; Linda Edmondson, 'Women's Emancipation and Theories of Sexual Difference (1850–1917)', in Marianne Liljeström, Eila Mäntysaari, and Arja Rosenholm (eds.), *Gender Restructuring in Russian Studies* (Slavica Tamperensia, 11; Helsinki, 1993); (on legal rights) *Svod zakonov Rossiiskoi Imperii*, ed. I. D. Mordukhai-Boltovsky (16 vols. and index; St Petersburg, 1912); M. Brun, 'Razvod', *ES* xxvi. 135–6; (on social history) F. Vigel', *Zapiski* (2 vols.; Leningrad, 1929); V. Davydov, *Iz proshlogo* (Moscow, 1913); M. I. Pylyaev, *Staryi Peterburg* (St Petersburg, 1887); *idem*, *Staroe zhit'e* (St Petersburg, 1892); Anon., *Russian Chit-Chat* (London, 1845) (the memoirs of an English companion to a Russian aristocratic lady); Anon., *An Englishwoman in Russia* (London, 1855) (the memoirs of a long-time resident).

the eighteenth-century association of literary composition with good manners and linguistic facility, matters also emphasized in girls' education of the day. So far, matters are simple enough. But the effects of political, social, and cultural factors were not always quite so straightforward. To take one central, and important point: whilst undoubtedly in part the *result* of educational opportunity and economic advantage, women's writing could also, paradoxically, function as a *substitute* for these. For women, writing could be not only a route to power, but also a compensation for powerlessness.

Over-simplifying the relations between literary composition and social background, the progressive hypothesis also gives an unduly simplistic account of that social background in itself. Certainly, the nineteenth century did see women gradually gain access to institutionalized education (a landmark here was the founding of a state secondary system for women in 1858). However, it is misleading to survey this process in isolation from a broader historical context. In the late eighteenth and early nineteenth centuries, the education offered to the (admittedly few) girls who had any kind of educational opportunity was in no sense radically different to that which their male contemporaries would have been given. But from 1826, the reforming educational minister Sergei Uvarov initiated a drive to centralize and rationalize education for men, and to direct it to vocational ends. The result was that women's education at home or at a *pension*, with a curriculum emphasizing music, the arts, and social skills, began to seem increasingly anomalous. Changes in other aspects of women's lives were just as ambiguous. The second and third quarters of the nineteenth century certainly did see women of the gentry begin to make lives apart from their families, and to earn their own salaries. But there were also some set-backs in women's economic and family situations. Divorce was tightened up by a law of 1839, which was both extraordinarily restrictive on the grounds for the dissolution of marriage, and exceedingly vague on the procedures for administering this dissolution, and which in substance remained on the statute books until the Revolution. Upper-class Russian women had always enjoyed comparatively generous property rights; but the economic privileges conferred by this situation were to come under threat after the abolition of serfdom, which pauperized many landowners, and made wage slaves of some upper-class women. And in the more slippery area of family relations, the well-documented shift from extended family to nuclear family marked a change from one type of male-centred power-structure to another; if fathers played a lesser role in women's lives as the century wore on, husbands, brothers, and male peers played a greater one.

The second, explosive, hypothesis ignores the evidence for and against progress in women's history, arguing that women began writing seriously only in the age of Pushkin, the so-called 'Golden Age' of Russian literature, and that they were inspired by the cultural upsurge of the day.[3] This again is an argument which is at once helpful and something of an over-simplification. As we shall see, Russian women's writing of the 1830s and 1840s was indubitably part of a literary tradition shaped by the efforts of Pushkin and other male littérateurs. However, the years after 1820 also saw the formation, for the first time in Russian history, of an effective national literary ideology. This dictated particular kinds of subjectivity, often giving women the status of metaphors rather than agents. And, as the concept of 'national literature' evolved, there was an explicit drive to theorize women's role in this literature, and to represent this as marginal in order that the new professional class of male littérateurs might concomitantly emerge with enhanced status.

If the connections between women's writing and the social context are complicated, so too is the internal history of women's writing. The texts which women actually produced were riven with arguments about appropriate femininities, about the proper forms of expression for these, and the ethical and aesthetic standpoints which they display are very diverse. But despite this diversity, and despite the fact that women writers constantly engage with the work of their male colleagues, their work does have its own historical logic. Russian literature is convention- ally (if rather tediously) seen as a smooth progress from 'Sentimentalism' (c.1780–1810) to 'Romanticism' (1810–40) to 'realism' (from 1840).[4] This periodization is not remotely adequate to women's poetry, where 'Romanticism' in a positive, rather than a reactive, sense did not show itself until around 1840, but where its principles were to remain in force until the 1860s; nor is it appropriate to the discussion of women's prose, where the abstract distinctions of 'Romanticism' and 'realism' were of much less significance than varying attitudes to the 'woman question' and the overlapping differentiations of genre (broadly speaking, a proto- feminist 'provincial tale' faces an anti-feminist 'society tale').

Sensitivity to the agonistic and genre-centred character of women's writing does not mean, however, that chronology should be eschewed altogether. As we shall see, there is diachronic as well as synchronic

---

[3] The informative introductory survey to Hugh Anthony Aplin's Ph.D. thesis, 'Mariya Zhukova and Elena Gan: Women Writers and Female Protagonists, 1837–1843' (University of East Anglia, 1989), is one account which emphasizes the importance of the 'golden age'. See also M. Fainshtein, *Pisatel'nitsy Pushkinskoi pory* (Leningrad, 1989).

[4] See e.g. Charles Moser (ed.), *The Cambridge History of Russian Literature* (rev. edn.; Cambridge, 1992).

diversity. For a hint of how this manifested itself, let us turn to a text which is central to the ideology of Russian literary nationalism.

In 1843 the critic Vissarion Belinsky published a lengthy essay on the young woman prose writer Elena Gan. The essay was by no means the first publication concerned with women's writing to appear in Russia.[5] It does, however, represent an early and suggestive attempt to execute a survey of women's writing in a historical perspective. Belinsky divides Russian literature's past into two phases. He argues that in the first phase, writing had for the most part been an amateur activity. During this period, the profession of letters had been as open to women as to men. With the emergence of Pushkin and his generation, however, had come an appreciation of the need for 'real talent'. Without defining the criteria which lie behind the term, Belinsky suggests that the demand for 'talent' led to a recognition of the inferiority of pre-Pushkinian women's writing, and an improvement in standards amongst women writers.

Belinsky is not only concerned with the past; he is concerned, at least by implication, with the present and the future. His review begins with an extended comparison of the status of literature in Russia and in the West (Belinsky's notions of developments in 'the West' are, like those of most of his contemporaries, largely drawn from a knowledge of French literature). In Russia the purpose of literature is still commonly under-stood to be entertainment; in the West, by contrast, it is the vehicle of serious social issues. Belinsky asserts that the emergence of literature as a public, professional sphere has made it very difficult for women to be accepted as writers. Conservatives have dwelt on their private, domestic duties, and the incompatibility of these with a literary life. George Sand enjoys an exceptional reputation; any other women who aspired to her position would be greeted with hostility, no matter what her talents.

Though the significance of the parallel is not underlined, Belinsky's observations about the rise of 'professional' attitudes to literature in the West were intended to anticipate and encourage similar developments in Russia. 'Amateurism' and the Pushkin generation are to be succeeded by a third stage, where literature is to be a matter of social commitment and political engagement. The feeble poetic ramblings, and the graceful depiction of feeling, which Belinsky attributes to earlier women writers will no longer be acceptable. Rather, there will be a new demand for committed, thoughtful women writers of the 'George Sandian' type,

[5] V. Belinsky, 'Sochineniya Zeneidy R——' (1843), Polnoe sobranie sochinenii (13 vols.; Moscow, 1953–9), vii. 648–76. S. V. Russov, author of Bibliograficheskii slovar' rossiiskim pisatel'nitsam (St Petersburg, 1826), was a pioneer in the collection of data on women's writing in Russia. Russov's successors included Kireevsky, Verevkin, and Belinsky himself, in earlier reviews of earlier publications by women writers, such as Mariya Zhukova and George Sand.

concerned with women's sufferings in love relationships. The writer Elena Gan, though in every ideological sense inferior to George Sand, is for Belinsky the harbinger of something which might eventually develop into writing on a level with Sand's.

Belinsky's wishes in writing his review of Gan were fulfilled: this was a text which constructed history, as well as being constructed by it. As we shall see, this essay was an important contribution to the development of a 'committed' tradition of women's writing after 1840. The value judgements which he expressed here, and in his other essays on women writers, had ramifications throughout nineteenth-century criticism. They were only to be challenged (and then only implicitly) by the developing modernist movement at the turn of the twentieth century. Indeed, they retain their influence to this day in Russia, being used to legitimate the choice of which nineteenth-century women writers are to be republished, as well as buttressing attitudes to women writers which in some ways have not changed since the second third of the nineteenth century. Belinsky's historical analysis, combining the 'progressivist' and the 'explosive' hypothesis, was also to be hugely influential; it was adopted by literary historians of the twentieth, as well as the nineteenth, centuries. Soviet (and post-Soviet) commentators continue to follow Belinsky in assuming that women's writing in a serious sense began with the Pushkin generation, applying an aesthetic which does not question the assumptions underlying his remarks about 'real talent'.

The analysis of Russian women's writing before and after Romanticism which I give below is informed by recent feminist critiques of nineteenth-century literary ideologies. It will illustrate how far such apparently neutral categories as 'talent', 'commitment', or 'serious purpose' were constructed so as to give women writers a marginal or a secondary status. I shall argue that women writers had in some senses more freedom in the late eighteenth and early nineteenth centuries, at any rate in poetry, than they did after 1820. I shall show that Romanticism's cult of the 'genius' was explicitly gendered, and illustrate the new pressures which this placed on women poets after 1820. But I shall argue that the 'committed' tradition of prose ushered in by Belinsky after 1840, whilst apparently more accessible to women, could be even more constraining than the seemingly more hostile tradition of post-Romantic poetry. This was partly because of the associations between the Russian-language tradition of women's prose writing and the cult of sensibility; but it was also because of the special role which Belinsky, and other critics like him, assigned to women writers, who were assumed to be only properly concerned with depicting discrimination against women in society and in the family. These restrictions within the prose tradition do not mean that it is possible to argue that poetry invariably constituted an alternative and 'true' women's tradition in which women could find their way to autonomous expression of the self. But I shall argue that post-Romantic poetry did on occasion allow limited expression of an explicitly feminine self, by a kind of historical accident. The rise of committed prose pushed poetry from its pivotal position in Russian literary ideology; after 1840 women could adopt a central position in the marginal or peripheral tradition of poetry, which could be a stimulating alternative to the adoption of a marginal position in the central tradition of prose.

As these observations indicate, the traditions of prose and poetry at some points intersected and depended on each other; many individual women writers, besides, worked as both poets and prose writers. However, the different routes followed by prose and poetry are perhaps more easily appreciated if each is analysed separately; for this reason the two traditions are indeed treated in isolation here.

Muses, Daughters, Readers: Women's Poetry before 1820

In terms of literature and culture, eighteenth-century Russia offers a complex and contradictory panorama to a late twentieth-century specta-tor. A few writers, all men, produced writing of mandarinic rhetorical splendour whose sophistication was later to be matched by few Russian poets, but they were read and understood by a scarce handful of their contemporaries. For the most part, the community of Russian readers looked to reading for entertainment as much as enlightenment. Much of the material by which this community's omnivorous tastes were satisfied consisted of factual or quasi-factual texts, rather than of fiction, but there was also a steady demand for songs, poems, and tales. Until well into the nineteenth century, readers' needs for the latter genres were at least as likely to be met by Western literature as by Russian literature. 'Western' signified French literature above all: this might be read in the original, in translation, or in a Russian adaptation.[6]

There were frequent attempts to regulate and direct taste, most particularly in the years after the accession of Catherine II, and to impose

---

[6] On the élite character of neo-classicism in 18th-c. Russia, see Marinus Wes, *Classics in Russia 1700–1855: Between Two Bronze Horsemen* (Leiden, 1992), chs. 1–3; Evgeny Bershtein, 'The Solemn Ode in the Age of Catherine: Its Poetics and Function', in Joe Andrew (ed.), *Poetics of the Text: Essays to Celebrate Twenty Years of the Neo-Formalist Circle* (Amsterdam, 1992), 75–91. According to Vigel', *Zapiski*, i. 95–6, aristocratic Russian society's 'Versailles prejudices' meant only French 'pink books of amours' were read; on p. 101 he records that the upper classes attended only the French theatre.

formal canons drawn from French neo-classicism. For the most part, however, these attempts did not establish anything resembling a unified and prescriptive literary ideology. The conditions of literary production were haphazard, the products themselves various. In such circumstances, notions of literary authority, or of authorship, could not but be hazy and underdeveloped. Notions of the reader were also flexible: though the gulf between urban élite and urban under-classes was in socio-economic terms enormous, there was in some ways more congruence between literary preferences across classes than in the more 'democratic' nineteenth century.[7]

The embryonic nature of literary ideology, combined with the eclectic and catholic tastes of readers, meant that circumstances were not unfavourable to the appearance of works by women writers as such. Russian society was also familiar with the notion of women's writing in an abstract sense from early in the eighteenth century: contact with the poetic traditions of classicism and neo-classicism brought with it familiarity with the concept of the Muses, as well as with the figures of the Greek poets Sappho and Corinna.[8]

Another sign that conditions were likely to support the birth of Russian women's writing came in the publication of texts composed by Russian men whose addressees or narrators were women. In the 1750s the poet Aleksandr Sumarokov composed a series of elegies which describe the pains of separation from the female object of his desire, or of disillusion as she prefers another man, 'sitting upon his knee and kissing him'.[9] If the women in these elegies are mute, and refracted through a man's perception, other sources represented the female voice directly. The popular genre of songbook, or *pesennik*, for example, specialized in love-songs with female heroines.[10] All in all, the conditions of the literary

[7] The market for material in Russian covered a wide range of social ranks, from the lower echelons of the gentry downwards; these readers also had catholic tastes, as is indicated by Aleksandr Izmailov's turn-of-the-century parody of a gentleman's library offered for raffle. Besides such works of 'literature' proper as Izmailov's own *Evgeny*, the selection included works by Mrs Radcliffe and her imitators, histories, anecdote collections, divination manuals, textbooks, and salmagundis (*Polnoe sobranie sochinenii* (3 vols.; Moscow, 1890), i. 293–5).

[8] In his 'Mnenie o nachale poezii i stikhov voobshche' (1748), *Sochineniya* (3 vols.; St Petersburg, 1849), ii. 185, Trediakovsky speculates that the original poets may have been the 'Muses', the daughters of Pierus, taught by their father to sing; Lomonosov's 'O kachestve stikhotvortsa rassuzhdenie' (1755) names Sappho as a member of the poetic profession: *Izbrannye filosofskie proizvedeniya* (Moscow, 1950), 524. An amusing example of the persistence of such classical allusions into the early 19th c. comes in a letter of 6 May 1816 from A. S. Shishkov to Anna Bunina, in which she is addressed as 'Sappho Petrovna' (Saltykov-Shchedrin Manuscript Section f. N. 862 Shishkov, A. S. N7, 1.7).

[9] Aleksandr Sumarokov, *Trudolyubivaya pchela* (St Petersburg, 1759); see also *Elegii lyubovnye* (St Petersburg, 1774).

[10] Some material on song-books of the 18th c. may be found in Aleksandr Yakub, 'Sovremennye narodnye pesenniki', *Izvestiya otdeleniya russkogo yazyka i slovesnosti Imperatorskoi Akademii*

market and social and cultural relations in general were more receptive than otherwise to any of the Russian women who, emboldened by new educational possibilities and by a broadening role in the public sphere (as hostesses and leaders of salons), might choose to put pen to paper.[11] Hostility to women writers, where voiced, tended to be based on a suspicion that they might be neglecting housewifely tasks: 'Who's going to make the cabbage soup now?' as one jaded male observer commented.[12] But such objections had a routine and formulaic character, given the very large size of the domestic staffs in eighteenth- and early nineteenth-century aristocratic households: women who had the time and resources to write belonged to a class only dimly aware of the kitchen's very location, let alone of what mysterious alchemies might be perpetrated within it. Certainly, aristocratic ladies do not seem to have been deterred by such sallies, and the late eighteenth century sees large numbers of them enter publishing (albeit often anonymously). Many of them worked as translators, making use of the language skills then, as later, considered a requisite feminine accomplishment; but a significant minority produced original writings, by which I mean both that these writings were not translations, and that they were not purely imitative of extant texts.[13]

The Western women writers who became most popular in Russia during the late eighteenth and nineteenth centuries were specialists in prose. Between 1780 and 1825, more than fifty books by the French writer Madame de Genlis appeared in Russian translation, and some of the writer's *nouvelles* appeared in the French language in Paris and in St Petersburg simultaneously. In the 1790s the Gothic novelist Ann Rad-

---

Nauk (1914), 1: 47–92; an early 19th-c. selection is *Noveishii vseobshchii pesennik ili sobranie otbornykh i vsekh dosele izvestnykh pesen* (4 vols.; Moscow, 1822).

[11] On 18th-c. women's education see Madariaga, *Russia in the Age of Catherine the Great*, 493, 499–500; J. L. Black, 'Educating women', in *Citizens for the Fatherland: Education, Educators and Pedagogical Ideals in Eighteenth-Century Russia* (New York, 1979), 152–72; on salons see Gitta Hammarberg, *From the Idyll to the Novel: Karamzin's Sentimentalist Prose* (Cambridge, 1991), ch. 4. An indication of salon hostesses' importance is given also by the high numbers of 18th-c. texts by male poets which are dedicated to female patrons. (See the details given in *Svodnyi katalog russkikh knig XVIII veka (1725–1800)* (5 vols.; Moscow, 1962–1975); *Drammaticheskii slovar'* (Moscow, 1787; repr. St Petersburg, 1880).) A classic manual for salon poetry is N. G. Kurganov, *Pis'movnik, soderzhashchii v sebe nauku russkogo yazyka . . .* (5th edn.; St Petersburg, 1793).

[12] The cabbage-soup comment belongs to the poet V. I. Maikov, referring to Kheraskova: quoted in Aplin, 'Mariya Zhukova', 31.

[13] Aplin is possibly right to assert (ibid. 34) that in its early history Russian women's writing's 'archetypal representative would have been a weak, anonymous, verse translation from the French', but weak verse translations were by no means the only material published by Russian women before the 1830s. Apart from the authors mentioned below, women publishing original Russian verse before 1820 included Anna Naumova, author of *Uedinennaya muza zakamskikh beregov* (Moscow, 1819), Anna Volkova, author of *Stikhotvoreniya devitsy Volkovoi* (St Petersburg, 1807), E. Kheraskova, E. Khvostova, and Sarra Tolstaya.

cliffe likewise enjoyed a vogue.[14] But it was with lyric poetry that Russian women's writing began.

Why should this have been? Late nineteenth- and early twentieth-century commentators on the eighteenth century were inclined to attribute women's preference to the supposedly age-old traditions of folklore, and to trace the feminine love poem back to women's association with the formal lament, the most important women's genre of rural culture.[15] However, there are no records that any of the upper-class woman who turned to writing poetry took a serious interest in folkloric material. And in any case the literary taste of the day was not conducive to the expression of such material; most eighteenth-century poetry and song collections do not directly reflect the conventional formulae, lexicon, or rhythmic patterns of the orally transmitted convention.[16] It was not until the beginning of the twentieth century, in fact, that such material was to make any significant impact on Russian women's writing—a matter which may well have prompted literary historians of the day to their anachronistic suppositions. It would almost certainly be just as anachronistic to assume that these early Russian women poets saw their work as complementary to the French-language tradition, and perceived poetry to be a way of establishing a specifically Russian identity. The likeliest explanation for the earliest Russian women writers' orientation is the high status of poetry amongst their male contemporaries. And in fact, one of the earliest published works by a Russian woman writer, an 'Elegy' by Ekaterina Sumarokova, the daughter of Aleksandr Sumarokov, not only imitated the manner of her father's elegies, but was composed, like them, in the voice of a man speaking to a woman.[17] Sumarokova's successors' literary preferences also followed those of their male contemporaries. Women writers worked in most of the genres current in the late eighteenth and early

---

[14] See the entries on Genlis and Radcliffe in *Svodnyi katalog*, and in Grigory Gennadi and Nikolai Solko (eds.), *Spravochnyi slovar' o russkikh pisatelyakh i uchenykh, umershikh v XVIII i XIX stoletiyakh: spisok russkikh knig 1725–1825* (Berlin, 1880); A. Kirpichnikov, 'Zhanlis', *ES* xi. 720–1; Anon., 'Radklif', *ES* xxvi. 92.

[15] On the argument for folk traditions as a precedent, see for example S. Vengerov, *Russkaya poeziya: sobranie proizvedenii russkikh poetov* (7 parts; St Petersburg, 1897–1901), who attributes various song-book entries to Praskov'ya Kuznetsova-Gorbunova, later Countess Sheremet'eva, and to the actress Elizaveta Sandunova (see pt. 3, pp. 245–6, 360).

[16] A readily accessible modern collection of laments is *Prichitaniya*, ed. K. V. Chistov and B. E. Chistova (Moscow, 1960). On metropolitan ladies' hostility to Russian customs and beliefs, see e.g. Ivan Aksakov's portrait of his mother in his *Memoirs*. It is notable that the quasi-folkloric motifs employed by e.g. Naumova, *Uedinennaya muza*, are worked into metres drawn from literate poetry, not the oral tradition.

[17] E[katerina] S[umarokova], 'Elegiya', *Trudolyubivaya pchela*, 3 (1759), 191–2. See also 'E. Knyazhnina', Vengerov, *Russkaya poeziya*, pt. 3, pp. 218–22.

nineteenth centuries, with the significant exception of the verse play: formal odes, elegies, even the occasional epic, are found alongside epigrams and occasional verse.[18]

If Sumarokova wrote in the male voice, Catherine II's preferred genre, the play, obviated the need for reference to the composer's gender. But not all early poets were so reticent. In 1777 the poet Ekaterina Urusova published a volume entitled *Heroides*, in which she adapted the post-Ovidian tradition of the verse epistle narrated by an outstanding woman of the past to her own purposes.[19] Though she followed tradition in putting rhetorical complaints into the mouths of women deserted by their lovers, Urusova did not take her heroines from Ovid or from any of his neo-classical imitators; instead, she appears to have reshaped them from neo-classical dramas of her own day. In a further, and more important, gesture of independence, Urusova also placed an invocation to the Muses as the opening piece to the collection. She thereby adapts an epic convention to a lyric genre, showing a certain freedom with neo-classical tradition. Still more significantly, her 'Invocation' expresses a sense of female solidarity as an impulse of creation. Urusova exhorts the Muses to 'hear the voice of their own sex', and traces the origins of women's writing directly to Catherine II, a female ruler's, assault on ignorance. She speaks of the emergence of Russian 'Sapphos' and 'De La Suzes' (perhaps meaning Sumarokova and Kheraskova), as precedents whom she intends to follow. In the final epistle of the collection, Urusova re-emphasizes and reshapes this notion of poetry as communication between women: the narrator of the piece, Kliada, addresses herself to 'my fellow-sufferers amongst women' (*souchastnitsy muchen'ya moego*).

Urusova's successors did not always follow her in proclaiming poetry as the voice of woman speaking to women. But one of them, Anna Bunina, did pay heed to the claims of women readers on her as a poet, if only in a negative sense, by rebuffing them:

---

[18] Ekaterina Urusova, whose 'heroides' are discussed below, was also the author of an epic, *Pollion* (St Petersburg, 1774); odes were written by Khvostova, Kheraskova, Bunina; Catherine II composed entertaining opera libretti in verse, but her histories and comedies alike are in prose: *Dramaticheskie sochineniya*, ed. A. N. Pypin (4 vols.; St Petersburg, 1901).

[19] Urusova, *Iroidy: muzam posvyashchennye* (St Petersburg, 1777), 4. (See also ['Invocation'] in *Anthology*.) Ovid, *Heroides and Amores* (London, 1914); on Ovid and neo-classical tradition, see L. P. Wilkinson, *Ovid Recalled* (Cambridge, 1955), 96–9, 404–7, 424–7; Rachel Trickett, 'The Heroides and the English Augustans', in Charles Martindale (ed.), *Ovid Renewed: Ovidian Influences on Literature and Art from the Middle Ages to the Twentieth Century* (Cambridge, 1988), 192–204. Renata Carocci, *Les Héroides dans la seconde moitié du XVIIIᵉ siècle* (Paris, 1988), does not record any heroides with the same characters as Urusova's. On Henriette De La Suze, see *eadem* and P. Pellisson, *Recueil des pièces galantes en prose et en vers (1663)*: a biography is available in the edn. of Paris, 1748: vol. i, pp. i–xiii.

ЖЕНЩИНЫ

А ты пустилася хвалить мужчин!
Как будто бы похвал их стоит пол один!
Изменница! Сама размысли зрело,
　　Твое ли это дело?
Иль нет у них хвалителей своих?
Иль добродетелей в нас меньше, чем у них!

Я

Все правда, милые! вы их не ниже,
　　Но, ах!
Мужчины, а не вы присутствуют в судах,
　　При авторских венках,
И слава авторска у них в руках,
А всякий сам к себе невольно ближе.[20]

THE WOMEN

'Tis only men you honour with your lays,
As if their sex alone deserved your praise.
You traitress! Give our case some thought!
　　For is this what you ought?
Are their own founts of flattery too few,
Or can they boast of more than our virtue?

ME

It's true, my dears, you are no less,
　　But understand:
With men, not you, the courts of taste are manned
　　Where authors all must stand,
And all authorial fame is in their hands,
And none can help loving himself the best.

The sardonic tone in which Bunina evokes male literary power—and the witty device of evading the prohibition on talking about women by discussing the prohibition itself—indicate her adoption of a less conventional and restrictively genteel view of poetry than that suggested by Urusova, who had spoken of 'tender songs', 'the bestowing of laurels on virtue', and 'the pleasant piping of cheerful things'.[21] Bunina did bestow 'laurels on virtue', composing large-scale civic odes. But she was

---

[20] Anna Bunina, 'Razgovor mezhdu mnoyu i zhenshchinami', in her *Sobranie sochinenii* (3 vols.; St Petersburg, 1819–21), iii. 106–8. (See also 'Conversation between Me and the Women' in *Anthology*.) A similar half-joking taunt is directed at women in the preface to Bunina's *Pravila poezii, sokrashchenno-perevedennye iz abbata Blatë, s prisovokupleniem rossiiskogo stikhoslozheniya* (St Petersburg, 1808).

[21] It might seem tempting to view Urusova's emphasis on 'pleasantness' as gender-linked, but this is simply a conventional poeticism of the time: cf. Trediakovsky, 'Mnenie o nachale', 191, where poetry is seen as a form of persuasion to social consensus 'impossible without words, words of a kind that would be at once powerful and sweet'.

certainly not a singer of 'tender songs'. Her poetry is gracelessly conversational rather than melodious. It encompasses 'low' and hum-drum subjects: 'Poverty is no stain', for example, begins with a series of vignettes delineating the subterfuges of those without money. It then proceeds to a series of brilliant pictures of Bunina's childhood in which the familiar metaphor of poet as bee is placed in a very everyday context: Bunina is stung as a small child, and aided by her wet-nurse, who places earth on the wound, and gives her bread to chew. If the bee-sting is a punishment for Bunina's presumption in 'grasping' for a role to which she may not aspire, the rebuff is undercut and the wound healed, by a sense that women may co-operate.[22]

As the illustrations given so far suggest, the earliest Russian women poets are by no means unconscious of the peculiarity of female verse composition. Women poets who comment on their sex may do so in a mildly derogatory manner; the modesty topos figures frequently. That said, it should be borne in mind that the modesty topos was also incumbent on the male poets who chose to publish in this status-conscious aristocratic society.[23] And women poets, their ritual act of deference once out of the way, do not seem unduly restricted or inhibited by their sex. For example, Bunina's younger contemporary, Elisaveta Kulman, began her portrait of the Greek poet Corinna at a poetic contest by suggesting her submission to male authority: Corinna advances 'shyly' to the stand, and then asks Pindar to let her speak, and cast off the 'infancy' to which she is bound by sex. But the end of the poem sees the heroine welcomed simply as 'a young poet', and admitted to the company of her male contemporaries. Kulman herself, who died at the age of 17 in 1824, knew both Greek and Latin, and seemed perfectly at home in the 'masculine' world of neo-classical poetry. Yet her intricately allusive accentual verse 'Pindaric odes', or Alcaic and Sapphic strophes, also convey a positive sense of feminine identity: the divinity whose retinue she evokes is not Apollo, but the 'vengeful', yet affectionate, Diana.[24]

I would, of course, not wish to argue that eighteenth- and early

---

[22] Bunina, 'Khot' bednost' ne porok', in Yu. M. Lotman and M. G. Al'tshuller (eds.), *Poety 1790–1810 godov* (Leningrad, 1971), 467–71. (See also 'Though poverty's no stain' in *Anthology*.) Although this poem was not published during Bunina's lifetime, Lotman and Al'tshuller's note indicates that it was very widely circulated in manuscript. Bunina's lyric subjectivity and literary standing are to be extensively explored in the pioneering critical biography of the poet on which Wendy Rosslyn is now engaged.

[23] One significant instance of the use of a 'modesty topos' by a male poet is Yakov Knyazhnin's ode to Princess Dashkova, 'K knyagine Dashkovoi: pis'mo na sluchai otkrytiya Akademii Rossiiskoi' (1784), in his *Izbrannye proizvedeniya* (Leningrad, 1984), 649–53.

[24] Elisaveta Kul'man, 'Korinna', *Piiticheskie opyty* (3 vols.; St Petersburg, 1833), ii. 40–55; 'K Diane', ibid. iii. 55–6 (see also 'To Diana' in *Anthology*).

nineteenth-century women poets had any very strong sense of their mission precisely as women poets, or that their collections were hailed by others as the beginning of a grand new tradition of 'feminine poetry'. Nor do I mean to suggest that such women enjoyed a standing equal to that of their most successful male contemporaries. The point is that women's writing was served, at this stage, by its very unnoticeability. In an environment where most writers devoted only part of their time to writing, women could not be accused of 'amateurism'; given an aesthetic which placed more emphasis on felicity of style than on expression of psychological essentials, more stress on the nature of what was generated than on the character of its generator, women could be subject to no excessively obvious gender-based restrictions in an artistic sense. And so, whilst many women poets certainly participated fully in the 'amateurism' of the eighteenth and early nineteenth centuries, composing eminently forgettable jingles for the various 'ladies' journals', a small number were able to write lyrics expressing a diverse and remarkably confident sense of feminine identity.[25]

From about 1820, however, Romanticism, which had previously become *an* ideology in Russian poetry, was to become *the* ideology in Russian poetry. Its dominance brought a new emphasis on the process of creation; the result was that the question of whether women were capable of writing poetry—intellectually, spiritually, and even physiologically—was to be raised with a new urgency. And the raising of the question would bring with it a systematic denigration of women who had attempted to write poetry in earlier years, as Romanticism set up its poetic canon, honouring both the 'masculine' phenomenon of inspiration, and the great men of the past who had manifested it.

Poetry after 1820: Romanticism and the 'Man of Genius'

> Hail the new Sappho! Let not the lady
> Be fearful of the foaming sea;

[25] Lomonosov's 'O kachestve' is concerned with education and linguistic competence as prerequisites for poetry, and even Trediakovsky's 'Mnenie o nachale' is more preoccupied with the socio-linguistic origins of poetry than with the role of the poet as an individual. That poetry written by women was imaginable in 18th-c. Russia is suggested by listings in 18th-c. dictionaries: the *Teutsch-Lateinisches und Russisches Lexicon* [ed. E. Weismann] (St Petersburg, 1731), lists 'stikhotvornitsa' for 'Poetin'; P. Zhdanov, *Slovar' anglo-rossiiskoi* (St Petersburg, 1784), gives 'sochinitel'nitsa stikhov' for 'poetess'; G. Heym, *Novyi rossiisko-frantsuzsko-nemetskii slovar'* (Moscow, 1799), lists 'sochinitel'nitsa' for 'Schriftstellerin, Verfasserin, celle qui ecrit'. For 'forgettable jingles' by women writers, see e.g. V. Pokrovsky, *Damskoi zhurnal 1806–1906* (Moscow, 1906).

> Phaon would fling himself off Lefkas
> Rather than hear her poetry.
>
> (A. D. Illichevsky, 1827)

In some European countries, most particularly Germany, the rise of Romanticism as a literary ideology had been accompanied and buttressed by a reaction against the philosophical inheritance of the Enlightenment. A host of alternative philosophical and contemplative orientations had shown themselves; many were of a mystical character, some looking to the religious traditions of the Middle Ages.[26] It was natural that Romantic dualism, to which an 'I-Other' polarization was central, should be particularly concerned with that quintessential 'Other', the 'feminine principle' as an embodiment of mysterious and inexplicable other-worldly forces. Whilst 'the feminine principle' was sometimes evoked to celebrate women's roles as arbiters of morality and guardians of the hearth (so in Schiller's ode 'Dignity of Women'), it could also be associated with a new awareness of, and on occasion reverence for, the creative powers of women.[27] A famous, though relatively late, representation of the 'feminine principle' is the final scene of Goethe's *Faust* Part II (1832), which represents 'the eternal feminine' through the apotheosis not only of Gretchen, but also of other and various feminine beings. If 'the feminine' appears in this scene as the end-point of male striving, it has a rather different significance in some earlier, and equally influential, texts by Goethe. In Act III of *Faust*, Mephistopheles, transmuted into the Greek witch Phorkyas, adopts a directly authoritative role; in *Wilhelm Meister's Apprenticeship* (1795–6), and *Elective Affinities* (1808), 'the eternal feminine' and writing intersect. Mignon, *Wilhelm Meister*'s other-worldly heroine, is a maker of songs; Ottilie of *Elective Affinities*, who starves herself to become an object of popular veneration, thus puts into practice a course of self-transcendence anticipated in her diary, fragments from which are woven into the narrative's second part.[28]

[26] On the mystical aspects of German Romanticism, see Paul Roubiczek, 'Some Aspects of German Philosophy in the Romantic Period', Raymond Immerwahr, 'The Word *Romantisch* and its History', Siegbert Prawer, 'Introduction', in Siegbert Prawer (ed.), *The Romantic Period in Germany* (London, 1970), 305–26, 34–63, 1–16.

[27] This point is perhaps given insufficient attention in Sandra M. Gilbert and Susan Gubar's stimulating critical study of 19th-c. women's writing, *The Madwoman in The Attic: The Woman Writer and the Nineteenth-Century Literary Imagination* (2nd edn.; New Haven, Conn., 1984), which seamlessly assimilates Goethe's notion of the 'eternal feminine' into the high-Victorian domestic ideal, 'the angel of the house'.

[28] Goethe, *Faust: der Tragödie zweiter Teil*, Act V, final scene, *Werke: Hamburger Ausgabe in 14 Bänden* (10th edn.; Stuttgart, 1981), iii. 556–64; cf. Mephistopheles' appearance as the she-witch Phorkyas in Act III; *Die Wahlverwandtschaften*, ibid. vi. 242–490; *Wilhelm Meisters Lehrjahre*, ibid., vol. vii.

In Russia, however, interest in 'the feminine principle' was not to develop until nearly a hundred years after it had made itself felt in the West. One might attribute the slowness with which the ideology was transmitted to the relative unfamiliarity of German, compared with French, material amongst educated Russians; but in fact an interest in feminine creativity had shown itself there too: in her novel *Corinne* (1807), Madame de Staël, author of a study of German Romanticism, had represented a woman poet whose poetic creations conformed to the quintessential Romantic literary genre, the improvisation; the rhapsodic and ecstatic character of Corinne's verse was suggested by the costume in which she first appeared to the reader, that of the Sibyl of Domenichino.[29] Though Russian high society in the latter days of Alexander I's reign was embued with mysticism, and mediums with 'magnetic' skills, such as Madame Turchaninova, enjoyed considerable social triumphs, such enthusiasms were foreign to the literary world, where the notion of 'feminine creativity' hardly impinged at all.[30] For Russian Romantics such as Pushkin, as for their predecessors, such as Zhukovsky in his 'Svetlana', women's sense of the other-worldly was interpreted as a penchant for superstitious popular belief and ritual, their capacity for visions glossed as a sense of unsayable erotic desire; and, whilst Madame de Staël enjoyed considerable fame, she was more highly respected by the organizers of Romanticism as a political dissident and an essayist than as a creative writer.[31]

Russian Romanticism was, as we shall see, by no means free of mysticism, most especially during its later years. However, it is possible that the enthusiasms of Alexander I's court for women mystics played some role in discouraging the absorption of ideas about 'the eternal feminine' by Russian Romanticism, given the movement's anti-establishment character. But far more important was the fact that abstract debate on aesthetics played a less significant part in Russia than it had in Germany, France, or England; if literature was at first conceived by the Russian Romantics as *a* medium of politics, it was later to become *the* medium of politics. The idea that the literary role must necessarily be a public and political one was in turn to have direct effects on the Russian

---

[29] Germaine de Staël, *Corinne* (Paris, 1807).

[30] On Miss Turchaninova's activities as a prophetess, see Vigel', *Zapiski*, i. 67.

[31] V. A. Zhukovsky, 'Svetlana', *Sochineniya v 3 tomakh* (Moscow, 1980), ii. 17–24. In the same author's 'Kassandra', ibid. ii. 13–17, the prophetess, rather than presenting herself as a mouthpiece of the other world, laments that she cannot share Polyxena's fate, to be buried with the beloved. On Madame de Staël's role in Russia see S. Durylin, 'G-zha de Stal' i ee russkie otnosheniya', *Literaturnoe nasledstvo*, 32–4 (1939), 215–30. Where Staël was recognized as an author, femininity might be blocked out: Vyazemsky's poem 'Biblioteka' (The Library), quoted as a chapter epigraph, evokes her as having 'a woman's heart, the spirit of a man': *Stikhotvoreniya* (Leningrad, 1986), 188.

Romantics' attitudes to women's literary participation, to which the Romantics were consistently hostile, though their hostility took different forms and had different promptings at various times during the course of the movement.

In its first phase, which was brought to an end by the catastrophic defeat of the December 1825 coup aimed at pre-empting the accession of Nicholas I, and establishing a constitutional monarchy (the 'Decembrist Rebellion'), and the consequent defeat for any real hopes of reform, Russian Romanticism was associated with a politics hostile to autocracy and loosely founded on the aristocratic liberalism of the West. The radical stance of the members of the 'Decembrist' generation—born around the turn of the century, and rebelling against the standards of their parents and grandparents—dictated an acute reaction against the politics of the eighteenth century, and most especially against the rule of Catherine II, the century's most outstanding monarch. Disapproval of the venal despotism and misrule of her court—most particularly in its latter days—was encapsulated in disparaging references to the practice of favouritism, an institution which conveniently associated sexual domination with political domination, and so symbolized an era in which women had reversed normal power relations.[32] Satire was also directed at the women of Catherine's court who had survived her, whose despotism jarred with a new generation, and made them seem fantastic monsters. Memorably appalling eighteenth-century *grandes dames* stalk the pages of various memoirs written in the early nineteenth century. One might note in particular Anna Kern's terrifying maternal grandmother, who ran her estate with vast efficiency although she was unable to read or write, and who treated her guests like her servants; or the Princess Golitsyna remembered by Vigel, whose outbursts of rage, often expressed by physical means, terrified her entire household.[33] In a variety of literary texts written in the 1820s and 1830s, notably Griboedov's *Woe from Wit* (1824) and Pushkin's *Queen of Spades* (1833), such 60- and 70-year-old survivors appear as blood-curdling harridans, alternately bullying and patronizing their male and female dependents. Here, too, sexual and political motifs are intertwined. The central scene of *The Queen of Spades* insinuates the grisly details of the Countess's *toilette*, as the aged and festering belle puts off her carapaces of social and sexual authority;

[32] On favouritism see J. T. Alexander, 'Favourites, Favouritism and Female Rule in Russia, 1725–1796', in Roger Bartlett and Janet M. Hartley (eds.), *Russia in the Age of the Enlightenment: Essays for Isabel de Madariaga* (London, 1990), 106–24; cf. also Pushkin's remarks in *PSS* viii. 91–3, and his 1817 epigram imputing homosexual tendencies to A. N. Golitsyn, favourite of Khvostova: *Polnoe sobranie sochinenii v 10 tomakh* (4th edn.; Leningrad, 1977), i. 67.

[33] On real-life harridans, see Vigel', *Zapiski*, i. 72; ii. 22; Anna Kern, *Vospominaniya* (Leningrad, 1929), 25–32.

Griboedov's hero, Chatsky, advised to flatter a powerful woman for his own good, responds with a typical piece of Sturm-und-Drang-like innuendo, 'I can think of better uses for a woman than that'.[34]

The resentment inspired by women's institutional and sexual authority can also be sensed in the anxiety about marriage which haunted the young men of Pushkin's generation. The women of Woe from Wit use marriage as an instrument of subjugation; the disgust inspired by this spectacle in Chatsky was shared by Pushkin, who expressed concern that his friend, the poet Baratynsky's, marriage might have deleterious effects on his mind. 'Can Baratynsky really be married?' Pushkin enquired in 1826. 'I fear for his wits. A legal whore—that's a sort of warm fur hat with ear-flaps. Your whole head gets swallowed up.'[35]

The fact that the wives and mistresses of senior officials might wield considerable political power at second hand could only increase hostility to women in the political opposition; the prominent participation of women in conservative political and literary circles was likely to have a similar effect.[36] As for the opposition, its own serious conversation and exchange of ideas took place in meetings from which women were excluded: in the closed men's clubs and men's societies, many of them secret, of which dozens proliferated in the early 1820s.[37] The relative unimportance to the early Romantics of female company is also manifested in the fact that this generation's poems of male friendship often reveal considerably more emotional intensity than the care-

[34] On Pushkin, 'Pikovaya dama', see n. 94 below; Griboedov, Gore ot uma, III. iii: Polnoe sobranie sochinenii v stikakh (Leningrad, 1988), 106. The portrayal of such harridans also, of course, draws on the stereotypes of 18th-c. comedy: cf. e.g. Fonvizin's Nedorosl' and Sumarokov's Ssora muzha s zhenoi.

[35] Pushkin, letter to P. A. Vyazemsky, 24 May 1826: PSS x. 150.

[36] Among the women who wielded power at second hand in the 1820s and 1830s were P. Yu. Trubetskaya-Gagarina-Kologrivova, whose patronage extended over the civil service; and V. P. Pukalova, mistress of Arakcheev; a woman who made herself a public career within the autocracy was Antonina Bludova, who was an organizer of Orthodox Christian missions to Poland. (See Vigel', Zapiski, ii. 22, 35, 37). Zinaida Volkonskaya, whose cultural tastes were entirely Western, was one of the many upper-class women whose social contacts were with 'Slavophile' rather than 'Western' circles: see Nadezhda Gorodetsky, 'Princess Zinaida Volkonsky: An Approach' (1969; unpublished typescript held in the N. Gorodetsky archive, Taylor Institution Slavonic Library, Oxford); cf. the cases of Ol'ga Novikova, The M.P. for Russia: Reminiscences and Correspondence of Madame Ol'ga Novikoff, ed. W. T. Stead (2 vols.; London, 1909), and of Pavlova.

[37] On the political societies which flourished during Russian Romanticism see for example A. N. Pypin, Obshchestvennoe dvizhenie v Rossii pri Aleksandre I: istoricheskie ocherki (St Petersburg, 1900). On one of the most important all-male societies, Freemasonry, see S. P. Mel'gunov and N. P. Sidorov (eds.), Masonstvo v ego proshlom i nastoyashchem (2 vols.; Moscow, 1914–15); S[tephen] B[aehr], 'Freemasonry' in Victor Terras, A Handbook of Russian Literature (New Haven, Conn., 1985); idem, 'Freemasonry in Russian Literature: Eighteenth Century', MERSL viii. 28–36; Lauren G. Leighton, 'Freemasonry in Russian Literature: Nineteenth Century', ibid. 36–42. The experiences of Pierre Bezukhov in War and Peace constitute the best-known literary evocation of early 19th-c. freemasonry.

fully flattering poems which were written for the albums of 'young ladies'.[38]

As for the 'young ladies' themselves, they were expected to be decorative and to offer sexual companionship where required. 'Coquetry', by which was understood a complicated public ritual of flirtation not binding to the male participant, was regarded with favour. One coquette, the Moscow beauty Sofya Ponomareva, enjoyed an astonishing social success with radical literary society.[39] An unwarranted display of education would give women the reputation of being tedious bluestockings: 'Don't bother with being clever if you can be pretty,' Pushkin advised the young women of Kishinev.[40]

In such circumstances it was not surprising that the 'art' which was valued in women was above all conversation, which was to be of an entertaining, even risqué, but not at all learned or self-aggrandizing, kind. Vyazemsky categorized the skills of a society hostess in the following words, linking them with the intrinsic qualities of the female mind:

It is hard to positively quantify the female mind. The mind of a woman is often limited by its responsiveness to others; but that, too, is the source of its strength and power. The female mind is hospitable: it is quick to summon and welcome clever guests, and soon they are being put at their ease in the most solicitous and practised manner; even so does a perspicacious and experienced hostess behave, making no show before her guests, not fussing round them or imposing on them, but keeping just out of sight, as it were, so that they may have the maximum of space and freedom.[41]

Women who did not conform to this ideal faced a social opprobrium

[38] A thorough study of 'album culture's' formulae is L. N. Petina's doctoral dissertation: see her published abstract, *Khudozhestvennaya priroda literaturnogo al'boma 1-i poloviny XIX veka. Avtoreferat dissertatsii na soiskanie stepeni kandidata filologicheskikh nauk* (Tartu, 1988). Exemplary poems addressed by men to men are Pushkin, 'K Yazykovu', *PSS* ii. 172–3; 'Chaadaevu', *PSS* ii. 195; Baratynsky, 'N. I. Gnedichu', *Polnoe sobranie stikhotvorenii* (Leningrad, 1957), 93–5; Del'vig, 'Druz'ya: idilliya', *Sochineniya* (Leningrad, 1986), 58–60; cf. also Davydov's tribute to male company as against the hypocrisy and 'fat bellies squeezed into corsets' of mixed society: 'Gusarskaya ispoved'', *Stikhotvoreniya* (Leningrad, 1984), 101–2. On male bonding cf. also the brief observations in Sandler, *Distant Pleasures* (n. 6 to ch. 4), and Simon Karlinsky, *The Sexual Labyrinth of Nikolai Gogol* (Berkeley, Calif., 1976).

[39] On coquetry see e.g. Baratynsky's essay 'Istoriya koketstva' (1825), *Polnoe sobranie sochinenii* (2 vols.; Petrograd, 1915), ii. 204–7. Sofya Ponomareva and her circle are extensively discussed in V. E. Vatsuro, *SDP: iz istorii literaturnogo byta Pushkinskoi pory* (Moscow, 1989).

[40] Pushkin, 'Razzevavshis' ot obedni' (1821), *PSS* ii. 80–1. Conversely, various epigrams satirized empty-headed beauties: see e.g. M. I. Gippel'son and K. A. Kumpan (eds.), *Russkaya epigramma* (Leningrad, 1988), no. 234 (Khvostov, 1823), no. 399 (V. L. Pushkin, 1821)—though satire of this second kind has in fact a long prehistory, being manifested also by e.g. Knyazhnin's 'Ispovedovanie Zhemanikhi', *Izbrannye proizvedeniya*, 646–8.

[41] P. D. Vyazemsky, *Staraya zapisnaya kniga* (Leningrad, 1929), 217. A similar compliment to the receptive intelligence of women is paid by Pushkin, who writes in his 'Table Talk', dating from the 1830s, of their 'quickness of grasp and subtlety of feelings and intelligence' *PSS* viii. 67.

which was voiced more strongly than it had been in the eighteenth century. And writers were necessarily numbered amongst the non-conformists, offending not only by undue displays of intellect, but also by pretension to the 'masculine' world of politics and letters. The rules of polite exchange in mixed company might dictate that the poetic efforts sent by ladies to well-known poets received judiciously flattering responses; in private, or in the all-male company where opinion was really formed, these poets expressed overt contempt for female poetic ambitions.[42]

The change in women's status, from the relative tolerance they had enjoyed in 'reactionary' days, to the intolerance which was now their lot in 'radical' circles, resembles the shift in opinion described by Madame de Staël, who had given the following warning in her essay, 'Women who practise the art of letters': 'In monarchies women of letters have ridicule to fear; in the republics they must fear hatred.'[43] And, like the French women whom Staël had described, the women who appeared in the purview of the imagined republic of Russian letters could do no right, being caught between accusations of frivolity on the one hand, pedantry on the other. Small wonder that the early Romantic movement produced no woman poet whose output was anything like so wide-ranging and original as that of Bunina, Kulman, or even Urusova; nor were any women poets of the day sustained by the idea of female ancestors; nor did the sense of women's readership play much part in their writing.[44]

Circumstances altered little in the second phase of Romanticism, during which the political opposition withdrew into literature, and social engagement began to be supplemented by speculation on the poet's social role. The association of poetry with prophecy, and of creativity with an extraordinary state of inspiration, left in place the assumption that the poet must be masculine. Masculinity had previously been represented as necessary to the creation of poetry in a social sense; it now became something understood to be necessary in a mystical sense. In 1821 Pushkin had represented poetry as a private, playfully flirtatious encounter with the Muse. In two important poems written in 1826 and

---

[42] Aleksandra Fuks, a minor poet of the 1830s, was famously described by Pushkin as 'a certain bluestocking, a 40-year-old, intolerable hag with tallow-coloured teeth and filthy fingernails' (letter to his wife, 12 Sept. 1833: *PSS* x. 347; the immediately preceding letter is a flattering missive to Fuks herself). Baratynsky's honorific poem of 1832 to the same lady ('A. Fuksovoi'), contrasts with a private letter in which he complains of having to answer an 'epistle in bad verse sent to me by a lady of mature years with only imaginary claims to beauty' (*Polnoe sobranie stikhotvorenii*, 157, 364).

[43] Madame de Staël, *De la littérature considerée dans ses rapports avec les institutions sociales* (1800), ed. Paul Van Tieghem (2 vols.; Geneva, 1959), ii. 333.

[44] A representative selection of women's poetry from the early 1820s is available in V. V. Uchenova (ed.), *Tsaritsy muz: russkie poetessy XIX–nachala XX vekov* (Moscow, 1989): see the work by Volkonskaya, pp. 38–40, Timasheva, pp. 42–3, Gotovtseva, pp. 45–7.

1827, by contrast, he presents the poet's role as a 'priestly' one, prophecy and communication with the divine.[45] The sense that prophetic genius was proper to men emerges particularly clearly from a poem by Khomyakov, addressed to Zinaida Volkonskaya. On reading its first lines, any reader who has encountered the notion of the 'eternal feminine' assumes that the portrait of the Sibyl in the first half of Khomyakov's piece can only be meant as a compliment to Volkonskaya. But the second half of the poem makes it clear that this female prophet has in fact been evoked as a metaphor for the 'masculine' sphere of inspiration, a sphere from which Volkonskaya is to be excluded:

Кто, видя впалые ланиты,
И взор без блеска и лучей,
Узнал бы тайну силы скрытой
В пророчице грядущих дней?
И ты не призывай поэта!
В волшебный круг свой не мани!
Когда вдали от шума света
Душа восторгами согрета,
Тогда живет он.[46]

Who, seeing then her sunken lids,
The gaze without light or radiance,
Would guess the secret of the hidden power
In this prophetess of future days!
Neither should you provoke the poet,
Tempting him to your magic circle!
When, far from the racket of the world
His soul is warmed by ecstasy,
Then he may live.

The conviction that masculinity and writing were associated had not been declared so insistently in Russian culture before. Why should they have been now? The term *pero* (literally 'quill') is not a term so ripe for punning significance as its English equivalent 'pen', but some primary sexual association cannot be excluded. So much emerges, at any rate, from the saying 'the pen writes, the paper suffers [the pen to write on it, to be written on]'.[47] It is not anachronistic to attribute such associations to the Romantic generation: in a letter of 1824, for example, Pushkin was to utter the memorable dictum, 'When I'm in love, I write elegies in the way another man might rub his [prick] on the mattress', and the 1820s and 1830s were to see an increasing emphasis on the puissance and

[45] Pushkin, 'Muza', *PSS* ii. 26; 'Prorok', *PSS* ii. 304; 'Poet', *PSS* iii. 23.
[46] B. Murav'ev (ed.), *V tsarstve muz* (Moscow, 1987), 27.
[47] On *pero* see V. Dal', *Tolkovyi slovar' velikorusskogo yazyka* (4 vols.; Moscow, 1882), iii. 101.

vigour of 'the manly pen'.[48] Such metaphors were important, however, not for their own sake, but because the second-generation Romantics, in asserting the social and public value of writing as the mouthpiece of oppositional views, also needed to assert writing as a suitable full-time professional activity for gentlemen. The writer had to be made to appear as 'masculine' as the heroes of the Napoleonic War or the colonizers of the Caucasus, and far more so than a civil servant or a courtier. In a secondary and supporting manœuvre, writing, which was an activity carried out in the domestic sphere, had to be distinguished from those activities which were the responsibility of women in the domestic sphere. And so women's writing is lambasted as mere 'embroidery', whilst the male poet's act of writing is often represented as a withdrawal from the mixed society of the ballroom into a private space which is not only solitary, but gender-defined: the library or study (*kabinet*).[49]

The assertion of inspiration as a masculine phenomenon was accompanied by a growing insistence that women were inherently incapable of the effort of imagination involved in the composition of poetry. The young Belinsky, for example, stated the accepted formula in the following words:

The point is that man is by his very nature more universal than woman, being endowed with an ability to detach himself from his individual personality and transfer himself to many different situations, ones which he not only has not experienced, but never could experience; whilst woman is locked up in herself, in her female and feminine sphere, and if she leaves it, becomes some sort of ambiguous creature. This is why no woman can become a great poet.[50]

Belinsky's formulation implies a connection between 'imagination' and innate sexual characteristics, suggesting that departure from feminine norms will unsex the woman. In a leadenly satirical story of 1837, 'Lady Authoresses', the minor prose writer Verevkin had been much more direct, referring to an early eighteenth-century German gynaecologist as his authority for the assertion that the composition of poetry was

---

[48] Pushkin, letter to A. A. Bestuzhev, 29 June 1824, *PSS* x. 75; on 'manliness' and writing, see also B. A. Uspensky, *Iz istorii russkogo literaturnogo yazyka XVIII–nachala XIX veka: yazykovaya programma Karamzina i ee istoricheskie korni* (Moscow, 1985), 57–60.

[49] The association between masculine culture and the *kabinet* is represented in e.g. *Evgeny Onegin*, ch. 7, 18–22, which describes Tatiana's visit to Evgeny's study; a cancelled variant also had her reading his private album whilst there. (See Pushkin, *PSS* v. 128–9, 453–6, and Vladimir Nabokov's commentary to *Eugene Onegin* (4 vols.; rev. edn.; Princeton, NJ, 1975), iii. 99–102.) See also Vyazemsky, 'Biblioteka'. A link between inspiration and the masculine *déshabillé* of the dressing-gown is made in two famous portraits of Pushkin, by Vasily Tropinin and Orest Kiprensky, done in the late 1820s.

[50] Belinsky, '*Povesti* M. Zhukovoi' (1840), *PSS* iv. 115.

incompatible with the female biology of reproduction, and insisting that women's task was to *be* beauty, not to create it.[51]

The new essentialism left critics and cultural commentators with an obvious problem: how to explain those women who had written poetry, and those who were still writing it? The obvious solution was to accept that what women did was writing, but deny that it was poetry. The early poems of Elizaveta Shakhova were described by Belinsky as 'prose'; in his review of Elisaveta Kulman's *Poetic Experiments*, he reduces the poet to the status of spectator rather than actor, or indeed reader rather than writer, saying that 'an appreciation of beauty is not sufficient to ensure the creation of beauty'.[52] Other critics were more indulgent, but there were no suggestions that Kulman had been moved by real genius or genuine inspiration, and her work was forgotten within a decade. (In Germany, by contrast, Kulman's poetry ran into many editions, each prefaced by an introduction in which the poet's tutor described the development of this prodigy in the terms, and at the length, of a *Künstlerroman*.)[53]

For those women ambitious to be considered geniuses in Russia, one option was to adopt a male persona; this was the strategy employed in some early poems by the only post-Romantic woman poet to express an unwavering conviction of her own genius, Karolina Pavlova.[54] But in such cases opprobrium was likely to be earned for 'unwomanliness', unless work was published under a male pseudonym—a strategy not in fact adopted by women poets. Few of Pavlova's contemporaries were so bold as she. One of them, Nadezhda Teplova, could only imagine putting on the 'wings' of poetic inspiration after her own death ('Rebirth', 1835). And in another lyric, 'Advice', she offered the following caution to a young woman poet: rather than aspiring to the lyre of Apollo, she was to adopt modest and mundane ways of recording her thoughts:

> Брось лиру, брось, и больше не играй,
> И вдохновенные, прекрасные напевы

---

[51] N. N. Verevkin ('Rakhmannyi'), 'Zhenshchina-pisatel'nitsa', *Biblioteka dlya chteniya*, 23/1 (1837), 19–134. A would-be comic account of the pretentious Varvara, or 'Var'eta's', attempts to make herself a career in writing, this piece is at the same time, so far as I know, the first Russian attempt to invoke scientific or pseudo-scientific material in order to link women's psychology with their physiology.

[52] Belinsky, '*Piiticheskie opyty* Elisavety Kul'man' (1841), *PSS* iv. 571.

[53] On the reception of Kul'man in Russia, see G. I. Ganzburg, 'K istorii izdaniya i vospriyatiya sochinenii El. Kul'man', *Russkaya literatura* (1990), 1: 148–55, which points out that her work was set by Schumann; the German version of her works, Elisabeth Kullmann, *Sämmtliche Gedichte*, ed. K. F. von Grossheinrich (Leipzig, 1841), had already gone into a 3rd edn. by 1844; it had an introduction of over 100 pages describing the evolution of Kul'man's imaginative gifts.

[54] On Pavlova, see Ch. 3 below.

Ты в глубине души заботливо скрывай:
Поэзия—опасный дар для девы!

. . . .

Что девственно очувствовала ты,
Что думою осмыслила глубоко,
Брось изредка украдкой на листы,—
Да не убьет завистливое око
Твоей возвышенной мечты.[55]

Cast down, cast down the lyre, and play no more!
Conceal the notes of beauteous inspiration
Deep in your soul, take care, take care!
The gift of poetry is dangerous for maidens!

. . . .

The maiden feelings you have had,
The meditations you have made,
Set down on paper secretly,
And let no eye with envious gleam
Murder your elevated dream.

Teplova's advice was sound; pretensions to inspiration might well be received with annihilating scorn. Considerably more warmth was, however, likely to greet those women whose poetry could be seen as 'feelings set down on paper', or the material of prose in verse form. A satirical poem attributed to Pushkin, and published in 1838 in the journal which he had edited, *Sovremennik*, complimented a certain woman poet (unusually, the term *zhenshchina-poet*, rather than the preferred *poetessa*, poetess, is in fact adopted) for having achieved 'only a line of poetry, but so much prose!'[56] Ivan Kireevsky was to speak in more elegantly flattering terms of women's poetry as 'genuinely poetic moments from the lives of a few women of talent [. . .] so gracefully, so charmingly reflected in the mirror of their verses'.[57]

Kireevsky's phrase 'moments from the lives' is clear enough: like prose writers, women poets were supposed to describe what they had experienced, or rather, what they might have been supposed to experience. But the qualifiers, 'charmingly' and 'genuinely poetic' are also indicative:

---

[55] Teplova, 'Pererozhdenie', L. Ya. Ginzburg and V. E. Vatsuro (eds.), *Poety 1820–1830 godov* (2 vols.; Leningrad, 1972), i. 585; 'Sovet', ibid. i. 588.

[56] 'A. Pushkin', 'K zhenshchine-poetu', *Sovremennik*, 10 (1838), 177. This poem is a parodistic variant of the lyric 'K. A. Timashevoi' (1826) in Pushkin, *PSS* ii. 307. Belinsky's review of Kul'man also speaks of 'prosaic' verse, to similarly ironic effect.

[57] I. Kireevsky, 'Russkie pisatel'nitsy', *Polnoe sobranie sochinenii v 2 tomakh* (Moscow, 1911), ii. 68.

women poets must select material from their lives. The love lyric was the genre most likely to satisfy this proscriptive code, and it did indeed become the central mode of composition for many women poets of the post-Romantic generations. Perhaps the most significant among them was Yuliya Zhadovskaya, who referred to the process of writing poetry as 'an escape from grief through dreaming'.[58] But it *is* in fact grief, in the form of melancholy love, with all its attendant rites of passage such as meetings, partings, letters to the beloved, and meditations in solitude, which is the main theme of her poems.

The formulation 'prose in verse' was frequently understood in a narrow sense: women produced verses of little artistic ambition, reflecting different aspects of the expected life-cycle of ladies at the date. But from the beginning of the 1840s an alternative interpretation began to be available. 'Prose' was now increasingly used as a term of approbation, since this was held to be the medium most suited to the representation of social issues.[59] The new 'utilitarian' ethos demanded that the language of poetry should be transparent, as the language of prose was transparent. Colloquial lexical forms and intonations were now preferred to the elevated poeticisms of the past; and, as M. L. Gasparov has shown, there was an increasing emphasis on the need for metrics to be 'unnoticeable'. What this in practice dictated was a deliberate suppression of metrical inventiveness, and a selection of forms adapted from folk poetry, or drawn from the standard repertoire of literate poetry. Virtuosity was now regarded with disfavour; employment of the most obvious Russian metrical form, the four-line stanza of alternate rhyme in four-foot iambs, would attract the highest reward from a utilitarian critic, that of being passed over in silence.[60]

The direct result of this emphasis on poetry as a vehicle for social commitment was the development, after 1840, of a new tradition of politically committed verse by women radicals. Poets such as Anna Barykova followed the leading male radical poet, Nikolai Nekrasov, in their high-pathetic depictions of topics from popular life.[61] An alternative direction was the adaptation of confessional lyric to the delineation of political struggles. Nadezhda Khvoshchinskaya, later to be a successful prose writer, used her poetry in order to declare her commitment to 'hard

[58] Yuliya Zhadovskaya, *Stikhotvoreniya* (St Petersburg, 1858), 39. An important contemporary review of Zhadovskaya's work is A. M. Skabichevsky, 'Pesnya o zhenskoi nevole' (1858), *Sochineniya* (3 vols.; St Petersburg, 1903), ii. 230–47.

[59] See e.g. Belinsky, 'Literatura 1842 goda'; quoted in Gasparov, *Ocherk istorii russkogo stikha*, 161; see n. 60 below.

[60] M. L. Gasparov, *Ocherk istorii russkogo stikha* (Moscow, 1984), 161–2.

[61] A selection of Anna Barykova's lyrics is available in Uchenova (ed.), *Tsaritsy muz*, 167–72.

labour', and to assert that 'the word' should be devoted to making political opponents recognize their own ugliness.[62]

But the breakdown of Romantic consensus also had other, more unexpected, consequences. As the poetry of inspiration began to be seen as 'marginal', it became a genre which could more readily be appropriated by those whose gender automatically made them marginal to literary life. The greatest woman poet of the nineteenth century, Karolina Pavlova, was to be a beneficiary of this contradiction: her poetry generated hostility because of its Romanticism, not solely because she was a woman; she could therefore enjoy a sense of the community of poets denied to her immediate predecessors, such as Teplova. In the separate chapter devoted to Pavlova, I shall give a detailed analysis of the transition which this change in cultural circumstances brought about in her work.

Most of Pavlova's contemporaries amongst women poets remained more reticent; indeed, Pavlova's literary rival, Evdokiya Rostopchina, exploited the idea of a modest and unassertive 'women's poetry' as a manipulative gesture in their bitter poetic disputations.[63] But if the new status of Romanticism did not in itself necessarily affect women poets, many were affected by the new status of prose. The formulation 'prose in verse' now no longer seemed so disparaging, because prose was now the central literary mode; but women poets who chose to continue writing verse, rather than simply moving into prose, had to justify their choice in some way, and hence to explore the conditions of their position as women poets. If on the one hand women poets graduated towards the language and techniques of prose in representing their interior worlds, on the other, their uncertainties about the place of poetry in an abstract sense now made them self-conscious in the sense of self-analytical, rather than in the sense of hesitant about or embarrassed by their writing.

The glimmerings of self-consciousness are evident even in Zhadovskaya, whose love lyrics, thematically banal though they are, employ a studiedly 'prosaic' diction, hover between a first- and third-person mode, and employ such 'novelistic' devices as a direct commentary to the reader.[64] Another 'prosaic' poet of note is Elizaveta Shakhova, a former child prodigy, who later became an Orthodox nun. Her poem 'Autobiography from a Wilderness' is a memoir in verse which describes her retreat

---

[62] Nadezhda Khvoshchinskaya, 'Slovo', B. Ya. Bukhshtab (ed.), *Poety 1840–1850 godov* (Leningrad, 1972), 268–9.

[63] Evdokiya Rostopchina, 'Pesnya po povodu perepiski uchenogo muzha s ne menee uchenoi zhenoyu', in her *Stikhotvoreniya, proza, pis'ma* (Moscow, 1986), 372–3; Rostopchina speaks of Pavlova 'translating from Finnish into Sanscrit', and calls her 'a Corinna, a bluestocking'.

[64] See especially Zhadovskaya, 'Dve sestry' and 'Poseshchenie', *Stikhotvoreniya*, 15, 135; and cf. Mary Zirin, 'Iuliia Zhadovskaia' in *ECWR*.

from life in the world, but expresses a determination to continue composing poetry in despite of the hostile aesthetic values of her time. Shakhova manifests an ambiguous relation towards the received vocabulary of inspiration, which she both employs and rejects; she moves from a depiction of herself as an 'inspired' poet in worldly life, applying to this a public 'poetic' vocabulary, to a new 'internal' tradition beyond such formulae; her perspective vacillates between emotional histrionics and a concrete appreciation of her surroundings.[65]

Both Zhadovskaya and Shakhova are poets whose work is more interesting in terms of ambition than of execution. A poet who more successfully explored the contradictions of 'prose in verse' was Pavlova's enemy Rostopchina. Rostopchina's emphasis on the 'prosaic' character of her work, though outwardly the sign of an appropriate modesty, could on occasion conceal a clever and ironic manipulation of stereotypes. Her lyrics are presented as the thoughts of an imaginary heroine who moves, like her counterparts in prose, between the public social world, and the private world of feeling. But this is no simple contrast between outward pretence and inward sincerity. One poem refers to the adoption of costume as an important part of the ritual of transition to the public world. Rostopchina's heroine puts on the costume of an Albanian in order to attend a masked ball, a gesture which evokes Romantic narratives of escape to worlds of colourful exoticism. But the attempt to elude the constraints of public life, 'the urban woman's prison', is itself dependent on donning a mask manufactured for the appearance in public. The 'pretence' of society can be escaped only by a further pretence:

> Под красной фескою албанки
> Когда б забыть могла я вдруг
> Бал, светский шум, плен горожанки,
> Молву и тесный жизни круг![66]

> In the scarlet fez of an Albanian woman
> If only I might at once forget
> The ball, the worldly din, the malicious chat,
> The urban woman's prison, this cramping way of life!

---

[65] Elizaveta Shakhova, 'Avtobiograficheskii otzyv iz glushi', *Sobranie sochinenii v stikakh* (3 vols.; St Petersburg, 1911), ii. 117–19. (See also 'Autobiographical Response from a Provincial Wasteland' in *Anthology*.) Shakhova was an extremely prolific poet, the author of verse epics and a play in rhyming verse, *Yudif* (1876), as well as of much religious verse, some in the form of epistles to her confessors; she is of interest as a forerunner of the prolific tradition of religious writing by Russian women in the 20th c. For an informative, if distinctly patronizing, assessment see A. Beletsky, 'Turgenev i russkie pisatel'nitsy 30–60 godov', in Nikolai L. Brodsky (ed.), *Tvorcheskii put' Turgeneva* (Petrograd, 1923), 135–66.

[66] Rostopchina, *Stikhotvoreniya*, 59.

Another lyric, 'The Unfinished Sewing', deals with a different form of costuming the self. Emotional experience becomes the stuff not only of contemplation but also of transformation: the embroidered cloth at which the speaker sits stands not only for the remembered love-affair itself, but also for the process of remembering it. And in her cycle 'An Unknown Romance', Rostopchina distances herself from the love lyric by a highly original adaptation to poetry of a structural device current in prose of the period. The piece is a frame narrative beginning with a prose preface in which the (male) publisher introduces the poetry that follows as material discovered after the death of a provincial young lady, to the surprise of all her acquaintance. The conventional rituals of unhappy love are here presented in the context of a psychological case-study.[67] Though Rostopchina's contemporaries, with the exception of Chernyshevsky, failed to note any element of self-consciousness, identifying heroine and writer unquestioningly, her poetry is an interesting illustration of the new possibilities of 'prose in verse'.[68]

The end of the 1860s saw a decline in the fortunes of women's poetry, which were not to be revived again until the end of the century. But in the 1840s, 1850s, and early 1860s women's poetry in Russia (unlike women's poetry in England) could hold its own with prose. So far, the reasons behind this situation have been traced to the ambiguous status of poetry. But they should also be sought in the limitations of the prose tradition itself, which, as we shall see, suffered from being deemed suitable for women in certain ways, as poetry had gained from being considered unsuitable in most ways.

The Cult of Sensibility and Women's Prose before 1820

As my last remarks about 'prose in verse' suggest, the division between 'prose' and 'poetry' made here is to some extent artificial. The Romantics sometimes expressed hostility to the 'womanish' strands of prose, as they had to the feminine voice in poetry. The highest term of approbation by which Romantic and post-Romantic critics might commend the writing

---

[67] 'Nedokonchennoe shit'e', ibid. 114–15 (see also 'The Unfinished Sewing' in *Anthology*); 'Neizvestnyi roman', ibid. 172–201.

[68] On Rostopchina see N. G. Chernyshevsky, '*Stikhotvoreniya Grafini Rostopchinoi*' (1856), *Polnoe sobranie sochinenii* (15 vols. and 1 supp. vol.; Moscow, 1939–53), iii. 453–68, which takes issue with Belinsky's more simple-minded appraisal. More recent commentators, such as V. Khodasevich, 'Grafinya E. P. Rostopchina', *Stat'i o russkoi poezii* (Petrograd, 1922), 7–42, and Helena Goscilo, 'Evdokiia Rostopchina', *ECWR*, have also condemned Rostopchina for 'banality', and it is only fair to say that the world of her fictional heroine is never created with the linguistic originality which characterizes the early work of her infinitely more talented successor, Anna Akhmatova.

of a woman was to say that it manifested 'a firm manly hand'. Particularly warm praise was to be accorded to the prose memoirs of 'Aleksandrov', the pseudonym of Nadezhda Durova, whose literary existence as a man reflected her adoption of men's clothes and a manly role, as a cavalry officer, in life.[69] At the end of the 1820s, however, when the Russian literary establishment began turning to prose in large numbers, the genre was customarily opposed, in its 'humble' or everyday character, and in its moderate ambitions, to the visionary aims of poetry.[70] There was therefore no reason why the 'humble' concerns of women prose writers should not have formed part of its material. And indeed, the prose writing of women was generally received with more condescension than their poetry.

The association of women and prose writing was, as we have seen, to acquire a particular importance with Romanticism, but in fact it long pre-dated Romanticism. If the existence of women's poetry anticipated the evolution of systematic theories of 'the woman writer', the composition of prose fiction by Russian women followed on, and up to a point even developed out of, theory about women's place in literature. And there is greater continuity between this early tradition, underdeveloped as it was, and later tradition, than there is between women's poetry before and after 1820. The efforts of Pushkin's generation put an end to the loose and confused attitudes to poetry from which earlier women poets had occasionally benefited; the rise of prose in the 1830s, and especially the 1840s, was to reinforce certain proscriptive notions which had already been current in the late eighteenth and early nineteenth centuries.

Before we consider the development of the public tradition of women's prose, the composition of fiction, the importance of another, private tradition of women's prose writing should be noted. Before they began writing tales or novels, Russian women worked in the non-fictional genres of letter, diary, and memoir. It is these genres, and most particularly the memoir, which represent the most interesting direction of eighteenth-century women's prose for a modern reader. Two notable, and famous, early woman memoirists were Catherine II, and her courtier and adjutant in cultural matters, Princess Dashkova, whose life-stories display an attractive intellectual and sexual self-confidence. Both women were writers with a gift for barbed psychologicial encapsulation, who were able to describe the paranoic manipulations of court politics

[69] On the 'manly hand' of Aleksandrov, see Belinsky's review, *PSS* iii. 149. The note to the first translation into Russian of *Jane Eyre*, in similar vein, cites English rumours that the novel was the work of Thackeray's governess, and implies that Thackeray himself may have had a hand in the book, saying that 'many people quite justifiably suspect that a pen by no means of the feminine kind may have participated here': see editor's note to 'Dzhenni [*sic*] Eir', *OZ* 64 (1849), 175.

[70] On prose's 'modest' aims, see e.g. Pushkin, *Evgeny Onegin*, ch. 7 v. 43: *PSS* v. 118.

without any of the petty vindictiveness, excessive recall for detail, or verbosity which so often characterize the political memoirist. Their accounts have an immediacy whose origins may be defensive (it obviates the need for the detached moral commentary that might be expected to come with hindsight) but which certainly maintains narrative interest.[71]

For a variety of reasons, though, these fascinating documents were to have very little effect on the writerly tradition of their day, or on later writerly tradition. Publication history played some part in this. Catherine's memoirs, which were composed in French, as a private chronicle for the edification of her grandson, were not published until the 1850s—and then only abroad—though they had been circulating in manuscript prior to that.[72] Dashkova's memoirs also appeared a considerable time after their composition, in an English translation from the French original.[73] They could not, therefore, act as an inspiration to other women writers at the turn of the eighteenth and nineteenth centuries.

Even had the memoirs appeared in the late eighteenth or nineteenth centuries, it is doubtful how wide-reaching their effect could have been. It was mentioned earlier that even Pushkin's contemporaries, members of a generation not noted for its sexual prudery, had expressed disapproval at the lewd behaviour of women at the Empress's court; their censoriousness was reflected and intensified in the comments of Herzen, editor of the 1859 edition of Catherine's memoirs.[74] Any woman writer who had modelled herself on the authorial manner of Dashkova or Catherine, even (or perhaps especially) in works intended for a narrow family audience, would have courted opprobrium.

A memoir which *was* more to the taste of later generations was that written by Princess Natalya Dolgorukova in 1767, and published nearly fifty years later, in 1810. Dolgorukova, who came from one of the most powerful aristocratic families in Russia, followed her husband into exile after he was disgraced on the accession of the Empress Elizabeth, and her

[71] Ekaterina II, *Zapiski* (St Petersburg, 1907); the original French is available as *Mémoires de Cathérine II; écrits par elle-même*, ed. Dom. Maroger (Paris, 1953), and an Engl. trans. as *Memoirs of Catherine the Great*, ed. D. Maroger, trans. Moura Budberg (London, 1955); E. R. Dashkova, *Zapiski*, in G. N. Moiseeva (ed.), *Zapiski i vospominaniya russkikh zhenshchin XVIII–pervoi poloviny XIX veka* (Moscow, 1990), 67–281. On these and other memoirs by women, see also Barbara Heldt, *Terrible Perfection: Women and Russian Literature* (Bloomington, Ind., 1987), 64–102; on Dashkova, see A. Woronzoff-Dashkoff, 'Disguise and Gender in Princess Dashkova's Memoirs', *Canadian Slavonic Papers*, 33/1 (1991), 62–74.

[72] The first Russian edn. was *Zapiski*, ed. A. Herzen (London, 1859). On the text's history see p. v. On pre-publication readership, see for example an entry in Pushkin's diary for Jan. 1835: 'The Grand Duchess has borrowed Catherine II's *Memoirs* from me and has gone quite off her head about them' (*PSS* viii. 46).

[73] Composed in French between about 1804 and 1806, Dashkova's memoirs were first published in English, as *Memoirs of the Princess Dashkaw, Lady of Honour to Catherine II*, ed. W. Bradford (2 vols.; London, 1840).

[74] Herzen in Ekaterina II, *Zapiski*, p. vi.

memoirs describe the privations and terrors of their journey into Siberia. Though written in an appealingly conversational idiom quite free of the officialese found in some mid-eighteenth-century Russian prose, Dolgorukova's memoirs are far less lively and incisive than those of Catherine or Dashkova, but they were to have enormous resonance for later generations. Fifteen years after the first publication of the memoirs of this devoted wife, those Decembrist conspirators who were not executed (by far the majority) were to be followed into Siberian exile by their wives. For later generations, the link was obvious: Dolgorukova now seemed the ancestor of a long line of women who had provided staunch and self-abnegating support to a husband in time of political persecution, and who were obvious and appealing counter-images to the central official metaphor of wifely virtue, the Tsar's consort.[75]

The only memoirist of the early nineteenth century who dared to portray herself in an active professional existence was Nadezhda Durova; and in Durova, again, we see the representation of a female existence which was extraordinary, even freakish, to her readers. As she herself had put on male dress to avoid a stifling domestic life in the provinces, so her memoirs achieved a 'masculine' social range by discarding domestic and family concerns. Where Catherine and Dashkova had been able to reflect public and private worlds with relative impartiality, their successors were faced with a choice between the 'womanly' interior world and the 'masculine' outer world. Most of them, save Durova, opted for the former. And whilst these 'womanly' memoirs occasionally provide intriguing glimpses of the domesticity spurned by the women who wrote fiction, their main concern is usually the celebration of famous husbands, fathers, brothers, or friends.[76]

---

[75] Natalya Dolgorukova, *Sobstvennoruchnye zapiski*, in Moiseeva (ed.), *Zapiski i vospominaniya*, 41–66; English edn. available as *The Memoirs of Princess Natal'ja Borisovna Dolgorukaja*, ed. and trans. Charles Townsend (Columbus, Ohio, 1977). Very close in content and tone is the memoir written by Princess Mariya Volkonskaya, wife of one of the Decembrist leaders: *Zapiski*, ed. M. S. Volkonsky (St Petersburg, 1904) (parallel Russian and original French text). On the Tsaritsas, see e.g. Urusova's flattering poem, 'Ee Velichestvu Gosudaryne Marii Feodorovne', *Syn otechestva*, 24 (1815), 56. The canonical treatment of the Decembrist wives for later generations was to be Nekrasov's narrative poem *Russian Women* (1872): see his *Polnoe sobranie sochinenii v 15 tomakh* (Moscow, 1981–), iv. 123–86.

[76] Nadezhda Durova, *Devushka-kavalerist: proisshestvie v Rossii* (1836; repr. Leningrad, 1985); abridged edn., suppl. by other autobiographical frags. available in *Izbrannoe* (Moscow, 1984); there is also an excellent English edn.: *The Cavalry Maiden*, trans. and ann. Mary Fleming Zirin (London, 1990). Durova concealed, for example, the fact that she had been married and had a child before setting out on her military campaign. (See Mary Zirin in *The Cavalry Maiden*, pp. xix–xx.) 'Womanly' memoirs include those of E. Ya. Yan'kova, *Rasskazy babushki: iz vospominanii pyati pokolenii, zapisannye ee vnukom D. Blagovo* (1877), ed. T. I. Oriatskaya (Leningrad, 1989); Aleksandra Shchepkina, *Vospominaniya* (Sergiev Posad, 1915); Elena Khvoshchinskaya (Golitsyna), 'Vospominaniya', *Russkaya starina*, 89–91 (1897), 93–5 (1898); a representative selection of such material is also available in Moiseeva (ed.), *Zapiski i vospominaniya*.

If even the private tradition of the memoir could stress a genteel and rarified notion of the 'feminine', this notion was, logically enough, still more dominant in the public tradition of prose fiction. For a modern reader, perhaps the most interesting eighteenth-century representation of a woman is to be found in Mikhail Chulkov's entertaining picaresque novel *The Comely Cook* (1770).[77] This is the first-person history of a woman who recalls a Russian Moll Flanders in her frank depiction of a life lived by shrewd exploitation of opportunity, often of a directly sexual kind. But the robust vitality of this woman of the lower classes could hardly act as a model for the aristocratic lady or women of the gentry who alone had the education to attempt authorship in Russia. It was another fictional direction, Sentimentalism, which was to foster the development of women's prose writing.

Sentimentalism, or as it might less anachronistically be termed, the literature of sensibility (*chuvstvitel'nost'*), developed in Russia later than it did in the West, and arose directly out of an imitation of Western models.[78] Much of the philosophical and political sophistication of the Western movement was lacking in the Russian literature of sensibility, but one important idea which did make the transition was the idealization of women. Its first important effect, chronologically speaking, was the appearance of a new kind of heroine, one often more sensitive than her male counterpart. The most famous texts depicting such heroines were Nikolai Karamzin's *Poor Liza* (1792) and Pavel Lvov's *A Russian Pamela, or the History of Mariya, the Fair Village Maid* (1789).[79] However, considerably earlier than this, two Russian women had produced short stories in which heroines of the new type appeared. Anna Neelova's *Leinard and Termilia* (1784) was a conventional enough tale depicting the vicissitudes endured by two sentimental lovers.[80] But in

[77] M. D. Chulkov, *Prigozhaya povarikha* (1770), in his *Peresmeshnik* (Moscow, 1987), 260–325.

[78] 'Sentimentalizm', like the English 'sentimentalism', is a term whose origins go back to late 19th-c. literary history. It is not listed in 18th-c. dictionaries, such as Zhdanov and Heym (see n. 25 above), which do, however, record 'chuvstvitel'nost'', or 'sensibility'. The definitive history of sensibility in Russia still remains to be written, having been hindered to date by the use of 'sentimentalizm' as a term of abuse. Even apparently well-informed sources such as Lidiya Ginzburg's *O psikhologicheskoi proze* (Leningrad, 1977; Engl. edn. as *On Psychological Prose*, trans. Judson Rosengrant, Princeton, NJ, 1991), reduce the ideological apparatus of the movement to the celebration of emotion at all costs, and its aesthetic function to a phase of jejune experiment inevitably and naturally succeeded by the development of 'adult' realism. Hammarberg, *From the Idyll*, gives a broader and subtler treatment centred around narrative modes, but the sweep of the European movement is better gauged from such Western sources as the opening chapters by Marilyn Butler's *Jane Austen*, and Janet Todd, *Sensibility: An Introduction* (London, 1986).

[79] N. Karamzin, *Bednaya Liza* (Moscow, 1796); P. L'vov, *Rossiiskaya Pamela, ili Istoriya Marii, dobrodetel'noi poselyanki* (2 vols.; St Petersburg, 1789).

[80] Anna Neelova ('Devitsa N. N.'), *Leinard i Termilia, ili pokhozhdeniya dvukh lyubovnikov* (St Petersburg, 1784); see V. V. Sipovsky, *Ocherki istorii russkogo romana* (2 vols.; St Petersburg, 1909), i. 681.

1779 an anonymous 'Russian Lady' had published a rather more interesting piece, 'The Faithful Wife', which portrayed the trials of a virtuous woman. Her husband and children are kidnapped by bandits; a happy reunion eventually ensues, but before it does, the wife has various significant experiences. She is turned out of the house by her wicked brother-in-law, and is reduced to a despair so great that she repeatedly attempts suicide.[81]

For all its sketchiness, and its naïvety in literary terms, 'The Faithful Wife' is an interesting early example of how a Russian woman writer marks out territory. Lvov and Karamzin's heroines were to be from the peasantry; the 'Russian Lady' indicates how frail is the social position even of a woman from the country gentry. Where her male contemporaries had adopted a class-based perspective (the seduction as metaphor for social exploitation), she has a gender-based perspective (the loss of a husband as metaphor for women's lack of independent status). The narrative structure makes still clearer the 'Lady's' interest in relations between the sexes. The wicked brother in 'The Faithful Wife' is opposed to the virtuous husband, whose virtue is illustrated by his 'feminine' affective gestures, such as weeping. The contrast between incentive and disincentive models of male behaviour is much less marked in the work of Russian male writers. In Izmailov's *Evgeny, or the Fearful Consequences of a Bad Upbringing* (1799–1801) the adventures of two immoral rakes are represented in a narrative which, for all its moralizing tone, is markedly more concerned with the progress of the bad pair in lying, cheating, stealing, and sexual misbehaviour than with the fates of their victims.[82] The closest parallel to the 'Russian Lady's' work lies, in fact, not in high literary tradition, but in the late eighteenth-century Russian redactions of French and German romances, such as M. Komarov's *The Tale of the English Milord and the Countess of Brandenburg*, which depicts a 'feminized' and gentle hero. Tales of this type were to remain popular with women in almost all classes outside the intellectual and social élite right up to the Revolution.[83]

Once women had been established in literary practice as sensitive and

[81] 'A Russian Lady', *Raznye povestvovaniya, sochinennye odnoyu Rossiyankoyu* (St Petersburg, 1779). 'Vernaya supruga' is one of four moral tales collected here, of which two are political fables; a third deals with the agonizings of a virtuous heroine who feels that she cannot marry whilst her father still requires her care.

[82] Aleksandr Izmailov, *Evgenii, ili pagubnye sredstva durnogo vospitaniya* in his *PSS* iii.

[83] M. Komarov, *Povest' o priklyucheniyakh aglinskogo milorda i brandenburgskoi markgrafini Frideriki* (St Petersburg, 1782) and many subsequent edns., the most readily available edn. is that in A. Reitblat (ed.), *Lubochnaya kniga* (Moscow, 1990), 127–240. On 19th-c. readership see e.g. P. I. Bogatyrev, 'Moskovskaya starina', in N. S. Anushkin (ed.), *Ushedshaya Moskva: vospominaniya sovremennikov o Moskve vtoroi poloviny XIX veka* (Moscow, 1964), 115, which records that Old Believer merchant women were still reading such material in the 1860s.

virtuous, it was a short step to associating them with these qualities' aesthetic corrolaries, morality and decency. Russian literature of sensibility, like its Western antecedent, was to place particular emphasis on the role of women as arbiters of taste. For Nikolai Karamzin, writing in 1802, the defects and crudities of Russian literature were to be explained by its detachment from the language of upper-class women, who should ideally have functioned both as models and as readers. It was difficult to imagine how the situation might be corrected, however, since, as Karamzin observed, 'not with Russian phrases do those charming women bewitch us, on whose conversation we might hope to eavesdrop in order to embellish a novel or a drama with genteel and felicitous expressions'.[84] The loss was the greater for Karamzin since his association of women with gentility and with French culture was syllogistic: women are imbued with French culture, which is refined, and therefore they are refined. Such attitudes were pervasive amongst members of the metropolitan upper classes in the late eighteenth century, as the following passage from the memoirs of F. Vigel illustrates:

The preciosity which is so evident in literature of the day might also be found in the manners and behaviour of certain young men. Womanishness was by no means accounted shameful, and affectations of a kind which it might be unpleasant to witness in women, were considered the height of worldly refinement.[85]

The conjunction in Sentimentalist ideology of a perception of women as the vessels of emotion, and emotion as the prerequisite of writing, meant that female authorship could now be not only countenanced, but positively welcomed. The years after 1800 show a marked increase in the number and quality of Russian women prose writers. Some women writers continued and expanded the tradition initiated by Neelova or the 'Russian Lady', writing of women's tribulations in love and the family, and especially of the emotional hurt which they might suffer.[86] But a second, and distinct, prose tradition also emerged. Women from the top ranks of the aristocracy, as Karamzin rightly suggests, often had French, rather than Russian, as their first spoken language. Quite naturally, French was also the language in which they wrote.

Whilst Russian women's familiarity with French rather than Russian

---

[84] N. Karamzin, 'Ot chego v Rossii malo avtorskikh talantov?', *Sochineniya* (8 vols.; Moscow, 1803–4), vii. 311. On the prevalence of French, see also V. Alekseev, 'Yazyk svetskikh dam i razvitie yazykovoi normy v XVIII veke', in *Funtsional'nye i sotsial'nye raznovidnosti russkogo literaturnogo yazyka XVIII veka: sbornik nauchnykh trudov* (Leningrad, 1984), 82–95.

[85] Vigel', *Zapiski*, i. 110.

[86] For a survey of early women's prose in Russian, see Yael Harussi, 'Women's Social Roles as Depicted by Women Writers in Early Nineteenth-Century Russian Fiction', in J. Douglas Clayton (ed.), *Issues in Russian Literature Before 1917* (Columbus, Ohio, 1989), 35–48.

is a point routinely observed in historical commentaries, very little attention to date has been given to the French-language texts by Franco-Russian women writers. However, such texts are of considerable importance in the development of women's prose writing in Russian; three key instances will be considered here.

One early Franco-Russian text of note is Natalya Golovkina's epistolary novel, *Elisabeth de S, ou l'histoire d'une russe écrite par une de ces compatriotes* (1802). This concerns the tribulations of the eponymous heroine, a young Russian woman whose suitor is ensnared by a devious rival. Most of the correspondents in the book are women; their letters act as bulletins on the progress of the main affair, and also reveal the importance of the support and approval of other women in its progress.[87]

Elisabeth de S. is a rather laborious and lachrymose production; however, it comes to life when the wicked anti-heroine expresses her dislike for Elisabeth and her allies, or the male villain his hatred for a 'miserable mincing monkey' of a rival. One is tempted to see in such sudden surges of energy a degree of unconscious antagonism to the cult of sensibility; other French-language works were to develop Golovkina's buried distrust more openly. Julia Krüdener's novel *Valérie* (1801)[88] is also an epistolary work, consisting of a series of letters addressed to his friend Ernest by the hero, Gustave, who is infatuated with the eponymous heroine, a young married woman. So far, the book is an obvious imitation of Goethe's *Die Leiden des jungen Werthers*. But Gustave's obsession is so overwhelming that he is capable of none of Werther's digressions on the physical and metaphysical world. Where Charlotte remains the impassive object of Werther's obsession, a cypher who 'goes on cutting bread and butter' whatever happens (to quote W. M. Thackeray's verse parody of Goethe's plot),[89] the narrative of *Valérie*, as the title suggests, is a refraction of the heroine's inner life as much as of Gustave's. As Gustave dwells on his own agony, his letters, ironically, indicate the extent to which he is egotistically blind to Valérie's. A striking example of this effect occurs when Valérie miscarries her husband's child; Gustave is so eager to assure her that his grief is greater than hers that his visit simply augments her distress.

---

[87] Natalya Golovkina (publ. anon.), *Elisabeth de S., ou l'histoire d'une russe écrite par une de ses compatriotes* (3 vols.; Paris, 1802); Russ. edn. as *Elisaveta de S, ili istoriya Rossiyanki, napisannaya odnoyu iz ee sootechestvennits*, trans. I. Voeikov (St Petersburg, 1803). Golovkina (1769–1849), whose husband was the *kamerger* Fedor Golovkin, was also the author of *Alphonse de Lodère* (2 vols.; Moscow, 1807; 2nd edn.; Paris, 1809). (See Gennadi and Soiko, *Slovar'*.)

[88] Julia Krüdener (or Kridener), *Valérie* (1801), ed. Michel Mercier (Paris, 1974).

[89] W. M. Thackeray, 'The Sorrows of Werther', in J. M. Cohen (ed.), *A Choice of Comic and Curious Verse* (Harmondsworth, 1975), 45. The final stanza reads in full: 'Charlotte, seeing Werther's body | Borne before her on a shutter | Like a well-conducted person | Went on cutting bread-and-butter.'

Krüdener's novel shows how the idealization of women's emotional powers through the cult of sensibility could lead, not to the oppression of women's emotions, but to the oppression of women by means of their emotions. A text which makes a similar point, though it connects sensibility and self-indulgence more pointedly, is 'Laure' (1819).[90] Its author was Zinaida Volkonskaya, who, like Krüdener, was a cosmopolitan and much-travelled aristocrat. Volkonskaya's *nouvelle* employed a type of narrative in which the French writer Madame de Genlis had specialized: the plot of a novel of education in miniature is applied to a heroine. The heroine is a lively but rather vapid young girl, eager for success in the *beau monde*. Her amiable but naïve husband, whose human experience is entirely derived from books, can offer no moral guidance; Laure goes through a series of flirtations with different men, then with art, before finding a resting place in maternity: 'her tastes, which had always been extreme and changeable, were now enmeshed for ever by the delights of maternal love' (p. 66).

Volkonskaya's tale gives quite a vivid picture of a woman adrift, and of the world in which she moves, one in which nothing is taken seriously, and where social events, such as balls and parties, unfold in a stream of malicious chatter. Laure can find happiness only when she retreats to the interior life of child-bearing. Here Madame de Genlis's parables of female modesty and self-control are an obvious influence; like Genlis, Volkonskaya also takes an ironic view of the acquisition of accomplishments for its own sake. But her view of maternal love is ambivalent. The choice of the phrase 'enmeshed ... by the delights' (French *enchaîné*) is significant: the suggestion that maternity offers the possibility of independence is undercut by a hint of coercion.

Volkonskaya's tale criticizes self-indulgence, but holds back from analysing the full consequences of self-restraint: a genuine autonomy in maternity cannot be imagined.

By 1820, the date when 'Laure' appeared, Franco-Russian women had already established a tradition of prose writing which was both coherent and diverse. It was coherent in its emphasis on the female psychology, and especially on the capacity of this for sensibility; in its presentation of incentive and disincentive models of male and female behaviour; and in

---

[90] Zinaida Volkonskaya (as Zenaïde Volkonsky), 'Laure', *Quatre nouvelles* (Moscow, 1820); also available in Volkonskaya's selected works in French, *Œuvres choisies de la princess Zenaïde Volkonsky* (Paris and Karlsruhe, 1865) (citation in text to 'Laure' in this edition). Stories by Madame de Genlis which could be described as 'novels of education in miniature' include the three *contes* grouped as *L'Épouse impertinente par air, suivie du Mari corrupteur et de la femme philosophe* (Paris, 1804), as well as *Sanclair* (Paris and St Petersburg, 1808), and *Hortense* (on which see n. 141 below).

its recognition of literary activity as a possible pursuit for women. (Both the 'Russian Lady' and Volkonskaya use feminine forms of the first person in their narrative; Golovkina concentrates on female correspondents.) Important divisions had, however, developed between the Russian language tradition, whose narratives were generally set in a topographically and geographically undefined, but loosely Russian, location, and stressed the importance of giving vent to feeling; and the Franco-Russian tradition, where texts were set outside Russia and stressed the dangers of too great an emphasis on feeling. If the former tradition preferred the third-person omniscient narrator, the latter on the whole (though not invariably) inclined to epistolary forms.

On the whole (Krüdener's *Valérie* excepted) these early prose texts lacked sophistication; however, the conventions which they had established were to be developed and deepened by the next generations of women prose writers. If the concerns of the Franco-Russian tradition were to be maintained by the 'aristocratic' Russian prose genre of the 'society tale', the efforts of the earliest Russian-language writers were, conversely, to be distantly reflected in the competing genre of 'provincial tale'.

Prose 1820–1840: The Reign of the 'Society Tale'

When women from the 'beau monde' began to write in Russian, some of them worked under the direct and unmediated influence of Western women's writing. The Gothic manner of Ann Radcliffe's mysteries, popular in Russia since the late eighteenth century, was imitated in some of the tales written by Nadezhda Durova. In the story 'Nurmeka', for example, the grandfather of the heroine calls her to him on her death-bed and instructs her to lift her veil. When she does, he collapses and dies with a horror-struck expression. In 'Fate's Intrigue' (1839), Durova's description of the heroine's death from syphilis, a yellow, shrivelled and distorted wreck, owes at least as much to the hair-raising traditions of the horror-story as to any empirical observation.[91]

Durova's interest in Radcliffean intensity was, however, to remain an individual quirk, rather than become a general trend amongst Russian women writers. A similar idiosyncratic enthusiasm was Zinaida Volkonskaya's admiration for Madame de Staël. Volkonskaya composed a poetic paean to the French writer in 1814; she was later herself to become

---

[91] Durova, *Povesti i rasskazy* (4 vols.; St Petersburg, 1839): vol. i, 'Nurmeka'; vol. ii, 'Igra sud'by'.

known as 'the Northern Corinne'.[92] The unusually adventurous treatment which she accords to the female psychology in some prose texts of the 1820s depends on an appreciation, akin to Staël's, of the possibilities of female genius. In particular, the short story or prose poem 'The Dream' (1829) is original in its juxtaposition of the classificatory cultural storehouse of the male imagination, and the free-ranging, random intuition of the female fantasy. Whatever view one takes, in an absolute sense, of this binary opposition, Volkonskaya's work stands out in its immediate context through the confidence with which it asserts the equal value of 'feminine' intellectual strategies.[93]

Such occasional sports excepted, Russian women's prose writing after 1820 was not characterized by the straightforward appropriation of Western models. The pattern was, rather, one in which preoccupations already evident in the indigenous tales of sensibility were treated in ways which drew at one and the same time on Western women's writing, on the emerging Russian literary tradition, and on the adaptations of Western women's writing in Russian literary tradition.

The earliest sign of such developments came when women belonging to a class which might previously have written in French began to appropriate the new Russian literary genre of the 'society tale', a novella of upper-class life in the metropolis. The society tale, whilst not a genre indigenous to Russia, attained particular importance there from the late 1820s as an acceptable upper-class alternative to the 'bourgeois prose' narratives written by such social outsiders as Faddei Bulgarin, and concerning the lives of urban petty tradesmen. Famous examples of the genre include Bestuzhev-Marlinsky's 'Evening at the Bivouac' (1824) and Pushkin's 'The Queen of Spades' (1833). The genre's schematic framework juxtaposed the exterior and public world of the social event, such as the ball or party, with the interior world of the study or boudoir, the

---

[92] Volkonskaya, 'A Madame de Staël' (1814), in M. Azadovsky, 'Iz materialov "Stroganovskoi akademii" ', *Literaturnoe nasledstvo*, 33–4 (1939), 210. On Volkonskaya as the 'Corinne du Nord', and on other aspects of the biography of this fascinating figure, see Nadezhda Gorodetskaya, 'Zinaida Volkonsky'; some of the material from this biography is available in Gorodetskaya's 'Princess Zinaida Volkonsky', *OSP*, 5 (1954), 93–105, and 'Zinaida Volkonsky as a Catholic', *SEER* 39/92 (1960), 31–43; see also Fainshtein, *Pisatel'nitsy*; Murav'ev's biographical material in *V tsarstve muz* is much inferior.

[93] 'Snovidenie', *Galateya* (1829), 5: 21–31; see also 'The Dream: A Letter' in *Anthology*. Three years after the composition of this text, in 1832, Volkonskaya suffered a short nervous breakdown. Her devoted friend S. P. Shevyrev, formerly tutor to her son, collected her sayings in madness, many of which tended to a bizarre religio-mystical coloration ('ma sœur est douce et blanche comme du lait de Dieu'). Shevyrev's account is now filed with the case history of her illness, the latter providing fascinating insights into contemporary medical belief (the doctor felt she was suffering from a congestion of the blood). (See Saltykov-Shchedrin State Public Library, f. 850, Shevyrev, S. P. No. 16, 'Bolezn' knyagini', ll. 22–3; 'Otchet o bolezni', ll. 24–32.)

'pretence' of outward existence with the 'reality' of inner feeling. The satirical delineation of outward social forms was counterpointed by the emotional rhetoric with which interior worlds were depicted.[94]

The composition of society tales was not unique to women writers; the genre had, however, a particular significance for their work. The texts produced by the Franco-Russian tradition might be considered early examples of the 'society tale': *Elisabeth de S.* and 'Laure' both portray society as artificial, and the latter tale, at least, reveals some unease with the roles allowed by society to women. The society tale's binary framework allowed women writers of later generations to continue to depict their heroines' internal world with the affective intensity of Sentimentalism. At the same time, they could sharpen their attack on society, which might now be represented as a distortion of women's inner, or 'real', ambitions. They might also adopt Sentimentalism's critical attitude towards male behaviour. Where the lover heroes of society tales written by men are seen as polarized between feeling and convention, like their female counterparts, the heroes of society tales written by women are more often directly associated with social artificiality. The St Petersburg poet with whom Olga, heroine of Elena Gan's 'The Ideal' (1834) is obsessed is revealed as a perfidious philanderer, whilst in Evdokiya Rostopchina's epistolary story 'Rank and Money' (1838), a reworking of Krüdener's *Valérie* transferred to St Petersburg society, the hero's flair for emotive rhetoric proves merely a mask for his self-interest.[95]

The framework of the 'society tale' was so attractive to women writers that it was even adopted in tales to which it might at first sight seem inappropriate. In Durova's 'Nurmeka', for example, which is supposed to be set in the sixteenth century, the Tatar heroine retreats in moments of stress to her boudoir behind a pink curtain. Zinaida Volkonskaya's unfinished novel *The Tale of Olga* (written in the late 1820s) is less preposterously anachronistic than this. However, its representation of the heroine, Olga, the tenth-century princess responsible for the conversion of Russia to Christianity, shows her to be polarized between a public self, plagued by the spiteful gossip of her female courtiers, and a

---

[94] A. Bestuzhev-Marlinsky, 'Vecher na bivuake', *Sochineniya v 2 tomakh* (Moscow, 1988), i. 77–85; 'Vtoroi vecher na bivuake', ibid. i. 86–97; Pushkin, 'Pikovaya dama', *PSS* vi. 210–37. An exceptionally full survey of the 'society tale's' schemata and rhetoric is available in Elizabeth C. Shepard, 'The Society Tale and the Innovative Argument in Russian Prose Fiction of the 1830s', *Russian Literature*, 10 (1981), 111–61.

[95] On 'Ideal' see Ch. 4 on Gan below; Rostopchina, 'Chiny i den'gi', *Stikhotvoreniya*, 290–334; see also 'Rank and Money', trans. Helena Goscilo in her *Russian and Polish Women's Fiction* (Knoxville, Tenn., 1985).

contrasting private self of hidden emotional depths. (Here, it is true, these depths are religious rather than romantic in origin, as befits the subject's hagiographical associations.)[96]

This is not to say that writers of 'society tales' invariably regarded women's emotional outbursts with an uncritical eye, or that they necessarily portrayed men as unprincipled villains. Like the aristocratic writers of the earlier Franco-Russian tradition, the women authors of the 'society tale' sometimes, if not always, represented the cult of sensibility as a path to self-deception. Emotional outbursts might be handled ambivalently. The earlier epistolary forms were replaced by multiple-perspective narrative forms: the society tale ordinarily purports to be a confession made by a fictional character to an invented narrator, or a piece of authentic society gossip, which in the first case is related to, in the second overheard or witnessed by, a narrator who is herself, or himself, supposed to be a habitué(e) of high society.[97] In the most sophisticated 'society tales', such as Zhukova's 'Baron Reichman' (1837) or Karolina Pavlova's 'At the Tea-Table' (1859), a framework of intersecting narratives is used in order both to explore, and to ironize, sensibility's tradition of the exploited heroine. The central woman characters in these stories suffer affectingly, but the possibility that their suffering depends on an illusion is also raised.[98]

Despite the importance of the society tale in the initial phases of Russian women's writing, both in terms of the number of texts produced, and in terms of the literary interest which was sometimes attained by the genre, its dominance was soon to be challenged, and then overthrown, by another type of story, set in the Russian provinces rather than in the metropolis, and where schematism was employed to rather different effect.

Incentive Myths for Women: The Provincial Tale and the 'Escape Plot' (1840–1880)

> Why have so many lovely, gifted girls
> Married impossible men?
>
> (Robert Graves, 'A Slice of Wedding Cake')

[96] Volkonskaya, 'Skazanie ob Ol'ge', in *Sochineniya* (Paris and Karlsruhe, 1865); a full text is also available in Murav'ev (ed.), *V tsarstve muz*, an abridged one in *Dacha*.

[97] The confessional form is used e.g. in Bestuzhev-Marlinsky's 'Vecher'; the narrative-within-narrative by Pushkin in 'Pikovaya dama'.

[98] On these two tales see Chs. 2 and 3 on Zhukova and Pavlova below.

Unlike the society tale, a recognized term in Russian literary history, the 'provincial tale' is a coinage of my own. I use it to signify a medium- to full-length prose narrative set in the Russian countryside, and depicting a young female protagonist's struggles not to limit her life according to the accepted expectations for women from landowning families. Eschewing metropolitan glitter (though they are sometimes set in small towns rather than on estates), provincial tales are concerned with the country gentry, whether comfortably-off or impecunious, rather than with the rich aristocracy; their locus is the garden or sitting-room of a modest house, rather than the ballroom of a grand one. The emphasis is on external action: group scenes replace soliloquies, and a third-person omniscient narrator is normally deployed in place of the society tale's variety of writers or speakers.

The post-1840 fashion for tales of women's lives set in the provinces can be attributed in part to sociological factors. Many of the women authors of society tales (Rostopchina, Volkonskaya, Pavlova) were themselves aristocrats who had spent most of their adult lives in metropolitan high society; from the 1840s on, however, women authors increasingly began to be drawn from the provincial gentry, and often from the minor provincial gentry. The Khvoshchinskaya sisters and Nadezhda Sokhanskaya came from struggling landowner families, Sofya Soboleva was the daughter of an engineer; Avdotya Panaeva, daughter of an actor, married up into the provincial gentry.[99] Too much emphasis should not, however, be placed on the class of the writers involved. If the material that lay behind the society tale may be traced to sociological factors, the expression which was given to that material was shaped by a fusion of literary, cultural, and ideological trends, Western as well as Russian. Staël and Genlis had been central influences on the Russian society tale; the most significant non-Russian model in the development of the provincial tale was George Sand, or to be more accurate, one aspect of George Sand's writing. Her Russian admirers were not concerned with Sand as Romantic virtuoso; *Lélia* (1833), an imaginative evocation of the flexibility of gender boundaries, left them unmoved. It was Sand's denunciation of the oppressions inherent in the institution of marriage which carried weight; her work acquired exemplary status as interest in gender inequality, the 'woman question', as it was later to be

---

[99] On the Khvoshchinskaya sisters' background, see the memoir in N. Khvoshchinskaya, *Sobranie sochinenii* (5 vols.; St Petersburg, 1892), vol. i; on Sokhanskaya, see Mary Zirin, 'Nadezhda Sokhanskaia' in *ECWR*; on Soboleva see *Russkii biograficheskii slovar'*, vol. xix; on Panaeva, see her *Vospominaniya* (Moscow, 1956).

termed, developed in Russia, under the influence of French socialism, during the late 1830s and early 1840s.[100]

Marriage was important to the first generations of Russian feminist thinkers because it was seen as a metaphor of women's financial dependence within the family. A dependent of her father in childhood, the Russian woman without private means became a dependent of her husband after marriage; either of these male relatives was legally entitled to enforce her to reside with him, and his consent was necessary if she were to attempt to educate herself or to pursue a career.[101] If the first concern of early Russian feminism was inequality within the family, its second concern was women's inequality of opportunity in society: the assertion of the right to work, and the right to an education. Radical thinkers placed much emphasis on the inadequacy of girls' schooling, which was held to be no adequate preparation for any useful role in society.[102]

The main mouthpieces for Russian debates on women's rights were the so-called 'thick journals'. These heavyweight literary and political monthlies began from the late 1830s to play a central part in Russian literary life, edging into oblivion the more light-hearted miscellanies and almanacs which had dominated literate culture in the eighteenth and early nineteenth centuries. The most important thick journals included *Otechestvennye zapiski* (founded 1839), *Biblioteka dlya chteniya* (founded 1834), *Russkii vestnik* (founded 1856), and *Sovremennik*, which was begun by Pushkin in 1836, and edited from 1847 by Nikolai

---

[100] Sand, *Lélia* (1833), ed. P. Reboul (Paris, 1960). A full study of Sand's reception in Russia is urgently required. Some of the groundwork (though not that relating to women's writing) is covered in Carole Karp, 'Sand and the Russians', *The George Sand Papers: Conference Proceedings 1976* (Hofstra University, 1980), 151–61; *eadem*, 'George Sand in the Estimate of the Russian "Men of the Forties" ', *The George Sand Papers: Conference Proceedings 1978* (Hofstra University, 1982), 180–8; Lesley Singer Hermann, 'George Sand and the Nineteenth-Century Russian Novel: The Quest for a Heroine', Ph.D. thesis (Columbia University, New York, 1977). These sources suggest that *Jacques* was Sand's most influential work for Russians. Sand was also almost certainly an influence on the development of Russian regional prose by men and women, through such works as *Le Meunier d'Angibault* (1845).

[101] On women's legal rights, see, besides the sources given in n. 1 above, the brief, but exceptionally lucid, outline of marital status and inheritance law in the early 19th c. by William G. Wagner: 'The Trojan Mare: Women's Rights and Civil Rights in Late Imperial Russia', Olga Crisp and Linda Edmondson (eds.), *Civil Rights in Imperial Russia* (Oxford, 1989), 65–9.

[102] An outline of the early phases of Russian feminism is available in Stites, *Women's Liberation*, 3–315. How badly educated Russian women actually were is a ticklish subject: education for Russian men was none too efficient until at least the 1870s. Perhaps consequently, there is often a defensive flavour to assertions of women's ignorance. For example, G. Barratt, editor of Baratynsky's *Selected Letters* (The Hague, 1973), points out that 'Baratynsky's own pretensions to learning are piquant . . . His comment on Ezevsky's daughter's poor French, too, is thrown into relief by his own curious orthography' (note to letter no. 5). Alekseev, 'Yazyk svetskikh dam', takes carping comments similar to Baratynsky's, by Novikov and others, as evidence for the actual state of things in the 18th c., in my view, naïvely.

Nekrasov and Ivan Panaev, members of a group of St Petersburg radicals actively involved in the campaign for women's rights.[103] The thick journals' commitment to women's rights was manifested not only or even mainly in the publication of factual and discursive pieces about women's rights, but also, and indeed largely, in a preference for fiction in which the obtaining conventions in women's upbringing, and the current conditions of their lives, were questioned either in terms of the plot, or through a direct authorial address to the reader, or both. Besides being pro-feminist in their coverage, these 'thick journals' also gave a great deal of space to writing by women. Before 1840 many women writers had made their débuts by the publication of a book; after 1840 it was increasingly the publication of a piece of fiction in a journal which would bring a writer to Russian readers' attention.

The new rhetoric of women's liberation could not be served by just any literary publication. Effective propaganda for the emancipation of women demanded that they be represented as unfree, yet capable of freedom. The provincial tale was, accordingly, an incentive as well as a representative tradition; it dealt with a woman of unusual sensitivity, above the common run of provincial womanhood. Some examples of the genre, such as Zhukova's 'The Medallion' or Gan's 'A Futile Gift' emphasize the likely wastage of such sensitivity and talent in stagnant provincial backwaters. The most impressive example of this interpre-tation of the provincial tale was perhaps Nadezhda Sokhanskaya's 'A Conversation after Dinner' (1858). The anonymous woman narrator meets a young married woman after dinner, and the latter relates how her idealistic hopes of choosing her own destiny came to nothing. Though she describes herself as happy, and emphasizes the possibility of reconciliation within an arranged marriage, the emotional fervour with which her youthful experiences are related undercuts her pose of resigna-tion and stoicism.[104]

But the provincial tale was just as often understood as a narrative of success. The narrator-protagonist of Avdotya Panaeva's 'The Talnikov Family' (1848) describes her upbringing in nightmarish family circum-stances: her parents are callous yet full of moral cant, her grandparents more benign, but also more benighted. However, the heroine is able to liberate herself by marriage to a sympathetic young man, and her

---

[103] On the thick journals (tolstye zhurnaly) see the entries in Terras, Handbook, and in Kratkaya literaturnaya entsiklopediya (9 vols.; Moscow, 1962–75).

[104] N. Sokhanskaya ('Kokhanovskaya'), 'Posle obeda v gostyakh', RV 16 (1858), 641–96; a rather similar story is the same author's 'Lyubila', Biblioteka dlya chteniya, (1858), 7: 1–86, which also depicts the sufferings of a young woman hopelessly in love. Cf. Evgeniya Tur's stories 'Dolg', S (1850), 11: 5–60; 'Oshibka', S (1849), 10: 137–284.

departure for the wedding concludes the narrative.[105] Though views on the appropriate means of escape diverged—later examples of the provincial tale placed an emphasis on liberation from marriage, rather than on liberation through marriage—the 'escape plot' as such, that is, a plot illustrating obstacles overcome, was standard.

Not all the fiction produced by Russian women from the early 1840s conformed to the genre patterns of the provincial tale, but this narrative type was so dominant that Russian women writers were effectively confronted with a choice: they might either employ it, or they might not adopt young women as central characters at all. An example of the latter direction, the elision of young women, is Sofya Khvoshchinskaya's story 'Ordinary Mortals' (1858). This is a skilful piece of social realism cataloguing the debates preceding the Emancipation of the Serfs in 1861: the only women characters are some elderly ladies, who mutter anxiously and irrelevantly in the manner of a Greek chorus as the male narrator and his acquaintances thrash out their intellectual debates.[106] A similar displacement of focus from 'feminine' to 'masculine' concerns is evident in Sokhanskaya's 'Provincial Portrait Gallery', in which the narrative surveys the embitterment of a deserted patriarch, rather than pursuing his daughter into elopement.[107]

Adoption of men as central characters was not the only solution; another possibility, concentration on older women, was explored by Sokhanskaya in 'The Neighbours' (1862), a lively narrative which feminizes and reverses the plot of Gogol's story 'The Tale of the Two Ivans'. Gogol's male Ukrainian landowners plunge into a poisonous and interminable feud on a point of male honour; their female counterparts in Sokhanskaya's story are two middle-aged women who quarrel on an equally trivial point, but whose dispute is reconciled by the engagement of the son of the one and the daughter of the other.[108]

The dominance of the provincial tale did not mean that women writers had to write about young women; it did, however, impose particular patterns when they did. The result was a fair degree of stability and homogeneity in women's prose writing between the early 1840s and the late 1870s; a situation which had both its strengths and its limitations. The provincial tale was the first Russian genre which can be properly called a literature of women's liberation. It clearly articulated

[105] A. Panaeva, 'Semeistvo Tal'nikovykh', *Illyustrirovannyi al'manakh* (St Petersburg, 1848: in fact delayed for censorship reasons until 1866), 1–115.

[106] S. Khvoshchinskaya, 'Prostye smertnye', *OZ* 120 (1858), 1–39.

[107] Sokhanskaya, 'Iz provintsial'noi galerei portretov', *RV* 20 (1859), 61–157.

[108] Sokhanskaya, 'Sosedi', *S* (1850), 12: 161–244.

women's dissatisfaction with patriarchal society, and suggested ways in which the grip of that society might be loosened on individual women. But at the same time the teleological drive of the provincial tale, its dependence on the easy resolutions of the 'escape plot', made it, as I shall demonstrate, rather limiting in an artistic sense.

It was by no means only women who wrote the fiction emanating from the primary stage of Russian feminism. Indeed, two of the most famous texts of women's liberation, Herzen's *Who is to Blame?* (1842) and Chernyshevsky's *What is to Be Done?* (1863), were written by male authors.[109] The sense that it was men who were the ideological leaders is reflected, too, in the fact that many of the writers active from the early 1840s, unlike their predecessors, adopted male pseudonyms, and also in the fact that in Russia, in contradistinction to France, discursive material on feminism was produced by men alone.[110] However, when Russian women writers cast their reflections on women's liberation in fictional form, they did not merely parrot male opinion: much of the work produced by women manifested a high degree of intellectual independence. Some, at least, of the texts written by women were franker and more uncompromising in their denunciation of discrimination than the better-known texts written by men. And women's representations of the possibilities of change were in some senses more radical than those of their male contemporaries.

Let me substantiate these assertions by comparing Herzen and Chernyshevsky's work with some texts by women authors of similar date, and showing how a similar starting-point (an ignorant young woman seems to lack anything better to do than to marry a suitor who will not make a satisfactory husband), leads to rather different resolutions.

The first discrepancy is that not all the women authors nuance 'ignorance' in the same way as the men. When Herzen, in *Who is to Blame?*, draws a contrast between women's socially constructed lack of opportunity and their innate intelligence, he does it in terms that suggest less an active spirit of enquiry than a transcendence conferred by some mysterious unearthly power:

A girl either adapts to her surroundings from the first moment of her life, so that

---

[109] A. Gertsen [Herzen], *Kto vinovat, Sochineniya v 9 tomakh* (Moscow, 1955), i. 111–325; N. Chernyshevsky, *Chto delat'? Iz rasskazov o novykh lyudyakh*, in *Izbrannye proizvedeniya v 3 tomakh* (Leningrad, 1978), vol. i.

[110] e.g. Panaeva wrote as 'N. Stanitsky', S. Khvoshchinskaya as 'Ivan Vesen'ev', Soboleva as 'V. Samoilovich', and N. Khvoshchinskaya as 'V. Krestovsky'. Apart from fiction, women writers expressed their views on women's liberation through occasional reviews: see e.g. Evgeniya Tur, 'Zhenshchina i lyubov' po ponyatiyam g. Mishle', *RV* (1859), 6: 461–500.

at 14 she is already an accomplished coquette and a gossip [. . .] or, with the most extraordinary ease, she shakes off the dirt that mires her, overcomes external circumstances by dint of her inner nobility, attains an understanding of life by some process of revelation . . .[111]

There is no sense here of *how* women might achieve this remarkable process of maturation, in the apparent absence of resources. In Chernyshevsky's *What is to be Done?*, which supplies a rather more detailed account of the mechanics of the heroine's progress, education is seen as a gift which a sympathetic man may extend to a woman.

Women writers, by contrast, are both more interested in the mechanics of education than Herzen, and more cynical about male patronage than Chernyshevsky. Even Elena Gan, for all her emphasis on 'talent', or inherent characteristics, had dwelt, in 'The Ideal', on the formative effects of an educationally adventurous mother's choice of reading for two young girls. These girls have read 'Genlis, Staël and the lives of great men and women', by which is probably meant the various tales of Russian, French, and classical heroes, and adaptations of Plutarch that were considered suitable material for Russian schoolrooms in the 1820s, and Genlis's *The Lives of Famous Frenchwomen and their Influence on Letters*, as well as various fictional works.[112] And in 'A Futile Gift' Gan had shown that help from a sympathetic man, though it might play a considerable role in the initial stages of a provincial girl's quest to better herself, was at the same time likely to be a means of control, as well as, or instead of, a path to liberation.

Gan's successors broaden and deepen her portrayal of the various paths to enlightenment, and also suggest women are more likely to receive positive guidance from other women or from books than they are from men. In Sofya Soboleva's 'Another Broken Heart' (1862), the central character, Varvara, has developed her intellectual aspirations under the tutelage of a sympathetic mistress at a *pension* who has directed her reading; the same author's 'No Escape' (1864), describes a provincial town in which one young girl, Aleksandra Pavlovna, does in fact escape from the fate of her fellows through private reading, as well as through an independent existence as a music mistress; and Nadezhda Khvoshchinskaya, in 'The Meeting' (1879), represents a peasant mother who, by

---

[111] Gertsen, *Kto vinovat?*, 154.

[112] Gan, 'Ideal', *PSS* 9 (see ch. 4 n. 1). Cf. Genlis, *Histoire des femmes françaises les plus célèbres et de leur influence sur la littérature française* (2 vols.; London, 1811); Sergei Glinka, *Novoe detskoe chtenie, izdannoe Sergeem Glinkoyu* (Moscow, 1822); idem, *Moskovskii al'manakh dlya prekras-nogo pola, izdanyi [sic] na 1826–i god* (Moscow, 1825); N. Karamzin (ed.), *Panteon inostrannoi slovesnosti* (3 vols.; Moscow, 1798).

sheer self-sacrifice, manages to pay for her daughter's education.[113] Stories in which aid preferred by men turns out to be a form of manipulation include 'Another Broken Heart', again, in which a young St Petersburg man not only enlightens Varvara, but seduces her too. And Nadezhda Khvoshchinskaya's 'The Boarding-School Girl' (1860) shows how Lelenka, who is being educated at the unsatisfactory boarding-school of the title, encounters Veretitsyn, a young neighbour who at first supplies much-needed intellectual counsel and stimulation. But later Lelenka outgrows Veretitsyn's support, and resists the pressure put on her to repay it with emotional involvement.[114]

Often, too, women writers are more ambitious than their male fellows in their sense of the likely intellectual goals for women. Chernyshevsky's Vera Pavlovna graduates to activities that—however hedged about with Fourierian rhetoric—are not much more than philanthropic pastimes. By contrast, Lelenka of 'The Boarding-School Girl' uses her education to establish herself as a translator in St Petersburg, where she leads a wholly independent existence based on 'work, knowledge, and freedom'. Even a story published twenty years earlier, Mariya Zhukova's 'Self-Sacrifice' (1840) had concluded by showing an impecunious young woman of the gentry making her own way as the headmistress of a school.[115]

It is especially in the matter of male sexuality that male and female authors deviate. Chernyshevsky and Herzen prefer the positive male hero of Sentimentalism, who overflows with feeling for the female object of his affections, and whose attitude to his male rival (both texts, like Goethe's *Werther* and Krüdener's *Valérie*, deal with triangular relations between a married couple and an unmarried man) is all decent and respectful reticence. Their heroines are also impossibly virtuous: the question with which these narratives deal is whether adultery, a form of behaviour which society condemns, is, or is not, compatible with a true morality. Women writers deal with a different kind of triangle, and represent its members differently, being mostly a good deal more cynical about human behaviour. Their preferred pattern is one in which two women, one innocent, the other self-serving, compete over one man. In stories from the 1840s and 1850s, the two girls concerned are usually unmarried; in later stories, the self-serving woman is usually the wife of

[113] Sofya Soboleva, 'Eshche razbitoe serdtse', *Biblioteka dlya chteniya* (1862), 10: 223–312; 11: 101–93; 'Bezvykhodnoe polozhenie', *Russkoe slovo* (1864), 3: 117–58; 4: 29–79; N. Khvoshchinskaya, 'Svidanie', *Svidanie*, 363–415.

[114] N. Khvoshchinskaya, 'Pansionerka', in her *Povesti i rasskazy* (Moscow, 1963), 92–187.

[115] On Zhukova's 'Self Sacrifice', see also ch. 2 below. The ultimate 'liberation narrative', however, is perhaps Khvoshchinskaya's *Ursa Major* (see n. 117 below), in which the heroine rejects her vacillating admirer in order to make her own life running a smallholding and teaching children in a village.

the hero, who is in love with the virtuous innocent.[116] If women do not always act with the best possible intentions, men very rarely do. Women writers are concerned, on the whole, with male selfishness, rather than male self-sacrifice. In Khvoshchinskaya's novel *Ursa Major* (1872), the central male character, Verkhovskoi, is married to a caricature harpy of a wife, but fears that if he deserts her in favour of the young and charming Katya, he will sacrifice his career.[117] If Khvoshchinskaya's novel parodies the positive hero as vacillator, most women writers, by contrast, concentrate on another Sentimentalist figure, the rake. The narrator of Avdotya Panaeva's 'Young Lady of the Steppe' (1855) is revealed, in the course of the narrative, as a selfish egoist, whose relation to the child-of-nature heroine resembles that between hunter and quarry.[118] In the same author's novel *The Lot of Women* (1862), the heroine's wastrel father asserts his patriarchal rights to claim his daughter from her energetic mother, an excellent estate manager, and manœuvres her into marriage with a companion in debauchery.[119] In Mariya Tsebrikova's story 'Which is Better?' (1863), two different kinds of unsatisfactory man, a flaccid weakling and a preening poseur, are juxtaposed: the reader's answer to the question can only be, 'Neither'.[120]

The incompatibility within marriage which Herzen and Chernyshevsky depict is portrayed as more a matter of chance than the result of anything intrinsically unsatisfactory in the conditioning of men, or in heterosexual relations themselves. The possibility of contentment in a heterosexual relation is suggested by Herzen, though his novel in fact ends with the departure of the would-be lover, and the spouses' miserable reunion. It is directly portrayed by Chernyshevsky, whose Vera Pavlovna achieves ecstasy in her union with Kirsanov. Women writers are either more reticent or more ambivalent, or both. The conventional marriage is seen as a nightmare alliance of a sensitive and innocent young girl with a coarse and brutish older man. The heroine of Anna Pavlova's story 'The Stepmother' (1861), for example, who is pressurized by her stepmother into marriage with a debauched alcoholic, is successor to a whole series of heroines yoked to boorish, stupid, or boring husbands in stories by Durova, Gan, Panaeva, Sokhanskaya, and

---

[116] Such negative–positive pairings are made, for example, in Gan's 'Theophania Abbiagio' and 'Ideal', Zhukova's 'Medallion' and 'Self-Sacrifice', Panaeva's *A Woman's Lot*, N. Khvoshchinskaya's *Ursa Major*, Soboleva's 'Another Broken Heart' and 'The Story of Polya'; 'Tri doli' by M. Vilinskaya ('Marko Vovchok'), *Svidanie*, 17–93, increases the basic pair to three.

[117] N. Khvoshchinskaya, *Bol'shaya medveditsa*: see her *SS* iv. 146–404.

[118] Panaeva, 'Stepnaya baryshnya', *Dacha*, 343–413.

[119] Panaeva, *Zhenskaya dolya*, S (1862), 3: 40–176; 4: 503–61; 5: 207–50.

[120] Mariya Tsebrikova, 'Kotoryi luchshe?', *Svidanie*, 235–80.

Evgeniya Tur.[121] Given the fascination of many male writers (and painters) of the period with such marital asymmetry, this seems conventional enough; a much more striking point is that extramarital relations are not necessarily seen as a palliative. Even where they succeed, as in Soboleva's story 'The Story of Polya' (1863), a tale of relations between a married man and a young girl whose satire is directed solely at small-town society's hypocritical ostracization of the 'fallen woman', there is a marked reluctance to depict the happiness in detail. Soboleva eschews all reference to sexual pleasure, not showing even the watery enthusiasm with which Chernyshevsky depicts the sexual act.[122] More commonly, woman writers suggest that extramarital relations are likely simply to play into the hands of rakish villains: this is the case, for example, in Ekaterina Starynkevich's story 'They Are Not to Blame' (1871), in which the central woman character becomes estranged from her husband, only to fall for a worthless younger man.[123] Some women writers, notably the Khvoshchinskaya sisters, go so far as to suggest that celibacy is the only sensible course for women with a heightened sense of their own autonomy. In Sofya Khvoshchinskaya's 'Town and Country Folk', the innocent and intellectually commonplace provincial heroine finds the courage to resist a marriage being forced on her by a bossy woman neighbour.[124]

Post-1840 realist women's writing reveals the capacity of Russian women for levels of social criticism which go beyond those which male commentators wished to prompt in them. In the 1860s, when Dmitry Pisarev was lamenting the poor quality of Russian women's education on the grounds that it made them 'bad mothers', and another well-known radical, Nikolai Shelgunov, was telling women that if they had jobs they might just about manage to achieve the independence of their own chambermaids. Russian women writers had already developed

---

[121] Anna Pavlova, 'Machikha', *Russkii vestnik*, 33 (1861), 307–74, 637–743. Earlier stories in which unsatisfactory husbands appear are Durova's 'Igra', Gan's 'Ideal', Tur's 'Oshibka', and Panaeva's 'Stepnaya baryshnya'. Male literary texts which represent similar combinations are Aksakov's *Memoirs* and Dostoevsky's *The Gentle Woman* (Krotkaya); paintings include Vasily Pukirev's *The Unequal Marriage* (1862) and Pavel Fedotov's *The Major's Courtship* (1848). More unusual are women's portraits of other male relatives: a scathing sketch of a brother is given in N. Khvoshchinskaya's story 'Bratets' (1858), *Povesti i rasskazy*, 33–91; of a father in Soboleva's 'Dobroe staroe vremya', *Russkoe slovo* (1865), 4: 38–72; 5: 1–40.

[122] Soboleva, 'Istoriya Poli', *Svidanie*, 363–416. It should be said that my view of Chernyshevsky is not universally shared. Richard Stites, for example, describes him as manifesting 'an acutely sensitive appreciation of amorous eroticism' (*Women's Liberation*, 95); for an extended reading of Chernyshevsky in similar vein, see Joe Andrew, *Women in Russian Literature* (London, 1988), 155–80.

[123] Ekaterina Starynkevich ['Elena Sal'yanova'], 'Ne oni vinovaty', *VE* (1871), 1: 133–66; 2: 667–704.

[124] S. Khvoshchinskaya, 'Gorodskie i derevenskie', *Svidanie*, 95–233.

rather more ambitious views of the benefits that were to be derived from education and employment.[125]

Up to a point, then, Russian women achieved the transition to the prose of engagement without the marginalization which Belinsky had predicted. The prose of Russian women writers could compete on equal terms in the 1840s, 1850s, and early 1860s: some stories by Sofya or Nadezhda Khvoshchinskaya, or Sokhanskaya, Soboleva, and Panaeva, are at least as interesting and competently achieved as anything by their male contemporaries, with the notable exceptions of Gogol's 'The Overcoat' (1841) or Turgenev's 'First Love' (1860).[126] The problem is that the 1860s, the moment when the Russian feminist movement really began to take off, was also the decade at which real differences between men's and women's writing again began to show themselves.[127] In Russia, where the enthusiasm for women's liberation ran far beyond what was current in Western Europe, no major woman novelist was to emerge, even at a stage when Russian prose writers were turning to the novel *en masse*.

This is not to say that no Russian women attempted novels, for a good number of them did. But the extra length and space did not make significant contributions to their narrative practice. Large-scale works, such as Panaeva's *The Lot of Women* or Natalya Khvoshchinskaya's *Ursa Major*, simply give an account of women's escape from restrictive circumstances whose extra length is achieved by the iteration of certain set-piece scenes, or psychological motifs.[128] There is a reluctance to develop subsidiary characters into more than fleeting caricatures (though these are often portrayed with considerable satirical skill). If the heroine has any female counterpart (frequently she appears in splendid isolation, elevated beyond the lot of common 'femininity'), then this woman is simply her negative mirror-image, flirtatious and deferential towards men where the heroine is aloof and intellectual. Russian women writers do

[125] D. I. Pisarev, 'Zhenskie tipy v romanakh i povestyakh Pisemskogo, Turgeneva i Goncharova' (1860), *Sochineniya v 4 tomakh* (Moscow, 1955–6), i. 233–7; N. V. Shelgunov, 'Zhenskoe bezdel'e' (1865), *Sochineniya* (3 vols.; St Petersburg, 1892), ii. 209–63.

[126] The 1840s and 1850s were the triumph of the 'natural school', whose most noted representatives were Dal', Grigorovich, and the early Dostoevsky. Women writers did not work in this urban 'social exploration' mode. But some, such as Sokhanskaya, displayed a considerable interest in the ethnography of rural life, and their preferred genre of 'provincial tale' is in no sense inferior.

[127] Dostoevsky's *Crime and Punishment* came out in 1866, his last novel *Brothers Karamazov* in 1880; *War and Peace* and *Anna Karenina* date from 1869 and 1877 respectively. On feminism in the 1860s, see Stites, *Women's Liberation*.

[128] For details of Panaeva, *Zhenskaya dolya*; Khvoshchinskaya, *Bol'shaya medveditsa*, see above; cf. Tur, *Plemyannitsa* (4 vols.; St Petersburg, 1851). It is worth noting that where Tur worked as a writer for children, e.g. in the novel *Sem'ya Shalonskikh: iz semeinoi khroniki* (St Petersburg, 1880), she produced writing which was far more laconic, tightly structured, and closely observed than her work for adults.

not give us pairings of equals, like those in George Eliot's novels *Middlemarch* and *Daniel Deronda*; rather than presenting to the reader two different, autonomous types of world-view, each graduating to self-knowledge, a Dorothea and a Rosamund, they concentrate on a single heroine, invariably a Dorothea. And even the single heroines often seem poorly differentiated, almost interchangeable one with another, at one in their ambitions and in their means of achieving them.

The failure of Russian women to graduate successfully to the novel in fact also highlights the limitations of their shorter fiction. The escape plot of the provincial tale, with its concentration on external hindrances, on obstacles heroically overcome, meant that the world from which women sought to escape had necessarily to be represented in formulaic terms, and reduced to certain key objects or activities, which recur in text after text: the oppression of domesticity, for example, is almost invariably encapsulated by showing the heroine at her hated embroidery frame. The physical abstraction suggested by the near-absence of reference to things and customs is underlined by the elision of the body. Childbirth, the care of young children, women's indignation at the licensed lubricity of the male doctor's investigative gaze, are all matters foreign to the work of any woman writer—though recorded in that of the so-called arch misogynist Tolstoy.[129] And the interior, psychological world is just as elusive. The provincial tales display a striking wariness concerning psychological matters. The omniscient third-person narrators of most stories barely investigate their heroine's thoughts: once the escape route is embarked on, the possibility of doubt and confusion, of shifting perception, is excluded entirely. There is an emphasis on action, not on contemplation; the metaphysical and spiritual are absent, not figuring even in the representation of how the world is understood by individuals. In this sense, the Russian tradition of prose by women differs markedly from its Anglophone counterpart, in which even a novelist as committed to the representation of abstract philosophical problems as George Eliot can be fully aware of the psychological dramatism of ideas. Here, for example, is how she described the resolution of Dorothea's spiritual crisis in *Middlemarch* (1872):

On the road there was a man with a bundle on his back and a woman carrying her baby; in the field she could see figures moving . . . Far off in the bending day was the pearly light; and she felt the largeness of the world and the manifold workings of man to labour and endurance. She was a part of that involuntary,

---

[129] All the above issues are reflected in Tolstoy's *Anna Karenina*; cf. Heldt, *Terrible Perfection*, 38–48.

palpitating life, and could neither look out on it from her luxurious shelter as a mere spectator, nor hide her eyes in selfish complaining.[130]

The Russian prose passage which resembles Dorothea's epiphany most closely in fact comes from a text written by a man, and representing a male character: it is Dmitry's redemptive dream-vision of a starving baby in Dostoevsky's novel *The Brothers Karamazov*:

And he feels a melting in his heart never felt before, feels that he wants to weep, that he must do something so that the child should weep no more, so that its swarthy, emaciated mother should weep no more, so that tears should no longer exist from this moment on; and all this must be done right now, this very minute, without losing a single moment, stopping for nothing, using all the Karamazov energy.[131]

And, though Dostoevsky, in his reworking of the *King Lear* myth, turns his Regan, Goneril, and Cordelia into men, and so displaces his women characters from the centre of his tragedy (they are peripheral to the family conflict, and inspire others to action, rather than acting themselves), his women still manifest much richer, more surprising, and unpredictable patterns of behaviour than the women characters created by his women contemporaries.

Women writers' reluctance to examine the motivation of 'outstanding' women is underlined by the relative scarcity of women narrators in their texts. Perhaps because the first-person narrative had been used so effectively by women writers in order to ironize the motivation of men, it is on the whole avoided in the depiction of women. Where women narrators are used, they appear to efface themselves lest difficult questions are asked. In Starynkevich's 'They Are Not to Blame', for example, the narrator-heroine's withdrawal, at the end of the story, to Italy has been prefigured by different kinds of narrative reticence: she refers only in passing to the affair which has caused the split with her husband. And in Soboleva's story 'Pros and Cons' (1863), the narrator's lively account of her own upbringing as a spoilt, wilful only daughter switches half-way through to a third-person narrative about the harmful effects of education on an egotistical young woman, who uses her wiles to snatch a man in whom she is not really interested from an underprivileged, but worthy, rival.[132]

Reticence in a literary sense, an eschewal of literary opinion, seems to have signified not only a protection of the virtue of a fictional heroine,

---

[130] George Eliot, *Middlemarch*, ch. 80.

[131] Dostoevsky, *Brat'ya Karamazovy*, pt. 3, bk. 9, ch. 8: *Polnoe sobranie sochinenii v 30 tomakh* (Leningrad, 1972–90), xiv. 456–7.

[132] On Starynkevich, 'Ne oni vinovaty', see n. 123 above; Soboleva, 'I pro i contra', OZ 158 (1863), 295–448; see also 'Pros and Cons' in *Anthology*.

but a manifestation of the author's own probity. So much is suggested, at any rate, by the memoirs of Avdotya Panaeva, who constantly underlines her failure to participate in literary conversation, and dwells on the fact that she was valued amongst her male radical writer friends in the traditional feminine role of comforter and confidante, so that they could hardly believe this 'prosaic woman' was also the author of prose. Panaeva's main mode of a specifically literary kind, here as in her fiction, is satire. The reticent narrator acts as a literary *animatrice*, the backdrop to a series of ironic portraits of Turgenev and many other Russian literary greats. Only rarely does Panaeva portray herself as an actor in the drama, most notably in an anecdote about how she attempted to subvert Alexandre Dumas's expectation that she act as a perfect hostess by providing him with a meal of grotesque richness. (The attempt, however, was unsuccessful: Dumas's admiration of Panaeva's housekeeping skills was still further increased.[133])

Yet the literary deference of Russian women writers is not a straight-forward phenomenon; in its own way it could be as ostentatious as the behaviour of Jane Eyre, parading in her 'modest' grey wedding-dress. The linear narrative not only leaves awkward questions unasked, but works to distract the reader's attention from such questions; however, on closer scrutiny, many incentive narratives do manifest elements that run contrary to, rather than supporting, the standard plot of escape. For example, the managing older women who hold sway over marital arrangements represent a middle-aged female authority, obtained through conservatism, whose presence to some extent undercuts the aspirations of the youthful heroines. The reader is left to wonder what will happen to these heroines when they are 40, given that their society is one in which (according to the narratives themselves) the main source of power open to older women is manipulation of their descendants. Individual texts also manifest thought-provoking gaps and contradictions. In Soboleva's 'Pros and Cons', for example, the polarization of incentive and disincentive modes of feminine behaviour in the second part of the text seems straightforward enough in itself. However, the virtuous Lyuba is far less reminiscent of the narrator's own earlier self than the spoilt and wilful Zina. The resemblance raises questions about the narrator's own right to pronounce on what she witnesses, and gives her self-righteousness an ironic resonance. Panaeva's story 'The Fanta-sist' (1864) also gives an apparently standard plot of escape a new twist, though one of rather a different kind. The idealistic young 'fantasist' of the title discovers, quite in line with the usual conventions of the

---

[133] Panaeva, *Vospominaniya* (1890; Moscow, 1956).

provincial tale, that the man to whom she has looked for mental guidance is, in fact, entangled with her flirtatious and scheming sister. The discovery is made as she, directed by the maid, spies on the two of them through a key-hole. Though Panaeva attempts to play down the obvious connotations of sexual voyeurism by placing the spies, rather than those whom they spy on, in a bedroom, and referring only to the 'worldly polish' of the man's attire, the contrast between sexual innocence and sexual manipulativeness is called into question (who is the transgressor?)[134]

It is arguable that feminist criticism should concentrate precisely on such paradoxes, searching for hidden motifs and inner contradictions rather than following the obvious linear schematism of the narrative. But whilst one would not wish to deny the function of imaginative criticism in unlocking new meanings in women's prose, from a historical perspective it is requisite to point out that the socially engaged and morally incentive realist tradition which Russian women prose writers adopted from the 1840s was consciously shaped in a way that avoided speculation on the interior world and sexuality. Whilst in practice the 'escape plot' manifested doubts and incoherences, in theory it was not meant to: the expression of doubts and incoherences was something which Russian radicals considered a diversion from the matter in hand. In a review of 1871, 'English Authoresses', for example, the writer Mariya Tsebrikova, who was also an important activist in the feminist movement, argued that English women had little sense of how to liberate themselves. They could only write about their own wretched lives; it would not be they who would execute the requisite literary task, that of creating 'the image of a woman who is able to devote herself to serving mankind's great causes in both word and deed'. Tsebrikova's strictures reveal an astonishing proscriptiveness regarding the admissable material of fiction. Gaskell 'is a most striking example of the deadly influence of mysticism on a writer's talent'. The Brontës manifest 'the morality of the parsonage'. *Middlemarch* is 'over-long and under-unified'.[135]

Here we begin to see how the ideological gains of Russian women's writing could be made at the expense of some of the conceptual or

[134] Panaeva, 'Fantazerka', *S* 104 (1864), 169–219. If feminist criticism does not open out the realist text, it runs the risk of duplicating accusations customarily made by male critics against women. Cf. Yeats's poem 'In Memory of Con Markiewicz and Eva Gore-Booth' (1927), in Seamus Deane (ed.), *The Field Day Anthology of Irish Writing* (Derry, 1991), ii. 816, in which he asserts the essential incompatibility of the political and the aesthetic for women, opposing the 'two girls in silk kimonos, both | Beautiful, one a gazelle', to the crones of the present, and the 'vague utopias' of their politics to the 'gazebo', i.e. a perspective transcendent of spatial and temporal limitation.

[135] Tsebrikova, 'Anglichanki-romanistki', *OZ* 197 (1871), 403–60; 198 (1871), 121–72; 199 (1871), 175–205. On Tsebrikova see Stites, *Women's Liberation*, and also A. N. Mogilyansky, 'Novye dannye o M. K. Tsebrikovoi', *Russkaya literatura* (1971), 1: 102–11.

technical diversity achieved by such Western practitioners of the 'novel of ideas' as George Sand, Charlotte Brontë, Maria Edgeworth, or Elizabeth Gaskell. And Tsebrikova's interpretation, so far from being novel or idiosyncratic, in fact reflected ideas that had long been widespread in Russian radical criticism, which regarded adventurousness in prose no more favourably than virtuosity in poetry. Belinsky's recommendation of Elena Gan's writing as a model for woman writers had, for example, been based on a simplistic interpretation of Gan's work as the expression of an 'idea'; his critical analysis made no reference to the idiosyncrasies of her histrionic and self-questioning textual strategies. Later followers of Belinsky, such as Nikolai Nekrasov and Nikolai Dobrolyubov, were to display a similar indifference to the language of the text.[136] And the provincial tale's indifference to the physical world was traceable to the asceticism which characterized the Russian radicals in general, not simply women of advanced ideas. Domesticity was held to be incompatible with intellectual achievement, and intelligent women could not, it was felt, be interested in the management of households. In his observations on Elena Gan's writing, Nekrasov rains down abuse on cooking, child-bearing, and housekeeping, pellucidly conveying, for all his corkscrewing syntax, that women writers must write of something else if they are to be taken seriously:

Our women authoresses to some extent confirm the absurd view according to which, if woman has been made, as many think she has, for the kitchen, the nursery, and the maids' room, and if she is to be allowed to take up a manly pursuit—to grasp the author's quill, then she must do so only with the most modest and innocent purpose: to repeat worn-out *sententiae*, already known to everyone and interesting to no one, and to celebrate lace, shawls, and the 'dear torment of balls'.[137]

And so the conclusion irresistibly emerges that Tolstoy's freedom to depict women's private and interior concerns was derived not in spite of his hostility to women's liberation, but because of his hostility to women's liberation.

For all that, though, we should not see the feminist project of the

[136] Belinsky, '*Sochineniya* Zeneidy R'; cf. N. Nekrasov, 'Vzglyad na glavneishie yavleniya russkoi literatury v 1843 godu', *Polnoe sobranie sochinenii i pisem v 15 tomakh* (Moscow, 1981–), iii. 151–2; N. A. Dobrolyubov, 'Stikhotvoreniya Yulii Zhadovskoi (1859)', *Sobranie sochinenii v 9 tomakh* (Moscow-Leningrad, 1961–4), iii. 133–47. Cf. also Arja Rosenholm's detailed case-study, 'Auf den Spuren des Vergessens: zur Rezeptionsgeschichte der russischen Schriftstellerin N. D. Chvoščinskaja', *Studia Slavica Finlandensia*, 6 (1989), 63–91.

[137] Nekrasov, 'Vzglyad', *PSS* iii. 151–2. An example of sexual prudery in the radical tradition is Dobrolyubov's review of Avgusta Voronova's stories, 'Pervyi shag', *SS* ii. 279–80, which suggests that these stories, representing drunken assaults on women, are unsuitable reading material for young girls. See also Irina Paperno, *Chernyshevsky and the Age of Realism: A Study in the Semiotics of Behavior* (Stanford, Calif., 1988), esp. 90–1, 95–6.

provincial tale simply in terms of a homiletic elision of infinite possibility. The discourses of sexuality or of interiority were encircled with restrictions and prohibitions not of the radicals' own making; they could not simply be plucked and enjoyed, like fruit ready on a tree. There were compelling reasons, for example, behind the avoidance of sexuality as a topic. Russian women's unusual frankness about gynaecological matters in conversation had been noted by a Scottish doctor who visited Moscow in the early nineteenth century.[138] Frankness in *writing* is quite a different matter, however. We must remember the notion, first raised in the late 1830s, and resurfacing in misogynist texts at intervals thereafter, that women's biology was incompatible with literary activity. With no counter-arguments assigning a positive value to the female body at their disposal (for there were none in existence), women could only suggest the negative essentialism of misogyny by referring to their bodies in print; in the circumstances, their silence is only too understandable.[139]

Not only the obviously problematic domain of sexuality, but the apparently more neutral areas of lyricism and psychological exploration were also fraught with difficulty. In her recent comparative analysis of Evgeniya Tur's 'Antonina' and Turgenev's 'The Unhappy Woman', Jane Costlow has illustrated how a male writer's act of appropriating a woman writer's text becomes an act with aggressive overtones: the lyricism of Turgenev's treatment is at once a suspension of judgement and an act of possession, which refuses the overt affiliation evident in Tur's more didactic and less poetical treatment.[140] If this shows how a male writer could defuse the feminist text retrospectively, the wariness of women writers with regard to discourses of interiority had a prehistory as well. The deepest root of the provincial tale tradition is the tale of sensibility as developed by Russian women before 1820, with its stress on the oppression of women. But an important catalyst for the development of the tales of 'provincial misses' which poured from Russian presses in the middle decades of the nineteenth century was the publication of Pushkin's novel in verse *Evgeny Onegin* (1823–31). The figure of Tatiana, an unusually imaginative young girl from the country gentry, and later a woman whose independence is established by an act of

[138] Robert Lyall, *The Character of the Russians, and a Detailed History of Moscow* (London, 1823), 121–4.

[139] On the biological argument, see observations on Verevkin, above; an additional obstacle to the expression of sexual material by women was the idea that writing might in itself be a form of sexual display, an idea which is referred to obliquely in the work of Elena Gan. Interesting comparative possibilities are suggested by Helena Michie, *The Flesh Made Word: Female Figures and Women's Bodies* (New York, 1989), a study of prohibitions on the body in Anglo-American written culture.

[140] Jane Costlow, 'Speaking the Sorrow of Women: Turgenev's "Neschastnaia" and Evgeniia Tur's "Antonina"', *SR* 50/2 (1991), 328–35.

principled self-abnegation, was to become the pattern for their heroines; her frivolous and self-centred sister Olga was the origin for the heroine's negative counter-image, a scheming flirt.[141]

The readiness of women writers to accept Tatiana as a model was striking; it is possible to see the central project of the provincial tale as an attempt to prove that Tatiana's dignity was attainable by women who did not accept Tatiana's destiny as a faithful wife. The obvious question now is: why should *Evgeny Onegin* have become canonical? One reason for this was the insistence by nineteenth-century commentators (almost always male) that Tatiana was the ideal of national womanhood.[142] But another, and less obvious reason lay in *Evgeny Onegin*'s mediated dependence on the traditions of French women's writing.

Like his heroine, Tatiana, Pushkin had read not only Richardson's *Charles Grandison*, but also a variety of women writers, among them Mrs Radcliffe and Madame de Staël. His representation of the 'dark' aspects of femininity (brunette, rich, and eloquently emotional) in Tatiana alongside its 'light', blonde, matter-of-fact aspects in her sister Olga recalls the contrast between the 'dark' heroine Corinne and her fair rival Lucille in Madame de Staël's novel *Corinne* (1807). The polarization of Pushkin's heroes Onegin and Lensky is also anticipated in Staël's treatment of her Northern Sentimentalist baron Oswald, who is opposed to the cynical and worldly French rake, the Comte d'Erfeuil.

There is an important matter in which Pushkin departs from Staël in appropriating her, however: the treatment of the central figures in *Evgeny Onegin* is explicitly ironic. That there was nothing intrinsically 'unfeminine' in satirizing Staël had been demonstrated by Madame de Genlis's humorous tale *Hortense* (1808), wherein the eponymous heroine makes 'un sot marriage', and a fool of herself, whilst retracing the steps of Corinne in Italy. However, Russian women writers had some reason to be suspicious of irony applied to the text of sensibility, since it had, historically, been Sentimentalism's criticism of male sexual abuse of women which had been targeted by the ironizers. To put it schematically, Russian women readers and writers were faced with a choice between Karamzin's 'Poor Liza', which portrayed the seduction of a socially defenceless woman in negative and pathetic terms, or Pushkin's parody-revision 'The Station-Master' (1829), which indicated that surrender to such a seduction might be the best that such a woman could

---

[141] Pushkin, *Evgeny Onegin*, *PSS* v. On Tatiana see also Diana Burgin, 'Tatiana Larina's Letter to Onegin and *la plume criminelle*', *EP* 16/1 (1991), 12–23.

[142] On Tatiana as the ideal of national womanhood see, for example Belinsky, 'Evgeny Onegin: stat'ya devyataya', *PSS* vii. 480–500; cf. the amusing remarks of Nabokov in Pushkin, *Eugene Onegin*, ii. 280–1.

expect to do with her life.[143] Women and men sympathetic to feminism continued to support the central tenets of Sentimentalism: they held that the exercise of self-control by men in marital and extramarital relations was a pre-condition of a just society, and they believed in the 'perfectibility' of human nature by means of moral education. How could they agree with a reviewer of 1831, who had declared, in his analysis of Evgeny Baratynsky's narrative poem 'The Concubine', that expression of moralism in literature was boring and old-fashioned?[144]

In eschewing irony, the authors of provincial tales did not dissociate themselves only from texts written by male writers which subordinated female sexuality to male desire. They also dissociated themselves from the questioning attitudes to the cult of sensibility expressed by the 'aristocratic' authors of the society tale, whose work was increasingly associated with reactionary politics after 1840. Overt affiliation to the cult of sensibility allowed provincial-tale authors to concentrate on emotional confusion, and hence to escape from the contemplation of intellectual confusion (a heroine's doubts and fears about her own actions and motives). But at the same time, provincial-tale authors also committed themselves to the limited psychological vocabulary associated with the cult of sensibility. The internal world is expressed by means of external gestures, especially tears, or by means of melodramatic speeches; or represented in the authorial narrative by hackneyed phrases ('her breast was torn with anguish', and the like). It is scarcely surprising that many women writers preferred to represent their heroines as staunch, dignified, and resolute.

There was a further problem, too, which lay in the issue of privileged knowledge. When Tolstoy's narrator in *Anna Karenina* crosses the forbidden boundary into Kitty's bedroom, and eavesdrops on her conversation with her sister Dolly, the reader has absolute confidence, for here is an observer who is an outsider, yet who parades intimacy, who is simultaneously involved and distant.[145] A Russian woman writer who made such a leap would attain no private information or secret knowledge; she would simply convey what everyone expected her to know in any case. In other words, by dwelling on the particular experience of women, Russian women writers revealed 'femininity' in an undesirable sense; the cause to which they had committed themselves, on the other

---

[143] Madame de Genlis, *Hortense, ou la victime des romans et des voyages, par faire suite à Sainclair* (Paris and St Petersburg, 1808); unlike Genlis, Pushkin's *Onegin* however also parodies Staël's epistolary novel *Delphine* (Paris, 1805). Pushkin, 'Stantsionnnyi smotritel', from *Povesti Belkina, PSS* vi. 88–98.

[144] N. Polevoi, 'E. Baratynsky, *Nalozhnitsa*', *Moskovskii telegraf*, 38 (1831), 235–43.

[145] Tolstoy, *Anna Karenina*, pt. 2, ch. 3, *PSS* xviii. 130–2.

hand, consisted in liberation from femininity. Or, as the heroine of Khvoshchinskaya's *Ursa Major* puts it: 'A woman should be a woman for one man alone; for everyone else she must be simply a human being' (p. 232).

The women authors of the provincial tales were not bedevilled by didacticism as such; didacticism, after all, can be exhilarating (one has only to think of Alexander Pope or of Jane Austen). It was the association of that didacticism with rigidly puritanical opinions, and its location in a generally prohibitive cultural context, which caused problems. The provincial tale argued a case for the liberation of women which assumed that *exceptional* women deserved to be liberated; part of the project, therefore, consisted in the denigration of 'ordinary' femininity. And, for a variety of reasons, the motivation of the exceptional women themselves could not be scrutinized. But given the homogeneity of the radical press, the fact that the case for women's liberation was ubiquitously argued (in literature, in literary journalism, and in political articles) to an audience already persuaded of that case's merits, it is perhaps surprising that the provincial tale allowed the expression of even the limited amount of variety and uncertainty which it does reveal.

The hostility to imaginative writing and to ambivalent narrative stance amongst those committed to women's emancipation was to resonate in the years after 1880 as well. The era was to see a tremendous expansion of the issues handled in realist literature, and a re-examination of established literary practices. However, interiority was to remain, in some senses, a problem for women's realist prose, and the tradition was to remain aloof from some technical innovations that came with the rise of Symbolism. Even as late as the 1890s, the work of Anne and Emily Brontë, for instance, was to be criticized for its 'excessive fantasy'.[146] For its part, the Symbolist movement was to have little patience either with the political feminist movement, or with the depiction of the 'dreariness of grey lives', which was believed to be the concern of Russian realist writers, women as well as men; whilst the understandable reaction against the conceptual crudities of the radical aesthetic was to provoke some rather naïve assumptions about the absolute freedom that might be attainable outside that aesthetic.[147]

---

[146] See Anon., 'Bronte (Sharlotta Bronte)', *ES* iv. 723–5.

[147] For criticism of realist writing as 'grey' and artistically unskilled, see for example the decadent poet Mikhail Kuzmin's review of E. Militsyna's *Rasskazy*: 'Zametki o russkoi belletristike', *Apollon* (1910), 4: *khronika*, 66; on the limitations of the decadent view of 'freedom', see especially Charlotte Rosenthal, 'Zinaida Vengerova: Modernism and Women's Liberation', *ISS* 8 (1987), 97–106.

2

Mariya Zhukova (1804–1855)

WHILST by no means the first woman prose writer in Russia, Mariya Zhukova was one of the first women who produced a substantial body of work in the Russian language, and the first to be given significant honours in her own country. Zhukova began publishing work in the late 1830s, at a time just before prose finally put an end to the hegemony of Romantic poetry. Since the majority of prose writers of the day were also poets, and Zhukova, by contrast, worked in prose from the beginning of her career, she was also one of the earliest serious nineteenth-century writers, irrespective of gender, to declare herself as a prose specialist right from the start. Zhukova herself, however, seems to have been little conscious of her status as a literary pioneer. She appears, rather, to have taken to writing for pressing practical reasons. In the late 1820s she had become estranged from her husband, being left to bring up her son alone. Having no substantial private means (she came from a respectable, but by no means grand or wealthy family of the provincial aristocracy), she was forced to consider her own resources. A good draughtswoman, she could produce pleasing sketches; writing seems to have suggested itself as a parallel, and comparable, activity likely to appeal to the circles of the St Petersburg upper classes in which she moved.[1]

Supported by her friend and patron, Princess Golitsyna, Zhukova made her first publication, a group of short stories under the title *Evenings by the Karpovka*, in 1837. (The fact that she chose to begin

[1] The best source on Zhukova's biography is Hugh Aplin's thorough and well-annotated survey of her life in 'Mariya Zhukova and Elena Gan. Women Writers and Female Protagonists, 1837–1843', Ph.D. thesis (University of East Anglia, 1989), 81–98. See also the anon. obituary in OZ 100 (1855), sect. 5, 57–8. Zhukova's connection with the Apothecary's Island in St Petersburg, the setting for *Evenings by the Karpovka*, is charmingly described in V. N. Toporov, 'Aptekarskaya ostrov': see N. V. Zlydneeva, V. V. Ivanov, V. N. Toporov, and T. V. Tsiv'yan (eds.), *Noosfera i khudozhestvennoe tvorchestvo* (Moscow, 1991), 200–73.

with an individual volume, rather than place one of her stories in a journal, is probably an indication that financial remuneration was of more consequence than literary prestige.)[2] *Evenings* consisted of brief tales supposedly narrated to Natalya Dmitrievna, an elderly upper-class woman in poor health, by friends gathered in the *dacha* which she had taken for the summer in a fashionable resort, the Apothecary's Island near St Petersburg. The audience's indulgence was sought with a suitably modest formula of patronage, suggesting that the narrator of the introduction had acted simply as recorder of stories written by other people, and that more material would become available were it requested:

I should warn the reader that Natalya Dmitrievna has granted me the especial favour of allowing me to collect and publish the stories whose acquaintance I first made in her drawing-room. I have not changed a word in them, but am publishing them in the exact form in which they were originally composed, to amuse an elderly invalid lady. Whether I shall continue with the publication will depend on the attention with which the public may be inclined to favour these, the fruits of my first labours.[3]

These hints provoked a gratifyingly appropriate response: Zhukova's tales became very popular. She was able to continue her first collection, and to follow it with another, *Tales* of 1840, which had gone into a second edition as early as 1841. Thereafter, Zhukova did begin publishing in journals, which was also an indication of the rise of her reputation. Between 1841 and 1845, she published a number of substantial stories in such prestigious locations as *Sovremennik* and *Otechestvennye zapiski*, including 'Dacha on the Peterhof Road' (1845), as well as a book of travel impressions, *Sketches of Southern France and Nice* (1844). But from the mid-1840s, Zhukova's productivity began to tail off: she produced only two more pieces, 'An Episode from the Life of a Country Lady' (1847), and 'Nadenka' (1853); a third story, 'Two Weddings', was published posthumously in 1857. Biographical materials relating to Zhukova are so scanty that it is impossible to say whether Zhukova's drop in productivity was the result of the poor health from which she was

---

[2] Zhukova [as 'M. Zh——va'], *Vechera na Karpovke*, vol. i (St Petersburg, 1837); vol. ii (St Petersburg, 1838). On financial remuneration, see e.g. the warning by Gan's fictional character Heilfreund to Anyuta that as a novice author, she will either have to publish for nothing in the journals, or bring out a volume at her own expense (Gan, 'Naprasnyi dar', *PSS* 758—full details under Gan, Ch. 4 n. 1 below).

[3] Zhukova, *Vechera na Karpovke*, vol. i; see *Vechera na Karpovke* (Moscow, 1986), 11; further citations to this edn. in text as *VK*.

suffering in the last few years of her life, or of the fact that she had now been able to secure her future in a material sense.[4]

As this account suggests, Zhukova turned to writing in much the same way that a modern upper-class European woman, left hard-up after a divorce, might start an interior-decoration or party-catering business. Rather than a vocation, writing was for her a profession, or even a job. And, in turn, this social position had particular effects on her work. Some women writers of her day saw writing as a one-way process of emotional communication; where a readership is imagined, it is visualized as hostile, but passive—the attitude is very much, 'you can listen to this whether you like it or not'. This was an attitude expressed in the work of such poets as Teplova, and in the narrative manner of Elena Gan, as well as in the latter's portraits of fictional heroines such as Anyuta and Theophania.[5] Zhukova, by contrast, could not but be conscious of the need to shape and direct her material in order to ensure its appeal.

The need to accommodate public taste had various results, some of which are obvious at a superficial level, but others of which become evident only after deeper consideration. At first sight, Zhukova's work seems to have a reassuring, even a palliative character; it appears conservative both in an aesthetic and in a political sense. Only on closer scrutiny does it become evident that the constraints of her sensitivity to readership might have positive effects, giving her writing a strong measure of professional discipline—a discipline already suggested in the choice of the word 'labour' [*trud*] to describe the act of writing up the stories in *Evenings by the Karpovka*. Zhukova was well aware that emotional intensity was not the only, or even the most important, criterion by which literature might be judged. She was disinclined to confuse 'feelings' with 'words', emotions with the textual expression of emotions; she was, as we shall see, more concerned with examining the conventional understanding of behaviour and psychology than with representing behaviour and psychology in their own right. All this means that, though Zhukova was an early exponent of the provincial tale, her work is best suited to the formal and symmetrical narrative patterns of the society tale.

I shall demonstrate this point by giving a brief general survey of Zhukova's work, including her provincial tales, before going on to look

---

[4] Zhukova [as 'M. Zh——va'], *Povesti* (2 vols.; St Petersburg, 1840); repr. as *Russkie povesti* (St Petersburg, 1841); *Ocherki yuzhnoi Frantsii i Nittsy* (2 vols.; St Petersburg, 1844); 'Epizod iz zhizni derevenskoi damy', *OZ* 52 (1847), 1–116; 'Dacha na Petergofskoi storone', *OZ* 39 (1845), 225–326 (see also *Dacha*, 245–321); 'Naden'ka', *S* 40 (1853), 137–82; 'Dve svad'by', *OZ* 112 (1857), 591–663; 113 (1857), 51–138.

[5] On Teplova, see Ch. 1 above; on Gan, see Ch. 4 below.

in more detail at her society tale, 'Baron Reichman', and at the structure of *Evenings* as a collection.

Whether in her society or provincial tales, Zhukova's essential subject-matter is the relations between men and women before and during marriage, according to the traditions of 'feminine prose' already established in Russo-French and Russian literature. In comparison with her immediate predecessors and contemporaries in the Russian tradition, however, she is relatively cautious in her criticism of the family tie. Most of her fictional husbands and suitors act with the best intentions (or appear so to act—as we shall see later, more than one interpretation can be put on some stories); only one of her male characters, the protagonist of 'The Monk', the first story in *Evenings*, is represented as dangerously aggressive; and this character is anomalous on class grounds, since this story deals with a merchant family, rather than the circles of the gentry which Zhukova normally portrayed. Even in her later narratives, some of which do directly raise issues of female emancipation, narrative resolutions are often (though not always) quiescent. In 'My Friends at Kursk' (*Povesti*, ii. 181–283), the spirited heroine mounts a direct attack on Verevkin's scurrilous publication 'Lady Authoresses', but her rebellion remains verbal. By the end of the story she has succumbed to unhappy love, and is consoling herself with the solaces of religion.

Zhukova's caution is also evident in her general preference for scrutinizing incidental customs in the family, rather than the institutional structures themselves. This tendency to criticize peripheral, rather than central, aspects of marriage and the family is exemplified in her fascination with figures on the fringes of the family, above all the *vospitannitsa*. The *vospitannitsa* was the term used for a poor relation who was the recipient of charity in the households of richer relatives, and who occupied a position not too far removed from that of a companion or upper servant. (The parallel in English women's writing would be the governess; in Russian fictional households, as in the aristocratic households of reality, governesses are almost invariably of non-Russian origin, and make only fleeting appearances, normally as rather comic old-maid types.) The *vospitannitsa* is not a type originating in, or unique to, women's writing in Russia. Well-known examples from Russian literary texts written by men are Liza in Pushkin's 'The Queen of Spades', and later Sonya in Tolstoy's *War and Peace*. In both these cases the reader's sympathy for an apparently victimized figure is later undermined: Liza, an amusing illustration of institutionalized aggression, marries and herself begins to bully a *vospitannitsa*; when Sonya's infatuation for her cousin Nikolai proves fruitless, we are assured by the narrator that her position should not be sentimentalized, for 'she was one of those people who attach themselves to the whole household, rather than to anyone in it, just like a cat'.[6]

In Zhukova's fictions the misfortunes of the *vospitannitsa* are not so easily dismissed. In 'The Medallion' (*VK* 75–110), for example, this woman character is the central female figure, a gentle and self-sacrificing individual whose secret and hopeless love for the family doctor subjects her to a series of terrible emotional upheavals. This image of silent suffering is heightened by its juxtaposition to a negative counter-heroine, the spoilt daughter of the house. 'Self-Sacrifice' (*Povesti*, i. 111–257) also depicts the difficulties of a *vospitannitsa* heroine, and here, too, a negative counter-heroine is juxtaposed. Liza, adopted as a companion by a rich young countess, is taken into a social circle very different from that of her retiring and respectable provincial parents; but her rise in social status is illusory, and before long she is manipulated into a situation where she finds that she must cover for the intrigues of her self-centred friend. For all the similarities in plot and structure, the two stories are very different in effect. Where the protagonist of 'The Medallion' is left disconsolate, the central character in 'Self-Sacrifice' reacts to her situation self-consciously, preferring a single existence to the offer of financial support (that is, dependence) within marriage.

Zhukova's presentation of Liza suggests very clearly that a resolution to the problems of women's economic dependence in the family might lie outside the family. But in illustrating this formula of independence by portraying a woman whose status *already* lies outside normal family relations, she can avoid an all-out attack on marriage. Those women whose position in the family is already secure, and whose allegiance to the patriarchy is 'natural', the daughters of the house, have no need to avoid marriage; instead, they exploit their negotiating capacity within it. And Zhukova does not represent the solution of her anti-heroines as a form of independence; it is to be understood as a manifestation of wilfulness or even of immorality.

Zhukova's successors amongst women writers were to be much less hesitant in their approach to family life: melancholic fatalism was to be replaced by sustained anger, and the upbeat ending of 'Self-Sacrifice' was to be transferred to plots which involved actual daughters of the house. But if Zhukova's ideological framework was later to be replaced by one that was less cramping, her tales illustrate in embryo many of the aesthetic problems which were to beset later practitioners of the provin-

---

[6] Tolstoy, *War and Peace*, Epilogue, pt. 1, ch. 8. On the subject of the *vospitannitsa*, see also Svetlana Slavskaya, '"Everyone Knew Her and No-One Noticed Her": The Fate of the *Vospitannitsa* (Female Ward) in Nineteenth-Century Russian Literature', Ph.D. thesis (Columbia University, New York, 1991).

cial tale. The abstract, formulaic setting, the contrast between upright heroine and self-serving anti-heroine, the narrator's sometimes leaden didacticism—all these elements are present in these early provincial tales, as they are in later examples of the genre. It is true that Zhukova attempts a more extensive depiction of her central characters' interior world than some of her successors would. Her late story 'Dacha on the Peterhof Road', for example, is one of the few early nineteenth-century stories by a Russian woman to deal with the subject of madness. But the attempt to capture interiority is vitiated, for the emotional rhetoric at her command is limited and conventional: it does not go beyond a range of affective gestures, such as chins leant on hands, paling cheeks, floods of tears, fainting, and so on. Rather than illustrating how one woman writer could find a language of inner feeling, she conclusively demonstrates the difficulties of this language for women writers.

All this might seem to belittle Zhukova, making her sound a palatably derivative writer, one pandering to the taste of those who unthinkingly accepted the status quo. Such suspicions might well be heightened by the patronizing tone of contemporary reviews. For Belinsky, who (when in his bourgeois rather than anti-bourgeois phase) gave her first collection an approving write-up, Zhukova was the true example of what 'feminine prose' should be: modest in its ambitions, describing material appropriate to a lady, and graceful in its achievements. He was almost equally complimentary on the subject of her second collection, pausing only to voice some doubts about the emancipated heroine of 'My Friends at Kursk'. Yet only two years later, he was to brand her a 'feminine' writer in the worst sense of the word: one whose work was sentimental, 'idealistic', and had no relevance for new, socially aware, generations.[7]

Amongst later critics, Zhukova's work has attracted interest mainly as a sampler of fashionable genres: she has been accorded a tiny niche as one of the very minor writers of the post-Pushkin generation, one typically 'feminine' in her microscopic concerns. In a recent example of such an assessment, R. V. Iezuitova, editor of the 1986 republication of *Evenings by the Karpovka*, argued that the treatment of adultery in 'Baron Reichman' was far inferior, in profundity and subtlety, to that in Tolstoy's *Anna Karenina* (VK 281).[8]

The transparent absurdity of this comment (comparing as it does a

---

[7] Belinsky, '"Vechera na Karpovke" M. Zh——voi', *PSS* ii. 356–65; *idem*, '"Povesti" M. Zh——voi', *PSS* iv. 110–18; for his later attack on her, see 'Povesti Zinaidy R——va', *PSS* vii. 656.

[8] For an English translation of 'Baron Reichman', see Joe Andrew, *An Anthology of Russian Women's Writing 1830–1855* (forthcoming); and on this and other stories by Zhukova, see Andrew's essay, 'Mariya Zhukova and Patriarchal Power', in his *Narrative and Desire in Russian Literature 1822–1849: Feminine and Masculine* (London, 1993), 139–83.

story of only just over thirty pages with a novel of over seven hundred) already indicates the necessity for a rereading of Zhukova's work, one which would not simply search for manifestos of liberation and find them lacking, but which would see her work in terms of broader issues of representation and autonomy. The preliminary point of entry for such a reading is suggested by Iezuitova's substantiating comments on 'Baron Reichman': she finds the plot of the story, in which two male rivals, a husband and his friend, collude in order to curtail the wife's growing infatuation for the friend, improbable:

The errant heroine is opposed by the virtuous Baron Reichman (a man with an unblemished biography, a war hero, a man admired by his subordinates) who is willing to forgive his wife her mistakes. Since he cannot force himself to impugn the honour of the noble Baron, Levin renounces his love. (*VK* 281)

To argue in this manner is entirely to misrepresent the virtues of Zhukova's text, which is made to appear a great deal more simple-minded than it in fact is. Whilst in some ways a conventional society tale (the catalyst of the plot is the malignant rumour, a topos of Russian aristocratic fictions from Griboedov on), 'Baron Reichman' is simultaneously an original piece precisely *because* of its resolution, which shows how male codes of behaviour isolate women. Romantic love, we are led to see, is a fiction which men are prepared to entertain so long as it does not threaten 'honour', the hierarchical network of relations cementing male society.

The story takes an unusually clear-sighted view of the illusory freedom which women are offered by extramarital heterosexual relations in a patriarchal society. It shows that such relations depend on a husband's co-operation, as well as on the unpredictable inclinations of other men. It is Baron Reichman who first excites his wife's interest in Levin; it is he who curtails the affair when it has begun to break the rules of what he first set up as a pleasant game. And the restoration of the status quo in marriage leaves the reader with deep feelings of unease, since it is achieved by a transparent threat on the part of Baron Reichman. He asserts his rights to determine the fate of his 'son and heir', and thus appeals, we are told, to the Baroness's 'maternal feelings' in order to pressurize her into severing the connection with Levin. But the epilogue to the story sees her living abroad, and accordingly separated from both suitor *and* son; the latter, like the former, is now appropriated to her husband's cause.

'Honour' in this story should not be understood too simply, when its main mouthpiece is a man who (we are told) might have prevented his wife's affair, had he not spent so much time on grooming his own whiskers in order to pluck out the grey. The narrator does not dwell on the point, but the scene raises some uneasy questions: how can a man who so despises the outward signs of seniority then lay claim to its authority? And may his emphasis on 'honour' not perhaps be simply a further form of vanity? Yet another layer of ambiguity comes from the fact that the Baron's 'honourable' attitude to marriage is attributable, at least in part, to self-interest. We know that his wealth is his wife's, and so his preservation of the marriage is also a preservation of his own financial security; we also know that he has been rescued by her fortune from the gambling debts which he brought with him to the marriage.

'Baron Reichman' does not suggest, however, that the 'feminine' answer to honour, which would be to sacrifice social relations to love, is necessarily to be preferred. Baroness Reichman is a character undone by her own imagination; imbued with the cult of sensibility, she cannot help preferring her husband's 'poetic' lieutenant to his prosaic self. Yet the story is not simply a fable advocating sexual self-control in married women. It pairs an 'innocent' woman (Levin's 'natural' choice, the nubile Eleonskaya) and an 'experienced' woman (the Baroness), but this framework is used to represent a problem, not to suggest its solution. The 'innocent' Eleonskaya turns out to be the pawn of her mother; she is the instrument of a sexual predation which is socially acceptable, since its aim is marriage, but which can hardly be condoned in moral terms. The 'experienced' Baroness is undone by a piece of innocent, but socially unacceptable, behaviour, a failure of manners, not a failure of morals. Her relationship with Levin is not a love-affair in the full physical sense—the two spend most of their time singing arias from Italian opera together. The offensive nature of the relationship lies, rather, in the fact that it is more public than any love-affair would be, and hence a greater threat to the accepted forms of social organization.

The way that this apparently didactic contrast between two different women is nuanced might in itself make one wonder about the moral which the narrator derives from the story, which is that marriage would work if only women would try harder to please their husbands. Such doubts are enhanced by what we are told about the narrator, Pronovsky, in the introduction to *Evenings by the Karpovka*. This gentleman, we learn, has 'never been married' (though he has been unhappily in love); his pontifications on the proper behaviour of married women hence have an obvious irony. Besides, Pronovsky emerges as a remarkably unsuitable commentator on any serious subject:

He was in general one of those people who rarely voice their thoughts in public, and who speak of themselves still more rarely, who jokingly decline to settle any question of importance, or else content themselves with expressing borrowed opinions of what can be said pro et contra, saving their true thoughts for a few close friends. All in all, he conducted himself like a true philosopher, who can live happily anywhere and in any situation. (*VK* 10)

In 'Baron Reichman', then, we see women manipulated at various levels. The society which is represented manipulates them, they manipulate themselves by their own acceptance of certain subject positions, and the way in which they are represented within the text is also manipulative. If they are cyphers, then that is because their situation allows nothing else to them. Apparently more 'optimistic' than Gan's stories, 'Baron Reichman' is in fact more pessimistic. Escape from social constraints may prove beyond the earthly powers of Gan's talented heroines, but the reader is left in no doubt that their goal is worthwhile. In this story, by contrast, Zhukova illustrates that the very imagination of 'escape' is socially constrained, and that the apparent blandishments of freedom may be as ensnaring as the dull dictates of conformity.

Zhukova's reflections elsewhere indicate that for her freedom for women was a problem, not a given. In her travel book, *Sketches of Southern France and Nice*, she appears to endorse the idea that women are victims rather than agents, advocating, for example, a programme of strict control and moral guidance for 'those who have strayed from the path of virtue'. But the *Sketches* also contain some more abstract reflections, which illustrate that freedom and responsibility are context-dependent for Zhukova. Rail travel, she argues, is a surrender of the traveller's will to the inevitable, in contrast to the direct exercise of power which may be enjoyed in a carriage (*Ocherki Yuzhnoi Frantsii*, 26). Her views on women's social power went along similar lines. She was a collectivist and not an individualist, and held that changes of cultural direction were only possible in particular circumstances. This holds not merely for her views on the family (as we have seen, the only people who can move outside the family are those who are already outsiders), but also for her views on society in general. If she does project a sense of emancipation in *Evenings by the Karpovka*, then this is through the easy-going mixed-sex circle of Natalya Dmitrievna, represented in the frame narrative, in which women and men meet on equal terms, rather than through the actions of any individual heroine. And that 'emancip-ated' society, we should note, is one both spatially and conceptually removed from the metropolitan circles in which Baroness Reichman revolved. In unfree societies individuals are unfree; and freedom lies in the construction of society at large, not in the acts of isolated persons. The formulation which Zhukova reaches in *Evenings by the Karpovka* is diametrically opposed to the provincial tale's assertion that gifted individuals are able to overcome unpropitious circumstances, but it is in itself neither less sophisticated nor less convincing.

It is perhaps not surprising that Zhukova should have decided to ponder the notion of society in the abstract, given that readership was so important to her. Her concern with readership also had effects on her style. The need to entertain the leisured public which Zhukova visual- ized may have given her language a certain conservatism—beautiful women are always like the portraits of Albani, the sun is said on at least two occasions to resemble a spoilt beauty, and so on—but it also dictated that this language should be lively and aphoristic. It is doubtful whether Baron Reichman would have loved his wife so much had he made her acquaintance in a hut, we are told, 'for the Baron cared but little for eclogues' (*VK* 42); elsewhere it is drily observed that, 'It cannot be said that the mazurka is an entirely convenient dance for declarations of love'. Metonymy is skilfully used to encapsulate. For example, the character of the Reichmans' marriage is established in a passage linking the Baron's 'luxuriant epaulettes' and the Baroness's 'straggly villages', which together make up the 'foliage on the world's tree'. And in a later scene barges bob down the river carrying the luggage of the *beau monde* back from the country villas, with a jumble of fashionable objects heaped together on board:

Flower-pots stood on tables, which themselves were stacked on divans; armchairs peeped out from under screens heaped high with mattresses and pillows; a bay tree stuck up in the midst of piles of hat-boxes, whilst copper saucepans gleamed next to a marble bust of Venus. On a stool with satin upholstery a cook sat stiffly, and chatted to a footman in blue livery. (*VK* 66)

There is little attempt to distinguish the style of the different narrators in *Evenings*, but there is a general gloss of easy-going wit both in Zhukova's early stories, and in her travel notes. Like the prose of Pushkin, Zhukova's work shows the lessons learnt from French. (The deterioration into a less competently shaded melodramatic narrative mode in Zhukova's later stories may be another, but here more unfortu- nate, indication of her rapid response to a likely readership: this time, one that expected instruction before all else. No doubt the enormous success of Elena Gan went some way towards pushing her in this direction.)

But it is above all in the frame narrative form of *Evenings by the Karpovka* that the felicitous results of Zhukova's professionalism are evident. She uses this well-worn convention to achieve effects which are very much her own. Her pairings of tale and teller are as likely to be mis- matches as affinities. A bachelor, as we have seen, lectures the company about marriage; a man happily in love tells a lachrymose tale of tragic love; a secure middle-aged widow contributes a story about the trials of a put-upon wife. Besides such obvious ironies, there are other, perhaps less immediately striking, virtues in Zhukova's schema. The first such virtue lies in the particular grouping and arrangement of material which the cycle form makes possible. Zhukova's portrayal of women locked into social and family relations which are emotionally unsatisfactory is not new. But by assembling a collection of narratives which represent women in various, rather disparate settings, she is able to argue that dissatisfaction is not unique to the narrow set of women represented in the 'society tale': very similar problems are faced by women from different historical periods, and from different social backgrounds. The heroine of 'The Monk', like the heroine of 'Baron Reichman', is trapped between her society's conventional reading of circumstantial evidence and her husband's jealousy: the mechanics of marital repression are similar in the merchant classes and in the aristocracy, though in the former social stratum patriarchal authority is allowed more violent expression. 'The Dumb Girl' (*VK* 118–86) is a historical tale, set at the time of the palace coup engineered in 1740 by Russian noblemen hostile to the future Empress Elizabeth. The story attracted much criticism when first published on the grounds that it lacked historical authenticity. But in fact the reconstruction of historical events as such is of quite peripheral narrative importance; the main concern in the text is to depict the life of the eponymous heroine, who is attached to an aristocratic household in a position resembling that of a court fool. Though her situation is more desperate than that of any of Zhukova's *vospitannitsa* figures, this girl's relationship with a household of more privileged people than she is not dissimilar.

By grouping, in *Evenings*, several narratives with quite different settings, Zhukova raised more directly than any of her contemporaries or immediate successors the question of whether women from different classes and eras had similar interests, and suggested a considerable variety of 'feminine' experience. By placing these narratives in the frame of conversation at Natalya Dmitrievna's, Zhukova also suggested her concern with the representation of women according to different literary conventions, and raised the issue of how these literary conventions were to be interpreted. The tales themselves, as we have seen, raise serious problems; they are as likely to be pathetic as racy in tone, yet all of them are received light-heartedly by the assembled company. And at the end of the collection, the idea that exposure to literature may have beneficial effects on society is raised only to be exploded. Two young dependents of Natalya Dmitrievna, the elderly lady in whose social circle the tale-telling takes place, exploit the favour with which the various tales of romantic love have been greeted in order to beg permission to give their love a happy ending. There is considerable irony in the cementing of a marriage by a series of tales in general so remarkably pessimistic about the likely success of matrimony. Contact with literature apparently does have definite effects, but it is not always clear that these will be therapeutic; here it has communicated a sense of self-interest, but hardly a sense of self-preservation.

For all the concentration on defenceless young girls in *Evenings on the Karpovka*, the collection's most memorable character is Natalya Dmitrievna herself, who is financially and socially independent, enjoys friendships of intellectual equality with male companions, and has a tartly dry sense of humour. For once, a female survivor of the eighteenth century is portrayed as a benevolent matriarch, rather than as a terrifying virago. Indeed, the text itself appears to owe much to eighteenth-century tradition. The story-telling contest is set up in order to present a Russian challenge to French literature; and there is one particular author to whom the results of the contest seem particularly indebted: Madame de Genlis. As the similarity of title suggests, Genlis's *Evenings at the Château*, a collection of narrative material arranged as tales told on a series of evenings, has parallels with Zhukova's *Evenings*: these do not so much lie in the realization of the individual narratives, which in the case of the Genlis text are explicitly didactic tales directed at the children in a family group, as in the handling of the frame section of the narrative (a benevolent grandmother organizes story-telling to keep the family amused).[9]

There seem to be some general affinities between Zhukova and Genlis—not Genlis in her high preaching mode, that is, but Genlis the shrewd and wry social commentator of *Sainclair* or *Hortense*, whose paradoxical aphorism is borrowed for a chapter epigraph in 'Baron Reichman': 'La faiblesse prend souvent des résolutions plus violentes, que l'emportement' (*VK* 67). What Zhukova shares with this Genlis is an amused detachment from events. Like the latter, she argues the primacy of emotion in women; but she, too, is concerned with the need for rational resolutions to its dictates, and relative moderation in its expression.

The best of Zhukova's work illustrates that women writers' sense of autonomy could exist independently from melodramatic representations

---

[9] Genlis, *Les Veillées du château, ou cours de morales à l'usage des enfants, par l'auteur d'Adèle et Théodore* (Paris, 1784) [one of many editions]. The title of *Evenings*, however, has an obvious Russian precedent too in Gogol's *Vechera na khutore bliz Dikanki* (1830); but Gogol's text has a single, male narrator, speaking to a reader, rather than being a set of tales narrated in company, as Genlis's is.

of the oppression of women. If Elena Gan resembled the 'tormented writer' of Italo Calvino's fable *If on a Winter's Night a Traveller*, Zhukova resembled the 'productive writer'. Belinsky's attack on her achievements as a foil to his elevation of Elena Gan was to discourage her immediate successors from contemplating the virtues of this particular 'productive writer', which were only to resurface again at the turn of the nineteenth century. This was unfortunate for two reasons. A combination of the concerns of both Gan and Zhukova, like the shuffling of the manuscript pages produced by the 'productive' and 'tormented' writers imagined by Calvino, might have produced 'a single book, a great book . . . the book that both the productive writer and the tormented writer [had] always dreamed of writing'—the great novel that, in fact, no Russian woman writer ever wrote.[10] If this seems unduly fanciful, one may safely make the more humdrum assertion that Zhukova's career was a turning-point in the history of Russian women's writing. In her early work, there is uncertainty about precisely what the audience *does* want; and so the entertainment imperative may undercut the didactic imperative, whilst the ends preached by didacticism itself may be quite diverse. But with increased certainty about precisely what was wanted from her, Zhukova, like many of her successors, was to take the sympathy of her readership as a given: she was to construct the reader as a passive listener, rather than as something approaching a co-creator.

[10] Italo Calvino, *If on a Winter's Night a Traveller*, trans. William Weaver (London, 1988), 138.

3

Karolina Pavlova (1807–1893)

LIKE Elisaveta Kulman, Karolina Pavlova, whose maiden name was Jänisch, was partly of non-Russian descent; her father was of German extraction, and Pavlova was to grow up trilingual in German, Russian, and French. Her earliest published collection was a volume of original German poetry, and translations of Russian poetry into German, *Northern Lights* (1833); her second collection was a similar mixed edition of original French poems and translations, *Preludes* (1839). It is tempting to attribute her remarkable, even unique, achievement in creating herself as a Romantic woman poet to her mixed origins, and to speculate that her status as an *étrangère*, a woman outside the society in which she moved, may to some extent have insulated her, at a subjective level, from the general belief that the composition of poetry was anomalous for women.[1]

There certainly seems some evidence that Pavlova was aware of the German Romantic emphasis on the creative powers of 'the eternal feminine'. Amongst her translations, for example, was a version of a song from a long narrative poem, *Cäcilie*, written by the minor German Romantic poet Ernst Schulze, which relates the adventures of the heroine of a religious crusade in tenth-century Denmark. Though Cäcilie is observed from the outside in the servile terms of medieval courtly poetry, and her interior world is little explored, Schulze's poem is remarkable as an extended treatment of 'feminine' spirituality as an active, not simply as a passive entity.[2] The instinctive poet, Cecilia, who is the protagonist of Pavlova's story-poem *A Double Life* (1844–7), may be named for

---

[1] Pavlova, *Das Nordlicht* (Dresden, 1833); *eadem, Les Préludes* (Paris, 1839).

[2] Ernst Schulze, *Cäcilie: ein romantisches Gedicht in zwanzig Gesängen* (2 vols.; Leipzig, 1818–19); Pavlova's extract appears in *PSS* (see n. 3 below), 388–9. Another figure from early 19th-c. German literature borrowed by Pavlova was Schiller's St Joan, whom she made the subject of a poem in French written shortly after translating the play: Pavlova, 'Jeanne d'Arc', *Polnoe sobranie stikhotverenii* (Moscow-Leningrad, 1964), 500–2. (References to this edn. henceforth in text as *PSS*.)

Schulze's heroine; she certainly has an affiliation to German Romantic tradition in a general sense, being a half-German girl whose earliest poetic works are mostly balladic evocations of mysterious erotic encounters in the manner of Goethe's 'The Erl-King' or of Pavlova's own early poem 'The Phantom Hour'.[3]

For Pavlova, as for Elisaveta Kulman and Zinaida Volkonskaya, the diversity that came from her multilingual and multi-cultural background was of great importance in making her a writer. But in Pavlova's case the diversity worked to quite different effect; writing in a less generously cosmopolitan era than Volkonskaya's or Kulman's, she had a relation with non-Russian tradition that was often antagonistic, rather than harmonious. She was sensible of, and sensitive to, the negative resonance of her status as a foreigner. In her middle years she increasingly began to gravitate towards the Slavophile movement, and her proclamations of zeal for the cause have a flavour of anxious protestation, as if she wished to prove herself more Russian than the Russians. In 'Conversation in the Kremlin' (1854: *PSS* 158–68), for example, a Russian is challenged by a Frenchman and an Englishman, who argue that Russia has always been outside the mainstream of European culture and history. The Russian's response is to assert the grandeur of his own historical tradition: in the past Russia has followed a truly Christian path of asceticism and suffering, whilst 'in your Babylon | You defied God in your debauched feasts'. The future too belongs to Russia, for:

> Для прежних подданных татарских
> Настанет день, придет пора
>
> .   .   .   .   .   .
>
> И мы, теснимые жестоко
> Напором злым со всех сторон,
> Одни без лжи и без упрека,
> Среди завистливых племен,
> На Бога правды уповая,
> Под сению его щита,
> Пойдем на бой, как в дни Мамая,
> Одни с хоругвою креста!

> For the former subjects of the Tatars
> The day will dawn, the time will come
>
> .   .   .   .   .   .
>
> And we, who are oppressed so cruelly
> By fierce incursions on all sides,
> We, who alone lack sin and falsehood,

---

[3] On *A Double Life*, see below, n. 16; Pavlova, 'Die Geisterstunde', *PSS* 470–6.

Though envy gnaws all other tribes,
We, who are confident in the God of justice,
Will walk beneath his sacred shield,
As in Mamai's time, to fight the battle,
Our banners alone bearing the cross!

What is more, this impassioned argument is directed by a speaker whose mien is 'lively' and 'thoughtful', at a 'gloomy' 'awkward' and 'arrogant' English 'lord', and a 'veteran of Napoleon's eagle'—that is, a representative of a power already once defeated by the Russian army. The patriotic case is so overstated that it is no surprise to learn that Pavlova wrote this celebration of a mystical Slavonic community at a time when she herself was living outside the Russian borders, and had been before her departure ostracized by much of the Russian community in a real sense—that is, by the Moscow society to which she had formerly belonged.[4]

However, self-dissolution in a touchy and defensive assertion of Russia's God-given superiority was by no means Pavlova's only way of reacting to her culturally ambiguous status; 'Conversation in the Kremlin' is exceptional even in terms of her civic verse. And in any case, her mixed descent was only one factor in her development as a writer. It may explain why she, unlike other upper-class women, became a poet; it does not explain why she became a poet unlike other upper-class poets. A much more important prompting for Pavlova's later career was that her ironic and watchful intelligence was particularly well suited to the introspective and analytical phase which Russian Romanticism entered in the 1840s.

That said, one should not overstate the simple congruence of personality and background. As has just been mentioned, Pavlova was the subject of great hostility in Russian society, some of which was in fact provoked by her intellectual ambitions. On the publication of her early translations, Belinsky attempted to reduce her efforts to the standard measure of 'feminine talents', linguistic felicity: he considered that this was in evidence, but that larger demands of taste and discrimination were left unsatisfied.[5] Later, Pavlova's financial independence and her

---

[4] There were two reasons why Pavlova's unpopularity had reached a peak in 1854. First, she had become estranged from her husband, a minor writer named Nikolai Pavlov, who came from a much lower social class than she (he was the illegitimate son of a serf and a nobleman), and who had been living off her money. Her failure to support him was considered outrageous, and she was held responsible for his arrest by the police, and consequent imprisonment, on a political charge. Secondly, she had left St Petersburg without attending her father's funeral in 1853. (See Heldt in *A Double Life* (n. 16 below), pp. v–vi; Boris Rapgof, *Karolina Pavlova: materialy dlya izucheniya zhizni i tvorchestva* (Petrograd, 1916).)

[5] Belinsky, 'Povesti Zeneidy R——', *PSS* vii. 655.

position as the leader of a Moscow literary salon did not protect her from accusations of being a bore and a bluestocking, which were viciously expressed, for example, in the following epigram by S. Sobolevsky:

Забыв о милой Каролине,
О прелести ее стихов,
Я уезжал вчера ins Grüne
Послушать майских соловьев.
А бывшие в собранье лица
Единогласно говорят,
Что эдак воет лишь волчица
Когда берут у ней волчат.[6]

Neglecting my dear Karolina,
And all her verses' sweet delights,
I betook myself *ins Grüne*
To listen to the nightingales.
But those who *did* attend the reading
Described it to me afterwards:
She wailed far worse than any she-wolf
Whose little cubs have all been snatched.

The expression 'she-wolf' makes matters clear: here is a woman whose unmusical rampages are unfit for civilized society, and who is capable of expressing only a 'wail' deriving from the perversion and frustration of her maternal instinct. One of Pavlova's severest critics was another woman poet, Evdokiya Rostopchina; and she, too, was to dwell on the 'unwomanliness' of her rival, whom she represented as a fright and a bluestocking.[7] Even a commentator writing seventy years later, Vladislav Khodasevich, was to argue that Pavlova's case proved how impossible it was for women to write intellectual poetry. In his article, 'A Woman Rescued from Oblivion', he summed her up as an embittered failure: 'Unloved, unattractive, reserved, Pavlova did not lead the life proper to women; no doubt that was why she so disliked her more successful contemporary, Rostopchina.'[8]

In 'Three Souls', written in 1845, Pavlova was apparently to acknowledge the justice of such assessments. The poem not only addresses the difficulties of composing poetry in a hostile society, but suggests that these difficulties are insuperable, frustrating and vitiating the act of composition itself. Reworking (consciously or unconsciously) a poem by Anna Bunina entitled 'To A. L.', which had evoked the lives of three

---

[6] S. Sobolevsky, 'Karolina Pavlova', *Russkaya epigramma*, no. 311.
[7] On Rostopchina's views of Pavlova, see Ch. 1 above.
[8] Vladislav Khodasevich, 'Odna iz zabytykh' (1916), *Sobranie sochinenii*, ii (Ann Arbor, Mich., 1990), 218.

women friends, one claimed by death, one by Hymen, and one by the Muses, Pavlova juxtaposes the fates of three different women poets.[9] One has forgotten her early gifts in the vacuous whirl of the social round, a second has 'remained faithful to hopeless ecstasies | And to unfulfilled dreams', but has died at an early age, and a third has suffered a still more dismal fate, since her hopes and dreams have had no outlet, and her spiritual world has inspired no poetry:

> И в душе, созрелой ныне,
> Грустный слышится вопрос:
> В лучшей века половине
> Что ей в мире удалось?
> Что смогла восторга сила?
> Что сказал души язык?
> Что любовь ее свершила,
> И порыв чего достиг?—
> С прошлостью, погибшей даром,
> С грозной тайной впереди,
> С безполезным сердца жаром,
> С волей праздною в груди,
> С грезой тщетной и упорной,
> Может, лучше было ей
> Обезуметь в жизни вздорной
> Иль угаснуть средь степей.   (*PSS* 126–7)

And in her soul, now come to ripeness,
A melancholy doubt resounds:
In the better half of her apportioned years,
What has she accomplished here?
What have her inspirational powers achieved,
When did her spirit's tongue speak out?
What has her love managed to do,
What has her energy attained?
With her past life all gone for naught,
With that fearful mystery ahead,
With that useless ardour in her heart,
With that pointless freedom in her breast,
With those futile, but incessant dreams,
It might have been better had she too
Been stupefied by frivolity
Or wasted in the bare bleak steppes.

But unlike some of her predecessors, such as Teplova, Pavlova was to

---

[9] On 'Tri dushi' see also Diana Greene, 'Karolina Pavlova's "Tri dushi"': The Transfiguration of Biography', *Proceedings of the Kentucky Foreign Language Conference: Slavic Section* (Lexington, Ky., 1984), 15–24. Bunina, 'Tri druga', *SS* iii. 51–2.

move beyond such generalizing statements of feminine impotence. If her earlier work often expresses suspicion of the feminine, her later work expresses a confidence in her own genius which escapes the established traditions of feminine poetry, yet embraces femininity as part of identity. In fact, Khodasevich's analysis was a travesty of Pavlova's biography, and of her career. So far from being 'unloved', she was sustained during her childhood and early adulthood by the very great devotion and admiration of her father. As she wrote of herself in 'Three Souls', 'Love was from the cradle | Her faithful guard' (*PSS* 126). She was very far, too, from 'not living as a woman'. In a poem of 1847 addressed to Rostopchina, she attacked the latter's 'George Sandisme', and contrasted the modest conservatism of her own life:

> Мой быт иной: живу я дома,
> В пределе тесном и родном,
> Мне и чужбина незнакома,
> И Петербург мне незнаком.
>
> По всем столицам разных наций
> Досель не прогулялась я,
> Не требую эманципации
> И самовольного жития.   (*PSS* 134)

> Not so my life: I live at home,
> Mixing with my own family;
> I have not been to foreign lands,
> And Petersburg is strange to me.
>
> I have not gone a-gallivanting
> Around all Europe's nation states;
> I do not need emancipation,
> Or to live as wilfulness dictates.

In her later work, Pavlova did not take refuge from the 'narrow world' of femininity in a world purportedly above gender, as the women prose writers of radical tradition did; but nor did she, like women poets of the 1830s, lament the limitations of 'the feminine world'. Her later work responded to cultural pressures in an active as well as a passive sense, not simply reflecting, but also confronting, contemporary attitudes. When radical critics nominated prose as the key tradition of public and socially committed composition, and Romanticism became marginal, Pavlova managed to construct a sense of belonging to a threatened literary borderland where men and women were in some ways inhabitants of equal status; she was able to interweave gender politics with aesthetic and political concerns.

In 'Three Souls' Pavlova had still represented women's composition of poetry in a melancholy and resigned tone rather like that which Teplova had used in her poem 'Warning'. But a poem written in the following year, 1846, marked a turning-point in her career. In the magnificent elegy 'Life calls us' (which in manuscript bears the cancelled titled 'Meditations', *PSS* 128–31), Pavlova contemplates the tragic deaths of various Russian poets, and the neglect to which their memory is subjected; through the scrutiny of this material, she also creates her own poetic autobiography, reshaping themes from her own past, and working towards a positive and enabling sense of her own apartness.[10]

'Life calls us' begins by describing a moment of recollection snatched from the struggle of everyday existence. Like the traveller who looks from a pastoral valley in early summer towards the chilly heights of a mountain, she who looks back on her own life prefers the past to the present. The act of 'looking back' here proves to be a vision of 'shades of the past', the recollection of friends and acquaintances dead or departed. The expected motif of lost youth plays some part, but it is subordinate to another and more important motif. Most of the friends have offered literary as well as personal companionship; Pavlova herself pays tribute as a poet speaking of poets. Indeed, in a key stanza dedicated to one dead poet, Evgeny Baratynsky, she presents herself as the last of the line, a voice speaking alone:

> И неужель, любимец вдохновений,
> Исчезнувший, как легкий призрак сна,
> Тебе, скорбя, своих поминовений
> Не принесла родная сторона?
> И мне пришлосъ тебя назватъ, Евгений,
> И дань стиха я дам тебе одна? (*PSS* 130)

> Can it be true, favourite of inspiration,
> Who vanished like a dream's sad paling ghost,
> Can it be true the land where you were born,
> Grieved not for you, and paid no last respects?
> And is it I, Evgeny, who must name you,
> Do only I give you the gift of verse?

Pavlova has in fact 'named' Evgeny quite specifically: by referring to him as the 'faint ghost of a dream' she has absorbed him, even in life, into her own 'chorus of ghosts'. By means of a repeated image, the life of one poet becomes the metaphor for the creation of another.

Thus far Pavlova's insistence that she is sole inheritor to a line of poets (apart from Baratynsky, she alludes to Mickiewicz, Pushkin, and Lermontov) seems to suggest an acceptance of the early Romantic idea of inspiration as necessarily masculine. In many of her early poems, such

---

[10] For a translation of 'Life calls us' see *Anthology*.

associations had in fact been taken for granted. Her earliest surviving poem in Russian, 'The Sphinx' (1831; *PSS* 75) represents this beast as a mysterious male figure, albeit one who wears a female mask; 'The Poet' (1839; *PSS* 77) is a portrait of a male writer; and in 'To Baratynsky' (1841; *PSS* 112) Pavlova accepts the title of 'poet' only because it has been conferred on her by Baratynsky, who has acted as her sponsor.

In Pavlova's early poems, any revisions to received Russian Romantic tradition had been hesitant or allusive. In 'The Miner' (1841; *PSS* 97–103), the hero, a transparent metaphor for the artist-craftsman, is offered forbidden knowledge by a voice from the cleft; the promise of enlightenment alienates him from the everyday world, but his decision to break with the mine is pre-empted by a rock fall, swallowing him up for ever.[11] If the association between femininity and oblivion is indirect and symbolic here, an overt link between the two is made in another early poem, 'The Crone' (1840; *PSS* 85), which depicts a witch-like figure who lures a young man into her hut.[12] Here she tells him fantastic stories of a beautiful but heartless young woman, making her strange narrative from the strange material of 'other-worldly language'. Eventually the fascination of the tales told by the hag renders the young man himself 'dumb', unable to do anything but listen. His mingled horror and fascination are shared by the narrative itself: the hag's stories 'wither' the young man, her glance before she lures him in 'pierces to his heart's wounds like an arrow'. And the stories told by this emasculating virago are so dangerous that they are not narrated directly, but given in the third person. Rather than a celebration of female narrative powers, the poem is a fastidious dissection of these powers, and a warning to the (male) reader to beware of them.

In a sense, 'Life calls us' shares the perspective of such pieces, reasserting the link between masculinity and creativity. Yet at the same time the elegy dissolves this link. The recognition of Pavlova's particular place in a beleaguered poetic tradition ends her earlier, anxious separation of 'masculine' and 'feminine' creators. The poem's first, and most emotional, recollection, is of another woman, whose 'path the merciless Creator chose', but who, in submitting to this fate, has also herself risen to a saintly act of self-transcendence (*podvig*), indeed to a Messianic destiny (she has put upon herself 'the crown of thorns'). It has been plausibly argued that this woman addressee may be one of the wives of the Decembrists, since the separation between Pavlova and her occurred twenty years prior to the composition of 'Life calls us', but the usual

---

[11] On 'Rudokop' see also Heldt, *Terrible Perfection*, 113–14.
[12] For a translation of 'The Crone' see *Anthology*.

interpretation of the Decembrists' wives as metaphors of wifely self-abnegation is subordinated here to the idea of self-realization in suffering. The anguish of this addressee, we are told, was 'unuttered'; but the feminine voice in general has not been silenced. Throughout the elegy, Pavlova speaks in the first person, employing feminine verbs and adjectives; this is the voice not only of a poet, but of a woman poet, appropriating to her own gender the tradition of the 'lament for the makaris', the elegy for fallen poets.[13]

'Life calls us' was a breakthrough in Pavlova's poetic career because it applied an explicitly feminine first person to a biography which was expressly that of a poet, rather than simply that of a woman of high society, however sensitive and intelligent; it was also an advance in terms of its intellectual profundity and of its aesthetic maturity. Though still perceiving fancy as 'murderous', just as 'Three Souls' had, the poem ends with acceptance of fancy's subsidiary place to 'life', representing the end of a 'dream' not only as the demise of beauty, the disappearance of the 'diamond row of stars', but as 'sobriety' and 'labour',

> Белеет день, звезд гасит рой алмазный,
> Зовет к труду и требует дела;
> Пора свершать свой путь однообразный,
> И всё забыть, что жизнь превозмогла,
> И отрезветь от хмеля думы праздной,
> И след мечты опять стряхнуть с чела.

> The pale day rises, the diamond stars are fading,
> Day calls to work, demands that things be done;
> It is high time this dreary road was ended,
> Time to forget what life has overcome,
> And sober up intoxicated fancy,
> Cast off the trace of day-dreams from my brow.

The results of Pavlova's daytime labours are evident in the poem's high level of technical accomplishment; she manipulates a relatively complex stanza form, the sestet, with ease and accomplishment. There are also two examples of what were, for the 1840s, innovative rhymes (the split rhyme *vse my/nemy* in the first stanza, and the augmentative rhyme *odnoobraznyi/prazdnoi* in the final stanza).

For reasons which are unclear, the elegy remained unpublished during

---

[13] The hypothesis about the Decembrist wife was first advanced by Bryusov in Pavlova, *Sobranie sochinenii* (2 vols.; Moscow, 1915), 313; see also Gromov in Pavlova, *PSS* 558. Gromov makes no suggestion as to the woman's identity, but the likeliest candidate is Aleksandra Grigorievna Chernysheva (1804–32), a Muscovite of similar age to Pavlova, who followed her husband, Nikita Mikhailovich Murav'ev, to Siberia, and died there aged 28. On 'Life calls us' as a 'lament for the makaris', cf. the medieval Scottish poet William Dunbar's famous elegy, 'Lament for the Makaris'.

Pavlova's lifetime, not being included even in her collection of 1863, *Poems*.[14] But Pavlova did not go back on her declaration of independence in a poetic sense. The understanding of poetry as first-person female utterance, once arrived at, was to persist in her later poetry. Some of her later pieces of poetic autobiography were still resigned or despairing in tone: in 'Meditations' (1847), for example, the assertion that 'the company of poets is silent' provoked her to question the purpose of writing once more:

> Пришлось молчать мечтам заветным;
> Зачем тому, кто духом нищ,
> Тревожить ныне словом тщетным
> Безмолвный мир святых кладбищ!

> The fatal day-dreams must be silent;
> For why should the beggarly of soul
> Disturb the sacred peace of graveyards
> And break the silence with vain words?

But elsewhere Pavlova expresses no such scruples. In her most famous poem, 'You who have lived on in my beggarly heart' (1854), she lifts a defiant voice to 'break the silence', and names herself with the word *izbrannitsa*, 'the chosen one', a term which borrows from the quasi-religious mythic vocabulary of Russian Romanticism, but which, in a radical gesture, also feminizes the notion of the inspired being. Similarly, in 'What is past, what is lost, what is gone' (1854; *PSS* 170), Pavlova represents her life and work in terms of self-conscious risk: she is a 'gambler' who stakes her own 'treasures'. The end of the poem opposes this sacrifice of happiness to the 'greedy, venomous' gazes of 'those in luck', and thus implies both the inferiority and slavishness of a seeming happiness, and the nobility of an apparent defeat.

Between 1846 and 1858, Pavlova wrote many of her finest lyric poems; though apostrophes of exile and parting are increasingly frequent in poems of the late 1850s, prefiguring the silence which was to descend on her from 1860, a sense of resolution still breaks through. 'It is not time' (1858), for example, expresses a determination to endure the 'lies' of tomorrow, as the 'falsehoods' of yesterday and today have been endured (*PSS* 197). And even in her most pessimistic poems, her sense of poetry as an intellectual utterance, rather than simply an outburst of feeling, distinguishes her voice from that of her female contemporaries. For Pavlova, if poetry is 'pointless', it is pointless from a philosophical perspective (because communication itself is either impossible or futile),

---

[14] *Stikhotvoreniya* (Moscow, 1863), 'Zovet nas zhizn' was first published in the Symbolist almanac *Severnye tsvety* in 1901.

not because writing is an activity improper to those of the wrong sex. In the late cycle 'Phantasmagoria' (1858; *PSS* 210–17), for example, an account of lost love becomes an illustration of the deceptions wrought by imaginative remembrance, and also of the 'inappropriateness' of such remembrances, rather than simply a lament for emotional deprivation. Where Zhadovskaya and Rostopchina speak in the voice of one immediately involved, Pavlova speaks from an—often ironic—distance. The interplay, or contrast, between event and recollection is evident at once, requiring no qualification of enclosing frames.

None the less, Pavlova did make excursions into genres where prose and verse intersect, and with notable success. Her most conventional piece is the short story/poem, which she herself labelled a 'sketch', thus stressing its link with psychological prose of the day, *Phantasmagoria* (1856–8; *PSS* 373–8). We are presented with the thoughts of 'someone' sitting in a carriage; later this 'someone' is stated to be a woman leaving Russia. As in Rostopchina's 'Unknown Romance', objective third-person description is succeeded by the emotional immediacy of lyric verse: but the opposition of genres at this level is undercut by the fact that Pavlova's prose introduction is oblique and fragmentary, her verse considered and stately, so that here prose seems in some ways closer to its subject than poetry. Two other texts from Pavlova's mature period also handle the 'prose-verse' distinction in a manner that goes well beyond the ordinary equation of verse with the inner world, prose with the outer. *Quadrille* (1843–57; *PSS* 308–72) is a long poem which combines the subject-matter of the society tale, and its use of the frame narrative, with the prosody of the narrative poem. Three visitors, Nadine, Olga, and Liza, gather at the house of their friend the Countess. The conversation soon turns to expected topics, as the narrator slyly reveals:

> Всегда в беседе мы своей
> Невольно в речь впадаем ту же:
> Молчим почтительно о муже,
> Но вообще браним мужей.   (*PSS* 312)

> Inevitably when we converse
> One subject always draws our talk;
> Too polite to name our husbands' faults,
> We brand 'all husbands' as perverse.

But the talk that results is less about the faults of men, than about women's degree of responsibility for their own fates. Each of the four women in turn tells the story of a crucial event in her life, and in each case the notion of 'responsibility' is differently nuanced. At the end of the poem, the four friends ponder in silence what they have heard; the reader is likewise left to meditate on whether 'power' and 'responsibility' can be identically comprehended in the case of a spoilt heiress who provokes a duel, a poor provincial girl whose love-match is precluded by her inferior dowry, and two other women whose comic, rather than tragic, contributions show them displaying quick wits and a sense of self-irony in adversity.

Since *Quadrille* is entirely composed in verse, the narratives are not so obviously separate from the frame as they would be in a cycle of lyrics associated with a prose frame. Instead, the movement to the inward, confessional narrative is linear: ironically, it is the Countess, apparently the most worldly of the women, who narrates the most tragic series of events. In other words, rather than marking the hierarchy by which inward feeling is distinguished from outward show, the use of verse here acts as a unifying device, pulling against such a hierarchy. Perhaps more importantly, the use of verse undermines the distinction between narrator and fictional characters which would be conventional in a 'worldly tale': the narrator is not simply the interested or disinterested chronicler of circumstances, but herself digresses in confessional mode.

There is also another sense in which *Quadrille* is a mixed-genre text. The question of how far women might be responsible for their own fates, and the emphasis on responsibility as a pre-condition of autonomy, had been explored by Pavlova in two important pieces whose heroines are parallels to, or even doubles of, the countess in *Quadrille*. 'Scene' (1855; *PSS* 175–84) is a verse dialogue which represents an aristocratic lady and her lover engaged in a game of chess, whose complicated moves are paralleled by their acid conversational interchanges, and by their attempts to win emotional victory one over the other. A more substantial treatment of similar material is *At the Tea-Table* (1859), a society tale in prose, which is both a very late example of the genre, and a particularly fine one.[15] Like Mariya Zhukova's 'Baron Reichman', *At the Tea-Table* deals with the consequences of romantic self-indulgence; and it, too, is a frame narrative, the telling of which is prompted by an argument at the eponymous tea-table, as a countess and her guests rehearse the various arguments about why women should be disadvantaged. But the Princess, the heroine of Andrei Petrovich's tale, is more complex than Baroness Reichman. She is articulate and highly intelligent, and has her own feelings well under control—or at any rate, it is rumoured in society that she does. Out of boredom she plays with a young man, Khozrevsky, whose inferior social position makes him more defenceless than she, and

[15] 'Za chainym stolom', *RV* 12/2 (1859), 797–827; see also Pavlova, *Sobranie sochinenii*, ii. 335–412; 'At the Tea-Table' in *Anthology*.

then rejects him when he confesses that he has spent three years affecting sweet-natured stupidity because his social position—he is penniless and desperately needs a place as private secretary to a wealthy old man— demands that he should. 'I cannot be the wife of a man who is so skilled in the art of deception', the Princess informs him (*SS* 409).

The tale is presented by its male narrator before he tells it as an illustration of intrinsic, 'natural' gender qualities; but after he has told it he insists that it is a moral conundrum (asked what he wants to prove, he replies, 'Nothing'). Certainly, the piece refutes the idea that women are intrinsically subordinate, reversing the sense of man as predator, woman as quarry, which had been borrowed by the provincial tale from the literature of sensibility. But at the same time it illustrates the asymmetrical attitudes which society adopts towards the behaviour of men and women: Khozrevsky is accepted when he dissembles, whilst even the Princess's wealth and position do not guard her against charges of pretence. Deception is so fundamental to this society that its effects are inescapable: all revelations can be perceived only as fresh affectations, fresh poses. The seventh veil is dropped to expose an eighth veil.

Quadrille incorporates elements of role reversal and moral ambiguity similar to those which are used in 'At the Tea-Table', and displays a command of dialogue equal to that in 'A Scene'. Pavlova's citation of her own material makes it a text that mixes genres at many different levels. But Pavlova's most wide-ranging mixed-genre text is the prose and verse tale *A Double Life* (1844–7; *PSS* 231–304), which is at once lyric diary, society tale, *Künstlerroman*, and contribution to the debate on women's place in the public and private world.[16] The protagonist, Cecilia, is a naïve young girl who is caught between her own half-formed emotions and the social ambitions of her mother. Barely sensitive to her manipulation by the latter, she can scarcely be aware of how she is deceived by the former. The narrator, however, leaves the reader with no illusions, attacking Cecilia's comfortable ignorance in the following words:

By now Cecilia was 18 years old, and was so used to wearing her mind in a corset that she felt it no more than the light silk one which she would take off at night. That is not to say that she had no talents; she certainly did, but they were modest ones, decorous ones, *les talents de société*, as the language of society so accurately terms them. She sang very prettily, and drew very prettily too. Poetry, as we mentioned before, was something which she knew more by reputation

---

[16] For a translation see Pavlova, *A Double Life*, trans. and ed. B. Heldt (2nd edn.; Oakland, Calif., 1986). (For the reader's convenience, parallel citations are made to this edn. in text as *DL*; however, the English versions here are my own.)

than in actuality, and which she knew to be something wild and not at all compatible with a decent life.   (*PSS* 249–50; *DL* 26–7)

But *A Double Life* is more than simply an exercise in depicting how women are socially disadvantaged by their upbringing. Cecilia derives genuine enjoyment from the pursuits considered suitable to a young woman: she takes commonplace pleasure in ribbons, dresses, and flirtations, as well as in such physical exercises as dancing and riding. Unlike the conventional heroine of prose narratives, she is not above, but of, her own milieu. Yet at the same time Cecilia, like the heroine of Christina Rossetti's comparable story 'Maude', is also a poet, though one who, unlike Maude, does not write verses for an audience, even one made up of her friends.[17] She composes for herself in her room at night poems flowing from her semi-conscious mind in torrents, 'rocking her as though she were in a boat' (*PSS* 249; *DL* 27). These poems are not consciously crafted, and we are told of no attempt to record them to paper; they narrate themselves to Cecilia like dreams. And, like dreams, they consist of inchoate fantasies of mysterious and magical male objects of desire, who appear, not to Cecilia herself, but to a series of anonymous and undifferentiated young girls.

Just before Cecilia's marriage, the process of harmless fantasy is arrested. She begins to fear severance from what she has known, and the foreboding is so great that she feels that 'someone has died'; we are told by the narrator that she herself lies 'like the marble statue on a tomb'. It is at this moment that she begins to realize that the origins of her fantasy lie in the past, rather than the future:

She looked round at this humble, chaste room, which tomorrow she would have to leave for ever, and many things began to become dimly comprehensible to her. All her childish happiness, which she had so arrogantly spurned, flashed before her as a priceless treasure now lost. Her chest felt as if a great stone were weighing it down.   (*PSS* 300; *DL* 101)

That night, her poetic vision informs her that she has 'recognized the longed-for gift too late', and warns her of pain and struggles to come. The reader has been given to understand exactly why this should be: in a not entirely subtle piece of montage, we have been shown her sitting alone in her narrow room on the night before the wedding, whilst her future husband carouses with his male friends. But what appears at first to be an unambiguous loss of autonomy then proves to have less straightforward effects. It is only on her marriage that Cecilia is able to know herself: for the first time a poetic fit comes on her in which she can

---

[17] Christina Rossetti, 'Maude: A Story for Girls', *Selected Poems*, ed. C. H. Sisson (Manchester, 1984), 136–61.

speak in the first person. She is now able to tell her own story, rather than having it told by others for her; but there the story ends. Whether she has used her new powers is left unclear:

> Последняя, быть может, песня зта;
> Скорей годов уносятся мечты!
> Признать и мне ль власть суетную света?
> Забыть и мне ль служенье красоты?

> And this may be the last of all my songs,
> Soon all the dreams of youth will fly away!
> Shall I too succumb to the powers of frivolity?
> Shall I too forget the service of beauty?
> (PSS 306; DL 110)

The doubling in *A Double Life* does not end with the psychological ambiguity of Cecilia's own journey to enlightenment. The process by which this heroine learns to speak as 'I' parallels and prefigures Pavlova's own development as a writer, whilst at the same time marking the distinction between writer and heroine. For if the discovery of the directly subjective utterance marks the end of this narrative, and hence the beginning of Cecilia's silence, a similar discovery on Pavlova's part was, as we have seen, to signify the beginning of her maturity as a writer. Begun before Pavlova's own poetic perepeteia, *A Double Life* was completed after it; in this sense (though not in the sense of any immediate identification between heroine and author) this mixed-genre text can be seen as autobiography, a piece of self-recognition contemporary with, and parallel to, her great elegy 'Life calls us'. Crucial in terms of her own work, Pavlova's rite of passage was also to have a more than personal significance. By refashioning herself, she became Russian poetry's first important woman Romantic poet, a writer whose preeminence was recognized, however reluctantly, by the vast majority of contemporary literary critics.[18] Though her reputation went into a decline from the end of the 1860s, at the turn of the century, when the Russian Symbolists revived Romanticism on the one hand, and began a cult of women's creativity on the other, Pavlova was to be rediscovered. And, as a result, her feminine, but uncompromisingly intellectual, version of Romanticism was to be an inspiration to three of the most important women poets of the early twentieth century, Marina Tsvetaeva, Sofiya Parnok, and Anna Prismanova.

---

[18] On the reception of Pavlova, see Heldt in *A Double Life*, pp. ix–x, xvi.

4

Elena Gan (1814–1842)

WHEN Elena Gan died from tuberculosis at the age of 28, Russian literature was still sufficiently embued with the spirit of Romanticism, with its cult of the prodigy, to ensure something resembling a posthumous sensation. This sensation was not on the scale of that represented by the German-language tributes to her predecessor, Elisaveta Kulman, or by the later Russian celebration of her successor, the prose-poet Elena Guro. And the tributes offered to Gan differed from those offered to Kulman or Guro in that the theme of artistic self-martyrdom as such was relatively muted, for all that Gan had been one of the few immediately post Pushkinian women writers to expand on the idea of feminine genius, most notably in her story 'A Futile Gift' (1842).[1] For radical critics such as Belinsky, whose mystical inclinations were now honed to a social purpose, Gan's life and work were exemplary for other reasons. As pointed out in Chapter 1, Gan was held up to Russian women writers as a model for their endeavours; her immaturity in years made her a symbol of the immaturity of Russian women's writing in general; but her critical attitude to her environment was also symbolic. Moreover, the death of this young woman, cut off whilst still energetically producing work, was an illustration of how social conditions in the Russian provinces worked to frustrate the talent of young women. The chronicler of

---

[1] Gan's early works had been well received and she had become popular with a general readership, but the publication of her posthumous *Sochineniya* (1842) was greeted with unprecedented interest. Reviews appeared in most of the major journals of the day, and Gan attracted favourable comment not only from radical critics such as Belinsky and Nekrasov, but also from conservatives such as Polevoi (see *Severnaya pchela*, 227 (1843), 907: cited in H. A. Aplin, 'Mariya Zhukova and Elena Gan', Ph.D. thesis (University of East Anglia, 1989), 380). Thereafter, interest in Gan faded, and was revived only towards the end of the century, with the publication by Starchevsky (see n. 2), and also of Gan's *Polnoe sobranie sochinenii* (St Petersburg, 1909); cited henceforth in text as *PSS*.

provincial heroines, Gan was herself made the archetype of the provincial heroine.[2]

Later commentators too have been inclined to follow this treatment of Gan as an emblem: her life and work (which are never sharply distinguished) have been interpreted as the tragedy of talent confined by uncongenial provincial society, or alternatively as a manifestation of Russian womanhood's heroic ability to achieve autonomy despite provincial dullness and prejudice. Whether Gan is seen as someone who broke free from, or was brought down by, the typical, the circumstances of her life have been rendered in much the same way. Emphasis has been placed on her marriage, seen as an unsatisfactory union with an unimaginative German officer; thence is derived the hypothetical source of her fictional treatments of marriage. She has also been seen as someone who bravely, if not always successfully, struggled against the necessary marginalization from the literary mainstream which confinement in her provincial fastness brought her.[3]

How far such interpretations of Gan's life reflect historical fact is questionable. She was born Elena Fadeeva, and came from a family of the gentry with wide-ranging cultural interests; she appears to have been well educated, and had a reading knowledge of at least five European languages. Her mother, born Princess Dolgorukaya, came from one of the most distinguished and ancient aristocratic families in Russia; in her own right, she was a woman of considerable intellectual accomplishment, with many publications on botany to her credit. Socially and intellectually, therefore, Gan's background was not such as to make her the obvious inferior of many writers, critics, or editors of her day, or of her husband's military colleagues. On the contrary: if she did encounter social difficulties, one may suppose that these are likely to have derived from inverted snobbery, and that she was an outsider because her antecedents were rather grander than those of most people in the small provincial towns where her husband was billeted, or those of the members of the St Petersburg literary circles which ran the journals where she published.[4] Hence, it is inappropriate to see the social misfits

---

[2] Most of the Gan obituaries dwell on her provincial origins, none mentioning either her distinguished pedigree or her excellent education. Cf. also the late 19th-c. biographical article of A. V. Starchevsky, 'Roman odnoi zabytoi romanistki', pt. 1 *IV* 25/8 (1886), 203–34. A recent example of such mythologization is Cathy Porter, *Fathers and Daughters: Russian Women in Revolution* (London, 1976), 49–50.

[3] Recent comments on Gan as an 'exceptional woman' include the assessment by Richard Stites, *The Women's Liberation Movement in Russia* (Princeton, NJ, 1978), 23–5.

[4] The fullest and most careful survey of Gan's biography and antecedents is Aplin, 'M. S. Zhukova and E. A. Gan', 236–64, which also notes the paucity of direct information. Even Aplin, however, makes some fairly questionable interpretations of Gan's life: take e.g. his suggestion that she would probably have stopped writing had her marriage been happy (p. 244).

amongst Gan's heroines, such as Anyuta, the daughter of an aristocrat's factor in 'A Futile Gift', or the heroine of 'Theophania Abbiagio' (1841; *PSS* 424–520), who is descended from a line of decayed Italian aristocrats, as reflections of her actual social status; they are characters consciously invented to represent a particular view of feminine heroism in adversity. In several tales—'A Futile Gift', again, or 'The Ideal' (1837; *PSS* 1–48) or 'Society's Judgement' (1842; *PSS* 300–67)—the lives of such women, endowed with sensibility and talent, yet socially disadvantaged, are explored through the eyes of a narrator who herself is a woman of some self-confidence and independence.

With Gan, as with other writers of whose life little is known, the biographical interpretation rests on a circular process: supposedly factual details are extracted from the work, and then used as evidence to show how she based her work on her own life. We have no direct evidence that her marriage was unhappy; certainly, it does not seem to have been forced upon her in the way that marriage is forced upon some of her heroines. We cannot simply assume, at any rate, that the marriage in, say, 'The Ideal', which shows a sensitive young woman espoused to a dull older man, derives directly from Gan's own experience. Her own letters, and the reminiscences of close relatives and friends, suggest that her life had its difficulties, which Gan herself attributes to financial causes, whilst her relatives are more inclined to deduce marital incompatibility (but an incompatibility coloured by indifference, rather than melodramatic hatred). Gan's letters also provide some evidence of a tendency to self-dramatization. But at the same time both these letters, and the memories of those who knew her well, give reason to suspect that Gan herself was a great deal shrewder, more intelligent, and more self-ironizing, than any of her heroines.[5]

What *is* clear, however, is that there is an internal link, in Gan's own stories, between her social misfit heroines, and her representations of the woman author. 'Society's Judgement' opens with an introductory section which argues that a writer is perceived by casual acquaintances in the provinces as a monstrous prodigy, a social freak show. Superficially the argument resembles that in Madame de Staël's early feminist text, 'Women who practise the art of letters'. However, Staël's position was assimilationist (her ideal society would have been one in which educated women, including women writers, were treated disinterestedly, according to the rational principles of the Enlightenment), whilst Gan's is not. In

---

[5] A selection of Gan's letters is published in Starchevsky, 'Roman odnoi zabytoi romanistki', pt. 2, *IV* 25/8 (1886), 509–31. For the family reminiscences, see V. I. Zhelikhovskaya (her daughter), N. A. Fadeeva (her sister), and E. N. Akhmatova, 'Po povodu stat'i "Roman odnoi zabytoi romanistki"', *IV* 26/11 (1886), 456–64.

the latter's work, the social exile of the woman writer emerges as the distant equivalent of the political exile of the male writer, as celebrated by Russian Romanticism.[6] To be marginal is a tragedy, but it is also a mark of social distinction.

And that was precisely the central paradox of Gan's work: whilst lamenting the writer's social marginalization, she at the same time fostered it. Her own position as a writer is deliberately and consciously antagonistic. In 'Recollections of Zheleznozavodsk' (*c.* 1841; *PSS* 49–62), she plays a literary joke on the reader. The woman narrator, on holiday in the Caucasus, waits for friends to arrive and take her out riding, and whiles away time with a lurid novel. The ride itself soon provides her with excitement to rival any fictional sensation: kidnapped by Caucasian bandits, she and her male companions are held prisoner in an *aul* (mountain village). Aided by a sympathetic woman in the village, the narrator attempts escape, but is discovered by the chief of the *aul*. The scene invites half-voyeuristic, half-shocked expectations of rape, but these are abruptly disillusioned: the whole tale is revealed to be a dream, the narrator's post-prandial indigestion after a blow-out of French fiction. This revelation is accompanied by a challenge to the reader in the form of a provocative statement of the author's 'right' to dream and disappoint in this way:

So why do you cast doubt on my dream? If you do not have dreams like it yourself, then in very truth I cannot be blamed for that! ... There is more gunpowder in my soul than in yours, there is an abundance of inflammable substances in it, so it is scarcely wonderful that, when I am loaded with [the cannon-ball] of imagination, my soul should fire a more powerful shot than yours ... Truly, you must cease your doubting now, or else, as a demonstration of the power of my soul and of the speed of my imagination, and also in order to spite you, I shall go on having dreams of that kind and shall describe them in even greater detail!   (*PSS* 62)

The intended irritation is fully achieved: the story leaves one annoyed with this expression of narratorial egotism, and still more annoyed with the hackneyed device of disillusionment, 'it was all a dream', which has preceded it.

But Gan's writing is not simply display for its own sake. As her military metaphor suggests, her fiction may be a contest of imaginative

---

[6] The Romantic theme of political/social exile is particularly extensively developed in the early work of Pushkin: see for example his so-called 'Southern Poem', *Kavkazskii plennik* (1820–1), *PSS* iv. 81–105, and cf. Stephanie Sandler, *Distant Pleasures: Aleksandr Pushkin and the Writing of Exile, 1820–1824* (Stanford, Calif., 1989); Baratynsky (see e.g. his 'Northern Poem' *Edda* (1824), *PSS* 227–43); and Lermontov: see e.g. his narrative poem *Mtsyri* (1839), *Sobranie sochinenii v 4 tomakh* (Leningrad, 1980), ii. 405–24.

powers, a challenge to the reader; but it also argues a specific case. The cannonball is aimed at a target. Though several stories, such as 'The Ideal' and 'Theophania Abbiagio', deal with unsatisfactory marriages, it is not quite correct to suggest, as Belinsky did, that her primary concern is the denunciation of women's imprisonment within the hypocritical institution of the conventional marriage. Nor does she campaign for education in an institutional sense. Her emphasis is, rather, on the sentimental education of women, the development of their interior world, in unfavourable conditions. The dullness of husbands can be an obstacle; but a far more fundamental problem is the self-interest, vanity, and sexual predation of suitors, lovers, or friends. Olga, of 'The Ideal', becomes infatuated with a young literary lion, and is then horribly disillusioned; visiting his St Petersburg flat, she reads a letter which he has written, and discovers him to be an unfeeling rake. Anyuta, of 'A Futile Gift', is aided in her literary ambitions by her brother's German tutor, Heilfreund. His 'speaking name', signifying both 'friend' and 'saviour', develops an ironic resonance: his support for Anyuta's writing rapidly becomes interference with the natural development of her genius. His desire to protect her from the exigencies of the literary world means that he himself acts as a preliminary censor, ensuring her continued obscurity. 'Society's Judgement' depicts a spirited and independent woman brought down by the paranoiac jealousy of an unstable and self-centred admirer. In 'Theophania Abbiagio' the heroine despairs of her young and well-intentioned, but weak, fiancé's vacillations; she is eventually given in marriage to a fat and lame old man.

Gan's male characters rework the types of the eighteenth-century didactic fable, but she associates none of them with an incentive myth of male behaviour, portraying instead different gradations of the unsatisfactory. However, she does follow the traditions of sensibility in making the female characters the index of morality and emotion. In one of her most interesting stories, 'The Medallion' (1839; *PSS* 210–99), a woman uses coquetry as a weapon with which to avenge the ill-treatment that her sister has suffered at the hands of a spoilt and flirtatious young prince. She subjects him not only to erotic disappointment, but also to scalding invective. But on the whole Gan's female characters react more passively to adversity; their high principles are frequently expressed in resignation, which may sometimes have a religious character. If real men disappoint, women can find comfort in a male divinity, casting themselves before an icon of the Saviour and thus achieving a vision of comfort in another world (so at the end of 'The Ideal', for example). 'Resignation', however, often applies to outward, rather than inward surrender, to a furious, rather than a smiling or gently melancholic, passivity. Where Zhukova's tone in describing the trials of her heroines is muted, Gan's is ferociously emphatic and histrionic. Her heroines do not merely suffer: they also rage against circumstances. Theophania, for example, realizes that her fiancé, Doligni, has become engaged to her out of a sense of duty, but is in fact in love with her friend Olga; her immediate reaction is a rush of fury:

As Alexander rebuffed all Olga's pleas and blandishments, Theophania's heart leapt for joy in her breast, joy caused not by her hopes of future happiness, but by her delight in the humiliation and despair of her hated rival.

'He is mine! Mine!' she repeated to herself, filled with triumphant malice, as she dashed like a young doe through the bushes, down the avenues and past the flower-beds, trembling in her fury.   (*PSS* 518)

The narrator hastens to tone down this impression, saying 'angry and vengeful feelings were foreign to Theophania's character', but in fact it is clear that her eventual decision to surrender Doligni sublimates anger and revenge in more appropriate and decorous emotion. She debates internally how her self-sacrifice can be made more pure, more perfectly disinterested. The process of her self-betterment can only diminish Doligni, an equation which the end of the story makes transparent as he, by now a careerist in the civil service, and entirely compromised by a socially ambitious wife, learns of the nun-like existence which Theophania has constructed for herself within marriage, making her room into a shrine of Platonic love.

If the image of Theophania cloistered in her bare attic room suggests a withdrawal into the better and more beautiful world of celibacy, there are often strong overtones of sexual revulsion in the intensity with which Gan describes relations between men and women. This revulsion emerges, for example, in the ironic description of a provincial dance at the beginning of 'The Ideal':

O waltz, you who have been so much denounced in society, yet who remain society's favourite dance, if you have preserved your innocence anywhere, then it must surely be in the cramped salons of provincial towns, where the deft cavaliers do not so much support their ladies, as clutch on to them for support, so as to keep in time and not get their legs caught up with the following couple; where the long spurs of those same cavaliers mercilessly puncture the delicate limbs of the ladies; where the thick scent of the pomade with which so many of them smear their locks in such generous quantities causes their lady partners to turn their heads aside and await the end of the set with most passionate anticipation.   (*PSS* 4)

The fastidiously coloured juxtaposition of the intrusive grossness of the male, the shrinking frailty of the female, makes its point effectively. And it is sexual disgust, too, which gives Gan's polarizations of heroine and anti-heroine their particular force. The female characters who are her heroines' counter-images are distinguished not only by the social self-confidence which goes with independent income, but also by sexual rapacity. Olga, Theophania's rival, is a young aristocratic woman whose widowhood has not only conferred on her financial independence, but also a sexual manipulativeness absent in the heroine. In 'Ideal', a still more hostile portrait appears. The rival of the idealistic heroine is a mature woman whose morals are cynically lax; it is her sexual charms which have endeared her to the rakish Anatoly: 'In his mind he saw the splendid bosom of the Italian countess and heard, not the sobs of the deceived woman, but the passionate babble of the triumphant one' (*PSS* 43). Rather than financial independence being the prerequisite of social or sexual success, the feeling is that it is the *reward* of such success; the apparent freedom of a nubile widow is bought at the cost of something very like prostitution.

Gan's conviction that sexual autonomy can be guaranteed only by abstinence appears to underlie the ambivalence towards the act of writing which is expressed in some of her stories. It is the notion of writing as sexual display which is frightening. The idea of exposing herself in the literary market-place excites horror in Anyuta:

'Did you think that I would accept such a proposal?' she demanded, with dignified hauteur. 'Could you possibly imagine that I would agree to sell my thoughts, my feelings, those glimpses of my inner paradise, the best part of myself—to sell them, as I might sell my knitting or embroidery? Do you know what you are asking of me? To open my soul and heart to the world, to solicit crowds and pleasure them by my inner joys, my tears, my sufferings, as though I were putting on a puppet show for some paltry remuneration? . . . O God, O God!' Anyuta added bitterly, 'to think that such a sinful thought could be born in even your head, and that your tongue could utter such an insult to me!' (*PSS* 754)

The words 'solicit' (*sozvat'*) and 'pleasure' (*teshit'*), with their connotations of prostituted sexuality, make matters clear: creation for its own sake is one thing, but the act of communication is fraught with dangers.

How are these dangers to be controlled? The answer lies in the refusal of certain kinds of relation with the reader: antagonism is safe, but narrative pleasure must not be granted. Unlike Zhukova, Gan employs the frame narrative not as an indication of how literature may entertain, nor as a way of keeping social criticism respectably veiled in layers of circumvention; it functions as a device for underlining the verisimilitude of what is depicted. Her internal texts are not stories told to amuse, but human documents of an explicitly confessional character. 'The Judgement of Society' is made up of three different layers of such documents: an introductory piece by a narrator who is a woman writer, a memoir left by a provincial landowner after his death, and a letter from the woman who has been the subject of his infatuation. All three documents are accusations directed against the hypocrisy of society. Their style is barely differentiated—indeed, it does not need to be, for, as with the letter written by Theophania Abbiagio, 'not words, but living thoughts pour from the soul on to the page' (*PSS* 521).

Inevitably the result is that Gan's fiction has a rather monochromic character. Any ludic literary qualities, such as humour, appear in the service of a moral purpose. Irony is not a pervasive narrative strategy, but one directed against the worldly characters. In 'The Ideal', it is the worldly norm which appears absurd, not the heroine's reaction to it; self-imposed apartness is never made to seem ridiculous. When the heroine, Olga, hearing that Anatoly, the poet with whom she is romantically infatuated, is ill, she rushes over to his flat. But this extravagant behaviour is presented without comment; irony is directed, rather, at Anatoly himself: Gan makes the letter which Olga discovers an expert parody of the frivolous and careless tones adopted by the St Petersburg blade:

My kind friends have put about the rumour that I am *desperately ill*. Why should they do that, do you think? Laugh as much as you choose, dear count; it is all for the sake of my misty-mystical Madame Golzberg. I confess that she quite bores me already, but I have no wish to leave the business unfinished; rather, my sympathy for the creature compels me to turn her thoughts to more earthly matters.   (*PSS* 42)

Another kind of discourse leaks in here, hostile to the sensibility which Gan is otherwise concerned to display; but its effects are quickly curtailed by a shift to the emotional upset felt by Olga herself.

Received opinion has assumed that Gan's writing displays the influence of George Sand, but technically she is much Sand's inferior. This is clear, for instance, if one compares 'The Judgement of Society', with its multiple narrators all used to make the same point, and its rather clumsy verbosity, with the immense imaginative virtuosity of *Lélia*, a many-layered text in rhythmic prose; Gan's work also lacks the technical expertise of *Indiana*, a text whose socially critical standpoint and thematic concerns may be more fairly compared to hers.[7] There is something slightly amateurish and distinctly adolescent in Gan's fictional manner; the claustrophobic annoyance provoked by reading her stories can recall the experience of being stuck in a lift with a stranger who launches into a long monologue about how exceptional she (or one of her friends or family) is. The first Russian women writer to insist on

    [7] Sand, *Lélia*, see ch. 1, n. 100; *Indiana* (1832), ed. Pierre Salomon (Paris. 1983).

her own talent, Gan was also the first to illustrate that there can be a significant gap between the conviction that one is talented and what objectively appears to be adequate performance as a writer.

And yet Gan did have a more characteristic and memorable style than some of her successors, and her stories are in some ways stronger as problem pieces. Her violent hostility to sexual relations makes her writing, in a nice paradox recalling that expounded in Foucault's *History of Sexuality*, less reticent than that of many later women writers (her closest successor in this is Panaeva); in a bizarre way, she is also more sexually explicit than such sexual liberals as Chernyshevsky.[8] If her use of emotional rhetoric is hyperbolic, it does contribute to her idiosyncratic manner of depicting interiority, taking her work beyond the range of affective gestures and vocabulary employed in much mid-nineteenth-century women's writing. And, whilst her rough use of narrative layers makes it understandable that later writers preferred a smoother and more anonymous third-person discourse, this very roughness can also leave a pressing sense that uncomfortable questions have been left unanswered. In 'Recollections of Zheleznozavodsk', for example, the final insistence that the story is a 'dream' is such a clumsy cliché that it indirectly draws attention to the—most undream-like—concrete detail with which the tale is furnished. And this detail in turn makes some rather subversive points about accepted notions of heroism. There is indirect satire of the masculine code of honour. One of the narrator's male companions has dressed himself up as a Circassian warrior for the expedition, but he totally fails to defend his party when it is ambushed by real warriors. Where male authors of her generation, such as Lermontov in *The Hero of Our Time*, saw the Caucasus as a place where the valour of the colonizers was enhanced by the bravery of the conquered people, Gan represents it as a place where Russian tourists play at valour, but succumb absolutely when faced with real danger.[9] Yet, unlike Gan's other stories, this is not simply a polarization of 'masculine' self-deception and 'feminine' bravery and frankness; the female narrator here is as compromised as her male companions. Whilst in captivity, she goes on hunger-strike for a while, but has to give in when overcome with physical weakness. And the refusal of the *aul* chieftain to believe that she is not married to either of her male companions, besides suggesting the freedom of Russian women compared to the seclusion of their Oriental

---

[8] See particularly Foucault, *History of Sexuality*, vol. i: Intro. (London, 1986). On sexuality and Gan, see also Joe Andrew's excellent introductory essay, 'Elena Gan and *A Futile Gift*', in his *Narrative and Desire in Russian Literature, 1822–1849: Feminine and Masculine* (London, 1992), 85–138.

[9] Lermontov, *Geroi nashego vremeni* (1841), *Sobranie sochinenii v 4 tomakh*, iv. 7–142.

sisters, also draws attention to a certain ambiguity in the narrator's situation—an ambiguity which is underlined when she begins to worry about the fate of her children, left behind when she set off.

It was not, however, as a writer who (albeit unconsciously) expressed an internally divided and contradictory didacticism that Gan was significant for her readers. Her work was seductive because it showed women who were unhappy because they had unusual qualities; it therefore simultaneously suggested the possibility of liberation from unhappiness, and provided a rationale for unhappiness (which could be borne more easily if it appeared to be a mark of exceptional talents). And, as a writer who eschewed compromise, she was suitably inspiring in the absolutist conditions of Russian culture. The sensitive provincial girls whom she represented were the forerunners and to some extent the initiators of the heroines who became canonical in mid-nineteenth-century women's writing. But if the themes of her writing found expression there, the querulous and antagonistic aspects of her prose did not. Later women writers were to be less verbose, but also blander, more schematic, less idiosyncratic than she. Only much later, in the work of Dostoevsky, a writer quite outside the traditions of emancipatory prose, were her stylistic strategies to find a form of belated and bizarre kinship.[10]

---

[10] The mature work of Dostoevsky shares Gan's rhetorical intensity and her clumsiness (see especially *The Idiot*, and compare Malcolm Jones's recent study, *Dostoevsky after Bakhtin* (Cambridge, 1990), *passim*).

PART II

5

Configurations of Authority: Feminism, Modernism, and Mass Culture, 1881–1917

> The Woman Question will be solved
> By something in the *Lesbos* mould.
>
> (Vladimir Solovyov)

IN the years which succeeded the assassination of Alexander II in 1881, state repression reached heights unattained since the reign of Nicholas I. Assaults were launched on every possible forum of opposition, most particularly the universities and the press. As a consensus on liberal reforms within the autocracy came to seem a less and less likely prospect, attitudes within the opposition also hardened; the arguments in favour of revolutionary struggle began to carry increasing weight, and hostility to Tsarism started to take on the purposive forms of mass organization. The efficacy of revolutionary politics seemed confirmed by events in 1905, when major insurrections all over the Russian Empire succeeded in forcing a variety of important concessions from the Tsarist government. Among them were changes in agrarian policy, university administration, literary censorship, and political institutions (most importantly, the foundation of an elected central assembly, the State Duma). But these changes did nothing to heal the split in the Russian cultural élite; rather, they exacerbated it, by confirming the fears of conservatives on the one hand, the hopes of liberals and radicals on the other.[1]

---

[1] On political, social, and intellectual change between 1880 and 1917, see Hugh Seton-Watson, *The Russian Empire 1801–1917* (Oxford, 1967); J. N. Westwood, *Endurance and Endeavour: Russian History 1812–1980* (4th edn.; Oxford, 1992); Franco Venturi, *Roots of Revolution; A History of the Populist and Socialist Movements in Nineteenth-Century Russia*, trans. F. Haskell (London, 1960); V. R. Leikina-Svirskaya, *Intelligentsiya v Rossii vtoroi poloviny XIX-go veka* (Moscow, 1971); *eadem, Russkaya intelligentsiya v 1900–1917 godakh* (Moscow, 1981); R.

Yet despite an official and public atmosphere which could range from the sclerotic to the hysterical, and a private atmosphere imbued with a melancholy which often verged on the suicidal, these years were also the time when, from certain points of view, Russian women's experience was most complex and diverse. The era offered the middle-class women who made up the bulk of the reading and writing public more pluralism of opportunity than they had previously enjoyed—and arguably, more than they would enjoy thereafter. The debate on women became increasingly sophisticated, helped by the emergence, from the mid-1890s, of a full-blown feminist movement, which kept in touch with its international counterparts. This movement manifested a far greater diversity than previous campaigns for women's liberation. It was divided into several different factions, all of which fought for change on numerous fronts: the most notable distinction was between the socialist women's movement, which subordinated liberation for women to the fight for social revolution in a larger sense, and the feminist movement proper, which regarded the campaign for gender parity as a matter of primary importance and urgency.[2]

All in all, we could say that after 1881 'the woman question' became a whole series of questions about women. This did not mean that traditional concerns ceased to be of importance. Education was still one of the various women's groups' main preoccupations, though the emphasis had shifted, now that institutional education to secondary level was generally available (to women outside the working classes, at any rate); the main concern was now broadening of opportunity at tertiary level. Official policy right up to the Revolution followed an erratic progress; reversals were as frequent as gains. But, despite many setbacks, the period saw a considerable expansion in the availability of higher education for women, and also of professional training in many different spheres, notably medicine. Opportunity for those who completed training was another area where expansion was marked, though slow. Few women gained access to the real power centres of the Russian Empire (the civil service and the industrial sector). But a growing number of women did take up employment in white-collar and intellectual

Manning, *The Crisis of the Old Order in Russia: Gentry and Government* (Princeton, NJ, 1981); Dominic Lieven, *Russia's Rulers under the Old Regime* (London, 1989); Maureen Perrie, *The Agrarian Policy of the Russian Socialist-Revolutionary Party from its Origins through the Revolution of 1905–7* (Cambridge, 1976).

[2] The two most comprehensive sources on the women's movement in late 19th-c. Russia are Linda Harriet Edmondson, *Feminism in Russia 1900–1917* (London, 1984), and Richard Stites, *The Women's Liberation Movement in Russia: Feminism, Nihilism and Bolshevism 1860–1930* (Princeton, NJ, 1978), chs. 6–9. See also Anon., 'Emantsipatsiya zhenshchin', *ES* xl. 706–8; P. Mikhnuev, 'Zhenskii vopros', *NS* xvii. 772–84.

professions. Some impression of this expansion of professional activity can be gained from women's magazines and journals. The journal *Drug zhenshchin*, which began to be published in 1882, carried articles on women in journalism, education, literature, medicine, and white-collar employment. This first sign of growing pluralism was to survive for only two years, but with the end of the century the feminist press became established on a firmer footing. Several journals, perhaps the most important of which were *Zhenskii vestnik* and *Zhenskoe delo*, were founded; and a diary-annual, *Pervyi zhenskii kalendar*, began appearing. This last published yearly profiles of women activists, women writers, and successful professional women, articles on women's position in the labour market, and details of professional organizations and support groups, as well as advice on matters medical, legal, social, and domestic.[3]

If education and employment represented main themes carried over from the early days of 'the woman question', and continuing right up to the Revolution, there was also a proliferation of other issues. One of these was suffrage, a burning issue for the women's movement all over Europe. The constraints dictated by the autocratic nature of Russian society slowed down the franchise debate, and hindered its extent, since the campaign for women's suffrage was naturally dependent on the long and slow campaign for suffrage in general. Until the turn of the century, indeed, discussion about women's suffrage in Russia was a matter of more or less abstract speculation on such points as whether women were psychologically suited to achieving the vote. In the 1880s and 1890s, as in the 1860s and 1870s, the most active and visible female political activists were participants in small underground political groupings, especially those of revolutionary populist inclinations, who made prominent contributions to gesture politics, but whose effect on ideology and policy was slight.[4]

From the early 1900s, however, the suffrage question acquired a new significance. Contact with women's movements campaigning abroad, in America and in Western Europe, undoubtedly played a part in this, but just as important were events at home, as it began to seem that there might be genuine prospects of participatory government. During the

[3] On education see Edmondson, *Feminism*, 146–7; Stites, *Women's Liberation*, 157–77; Christine Johanson, *Women's Struggle for Higher Education in Russia, 1855–1900* (Kingston, Ontario, 1987); 'A.Ya.', 'Zhenskoe obrazovanie', *ES* xi. 869–72; N. Ivanov, 'Zhenskoe obrazovanie', *NS* xvii. 786–813.

[4] On the revolutionary populists see Margaret Maxwell, *Narodniki Women* (Oxford, 1991); Barbara Engel, *Mothers and Daughters: Women of the Intelligentsia in Nineteenth-Century Russia* (Cambridge, 1983); Stites, *Women's Liberation*, 126–54. The early debate on suffrage is covered briefly in ibid. 44–5.

revolutionary upheavals of 1905, women campaigned for the right to vote in elections to the local administrative bodies, the zemstvos. Later, when the Tsar conceded the creation of a constituent assembly, the Duma, and promised to extend the vote to groups which had not previously enjoyed it, feminists switched their efforts in this new direction. Heated lobbying and petitioning went on for some years, ebbing and flowing with the fortunes of the Duma itself, until the defeat of a bill brought by P. Milyukov at the Fourth Duma in 1913 finally routed suffrage efforts in the mean time. Efforts were only resumed after the Revolution of February 1917, and were finally rewarded five months later: a decree granting universal suffrage to those over the age of 20 was proclaimed on 20 July.

The crusade for suffrage was important not only in its own right, but because the lobbying by women which accompanied it dictated a level of co-operation with some of the new political parties which came into being after 1905. Even the parties bitterly opposed to suffrage had now to contemplate the possibility, and on occasion the actuality, of new public roles for women; in those parties which supported women's rights, women might make genuine contributions to ideological debate, rather than simply acting as figure-heads for symbolic rebellion. The extent of women's direct influence on politics remained relatively small, but the indirect effects of their increased prominence were rather larger.[5]

The changes mentioned so far—with the exception of the final granting of suffrage—increased the opportunity of a very small number of women, all from privileged backgrounds. But they took place against a broader background of enormous social upheaval. Throughout the nineteenth century, the population of the major Russian cities had been rising rapidly: that of St Petersburg, for example, had more than doubled between 1800 and 1840 from 220,208 to 472,800, and between then and 1898 had risen nearly three times, to 1,193,825. However, before 1880 these increases had mainly affected the numbers of men in the cities: at first because of the arrival of large numbers of civil servants, later through the in-migration of factory workers and artisans. After 1880, though, the proportion of women to men in the cities rose by more than 50 per cent, from a ratio of 26.06 women to 100 men in 1881 to a ratio of 39.36 women to 100 men in 1900. The climb in the number of women affected numerous occupations which had formerly been overwhelmingly masculine: the most marked rise in their representation was in white-collar

---

[5] For a detailed account of the complexities of the suffrage campaigns after 1900, see Edmondson, *Feminism*, esp. chs. 3, 6.

professions, but the number of female factory workers and servants also went up steadily. Unlike their male counterparts, female migrants to the cities were likely to stay put, once moved, still further increasing the weight of their influence in the urban population. Conversely, those women who remained in the countryside began to make up the only stable element in the adult working population of some villages.[6]

These changes were to make Russian intellectuals aware, effectively for the first time, that rural and urban working-class women had specific problems and a distinct culture. In the 1880s an increasing number of articles and commentaries by observers on all sides of the liberal and left intelligentsia began to survey the situation of such women, devoting themselves to such diverse areas as marital law, passport regulations, property rights, child care, working conditions, and the representations of women in folklore. The material published was sometimes of a generalizing or speculative kind, but it just as often rested on a firm foundation of empirical observation and ethnographical research. And interest in such questions was not merely passive: both members of the socialist women's movement and feminists in a broad sense, as well as populists and radicals of all hues, made strenuous attempts to better the conditions of working women through various measures, including the institution of 'Sunday schools' for workers' education and political consciousness-raising, the organization of health support, the provision of charitably funded child-care and welfare networks, as well as through campaigns for changes in the legal status of women and in the social policy affecting them.[7]

[6] On the overall population of St Petersburg, see *ES* xxviii. 312–13. The male–female population ratio is given in Ariadna Tyrkova, 'Zhenskii trud i prostitutsiya', *Russkaya mysl'* (1910), 6, sect. 2, 125; the article also gives general details of women's employment. On women's occupations in the cities see also Rose Glickman, *Russian Factory Women: Workplace and Society, 1880–1914* (Berkeley, Calif., 1984); Diane Koenker, *Moscow Workers and the 1917 Revolution* (Princeton, NJ, 1981), 31–41; S. A. Smith, *Red Petrograd* (Cambridge, 1983), 23–35. Figures for the number of women employed in individual industries can also be found in *ES* and in Granaty, *Entsiklopedicheskii slovar'* under *prisluga, sluzhashchie, fabrichnye*, etc. On women in the villages, see Barbara Alpern Engel, 'Transformation Versus Tradition', in Barbara Evans Clements, Barbara Alpern Engel, and Christine Worobec (eds.), *Russia's Women: Accommodation, Resistance, Transformation* (Berkeley, Calif., 1991), 138–40.

[7] Amongst such first-hand accounts touching on working-class and peasant women's lives were Aleksandra Efimenko, *Issledovaniya narodnoi zhizni* (Moscow, 1884); Minna Gorbunova, 'Zhenskie promysly v Moskovskoi gubernii', *Sbornik statisticheskikh svedenii po Moskovskoi gubernii*, 7/4 (1882); Ya. Ludmer, 'Bab'i stony', *Yuridicheskii vestnik* (1884), 11: 446–87; 12: 658–75; V. Ovtsyn, 'K istorii i statistiki gorodskogo proletariata v Rossii', *RM* (1891), 5, sect. 2, 60–85; 'M' and 'O', 'Tsifry i fakty iz perepisi Sankt Peterburga v 1900 godu', *RM* (1902), 11, sect. 2, 72–92; M. I. Pokrovskaya, *Po podvalam, cherdakam i uglovym kvartiram Peterburga* (St Petersburg, 1903); E. F. Budde, *Polozhenie russkoi zhenshchiny po bytovym pesnyam* (Voronezh, 1883); M. Eleonskaya, *Russkaya chastushka* (Moscow, 1910). Efimenko and Pokrovskaya were amongst the many Russian chroniclers of working-class life who also took an active part in the feminist movement: further details are given in Edmondson, *Feminism* and Stites, *Women's Liberation*.

The impulses which prompted such campaigns were undoubtedly genuine, and their effects often ameliorative. But the aid provided was, inevitably, never adequate to the huge problems of the deprived in the inhumane conditions of Russian cities. Often, too, there was a blindness to the needs of particular groups (such as domestic servants). In certain cases the organization of charitable efforts was based on rather woolly-minded notions of aiding the unfortunate (like their Western counter-parts, Russian feminists made notably unsuccessful excursions into the promotion of temperance and the discouragement of prostitution).[8] But, most importantly of all, and perhaps unavoidably, given the vast divide in living standards and educational opportunity between the élite and the lower classes in Russia, the intellectual women who organized such efforts were guided by a *dirigiste* mentality. The feminists on the one hand, the female socialists on the other, had an equal disinclination to treat working-class women as equals. The thinking of both groups placed their problems at the bottom of a hierarchy, subordinate to those of working-class men on the one hand, middle-class women on the other.[9] This was in its turn to have important effects on the representa-tions of working-class women in stories by Russian writers—though, as will be illustrated, some women writers did succeed in drawing on the internal traditions of women's writing in order to establish an alternative, anti-*dirigiste*, direction of representation.

As we shall see, the involvement of Russian women in major public political campaigns was of limited significance to the development of women's writing, though women's involvement in revolutionary acti-vism did leave some traces. But several talented realist writers of the period (notably Lyubov Gurevich and Olga Shapir) were also active feminists, and the development of new feminist ideologies more sophis-ticated and complex than those of the past was to make itself felt throughout the realist writing of the period. Outside the realist tradition, however, institutional feminism was to have little influence. It was another kind of public debate, that around sexuality, whose effects were to be more pervasive. No longer was discussion of sexuality focused on the customs and legal regulation of marriage, or dictated by the

---

[8] Domestic servants were the subject of very few studies by Russian feminists; the general conviction was that the perpetuation of service was inevitable if women were to be freed to work. See for example E. Turzhe-Turmanskaya, *Belye nevol'nitsy: domashnyaya prisluga v Rossii* (Smolensk, 1906). On feminists' campaigns against alcoholism, see Stites, *Women's Liberation*, 197; against prostitution, Edmondson, *Feminism*, 143–6. On prostitutes see also Barbara Engel, 'St. Petersburg Prostitutes in the Late Nineteenth Century: A Personal and Social Profile', *Russian Review*, 48 (1989), 21–44.

[9] On the relative priorities of socialist feminists and non-socialist feminists, see especially Glickman, *Russian Factory Women, passim.*

Chernyshevskian piety of serial monogamy based on spiritual affinity. The right to free monogamous liaisons was now taken for granted by most Russian intellectuals; what was at issue was libertarianism in the widest sense, its pleasures and its dangers. Discussion of this topic led to a vast proliferation of discourses on sex, from the psycho-pathological to the medical to the philosophical and literary.[10]

In his authoritative study of developments within the latter two discourses, the Danish Slavist Peter Ulf Møller has argued that the broadening of discussions on sex can be directly attributed to the influence of Tolstoy's famous story *The Kreutzer Sonata* (completed in 1889, and widely circulated in manuscript prior to its official publication two years later). Møller divides the years following *The Kreutzer Sonata*'s appearance into two periods. In the first, which lasted until 1895, there was emphasis on the dangers of the sexual instinct; in the second, puritanism and asceticism were replaced by a stress on erotic liberation and the rehabilitation of the body, and 'the raising of sexual morality was not nearly as topical as the question of sexual liberation without any kind of religious justification'.[11] I would argue, however, that the process was less one of substitution than of augmentation. The years after 1895 certainly saw an increasing admission of explicitly erotic material to philosophical debate and to literature, most particularly in the years after 1906, when official censorship of books and journals had been relaxed. But the new eroticism by no means put paid to Russian culture's earlier asceticism; political radicals, including most socialists, continued to voice doctrines of sexual continence, which were in turn buttressed by scientific or quasi-scientific debate on such matters as sex crime and sexually transmitted disease. For their part, many of the proponents of 'sexual liberation', notably Vasily Rozanov, continued to justify their pronouncements in religio-mystical terms, if not necessarily in the terms of a narrowly orthodox (or Orthodox) Christianity, well after 1895. The turn of the century witnessed a massive upsurge of religious interest amongst the Russian intelligentsia, above all in a post-Dostoevskian revisionist version of Russian Orthodoxy; and sexual mysticism, as Rozanov himself argued, could be more easily harmonized with Ortho-

[10] On sexual questions see for example V. Agafonov, 'Polovoi vopros', *MB* (1908), 3, sect. 2, 1–38; 4, sect. 2, 1–28 (general); A. Zhbankov, 'Polovaya prestupnost'', *SM* (1909), 7: 54–91 (on sex crime); A. S. Izgoev, 'Po st. 1001', *RM* (1908), 9, sect. 2, 187–93 (on pornography); A. N. Bernshtein, 'Voprosy polovoi zhizni v programme semeinogo i shkol'nogo vospitaniya', *RM* (1908), 3, sect. 2, 51–71 (on sex education); Laura Engelstein, 'Morality and the Wooden Spoon: Russian Doctors View Syphilis, Social Class and Sexual Behavior, 1890–1905', *Representations*, 14 (1986), 169–208; O. Sh., 'Sifilis', *ES* xxx. 113–24; G.M.G., 'Prostitutsiya', *ES* l. 479–86; Anon., 'Venericheskie bolezni', *NS* x. 121–2 (on disease).

[11] Peter Ulf Møller, *Postlude to the Kreutzer Sonata: Tolstoy and the Debate on Sexual Morality in Russian Literature in the 1890s*, trans. John Kendal (Amsterdam, 1989), pp. xiii–xiv.

dox teaching on the sacrament of marriage than could sexual abstinence or random promiscuity.[12]

Where sexual libertarianism did develop, its effects were rather limited. Often it amounted to little more than an inchoate mixture of hedonism and self-interest, as deliciously satirized by Nadezhda Teffi in her story 'Changing Values', which portrays a riot by school boys in 'the year of revolutions', 1905:

'What's more, we demand universal and secret rights for women. We express our outrage, we protest! Ivan Semenych keeps giving us rotten marks, but the girls get "excellent" whatever rubbish they write. Manka told me so.' ...

   'I demand that mowality be dithcuthed! I want to dithcuth mowality, but Thenka keepth blowing in my ear! I want mowality abolithed! We thould be allowed to do just what we like! Why thould we "honour our father and mother": ith degwading!' ...

   'Right, go on.'

   'That we thould be allowed to get married!'

   'No, no, you've got it all wrong, universal and secret rights.'

   'All right, then put this in. "We demand free love, and that everyone should be able to get married, and secret rights for ladies, women and children." Is that it?'[13]

The fact that Teffi's story shows these callow demands being made by school *boys*, not school *girls*, indicates her nice appreciation of events in the adult world. Manifestos for the new libertarianism likewise emphasized male desire at the expense of the female, presenting women as artefacts designed for the pleasure of men, selectively sculpted in order to omit any alienating biological details.[14] Female desire was acceptable only where it could be presumed to depend upon, and collude with, male desire. Whilst views permissive of male homosexuality—if only in a

[12] For Russian radicals the emphasis, after 1900 as before, was on liberating women from their sexuality and biology, rather than on achieving the free expression of women's sexuality and biology. For example, Aleksandra Kollontai, *Novaya moral' i rabochaya klass* (Moscow, 1918) (a collection of articles first published in 1911–14) stresses a free union based on comradeliness, and not on hedonism; a more unusual vision of the benefits of sexual control is voiced by a doctor, S. Mikhnov, *Zhenshchina s biologicheskoi tochki zreniya* (Yurev [i.e. Tartu], 1904), who suggests that with the introduction of birth control women's gender-based disadvantages will disappear. The persistence of religio-mystical views on sexuality is illustrated by V. Rozanov's article 'Afrodita-Diana', *Mir iskusstva* (1899), 2: 85–8, and by his large-scale study *Lyudi lunnogo sveta* (St Petersburg, 1913). See also Stites, *Women's Liberation*, 258 ff.; Eric Naiman, 'Historectomies: On the Metaphysics of Reproduction' in Jane Costlow, Stephanie Sandler, and Judith Vowles (eds.), *Sexuality in Russian Culture* (Stanford, Calif., 1993).

[13] Nadezhda Teffi, 'Pereotsenka tsennostei', *Nostalgiya: rasskazy, vospominaniya* (Leningrad, 1989), 26.

[14] The aestheticization of women's bodies for the male gaze is found e.g. in Serov's nude portrait of the dancer Ida Rubinstein, and Somov's Beardleyesque illustrations to *Pokhozhdeniya markizy*, as well as in two notorious novels of the 1900s, Artsybashev's *Sanin* (1908) and Kuprin's *Yama* (1907). See also Eva Buchwald, 'Ideals of Womanhood in the Literature of Finland and Russia, 1894–1914', Ph.D. thesis (London University, 1990).

restricted sense—did develop, female homosexuality was generally either the subject of thunderings about 'perversion', or else was equated with the *absence* of libido, rather than with a change of direction by the libido. The most famous advocate of sexual liberalization, Rozanov, argued in his long essay *People of the Lunar Light* (1913), that the sex drive was an inevitable and sometimes uncontrollable part of human existence, in women as well as men. But Rozanov's ideal of sexual relations was one in which a slightly more libidinous man was conjoined with a slightly less libidinous woman, and the couple monogamously engaged in rational sexual activities (once every Saturday night, he recommends). Excessively active women were regarded by him with disfavour. So, too, were homosexual practices, which he regarded as resulting from the frustration of ordinary desire; and his depiction of these practices again reveals how normative the sexual assumptions of this supposedly revolutionary thinker in fact were. The two case-studies which back up his theoretical argument portray a practising male homosexual—a monk addicted to masturbation and pederasty—and a female medical student whose 'Uranian' tastes are a matter exclusively of the mind: she is a bluestocking girl in whom 'masculine' intellectual tastes are accompanied by an absence of womanly qualities.

The prohibitive libertarianism of turn-of-the-century attitudes was, as we shall see, to dictate to women how they might themselves contemplate their sexuality. Whilst female desire was no longer a totally unmentionable subject, it was one which might be mentioned (in print at least) only in certain ways. Unlike Rozanov or the medical establishment, literary decadents attached a positive value to overt sexual behaviour by women, including 'perverted' behaviour such as lesbianism. But in doing so they ascribed a transgressive character to feminine sexuality (which is to say, one that is normative in a mirror-image sense, where the possibilities of deviance are predicted and proscribed), which by no means all women found helpful. This was particularly evident in the case of lesbianism, whose 'decadent' connotations tended to appeal more to writers, such as Zinaida Gippius, who wished to toy in public with 'deviance', and so emphasize their own daring, than it did to writers, such as Sofiya Parnok, who were lesbian in terms of their actual biographical sexuality.

Apart from changes in attitudes to sexuality, and concomitant shifts in conceptualization of the self, it was changes in the literary institutions of the period which were of most significance to women's writing. These also increased considerably in diversity between 1880 and the Revolution.

A central point made in the first part of this book was the great power wielded by the thick journals, the literary and political monthlies. These could offer those authors whom they selected a wider circulation and a more assured success than would have been available had they published individually. These thick journals continued to be a major force after 1880 too. Individual components of the bloc had changed. *Sovremennik* had been closed down in 1866, *Otechestvennye zapiski* had folded in 1884, *Russkii vestnik* was to close in 1906; though *Vestnik Evropy* continued publication right up to the Bolshevik suppression of the press in 1918, several new titles were founded in the mid-1880s, the most important amongst which were *Russkaya mysl, Russkoe bogatstvo*, and *Mir bozhii*. But the ideological and cultural position of the thick journals remained, collectively speaking, very much what it had been. The continuing commitment of the Russian left, in the broadest sense, to the cause of women's liberation led such journals to publish not only factual articles, but also the work of politically committed women writers, including feminist writers. And after 1880 as before, the speciality of the thick journals was prose fiction of medium length (short stories and novellas) in the established realist manner. Amongst the many writers who supplied the demand were Olga Shapir, Ekaterina Letkova, Anastasya Krandievskaya, Valentina Dmitrieva, Olga Runova, Varvara Tsekhovskaya, and Marya Krestovskaya. (The overwhelming dominance of fiction meant that the thick journals gave only a small amount of space to poetry, and that most of this was pretty undistinguished; until the rise of the 'new arts' movements, of which more later, editors' tastes were for love and nature lyrics of the harmlessly melodious kind that formed the staple fodder of after-dinner recitations, or, when set to music, concerts, in the drawing-rooms of the Russian upper classes and bourgeoisie.)[15]

Traditionally for the Russian left, the thick journals tended to perceive women's rights in institutional rather than in personal terms; accordingly, women's writing was not guaranteed special coverage, any more than it had been before 1880. And the literary assumptions reflected in the occasional articles that did deal with the subject continued to be rather pedestrian and primitive. Women's contributions to non-realist

---

[15] The thick journal whose coverage of the 'woman question' was most extensive was probably *Severnyi vestnik*, on whose editorial staff women occupied important positions. But other journals also carried much material: see e.g. L.L.F., 'Materinstvo i umstvennyi trud', *MB* (1902), 9, sect. 2, 7–20; T. Bogdanovich, 'Zhenskoe dvizhenie za poslednie pyat'desyat let', *MB* (1903), 9, sect. 2, 204–37; O. Volkenshtein, 'Itogi pervogo vserossiiskogo zhenskogo s"ezda', *RM* (1909), 2, sect. 2, 146–53. For a sample of the kind of women's poetry the thick journals preferred to carry see e.g. Glafira Galina [Rinks], *Stikhotvoreniya* (St Petersburg, 1902), and Mariya Davydova, *Stikhotvoreniya* (St Petersburg, 1899).

writing were in general either ignored, or ridiculed; and even realist writing was usually treated to stodgily synopsis-heavy and tediously judgemental analyses, which frequently manifested the established tendency to denigrate women writers for devoting too much time to specifically women's concerns, yet assumed that women's concerns were the sole appropriate material of women's writing. One significant change, however, had taken place. Survey articles, such as M. A. Protopopov's 'Women's Writing' (1891), no longer champion a single author as the sole model for women's writing, as had been the practice earlier in the century; the change does indicate a certain, however ungracious, recognition of the diversity of their material.[16]

After 1880, as before, the thick journals remained the forum from which the vast majority of Russian intellectuals would have become acquainted with debate on the woman question and with new woman writers. But for all their continuing importance, their supremacy in Russian publishing had come under assault from two sides by the turn of the century.

On one side lay the commercial book publishers. The increasing importance of manufacturing industries, and the rise in the proportion of those employed in them, led Russian society, like other industrializing societies, to look with new attention not only at the issue of conditions at work, but at the issue of conditions outside work. As in Britain, France, and Germany, it was felt that an important factor contributing to the 'quality of life' for working people was access to modes of 'rational leisure'. In Russia as abroad, the campaign to get free time used rationally led to the institution of many different kinds of activity. A proliferation of public spectacles—magic lantern and film shows with temperance refreshments, zoological gardens, instructive exhibitions in museums and galleries, music-hall programmes made up of edifying and wholesome songs and dances, and of the Russian classics in simplified adaptations—was matched with an increasing emphasis on reading as a rational private activity. The production of cheap books had formerly been in the hands of a few dozen family firms, mostly based in Moscow; now, with the upsurge in city populations on the one hand, and the

---

[16] M. A. Protopopov, 'Zhenskoe tvorchestvo', *RM* (1891), 1: 98–112; 2: 161–81; 4: 123–41 [all sect. 2]; see also N. M. Mikhailovsky, 'Literatura i zhizn'', *RB* (1899), 8, sect. 2, 157–66, in which women writers such as Letkova and Gippius are treated alongside such well-known male writers as Chekhov, Gorky, and Mamin-Sibiryak. See also E. A. Koltonovskaya, *Zhenskie siluety* (St Petersburg, 1912). N. Ya. Abramovich's pedestrian comments on women poets in *Istoriya russkoi poezii ot Pushkina do nashikh dnei* (Moscow, 1915), 298–311, indicate that early 19th-c. stereotypes persisted in the traditional intelligentsia where literature other than prose was in question: he commends 'grace' and slams intellectual pretension. For all that, though, he mentions quite a substantial number of different poets.

growth of literacy in the countryside on the other, a mass market for books opened up, and a hugely expanded printing industry poured out editions at low prices and in large print runs. Female literacy was still much lower than male—though young urbanized factory workers did not lag all that far behind their male colleagues—so that the proportion of women readers in this mass market is a vexed question, their putative choice in reading matter still more so. However, the cheap educational libraries did publish some specially written work in which women writers addressed a working-class female audience, including Valentina Dmitrie-va's *Lipochka the Priest's Daughter* (1902), a tragic story of a woman raped during her political interrogation, and, more famously, Aleksandra Kollontai's *Working Mother* (1914), a tract contrasting the conditions of motherhood amongst the idle rich and the toiling poor. These works were as uplifting as the average temperance lecture; but a very different kind of mass-audience publishing also began to make itself felt at the turn of the century. Block-busting novels such as Artsybashev's *Sanin* and Kuprin's *The Pit*, whilst far too didactic in tone to be read with one hand, were, by the standards of Russian literature, unusually titillating, and were to find an eager readership amongst a whole variety of social classes. The absorption of such material was undoubtedly facilitated by the preoccupations of the massive popular entertainment sector, whose racy improprieties offered a broad public a diverse and contradictory set of fictional sexual roles. If the *myuzik-kholly* and *kafe-shantany* paraded before their audiences singers of a Mae West-like outspokenness, singing such ditties as 'Come up, come up and sweep my chimney', female sensuality was also to be reflected (although more pallidly) in the work of the two most notorious women writers of the early twentieth century, Evdokiya Nagrodskaya and Anastasiya Verbitskaya, whose 'sensational novels', to be analysed in detail later, brought them a success equal to that enjoyed by Kuprin or Artsybashev.[17]

The development of the literary mass market was recognized in the thick journals, which carried book reviews and survey articles reflecting a range of emotions, from sorrow to anger. A more potent sense of outrage was, however, inspired in these journals by enemies on the other flank: that is, the new literary and arts journals and almanacs which began to

---

[17] On rational leisure see esp. Daniel Brower, *The Russian City: From Tradition to Modernity* (Berkeley, Calif., 1990); on the growth of the printed books market, see Jeffrey Brooks, *When Russia Learned to Read* (Princeton, NJ, 1984), which includes some rather superficial observations on women's readership, pp. 161–2; on Valentina Dmitrieva's popular books, see O. Lasunsky in Dmitrieva, *Povesti. Rasskazy* (Voronezh, 1983), 21–3. On the character of commercial popular culture, see Catriona Kelly, '"Better Halves"? Representations of Women in Russian Urban Popular Culture, 1890–1910', in Linda Edmondson (ed.), *Women and Society in Russia* (Cambridge, 1992), 5–25.

be published from about 1900. These were short-lived in comparison to the thick journals proper (*Mir iskusstva* ran from 1899–1904, *Vesy* from 1904–9, *Zolotoe runo* from 1906–9, *Severnye zapiski* from 1913–17; the longest run enjoyed by an arts journal, *Apollon* (1909–17), is significantly shorter than that of the shortest-lived thick journal, *Severnyi vestnik*, (1885–98). But their notoriety and influence was out of all proportion greater than the years of their existence, and also than their official circulation figures, which were considerably lower than those for the thick journals.[18]

In contrast to the thick journals, the arts journals dealt with political and social issues only in abstract terms, and frequently only briefly even then (as snippets or short reviews in their 'chronicle' sections). They were concerned instead with the theory and practice of Symbolism, the most important literary school, or rather series of literary schools, in Russian twentieth-century literature. The hegemony of Symbolism and its post-Symbolist successors, such as Acmeism and the various brands of Futurism, was more or less coterminous with the existence of these journals. And it was these journals which were responsible for disseminating Symbolist ideas on the creativity of women, and for making the reputations of almost all the Russian women writers associated with Symbolism and post-Symbolism: Lyudmila Vilkina, Lyubov Stolitsa, Anna Akhmatova, Adelaida Gertsyk, Sofiya Parnok, Nadezhda Lvova, Elizaveta Kuzmina-Karavaeva, and the pseudonymous 'Cherubina de Gabriak' (Elizaveta Dmitrieva). An important role was also played by the almanacs published in affiliation with the journals, amongst which the most important was perhaps *Severnye tsvety* (1901–14).[19]

The gap between thick journals and arts journals was not unbridgeable. One thick journal, *Severnyi vestnik*, acted as an early forum for the 'new arts' debate. Some of the earliest Russian Symbolist poems and essays were published in it. Prose still made up its backbone, but some of its authors, notably Olga Shapir and Lyubov Gurevich, produced more

---

[18] The statistics on subscription numbers for Russian journals give some indication of their official circulation figures. In 1909 *Vesy* had 1,000 subscribers (see T. J. Binyon, 'Valery Bryusov: Life, Literary Theory, Poetry', D.Phil. thesis (Oxford University, 1969), 112); in 1906 the print-run of *MB* and *RM* was around 10,000 each (see L. N. Belyaeva, M. K. Zinov'eva, M. M. Nikiforov, *Bibliografiya periodicheskikh izdanii Rossii 1901–1916* (3 vols.; Moscow, 1958–60), vol. ii, no. 4733, vol. iii, no. 6860.

[19] Most of the important theoretical essays and much of the poetry associated with Acmeism (also known as 'Adamism') were published in *Apollon* from 1913; Futurist work, on the other hand, was more commonly brought out in one-off editions or almanacs, such as *Sadok sudei*, 1 and 2 (Moscow, 1913, Moscow, 1914); *Rukonog* (Moscow, 1914). Occasionally, women poets began their careers by publishing collections independently: so with Marina Tsvetaeva's *Vechernii albom* (Moscow, 1910), or Sergei Gedroits, *Stikhi i skazki* (St Petersburg, 1910), but in such cases the new arts movements still exercised a crucial influence on literary standing.

innovative work than that encouraged by other thick journals. After 1910, by which time Symbolism had become an established literary force, the liberal journal *Russkaya mysl*, under the literary editorship of Valery Bryusov, performed similar services to the movement in its later stages. And if commentators in the 'thick journals' began to take Symbolism more seriously with the course of time, it was also the case that Symbolism itself became more ideologically engaged in its later phases, acquiring elements of a loosely socialist populism, the revolution of 1905 being a watershed for many. Even before this, individual figures had sometimes crossed the divide. Zinaida Gippius had begun her career as a fiction writer with stories, such as 'In the Drawing-Room and the Servants' Hall' (1893), which were in no sense immediately distinguishable from many others published in the thick journals (though her early poetry did stand out from the dross which surrounded it). But with the formation of the arts journals, her allegiance was firmly established on that side. She began to publish her work in these new organs; besides poetry and (by now more adventurous) fiction, her contributions included critical articles in which, under the pseudonym Anton Krainy (Extreme) she discussed the literary endeavours of the thick journals in mercilessly disparaging tones.[20]

Such fluctuations and rapprochements mean that one should not overstate the breadth of the gulf between the new arts movements and the rest of Russian literary life. So far as women authors were concerned, however, such developments had relatively little effect. Whether attached to the thick journals or to the new arts journals, they remained relatively static in their literary tastes, no doubt because they tended to follow rather than to lead in literary splits and disputes; and it is not possible to trace the development of a specifically feminine contribution to committed Symbolism after 1905. The burgeoning politicization of such male writers as Bryusov or Blok had no parallel amongst their female contemporaries.[21]

So, in general, it is reasonably safe and convenient to trace a separate history for three distinct institutional and ideological traditions: the realist narrative, as practised in the thick journals, the 'sensational novel', as represented by various mass print-run individual publications, and the Symbolist and post-Symbolist text (mostly poetry, but including some

[20] Z. Gippius, 'V gostinoi i v lyudskoi', *VE* (1895), 3: 91–139; *Literaturnyi dnevnik 1899–1907* (St Petersburg, 1908); on her prose and poetry see also Temira Pachmuss, *Zinaida Hippius: An Intellectual Profile* (Carbondale, Ill., 1971).

[21] An early expression of Symbolism's new social commitment was the journal *Novyi put'*, an organ of the 'mystical anarchist' movement which published from 1903–4; later, arts journals such as *Vesy* were to give brief reviewing space to books by the likes of Bebel and Kautsky.

fiction and drama too), as published in the arts journals and literary almanacs. Each tradition in turn reflected external political and social events and interests rather partially. The political and economic battles for franchise and equal pay figured rarely, if at all, as the subjects of any kind of women's imaginative writing; the remaining issues which preoccupied public debate were, however, differently reflected within each different tradition.

The realist tradition was little concerned with self-expression as such; women writers were understood, as they had been before 1880, to be persons whose sex played an incidental, rather than a crucial, role as they produced their social commentaries and visions of a better life. The nature of such commentaries had, however, now changed. Education and self-betterment remained very important topics, and the 'aspirant myth' retained its hold, but there was now more concern with women's struggles *in* their careers, rather than their struggles to achieve careers. Other new elements were a higher level of reference to *realia*, and a much greater concern with the lives of women outside the upper classes. Sexual matters were also discussed more frankly than in realist writing of the past, though they occupied a much less prominent place than in the 'sensational novel', where, conversely, issues of education and self-betterment, whilst being in no sense ignored, had a secondary place.

Education and self-betterment were not issues of great importance to the Symbolist and post-Symbolist movements; these, as we shall see, were not dynamic, but essentialist, in their view of women. But these movements did give a particular prominence to sexual material; they also drew, in their own idiosyncratic way, on material from popular life. Folkloric texts and masks from Russian rural life were appropriated by women poets—who were themselves invariably of bourgeois or even haut bourgeois origin[22]—not for their own sake but in order that they might act as metaphors for poets as marginal, yet authoritative, cultural figures.

Realism and Feminist Writings

The backbone of the realist tradition as practised by women writers, after 1881 as before, was the escape plot. Many writers working for the thick journals still produced substantial tales centred on the struggles of young girls, often of provincial origin, to break their domestic chains, and make

---

[22] For example, Gedroits, Gertsyk, and Gippius came from provincial landowning families; Akhmatova, Kuzmina-Karavaeva, and Tsvetaeva were the daughters of high-ranking Tsarist officials; Parnok and Dmitrieva, whose family origins were more humble, were still far from being of proletarian descent.

themselves socially useful. Some 1890s heroines are almost indistinguishable from the earlier prototype, though there may be a new resonance to
their actions. Women's potential for violence in achieving their ends
may, for example, now be emphasized. In Dmitrieva's long tale 'The
Prison' (1887), the heroine, Lenochka, struggles, like a heroine of the
1840s or the 1850s, to educate herself, despite the hostility of her narrow-
minded provincial parents and of her wicked brother. The one bright spot
in her life is contact with her stepbrother, a political radical. The story
ends when Lena is forced by her brother's theft of her diary into shooting
him—though Dmitrieva's aesthetic, like that of Attic tragedy, dictates
that this violence should happen off-stage.[23]

Lena's crime has personal, rather than political, promptings; but her
half-brother's connections, and her brother's activities as amateur secret
policeman, give the story revolutionary overtones, making her a parallel
to the women terrorists, such as Vera Figner and Sofya Perovskaya,
whose acts of violence had reverberated through Russian society in the
1870s and 1880s. These women revolutionaries had themselves behaved
like the principled heroines of prose fiction or radical poetry (and in the
case of Figner, had also written of themselves in such terms); in a
continuation of the circularity of life and art, their actions were to inspire
the women writers of the 1890s and 1900s. The material at which Sofya
Kovalevskaya's story 'The Nihilist' (1892) had hinted was made explicit
in Tatyana Shchepkina-Kupernik's 'Her First Ball' (1907), whose idealistic heroine liberates herself from her petty-minded mother's ambitions for
her future; at the occasion supposed to announce her nubility to the
world, she withdraws a revolver from her corsage and shoots her dancing-
partner, a figure-head of reactionary politics.[24] In her novel of 1903, *The
History of a Life*, Anastasiya Verbitskaya (then in her pre-sensationalist
incarnation as a standard realist writer), represents a young woman,
Olga, who is involved with a revolutionary populist group of the 1870s:
she is eventually imprisoned for her crimes, but not before a long series of
scenes have depicted her estrangement from her family and her various
emotional and sexual entanglements.[25] A very similar text is Shapir's
long novel *The Stormy Years* (late 1880s), which will be discussed in

[23] Valentina Dmitrieva, 'Tyur'ma', *VE* (1887), 8: 543–96; 9: 5–67; 10: 502–63.

[24] Sof'ya Kovalevskaya, 'Nigilistka', *Svidanie*, 417–500; Tat'yana Shchepkina-Kupernik, 'Pervyi bal', *Tol'ko chas*, 317–33. The memoirs of Vera Figner are akin to the stereotypes of the 'provincial tale' in their emphasis on biography as chronicle of escape: see 'Moya nyanya', *Sbornik Znanie*, 14 (1906), 199–212; *Zapechatlennyi trud* (2 vols.; Moscow, 1920); her poetry is available in *Poety revolyutsionnogo narodnichestva*, ed. A. Bikhter (Leningrad, 1967), 217–44. An interesting study for comparative purposes is Margaret Ward's book on Irish women revolutionaries, *Unmanageable Revolutionaries* (2nd edn.; London, 1989).

[25] Anastasiya Verbitskaya, *Istoriya odnoi zhizni* (Moscow, 1905).

detail later: it, too, concerns a confident, independent, idealistic heroine, a member of a revolutionary populist group, who is here contrasted with a bored and emotionally confused high-society lady engaged in a more socially acceptable, but less worthy, activity: charitable work. A similar contrast is central to Letkova's story 'The Superfluous Woman', dealing with a woman who has left husband and daughters to go abroad with her political activist lover. After the death of both husband and lover, she returns to Russia, where she is shocked by the prevailing atmosphere of cynicism, anti-Semitism, and materialism. Her own daughters turn out to be interested only in crochet and clothes, express themselves shocked by the 'depravity' of her behaviour, and ask her to leave. She obeys, vowing to dedicate her life to the enlightenment of other, more promising, followers. The contrast between the social concerns of the past and the self-interest of the present could not be more marked, and it is only too obvious where Letkova's own sympathies lie.[26]

As the above examples suggest, narratives of revolutionary self-fulfilment are frequently associated, in fiction of the 1890s and 1900s, with sub-plots concerning sexual liberation. Sexual liberation is, however, also important as an independent topic. Here again, the post-1880 realist tradition preserves some aspects of plot dynamic and psychological categorization as practised prior to 1880. But the context and details of the action have undergone some changes.

For example, marital relationships, whilst still of central importance to women writers, are now treated rather differently. The new emphasis on the centrality of sexuality to human existence had contradictory effects on women's writing. The first effect was to render redundant a favourite theme of the past, in which women discovered fulfilment in an existence without men. Turn-of-the-century writers could no longer contemplate celibacy as a mode of autonomy: it is, rather, seen as a way to frustration and unhappiness. Lyubov Gurevich's story 'The Errand' (1890s), for example, shows how the false hopes of one woman are cruelly disappointed when an apparently promising male visitor turns out to have been merely an emissary to raise funds for her prodigal brother.[27] In other stories, an offer of marriage is seen as an honour rather than a social trap. In Sofya Smirnova's long story 'The Chimera' (1893), for example, the idealistic Shura is involved with Ivan Sergeevich, a much-travelled older

[26] Ekaterina Letkova, 'Lishnyaya', *RM* (1893), 7: 77–109.

[27] Lyubov Gurevich, 'Poruchenie', *Sedok i drugie rasskazy* (St Petersburg, 1904), 36–89; cf. 'Shurochka', ibid. 90–134, and the scene in Verbitskaya's *Istoriya odnoi zhizni*, 105–6, in which Olga, the heroine, mocks a woman doctor for diagnosing her problems as linked to sexual repression, but finds her thoughts turning to a man none the less.

man to whom she looks up unquestioningly; despite the 'chimera' created by malicious gossip, the two are eventually united, something which affords them 'genuine happiness'.[28]

In such narratives one can see that the new emphasis on sexual fulfilment might lead to the representation of heterosexual relationships as a requirement, rather than an option. But this emphasis could, conversely, provide further ammunition to women writers assaulting the institution of marriage from within. In some post-1880 texts, the former emphasis on lack of congruence in sentiment has been supplemented by a relatively frank expression of sexual discontent or even revulsion. In Marya Krestovskaya's 'The Wail' (1900), for example, the narrator, Natasha, describes her horror of sexual contact with her husband in graphic phrases:

Sometimes he would still turn up, with his caresses long gone cold, and take me, as one might take a glass of tea from the hand of a housemaid, not looking at her face and scarcely noticing that she was there at all.

And yet I remained his wife, and was supposed to have no right of refusal, but every time anger would boil within me and a sense of offence well up, and I would feel such shame, as if . . . as if I were submitting to a stranger who was taking me by force. In these shameful moments I felt contempt for myself and something near to hatred for him.[29]

At this point, however, the weight of tradition makes itself felt. Though sexual reasons, rather than emotional reasons, now prompt the break-down of her protagonist's marriage, Krestovskaya's psychological delineation of that protagonist follows the conventions of the escape plot, in that Natasha is shown to be aloof from her own situation, apparently considering that she bears no responsibility for it. Her disgust is represented in a series of passive constructions; she is unable to control even her reactions to circumstances, let alone circumstances herself, or to translate her definite sense of contempt for herself into more than a muted aggression (*near to* hatred, but not hatred) for her husband. But by the end of the story, apparently without undergoing any process of internal change, she is able to 'escape', and what is more, escape in a more positive way than has her friend Sonya, a woman who is sucked into a life of depravity culminating in suicide. Again, we see the didactic

[28] Sof'ya Smirnova, 'Khimera', *SV* (1897), 1: 1–39; 2: 3–27; 3: 1–24.
[29] Mari'ya Krestovskaya, 'Vopl'', *Tol'ko chas*, 187–8. With certain notable exceptions, such as Krestovskaya's 'Artistka', *VE* (1891), nos. 4–12, the tendency in much women's fiction of the 1890s–1900s is to represent sexually active women in disapprobatory terms; in Tsekhovskaya's 'U teplogo morya', for example, the central male character is made deeply uneasy by the machinations of an attractive widow.

novel's linear plot combined with a schematic pairing of heroine and counter-heroine, and a concentration on the outward manifestations, rather than the psychological deep structure, of oppression.

Another story which also depicts the problems of sexual dissatisfaction, yet suggests that these are easily resolvable, is Dmitrieva's 'The Picnic' (1892).[30] Liza, the young wife of a dull schoolmaster, becomes increasingly bored; the arrival of Unzhakov, a bounder from St Petersburg, exacerbates her marital malaise, in which compulsive sexual interest, 'the foreknowledge of unknown pleasures' (p. 44), plays a large part. Dmitrieva, a more puritanical writer than Krestovskaya, places the solution within marriage: confronted with the naked sexual interest of her admirer, Liza returns in distress to her husband, who has in the mean time himself undergone a surprising, but convenient, conversion to a garrulous brand of feminism: 'We throw you crumbs from our table and wonder why you should be so feeble and puny' (p. 63).

As both these stories illustrate, sexual dissatisfaction often functioned for women writers in an instrumental sense: it was a metaphor for other kinds of dissatisfaction, rather than an area of investigation in itself. Caught between the doctrine imposed by contemporary thinking, that sex was a necessary part of being a 'full woman', and the conviction, inherited from earlier generations of women writers, that sexual activity was likely to expose women to exploitation by men, women writers not unnaturally manifest the urge to drop the subject and move on to 'something else'. Quite what this 'something else' should be is not always clear, however since other types of 'pleasures', in the physical sense, are still more problematic than sexuality. Eating and drinking are activities which please only brutish individuals;[31] another visceral occurrence, pregnancy, hardly ever overtakes even brutes. Late nineteenth-century women writers are almost as chary of representing the gravid state, and its sequence, maternity, as their predecessors were. Runova's story 'Nothing Sacred' does deal with the subject obliquely, in that its topic is abortion, but birth is represented as an imposition, a duty, rather than a joy, advocated by a dictatorial male gynaecologist, and avoided by his women patients.[32] Verbitskaya's 'Sara Eizman' relegates pregnancy to the margins, being concerned with the struggles of a young

[30] Dmitrieva, 'Progulka', *RB* (1892), 9: 1–64.

[31] In Dmitrieva's 'Progulka', for example, the picnic is the scene of extravagant displays of eating and drinking by the coarsest and most unintellectual characters; the 'merry widow' of Tsekhovskaya's 'U teplogo morya' offers hospitality as ample as her own person.

[32] O. Runova, 'Bez zaveta: rasskaz', *SM* (1913), 10: 29–69; see also Laura Engelstein, 'Abortion and the Civic Order: The Legal and Medical Debates', in Clements, Engel, and Worobec (eds.), *Russia's Women*, 206.

Jewish woman to make a career as a midwife.[33] The story begins by representing the fears of a young woman on the point of giving birth; her sense of claustrophobia is captured in a scene in which white butterflies fall on the dining-room table, becoming entangled in the food, and drown in the milk. The anxieties of representing reproduction are further underlined by the fact that heroines' relationships with their mothers either play a very insignificant role, or a role which is made significant by the presence of a single emotion: enmity.[34]

The effacement of maternity does not, however, mean that women's relationships with their husbands or lovers are women realists' only field of enquiry. The broader family does appear, even if often in a negative context. There is a new sense of the way that family responsibilities may drain small children and middle-aged women, as well as dewy-eyed young girls. In Olga Shapir's lively story 'Veteran and New Recruits', for example, the cosy and ordered life of two sisters, a tart spinster and a more sentimentally expansive widow, is disrupted when the latter's son arrives complete with wife and baby. Mother and—to a lesser extent—aunt soon get bogged down in the child-care arrangements (which at this era of course means problems with nurses, rather than actual baby-sitting).[35]

If turn-of-the-century representations of revolutionary liberation, and sexual or family relations, renuance the conventional history of the well-to-do provincial heroines of the past, another popular type of narrative broke more radically with the traditional aspirant myth by changing its class base. The generally accepted notion of professional activity as an escape was now transformed by being applied to working-class women. An early example of this trend was Nadezhda Khvoshchinskaya's story 'The Schoolmistress' (1880). Khvoshchinskaya's heroine is the daughter of a cook, whose education has given her the opportunity of escaping from the squalor of her mother's existence. The narrative shows her campaign to establish herself in the provincial village where she is employed, and her resistance to the hostility of a narrow-minded family of landowners.[36] Khvoshchinskaya's heroine's class origins were inciden-tal to the narrative; in later texts, such origins were to play a larger part in heroines' aspirations. One remarkable example of the genre is Shapir's

[33] Verbitskaya, 'Sara Eizman', *Schast'e: novye rasskazy* (Moscow, 1905), 111. Cf. the same author's *Istoriya odnoi zhizni*, in which great prominence is given to the physical trials of pregnancy, such as vomiting, anaemia, and fainting.

[34] Other characters without mothers include Margot, the heroine of Tsekhovskaya's 'Dinastiya', *Tol'ko chas*, 383–479, and the central characters of Gurevich's stories 'Toska', *Sedok*, 141–67, and 'Rasseyanost'', ibid. 187–215.

[35] On Shapir, 'Invalidy i novobrantsy', see Ch. 6 below.

[36] Khvoshchinskaya, 'Uchitel'nitsa', *Povesti i rasskazy* (Moscow, 1963) 366–477.

long story about a servant family. 'Avdotya's Daughters' (1898), which will be analysed in detail later. Another is Anastasiya Krandievskaya's short text 'Daughter of the People', in which two do-gooding upper-class women patronize a working-class girl in her search for self-betterment, until they realize that she is determinedly independent, rather than abjectly grateful.[37]

In terms of the female protagonist's psychological characteristics, the concentration on working-class heroines did not always bring about change; familiar, too, was the pairing of a rebellious 'positive heroine' with a negative counter-image, who in this case was invariably a class antagonist. A determined working-class woman faces a feeble or complacent *bourgeoise* or (considerably less frequently) a woman intellectual. It is the working-class woman who carries the torch for militant feminism. Two decades later, in the context of the crude 'class-war' fictions of the early Soviet years such confrontations were to acquire sinister overtones.[38] But in the context of their own time, they were more provocative than superficial analysis of their formal characteristics might suggest. They allowed a more independent spirit to working-class women than was allowed by many feminist non-fictional articles and tracts of the day (or to be more accurate, they acknowledged such a spirit in working-class *girls*—the women in such stories are always unmarried and in their early twenties, as their provincial tale predecessors had been). They also provided an alternative tradition to that evident in a prominent genre of the 1890s and 1900s, the 'upstart fiction'. By this term I mean stories of the kind very popular around the turn of the century, in which the campaign of workers, or more particularly of servants, to better their lot is seen as a surrender to the worst sort of materialistic greed. The anti-capitalist sympathies of most Russian intellectuals meant that 'upstart fictions' were far more common than adaptations of the 'aspirant myth'. Women writers as well as men wrote stories attacking such 'upstarts' (one is Zinaida Gippius's 'In the Drawing-Room and the Servants' Hall').[39] However, some, if not all, of them described the struggles of working-class women to escape domestic slavery more

[37] Anastasiya Krandievskaya, 'Doch' naroda', *RM* (1904), 4: 98–111.

[38] On 'class war' fictions, see Ch. 9 below.

[39] Amongst the many turn-of-the-century fictions dealing with social upstarts are Boborykin, 'Goluboi lif', *Sobranie romanov, povestei i rasskazov*, vol. iii (St Petersburg, 1897), 146–80; Chekhov, 'V ovrage', 'Anna na shee', 'Sluchai iz praktiki', *Tri sestry*; Gorky, *Vassa Zheleznova*. It is worthy of remark that women writers give sympathetic portraits of social mobility where they deal with women from the working classes in a strict sense, but rarely diverge from their male colleagues' hostile portraits of merchants and servants: cf. Dmitrieva, 'Gomochka', *SV* (1894), 8: 260–80; 9: 1–44; 10: 65–98; and contrast Smirnova, 'Lichnoe oskorblenie', *Povesti i rasskazy* (St Petersburg, 1897), 355–411, and 'Peterburgskaya prisluga', ibid. 43–52; L. Nikiforova, 'Dve lestnitsy', *Sbornik Znanie*, 30 (1910), 1–118.

sympathetically, and more effectively, than their male colleagues. Still more importantly, some women writers were able to combine the dynamics of the escape plot with the broadly-based empiricism that had come with the naturalist traditions of their day in order to compose complex and ambivalent studies of working women. After 1880 we see the development of fictions in which the 'horizontal', descriptive axis is as important as the 'vertical axis' of onward-moving narrative, and where incidental details function as psychological or social signals rather than as obstacles to be overcome, or as symbols of unenlightenment versus enlightenment.[40] If the realist tradition as practised by women prior to 1880 might be described as 'theoretical' (what *might* be possible), the tradition after 1880 could be described as 'empirical' (what *is* possible). In some senses the 'empirical' direction might be described as a return to the practices of Zhukova or Sokhanskaya; however, the pervasiveness of institutionalized feminism ensured that post-1881 fictions had a more focused sense of why they were criticizing the status quo than either of these two writers.

By the term 'empirical' I do not mean to suggest that turn-of-the-century women's realism was necessarily inadequate in a theoretical sense. On the contrary, it was usually underpinned by sophisticated notions of the causes and functioning of discrimination against women; it displayed sensitivity to economic and to cultural, as well as to political, social, and legal factors. Nor is 'empirical' meant to suggest that these stories necessarily depended upon 'experience' in the sense of fieldwork as such. On the contrary: it is likely that printed documents often played a larger role than face-to-face contact. The late nineteenth-century empirical fictional tradition developed alongside ethnography; fictional accounts drew some of their authority from their congruence with ethnography proper. Conversely, ethnography was itself dependent on many of the perceptions and stereotypes of 'fiction' for *its* persuasiveness; textual circulation went in more than one direction.[41] That is not to say that the two directions were entirely interdependent. The style of fictional texts was, as we shall see, more diverse than that of scholarly or journalistic practice; the range of techniques which could be used in order

---

[40] The terms 'horizontal' and 'vertical' axis are used by Roland Barthes in 'Introduction to the Structural Analysis of Narratives', *Image—Music—Text*, trans. Stephen Heath (London, 1977), 79–124.

[41] There is a direct correlation, for example, between texts representing factory workers and peasants from an ethnographical point of view such as Pokrovskaya's essays, and realist stories such as Bezrodnaya's 'Pyatyi akt', *RB* (1909), 4: 1–41; 5: 3–36, or Smirnova's 'Syn soldatki', *Povesti i rasskazy*, 412–35; or Aleksandra Efimenko's study and the representations of peasant women in the stories by Letkova *et al.* cited below. On this point see also Kelly, 'Life at the Margins: Women, Culture and *narodnost'* 1890–1920', in Marianne Liljeström, Eila Mäntysaari, and Arja Rosenholm (eds.), *Gender Restructuring* (Helsinki, 1993).

to evoke interiority was also greater. But both fiction and scholarly or documentary work shared a determination to observe in detail an absorption in the incidental as well as in the significant.

The new concern with processes rather than with results, and with messy, irreducible detail, is already visible in a story by Kapitolina Nazareva written in 1879, 'The Specialist'. A naïve young woman, estranged from her husband, attempts to make use of her new legal freedoms: she applies for a divorce, intending to name herself as the guilty party. Though an older woman whom she befriends in a legal fixer's waiting-room warns her of the approaching difficulties, including the fact that cases depend on the weight of bribes rather than of evidence, she blunders on with her application. The story ends with a scene showing the court case itself: the woman is ensnared by moral double standards on the one hand (she is systematically humiliated on account of her supposed adultery by her husband's lawyers) and legal corruption on the other (the divorce is refused in any case, since she has failed to oil the right palms in advance).[42]

Rather than illustrate the termination of an unsuccessful marriage, this story illuminates the contrast between *wanting* to divorce and achieving a divorce. In the same way, several later stories explore the irresolvable tensions of unsatisfactory marriages or liaisons which cannot be easily and ruthlessly terminated: in Verbitskaya's story 'The Snuffed Candle' (1905), for example, Radishchev and Katya, meeting after a separation, both prove too dispirited to break out of the emotional stagnancy in which they live.[43]

There is a comparable departure, in many stories describing women's professional lives, from the earlier emphasis on the *desire* for a profession in the abstract to an exploration of what professional life actually means. Many realists are now concerned with women's problems *in* their jobs, rather than with women's struggles to obtain jobs. The early stories of Anastasiya Verbitskaya cover a particularly wide range of different professions: here we see women working as midwives, running employment agencies for servants, and in a range of other white-collar jobs.[44] Ekaterina Letkova is another writer who deals with comparable subjects: her story 'The Holiday' shows how Masha, a telegraphist, is provoked by the breathing-space allowed to her by a cruise on the Volga to contemplate her dead-end existence.[45] Her work is dull, her private life,

[42] Kapitolina Nazar'eva ['K. Nikulina'], 'Spetsialist', *VE* (1879), 1: 63–94.

[43] Verbitskaya, 'Zaduli svechu', *Schast'e*, 61–106.

[44] e.g. Verbitskaya, *Schast'e*; cf. several stories in Smirnova, *Povesti i rasskazy*, and the work of Ol'ga Shapir, to be discussed below.

[45] Letkova, 'Otdykh', *RM* (1896), 1: 180–96.

which is largely occupied with mending and other domestic tasks, still duller. Her mother, whose bullying has alone ensured that Masha completed her education at a high-pressure girls' school, is dead; for all the lack of spiritual contact between them, she was until her death Masha's only real companion. Contact with the other passengers on the boat, who appear more relaxed and confident, erodes Masha's self-respect; eventually she decides to end her life. Even this apparently momentous incident has an inescapable flavour of banality, however: 'Marya Nilovna squeezed through the railings, walked to the edge of the deck and stepped forward. No one heard her fall. She disappeared as unnoticeably as she had lived' (p. 196). Letkova was an unusually lucid writer, and her story directly articulates an anxiety which can be sensed in many other narratives of the period, concerned as they are with *schast'e* (happiness). What exactly do women want? Is employment always a guarantee of their satisfaction, when so many jobs for women promise so little in the way of economic security, or prestige?[46]

Prior to 1881 the traditions of memoir and fiction had to a large extent diverged; the concerns of the provincial tale had only occasionally been evident in the less elevated, but often livelier, genre of autobiography. After 1881 there is increasing convergence between the two genres; fiction's concentration on *realia*, and its preoccupation with women's professional lives, are also characteristic of the memoir. A typical, and interesting, example of the trend is a memoir written by the fiction-writer Valentina Dmitrieva, 'Round the Villages' (1896). Dmitrieva's first profession was that of a doctor, and this text recounts her trip to a group of small villages in the course of a diphtheria epidemic. But as well as illustrating the common interests of memoirs and fiction, this text also shows where they diverge. It is striking not only for its vivid depiction of the appalling squalor of Russian rural life, and because it shows the difficulties of working in the teeth of prejudice against women and of social hostility, but also because it portrays a woman who has to confront the problems of her own professional responsibility. Dmitrieva relates how, knowing that doctors are supposed to be detached and hardened, she could not herself manage this; and she reveals that she had an attitude to her own medical skills which was almost as fatalistic as that of her patients. When the cure of one desperately sick child overcame the peasants' hostility, she could not avoid the feeling that the

---

[46] The theme of 'happiness' is foregrounded in the title of Verbitskaya's *Schast'e*, and the word also appears in the titles of several individual stories in that collection; other texts where discussion of 'happiness' is just as important include Smirnova's 'Lichnoe oskorblenie', Tsekhovskaya's 'Dinastiya', Dmitrieva's 'Progulka', and Krestovskaya's 'Vopl''.

whole affair was simply a matter of good luck: the patient might just as well have died.[47]

This readiness to recognize vulnerability, the possibility of human error, is rarely so directly evident in fiction as such (and certainly not in Dmitrieva's own fiction). The reluctance to acknowledge unsureness may be one reason why the more adventurous techniques of the interior monologue and the epiphany, which were just becoming fashionable in Russia around the turn of the century, are adopted by many women writers only in the portrayal of male characters. Lyubov Gurevich's striking story 'The Cabby', for example, is narrated through the shifting consciousness of Ivan, a working man driven to a drinking bout after witnessing the murder of his sister-in-law by his brother.[48] Varvara Tsekhovskaya (Olnem) was another instance of a writer who applied her gifts for psychological portraiture to male characters by preference; 'By the Warm Sea', for example, is a subtly nuanced and lyrically fluid account of a doctor's contemplative days spent during convalescence at Yalta. Tsekhovskaya was no slavish imitator of Chekhov, but she had learnt from him; significantly, however, it was the 'masculine' interior monologue of such stories as 'The Student' that she followed, rather than the 'feminine' interiority of 'The Name-Day', which represents the perceptions of a woman in late pregnancy.[49]

But if a limited place is given to psychological expression in turn-of-the-century realism, it does still play a larger role than in the escape plot of the past, and authorial interventions are less overtly judgemental. A typical instance of the new manner is Letkova's 'The Holiday', which shows that the central character is deceiving herself, rather than simply stating that she does:

Her bad mood would not leave her. She went to her cabin and got her best dress out of her trunk. What was she keeping it for? It was three years now since she'd

---

[47] Dmitrieva, 'Po derevnyam', *VE* (1896), 10: 521–65. An extract under the title 'After the Great Hunger' appears in *Anthology*. Other interesting contemporary memoirs include Mariya Skavron-skaya's account of her work-induced nervous breakdown in *Drug zhenshchin* (1883), no. 1; E. Vasil'eva's memoirs of her work as a doctor in an insane asylum, 'Desyat' mesyatsev v zemskoi psikhiatricheskoi kolonii', *RB* (1900), 11: 187–215; 12: 167–84; and Elizaveta D'yakonova's diaries kept during her studies on the women's higher education courses in St Petersburg and later in Paris, and her treatment for psychological problems by an associate of Charcot: *Dnevnik na vysshikh zhenskikh kursakh (1895–1899)* (St Petersburg, 1904), and *Dnevnik russkoi zhenshchiny (Parizh 1900–1902)* (St Petersburg, 1905). Of interest too are the memoirs of turn-of-the-century writers: see esp. Verbitskaya, *Moim chitatelyam: Avtobiograficheskie ocherki s dvumya portretami* (Moscow, 1908), and the memoirs collected in *Sbornik na pomoshch' uchashchimsya zhenshchinam* (St Petersburg, 1901), and in F. Fidler (ed.), *Pervye literaturnye shagi* (St Petersburg, 1911).

[48] Gurevich, 'Sedok', *Sedok*, 1–12.

[49] Cf. Lidiya Avilova, who also applies interior monologue to men, or on occasion children, rather than to women; e.g. 'Obman', *VE* (1901), 7: 53–93; 'Po sovesti', *VE* (1901), 12: 532–45; 'Pervoe gore', *RB* (1900), 8: 240–50; *Rasskazy, vospominaniya* (Moscow, 1984).

made it, and she'd hardly worn it once; it seemed a pity. No, not that: she just wasn't used to 'dressing up', she wasn't used to thinking about herself. But now she did want to dress up, did want to look her best. She went to the mirror to comb her hair, and stared at herself.

'I'm so tanned!' she thought anxiously. 'A tan spoils everything.'

A grey, exhausted face looked back at her out of the mirror.   (p. 186)

The rather more empathetic and contemplative standpoint of late nineteenth-century realism is particularly evident in some portrayals of the Russian peasantry. The remoteness of this material from the eye of its beholder meant that the escape plot was not generally applied to peasant women, which could in turn mean that tales of peasant women became no more than bleak catalogues of victimization. An early example of the genre, Nadezhda Bashkevich's story 'Masha's Fate', depicts the sexual, economic, and social exploitation and brutalization suffered by one peasant woman.[50] Letkova's 'A Peasant Woman's Tears' (1898) represents a wet-nurse forced to make a commodity of her own body in order to survive.[51] A more sophisticated treatment of exploitation is the same author's 'Lushka' (1894), where the central character is a small peasant girl exploited by her dissolute mother as an unpaid nursemaid for baby after baby. Most survive only a few weeks, but one is more hardy, and for months Lushka is hindered from playing with other children in the village. Eventually her pent-up frustration and humiliation provoke a tragic denouement; her mother's indifference is only one factor in a social milieu equally marked by the thoughtless cruelty of the other small children, and the patronizing frivolity of some upper-class visitors who occasionally pull up their horses whilst riding through the village in order to pet the children. Letkova is particularly skilled in suggesting the mind-numbing repetitiveness of village life, and conveying through this a sense of moral stultification. As the children tell one another about an occasion on which one of them has been given some sweets, for example, she informs the reader that the narration of this piece of information has become a ritual; the children repeat it endlessly, having nothing else to talk about.[52]

But women writers' distance from their material did not always lead them to emphasize the inevitability of oppression in villages. Sometimes, remoteness of perspective also made it possible to explore mentality more extensively than it might be explored in stories about intellectual women. This process is illustrated by Dmitrieva's tale 'The Turkish

---

[50] Nadezhda Bashkevich, 'Mashkina dolya', *Drug zhenshchin* (1883), 2: 43–54.

[51] Letkova, 'Bab'i slezy', *MB* (1898), 5: 26–40.

[52] *Eadem*, 'Lushka', *SV* (1894), 3: 87–97.

Soldier's Wife' (1881), which represents a *soldatka*, the wife of a conscript, one of the most underprivileged social groups in the Russian peasantry.[53] When her husband is reported missing, presumed dead, Agafya, the protagonist, first finds herself work in town, and then returns to the village, where she takes a second husband. The story ends with the return of Agafya's first husband, who has been a prisoner of war; finally, a reconciliation takes place, and she continues to live with both husbands. The apparently eccentric arrangement works, Dmitrieva demonstrates, because the two adult men are no less Agafya's dependents than are her stepchildren, and because 'a husband', in peasant understanding, is more a repository of social status than an erotic companion.

Herself a woman of peasant origins who had made her way to medical school by dint of sheer determination, Dmitrieva had good reason to stress that women in villages had more than one way of reacting to their tough lives.[54] The unorthodox plot of her story is combined with an eye for unusual detail. There is a memorable episode in which Agafya, working as a servant, begins a liaison with an army officer, then terminates it, noticing his growing coolness, both matter-of-factly and definitively:

'If you've been deceiving me, to hell with you ...' For a minute her heart tightened painfully ... After all she had grown used to the Captain, she loved him. But there was no time for reflection. Agafya cut up all the dresses the Captain had given her, so that they shouldn't 'fall into the hands' of another woman, then she picked up her bundle and walked out. (p. 26)

Dmitrieva's story is also an early example of a text using non-standard language for parts of the narrative in order to mark interior monologue, a technique developed later by other writers, such as Shapir and Gurevich. Agafya's behaviour is refracted in an idiom which is imbued with peasant formulae. The fecklessness of Agafya's second husband, for example, is described as it might have been in the village itself:

Nothing seemed to go right for him; his barns were all tumbledown, his cow was so wretchedly fed she looked set fair to peg out, his cottage was freezing cold, and by the time his neighbours had the whole field ploughed, he'd have done only half, and even that not so much ploughed as churned up. (p. 28)

The new confidence and technical accomplishment of second-genera-

[53] Dmitrieva, 'Akhmetkina zhena', *RB* (1881), 1: 1–59.
[54] For Dmitrieva's background, see her autobiographies in *Sbornik na pomoshch'*, 191–3, and her *Povesti i rasskazy*, i (St Petersburg, 1916), 5–51.

tion women realists shows in their use of detail and in their psychological adventurousness; it is also evident in the fact that they no longer shun irony and humour. The stories of Sofya Smirnova are remarkable for their aphoristic dialogue; in the best work of Olga Shapir, as we shall see, a sense of the ridiculous emerges to notable effect. But the most significant use of humour is made by Nadezhda Teffi, whose anecdotal short stories (also to be discussed in detail in Chapter 7) structured the accepted material of realist fiction in narratives which were not only witty, but which also showed a sensitivity to the contingency of meaning and the variables of communication that subtly altered the assumptions and ambitions of women's prose, pushing them in the direction of modernism.

The years after 1880 saw women realists attain, for the first time since 1860, an equivalent standing to that enjoyed by their male peers. Certainly, the women realists have different preoccupations from those of their male colleagues; equally certainly, they are on the whole less successful where they venture into 'masculine' territory. When women writers produced stories about male workers, labourers, or street characters (as, for example, Yuliya Bezrodnaya and Anastasiya Krandievskaya did) their texts reproduced patterns familiar from the stories of urban or semi-urban life of better-known male writers, such as Gorky, Gleb Uspensky, or Chekhov.[55] When on their own ground, however, women realists did not need to imitate: in terms of thematics, at least, stories such as Shapir's 'The Settlement' or Letkova's 'Lushka' were precedents, not successors, to such famous Chekhov stories as 'Sleepy'. And if women writers' sense that literature should be politically engaged made them reluctant to surrender direct narratorial involvement in such techniques as interior monologue, their contradictory commitments to observation and to explication could lead them to shift unpredictably between external commentary and individual psychological perspective. Less preachy than the provincial tale, the late nineteenth-century empirical realist text also has a harder analytical edge, yet at the same time its complexity in technical terms is greater; more concise than their predecessors, such tales also have more to say. The sophistication of argumentation and problematics achieved in some 1890s and 1900s fiction is akin to that attained in the best society tales; the social and political range is far broader. Through the empirical realist tradition, women's prose had gained a new confidence; and, though new directions were soon to challenge its achievements, these were not in any sense to vitiate them.

[55] See e.g. A. Krandievskaya, 'Tol'ko chas', *Tol'ko chas*, 241–58; Bezrodnaya, 'S ulitsy: rasskazy', *VE* (1894), 5: 255–81 (the latter story does, however, deal with women characters).

The 'Sensational Novel': Block-busters of the 1900s

In *A Literature of Their Own*, Elaine Showalter argued that the best-selling novels written by such successful nineteenth-century English women novelists as Mrs Henry Wood, Ouida, or Mrs Humphry Ward belonged to a separate and distinct genre, that of the 'novel of sensation'. Though such novels brought considerable material success to their authors, they were important for far more than economic reasons: they had worked to subvert earlier stereotypes of 'women's writing':

Sensation novels expressed female anger, frustration and sexual energy more directly than had been done previously. Readers were introduced to a new kind of heroine, one who could put her hostility toward men into violent action.[56]

The Russian best seller developed rather later than its Western counterpart (which is to say, around 1910), so that the ground for its appearance had already been prepared by the appearance of the English 'novelists of sensation' in translation, and also by the circulation (in French until the censorship was relaxed) of the *fin de siècle* novelist Rachilde. Once emerged, the main Russian exponents of best-selling fiction, Verbitskaya and Nagrodskaya, soon began to build up a readership which, allowing for the smaller potential numbers, was of a comparable size to that enjoyed by their Western colleagues, and which brought them a comparable material success.[57]

In terms of how much they offended critics in all parts of the critical spectrum, Verbitskaya and Nagrodskaya were certainly 'subversive'. They were greeted with shocked and hostile reviews, which attacked the calibre of the material selected, and the quality of its presentation. How far they manifest the violent feelings, the anger and frustration, which Showalter finds in their English counterparts is a rather more difficult question. Certainly, their work has its share of melodrama. In the two most famous block-busters, Verbitskaya's serial novel *The Keys of Happiness* (1909–1913) and Nagrodskaya's *The Anger of Dionysus* (1911), scenes of confrontation, accusation, and recrimination abound. However, though undoubtedly sensational novels, these are not quite

---

[56] Elaine Showalter, *A Literature of Their Own* (London, 1977), 160.

[57] Though the 'novel of sensation' discussed by Showalter was a phenomenon of the 1860s–1870s, Ouida's story 'The Faithful Maid', for instance, appeared in *RB* as late as 1902. On Rachilde, cf. Blok's review in *SS* vi. On the material success of Verbitskaya and Nagrodskaya, see Brooks, *When Russia*, 158–67. Verbitskaya, *Klyuchi schast'ya* (6 vols.; Moscow, 1909–13); Evdokiya Nagrodskaya, *Gnev Dionisa* (St Petersburg, 1911). Another popular woman writer, Lidiya Charskaya, has been excluded here because her genteel stories were aimed at children and adolescents, rather than adults; an accessible edition of a representative story is *Sibiryachka* (Moscow, 1992).

'novels of sensation' in the sense described by Showalter. For one thing, their shock value did not lie in anger and intensity. As has been demonstrated, the perfectly respectable fiction of women's liberation contained far more hair-raising scenes of destruction and self-destruction than were penned by Nagrodskaya and Verbitskaya. The heroine of *The Keys of Happiness*, Manya, does attempt suicide, but she lives to emote another day; the heroine of *The Anger of Dionysus* remains detached amidst the hubbub of male emotion boiling all around her.

It was rather different reasons which made these novels send ripples through Russian literary life. Their popularity provoked anxiety that they might be corrupting the morals of the lower classes, who were always assumed to take an absolutely literal view of whatever they read. The books also trotted out some favourite ideological hobby-horses of the day; however, these were represented in a way that unintentionally simplified them to the point of absurdity. For example, Verbitskaya's heroine, Manya, has an insane mother, and so the role of heredity, a matter much debated in the late nineteenth-century, figures large in *The Keys of Happiness*; but its effects are grotesque and ridiculous, rather than soberly threatening, as the fear of inherited madness spurs one of Manya's lovers to Pavlovian spasms of irrational revulsion. And heredity is by no means the only contemporary orthodoxy that appears to disadvantage in the book. The two male members of its central love triangle are Nelidov, a would-be Nietzschean superman and anti-Semite, and Steinbach, a sensitive, cultivated Jew. Apart from reworking those hoary types, the 'rake' and the 'man of feeling', the two characters also represent, baldly and obviously, ideas about national characteristics which were more subtly (and also more insidiously) represented elsewhere. For her part, Nagrodskaya makes her *raisonneur*, Lazinov, state contemporary theories of the sexual continuum in words of one syllable. The heroine, he says, is a 'masculine woman', whilst her intense lover Stark is a 'feminine' man; this explains their insuperable, but vexed, attraction to each other.[58] The readers of thick journals, in which such ideas were discussed with the most pedestrian reverence, can scarcely have been delighted to see cherished material treated in a manner that one might well, were it not for these books' ingenuous tone, assume to be mercilessly flippant.

Such considerations aside, what might have shocked early twentieth-

---

[58] On the ubiquity of 'Nitssheanstvo' (Nietzscheanism) in turn-of-the-century Russian culture, see Beatrice Glatzer Rosenthal (ed.), *Nietzsche in Russia* (Princeton, NJ, 1986); on heredity see V. Shimkevich, 'Nasledstvennost', *NS* xxviii. 26–38.

century Russian readers in these books? In both cases, the central conflict hinges on the fact that the heroine is in love with two men. But so did the plots of many post-'Kreutzer Sonata' books published in the 1890s and 1900s; and, like many of their predecessors in the thick journals, Verbitskaya and Nagrodskaya select heroines who are artists (or in the former case, an 'artiste'), which makes it clear that their behaviour is not to be judged by ordinary standards.[59] Granted, Nagrodskaya and Verbitskaya make it clearer than many of their female predecessors that their heroines' triangular relationships are sexual, and dwell on these heroines' passionate impetuosity. (In Nagrodskaya's book, Stark and Tanya retreat to Tanya's bedroom for carnal purposes almost as soon as they have shaken hands for the first time; Verbitskaya's Manya and Nelidov take a much larger number of pages to reach their first encounter, but then reward the reader's impatience by thrashing about in the open air.) But if they are explicit in terms of what happens, these books are less explicit in terms of how it happens; indeed, the sex is a good deal less lurid than the quarrels, or even than the intellectual, or pseudo-intellectual, debates.

The real innovation of these books, in fact, did not so much lie in their depiction of intense sexual experience as in their representation of women whose sexual appetites were not constrained by guilt. It was Verbitskaya and Nagrodskaya's relative underemphasis on the remorse felt by a woman in love with two men, rather than their overemphasis on that woman's feelings of anger or even of desire, which made their work new in a Russian context. Otherwise, these texts were anything other than radical. Long-winded, clumsily written, and employing the Gordian knot approach to psychological problems, they exemplify the difficulties of Russian women writers in dealing with large-scale genres. At only a few hundred pages long, Nagrodskaya's book has a greater laconicism to recommend it; but in compensation, Verbitskaya's book has a greater gift for narrative suspense, and a more winning line in emotive rhetoric. Those qualities were to keep *The Keys of Happiness* popular for long after the Revolution, so that it began to stand for the character of pre-Revolutionary women's writing in general—a symbolism which was misleading not only because it reduced a very diverse tradition to one of its less significant constituent parts, but also because the new arts prose of the 1900s was to present a more exclusive public with a far more significant departure from monogamous rectitude, and from the aesthetic

---

[59] For an *artiste* heroine, see e.g. Krestovskaya, 'Artistka': n. 29 above.

values of the thick journals, than the sensational novel had even dreamed of.[60]

Women Writers and the 'New Arts'

In Russia, as in other European countries and America, the turn of the century was the time when the feminist movement reached its peak. In Russia, as elsewhere, it campaigned widely and actively for a range of civil and economic rights (franchise, family law reform, educational opportunity, equal pay, and welfare support). But if the historical development and the orientation of the Russian feminist movement resembled those of feminist movements in other countries, the Russian movement did differ in its relation to the general national cultural context. The movement itself, as mentioned earlier, was split into factions; in particular, it was increasingly riven, after 1900, by acerbic disputes between socialist feminists and liberal feminists. But, what was more important to the history of women's writing as such, there was a complete dislocation between the writers associated with the feminist movement, in any of its manifestations, and the writers associated with the various 'new arts' movements: Symbolism and its post-Symbolist successors Acmeism and Futurism. There is no Russian woman writer who can be equated with Virginia Woolf or Alice Meynell. To elucidate: not one Russian woman author of modernist prose or poetry manifested any interest in, or sympathy for, the debates around female emancipation in the feminist movement itself.[61]

On 19 March 1917, Zinaida Gippius watched women's groups process past her window, on their way to a mass demonstration at the Tauride Palace in support of demands that women should be given the vote by the Menshevik government. Her comments were characteristically acerbic: 'I shall be very glad if the "woman question" is solved simply and radically, as the "Jewish question" was, and then vanishes. For it is

---

[60] There are, so far as I know, no statistics indicating the popularity of *The Keys of Happiness* after 1917, but written sources record that it continued to be a favourite amongst working women (Brooks, *When Russia*, 160). The copy of the first two volumes in the Taylor Institution Library, Oxford, contains a gift inscription of 1927. A caricature of Verbitskaya, holding a large cardboard dummy of her novel, appears in the rogues' gallery published by the avant-garde journal *LEF: Zhurnal Levogo fronta iskusstv*, 1/5 (1924), 20.

[61] The socialist-feminist dispute boiled up with particular vehemence at the All-Russian Women's Congress in 1908; Aleksandra Kollontai played a leading role in provoking the confrontation. (See Volkenshtein, 'Itogi', Edmondson, *Feminism*, Beatrice Farnsworth, *Aleksandra Kollontai: Socialism, Feminism and the Bolshevik Revolution* (Stanford, Calif., 1980), 29–39.) A useful collection of Virginia Woolf's feminist political and aesthetic work is *A Woman's Essays* (Oxford, 1991), though it is only fair to point out that the bulk of her explicitly feminist work dates from the period after the First World War. On Alice Meynell see entry in Claire Buck (ed.), *The Bloomsbury Guide to Women's Literature* (London, 1992).

really quite revolting. Women who concentrate on it simply reveal themselves as bad human beings.'[62]

It is safe to assume that the forty thousand women demonstrators on 19 March did not include any of the major Symbolist and post-Symbolist women poets. As well-educated, and in many cases reasonably well-off, members of the bourgeoisie or haute bourgeoisie, they came from the same background as the Russian feminists, whether socialist or liberal. However, the female Symbolists and post-Symbolists took little interest in politics of any kind. The two exceptions to this generalization were Lidiya Zinoveva-Annibal and Elizaveta Kuzmina-Karavaeva, both sympathizers of a radical populist party, the Socialist Revolutionaries. Indeed, Kuzmina-Karavaeva was more than a sympathizer; she was a party activist, who was to serve as the Socialist Revolutionary mayor of a town in the Crimea for a few months after the Revolution; although she ceased contact with party politics thereafter, she was to retain her socialist beliefs all her life.[63] But such commitment to politics stood out against the general indifference. Still more overwhelming was women Symbolists' and post-Symbolists' boycott of feminism in a political sense. Few even voiced Gippius's overt hostility; a total silence on feminist issues was the norm.

The crux is, though, that the Symbolist and post-Symbolist writers *were* concerned, directly or indirectly, with the issues of self-expression and sexuality which have been so extensively explored by recent feminist writing in the West. Hence, they were in some senses more 'feminist' in the modern sense (though they would have been shocked to learn it) than were those of their contemporaries who belonged to the official feminist movement, or who accounted themselves socialist feminists. Granted, the new arts movements seldom articulated issues of self-expression in a choate form, or integrated them with theories of gender; but as time went on, women writers associated with the 'new arts' developed a poetics, if not always an aesthetics, which, in however limited a sense, confronted the issue of how to write as women, given the current general under-

---

[62] Gippius, *Peterburgskie dnevniki* (New York, 1982), 195. Cf. Gippius's anthology of 1917, *Vosem'desyat vosem' sovremennykh stikhotvorenii* (St Petersburg), which represents little work by women, besides Akhmatova and Gippius herself. The critic and writer Zinaida Vengerova, one of those most instrumental in introducing Western European modernist ideas to Russia, was another example of how the supporters of 'new arts', also had little interest in feminism: her two substantial articles, 'La Femme russe' (1897) and 'Zhenskaya svoboda' (1898) both prefer an individualist notion of 'freedom' to a collective or institutional one. See Rosenthal, 'Zinaida Vengerova: Modernism and Women's Liberation', *ISS* 8 (1987).

[63] On Zinov'eva-Annibal's sympathy for the Socialist Revolutionaries, see Lidiya Ivanova, *Vospominaniya* (Paris, 1990), 16–17; on Kuz'mina-Karavaeva's political activities, see T. Stratton Smith, *The Rebel Nun: The Moving Story of Mother Maria of Paris* (London, 1965), 80–97; Sergei Hackel, *One of Great Price: The Life of Mother Mariya Skobtsova* (London, 1965), 83–6.

standing of what the word 'woman' meant. And there were occasional pioneering contributions to the aesthetics of women's writing by women writers themselves. Sofiya Parnok, Nadezhda Lvova, Anna Akhmatova, and Adelaida Gertsyk all produced reviews or essays in which this subject is explicitly, and seriously, discussed; the collections of Kuz-mina-Karavaeva contained forewords discussing the woman poet's way into poetry, albeit in terms which were both abstract and markedly mystical.[64]

We can trace three stages in the process by which a poetics of women's writing was developed. In the first, from about 1890, an interest in the 'decadent feminine personality' began to manifest itself, and soon began to inspire women writers. The second phase, beginning in about 1905, was characterized by the emergence of new religio-mystical ideas about the nature of woman, or the 'feminine principle'. Some women writers were able to use these ideas in order to break with nineteenth-century limitations on women's writing; but views that women's language was 'irrational', and hence inexplicable, in turn produced a new set of constraints on the expression of feminine identity. In the third phase, after 1910, an anti-Symbolist backlash on the one hand restores the traditional link between women's writing and expected female experi-ence, but on the other furthers the development of a new self-conscious-ness amongst women writers, who can now not necessarily expect automatic approval if they adopt a feminine persona. The result is that many begin to emphasize the contingency of poetic personae, and to inscribe a new kind of feminine identity, one that is fractured, varied, and flexible.

The diversification of women's writing was directly connected with the breadth and sophistication of turn-of-the-century debates on the function of art. If Russian Romanticism had depended on a few rather vague and half-baked formulations, and on an assortment of ideas borrowed from abroad, Russian Symbolism, by contrast, was a complex and often contradictory fusion of different intellectual currents, sharing the inter-nationalism of early Western European modernism, yet profoundly nation-alist in its religio-mystical overtones. A general study of the Symbolist movement still remains to be written, and it is out of the question for me

---

[64] Nadezhda L'vova, 'Kholod utra: o novom zhenskom tvorchestve', *Zhatva* (1914), 5: 250–6; Anna Akhmatova, 'Nadezhda L'vova: *Staraya skazka*', *RM* (1914), 1, sect. 2, 27–8; Adelaida Gertsyk, 'Iz detskogo mira', *SZ* (1915), 9: 6–13; 'Moi bluzhdaniya', *SZ* (1915), 10: 22–38; 11–12: 52–68; 'Moi romany', *SZ* (1913), 2: 77–89; 4: 47–53; (trans. as 'My Loves' in *Anthology*) 'O tom, chego ne bylo', *RM* (1911), 5: 130–46; Elizaveta Kuz'mina-Karavaeva, forewords to *Ruf'* and *Skifskie cherepki*, see nn. 127, 128 below.

to attempt to characterize the movement's history in depth here.[65] I shall simply give an outline of the aspects of Symbolist and post-Symbolist thinking which were most important in the development of the three main phases of women's writing—or three main strands might be a more accurate term, since the development of discourses on art and literature, like the development of discourses on eroticism, was characterized by augmentation rather than by substitution.

The earliest strand of Russian Symbolism began to show itself in the early 1890s, and was characterized both by an insistent aestheticism, and by an extreme individualism. It borrowed both its general orientation and its title, 'decadence', from French culture. Its main movers and ideologues were men (Valery Bryusov, Dmitry Merezhkovsky), and the hedonist and aesthete heroes of many of its literary productions were also men.[66] But the decadent direction was also of great importance to women's writing; conversely, women's writing was also of significant importance to this direction, since the licence which decadent writing granted to the expression of active female desire was, for Russian society, one of its more scandalous features.

A major catalyst in the development of Russian decadence was the publication, in 1892, in Lyubov Gurevich's translation from the original French, of diaries written by the Russian painter Mariya Bashkirtseva (1860–84).[67] Bashkirtseva's account of her life from the age of 13 presented the author as someone obsessed, even in her earliest youth, with the idea of her own greatness. In the first instalments of the diary, this feeling was mostly subsumed in a regret that the writer's birth was not as aristocratic as she felt her talent deserved, and in an obsession with

[65] There is still no authoritative general analysis of Russian Symbolism to equate with, say, Guy Michaud's study of French Symbolism, *Message poétique du symbolisme* (Paris, 1961). In Russia itself, Marxist-Leninist hostility to 'idealism' and 'decadence' long hindered, and to some extent still does hinder, serious treatments of turn-of-the-century writing; ignorance of Western tradition is also an obstacle; whilst in the West study has tended to concentrate on the work of a few well-known figures, at the expense of a general understanding. The work-in-progress of Hansen-Löve (see n. 66) promises to be one of the fullest histories to date: at present the most useful introductions are perhaps Z. G. Mints, 'O nekotorykh "neomifologicheskikh" tekstakh v tvorchestve russkikh simvolistov', *Blokovskii sbornik, 3* (Tartu, 1979), 76–120; Pavel Gromov, *A. Blok, ego predshest-vennniki i sovremenniki* (Moscow-Leningrad, 1966); Georgette Donchin, *The Influence of French Symbolism on Russian Poetry* (The Hague, 1958). See also Pyman, *Aleksandr Blok* (n. 132), Davidson, *Vyacheslav Ivanov* (n. 77), and Grossman, *Valery Bryusov* (n. 66).

[66] On the initial phase of Symbolism, see A. A. Hansen-Löve, *Der russische Symbolismus: System und Entfaltung der poetischen Motive*, i (Vienna, 1989); Joan Delaney Grossman, *Valery Bryusov and the Riddle of Russian Decadence* (Stanford, Calif., 1985).

[67] The first publication of Mariya Bashkirtseva's diary in Russian was in *SV* (1892), 1–12. However, Russians with a knowledge of French would have had access to the original French edition, published in 1887. See Gurevich, 'M. K. Bashkirtseva: biografichesko-psikhologicheskii etyud', *RB* (1888), 2: 73–122; and O. Chyumina's poem 'Pamyati Bashkirtsevoi', *RB* (1888), 7: 115. Bashkirtseva's diary is available in English translation from the French as *The Journal of Marie Bashkirtseff*, trans. Mathilde Blind (repr.; London, 1985).

her personal appearance and precocious erotic triumphs. But then came a peripeteia, in the form of a prophetic dream in which Bashkirtseva soared on a cloud, holding a lyre, into the Empyrean heights: this vision dictated that her ambition should now be to realize her own genius. Thereafter, Bashkirtseva's dawning confidence in her artistic ability gave her narrative a new purposiveness, which was only to be curbed by her premature death.

Though Bashkirtseva's talent was for the visual arts, her diaries immediately attracted interest amongst littérateurs. Whilst the liberal press treated her with disapproval (an early review article appeared under the heading 'A Fair of Feminine Vanity'), she became a heroine for young aesthetes such as Valery Bryusov.[68] The appeal of Bashkirtseva for the decadents was ensured by her talent for vivid self-mythologization, her febrile egotism, and her buoyant arrogance. Her work challenged both the moral values of the conventional Russian intelligentsia, and realist literature's traditional expression of this morality: here was a writer who, like the empiricist realists, emphasized that she was telling 'the truth', but who saw this truth in terms of granting the reader unpalatable (or conversely, all too palatable) revelations of pubescent sexual experience.

From the mid-1890s until the Revolution, dozens of decadent fictions, some good, some bad, and a good many awful, were to elaborate different representations of the decadent heroine. A good many of these fictions were composed by men.[69] But Bashkirtseva was an inspiration to women writers as well, and for good reason. In her work, the radical insistence that women should be liberated in order to serve the community was replaced by an emphasis on service to self alone. And so she at one and the same time reassured her readers by stressing the traditional motifs of escape and emotional intensity, and excited them by placing these motifs in an ethical and social (or to be precise, anti-ethical and anti-social) context which was quite new.

A significant early instance of the effects on women writers of reading Bashkirtseva is to be found in the work of Zinaida Gippius. In the early 1890s Gippius, as mentioned before, produced rather run-of-the-mill prose fictions. The poetry which she began writing in 1892–3, however, was quite different in character. In most of her lyrics Gippius adopted a masculine persona, often speaking as a male libertine; but she also

[68] M. Protopopov, 'Yarmarka zhenskogo tshcheslaviya', *RM* (1892), 4, sect. 2, 178–203; on the decadents' admiration for her work, see Ulf Møller, *Postlude*, 260–1; Rosenthal, 'Zinaida Venger-ova', 99.

[69] On the decadent heroine, see also T. L. Nikol'skaya, 'The "Contemporary Woman" in Early Twentieth Century Russian Literature', *ISS* 8 (1987), 107–14, which, however, draws largely on works by men, and eccentrically nominates Bryusov's very second-rate story 'Dnevnik zhenshchiny' as the most impressive treatment of feminine decadence in fiction.

represented heroines who recall Bashkirtseva's naïve but manipulative *femme fatale*, and some of whom indulge their erotic feelings up to the point of demonism in a literal sense (involvement with the Devil). It was this heroine, rather than Gippius's masculine persona, which was in turn to become canonical amongst later women poets, many of whom also adopted Gippius's use of blood-letting imagery, of artfully contrived accentual metres, and of striking rhymes.[70]

If Gippius was perhaps the most influential poet of the pre-Revolutionary years, a still more vivid elaboration of a Bashkirtsevian persona than hers is to be found in Lidiya Zinoveva-Annibal's two collections of stories, *Thirty-Three Freaks* (1907) and *The Tragic Menagerie* (1907). The earlier collection is one of the first explicit portrayals of a lesbian relationship in Russian literature; it represents a physically and emotionally absorbing affair between an older and a younger woman. Though both this subject-matter and its sensational reception when it was first published make *Thirty-Three Freaks* worthy of note, the story exemplifies the constrictions which lesbianism's transgressive connotations could impose on women writers. The climax of the piece is a session in which the young inamorata is captured on canvas by thirty-three male painters. It is possible to read this scene ironically, since the masculine view of women generates thirty-three images which are inadequate to their task, the 'thirty-three freaks' of the title; but the text is otherwise entirely in line with the long tradition of erotic writing for men that represents lesbian sexuality as the stuff of titillation and no more. *Thirty-Three Freaks* places lesbianism in an impoverished spectrum of sexual behaviour made up solely of dominance and sado-masochism: the narrator of the story fantasizes, for example, about the 'blissful, blissful, blissful' expression of St Agatha, whose breasts have been sliced off by her torturers.[71]

The Tragic Menagerie, like *Thirty-Three Freaks*, is composed of short fragments or episodes, which are taken this time from the autobiography of a young landowner's daughter, Vera, whose memories draw her from childhood (she is about 9 when the book begins), through puberty, and leave her at 18.[72] As in *Thirty-Three Freaks*, there is a

---

[70] See e.g. Gippius, 'Posvyashchenie', *Sobranie stikhov*, i (Moscow, 1904), 3, which declares, 'I love myself as I do God'.

[71] Lidiya Zinov'eva-Annibal, *Tridtstat' tri uroda* (St Petersburg, 1907); see also 'Thirty-Three Abominations', trans. Sam Cioran, *Russian Literature TriQuarterly*, 9 (1974), 94–116. For a trenchant critical reading, see Diana Burgin, 'Silver Age Perceptions of Lesbian Sexuality and Sofiya Parnok's Poems', in Costlow, Sandler, and Vowles (eds.), *Sexuality*.

[72] Zinov'eva-Annibal, *Tragicheskii zverinets* (St Petersburg, 1907). (Extracts trans. T. Pachmuss in *Women Writers in Russian Modernism* (Urbana, Ill., 1978).) One of the most talented Symbolist prose writers, Zinov'eva-Annibal was also the author of a Symbolist drama, *Kol'tsa* (St Petersburg, 1903), a comedy parodying *Midsummer Night's Dream*, 'Pevuchii osel. Trilogii pervaya chast':

strong emphasis on sado-masochistic sexuality, but here the erotic elements in the narrative are grounded in a much more extensive psychological analysis, and so emerge to more than titillatory effect. Even more than Bashkirtseva's *Diary*, *The Tragic Menagerie* is the story of a provincial-tale heroine gone to the bad, of a protagonist who transgresses convention in search of erotic satisfaction, and undergoes an education in self-obsession rather than in social commitment. Vera's amorality is summed up by one of her many tormented governesses in an impassioned speech: 'You cry over canaries and lap-dogs, but when other children die without ever knowing what happiness is, you don't care. You don't even notice' (p. 232). By the time she reaches adolescence, Vera has finished with God; she soon proceeds to dispense with the proprieties also. With a young male relative, Volodya, she becomes fascinated by 'what the adult world assumes not to exist'. This is meant in a specifically sexual sense: she acquires a taste, first for being stripped naked and spanked by her cousin, later for nude bathing and other sexual games. When this starts to bore her, she starts to feel an overwhelming desire for further erotic experience, which is handicapped only by her own failure to determine the nature of absolute intensity:

I wanted something worse. Worse. I wanted the worst thing in the world. I began to wonder what that might be, and I was surprised that I didn't get what I wanted, that what should have happened didn't. And if it had been even worse than that, something really shameful, then that would have been just what I wanted.   (p. 209)

Vera then becomes fascinated by the idea of purchasing a whip, but she is disappointed when this purchase is accomplished, and the expected erotic epiphany fails to come about. Further stages in her rake's progress are marked by an obsession with self-destruction, increasingly hot-house relationships with other girls at the *pension*, and, finally, a scene in which she visits a childhood playmate, now a peasant wife, who has died in childbirth, and observes dispassionately the latter's black lips, contorted mouth, and upraised knees.

Vera's decadent personality is set off by no alternative moral viewpoint, except when she cites the comments of the shocked women who care for her in order to mock them; no motives for her rebellion are set down. The obsessive egotism of *The Tragic Menagerie*, the heroine's

altsvet', *Tsvetnik or: koshnitsa pervaya: stikhotvoreniya* (St Petersburg, 1907), 121–69: and of prose poems, which appeared posthumously as 'Teni sna', *Severnye tsvety: assiriiskii al'manakh*, 4 (Moscow, 1915), 134–46, and in Zinov'eva-Annibal, *Net!* (St Petersburg, 1918). For an account of her biography and literary career, with particular emphasis on her indebtedness to Ivanov's theories of the Dionysiac, see T. L. Nikol'skaya, 'Tvorcheskii put' L. D. Zinov'evoi-Annibal', *Blokovskii sbornik*, 8 (Tartu, 1988), 123–38.

claustrophobic self-absorption, make it repellent reading. But it is also a powerful and original book, whose depiction of desire and frustration is far less callow than Bashkirtseva's. And Zinoveva-Annibal entirely departs from the euphemistic and reductive traditions according to which feminine interiority had customarily been represented in women's prose writing. Unlike the heroines of realist literature, Vera is open to a huge range of sensory impressions, which are captured by means both of symbolism and of stylistic features such as repetition and intonation. The following passage represents the powerful feelings excited by a landscape:

The sight of the sloping ground excited me terribly. I left my friends and hurled myself down. My heart gave staccato thumps, I was gasping for breath. I had to do something. I had, I had to do something.

I ran, one leg catching on the short, thick grass of the slope.

Something sliced the meadow in two: a straight line, with two shining stripes across it.

And suddenly there came a wail, echoing across the emptiness of those distant, quiet valleys—a wild, penetrating, long-drawn-out wail, with a kind of bestial despair in it. A hissing serpent rushed towards me, and I flung myself towards it, forgetting myself completely.

Across the fields, across the fields, across the flat, smooth fields, the endless fields, past the woods, past the clearings, past the tame brick houses, where the sisters are, all the sisters live, the deaconess-sisters: and peace, and boredom, and stifling goodwill—away, away, take me, you hissing monster with your mane of steam, on your shining path! Away, away, to the distance, the furthest, freest, the impossible distance! (p. 257)

The symbolism of the book is often overtly sexual in character. Zinoveva-Annibal's story is one of the few pieces of women's writing in Russian which has any references to the discovery of the body in puberty. In one of the stories, 'The Red Spider', Vera visits a beach to swim. Immersing herself in the water, where she notices a 'mossy rock' and 'sea urchins', she swims and then returns to the shore:

There was a crack between two cliffs. I slithered into it without pause for thought, scratching my shoulders as I forced myself in. For some reason my head was swimming, I was holding my breath.

At the far end of the passage was a cave: it was moist, quiet, and dark. First my head and shoulders went through. Then everything else.

I lay in silence. I felt happy.

Perhaps the crab has a cave for a lair, too?

I lay, eyes screwed up. Smiling, I should think. It felt good there in the cool damp, so quiet.

I opened my eyes. Nearby is a black smooth rock, the wall of the cave. I like staring at things close to.

Suddenly I sense a movement. My eyes are so close to the smooth wall that I can see each tiny movement. A tiny red spider is crawling down the wall, just like a little scarlet bead. It is minute, but I can see it clearly.   (p. 277)

After this encounter Vera is able to see the spider, which had previously existed as a fearful mythical monster in her fantasy, as something familiar and comforting. The emphasis on the female body (with overtones of auto-eroticism at that) in *The Tragic Menagerie* makes the text unique amongst the work of turn-of-the-century women prose writers.

If Zinoveva-Annibal and Gippius, and many of Gippius's imitators, placed their decadent heroines in settings which represented transmutations of the provincial tale's country estate, it was equally common for women poets to exploit the turn-of-the-century fashion for Greek culture in order to appropriate socially acceptable masks for alternative eroticism. The maenad and the hetaera are so used in Lyudmila Vilkina's poem 'Contradictions', for example, in which the speaker takes imaginative flight into the world of sacred prostitution.[73] But such costuming was not universal; traces of decadent egotism and the transgressive mentality can also be seen in apparently more conventional feminine personae. Mirra Lokhvitskaya, a young poet of whom various male Symbolists began a cult around the turn of the century, was a technically adept practitioner of love poetry in which a variety of more or less defiant heroines appeared. Sometimes the speaker of her poetry is characterized as a Babylonian reveller, a medieval lady, or a rebellious nun, but sometimes, more shockingly, such safe masks are discarded, and the traditional language of the love poem becomes an expression of desire. In the short poem, 'Why should I care', for example, the cliché vocabulary of emotional involvement ('torment', 'bliss') is undercut by the much franker terms, 'pleasure' and 'excitement', and by the opening line's carelessly defiant tone:

> Что мне в эом, что с меня ты не сводишь очей?
> Я измучена тайной борьбой.
> В мраке долгих ночей, в мраке зимних ночей.
> Я хочу быть любимой тобой.
>
> Целый мир упоенья во взоре твоем,
> Что-ж легло между нами стеной?
> Ведь с тобою вдвоем, в наслажденье одном,
> Мы-б узнали восторг неземной![74]

---

[73] L. Vil'kina, 'Protivorechie', *ZR* (1906), 3: 46. The classical tradition is used in a similar manner by Lyubov' Stolitsa in 'Moya muza' and 'Zhrebii', *SZ* (1916), 7–8: 41–2; 'O krasnom plyushche' and 'V nemuyu noch'', *ZR* (1907), 2: 23; 'Vesennyaya girlyanda' and 'Levkoi', *ZR* (1907), 4: 30–1.

[74] Mirra Lokhvitskaya, *Stikhotvoreniya* (5 vols.; St Petersburg, 1903–14), i. 98.

Why should I care that your eyes never leave me?
I feel the torment of a secret fight,
In the dark of long nights, the long winter nights,
I want you to love me.

There's a whole world of bliss in your slightest glance,
So why should a wall lie between us?
If I could be alone with you, united by pleasure,
What heavenly excitement we'd feel!

Lokhvitskaya's erotic rebellion, and that of women's decadent poetry in general, had carefully marked limits, however: the only acceptable forms of erotic interest were heterosexual. For all the dependence of Russian decadence upon French precedent, the work of the women poets and writers known as the 'Sappho 1900' group had no direct eastward reverberations. The figure of Sappho was used to facilitate the publication of some discreetly lesbian lyrics by Poliksena Soloveva, but most early twentieth-century women poets wrote of love between women by speaking in the voice of a man addressing a woman.[75]

The earliest phase of Symbolism reinforced nineteenth-century tradition by keeping the love lyric as the central women's genre, though emphasis on active female desire did bring about significant alterations in the character of this love lyric. The poetry of heterosexual love was also to be of considerable significance in the second phase of Symbolism, during the rise of mysticism; but it now became the expression of metaphysical, rather than physical, desire, and of philosophical, rather than sensual, concerns. The work of Vyacheslav Ivanov, Aleksandr Blok, and Andrei Bely, the most important of the poets who began publishing after 1900, preached mystical union with other worlds rather than hedonism in this. The sources of this new, religio-mystical aesthetic lay less in the French Symbolism that had inspired the 'decadents' than in German philosophy and poetry (the mystical writings of Jakob Boehme, the writings of Novalis, Schopenhauer, and Nietzsche, the late poetry of Goethe). This German material was fused by the Russian Symbolists with material from indigenous Russian tradition, most notably Slavophile philosophy and the mystical poetry of Tyutchev; the process of

---

[75] On homosexuality in France, see Peter Gay, *The Bourgeois Experience: From Victoria to Freud*, ii (New York, 1986); George Stambolian and Elaine Marks, *Homosexualities and French Culture* (Ithaca, NY, 1977). Poliksena Solov'eva (Allegro), 'Ty mne tak doroga', *Stikhotvoreniya* (St Petersburg, 1899), 22; 'Zhemchuzhina', *Plakun-trava* (St Petersburg, 1906), 13–15; 'Ya tekh slov, chto ty mne prosheptala', *RM* (1911), 3: 184; and see also Burgin, 'Silver Age Perceptions'. The masculine form is used in love poetry addressed to women by Solov'eva, and by Gippius (see e.g. 'Tikhoe plamya', *Sobranie stikhov*, i. 81, 'Lestnitsa', ibid. i. 59); Sergei Gedroits, 'Kamnem kosnulsya' and 'I polon schast'ya', *Veg* (St Petersburg, 1913), 1, 19.

fusion involved both the combination of German and Russian elements, and the perception of the former through the latter.[76]

Though different Russian Symbolist poets interpreted their source material very variously, generating mythic frameworks of considerable diversity, both idealism and dualism were ubiquitous. Second-generation Russian Symbolism hinged on a binary opposition between 'the real' and 'the ideal', in which the latter was invariably accorded a greater value than the former. There was a feeling amongst some Symbolists that the love lyric was the central genre allowing access to 'the ideal'.[77] Because love poetry was such an important orientation in 'feminine poetry', women poets associated with Symbolism often simply transferred its established stereotypes to a new purpose, and produced lyrics whose main novelty lay in the fact that they might now be read in a new manner, deciphered according to a new aesthetic, rather than in their discovery of new forms, new lyric heroines, or a new language.[78]

For all that, the love lyric was by no means the only, or even the main, genre in second-generation women's Symbolist writing. The new mysticism pushed gender to the forefront of aesthetic debate: the binary opposition between 'real' and 'ideal' was reflected in an opposition between 'masculine' and 'feminine' principles, so that the feminine principle was associated with the ideal world—or at any rate, a privileged access to the mythic domain. This association in turn meant that the character of the 'feminine principle' became the subject of intense enquiry and speculation, and that the Russian literary world became receptive, for the first time in its history, to the German Romantic idea of the 'eternal feminine' as an element of positive value. As with other aspects of Symbolist aesthetics, indigenous and foreign thought both played a role here: German Romanticism's mystical cult of the feminine was familiar to most Russians not directly, but in the interpretation which it had been given by the mystical philosopher Vladimir Solovyov.

[76] On religio-mysticism, see Jutta Scherrer, *Die Petersburger Religiös-Philosophischen Vereinigungen: die Entwicklung des religiösischen Selbstverständnisses ihrer Intelligencija-Mitglieder (1901–1917): Forschungen zur Ost-Europäischen Geschichte*, 19 (Berlin, 1973); Frederick C. Coplestone, *Russian Religious Philosophy: Selected Aspects* (Tunbridge Wells, 1988); Jonathan Sutton, *The Religious Philosophy of Vladimir Solovyov: Towards a Reassessment* (London, 1988).

[77] On the love lyric as communication with an ideal world see e.g. Aleksandr Blok, 'Poeziya zagovorov i zaklinanii' (n. 91 below); on Vyacheslav Ivanov's theories of mystical love, see Pamela Davidson, *The Poetic Imagination of Vyacheslav Ivanov: A Russian Symbolist's Perception of Dante* (Cambridge, 1989).

[78] Among the poets who continued to produce love lyrics traditional but for the new way in which they might be read were Lyubov' Stolitsa (see 'Na kachelyakh', 'Zhizn' nochi', and 'Plamenem odetye', *ZR* (1906), 10: 33–4); Margarita Sabashnikova (see the selection from her work, 'Lesnaya svirel'', *Tsvetnik or*, 203–13); see also Mirovich, 'Pamyati vstrechi', *Severnye tsvety* (Moscow, 1902), 102.

In Solovyov's religious philosophy, the 'Eternal Feminine' had been represented as a power mediating between the (masculine) Deity and the material world, between creator and created.[79] The cosmogonic and theurgic functions which Solovyov sketched for the 'Eternal Feminine' in his theology were, however, less influential in Russian poetry than were the portraits which he drew, in his poems of the 1890s, of the principle as concrete vision. Of particular importance was a text entitled 'Das Ewig-Weibliche', which conjured up the feminine principle as a nameless, dark, mysterious, other-worldly and irresistibly powerful force which is able to overcome even the machinations of demons.[80] Following Solovyov, later Symbolist thinkers, such as Vyacheslav Ivanov, Aleksandr Blok, Andrei Bely, and Maksimilian Voloshin, were to associate 'the feminine' with everything that lay beyond, with occultic forces communicating themselves in strange new languages to the bewitched male listener.[81]

There was some argument amongst Symbolist thinkers about how far 'the eternal feminine', or ideal, was to be associated with the real, the lives of actual women. Solovyov himself had irritably observed, in the preface to the fourth edition of his *Poems* (1900), that it was 'the most perfect insanity' to pay honour to 'female nature in its own right'. This was a deeply ambivalent and fallible entity, and in no sense to be confused with the unambiguous, divinely perfect, unchanging Eternal Feminine.[82] Yet Solovyov's own poem 'Three Meetings' had muddied the waters by suggesting that the 'feminine principle' might incarnate itself in biographical experience; whilst in 'Aphrodite-Diana' (1900) Vasily Rozanov had determined the possibilities of feminine identity through a set of eternal and transcendent archetypes.[83] The practical results were that real women, including women writers, were expected to comport themselves as befitted incarnations of the 'eternal feminine'.

This brought its own difficulties, since 'the feminine principle' was always perceived as something ready-made, static, rather than dynamic. Sometimes the principle was associated with women's biological identity: Rozanov, for example, was to assert that the prophetic powers of women were indistinguishable from the 'fragrant, moist' qualities of their

[79] Vladimir Solov'ev, 'Smysl lyubvi' (1892–4), *Sobranie sochinenii*, vii (Brussels, 1966), 3–62.

[80] Solov'ev, 'Das Ewig-Weibliche', *SS* xii (Brussels, 1969), 71.

[81] Rozanov, 'Afrodita-Diana'; Sergei Krechetov, 'Arnol'd Ariel', *Doloi zhenshchin!*, Moscow, 1905 . . . Georg Groddek, *Problema zhenshchiny*, St Petersburg' [review-article], *Vesy* (1905), 3: 68–71; E. Gertsyk, 'Vyacheslav Ivanov. *Eros*' [review], *ZR* (1907), 1: 90–1; Vyacheslav Ivanov, 'O dostoinstve zhenshchiny' (1908), *Sobranie sochinenii*, iii (Brussels, 1979), 136–45; 'Drevnii uzhas', ibid. 91–110.

[82] Solov'ev, 'Predislovie avtora k tret'emu izdaniyu stikhotvorenii', *SS* xii. 4.

[83] Solov'ev, 'Tri svidaniya', *SS* xii. 80–6; Rozanov, 'Afrodita-Diana'.

sexuality.[84] Even where such biological analogies remain latent, Symbol-ist thinkers invariably argue that 'the feminine principle', and hence the expression of feminine identity, is conferred on the female writer by the wise tradition of ages, rather than invented by her. Vyacheslav Ivanov, for example, compared women's spiritual powers to a ship alight upon an ocean: a conflagration whose origins are unknown, and which never consumes its object entirely.[85]

The male theorists of feminine creativity aimed to predict, and predetermine, the emergence of a new kind of women's writing, and to a great extent they succeeded in this. From about 1905, the new Symbolist emphasis on woman as prophet began to have a considerable impact on essays and poetry by women. The aesthetics of Symbolism not only dictated the primacy of prophecy; it also prescribed the manner in which prophecy should be communicated, and the authoritativeness of the poetic utterance signalled. A supra-individualist mask, steeped in the mystery of centuries, was held to be prerequisite. For male Symbolist poets, an important source for such masks was classical tradition—or to be more accurate, pre-classical tradition: the religious cults of archaic Greece.[86] For women poets, by contrast, the most popular place to look for mythic figures who might be adopted as personae was Russian folklore.

This gender distinction may in part be extrapolated from the essential-ist character of Symbolism. The argument that women's capacity for prophecy was directly dependent on their nature ruled out the possibility that women might appropriate male masks, since that would have knocked down the equation between nature and expression. But women writers did not need to associate themselves with Orpheus, as male Symbolists did, in order to evoke archaic Greece; in principle, many feminine masks were also available. The role of women in early religious cult had been much emphasized by turn-of-the-century scholars and writers. The theory that primal societies had been matriarchies, and that mother-goddess worship was the fundamental form of belief, was familiar to Russians both through such Western sources as Engels and Frazer, and through Russian sources. The essays and poetry of Vyaches-lav Ivanov, for example, had invoked such Hellenic rituals as the Eleusinian Mysteries, the cultic celebration of the fertility goddess

[84] Rozanov, *Lyudi lunnogo sveta*, 40.

[85] Ivanov, 'O dostoinstve'. Cf. Rozanov, 'Zhenshchina i predstavitel'stvo', *Kogda nachal'stvo ushlo* (St Petersburg, 1910), 87–95.

[86] One of the most popular Greek masks was that of the poet-priest Orpheus: see for example Ivanov, 'Tvorchestvo' and 'Orfei', *SS* i (Brussels, 1974), 536, 577.

Demeter.[87] Yet, for all the ubiquity of such material, Greek and Roman feminine divinities and prophetic figures were ignored by Symbolist women poets. No doubt part of the reason for this is that Russian women who grew up in the 1890s and 1900s, unlike Russian men of that generation, were not routinely taught classical languages at school.[88] As we have seen, Russian women were capable of using classical motifs in erotic poetry, but that was rather a different matter. References to 'maenads' might be in tune with contemporary scholarly and intellectual interest in the cult of Dionysus, but that did not mean that specialized academic interest was essential to those who appropriated such material, since there was a well-established indigenous Russian tradition of using bibulous 'fauns' and flirtatious 'Bacchantes' as the symbols of a comfortably containable transgression.[89] Those interested in women prophets, however, could not satisfy their curiosity by referring to familiar Russian material; either an academic training, or an emphatic autodidactic bent, were required. Women writers did not have the former qualification as of right; if they referred to the classical tradition as mediated by their male contemporaries, such as the erudite Vyacheslav Ivanov, they risked being thought bogus as well as ostentatious. It was not until after the Revolution, when classical education had been abolished in Russia, and classicism had accordingly been pushed to the margins of cultural life, that Greek myth became belatedly accessible to women.[90]

No doubt its association with privileged knowledge made classical myth daunting for Symbolist women poets; if they allude to this mythic tradition at all, they do so only glancingly, so as to suggest the

---

[87] As long ago as 1883, *RB* had run Elisée Reclus's study, *Matriarchy in the Primitive Family*; Engels's *The Origins of the Family, Private Property and the State* (1884) was also standard reading amongst Russian intellectuals. Two Western sources with material on women's role in cult, Emil Rohde's massive study of archaic Greek religion, *Psyche: Seelenkult und Unsterblichkeitsglaube der Griechen* (1890–4) and James Frazer's *The Golden Bough* (1st edn., 1890) were familiar in Russia; indigenous sources on women's roles in religious cult include Ivanov, 'Ellinskaya religiya stra-dayushchego boga', *Novyi put'* (1904), 1: 110–34; 2: 48–78; 3: 38–61; 5: 28–40; 8: 17–26; 9: 4–70; cf. also *idem*, 'Drevnii uzhas', 'O dostoinstve'; F. F. Zelinsky, *Iz zhizni idei* (St Petersburg, 1904 and many subseq. edns.); the plays of Innokenty Annensky, *Melanippa-filosof* (St Petersburg, 1901), and especially 'Laodamiya: liricheskaya tragediya', *Al'manakh Severnaya rech'* (St Petersburg, 1906), 137–208, were also influential treatments of women and the Greek spiritual world.

[88] The comparative programmes for the men's and women's *gimnazii* are given in *ES*, 'Gimna-ziya'. See also Kelly, 'Innokenty Annensky and the Classical Ideal: Poetry, Translations, Drama and Literary Theory', D.Phil. thesis (Oxford University, 1985), ch. 1. Greek and Latin were available as an optional course at certain women's *gimnazii*; those taking this course did a reduced programme of foreign languages.

[89] On the 19th-c. Russian neo-classical tradition of fauns and bacchae, see Catriona Kelly, 'Bacchic Revels: Innokentii Annenskii's *Famira-kifared* and the Satyrs', *EP* 10/2 (Autumn 1985), 76–92.

[90] On the use of classical masks for poetic activity after the Revolution, see Ch. 9 below.

universality of archetypes, whether Russian-folkloric, medieval, or Greek (compare my observations on Gertsyk below). But a still more important reason behind the preference for folklore amongst Russian women writers was the fact that personae from Russian folklore came with their own ready-made sign systems, as personae from Greek myth did not. Turn-of-the-century Russian folklore collectors had begun to give increasing attention to such women's genres as the *prichitanie* (formal lament) and *liricheskaya pesnya* (folk love-song), and commentators were increasingly sensitive to women's roles in peasant spiritual culture, taking account of such figures as the *znakharka* (wise woman), and of specifically feminine types of spell and incantation. Women's contribution to the applied arts was also coming under scrutiny, as collectors began to take an interest in such traditional occupations as embroidery. Considerable attention was also paid to the part played by women in various Orthodox sects, such as the *Khlysty* (self-flagellants), and to the popular cults of female 'counter-cultural' saints (such as women *yurodivye*, or holy fools).[91] By the early years of the century, therefore, most educated Russian readers had a considerable grasp of women's roles in the rural popular culture which neo-Slavophile ethnography celebrated; allusions, even of the most superficial kind, to traditional activities, and mimicry, even in the most distant manner, of the formulae from which traditional texts were constructed, were bound to have powerful effects on such readers.

On the whole it was less traditional activities than traditional texts that were invoked. Very occasionally, women poets referred to the act of sewing as a metaphor for female creativity. Where Zinaida Gippius's 'The Seamstress' (1901) had used allusions to sewing as a way of introducing the colour and blood imagery that was ubiquitously associated with other-worldly experience in her poetry, a poem by Adelaida Gertsyk, 'The Tower', placed the practice of needlework itself centrally, drawing on sewing's connotations of spiritual manipulation (the threads played by the Parcae), and connecting the act of weaving and the act of the imagination. Another poet who exploited such material was Elizaveta Kuzmina-Karavaeva, who was herself also an expert practitioner of

---

[91] Amongst the many contributions on women as marginal figures in rural communities are: Nikolai Rudninsky, 'Znakharstvo v skopinskom i dankovskom uezdakh ryazanskoi gubernii', *Zhivaya starina* (1886); T. Popov, *Russkaya narodno-bytovaya meditsina* (St Petersburg, 1903); E. V. Barsov, *Prichitaniya severnogo kraya: antologiya* (2 vols.; Moscow, 1872–82); Blok, 'Poeziya zagovorov i zaklinanii' (1908), *Sobranie sochinenii v 8 tomakh*, v. 36–65; see also T. L. Nikol'skaya, 'Tema misticheskogo sektanstva v russkoi poezii 20-kh godov', *Puti razvitiya russkoi literatury: Uchenye zapiski Tartuskogo gosudarstvennogo universiteta*, 883 (1990), 157–69. On women and crafts, see particularly I. Bilibin, 'Narodnoe tvorchestvo Severa', *Mir iskusstva* (1904), 11: 303–18 (with abundant illustrations); *Mir iskusstva* (1901), 7 also carried plates of late-medieval Russian ecclesiastical embroideries.

embroidery, and who also executed exquisite small illustrative paintings in the manner of her embroideries.[92] But these are exceptions. The Symbolist preference for socially marginal figures as metaphors for the poet, added to the uncomfortably close connection between traditional women's work in villages and the despised sphere of domesticity, meant that poets generally took fringe figures, rather than ordinary women, as their personae. Zinaida Gippius, for example, reworked her earlier theme of demonic transgression in a new, more commanding manner in 'Incantation', a poem whose title and formulaic language marks its affinities with the Russian traditions of popular sorcery, and which uses references to the power of language ('secrets', 'vows', 'curses') in order to command the speaker's passage into another world.[93] If Gippius assimilates both the manner and the purpose of her source material here, sometimes allusions to popular tradition were less direct. In the poetry of Adelaida Gertsyk, for example, formulae reminiscent of Russian folklore are appropriated to narratives which create a world of myth that is not immediately definable in national terms. The narrative of three sisters imprisoned in 'The Tower' touches off allusions to classical tradition, to Western medieval romance, and to German *Märchen*, as well as to Russian popular material; a particularly fine poem, 'Silent, draped in the garments of sacrifice' at once evokes the seasonal rituals of the Russian countryside, and their archaic Greek equivalents.[94] Other of Gertsyk's poems are still more vague in setting and plot: they represent mysterious dyads or triads of women, whose question-and-answer interchanges suggest the formulae of riddles, of incantations or of fortune-telling. In 'Spring' (1910), a woman narrator tells a woman addressee/interlocutor about the behaviour of a third woman, who has sworn a pact with the cosmos from her 'unknown grave'. Incantatory formulae are used not only to characterize the third woman, but also in the dialogue of those who discuss her, eroding the reader's sense of any ultimate reality, whether as the starting-point of the poem, or as its objective.[95]

Not strictly binary-oppositional in the manner of Symbolist philosophy, Gertsyk's work uses folklore in order to create its own world, neither 'real' nor 'ideal' but fused from both. As one might expect from

[92] Gippius, 'Shveya', *Sobranie stikhov*, i (Moscow, 1904), 115–16; (see also 'The Seamstress' in *Anthology*); Adelaida Gertsyk, 'Bashnya', *Stikhotvoreniya* (St Petersburg, 1910), 20–4; on Kuz'mina-Karavaeva, cf. L. Shustov, 'Doch' Rossii', *Belye nochi* (Leningrad, 1985), 215. One of Kuz'mina-Karavaeva's paintings is reproduced in *Twilight of the Tsars: Russian Art at the Turn of the Century* (London, 1991), 131.

[93] Gippius, 'Zaklinanie', *Sobranie stikhov*, ii (Moscow, 1910), 95. See also 'Incantation' in *Anthology*.

[94] Gertsyk, 'Opyat' v tkanyakh belykh, zhertvennykh', *Stikhotvoreniya*, 27–8; see also 'Silent, draped in the garments' in *Anthology*.

[95] Gertsyk, 'Vesna', *Stikhotvoreniya*, 11; see also 'Spring' in *Anthology*.

the only woman Symbolist to produce any original thought on the function of the poetic word, Gertsyk's poetic language was also innovative: she used not only dialect words, but also archaic forms, 'boyars in their tall hats', as she called them herself, to create a voice at once sonorous and stylistically specific.[96] How ironic, then, that it should have been precisely the reviews of Gertsyk's work which made clear the dangers for women in passively accepting Symbolist male theorists' attempts to define and determine their poetry.

In these reviews, we seem to hear these male theorists heaving sighs of relief as their prophecies, or dreams, are fulfilled. The poet Konstantin Balmont, for example, writes:

I listened, bewitched. Yes, I too had dreamt of her, this Sibyl. In just this form ... How much maidenly, eternally-virginal longing there was in her. How much secret recognition, foreboding, lack of fusion with that which moves and passes, with that which dies, as we call it. An earthly girl-woman. And yet she is lunar, not earthly: the Sibyl.[97]

For Balmont, Gertsyk exists simply as an embodiment of his own dream, a mouthpiece of his own words. The following year, Vyacheslav Ivanov commended Gertsyk's poetry in similar terms; he was as keen to press interested readers to read his own poem addressed to Gertsyk and Balmont's review of her poetry, as to encourage them to read her own work:

A psychological characterization of the idiosyncratic talent of this young poetess ... has already been given by the present writer in the lyric 'Is it the rustle of a snake or the whisper of the Sibyl' ... and by K. Balmont.[98]

Such statements were clear enough signals that male Symbolist poets were only really interested in women's creativity as primary material that might be decoded and rewritten in a more appropriate form, as the priest at Delphi had transcribed the incomprehensible ravings of the Sibyl herself.[99] And even in the heyday of Symbolism, a few women poets writing in the mode of philosophical Symbolism expressed discomfort with the poetic masks which Symbolist theory had granted them. The most common reaction was to vary representations of 'the eternal feminine' by integrating it into a theory of 'creative androgyny', according to which the soul was seen as split between male and female halves.

[96] Gertsyk, 'Moi romany', pt. 2, 52.

[97] Konstantin Balmont, 'Sibilla', ZR (1909), 10: 29.

[98] Ivanov, *Stikhotvoreniya* Adelaidy Gertsyk', *Apollon* (1910), 7: *khronika*, 41.

[99] The Delphic oracle analogy was made by a contemporary of Ivanov's, Evgeniya Gertsyk, in her memoirs (*Vospominaniya* (Paris, 1973), 53), but precisely so as to suggest the superior expressive powers of men.

But in such cases the 'male' was usually understood, quite traditionally, as the active, striving aspects of spirituality (*Dukh—Geist*), whilst the female stood for passive contemplation (*Dusha—Seele*). Zinaida Gippius is a notable example of a poet whose 'androgyny' usually, though not invariably, takes the form of this conventional polarization: many of her love poems oppose a predatory masculine speaker to a shrinking feminine one, or vice versa. Some poems do, however, handle the issue of androgyny more ambiguously, representing internal conflicts whose oppositions are not resolved by a central governing construct. In a famous poem of 1908, 'She', Gippius represents her 'soul', a grammatically feminine noun, as the predatory serpent which Christian mythology associates with Satan; and in 'The Wedding Ring' (1905), a masculine speaker has a vision of an androgynous union with Christ, who himself has both feminine and masculine attributes: he extends the 'Protection' which Orthodoxy traditionally associates with the Virgin, but this feminine attribute is here linked with the 'active' adjective 'fiery'.[100]

If Gippius's myths were not always those which Symbolist authorities might have sanctioned, she did not, however, question the Symbolist doctrine that poetry must put forward appropriate archetypes. A response to Symbolism which is more radical in this latter sense is Mirra Lokhvitskaya's poem 'Fairy Tales and Life'. Here, the familiar narratives of Snow White, Cinderella, and the Sleeping Beauty are subversively parodied in order to suggest the deceptive qualities of myth. To each stanza, Lokhvitskaya appends a moral *envoi* instructing her readers to distinguish between 'life' and 'fairy-tales', but the deeper moral is that those who dream of being rescued by a prince will spend their whole lives in thrall to others.[101] Still more remarkable were two pieces of poetic prose by a writer called Anastasiya Mirovich, which were published in the second volume of the Symbolist almanac *Northern Flowers* (1902), and which suggested that the fashionable emphasis on 'the feminine principle' as other-worldliness or irrationality might be an instrument of male control, as well as a means to new writing by women. In the first prose text, 'Lizards', a young girl is recovered from a well. She has had visions, but cannot communicate them, and a sorcerer is called in to explain how she may be 'cured' by depriving her of the visions, but without restoring her power to speak. In the second piece, 'Elsa', a German pastor's young daughter who has taken part in a revolutionary

---

[100] Gippius, 'Ona', *Sobranie stikhov*, ii. 70; 'Brachnoe kol'tso', ibid. ii. 10. See also 'The Wedding Ring' in *Anthology*; cf. 'Zhenskoe', ibid. ii. 108. On androgyny in Gippius, see also Olga Matich, 'Dialectics of Cultural Return: Zinaida Gippius' Personal Myth', in Boris Gasparov, Robert Hughes, and Irina Paperno (eds.), *Cultural Mythologies of Russian Modernism* (Berkeley, Calif., 1992).

[101] Mirra Lokhvitskaya, 'Skazka i zhizn'', *Stikhotvoreniya*, iv. 93–4.

outrage, sinks into a similar state of mystical non-communicativeness. As she and her family sit silent, a male revenant, the spirit of her victim, comes to join them. Contact with 'other worlds', it is implied, destroys female language as readily as it brings it into being; assertion of female authority through language may provoke revenge on the part of men just as easily as submission.[102]

Mirovich's stories were, in a sense, prophetic of the literary future. By the end of 1910 the tide of enthusiasm for 'the feminine' was beginning to turn. According to Evgeniya Gertsyk, even by the end of 1909 Vyacheslav Ivanov was going through a sharp case of reverse transference, and getting to work on 'combatting his enthusiasm for the female element'.[103] Though Ivanov did not rush into print with his change of heart, some other Symbolists were less reticent. In 1912, for example, Valery Bryusov published, under the title 'Women poets', a compilation of reviews which had mostly been written much earlier. Since the majority of the reviews were hostile, their combined effect was such that the article might just as well have been called 'The Empress's New Poetical Clothes'; its effect was to suggest a very different interpretation of the 'special feminine language' that had been praised (if never analysed) by the mystical Symbolists, as Bryusov pinned down case after case of metrical incompetence or stylistic infelicity.[104]

What was more important was that the decline in the prestige of women's poetry also coincided with what is generally known as 'the crisis of Russian Symbolism'. In the years between 1910 and 1913, conflict between the 'spiritual' and 'decadent' strands in the Symbolist movement became explicit, and the raising of voices against both strands more general; the quarrel was followed by the fragmentation of the movement, and the formation of various post-Symbolist schools. The most important of these were Acmeism, or Adamism, and Futurism (which was in fact not one movement, but several, among them Cubo-Futurism, Ego-Futurism, and Centrifuga).[105]

No women poets were numbered amongst the ideologues of Acmeism and Futurism, and their membership of groups was usually incidental, depending on whom they were married to or living with at the time. But,

---

[102] Anastasiya Mirovich, 'Yashcheritsy' and 'El'za', 'Izmena', *Severnye tsvety na 1902 god*, 80–3. See also 'Lizards' and 'Elsa' in *Anthology*.

[103] Gertsyk, *Vospominaniya*, 53.

[104] Valery Bryusov, 'Zhenshchiny-poety', *Sobranie sochinenii v 7 tomakh*, vi (Moscow, 1974), 318–21.

[105] On the post-Symbolist schools, see Vladimir Markov, *Russian Futurism* (London, 1969); Justin Doherty, 'Culture of the Word: Aspects of Acmeist Poetic Theory and Fiction', D.Phil. thesis (Oxford University, 1989); R. D. Timenchik, 'Zametki ob akmeizme', *Russkaya literatura*, 7–8 (1974), 23–46; 5/3 [*sic*] (1977), 280–300; 9 (1981), 179–89.

like all other poets of the day, even non-affiliated poets, the women poets who worked in the wake of Acmeism and Futurism were deeply affected by the new theories which the two movements evolved. In rejecting (or purporting to reject) Symbolism's religio-mystical apparatus, the Acmeists and Futurists formulated a view of the place of women which was, at first sight, considerably more restrictive than that of the Symbolists. For Gumilev and Gorodetsky, the authors of the Acmeists' first manifestos, this place was something peripheral to the new manliness which was the movement's main concern. Poetry was formulated as the 'naming' of objects by the poet, who would speak 'like Adam on the first day'. The proper task of the woman poet could only be the delineation of ordinary Russian society, and the broken, effeminate men who were its normal members.[106] If the Acmeists allowed women a marginal position, even this much could not be said of the Futurists of whatever grouping. The early manifestos of the movement's various groups placed even more emphasis on 'virile' language than did the Acmeist manifestos. And all of the groups gave central place to a male hero engaged in a rebellion against 'bourgeois' values, including those of courtesy and domestic harmony, in the name of a new ethic of masculine self-assertion.[107] Often this hero was placed in a mythologized urban landscape, though some of the post-Symbolists preferred 'primitive' Russian figures such as the shaman (Khlebnikov), or chose the more exotic setting of colonial Africa (Gumilev).

The determinedly masculine character of Russian post-Symbolism is very much in keeping with that of modernist groups in Western Europe (for example, the Italian Futurists, the Vorticists).[108] The correspondence seems likely to be partly the result of direct influence. There was a very extensive Russian audience for the ideas of the Viennese philosopher Otto Weininger, whose aphorisms, collected in *Sex and Character* (1903), *Last Things* (1904), and *Thoughts on Sexual Problems* (1908), had suggested that women 'could not speak, only prattle', were incapable of rational cogitation, and were wholly defined in terms of their desire to reproduce or to experience sexual pleasure.[109]

---

[106] Sergei Gorodetsky, 'Nekotorye techeniya v sovremennoi russkoi poezii', *Apollon* (1913), 1: 46–50; Nikolai Gumilev, 'Zavety simvolizma i akmeizm', ibid. 42–5.

[107] See particularly *Poshchechina obshchestvennomu vkusu* (Moscow, 1912), on the linguistic aims of futurism, see the introductions to *Sadok sudei* 1 (St Petersburg, 1913), *Sadok sudei*, 2 (St Petersburg, 1914). A useful compendium of materials from these very rare editions is V. Markov (ed.), *Manifesty i programmy russkikh futuristov* (Munich, 1967).

[108] On misogynist elements in Western European modernism, see Wolff, *Feminine Sentences*, 34–56.

[109] Otto Weininger, *Geschlecht und Charakter* (Vienna, 1903); *Über die letzten Dinge* (Vienna, 1904); *Gedanken über die Geschlechtsprobleme* (Vienna, 1908: citations below to 4th edn.; Vienna, 1922).

Weininger's work was first translated in 1909, but prior to that Russians ignorant of German might have acquainted themselves with his work by reading one of the many articles devoted to discussion of his ideas which appeared in the periodical press and elsewhere—or they might have heard of him by more indirect means. As Teffi, again acting as an ironic observer of *idées reçues*, put it in her story 'The Lady Translator', 'In the old days there were no Weiningers, and so no one had any idea how low and how pernicious a being woman is. . . . But nowadays any fiancé, no matter how in love he may be, has had a taste of Weininger—albeit at tenth hand, from his sister's nephew or great-uncle's tutor'.[110] Whether at first, second, or tenth hand, Weininger's views on the 'speechlessness' and necessary inferiority of women were ammunition to the post-Symbolist backlash against women's writing, which was to have far-reaching effects, attaining its apogee after 1917, in the writings of the left avant-garde.[111]

But the Weininger heritage was complex; it did more than simply facilitate misogyny. The crux of Weininger's argument on women had been that nobility in women was a projection of the male fantasy, that men invented women through love; but at the same time he had concluded 'amo, ergo sum' (I love, therefore I am).[112] This declaration of masculine solipsism was at one level an extreme statement of the link between creativity and gender already made in Romanticism. However, the emphasis on all-powerful masculinity now had a new note of anxiety. Like all solipsists, Weininger was faced with an impossible burden of proof. If the 'ennobling' aspects of femininity were a matter of fantasy, why should its degraded aspects not be an illusion? Did 'femininity' really exist at all? If it did not, then what was to happen to its opposite, 'masculinity'? If love was an illusion, and love was the proof of existence, what then?

In Western Europe questioning of 'femininity' did in time indeed provoke scrutiny of 'masculinity'; this scrutiny was in turn to be one factor behind the crisis of identity which underlay the modernist movement.[113] In Russia, the progression was a little different. Though less sure of itself than in the early nineteenth century, Russian imperial-

---

[110] Teffi, *Yumoristicheskie rasskazy*, 247. Among the articles introducing Weininger to the Russian public before 1909 were Count Polonsky, 'Filosof pola i kharaktera' *MB* (1908), 9: 111–48, 'G.Sh.', 'Filosofiya polov Otto Veiningera', *RM* (1908), 6, pt. 2, 147–59; an early encyclopedia article is N. Lapshin, 'Otto Veininger', *NS* ix. 840–3. See also Naiman, 'Historectomies', n. 22.

[111] On the left avant-garde, see Ch. 9 below.

[112] Weininger, *Über die Geschlechtsprobleme*, 53–5.

[113] For material on 'the crisis of masculinity' in Western countries, see Sandra Gilbert and Susan Gubar, *No Man's Land: The Place of the Woman Writer in the Twentieth Century*, i (New Haven, Conn., 1988), chs. 1 and 3.

ism was not so obviously in retreat as the Austrian imperialism of Weininger's Vienna, and assertive masculinity was still perfectly congruent with a national identity whose key representations were visions of Russia as a horde of barbarian warriors in full cry, or a sodality of broad-chested *muzhiks*.[114] For the time being, 'masculinity' was safe enough. Understanding of the 'feminine', however, did become less stable, more contradictory, and more diverse. In an important essay written in 1909, 'On Contemporary Lyricism: the Shes', the poet Innokenty Annensky had given an early airing to many of the confusions which shot through the post-Symbolist era. On the one hand, Annensky argued that 'the eternal feminine' was nothing more than a symbol, a construct. But on the other hand, he asserted that the origins of recent Russian women's poetry lay in the fact that women had been 'written out' of men's poetry by such constructs; and he urged women writers to use 'women's language', which he saw in conventional Symbolist terms as mysterious, magical, other-worldly; alienating, yet of great power.[115]

Even for a Russian writer as steeped in European thought as Annensky was, post-Nietzschean idealism's problematization of human identity could not be fully absorbed. No Russian early twentieth-century thinker was to evolve anything analogous to the Freudian revelation that sexual archetypes might be realized through immediate and individual psychological factors, and have their own dynamic history. But even the partial absorption of this new material meant that it was now no longer possible to take refuge in the idea of women's prophetic powers, or indeed in any totalizing view of the feminine, heedlessly and without further thought. The drive to a more analytical appreciation of the act of writing by women was made still more compelling by the fact that the manifestos of the post-Symbolists, puerile as they in some respects were, did initiate a discussion of the nature of poetic language that was more complex and sophisticated than that which had been kept up by the Symbolists in their literary essays. All the post-Symbolist groups were united in discarding (for the mean time at least) the Symbolist emphasis on the mysterious origins of poetry (which had led to endless analogies with music, prayer, and so on), and concentrating instead on poetry's contexts and functions once it had come into being. For the Acmeists, whose quasi-realist perspective was akin to that of the *Neue Sachlichkeit* in Germany, the poetic word was to revert to depicting the perceivable

[114] Among the many neo-pagan texts of the post-Symbolist era is Khlebnikov's narrative poem 'Venera i shaman', *Tvoreniya* (Moscow, 1988), 230–6. After the Revolution, such expressions were to culminate in a view of Russia as a powerful barbarian nation: see particularly Blok's narrative poem 'Skify' (1918).

[115] Innokenty Annensky, 'O sovremennom lirizme: One', *Apollon* (1909), 3: 5–29.

world, and was to have readily recognizable (though always aesthetically assimilable) referents; for the Cubo-Futurists, the word was to be elevated for its own sake, and was to become the referent in its own right.[116] How far the poets who actually evolved such theories followed them in practice is debatable; the point is that, through their emphasis on the word as well as through their scepticism of the 'eternal feminine', Acmeism and Futurism offered a way out of Symbolism's assumption that women's writing was necessarily passive and automatic.

This complicated background meant that the breakup of Symbolist uniformity had diverse and ambiguous effects on women's writing. One of these was a retreat to a pre-Symbolist understanding of 'the feminine'; as Annensky's remarks suggest, this was accompanied by an emphasis on women's real experience, or rather, the part of that experience which was generally understood to be appropriate to poetry. Women poets now again began to comply with Kireevsky's demand of 1834 that women should express genuinely poetic moments from their lives in the mirror of their verses. As in the 1830s, representations of the life cycle of genteel Russian women became crucial; an especial prominence was given to the chronicle of love, with its meetings and separations, its letters received and answered. The poetry of Nadezhda Lvova, and some early poems by Anna Akhmatova, depicted the sufferings of a subdued and often submissive heroine in a variety of recognizable contemporary settings.[117]

The conventionality of such work should not be exaggerated. For one thing, the resurrection of the 'prose in verse' tradition could make women poets as productively cavalier with genres as they had been in the nineteenth century. In *The Crossroads* (1913), for example, Poliksena Soloveva produced a 'novel in verse' which, unlike most Russian texts so denominated, was no pallid imitation of *Evgeny Onegin*, but a properly independent work.[118] A polymetric epistolary novel composed in short sections, it dissected the upheavals of some provincial landowners' modern marriages in a way that gave weight to, and yet revised, the peculiar traditions of women's writing: the characters included an unmarried and emancipated woman who recalled the heroine of the provincial tale, but also a rebellious wife whose assertion of self in her marriage was the mainspring of the plot.

For another thing, the 'life cycle' was not always now understood as restrictively as it had been in the nineteenth century. Several women poets now adopted forms of poetic discourse modelled on the language

[116] On Acmeist and Futurist theory, see nn. 107, 108 above.
[117] See e.g. L'vova, 'Ya odenus' nevestoi v atlasnoe beloe plat'e', *RM* (1911), 11; Akhmatova, 'Szhala ruki', *SP* (see ch. 8, n. 4), 28.
[118] Solov'eva, *Perekrestok: povest' v stikakh* (St Petersburg, 1913).

of childhood. Here we can see how disparaging references to women's language as 'prattle' could actually have positive effects when interpreted in the context of the primitivism that was cultivated by various post-Symbolist movements, notably the Cubo-Futurists. Though women poets did not gravitate to the *zaum*, 'transrational language', the incantatory nonsense language which was developed by some men (Khlebnikov, Kruchenykh, Burlyuk), use of the discourse of childhood was in a sense a substitute for this. An important instance was the work of the young writer Elena Guro (pseudonym of E. von Notenburg), whose collections of little fragmented stories and short poems were published under whimsical titles, and illustrated with drawings of a childlike primitivism.[119] Marina Tsvetaeva's first collections, *The Evening Album* (1910) and *The Magic Lantern* (1912), whilst more knowing, indeed affected, than Guro's work, represented the lyric protagonist as a small girl, whose infantilism showed every possibility of lasting well into adulthood:

> Я только девочка. Мой долг
> До брачного венца
> Не забывать, что всюду—волк
> И помнить—я овца.
>
> Мечтать о замке золотом,
> Качать, кружить, трясти
> Сначала куклу, а потом
> Не куклу, а почти.[120]

> I'm only a small girl. My duty is
> To remember till I marry
> That the wolf is everywhere
> And I'm a little sheep.
>
> To dream about a golden castle,
> To rock, to spin, to shake
> A doll at first, then later on
> Something much the same.

The conservatism of some post-Symbolist poetry was again evident though, in the selection of constructs for the woman poet. Where Symbolist women poets had introduced new symbols of the writer, the

---

[119] Elena Guro, *Sharmanka* (St Petersburg, 1909); *Nebesnye verblyuzhata* (St Petersburg, 1914); a selection from the latter also appears in *Sadok sudei, 2.* See also her private diaries, collected in Elena Guro, *Selected Prose and Poetry*, ed. Anna Ljungren and Nils Ake Nilsson (Stockholm, 1988). For an extensive bibliography of Russian-language sources on Guro, see Toporov, 'Aptekarskaya ostrov'; two English-language sources of note are Kjeld Bornager Jensen, *Russian Futurism, Urbanism, and Elena Guro* (Arhus, 1977), and Vera Kalina-Levina, 'Through the Eyes of the Child: The Artistic Vision of Elena Guro', *SEEJ*, 25 (1981), 30–43.

[120] Marina Tsvetaeva, 'Tol'ko devochka', *SP* (see ch. 11, n. 1), i. 100.

post-Symbolists revived the nineteenth-century neo-classical tradition of the Muse: in Akhmatova's narrative poem 'By the Very Edge of the Sea', for example, Pushkin's Muse-Mistress appears as the Muse-Sister and Akhmatova's double.[121] It is scarcely surprising that several women poets, notably Sofiya Parnok, expressed some irritation at the new fashions in women's writing (their male colleagues, on the other hand, were on the whole more approbatory).[122]

Even where post-Symbolist poetry of this kind apparently contributed little that was new in its own right, it was affected by the fact that its literary context was now quite different to that in which the nineteenth-century tradition of 'prose in verse' had functioned. As we have seen, post-Symbolist thinking expressed confused and contradictory attitudes to the expression of femininity. On the one hand, overt constructs of identity were attacked as obstacles to the expression of reality; on the other, they were celebrated as a means of expressing the diversity and flexibility of artistic authority. The result was that there was no longer a schematic division between 'feminine' and 'unfeminine' verse; rather, there was a huge proliferation of the feminine personae which women writers might adopt. The restoration of 'feminine' verse in a conventional sense did not replace Symbolist and decadent personae, but augmented them; the notion of 'feminine' verse was itself profoundly altered by the new relativism. Women writers of the post-Symbolist period move freely between the 'positive' and 'negative' aspects of femininity, yes, but they also move beyond dualism altogether: neither the established patterns of polarization between positive and negative femininities, nor those of a conventional active male–passive female androgyny, now circumscribe the possibilities open to women.

Sometimes fluidity or inconsistency may be established over a collection or a cycle. This is so, for example, in the work of Elizaveta Dmitrieva, who wrote under the name 'Cherubina de Gabriak'. Dmitrieva's pseudonym, which had been invented by Maksimilian Voloshin and his circle, purported to belong to an exotic Hispano-French countess: it was an obvious fiction, and fictionality was also suggested by the speaker's adoption of incompatible poses: much the same tone is adopted whether she is waiting for a romantic assignation or waiting outside the confessional, and her attitude moves from haughty to light-hearted to melancholy in unpredictable sequence.[123] And in the poetry of

---

[121] Akhmatova, 'U samogo morya', *SP*, 339–46; cf. 'Muze', *SP*, 40.

[122] Sofiya Parnok (as 'Andrei Polyanin'), 'Otmechennye imena', *SZ* (1913), 4: 111–15.

[123] 'Cherubina de Gabriak' (E. Dmitrieva), 'Stikhi', *Apollon* (1909), 2: 3–10; (1910), 10: 3–14 (This was a 'women's number', also including: Sofiya Dubnova, 'V moei dushe'; M. Pozharova, 'Lesnye kacheli'.)

Nadezhda Teffi, a vast number of alternative masks (nuns, witches, *demi-mondaines*) were used to effect both amusing parody and linguistic variety for its own sake.[124] Other poets may move from identity to identity within a poem. Mariya Veselkova-Kilshtets's charming collection *Songs from a Deserted Manor-House*, for example, shifts between the perceptions of a young girl of the early nineteenth century, who lays out patience, tells her own fortunes, and watches mythical beasts grow on her embroidery frame, and a contemporary speaker who remembers the time of her great-grandmother.[125] The most sophisticated orchestrator of different personae both intra-textually and inter-textually, however, was Anna Akhmatova, whose poetry after 1913, as we shall see, exploits the full panoply of post-Symbolist resources; Akhmatova fragments the lyric speaker's identity by internal irony and contradiction and by reworking material from her own early poetry as well as material from an array of other literary and cultural sources.

Still more significantly, the revolt against Symbolism led to a new questioning of the automatic association of persona and language. In her important review, 'Feminine Poetry', Nadezhda Lvova (herself an entirely conventional poet) criticized the work of Akhmatova and Kuzmina-Karavaeva on just this point. Lvova asserted that 'women have not yet been able to find a language of *"their own"* adequate to these, *their own* "feminine" experiences'. (The emphasis and quotation marks are hers.)[126] In the second phase of post-Symbolism, we see women becoming increasingly conscious of the need to develop this 'language of their own'. The development can be seen, for example, in the work of Kuzmina-Karavaeva. Her first collection, *Scythian Sherds* (1912), works as an extended cycle narrated through the eyes of a Scythian princess. The colourful historical and mythic associations of the persona are, however, only partially translated into the language of the poems themselves, which is directly derivative of Gippius's work.[127] In her second collection, *Ruth* (1916), Kuzmina-Karavaeva was to discard the posing of her first collection, a feminine reflection of the fashionable interest in the barbarian world of Scythian prehistory. The reference to the biblical prophetess of *The Book of Ruth* is used to suggest a perspective, rather than to dictate it; the opening poem demonstrates the alienation of the poet *as* 'Ruth', as well as referring to it *through* Ruth, by shifting between first-person and third-person narrative; the

[124] N. Teffi, *Sem' ognei* (St Petersburg, 1910); a selection of poems appears in *Yumoristicheskie rasskazy*, 346–71.

[125] M. Veselkova-Kil'shtet, *Pesni zabytoi usad'by* (St Petersburg, 1912).

[126] L'vova, 'Kholod utra', 206.

[127] Kuz'mina-Karavaeva, *Skifskie cherepki* (St Petersburg, 1912).

'strangeness' of the protagonist is also suggested by the use of repeated references (the flight of cranes, the action of gleaning) in divergent contexts.[128]

One should not over-stress the pluralism of identity which post-Symbolism allowed women. The various personae which were accessible to women all depended on a fairly constrictive code in which obviously aesthetically or ethically loaded criteria were used to signal poetic authority. For all the Acmeists' and the Futurists' emphasis on 'the word for its own sake', thematic prohibitions remained in force. Abstract philosophical reflection for its own sake and intense, *realia*-heavy autobiography were both problematic genres. The publication of, say, explicitly lesbian poetry was still a rarity. That said, the years after 1910 were the only era of Russian literary history when explicitly lesbian poetry was composed for private purposes in any quantity. The on-off relationship which Marina Tsvetaeva and Sofiya Parnok had in 1915–16 was accompanied by the composition, on Tsvetaeva's part at least, of some especially fine love lyrics, in which, for once, the object of adoration proves as irreducible and as fully realized as are the emotions of the adorer.[129]

Before rounding off, I should briefly mention one last literary phenomenon of the pre-Revolutionary years: the development of a 'committed Symbolist' tradition, above all in drama. In two of her plays, *The Green Ring* and *The Colour of Poppies*, Gippius dealt sympathetically with various utopian shadings of Russian revolutionism, pointing to a new society which was to be formed by the idealistic younger generation. There was a distinctly decadent flavour to these plays, which dwelt on the inevitability of suicides in those hopelessly wrecked by social stagnation, and the poetry of spilt blood as armed uprising went its course.[130] In *Atlantis*, Larisa Reisner gave a still more voluptuous treatment to historical material, portraying the fate of a hero on the mythical Greek island who foresees catastrophe and is persecuted by the priestly caste as he tries to avert it.[131] Similar in their mixture of decadence and a utopian socialism at once vague and colourful, these plays were also linked by their recognition of women characters as ancillary to the main struggle. In *Atlantis* the hero is succoured by a young girl, whose role consists exclusively of sexual companionship. Gippius's young

[128] Kuz'mina-Karavaeva, *Ruf'* (St Petersburg, 1916). (Translations of 'Ruth' and of 'Long-Barrow Princess, ii' from *Scythian Sherds* appear in *Anthology*.)

[129] On Parnok and Tsvetaeva, see Sofya Polyakova, *V zakatnye oni dni: Tsvetaeva i Parnok* (Ann Arbor, Mich., 1983).

[130] Gippius, *Makov tsvet* and *Zelenaya kol'tso* are available in *P'esy*, ed. Temira Pachmuss (Munich, 1972).

[131] Larisa Reisner, 'Atlantida: p'esa v 5-i deistviyakh', *Shipovnik*, 21 (Moscow, 1913), 143–219.

female characters, though less indulgent with their bodies, are dewy idealists happy to play second fiddle to their male coevals, and take no part in the ideological debates of the play.

The interplay of socialism and decadence to the exclusion of women was indicative. It was clear even before the Menshevik Revolution that some rapprochement between the left avant-garde, the left Symbolist rump, and socialism, was not only possible, but likely. Whatever their differences in interpretation or understanding of the function of art, Lunacharsky, Mayakovsky, and Bryusov (to name but three) did have points of agreement, and even shared platforms. After the Bolshevik Revolution, the map of rapprochement was to shift slightly; some writers, such as Gippius, became violently anti-Revolutionary, and departed for the West. But many ex-Symbolists were at first happy to assimilate to Bolshevik policies; some, such as Valery Bryusov, even ended up as Bolshevik *apparatchiks*.[132] The bifurcation between women's writing as self-expression and the women's rights movement, in its various colorations, was to prove more lasting and more destructive. Bolshevik policy on women settled many, or even most, of the demands of the latter movement; but in reducing gender issues to a few relatively simple economic and social formulae, it also marginalized women's writing. Not surprisingly, the years after 1917 witnessed the emigration of many established modernist women authors, and the neglect or vilification of those who stayed. And, as cultural centralism went forward, it was accompanied by the institution of an aesthetic peculiarly hostile to the forms of expression which modernist women writers had evolved.

The antagonistic character of turn-of-the-century Russian feminism was in part responsible, then, for the pressure on women's writing after the Revolution. But on the other hand, it is arguable that it was precisely the diversity represented both by and within turn-of-the-century feminism on the one hand, and Symbolist and post-Symbolist writing on the other, which was to ensure the survival of women's writing, which was to give women writers the strength to continue writing despite the fact that the disincentives were now to be greater than ever before. In particular, the assault on unified notions of femininity which had been ushered in by post-Symbolism had allowed women to contemplate the

---

[132] On Blok's participation in the Bolshevik cultural establishment, see Avril Pyman, *The Life of Aleksandr Blok*, ii (Oxford, 1980), 312–25; on Bryusov, see T. J. Binyon, 'V. Ya. Bryusov'; N. Apushkin (ed.), *Valerii Bryusov v avtobiograficheskikh zapisyakh, pis'makh, vospominaniyakh sovremennikov i otzyvakh kritiki* (Moscow, 1929), 345–400. The only possible exception to my generalization on women is Larisa Reisner, but her involvement in 1920s revolutionary politics was more a question of play-acting than of real power. See Alla Zeide, 'Larisa Reisner: Myth as Justification for Life', *Russian Review*, 51/2 (1992), 172–87.

act of writing and set it against a recognition of society's expectations of how they should behave; this analytical process was to be of great value to those women writers who were, one way or another, later to emerge as dissident voices.

Besides its hypothetical role as insurance against future set-backs, the diversity of women's writing between 1880 and 1917 was an extraordinary phenomenon in its own right. More than anything else, the achievements of this generation of writers illustrate the importance of a sophisticated and ramified tradition of political feminism as a *background*, if not necessarily an inspiration, to a positive sense of women's writing as gender-explicit, but not necessarily limited by gender.

6

Olga Shapir (1850–1916)

OF all the nineteenth-century writers selected for separate analysis in this history, Olga Shapir is in some ways the most 'typical'. She was a prolific writer who published in the thick journals, who enjoyed a considerable reputation in her own lifetime, and was quickly forgotten thereafter. Politically, she was on the left, as women prose writers have generally been, and her work spans both the early phase of 'theoretical realism' in prose, with its 'escape plot', and the later phase of 'empirical realism', with its concentration on treatment in depth rather than at length. Like several other realist writers of her day, she was an active feminist: she was a member of The Russian Women's Mutual Philanthropic Society, a group of moderate feminist stance which was founded in the early 1890s, and which, despite fluctuating membership, continued to play a significant part in campaigns for legal and political reform until 1916. But Shapir's fiction, like the work of other women realists of the 1890s and 1900s, is concerned with feminist issues in an abstract sense, rather than with institutional feminism *per se*. Like many of her contemporaries—Letkova, Dmitrieva, Verbitskaya—she long retained a sentimental affection for the revolutionary politics of the 1870s and 1880s, to which she had devoted one of her longest works, the novel *The Stormy Years*.[1]

However, if Shapir's career is evidence of common concerns in the realist tradition as practised by women writers, it also manifests some of the contradictions within that tradition, providing evidence both of its possibilities and of its dead-ends. In common with many women realists,

---

[1] On Shapir's membership of the Russian Women's Mutual Philanthropy Society, see E. Chebysheva-Dmitrieva, 'Olga Andreevna Shapir: ee zhizn' i deyatel'nost'', *VE* (1916), 10: 375–95; on the society itself, see Linda Edmondson, *Feminism in Russia 1900–1917* (London, 1984) per index. Shapir's *V burnye gody* was published in *RM* during 1906 in 9 parts: *RM* (1906), 1: 1–55; 2: 49–82; 3: 67–108; 4: 57–106; 5: 96–156; 6: 87–116; 7: 1–44; 8: 70–109; 9: 108–49. Most of Shapir's shorter work is collected in her *Sobranie sochinenii* (10 vols.; St Petersburg, 1910). 'The Settlement' is included in *Anthology*.

Shapir wrote far too much, both in terms of the number of stories she produced, and in terms of their length. Undoubtedly, economic pressures were partly to blame for her excessive prolificity; Russian literary journals have traditionally paid their authors by the printer's sheet, and Shapir reveals in her autobiography that she commanded only a moderate rate per sheet even after she had established herself as a writer.[2] But Shapir could also manifest a curious lack of literary self-awareness. In her autobiography (written in about 1907), she describes *The Stormy Years* as the most important book she had written, laments the lack of critical interest on its appearance, and appears convinced that the intervention of an important male critic, Mikhailovsky, might have made matters different.[3] Alas for Shapir's self-judgement: *The Stormy Years* is in fact, for my money at least, one of the most tedious books ever penned by a Russian woman writer. Part of the boredom of reading it may be attributable to censorship matters: the necessity of referring obliquely and indirectly to the activities of the revolutionary group on which Shapir focuses means that much of the narrative is very difficult to follow, eddying in a wayward and unpredictable manner through a series of set-piece confrontation scenes. But the main problem lies in the traditional 'incentive' schematism of the plot. An upright, energetic, self-bettering heroine, Vera, is contrasted with a rich society woman, Baroness Olga, who moves uncertainly through various social and sexual encounters, and toys with philanthropy, rather than being properly involved in politics. The equal, comradely relationships to which Vera aspires have their counter-image in the sexual hypocrisy of the Baroness on the one hand, and of Polina, Vera's aunt, on the other.

To do her justice, Shapir allows both Polina and Olga a greater autonomy than is allowed to counter-heroines in works by earlier writers, such as Gan, Khvoshchinskaya, Soboleva, or Panaeva. Her novel also represents a brave attempt to combine an analysis of revolutionary politics with a critical overview of sexual possibilities (comradeship proves less easy for Vera in practice than in theory). The problems are stylistic rather than conceptual. Shapir's tone is insistently didactic, her handling of the love scenes melodramatic to the point of absurdity: traditional physical markers of intensity, such as fainting, are employed in abundance. The novel displays a fatal lack of self-consciousness or reflection in a *literary* sense, if not always in a political sense.

---

[2] Shapir, ['Avtobiografiya'], F. Fidler (ed.), *Pervye literaturnye shagi* (Moscow, 1911), 55. Shapir here states that her royalty was 'at most 200-250 roubles', presumably per printer's sheet; in order to earn a reasonable middle-class salary of say 3,000 roubles, she would therefore have needed to publish two substantial stories or a novel every year.

[3] Shapir, ['Avtobiografiya'], 54-5.

It is clear from Shapir's remarks in her autobiography that *The Stormy Years* was for her important as an excursion into 'large-scale' themes. Shapir states that it was drawn from her own experience as a fringe member of Sergei Nechaev's revolutionary terrorist group, which perpetrated a number of atrocities in St Petersburg during the early 1870s. She also asserts that she wrote the book in the late 1880s in order to combat the effects of the 'slanderous distortions and caricatures' of the Russian revolutionary movements which had hitherto appeared in print (p. 54)— a statement which implicates, first and foremost, Dostoevsky's famous novel *The Devils*.[4] In reversing Dostoevsky's political attitudes, Shapir does not, however, confront the gender issues raised by his representations (which show women duped by male revolutionaries), but simply voices her opposition to Dostoevsky in the conventional language of Russian radical politics when fighting for the moral high ground. She articulates no independent, feminized tradition of political fiction, a fiction which she can visualize only in terms of true portraits, or caricatures, of the male elect.

The Stormy Years shows Shapir at her feeble, prosy, and didactic worst. But, whilst few of the other texts which she produced in the late 1870s and early 1880s were quite so mind-numbingly verbose, many of them were just as clumsy.[5] Her discovery of feminism in the early 1890s was to allow her to formulate views which were at once more incisive and more wide-ranging; it also gave her fiction a new sharpness and concentration.

For all its earnest efforts to persuade the reader that revolutionary politics were what had really mattered in her life, Shapir's autobiography in reality illustrates how relevant the populist feminism of the 1890s had been to her development as a writer. Like many feminist writings of the 1890s and 1900s, the autobiography is a document with significant omissions: Shapir refers to her marriage only as a union of two committed minds, relating how she single-handedly campaigned to get her husband's permit to reside in St Petersburg reissued, and stressing his role as her first and most important critic, and her chief ideologue; it was he, she asserts, who had maintained in her 'a strong and selfless attitude towards her work' (p. 52). In narrating the events of her early autobio-

---

[4] The Russian term Shapir uses in order to brand earlier treatments of revolutionary terrorism is 'klevetnicheskie iskazheniya i paskvili'. There is a certain amusement for later observers in noting that the hostile remarks about *The Devils* in the Stalinist 1947 edition of *Bol'shaya sovetskaya entsiklopediya* are almost identically phrased.

[5] Other comparable texts by Shapir dating from the 1870s–1880s are 'Na poroge zhizni' (1879), *Povesti i rasskazy* (St Petersburg, 1889), 305–91, and 'Bez lyubvi' (1886), *SS* (10 vols.; St Petersburg, 1910), v. 1–385.

graphy, however, she is more forthcoming, putting together an account which is at once a prehistory of, and a parallel to, her treatments of women's lives in fiction. Her portrait of her parents shows how her father's despotism was a defensive reaction to social inferiority as well as an unthinking repetition of his own upbringing in a serf family. Sensitive to the class resonances of feminism, she is also sensitive to the differences in women's perspectives depending on age; rather than showing herself as an exceptional girl growing up without important female company, she dwells on the influence of her mother and her grandmother on her own intellectual development. Her affectionate portrait of the latter shows particular awareness of the sacrifices made by older women for their younger relatives' sake: describing how her grandmother had acted as midwife and nurse for her daughter's many offspring, Shapir describes her situation as 'a form of *secondary* slavery in the family' (p. 46—her emphasis).

Besides ideological issues, Shapir touches also on problems of aesthetics. Responding to a question about criticism, she shows an informed appreciation of women writers' status in Russian society: her decision to write about women's lives has been made quite deliberately, and she is aware that her concentration on women may have endangered her reputation:

Neither praise nor blame could divert me from my decision never to counterfeit the 'male pen'; I recognized that the only way in which I could make a contribution of any value was to write from a woman's perspective, and to reveal what only women can see in the eternal problem of love, in family relations, and in women's lack of rights in society. The ironic label of 'ladies' *belles-lettres*' so obviously fits the programme which I have just outlined that, I must confess, I have on the whole been surprised when I have *not* encountered it in critical observations on my work.   (p. 54)

But Shapir is concerned to emphasize that literature is something pleasurable, as well as something instructive. She shows the importance in her upbringing not only of her energetic mother, an able estate administrator with a marked intolerance for literary pastimes, but also of her grandmother, an enthusiast for literature whose domestic duties left her no time for writing herself, but who introduced her grandchildren to a broad selection of fiction and poetry. Writing of herself, Shapir represents her character as a synthesis of these two directions, saying that she always found her household duties, such as sewing, particularly conducive to meditation. And the autobiography itself is a demonstration, as well as a declaration, of how she handles material: the careful empiricist emphasizes that she hardly knew her father at first hand, but the fantasist then weaves various family legends about his behaviour into a portrait that, whatever its veracity, is evocative, striking, and displays a pleasant sense of the absurd.

The qualities which characterize Shapir's autobiography were also evident in her writing. She displayed considerable versatility in her choice of topic and genre, and showed that she had a sophisticated sense, both of gender relations in themselves, and of how these might be inflected through class and family position. To these intellectual qualities, Shapir added a flair for shrewd and on occasion humorous psychological portraits, and a sense of appropriate detail; in her best stories a certain linguistic flexibility sometimes sets up interesting ambiguities of perspective, which run contrary to any simplistic didacticism.

Contemporary critics were wont to suggest, rather patronizingly, that 'the depiction of feeling' was Shapir's forte;[6] in the quotation from her autobiography cited earlier, she herself emphasizes the importance of 'love' as the main site of conflict in women's lives. But she cannot in fact be pigeon-holed as a chronicler of sentimental relationships, firstly because marital and extramarital affairs were a significant, but by no means exclusive concern of hers; and secondly because 'love' as such inspired writing which is far from her best. Where emotional attachments are placed in the centre of the narrative, her writing becomes schematic and so excessively insistent in its depiction of emotion that one suspects that the portrayal of feeling actually embarrassed her. 'They Did Not Believe Her' (1898), for example, is a lengthy and clumsily-written story constructed round the classic binary opposition between a high- and a low-minded sister: here, one of the two is a respectable married woman, whilst the other is kept by a man in a vulgar love-nest. After a series of melodramatic scenes in which husband and wife, wife and sister, and husband, wife, and sister confront each other, the dilemma is eventually resolved by the death of the sinner herself (*SS* viii. 1–230). 'The Return' (1892; *SS* iv. 335–440) is a slightly less long-drawn-out but equally high-pitched fiction in which a young woman returns from her higher education courses to the provincial town in which she was brought up, and gradually comes to recognize the barrier that has now been placed between her and her fiancé, a young man from a wealthy merchant family. Any potential interest in the situation is dissipated by the hackneyed terms in which Shapir depicts the wealthy family's *nouveau riche* opulence and tastelessness, and by the soggy-cardboard texture of the love scenes themselves.

The theme of 'love' is much more effectively treated, though, in

---

[6] The remarks on 'the domain of feeling' come from *ES* xxxix. 165; see also Protopopov, 'Zhenskoe tvorchestvo', *RM* (1891), pt. 2, sect. 2, pp. 135–6, which rather crassly argues that Shapir has libertarian views; and M. N. Nikolaeva, 'Prevysprennye geroini', *RB* (1891), 12: 101–64.

Shapir's portraits of women whose lack of any other daily occupation causes them to take an obsessive interest in sexual relationships, a situation of which they may themselves be uncomfortably aware. In the story, 'Indian Summer' (1885; *SS* iv. 1–128), for example, Marya Matveevna, a provincial landowner, is engaged in a desultory attachment to a much younger neighbour, a relationship whose dubious social standing Shapir illustrates by showing the servants engaged in gossip about it. The arrival of her niece Nata, a precocious flirt, provokes such rivalry in Marya Matveevna that she smothers her own doubts about her admirer; on Nata's departure she is left to realize how uncongenial her new lover in fact is. It is not 'love' as such with which Shapir is concerned in this story; rather, she is concerned with how 'love' as an obligatory pastime and ritual illuminates the social difficulties faced by middle-aged women who are not safely married. One of her more attractive aspects as a writer is, indeed, her awareness that women who were not 'exceptional' in the terms of Russian literary convention—who were not exceptionally beautiful or exceptionally gifted, or even exceptionally young—had also to struggle to make their own lives. In 'The Funeral' (1889; *SS* viii. 311–67), for example, she illustrates the bleak fate of a 'vospitannitsa' in middle age. The unfortunate relative being buried has 'put in hours of sweated toil at every birth, christening, wedding, funeral, bankruptcy, illness, journey, etc. etc.'; she has never been heard to talk about herself; worst of all, she has had to laugh dutifully at every single joke told by her relatives. Patronizingly referred to by everyone as 'Katya', she is only discovered at the funeral to have had a name which was more high-flown, not to speak of more symbolic: it was in fact 'Konkordiya'. In 'Veterans and Raw Recruits' (1903; *SS* ix. 379–470), another story narrated with humour as well as an eye for injustice, Shapir accords a fictional treatment to the lot of the grandmother, that 'secondary slavery' which she was later to describe in her autobiography. Two middle-aged sisters, Varya and Marusya, find their settled existence disrupted by the visit of Marusya's son, complete with wife and family. The story shows how these self-elected dependents make impossible demands on Marusya, clamouring for her adulation as well as her practical help, but repudiating all her advice after consultation with their oracle, an up-to-date book on child care, published in 1900. Her sister Varya meanwhile punctuates conversation with amusingly tart remarks, but stands on the dignity of childlessness, and gives Marusya no practical help of any kind. Eventually the exhausted grandmother determines not to waste the rest of her life, and removes herself from the scene, declaring her intention to have the education which she was never able to have before. An 'escape plot', certainly, 'Veterans and Raw Recruits' is transformed both by its choice of a middle-aged woman as heroine and by the fact that ironical scrutiny is applied to all of the characters, even the heroine herself.

These rather lively narratives are only spoilt by Shapir's intrusive anxiety to make the unremarkable remarkable: in 'The Funeral' she introduces a dreary male relative, a gamester and wastrel, who has been helped by Katya, whilst in 'Veterans' Marusya's desire to depart is legitimated by a highly-coloured description of her frustration in which every available emotional cliché is drummed into service.[7]

But if Shapir did not, *pace* contemporary observers, excel in 'the depiction of feeling', and if love as such seldom inspired her, she did show remarkable abilities in the area of fellow feeling or empathy. In her depictions of working-class Russian women, she came into her own as a writer, combining a thoughtful awareness of their immense practical problems with respect for their efforts to overcome these problems, and a sense of the unexpected and the serendipitous in their daily lives. Shapir's portrayals of the 'rich emotional lives' of her upper-class characters often seem stilted; her poverty-stricken, but dry, shrewd, and determined working-class women are drawn with humour and affection. Her didacticism, which in some of her stories is merely a tedious statement of the obvious, is used here to outline difficulties, rather than to offer solutions; a fluidity between authorial narrative and individual perspective adds to the drama of the stories, and also to their ambiguities.

Three stories which manifest these qualities from very different points of view are 'The Settlement' (1893; *SS* vi. 421–71), 'Dunechka' (1904; *SS* vi. 343–417) and 'Avdotya's Daughters' (1898; *SS* vi. 3–156). All three stories are tightly constructed, and written in a style whose deliberate stylistic unevenness adds to their appeal; in all three working-class women are central characters. But the tone and structure of each is quite different.

'The Settlement' is a classic piece of late nineteenth-century critical realism, a study of the Russian poor which reveals how complacent bureaucracy and poor people's own oppression of each other alike conspire to trap the inhabitants of a workers' settlement in deprivation all their lives. The central woman character, Dunya, a peasant woman who takes in dress making and mending, and who is the only wage-earner in her household, struggles to hold her family together and to ensure that her younger brother, Fedya, has the best available education, at a *gimnaziya*, the type of classical high school which acted as a feeder for Russian universities. Dunya's action subjects her to disapproval on all

---

[7] For a painstaking tabulation of Shapir's use of clichés in her writing on love, see Tatiana Antalovsky, *Der russische Frauenroman: exemplarische Untersuchungen* (Munich, 1987). However, Antalovsky's conclusions reveal a total insensitivity to the author's merits in other senses.

sides: from the Tsarist educational administration, eager to deny peasants anything more than a narrowly vocational education, and from her
neighbours, who are at once envious of Fedya's success, and concerned
that the ordinary conventions of behaviour in the settlement should not
be flouted. Dunya's plans for her brother also inspire the resentment of
her father, who feels that his place as 'head of the family' is now
threatened, little though he has done to justify retaining it.

The story ends in catastrophe, as all concerned revenge themselves on
Dunya's brother for his sister's temerity; for Dunya herself, the denouement brings moral collapse. But at no point does Shapir suggest that
Dunya's decision to educate her brother was wrong. The narrative is
prefixed by the Russian proverb, 'Kuda zh chest, koli nechego est', which
may be literally translated as 'whither honour when there's nothing to
eat', and paraphrased as 'morals can't live without bread'. Shapir
demonstrates that, in conditions as bad as those in which Dunya lives,
morality and honour in an absolute sense do in fact disintegrate; the
'right' action is impossible. She displays an understanding of the
function of 'custom' in peasant society which is unclouded by any
sentimental views about 'good old patriarchal ways'. Valentina Dmitrieva, writing from a different political standpoint in her memoir 'Round
the Villages', had attributed the moral decline of the peasantry to the
extinction of the old-style patriarchy; for Shapir, by contrast, 'custom'
signifies the irrational repetition of structures perpetuating discrimination
against women, even when these women are no longer dependent on
their male relatives in an economic sense. At the end of the story, Dunya
can only stand by whilst her father beats her brother: when the family is
dishonoured, it is only the representative of traditional honour, the head
of the patriarchal family, who can act to restore the status quo. Yet the
restoration of the patriarchy also brings down the patriarchy, since the
intervention of the father destroys the son, and hence the future of the
family in a traditional sense.

At this level alone, Shapir's representation of peasant society would be
worthy of note, since it puts into perspective the representations of
Russian villages which appeared in the work of some Bolshevik writers
during the 1920s, whose purpose was to demonstrate that women might
readily be liberated from the peasant family.[8] What is still more
remarkable is Shapir's ability to combine ideological breadth with a
careful and sensitive delineation of the physical fabric of peasant life.
Shapir is intensely aware of the objects and of the domestic rituals with
which bleak poverty is softened. She is interested in everything: the out-

---

[8] On the 1920s prose tradition, see Ch. 9 below.

of-date fashion prints which are pasted on Dunya's door, the patchwork quilt under which Fedya sleeps, the coffee-pot without a spout which the family uses, the stool out of place in the kitchen. She has an eye for the clothes which Dunya would wear at home with her own family (an old dressing-gown that she must pull close round her for decency), and for the more respectable garments which she would put on when visitors called; she observes the desiccated meat which Fedya is given for his special breakfast on the morning of his exams, and the desiccation of Dunya's own body, the symbol and the result of her self-abnegatory campaign.

The world in which Dunya and her family live is solid and material; it does not simply stand for some abstract set of social relations. Here Shapir makes a gesture with significance in terms of the general cultural context. Few Russian turn-of-the-century writers would have included so much fortuitous material in depicting this sort of semi-urbanized peasant milieu; they would, rather, have excluded all but certain key factors, intended to signal the 'vulgarity' of this milieu to the reader.[9] Shapir is more concerned to record how a class-bound society functions than to condemn or to commend its individual members. She includes one small, but telling incident, in which the young aristocrat who has accompanied Fedya home from school and made offers of help to Dunya in a tone of exquisite courtesy loses his temper and shouts at his own coachman.

For all its ethnographical richness, this text is not, however, simply a record of material culture and manners. Dunya and Fedya's imaginative lives, their hopes for the future, are sympathetically recorded. The third-person narrative slips, not always predictably, between a detached, slightly academic, documentary style and an involved, colloquial style. Dialogue and external description are supplemented by the language of gestures; Shapir manages to suggest the iteration of events through description of the present, as well as through flashback; and she unobtrusively conveys the unarticulated tragedy of a woman who can express affection only by bullying and driving her relatives, as she bullies and drives herself.

The second two stories, 'Avdotya's Daughters' and 'Dunechka', are a complete contrast in plot. They deal with the new 'aspirant heroine', the energetic lower-class woman who has determined on a life beyond that which her parents have lived, and whose sense of a well-defined goal differentiates her from the spineless middle-class women also portrayed in the stories. But here too Shapir's sense of exact social location, her

---

[9] For a quite different treatment of a 'vulgar' milieu, see e.g. Smirnova's 'Soldatka' or Chekhov's 'V ovrage'.

interest in the idiosyncracies of behaviour, and her sensitivity to shifting nuances of class and gender allegiance give her writing more subtlety than is often found in feminist fictions of the day. These two stories, whilst quite different in atmosphere to 'The Settlement', display a comparable involvement in their chosen milieu and an equal assurance of technique.

The slighter of the two stories is 'Dunechka', which is set during the long train journey made by a young midwife, the Dunechka of the title, to Port Arthur. There is very little plot, and most of the narrative is in the form of dialogue. From Dunechka's conversation with the other passengers, we learn that she is the daughter of a nanny who has saved up to have her educated. Naïvely self-confident, she has pithy answers ready for the men in the carriage who attempt to ingratiate themselves; she also assumes that other women must all share her history, saying at one point how 'a shiver goes down her spine' when she thinks of how women lived in the past. Another passenger points out that some of them still do live as they lived in the past, much to Dunechka's astonishment (*SS* vi. 373). The sole event in the story is that a bizarre friendship springs up between Dunechka and a nervous woman teacher; eventually Dunechka leaves the train before Port Arthur with this woman, much to the disappointment of one of the young men on the train. What might seem a straightforward fable of solidarity (as Dunechka puts it, 'Let's conquer the world together', *SS* vi. 390) is made interesting by the immediacy of the narrative: we move from Dunechka's perceptions to her speech and back again. Dunechka's unreflective character allows unanswered questions about the precise nature of the attraction between the two women and its likely outcome to hang in the air.

'Avdotya's Daughters' is a longer narrative, with a more ramified structure and a wider time span, which in some ways reads rather like the prehistory of 'Dunechka'. The daughters in question are, in fact, the two daughters of a cook, who are determined to avoid her fate, domestic service. One of them, Sasha, is training as a midwife (an opportunity ensured by a woman philanthropist), and has already established a degree of independence. When a suitor makes overtures, hoping to marry her, she negotiates on her sister Arisha's behalf, and contrives a bargain according to which Arisha will be set up as proprietor of a dressmaker's workshop. Sasha later displays a comparable resolution with her own suitor; her Despina-like machinations are comically counterpointed by the activities of her employer's daughter, a wilting *bourgeoise*, who spends her days fighting off neuralgia and reading novels.

The story is, however, less simple-minded than this bald summary would suggest. The contrast between 'servants' and 'mistresses' is sketched with a light hand, and there is every sensitivity to complicating factors. As children, the employer's daughters and the servant's daughters have played together, and none of them fully understands the alienation and dislike that has now set in. Shapir also shows a considerable command of detail, which she records in various registers. The story allows Arisha's indignation at being sexually harassed by the arrogant young son of the house to be directly appreciated; but other aspects of the household social relations are represented with irony and humour. This, for example, is a scene in which a roast burnt by Avdotya the cook is presented at table:

The boring Sunday lunch was fated to finish with still more misery. As it turned out, the general's wife might as well not have bothered trying to persuade her sick daughter to eat just one tiny piece of the delicious veal; in the event, she did not even taste it herself.

In the kitchen Avdotya, purple in the face with anxiety, flung the veal off the roasting dish on to the table and got to work with a knife on the frightful results of her conversation with Afanasy Ivanovich. A lot of use that was! Stripped of its proper rosy crust, the veal looked dreadfully unappetizing, even comic.

Arisha seized the dish of veal and carried it into the dining-room with a determinedly nonchalant air, as though she had no idea what was in her hand.

This was the last straw for the general's wife. At least ten times Viktor had to hear how, of course, there was no guarantee that if you paid thirty-five kopecks a pound for meat, you'd get anything worth eating. But veal was quite a different story. Pay thirty-five kopecks for that and you were *bound* to get something decent. You could only do one thing wrong with it—burn it, burn it, burn it, that was all! (SS vi. 35–6)

Another, comparably evocative, scene is one in which Sasha decides to stay the night; she and Arisha annexe the bathroom, where they then spend the first part of the night squabbling. Shapir gives a detailed description of how Arisha prepares the room first, in defiance both of her mother and of her employers. The narrative is not only well observed in terms of detail; it also shows every sensitivity to the symbolic resonance of this lower-class encroachment on a bourgeois space, yet gives this symbolism an unexpected twist. The invasion by a servant family of a bathroom would have been seen in a standard nineteenth-century 'upstart narrative' as the pollution of an area associated with cleanliness and purity. Here it becomes an eminently practical appropriation of an area which is normally wasted:

Arisha put leaves from the dining-table on top of the bath. It made an excellent bed. Flat as anything—not like those wretched trunks! She lit a tiny lamp and put it in one corner, then set a basket with a cloth over it on the floor, with a chair in front as a guard. Well, you'd never fit a bedside table in there.

Her mother wasn't best pleased: just wait till madam sees, then she's for it.
'"For" what? Why should she care?'
'So it's your room, is it?'
'Well, where *is* my room? I could do with a room of my own, like people get in some other places. This isn't anyone's room. They just put all junk in it . . .' (*SS* vi. 54–5)

Throughout, Shapir's narrative combines an exquisite sense of the ridiculous with an eye for the serious conflicts of gender and class interest. Separated by the spatial divisions of their environment—the servants are confined to the area around the kitchen, which their employers do not enter—the working-class and bourgeois women characters yet have much in common. All of them perceive marriage as a social necessity, but their society is one in which men are for the most part absent. The working-class women here are better equipped for marriage because they have a clearer appreciation of the likely future; they regard marriage as a contractual arrangement in which terms must be dictated at an early stage.

But unlike some of her contemporaries, Shapir does not represent working-class women's lives as a utopia of self-determination. Sasha's chance to escape life as a servant has come about through a fortuitous act of philanthropy, and the ripples of liberation can spread only so far: when she and Arisha escape, their mother is left in service.

The conditions which bind and entrap women on both sides of the baize door are, like the separations of class, represented metonymically. The employer's daughter and the cook's daughter are alike encased in corsets; both suffer the physical tribulations of 'headaches' (probably the nearest a Russian woman writer of this generation can get to mentioning the menstrual function). Both sets of women suffer extra stress when the son of the house visits: his mother feels compelled to organize special meals, the cook has to put herself out to create these meals; if Arisha endures sexual harassment, Katya suffers a different type of harassment at her brother's hands—being treated as though she had no brain.

Shapir's story represents gender and class relations as at once variable and inflexible. She has no illusions about the nature of class discrimination: unlike most Russian realist narratives dealing with servants, this story does not represent them as greedy and perfidious go-getters, or as hapless dupes. 'Avdotya's Daughters' is one of the few Russian texts to analyse the question of domestic labour with any subtlety. Certainly, there are limitations even in Shapir's analysis: the inevitability of domestic service as such remains unquestioned because of the 'escape plot's' inexorable onward drive, its concentration on individual and exceptional heroines. The fate of Avdotya herself, forever confined to her kitchen, is passed over in silence. But 'Avdotya's Daughters' is, for all that, an illustration of how the late nineteenth-century realist tradition, permeated by a far more sophisticated concept of the 'woman question' than the fiction of earlier generations, was able to build on early nineteenth-century tradition. It, and 'The Settlement' (which is in some senses a companion piece, a tragedy where 'Avdotya's Daughters' is a comedy) also illustrate that Shapir, who at her worst was an impossibly earnest, prolix, dogmatic, and yet incoherent writer, was also capable of producing well-conceptualized, technically accomplished, and impassioned problem pieces. These two stories are amongst the most significant contributions made by Russian women writers to the late nineteenth-century realist tradition. They indicate how much has been lost with the systematic effacement and obliteration of the Russian feminists' achievements from literary history and from artistic practice.[10] With knowledge of this tradition, the thematically and technically comparable (though ideologically less sophisticated) feminine version of critical realism which developed in the 1960s would have been able to build on history, rather than repeating it, and could have taken heart from the achievements of the past, rather than succumbing to anxious doubts about the necessary inferiority of women's writing.

[10] Shapir's feminism is not mentioned e.g. by Uchenova, the editor of *Tol'ko chas*, who instead simply defends the author against charges of being a 'petit-bourgeois writer' (p. 584).

7

Nadezhda Teffi (1872–1952)

Tragedy is only imperfectly realised comedy.

(Patrick Kavanagh)

HUMOUR, in the end-directed form of satire, had always held an important place in Russian female prose writers' battery of techniques. Some texts had displayed a command of satire rising to virtuoso levels: the rogues' gallery of credulous grandparents and hypocritical parents in Panaeva's story 'The Talnikov Family' is delineated with a hatred more unregulated even than that which Saltykov-Shchedrin lavished on his characters in his vitriolic chronicle *The Golovlev Family*. Panaeva allows her characters of the older generation no reconciliation amongst themselves or with their offspring, not even a *rapprochement* of the gruesome and maudlin kind which eventually overcomes the surviving Golovlevs. Effective as the feminine satiric tradition was, however, it was in one sense inhibitive: the consensus amongst women writers that humour best served the mockery of convention had been an obstacle to the development of another possible understanding of 'humour': as a domain allowing space to fantasy and to a sense of absurdity for its own sake. The first writer whose work could be said to manifest a humorous tendency in this sense was Nadezhda Buchinskaya, née Lokhvitskaya, who under the pen-name 'Teffi' produced poetry, memoirs, and humorous plays, as well as the dozens of short stories for which she is best known.

By no means all Teffi's work, to be sure, is 'humorous' in the meaning which I have just given the term. Her first publications were lyric poems; when she began her literary career in earnest, this was as a writer who was very much a satirist in the teleological sense, contributing short anecdotal narratives and *feuilletons* (satirical essays) to *Satirikon*, a left-wing humorous magazine set up during the post-1905 deregulation of censorship, and to other organs of the kind. When the Bolsheviks closed down *Russkoe slovo*, the newspaper on which she was then working, she retreated behind White lines, before being forced to emigrate; from 1920 she made her life in Paris, where she continued her writing career as a sharp-eyed chronicler of the foibles of *émigré* life. All her life Teffi maintained a journalist's productivity; even in old age she was still one of the emigration's most hard-working and successful writers.[1]

Sometimes the strain of weekly deadlines is evident in Teffi's work; the same jokes occasionally get repeated, and the brevity of her narratives could make them perfunctory just as easily as it rendered them explosive or pithy. Some of the jokes, too, have dated, with their flavour of an age when mention of, say, 'bloomers', or extramarital 'nooky', was enough to bring the house down. Her stories were said by Mikhail Zoshchenko to have been favourite reading for Russians going on long train journeys; but in fact her work gains from being dipped in to, rather than read end to end. The best of her stories, though, will bear being reread many times. In these, her insistence that laughter was a fundamental characteristic dividing 'human beings' from 'humanoids' comes to the fore, often taking her narratives in unexpected directions.[2]

The specific quality of Teffi's humour has been described by several commentators as 'laughter through tears', a phrase which might suggest a bad case of post-Gogolian sentimentality, of the sort that was expected fodder in early twentieth-century fiction magazines at Christmas or Easter time. Teffi herself took issue with just such expectations in 'The Festive Season':

The question of how to decorate Christmas trees and what ornaments to put on them was settled a very long time ago—several centuries or more, I should think.

Everyone knows what to buy.

A star for the very top, which hangs there so a lady authoress can write a story about a poor little boy whose grandmother promises to buy a star to put on the Christmas tree. But of course the grandmother hasn't the slightest intention of

---

[1] For accounts of Teffi's biography, see Elizabeth Neatrour, 'Miniatures of Russian Life at Home and in Emigration: The Life and Works of N. A. Teffi', Ph.D. thesis (University of Indiana, 1972); cf. the same author's intro. to Teffi, *Nostal'giya: rasskazy, vospominaniya* (Leningrad, 1989) (cited below as N), and D. D. Nikolaev in Teffi, *Yumoristicheskie rasskazy* (Moscow, 1990) (cited below as YR). Though these two recent editions are convenient and representative selections, there is no complete, or even substantial, edition of the works of Teffi, and the publication history of her writing is extremely complicated, since her huge popularity meant that her works ran into many editions; sometimes the same collections appeared several times under different titles. For a detailed bibliography, see Neatrour, 'Miniatures of Russian Life', 372–81. Teffi's story, 'Walled Up', and her farce, *The Woman Question*, appear in *Anthology*.

[2] See for example 'The Siding', mentioned below; some of Teffi's stories about servants, such as 'Pokayannoe', YR 28–30, also have a quaint creakiness to a modern reader. Zoshchenko's remark is cited by Nikolaev in YR 3. For Teffi's views on humour, see 'Chelovekoobraznye', YR 149–53.

doing as she said. The little boy dies and the grandmother learns her lesson and stops telling fibs. (*YR* 229–30)

Teffi did turn increasingly to 'straight' stories in her later years; many of the pieces written in emigration are of this type. But even her 'straight' manner was not precisely tearful: she is more concerned to excoriate cruelty than to dwell on its effects. This is clear, for example, in one of her Paris stories, 'Huron', whose plot has a superficial resemblance to the 'Christmas story' that had been the subject of her mockery. A lonely Russian boy's greatest wish is to possess a set of cards with pictures of American cowboys on them; his guardian promises to get them from a friend in the States, but never makes any attempt to carry out her promise. Unlike the 'lady novelist's' effort, however, Teffi's story does not exploit the sentimental possibilities of the boy's situation; the reader is left to take his misery for granted, and the poverty of imagination to which he has been reduced is described without any softening, as his guardian contemplates the pathetic group of documents which makes up his 'holy of holies' (*N* 205–9). An earlier story, 'Walled Up', deals with the relations of two middle-aged women, a stout, bossy landlady of German origin and her shabby-genteel lodger (*YR* 83–90). The former is coarse, unpleasant, and tippling, but the latter excites as great a contempt for her stuck-on eyebrows, her self-sacrificing table-manners, her pathetic attempts at polite conversation, and her wretched efforts to attract attention through a show of self-mortification. At the end of the story, Teffi sums up the lodger's feeble assertion of personality through self-destructive frailty by describing how the tear-soaked handkerchief which she has placed on a chair to dry flutters in the faint breeze that edges round the blank wall outside the window. In its dispassionate dissection of wretchedness, Teffi's manner looks forward to Katherine Mansfield's story 'The Daughters of the Late Colonel'.[3] In a national context she does indeed resemble Gogol; not, however, because of her lachrymose sympathy for her victims, but because she regards them with the ruthless eye of a Christian moralist. She follows the Gogol of *The Overcoat*, rather than the Gogol of *Old World Landowners*. In her memoirs of the White evacuation from Russia, Teffi describes her farewell visit to the Lavra and to the cathedrals in Kiev, where an icon of the 'stern Byzantine princess' St Irene, encrusted with precious stones, catches her eye (*N* 350). Her own practice as a moralist was informed by an equal severity; like St Irene, she turned a jewelled gaze on human folly.

[3] Katherine Mansfield, 'The Daughters of the Late Colonel' (1922), *Selected Stories* (Oxford, 1981), 252–72.

'Humour' in Teffi should, therefore, certainly not be understood as detached serenity, whether or not alternating with indulgent pathos: in several important ways this humour functioned as a weapon. Yet it was a weapon directed to different ends from those which had been selected in the provincial tales of her predecessors. In Teffi humour is not a technique adopted in order to illustrate the uniqueness of an outstanding heroine; rather than enhancing one kind of literary representation, it introduces a shifting set of perspectives in order to question the very basis of representation, at once enhancing, and undermining, the authority of a writerly utterance.

By adopting a humorous, trivializing tone, Teffi is able to establish her 'right' to discuss mainstream political subjects whilst employing a feminine persona. Her stories include studies of court procedure, underground politics, and political journalism, none of which is treated with any more reverence than such obvious 'feminine' subjects as the purchase of clothing or the organization of a home. The 'Lady Translator', the well-born but unemployable young girl who decides to set up as a translator, purchases two dictionaries, and steams ahead, grammar and common sense flung to the winds, has her counterpart in 'Scipio Africanus', the jack-of-all-trades journalist who can turn his hand to theatre criticism (without bothering to attend the plays on which he writes), but is equally happy working as a lobby correspondent, or as a weighty social commentator whose every other article consists of a piece correcting the 'trifling factual errors' in his article written a week previously (*YR* 247–50, 131–5). In 'The Importance of a Political Education' Teffi directs her mockery at the self-deceptions of anti-Tsarist politics, portraying an old revolutionary who is unable to discard the defensive strategies of his youth, though the political world is now different, and who displays an astonishing incomprehension of what is going on around him:

Whilst awaiting his turn [in the bank] my uncle began saying the strangest things about himself, speaking in an unnaturally loud voice:

'I won that money in my club, my dear,' he said, 'I was at the table for days and nights on end. As a matter of fact, I won a good deal more, but I drank the rest away. I may be putting this in my account for the time being, but I'll spend the rest on drink too, you see if I don't.'

'But Uncle!' I gasped. 'You never play cards, and you don't drink either!'

He tugged at my sleeve fiercely and muttered in my ear:

'Quiet, will you! I'm only saying it for *their* benefit! It's all meant for *them*; when they hear that they'll decide I must be an honest fellow!'   (*YR* 69–70)

Teffi's portrait, topical in its own day, is yet of more than immediate significance: the behaviour of some former dissidents in the post-Soviet period is not too different from what she delineates here. And this modern parallel also helps one to understand how provocative the impertinent view which she takes of underground political activists must have been its own time.

The contrast of 'weighty' subjects and 'light' tone is reinforced by Teffi's commentary on the authorial function, which may be direct or indirect. Satire directed at linguistically incompetent females (as in the cases of the 'lady authoress' and the 'translatoress' mentioned earlier) is used to offset, and heighten, the competence of an author whose peculiarly acute linguistic awareness is one of her most striking features. 'Domestic Harmony', for example, portrays a family group for whom 'conversation' consists in the endless iteration of private obsessions in monologue; awareness of other people in the room is limited to a sense of when they have finished speaking, so that another tirade may begin (*YR* 59–62). In 'The Siding' (*YR* 117–26), an otherwise rather dated farce about a young wife who, after a series of improbable events, is caught in a railway carriage with another man by her railway engineer husband, the use of linguistic clichés is well observed. As the door of the carriage opens and the wife sees her husband, '"Dinner's ready," she announced, for some unfathomable reason'.

In all the above stories, there is a direct and obvious polarization between the handicaps of language suffered by fictional characters, and the linguistic virtuosity of the narrator. But Teffi's use of humour can also have other, more ambiguous, effects. It works as a strategy of evasion, as much as of self-assertion. In the autobiography which she wrote for Fidler, for example, she responded to his set of bread-and-butter questions in a characteristically oblique way.[4] Where most other writers (for example, Olga Shapir) had used the questions as a skeleton structure for a full autobiography, Teffi answers them in a series of truncated sentences, as if she were filling in an official form. She parodies an unimaginative and literal-minded exercise by being still more strait-laced and literal-minded herself. But her dryness is interrupted by flashes of eccentricity. To the question, 'Have other writers ever published stories with the same plots as yours', she replies: 'Yes, my plots have quite frequently coincided with those of various works by foreign authors. For instance, I was just about to finish a play on the same subject as *Elga*, when Hauptman pre-empted me. But luckily my texts have usually managed to sneak into print before their twins have.'[5] By contrast, Fidler's other authors had either ignored the question, no doubt suspect-

---

[4] F. Fidler (ed.), *Pervye literaturnye shagi* (Moscow, 1911), 203–5.
[5] Ibid. 204.

ing *lèse-majesté*, or had negated it indirectly and defensively by emphasizing their early sense of their own *particular* talents. Teffi, though,
jokingly raises the possibility that authorship in an individual sense
might not even exist, and represents the creative process as six plots in
search of an author. Elsewhere in the autobiography, she again suggests
the fortuitous nature of talent by stressing that her parents had made no
great efforts to encourage her and her sisters' individual personalities.

In the same way, Teffi's intrusion into her own narratives can have
diverse, and even contradictory, results. If in some stories it acts as a form
of self-justification, asserts the right to comment, in others it questions
such self-justification, denies the right to comment. Many other critical
realists had placed themselves at an obvious social distance from the
scenes which they described, seeing the writer or narrator's non-involve-
ment in production processes as a central part of his or her right to
analyse them. In Chekhov's 'Case Notes', for example, a doctor visits a
factory; his sense of how exploitation fuels luxury is clarified by his total
alienation from that luxury, which he sees as tasteless, unnecessary,
vulgar.[6] A fundamentally different standpoint is adopted in Teffi's
'Tactless Gaffes' (YR 292–5), which represents a similar social polarization. Whilst the upper classes have only the haziest ideas about new
technology, their employees and social inferiors are up with the latest
developments, argues a colonel at a party attended by the woman
narrator. How tactless, everyone at the party agrees. On returning at the
end of the evening, which has been spent on games of roulette and the
singing of popular songs, as well as on desultory chat, the narrator
discovers that her own servant has been out playing a thoroughly
intellectual parlour game. How tactless, is the narrator's automatic and
private response, a response that ends the story. Every act of analysis, it is
illustrated, is part of the social processes which it seeks to criticize, and
imbued with the stereotypical and lazy modes of thought which those
processes engender.

Such shifts in standpoint are paralleled by a process in which imputed
autobiographical elements are communicated or withheld in the narratives. Teffi always adopts a friendly, conversational manner; she may
point to experiences that the reader is likely to share, often beginning a
story with such a phrase as 'we all know'. In some stories she
offhandedly introduces an anecdote of her own childhood, and this, too,
is done with the air of a reference to familiar details. But her apparently
unstudied frankness has strict and well-defined limits. Teffi's two
autobiographies (her note for Fidler and her memoir on the evacuation)

---

[6] Chekhov, 'Sluchai iz praktiki'.

are documents which are markedly lacking in personal information. The latter text is preceded by a note warning the reader of what is to come:

If the author does happen to talk about himself now and then, that is not at all because he thinks the reader might be interested in his own person, but only because he himself took part in the adventures here described and himself had these experiences of certain people and events; and if this pivot, this living soul, were to be removed from the story, then death would overtake it.   (*N* 268)

Teffi slides from metaphor to metaphor, each expressing a different view of the writer. 'He' [*sic*] is an actor ('took part in'), an observer ('had these experiences'), a structural device of a rather mechanical kind ('this pivot'), but at the same time something with its own vital existence ('living') and spirituality ('soul'). The nuances of this abstract definition are reflected in the diversity of Teffi's practice in the memoir itself. There are occasional confidences. One St Petersburg editor, we are told, has been the only friend brave enough to visit her during a period when she was unhappy, and to enquire what the cause for her misery might be. It is strongly hinted that this cause was an unhappy love-affair, but the topic is dropped immediately. And Teffi's reticence on other events of an emotional significance is remarkable: she does not refer to her marriage, to her children, or to her estrangement from her first husband.[7] The manner of the memoirs is likewise both engaging and disconcertingly anonymous: Teffi even avoids using her own name, referring to herself as 'so and so' ('"Are you so-and-so," she asked me',) rather than by name.

Teffi's vexed and ambiguous attitude to subjectivity underlines the difficulties of reading her stories simply as 'satires', or even as pieces in which unreflective and pleasurable laughter is followed by the painful recognition of underlying social or metaphysical truths. Several of her stories in fact point to the insidiously corrupting effects of didactic fictions. In one story, for example, she illustrates the necessary futility of improving works, pointing to the non-communication between German children's books and Russian children as readers:

Take the story about little Fritz, for example, who did thousands of good deeds, more, even, than the most perfect Buddha might manage. At the end of the story Fritz goes down the street and all the passers-by look at him and say, 'Here comes dear kind little Fritz.' That's it.

When Russian children read a story like that, and see how miserably rewarded good deeds are, they decide that they really might as well go on being just as badly behaved as they were before.   (*YR* 232)

As this story suggests, Teffi regards communication failure not only as

---

[7] On Teffi's reticence, see also Neatrour in *YR* 4.

an index of impropriety, but also as a mental activity allowing an escape from what is predictable or expected. The hiatuses of meaning give space to the imagination. This idea is perhaps most fully demonstrated in the absurd tale, 'When the Crayfish Whistles', which concerns a boy whose whole life has been determined by a misunderstanding in childhood:

'So when the crayfish whistles, will we get anything we want?'
   'Hmmph!'
   'When *will* he whistle?'
   Petya's father was about to explain, but then he remembered that it is a father's duty to be strict. He slapped Petya lightly on the neck and said, 'Time you were in bed, piglet!'   (YR 298)

In ordinary usage, 'when the crayfish whistles' is a cliché meaning much the same as 'pigs might fly'. But when this humdrum meaning is denied the boy, he devotes his life to the search for 'a whistling crayfish'. Eventually one of his descendants succeeds in breeding the creature, which, though it looks like 'a river boatman from the South West, with pop eyes, a thick moustache and a quelling gaze', proves to have magical powers: it has, in fact, the most dangerous skill of granting wishes, not of the proper and decent kind that may be formally and ritually uttered in threes, but of the subversive and impossible sort that can never be spoken at all.

   A good many of Teffi's stories, like 'When the Crayfish Whistles', are concerned with childhood, whose appeal lies precisely in its unanalytical, and therefore endlessly imaginative, view of the world. Reading, Teffi emphasizes, is for children a voyage of exploration, rather than a search for discovery. Her story 'Books' juxtaposes the dull categories which hamper the adult reader with the child's excitement over words:

'Yes,' one says. 'The end is a little over-extended. Such-and-such a chapter seems to add little, such-and-such a character could do with some trimming. The engineer's speeches are very well executed.'
   And once more one discusses, in still more detail, what is 'executed' and how.
   How impossibly boring it all is.
   But I remember a time when I didn't even know that books *were* 'executed'.   (N 79)

Having digressed to describe the remembered childhood pleasure of a juicy blot squelching out of her pen as she wrote, Teffi then goes back to the topic of imaginative reading, dwelling especially on the delights of misunderstanding:

I remember an illustration: a man standing with his arms folded. The caption read: 'Paganelle meditated'.
   Instead of 'meditated', in my haste I read 'medidiated'. For a long time I

pondered what this might mean. It was obvious it could only be some very complicated, difficult, and even slightly scary activity. (N 80–1)

The importance of verbal invention is also brought out in 'A Substitute for Political Conversation' (YR 38–42) which describes a silly and, so soon as one has learnt of it, rather addictive game of word substitution, made up of questions like this: 'Why dog-ma and not cat-ma? Why trans-mog-rification and not trans-mutt-rification? Why In-dia and not Out-dia?', and so on.

Linguistic anarchy often went further than such harmless jokes might suggest. Teffi was quite capable of insisting that disorder and irrationality were states which were both inevitable and admirable. 'Causes and Effects' (YR 282–6), for example, insists that there *is* no logical link of consequentiality, and that an object which sets off from A on course for C may just as well end up at Y, or for that matter R, by a series of processes each of which is itself unpredictable. Other stories illustrate Teffi's capacity to enjoy the deplorable. There is a flavour of conventional intellectual snobbery in some stories, such as 'Nanny's Story about a Horse's Head' (YR 75–9), or 'They're Singing' (YR 140–1), in which she describes the 'degeneration' of turn-of-the-century popular culture; yet regret about declining standards is mingled with an insidious enjoyment of the low. In the former tale, a mother earnestly boasts to her tea-time guests that she has now tracked down a Russian nanny for her children, who will be able to expand their imagination with 'proper' Russian fairy-tales. Tiptoeing to the nursery, the guests hear this nanny engaged in narrating 'The Story of the Horse's Head', a tale in which the absurd (a peasant family adopts a talking horse's head, and it then insists on marrying a princess) is as exquisitely combined with topical *realia* (the princess has a skirt with three ruffles trimmed in corduroy) as in any of Teffi's own stories. Similarly, 'Conversations' (YR 268–71), whilst affecting to criticize the 'meaninglessness' of many Russian street exchanges, actually makes it clear that these exchanges are a kind of art form in their own right.

Teffi's enjoyment of language at many levels emerges also in her gift for literary parody or pastiche. 'Observations on the Theory of Flirting' (YR 145–7), for example, is a burlesque of the popular-sociological commentary, a turgid genre much favoured by Russian essayists from the 1870s right up to the present. Other pieces, however, mockingly imitate more directly 'literary' material. Very well read in European literature, Teffi often, as she had gently hinted in her 'Autobiography', ran ahead of fashion in Russia itself. 'French Novels' (1910; YR 271–4) parodies the contemporary fashion for pre-pubescent female heroines in erotic novels, which was not to reach Russian literature until rather later; 'The Fatal Leap' (1910), which is dedicated to 'Hermann Bang and all the other authors writing stories about acrobats who die for love', prefigures the circus motifs which were to enjoy vast popularity in Russian literature from about 1912 until the mid-1930s (*YR* 101–6). Perhaps the most significant of Teffi's parodies, though, were her self-consciously stylized lyric poems, whose diverse and contradictory heroines, from pining nuns to dictatorial princesses, exploited the post-Symbolist direction in women's writing as effectively as did the now much better-known work of Akhmatova or of 'Cherubina de Gabriak'.[8]

The intersection of language as parody and as the medium of invention was demonstrated rather differently in Teffi's hilarious play *The Woman Question* (*YR* 372–89). This purports to be the dream of a young woman of feminist inclinations who, after a family argument about whether women should have the right to social and political equality, lies on a sofa, falls asleep, and has a vision of Russian society with all the gender roles precisely reversed. Women colonels, women professors, and women civil servants nag their compliant and stay-at-home husbands, whilst their rebellious sons mutter darkly about liberation for men. We see the women colonels and professors pinching maids' bottoms, patronizing their menfolk, boring them with pompous moral speeches, and relating greasy anecdotes. By showing powerful women who indulge in awful 'male' behaviour, Teffi is able to demonstrate effectively that women's role as the arbiters of morality depends on their subjugation. But the play cannot be glossed simply as an ironic vision of the results which would be likely to derive from crudely egalitarian theories of women's liberation. It is also concerned with linguistic invention, and with the limits of linguistic invention. The 'colonelesses' and 'professoresses' speak and act in a way that reproduces masculine clichés of behaviour and language, drinking champagne from top-boots, and speaking of 'gentlemen of easy virtue'; but there are subtle differences, too, since a degree of linguistic skewing to the masculine remains inescapable. The son of the house can talk of 'the man question', and say that he has heard that it is now 'possible, would you believe, for men to become lady doctors'; but even in this looking-glass world the male servant has to say, 'I'm working as a chamber maid', because the coinage 'chamber man' is impossible. Clothes, too, retain in part their original signifying function: the 'chamber maid' wears a frilly apron, but keeps on 'his' trousers.

Both neologistic and conventional, the language of Teffi's play reflects

---

[8] Teffi, *Sem' ognei* (St Petersburg, 1910); see also Ch. 5 above.

the limits of contemporary views on androgyny; but in her insistence that the 'woman question' had a linguistic dimension she was a rare transitional figure between realism and modernism. A good deal more politically conscious than most women writers involved in the 'new arts' movements, she at the same time did not share the realist view that literature was necessarily and invariably a vehicle for political concerns; instead, she emphasized all the dangers of using literature as an omnibus for such concerns. An apparently serious issue, such as the prevalence of murders committed out of jealousy, is handled in a story which appends the clinching 'human interest' anecdote of journalistic sociology to a sententious introduction. Concluding her tale of woe, the narrator observes: 'How did I know so many details about this sad event? I made the whole thing up' (*YR* 242). The many realist writers who pretended to a preternatural omniscience, whilst insisting on narrative 'truth', have the contradictions of their practice exposed.

Teffi was, however, also intelligent enough not to dwell too much on her own complexity. The pleasure of reading her work derives partly from its being apparently so straightforward and effortless. Her technique is defamiliarization in the most fundamental sense of the word: she takes a standard genre or literary strategy, and twists it in many directions, whilst at the same time encouraging the reader to revel in the pleasure of the apparently familiar. Similarly, she is able to combine an impression of winning candour with a demonstration of the fact that we are familiar with authors in an intellectual, formal, and linguistic, and not in a biographical sense. Though she was in no sense a trivial writer, or an advocate of unthinking hedonism, her work is so readable that she might be (and has been) mistaken for both. But it was her considerable achievement to create her own imaginative and lastingly enjoyable variant of modernist prose, presented in the ephemeral form of the anecdote.

8

Anna Akhmatova (1889–1966)

THOUGH her poetry owed much to the Symbolist myth of the poet as prophet, Anna Akhmatova confounded the saying that a prophet is without honour in his own country. In Russia, and in the Russian-speaking world beyond Russia's borders, she is unquestioningly acknow-ledged to be the most outstanding *poetessa* in the whole of Russia's history. But her status is far higher than 'poetessa', a word whose denigratory flavour she herself fully appreciated, would suggest. In the last years of her life and especially after her death, Akhmatova's contemporaries have honoured her as a heroine in the full original Greek sense of the word (meaning a woman of semi-divine powers), and have accorded her much of the reverence given a Christian saint. Later generations of poets have celebrated her as a muse, a celebration that has usually had nothing to do with pallid neo-classical convention, and everything to do with a mystical cult of poetry and of the poet. More remarkable still (since there are, after all, many Russian national heroines) is that she has been recognized as a major poet without any gender qualification. She and Marina Tsvetaeva are the two female denizens of the twentieth-century Russian Parnassus, and in many ways Akhmatova's place there is more secure than Tsvetaeva's. Tsvetaeva's life and poetry have aspects which are both threatening and embarrassing for Russian readers; such aspects are absent both from Akhmatova's own writings, and from the accounts of her life given by others.[1]

The fact that Akhmatova's official myth accords with propriety is not the only reason for her stature. Her poetry, which is for the most part less complex in thematic, lexical, and metrical terms than Tsvetaeva's mature work, is accessible to a much larger readership. Her early love

---

[1] One of the most illuminating inductions into Akhmatova's status in Russia is Pamela Davidson and Isia Tlusty's collection of poems dedicated to her, *Posvyashchaetsya Akhmatovoi* (Tenafly, NJ, 1991).

poetry has been enjoyed since its first publication by a broad, and overwhelmingly female, audience which includes schoolgirls and provincial teachers as well as aspiring poet(esse)s. The breadth of interest in Akhmatova can be sensed when one visits the museum dedicated to her life. Opened in 1989, and occupying part of the communal flat next to the Sheremetev palace in which she lived for some twenty years, it contains an eccentric assemblage of personal possessions, paintings of the poet, books belonging to her and to her various husbands, as well as manuscripts. The character of its visitors is equally varied: Akhmatova specialists are heavily outnumbered by amateurs, who include factory workers as well as members of the intelligentsia. Still more remarkably, amateurs of Akhmatova's work have also been responsible for the creation of a second, rival, museum at Tsarskoe Selo, and also for the compilation of an Akhmatova encyclopedia.[2]

Whilst Akhmatova is known to a broad section of the Russian public as a 'poetess of love', or as a chronicler of the Terror, a quite different audience, this time dominated by men, at the same time perpetuates a contradictory academic interpretation of her work. Sub-texts have been hunted down and cultural background laboriously established: Akhmatova's understanding of folklore and classical literature, her readings of (among many others) Dante, Pushkin, Annensky, Mandelstam, Pasternak, have all been extensively researched. The volume of scholarly material dedicated to her poetry is hardly inferior to the volume of material devoted to, say, Pasternak. No other Russian woman poet has ever been studied in such depth.[3] Nor, for the time being, is any likely to be studied in such depth, since the consequence of accepting Akhmatova's absolute authority is to take on trust her view, expressed in a barbed epigram, that she was herself the Alpha and Omega of poetry by Russian women:

---

[2] The Akhmatova museum opened for the poet's centenary in 1989; it is located in the house on the Fontanka where Akhmatova lived in the flat of her *de facto* husband Nikolai Punin from 1926 until 1952. My informant on other Akhmatoviana was Wendy Rosslyn.

[3] On the responses of ordinary women readers to Akhmatova, see the occasional accounts given of her correspondence by Lidiya Chukovskaya in her *Zapiski ob Anne Akhmatovoi* (2 vols.; Paris, 1976–80; vol. i repr.; Moscow, 1989). Academic material on Akhmatova is now quite extensive. A good guide to the secondary material in English is Garth Terry, *Anna Akhmatova in English: A Bibliography 1889–1966–1989* (Nottingham, 1989). Wendy Rosslyn's *The Speech of Unknown Eyes: Akhmatova's Readers on her Poetry* (2 vols.; Nottingham, 1990), is a well-annotated recent collection of essays. See also Michael Basker, 'Recent Akhmatoviana: Some Post-Centennial Publications and Prospects', *Scottish Slavonic Review*, 17 (1991), 168–72. On Akhmatova as a 'woman poet', see specifically Rosslyn, *The Prince, the Fool and the Nunnery: The Religious Theme in the Early Poetry of Anna Akhmatova* (Avebury, 1984); Sharon Leiter, *Akhmatova's Petersburg* (Cambridge, 1983); T. V. Tsiv'yan, 'Antichnye geroini—zerkala Akhmatovoi', *Russian Literature* 7–8 (1974), 103–19. The only general biography in English is still Amanda Haight, *Anna Akhmatova: A Poetic Pilgrimage* (Oxford, 1976).

Могла ль Биче словно Дант творить,
Или Лаура жар любви восславить?
Я научила женщин говорить,
Но Боже! кто их замолчать заставит?

Could Dante's Bice sing as well as he,
Or Petrarch's Laura praise the heat of love?
I was it who taught women how to speak,
But God! who'll stop their mouths?[4]

Akhmatova effaces both the past and the future of women's writing (not only Russian, but Western as well). Hers is the only voice, others are only echoes, and unimpressive echoes at that (women cannot 'sing' or 'praise', but must use the ordinary language of 'speech'). She at once approves the use of force to silence women—an act against which she had vehemently protested when it was applied to her—and herself commands that silence.

A further effect of Akhmatova's pre-eminence has been to make her versions of particular subjects canonical, even where these are actually indifferent pieces of writing. Her three portraits of biblical heroines, 'Rachel', 'Lot's Wife', and 'Michal' (*SP* 159–62) are meandering narratives fossilized by the use of language which is tortuously archaic and visually inexact: Lot's wife, for example, becomes a pillar of 'transparent' salt, her 'swift feet' (diluted Homer) 'grow into' the ground; seven years are 'as seven dazzling days' for Rachel's admirers; Laban's younger daughter 'groans and tears her fluffy plaits' in agony. Unlike Kuzmina-Karavaeva's shimmering reimagination of biblical legend in 'Ruth', these portraits carry the dusty smell of the Scripture class on them; yet they are reprinted and earnestly scrutinized, whilst Kuzmina-Karavaeva's work is not. The emphasis on Akhmatova as *the* martyr of Stalinism has also diverted attention from the sufferings of such other women poets as Anna Barkova and Olga Berggolts (both of whom were incarcerated during the purges), or Vera Merkureva and Sofiya Parnok (both of whom were reduced to total physical and psychological exhaustion by being forced to work the treadmill of hack translation). So far from being the only female victim of Soviet cultural politics, Akhmatova was in fact one

---

[4] Akhmatova, 'Epigramma', *Stikhotvoreniya i poemy* (Leningrad, 1976), 205. (There is still no definitive academic edition of Akhmatova's work; though subject to censorship cuts, this edition is both easier to use than, and in some ways textologically superior to, more inclusive editions such as *Sochineniya* (3 vols.; Munich, 1967–73), or the recent 2-vol. *Sochineniya* (Moscow, 1986), or *Sobranie stikhotvorenii* (Moscow, 1989). For convenience's sake it has therefore been cited here; citations henceforth in text as *SP*.) All Akhmatova's poetry is now available in English in *Complete Poems*, trans. Judith Hemschemeyer, ed. Roberta Reeder (2 vols.; Somerville, Mass., 1990); earlier translations include *Selected Poems*, trans. Richard McKane (Newcastle upon Tyne, 1989). Akhmatova's poems 'Sister, I have come to take your place', 'Solitude', and 'Fear turns objects over', as well as her essay 'Memories of Aleksandr Blok' appear in *Anthology*.

amongst many victims, though her greater fame has made her ill-treatment more notorious.

This is not said in order to belittle Akhmatova's work. To attempt 'cutting her down to size' (and what size?) would be a pointless exercise. But no poet is well served by the sort of unquestioning reverence which Akhmatova's work is now accorded; it is detrimental to the understanding even of her own biography and writing, let alone to the study of literary history in a general sense. We need to understand that Akhmatova's elevation was not natural and inevitable; it was the result of a process of self-creation and mythologization. And this in turn depended, not on her invention of a literary history for women, but on her expert synthesis and reimagination of possibilities already explored by other women poets, as well as on her reshaping of important texts by male authors in which women were represented. We shall see that other women, *pace* Akhmatova, in fact taught her a great deal about how to speak; she owes as much to the feminine tradition that she disowned or suppressed in her later work, as to the masculine tradition that she, by means of references to Dante, Pushkin, Mandelstam, and Pasternak, so prominently celebrated.

In the analysis which follows, I shall also try to make Akhmatova's poetry seem a little less safe, emphasizing the versatility, dynamism, and invention of which she was capable even in the most familiar of her writings, the work which she produced before 1917. I shall be concentrating on Akhmatova's shorter works, both for reasons of the small compass available to me, and because it is here, I believe, that her gift for the miniature (a word I use to suggest the hard intellectual and artistic virtuosity of Mogul painting, rather than the prettiness so often attributed to women poets) is most evident. Giving Akhmatova's remarkable talent its due, I also intend to show how closely connected with other women poets of her generation she in fact was. After an early phase in which she absorbed received material more or less passively, she then began to manipulate the feminine personae available to her quite consciously. Her career before and after 1913 was both a process of self-transcendence, and a striking illustration of the progression from Symbolism to post-Symbolism to modernism which other gifted women poets of her generation also executed.

Akhmatova's first work was published when she was only 18, under her own name Anna Gorenko. As she herself was later to say contemptuously, it was 'the sort of thing that got used as fillers in the little magazines'.[5] She first began to write more serious work after her marriage

---

[5] See Akhmatova's observation to Chukovskaya, 8 June 1940: cf. the remark of 6 May 1940.

to Nikolai Gumilev, who was already an established poet, and who gave her an entrée to literary circles. With the invention of her literary pseudonym, taken from the name of her Tatar great-grandmother, came the invention of a much more sophisticated literary identity and lyric subjectivity. If 'A.G.' was naïvely imitative, 'Akhmatova' was an adept stylizer from the first. Indeed, her first collections, *Evening* (1912) and *The Rosary* (1914) evoked a whole set of identities or personae, rather than a single persona. One strategem was to put words into the mouths of heroines taken from texts written by men. Several early poems represent *tête-à-têtes* recalling those shared by the hero of Blok's lyric poetry and mysterious feminine figures, such as the Strange Lady. Akhmatova's woman has all the accoutrements of the Symbolist heroine (lilac, ostrich feathers, string orchestras), but the perspective is now hers; the result is to demystify the heroine, and mythologize the hero, so that he becomes a 'ferner Geliebter'.[6] Another early heroine borrowed from a 'male text' is Ophelia, who in a very early poem, 'Reading Hamlet', addresses Hamlet directly, as an equal: recalling his injunction to 'get her to a nunnery', she observes dismissively, 'That is all princes ever say' (*SP* 52). The second part of the poem reworks Pushkin's 'Thou and You', a famous love lyric apostrophizing a lady who mixes up the formal and informal pronouns when speaking in a public place. Akhmatova's speaker transforms a blunder into a strategy, announcing, 'And *deliberately* mistaking my words | I said, "Thou" . . .' [my emphasis].[7]

The simple binary opposition 'male text/female text' is undercut by other kinds of opposition. Besides evoking women as represented by men, Akhmatova also appropriated traditions associated with women's writing. The most important of these was the mid-nineteenth-century tradition of 'prose in verse'. Akhmatova retains the melodramatic masochism of her nineteenth-century predecessors; but she employs similar devices in order to signal its contingency. In her exact placing within social setting, costume, and affected manners, Akhmatova's heroine is the early twentieth-century equivalent of the heroines of Rostopchina or Zhadovskaya. Where Rostopchina or Zhadovskaya's heroines compose letters and languish at balls, Akhmatova's heroine appends epigraphs to unfinished portraits, awaits assignations at the tea-table or in the café, or rustles and jingles in silks and necklaces. But, in line with the prose aesthetic of her day, there is now a higher incidence of *realia* other than the heroine's own attributes. References to such

---

[6] On Akhmatova and Blok, see also Introduction; a detailed and wide-ranging study of intertextuality in the work of the two poets is V. N. Toporov, *Akhmatova i Blok: k probleme postroeniya poeticheskogo dialoga* (Berkeley, Calif., 1981).

[7] Pushkin, 'Ty i vy', *PSS* iii. 58.

phenomena as 'oysters' would not have been possible in Rostopchina or Zhadovskaya: they give Akhmatova's verse a particular visual and tactile specificity.[8]

The idea of 'prose in verse' was, as I have suggested, a reversal to more traditionally 'feminine' personae than those employed by the Symbolists. Where Akhmatova does use Symbolist personae, they acquire a more earthbound, and textbound, flavour than they had in Symbolism. In 'Sister, I have come to take your place', for example, Akhmatova imitated the manner of Adelaida Gertsyk, evoking a mysterious dialogue between two women beside 'a bonfire', a locus whose spatial and temporal vagueness suggests the multiple symbolic connotations of the speakers. Like the dialogues in Gertsyk's poems, this may be a dialogue between mythic figures, or between abstract qualities, such as death and life, or between poet and muse, or between two halves of the same person. Akhmatova adopts the Dionysiac instruments of flute and tambourine, as well as the classic Dionysiac plant of Russian Symbolism, the lilac, as attributes of her two speakers; and in the mysterious last lines, 'And the one, like a snow-white banner | and the one, like a lighthouse', she draws on the other-worldly connotations which whiteness and radiance have in Gertsyk's poetry, as they have in the Symbolist mystical tradition in general. Gertsyk's resonant archaisms and complex metrical schema have, however, been eroded in favour of an intonationally unemphatic metre (the dolnik), and the lexicon of neutral everyday speech. In one phrase only does Akhmatova specifically suggest the rural folklore which pervades Gertsyk's style: in the refrain 'by the forest bonfire, by the high bonfire', where the repetition of the preposition borrows a stylistic marker of folk-song. But on the whole her lexicon and syntax eschews the language of rural folklore, let alone the language of rural folklore's most exceptional and elevated rituals, spells, and funerals. And as in Akhmatova's love lyrics, there is emphasis on material details, such as the exchange of garments, to suggest fluidity of identity:

> Мои одежды надень,
> Позабудь о моей тревоге,
> Дай ветру кудрями играть.
> Ты пахнешь, как пахнет сирень,
> А пришла по трудной дороге,
> Чтобы здесь озаренной стать.   *(SP 77)*

---

[8] The use of *realia* in Akhmatova's poetry is most nearly matched in the work of Mandelstam, rather than any woman poet of the day. Cf. for example ' "Morozhenno!" Solntse. Vozdushnyi biskvit', Mandel'shtam, *Stikhotvoreniya* (Leningrad, 1979), 86.

> So clothe yourself in my dress,
> Forget the disquiet I feel,
> Let the wind play in your hair.
> You smell like the lilac smells,
> The path you have walked is steep,
> You have stepped into radiance.

Mandelstam was to describe Akhmatova's early poetry as 'a vulgarization of Annensky', understanding her work as an imitation of Annensky's melancholic intonation, but not of his conceptual sophistication.[9] It would perhaps be more accurate to describe 'Sister, I have come to take your place' as a 'vulgarization of Gertsyk', and as an exercise displaying all a 'vulgarization's' virtues of apparent accessibility, drawing the reader in, yet proving that the apparently familiar may be equally as elusive as the self-consciously strange.

Another persona exploited in Akhmatova's early poetry (though she appropriates this to less interesting effect than she had appropriated Gertsyk's double image of woman as both representer and represented) is that of the 'decadent' female 'sinner' who had appeared in Gippius or Lokhvitskaya or Cherubina de Gabriak's poetry. In 'Confession', for example, a woman kneels before the priest at the moment of absolution, and feels 'the touch of a hand through fabric'. The undertone of sensuality is still further enhanced by the fact that 'the touch of a hand' is the ordinary synecdoche of sexual contact in early Akhmatova (*SP* 74). Generally, though, the early poetry entwines erotic and religious motifs to less florid effect than here. In such poems as 'You have come to console me' (*SP* 72) or 'I have seen my loved one nowhere' (*SP* 279), religious belief appears, as it had in the work of some women prose writers of the nineteenth century, as a vital refuge for the heroine, and an inseparable part of her world-view.

Akhmatova's first collections, indeed, neglect few of the personae established in women's writing; but the variety of different speakers contrasts with a relatively narrow range of vocabulary and rhetorical practices. The result is that psychological unity is an idea which is at once suggested and withheld. The idea of a complete or Protean feminine identity vies with a sense of split identity, which is occasionally underlined by overtly contradictory pairings. 'The Carriage Ride' and 'Evening', for example, juxtapose on the one hand a heroine who stares directly into her consort's eyes and notes his 'barely trembling' hand, and on the other a heroine whose interest is directed to how he looks at her, and who notes that her admirer touches her with as little sexual tension

---

[9] Mandel'shtam, 'Burya i natisk', *Sobranie sochinenii* (4 vols.; Washington/New York, 1967–81), ii. 345.

as he might touch a cat, or observes him summarizing her looks at a glance with detachment, 'as one looks at slim horsewomen' (*SP* 56, 57).

Akhmatova's work between 1910 and 1913 illustrated how one gifted woman poet responded to a general historical shift in perspective experienced by the followers of Symbolism at large. Her further achievement was that she was able, in some of the work which she produced from about the end of 1913 onwards, to move from this post-Symbolist fluidity across texts to a more sophisticated, 'modernist' notion of self-questioning within a single text.

An early sign of Akhmatova's development was her review of the work of another woman poet, Nadezhda Lvova. Whilst in no sense an outright rejection of Lvova's achievement, the review was at the same time a gesture of independence on Akhmatova's part. Where the manifestos of the male Acmeists, such as Gumilev and Gorodetsky, had declared that women's task was to talk about men, Akhmatova suggests that it is to talk about themselves, and asserts the contradictions between 'life' and 'poetry', rather than accepting the identification of the two implied by Gumilev. But the review is not a rejection of 'masculine' tradition in favour of 'feminine' solidarity with Lvova. Akhmatova distinguishes herself from Lvova's emphasis on submission, and efforts to achieve formal complexity, and evolves a contradictory theory of women's poetry as power attained through stoicism and simplicity.[10]

Akhmatova's own poetics is implied, rather than stated, in this review, which, like most statements on poetics made by Russian women poets in the early twentieth century, is not systematic in an aesthetic sense. But the very existence of the critique is interesting, marking as it does Akhmatova's dissatisfaction with her own former emphasis on the love lyric, as well as with Lvova's writing, and showing that she now had a new preoccupation with issues of representation as such. The imperfect and halting statement of such issues in the review was to be followed by a more confident assertion of their importance in a symbolic form. In 'No, tsarevich, I am not she,' for example, Akhmatova refuses the traditional 'feminine' identity as the lover of men, and opposes to it the Symbolist role of woman as prophet. But in contradistinction to Symbolist women poets, she sees the latter role as self-conferred, rather than given to her by unseen forces, as constructed or invented, rather than found:

> Нет, царевич, я не та,
> Кем меня ты видеть хочешь,

---

[10] Akhmatova, 'N. L'vova. *Starye skazki*', RM (1914), 1: 27–8.

И давно мои уста
Не целуют, а пророчат.

Не подумай, что в бреду
И цзмучена тоскою
Громко кличу я беду:
Ремесло мое такое.　　　　(*SP* 120)

No, tsarevich, I am not she
Whom you wish to see in me.
And for a long time since my lips
Have prophesied, they have not kissed.

Do not suppose that I am raving
And worn to wretchedness by grieving;
This is not a wail, oh no,
It is my craft to tell of woe.

Evoking a witch-like identity similar to that portrayed by Pavlova in 'The Crone', but confidently adopting it to herself, Akhmatova goes on to make herself responsible for the young man's fate, offering him blandishments whose value she then questions.

A still more interesting poem in which Akhmatova constructs herself an identity is 'Solitude', which not only asserts independence, but shapes it metaphorically. In the first line Akhmatova speaks of herself as the target of 'stones', like the adulteress in the Bible; but the heap of discarded missiles then becomes a 'tower'. This stone structure is at one and the same time the dwelling place, both refuge and prison cell, of a legendary princess, an ark where a dove may feed on corn, and, an association suggested by the adjective 'slender' (stroinyi), a metaphor for Akhmatova's own body. At the end of the poem, the image of the 'Muse', whose 'dusky hand' will complete the writing left unfinished by the speaker, inserts a metaphor of communication from isolation which parallels that of the feeding dove; at the same time, the synecdoche, 'hand', points up the notion of writing as a physical act that is latent in the tower image. The poem has two different dynamics which work separately and jointly so as to disrupt any unitary view of the feminine: the text sees feminine subjectivity as an act made in response to and in defiance of the world, yet at the same time it sees feminine subjectivity as proliferation of self-understanding and self-naming; the princess of medieval Western legend, the immured tsaritsa of Russian tradition, stand alongside a reworking, in the feminine, of Pushkin's muse as companion.

One of Akhmatova's great achievements was that she continued to contemplate identity in terms of modernist fragmentation after the

Revolution too, rather than retreating into national mythology. In a remarkable poem of 1921, 'Fear turns objects over in the darkness', for example, she uses criss-crossing layers of literary reference in order to suggest different locations of the feminine subject in history. The poem begins with a delineation of fear through what are evidently the reactions of a victim of the Terror; then it introduces a reference to an 'axe'. This is used to set up two disparate interpretations of the female victim's situation. On the one hand this victim shares the situation of the women slaughtered by Dostoevsky's axe murderer Raskolnikov, being destined to be butchered by someone creeping about amidst the squalor of a St Petersburg tenement; on the other she puts upon herself the identity of a queen awaiting execution:

> Лучше бы на пдощади зеленой
> На помост некрашеный прилечь
> И под клики радости и стоны
> Красной кровью до конца истечь.   (*SP* 168)

> Better by far to lie on a rough scaffold
> On the green grass of a city square
> Whilst amidst the groans and jubilation,
> Scarlet life-blood poured, then poured no more.

Even Akhmatova's apparently most 'personal' statements reflect a process of literary and cultural siting which takes account of alternative identities, as well as using the command of literary sub-texts as a weapon of authority. 'Spell' (1936), which was written to commemorate the anniversary of Gumilev's execution, and of his marriage to Akhmatova, is modelled on the folkloric incantatory genre whose 'feminine' associations, as we have seen, had been established by Symbolism.[11] The poem is, however, more than simply an assertion of feminine cultural authority. The reference to 'roads' and then to 'supper' suggests a precedent in the Gospels: the meeting of Christ's disciples with Christ on the road to Emmaus after the Resurrection. The two inherited texts reflect opposed processes: where the 'spell' wrenches the dead from the grave with a command, the Gospel legend reflects a process of revelation dictated by the dead. Further, the intersection of 'pagan' and 'Christian' motifs is also, as represented here, the intersection of 'feminine' and 'masculine' cultural traditions, which, in a nice reversal of the expected, are in fact a masculine tradition of (Christian) submission, and a feminine tradition of (pagan) command. Like 'The Muse' (*SP* 183–4),

---

[11] On 'Zaklinanie' from a rather different perspective, that of pagan ritual, see Mikhail Meilakh, 'Anna Akhmatova's poem "Zaklinanie"', in Rosslyn (ed.), *The Speech of Unknown Eyes*, ii. 173–82.

the poem in which Akhmatova imagined herself at once the Muse's double and Dante's successor, 'Spell' illustrates that she could imagine an 'androgyny' which went beyond a simple pairing of 'masculine' and 'feminine' qualities.

By no means all Akhmatova's mature poetry, however, is characterized by a similar emphasis on gender fluidity and self-consciousness. These were qualities which she *could* manifest, rather than qualities which she invariably *did* manifest. If some of her public verse is written in the post-Symbolist persona of a female prophet, much of it achieves authority by eliding the gender of the speaker, or surrenders authority by adopting a mask of compliant femininity. The poems which she wrote during the First World War, for example, are outstanding in the context of their time because of Akhmatova's total eschewal of the jingoistic patriotism with which many of her male contemporaries had greeted the outbreak of war. But they also avoid political controversy by speaking in the voice of one who has to mourn the fallen, rather than one who has a right to end the battle. In the poems which she wrote after the Revolution, she adopts a similar standpoint, conferring on herself the right to command only where she speaks without gender (this is so, for example, in the famous poem 'I am not with those who leave their country', which excoriates the *émigrés*, whilst acknowledging the injustice of the new regime). As in Gippius's civic poems written at the same time, there is a tacit recognition that the expression of political authority is incompatible with a feminine voice.[12]

It was above all these poems, and the events of the post-Revolutionary years, which made Akhmatova's reputation. Certainly, even before the Revolution she had been a 'noted name', as Sofiya Parnok put it in her review of 1913. Her first two collections had been widely praised in the literary press.[13] But at this stage, Akhmatova was no more than one amongst many talented and fêted young women poets, sharing the laurels with, among others, Elizaveta Kuzmina-Karavaeva, Nadezhda Lvova, Elena Guro, and Marina Tsvetaeva. After the Revolution, on the other hand, her standing became quite exceptional. Biographical matters played a large role in this. In August 1921 Nikolai Gumilev was executed

[12] On Gippius's civic poetry, see Catriona Kelly, 'Zinaida Gippius', in *The Encyclopedia of Continental Women Writers* (2 vols.; New York, 1990); on the importance of Akhmatova's First World War civic poetry in establishing her reputation, see for example Mandel'shtam's 1916 description of her as having turned from 'woman' into 'wife', and hence into a 'symbol of Russia': 'O sovremennoi poezii', *SS* iii. 30.

[13] Early reviews of Akhmatova include: (of *Evening*) Bryusov, in 'Segodnyashnii den' russkoi poezii', *RM* (1912), 7: 22; Georgy Chulkov, 'A. Akhmatova, *Vecher*', *Zhatva* (1913), 3: 275–7; see also Kuzmin, 'Predislovie', *Vecher* (St Petersburg, 1912), 7–10; (of *The Rosary*) Gumilev, ['Gorodetsky, Akhmatova i drugie]', *Apollon* (1914), 5: 34–42.

for his alleged participation in a monarchist plot. He and Akhmatova had separated, and then divorced, several years previously; but their connection in the popular imagination was still such that Akhmatova took on the role of his official widow—a role that she herself was to cultivate assiduously, disparaging all other women who had associations with Gumilev. By the early 1920s, too, almost all the other celebrated women poets of the Symbolist or post-Symbolist generations had died, emigrated, or been displaced from the literary capitals, so that there was no one left to challenge Akhmatova's literary pre-eminence. Her status was to be recognized in a tribute from an unexpected source, Aleksandra Kollontai, who directed Young Communists to read her work; it was also to be registered, in a negative sense, by a number of more or less virulent attacks on her, as the most significant representative of 'backwardness' in women's poetry, during the early 1920s.[14] These attacks could in turn only add to her status in the external and internal emigration, and make her seem a miraculously preserved representative of the old, pre-Soviet Russia.

Although Akhmatova was never herself arrested, in the years after 1925 she suffered a further series of personal tragedies and of *ad feminam* attacks. Both her third husband, Nikolai Punin, and her son, Lev Gumilev, were arrested in 1935; the latter was imprisoned between 1938 and 1945; both he and Punin were to be arrested again in 1949. In 1946 Akhmatova was made the subject of a vicious denunciation by Andrei Zhdanov, the Leningrad Party chief. Taking the abuse of the 1920s to new gutter levels, Zhdanov stigmatized Akhmatova as 'half-nun, half-whore'. Even earlier than this, Akhmatova, like other serious Soviet poets, had found it difficult to place her work; in the late 1940s and early 1950s, it became nearly impossible, and Akhmatova was left dependent on occasional royalties, translation payments, and personal charity. Only after the death of Stalin was Akhmatova to enjoy the public recognition which the Soviet cultural establishment had previously denied her, and to be granted the accompanying material benefits.[15]

[14] On Kollontai's recommendation of Akhmatova to the Komsomol, see Beatrice Farnsworth, *Aleksandra Kollontai: Socialism, Feminism and the Bolshevik Revolution* (Stanford, Calif., 1980), 323. Contrast however, Bryusov, 'Vchera, segodnya i zavtra russkoi poezii' (1922), *SS* vi. 509; Mandel'shtam, 'Zametki o poezii', *SS* ii. 262, where Akhmatova's behaviour, that of 'a stylite on a piece of parquet' is compared unfavourably with the (rougher and more powerful) 'prophecy from a log' of her (male) Symbolist predecessors; and Trotsky, *Literatura i revolyutsiya* (Moscow, 1925), i. 30–1. For a good summary of the general situation before and after 1925, see also Haight, *Anna Akhmatova*.

[15] On Punin and Gumilev, see Haight, *Anna Akhmatova*. On 'Requiem', see Ch. 9 below. The full Russian text of Zhdanov's peroration, with English trans., is reproduced in A. Zhdanov, *The Central Committee's Resolution on the Journals Zvezda and Leningrad*, trans. F. Ashbee and I. Tidmarsh (Royal Oak, Mich., 1978).

Official disfavour and covert adulation combined to make Akhmatova into something very like the poet laureate of the internal emigration, a role which she at once accepted and rejected. A poem of 1946 finds her already wondering about the survival of her reputation, as she witnesses the 'sly moon' spying on how her 'posthumous fame' is blacked out, and envisages a future when 'neither streets nor stanzas' will bear the name of Akhmatova (*SP* 296). But at the end of her life she laconically suggested the pain of surviving to see such a future, writing in an aphoristic fragment, 'Let your night prayer be | that you should not wake up famous' (*SP* 320). Ensuring a posthumous reputation demanded great personal sacrifice. Akhmatova devoted a good deal of the last ten years of her life to ghosting her own biography, insistently repeating certain key anecdotes to confidants and visitors alike; yet, as Anatoly Naiman's perceptive memoir of her last years shows, she would sometimes interrupt the recital of 'gramophone records', as she termed them, with some running joke or humorous catch-phrase, suddenly turning her listener from devoted disciple and chronicler to intimate.[16] Here the terrible loneliness of someone brought up in the far from reverential atmosphere of a large family can be sensed. The death or emigration of Akhmatova's siblings, and the friends of her childhood and youth, as well as her own construction of herself as a master of Russian poetry, had meant that there was no longer anyone who could respond in kind.

Akhmatova's ambiguous attitude to her own reputation also pervades the poetry which she wrote in her last three decades. She vacillates between obsessive self-mythologization and evasion, between construction of an acceptable public self and a refusal of this public self through the representation of a self-questioning and elusive subjectivity. The public and civic verse which she wrote in her middle and last years, she increasingly began to metaphorize herself as the voice of the 'true Russia', the suppressed nation. In Anna Barkova's poetry we hear the voice of a clever, difficult, and hostile social outsider; many of Akhmatova's poems, by contrast, speak with an authority gained from the insistence that her marginality is aberrant. Where Barkova expresses a dissident misanthropy, Akhmatova expresses the possibility of an alternative consensus, which is generally signified by the assignation of a female figure to an important, but subordinate, place within the consensus.

In contrast to her contemporary, Boris Pasternak, Akhmatova did not jettison modernism in her late poetry; indeed, *Poem Without a Hero* is

---

[16] Anatoly Naiman, *Rasskazy o Anne Akhmatovoi* (Leningrad, 1989); trans. Wendy Rosslyn as *Remembering Anna Akhmatova* (London, 1991).

one of the great Russian modernist works.[17] But when speaking from a modernist standpoint, she often eschewed modernism's linguistic strategies, such as shifts in register or syntactical fluidity. Her repertoire and rhetoric remained those of her early poetry. In 'Cinque', for example, the manner of her early love poetry is appropriated to an evocation of metaphysical communication with an absent lover. In a poem of 1959, Akhmatova spoke of 'making the empty silence speak unto ages' (SP 303). What this often meant in practice was pre-empting the future through the past by taking a time-honoured poeticism, and distancing it by use of a concessive conjunction such as 'almost'. This way of employing the familiar made it possible both to please the reader of limited horizons for whom sonorous platitudes were the expected order of things, and to placate the learned one by giving the literary equivalent of a wink. In 'Singing', for example, Akhmatova speaks of a woman's voice as both crystalline and rich, referring to 'many-coloured silks', 'diamonds', and so on; the poem is a perfectly conventional portrayal of music's spiritual sensuality, yet it also parades familiarity with the 'piano sonnets' of Innokenty Annensky, whom Akhmatova had made a cult figure amongst Russian *littérateurs* (SP 305).

The technique of distancing more or less verbatim citations is not an entirely comfortable one. There may be something in the aphorism, 'it is the dream of every honest cliché to end up in a great poem', but few poems, even great poems, can accommodate a whole collection of jostling clichés held back by the red rope of 'almost'.[18] Nor was this the only ill-effect of Akhmatova's self-imposed role as unofficial poet laureate. The late cycle *Northern Elegies*, for example, contains some very fine and memorable poetry, yet also some passages of rather ordinary writing. The cycle opens with an impressive prelude, describing 'the Russia of Dostoevsky' before Akhmatova's birth, and wittily suggesting how cities can only be perceived through images of themselves (St Petersburg in the 1960s still resembles 'a second-rate, but perfectly decent, water-colour of the 1870s'). But in later parts of the cycle, this wit and energy are on occasion dissipated by a process of uneasy iteration, in which the teasingly orutund alternates with the flatly mundane.

In the sixth elegy, for example, Akhmatova compares herself at the opening with a river 'turned' by her epoch and not knowing its own banks. This magnificent adaptation of a neo-classical poetic topos, time as a river, to imply the grandiose Soviet transformations of nature and human nature during the 1930s, blends, at the end of the poem, into

---

[17] On 'Poema bez geroya' see also Ch. 9 below.
[18] This aphorism of Charles Simic's is quoted in *Antaeus Jubilee Edition: Fiction, Poetry, Documents* (London, 1990), 1.

another metaphor for lost identity, the conceit that 'another woman' has taken Akhmatova's 'most legal name', and lived out her life in her stead, whilst Akhmatova has been left with 'a nickname'. 'I shall not lie in my own grave', she observes, before concluding with a reference to how the future, glimpsed from the past, might have made her at last 'know envy'. Personal history and national history are perfectly blended, and the temporal vertigo imparted by the sense of looking backwards in order to look forward exacerbates the feeling of self-loss with which the poem is concerned to project. However, these points in the poem's narrative progression are separated by a series of allusions which are not nearly so striking. Akhmatova introduces the standard (indeed banal) idea of identity as theatre: 'The curtain has gone up without me'. She then refers to her life as a procession of 'friends not met, towns not seen, poems not written'. Of these references, only the last appears to carry through momentum from the beginning of the poem to the end. Akhmatova evokes her 'unwritten poems' as a 'secret chorus' waiting to smother the speaker (there is a suggestion of the angry ghosts of unborn children). Generating a sense of claustrophobia in its own right, this line also creates a powerful image of maternal guilt, which is foregrounded by an encoded reference, at the end of the poem, to the *realia* of Akhmatova's biography. A woman with Akhmatova's own 'most legal name' (which is to say, her married name 'Anna Gumileva'), had indeed literally 'replaced' her: Gumilev's mother, Anna, had brought up Akhmatova's son Lev.[19] This powerful chain of images is matched by a link between the stark image of 'lying in the wrong grave' and the image of the altered river course at the beginning, which are immediately appreciable visual parallels. But some of the intervening lines seem just so much padding.

Occasionally Akhmatova could cite apparently hackneyed material so as to take the reader by surprise. In 'Despite your promises', for example, she conjures up an ambiguous vision from the past, a young man who 'sighs and weeps like a keener at a funeral', and who recalls the various sad shades of *Poem Without a Hero* or 'Cinque'. But rather than launch into yet another mythologization of her own biography, she moves into an ironic coda:

> Он больше без меня не мог,
> Пускай позор, пускай острог . . .
>
> Я без него могла.

[19] On Akhmatova, Lev Gumilev, and Anna Gumileva, see V. Sreznevskaya, 'Iz vospominanii', in Nikolai Gumilev, *Neizdannoe i nesobrannoe*, ed. Michael Basker and Sheelagh Graham (Paris, 1986), 163–4.

> He could not do without me. No!
> If that meant prison—be it so!
> I could not do *with* him.

But in other late poems, Akhmatova's insistence on commemorating material of private importance could sometimes become indulgence of the recondite for its own sake; conversely, her classicizing public manner could teeter towards pomposity. As Nadezhda Mandelstam put it, 'The raciness of her verbal portraits was breathtaking. Such power of language sometimes broke through in her poetry, but not as often as it should have.'[20]

In her later years, Akhmatova had to endure the ultimate frustration for any creative artist—the dogged preference of readers for her or his early work. There was a sense in which her unfair remarks on 'teaching women how to speak' were perfectly justified. Akhmatova the early love poet was to have scores of imitators; Akhmatova the modernist poet of *Poem Without a Hero* was not. If Tsvetaeva's writing has alienated readers by its obvious unconventionality, Akhmatova's writing has suffered a converse, but no less unfortunate, fate: that of a superficial and easy appreciation. At the same time, it is undeniable that Akhmatova's own preoccupation with her early work, and her perpetuation of its linguistic manner, played a large part in later interpretations and appropriations of her poetry. If her standing depended on her representation of herself, it was equally true that her representation of herself depended on her standing. The dichotomous interpretations of Akhmatova as 'feminine' love 'poetess' with huge popular following, and 'masculine' literary classic are not aberrant misapprehensions of a body of work whose 'real' value is there to be discovered by a feminist, or any other, critic. If she was not *simply* a diary poet who recorded the joy of assignations, the pain of partings, and the agonies of religious guilt, she was *also* a poet of this kind, and she did more than any other twentieth-century poet to shape the later history of 'prose in verse'. In my interpretation, I have not tried to recover some essential or definitive 'feminist' Akhmatova; but I have shown that her work emerges in a quite different way when it is placed against the diverse history of women's writing in the twentieth century. Though the best of her work, above all *Poem Without a Hero*, remains *sui generis*, and even her less good poems are often competent enough to make all imitators seem deficient, Akhmatova was a poet who, unlike Tsvetaeva, perpetuated rather than exploded tradition, the tradition of 'feminine poetry' included. Yet at the same time Akhmatova's career, over the course of which she applied

---

[20] Nadezhda Mandelstam, *Hope Against Hope* (see Part IV, Ch. 13, n. 65), 438.

ambiguous and various strategies of self-realization, definitively illustrates that 'conformity' and 'non-conformity' are not adequate categories for describing the work of women writers, ascribing as they do a pattern of incidental and momentary gestures to an inflexible system of once-and-for-all categories.

PART III

9

Class War and the Home Front: From the Revolution to the Death of Stalin (1917–1953)

I look to right, I look to left,
Folks all have medals on their chests.
Boys got theirs for victories,
Girls for work in factories.

(Rhyme from *Rabotnitsa*, 1947)

I believe like a village woman:
Hold my tongue, raise sons for the future.

(Natalya Krandievskaya)

WITH the coming to power of the Bolsheviks in October 1917, the cause of women's liberation in Russia seemed to gain an overwhelming victory. Amongst the earliest actions of the new regime was to put together a legislative programme which granted women fuller political, economic, and social rights than they enjoyed anywhere else in the world until after the Second World War. The Menshevik government had given women the right to vote; 1918 decrees on labour, marriage and the family, and the political system acknowledged women's right to full political participation, to equality within marriage, and to equal pay. In 1920 these measures were followed by the legalization of abortion; and the early 1920s saw the passage of numerous other laws and regulations, intended to promote as well as to ensure equality, and also to extend protection to women at work and in the home.[1]

---

[1] On legal changes in the first years of Soviet rule, see *Dekrety sovetskoi vlasti* (13 vols. and continuing; Moscow, 1957–); *Sistematicheskii sbornik uzakonenii i rasporyazhenii Rabochego i Krest'yanskogo pravitel'stva* (Moscow, 1919), especially 'Konstitutsiya RSFSR', 91–103, 'Kodeks zakonov o trude', 203–4, 'Dekret o brake i sem'e', 35–6. A useful guide to legislation after 1921 is M.

Yet the stuff of victory for women's liberation was also to be the substance of its defeat. This was partly because feminism, its demands satisfied, now appeared redundant. Crises of confidence in the women's movement were evident in other European countries, where women had secured the right to the franchise alone; in Russia, where legal reform was rapidly followed by radical changes in social policy (the provision of a welfare network dealing with child care and medical help, the institution of a service infrastructure), the loss of interest in liberation was, inevitably, still more marked.[2]

Apart from this generally applicable factor, however, there were additional and more idiosyncratic matters affecting the Russian case. First amongst these was the anti-individualist character which Russian socialism had inherited from Russian radicalism: individual interests were subordinated to collective interests, and civil rights were under-theorized. Theory had direct results on practice: like other manifestations of non-Bolshevik political expression, feminist organizations, newspapers, and journals were suppressed in 1918; and the granting of rights to women depended at least as much on notions of what was expedient to state and Party interests as on abstract ideas of justice. (For example, the first Bolshevik law on franchise guaranteed the vote to 'persons employed in the domestic sphere' only where they were supporting a person or persons engaged in 'productive labour'.) Over the next thirty-five years, equality for women remained a stable element of Party rhetoric, but actual policy on women was subject to a good deal of change; many of the central measures of early Bolshevism were reversed, or their effects transformed out of all recognition. Abortion was made illegal, and procedures for divorce tightened up, in 1936; in the same year, male homosexuality was outlawed. From then on, the nuclear family increasingly began to be institutionalized as the social norm, and the flexible attitudes to sexual liaisons that had been evident in the 1920s gradually disappeared. Emphasis on the interests of the State also meant that the so-called 'right to work' was increasingly glossed as a duty to

Bukov (ed.), *Okhrana zhenskogo truda: sbornik deistvuyushchego zakonodatel'stva i rukovo-dyashchikh ukazanii VTsSPS po prorabote sredi zhenshchin* (Moscow, 1926). See also Melanie Ilic, 'Soviet Protective Labour Legislation and Female Workers in the 1920s and 1930s', in Marianne Liljeström, Eila Mäntysaari, and Arja Rosenholm (eds.), *Gender Restructuring in Russian Studies* (Helsinki, 1993). Even in this early phase of Soviet rule, though, one notes that legislative formulae are more inclined to assume the equality of women than to articulate it, and that the duty of women to work was of central importance both in a conceptual sense (it is of primary narrative importance) and in a practical sense (cf. the 1919 decree making it incumbent on all women to sew underwear for the Red Army: *Dekrety*, xi. 142–4).

[2] On the reaction against feminism which succeeded the granting of suffrage, see e.g. Vera Brittain, *The Testament of Youth* (1933; London, 1979), 580–92, which also makes it clear, however, that the movement began to pick up again from the early 1920s.

work. All through the 1920s, 1930s, and 1940s, there were drives to bring women out of the home and into the labour force. At first some genuine ideas of the dignity of labour were in play; but later on the demands of the industrialization drive began to acquire overwhelming importance. Soviet enterprises were under-mechanized and hence labour-intensive; the capacity of industry could be expanded only by the participation of women; and so women came under increasing pressure to work, whatever their family circumstances.[3]

A further factor of significance, which existed right from the beginning of Soviet rule, was the unacknowledged gender bias of Bolshevism. Both before and after the Revolution, the pivot of ideology was not just 'the worker', but the politically conscious, skilled worker, whose dominance in metaphor was underpinned by hidden assumptions about what constituted productive and unproductive labour, and about the nature of skills. As in any capitalist society, domestic labour was presumed to be unproductive, and the operation of a lathe was classified quite differently from, say, the operation of a sewing-machine. The practical result was a continuing over-representation of women in jobs which were supposedly unskilled, and hence poorly remunerated; the ideological result was an emphasis on the 'backwardness' of women. Assumptions that women were more likely to be 'illiterate', both in the ordinary and in the political sense, led to the setting up of special Party women's sections (*zhenotdely*), whose ultimate aim was to recruit women to the Party, but which performed useful work in giving working-class and peasant women access to literacy classes, providing them with an elementary political education, informing them about their new legal rights, and propagandizing health care. But the assumption that women had special needs also generated crude positive and negative stereotypes of women's behaviour, polarizing 'enlightened' working women and 'backward' peasants or bourgeoises, and by a process of circularity at once labelling the 'feminine' backward, and stigmatizing 'backwardness' as feminine. Traditional 'feminine' activities, such as housework and child-rearing, were represented in derogatory terms; it was assumed that women were more likely to be drawn to 'backward' forms of belief, such as religion and superstition, and that they were a group sunk in false consciousness and incapable of perceiving their own interests independently.[4]

---

[3] A particularly clear summary of changes in ideology and social policy between 1917 and 1953 is given in Mary Buckley, *Women and Ideology in the Soviet Union* (Hemel Hempstead, 1989). On the 1920s, see chs. 1–2. On the limitation of voting rights for those domestically employed, see *Sistematicheskii sbornik*, 100.

[4] The Bolshevik hostility to housework and child-rearing as demeaning and irrational activities is evident e.g. in Lenin's observations of 1919, quoted in Richard Stites, *The Women's Liberation*

The crudities of ideology meant that policies intended in women's best interests might function haphazardly, and sometimes do as much harm as good. The campaign to provide child care and services for working women was associated with the creation of a new under-class of 'unskilled' service workers, overwhelmingly made up of women. The liberalization of marital regulations in the 1920s gave legal recognition to the fluid liaisons which urban members of the intelligentsia had themselves preferred even before the Revolution, but they deprived working-class and peasant women of the leverage and status which they had derived from the conception of marriage as a binding economic and social contract. And the assault on domesticity carried out in the 1920s ignored the fact that working-class and peasant women's sense of autonomy derived in part from a gender-based division of labour within the home. The result was a contradictory dynamic according to which gender discrimination persisted in the public sphere and in the home, yet any palliative effects deriving from the traditional divisions of labour were eradicated, since women could no longer feel a sense of pride in 'women's work'.[5]

Early Bolshevik policy depended on coherent notions of 'femininity' in a negative sense, which were in turn to make a narrowly traditional notion of femininity into a positive symbol for their opponents. But there was considerably more uncertainty in the early days, even amongst the ideological leaders themselves, as to what the positive models of femininity should be. Resolute women workers might be ubiquitous symbols in ideology, but the old Bolsheviks who occupied government posts were far from approving the sexual libertarianism advocated by

Movement in Russia, (Princeton, NJ, 1978), 378. Cf. (on child-rearing) Eric Naiman, 'Historectomies: On the Metaphysics of Reproduction', in Jane Costlow, Stephanie Sandler, and Judith Vowels (eds.), *Sexuality in Russian Culture* (Stanford, Calif., 1993); (on housework), Ol'ga Berggol'ts' poem of 1935, 'Novosel'e' (The New House), *Izbrannye proizvedeniya* (Leningrad, 1983), 126, which talks about handing over household items to a (female!) cook as a joyous rite of passage. In visual propaganda of the 1920s, images of women and children were used only in material aimed specifically at women (on health, domestic economy etc.): see Elizabeth Waters, 'The Female Form in Soviet Political Iconography', in Barbara Clements, Barbara Engel, and Christine Worobec (eds.), *Russia's Women* (Berkeley, Calif., 1991), 225–42. On denigratory images of 'traditional women' in agitprop theatre of the 1920s, see Catriona Kelly, 'A Stick with Two Ends: The Puppet Theatre *Petrushka* as a Case Study of Misogyny in Popular Culture', in Costlow, Sandler, and Vowles (eds.), *Sexuality*. As regards the effects of ideological bias, even the 'adjusted' statistics given in an official publication of the 1930s, *Zhenshchina v SSSR: statisticheskii sbornik* (Moscow, 1937), indicate that industrialization had led to a disproportionate representation of women in 'unskilled' jobs in heavy industry and in the service industries, besides intensifying their presence in already heavily feminized sectors such as the textile industry.

[5] Dissatisfaction in traditional working-class and peasant quarters to the new marriage legislation is analysed in Stites, *Women's Liberation*, 367–71; see also Buckley, *Women*, 40, 128; specifically on peasant objections, Beatrice Farnsworth, *Aleksandra Kollontai: Socialism, Feminism and the Bolshevik Revolution* (Stanford, Calif., 1980), 340–6.

young activists on the left fringes of the Party. Most of the Party leaders themselves had monogamous attachments which, if they sometimes continued the traditions of 'equal comradeship' practised by the Russian left since Chernyshevsky, just as often resembled the traditional marriages of high-ranking Tsarist officials, with wives as hostesses supported by staffs of servants.[6]

By the end of the 1920s, these undercurrents of traditionalism, both popular and official, began forcing their way through to the surface again. In 1930 Stalin dissolved the Party women's sections, and declared that 'The woman question has been solved'. The ensuing years were to see the creation of an increasingly coherent incentive model for women in official ideology: the Soviet woman was to be a fusion of worker, wife, and mother: a graceful and gracious Soviet superwoman, bathed in the light of a never-setting sun. In the 1930s and especially the 1940s, the view of women in Soviet ideology increasingly came to resemble that which was propagandized in other totalitarian states, Hitler's Germany and Mussolini's Italy. But there was an important difference. In the Soviet Union, the urgent demand for women's participation in industry meant that they continued to be valued in terms of their productive as well as of their reproductive capacities. Even in the late 1940s, when a variety of pro-natalist policies was instituted in order to compensate for the enormous population losses caused by the War (not to speak of the political purges of the 1930s), there was never a campaign to persuade Soviet women to go back to the home full time, on the pattern of the campaigns to this end organized in Italy and Germany. However, as we shall see, plenty of propaganda was put out in the cause of reinforcing traditional practices and attitudes within the Soviet home.[7]

Throughout the period from 1917 to 1953, there was a close attachment between literature and ideology, ensured on the one hand by a

---

[6] On differing attitudes to sexual libertarianism, see Stites, *Women's Liberation*, 346–91; Farnsworth, *Aleksandra Kollontai*, 246–7, 336–67. Élite marriages based on comradely principles included those of Lenin and Trotsky; the contrasting model is to be seen, however, in the marriage of Pyatnitsky and Sokolova (see her memoir in Vilensky, *Dodnes' tyagoteet* (Moscow, 1989) and to some extent also in Lunacharsky's marriage to the actress Natal'ya Rozenel' (see N. Lunacharskaya-Rozenel', *Pamyat' serdtsa* (2nd edn.; Moscow, 1965); this type of marriage was to become increasingly prevalent in the 1930s. Further insight into the persistence of traditional notions of femininity during the 1920s is also offered by Tatiana Strizhenova's fascinating study of the Soviet fashion industry, *Soviet Costume and Textiles 1917–1945* (Paris, 1991), which indicates that floaty dresses, high heels, and lipstick were just as fashionable with members of the Soviet élite in the 1920s as with bright young things in the West.

[7] Donald Filtzer, *Soviet Workers and Stalinist Industrialisation: The Formation of Modern Soviet Production Relations* (New York, 1986), 63–7, summarizes the situation with regard to women's participation and work conditions; see also Buckley, *Women*, ch. 3. On Germany during the 1930s, see Claudia Koonz, *Mothers in the Fatherland: Women, the Family and Nazi Politics* (New York, 1987); on Italy, Michel Ostenc, 'La Conception de la femme fasciste dans l'Italie mussolinienne', *Risorgimento* (1983), 3: 155–74.

censorship still more rigid than that of Tsarist days, and on the other by economic centralization and nationalization, so that the cultural establishment was progressively brought under state control. The pre-Revolutionary thick journals, like the rest of the non-Bolshevik press, were closed down in 1918; from the end of the 'New Economic Policy', the period of limited economic pluralism between 1921 and 1925, book-publishing was brought under ever tighter control, as were the activities of the various cultural groups not until then directed by the State. It became increasingly difficult for writers to survive without hand-outs from the State, and these were never granted disinterestedly. Finally, in 1932, all remaining informal groups were dissolved, and the Union of Soviet Writers became the only legal professional body. At its first congress in 1934, the doctrine of Socialist Realism was imposed. Whatever the possible ambiguities of this doctrine itself, which enjoined an authorial practice at once mimetic and mythic in its representation of 'reality', there was no doubt that the writer's first, indeed only, duty was to be a practitioner of 'Socialist Realism' in the sense of being an instrument of official ideology.[8]

The process of cultural centralization was to have particularly marked effects on women writers. Before 1925, their work had been disproportionately represented outside the prestigious organs of the Bolshevik literary establishment. And so, when the informal groups began to close, there was a marked drop in the numbers of women writers able to publish. And after 1932, when literary power became concentrated in the hands of a small number of union officials and journal editors—all of them men—the profile of women's writing dropped still further. The board of the Union of Writers did contain quite high numbers of women, who were in fact over-represented in comparison with their presence in the membership, but these women had token, rather than real, power. Equally token was the representation of women's writing in the prestige literary journals and publishing houses of the post-1932 period.[9]

[8] On cultural centralization, see Boris Thomson, *The Premature Revolution* (London, 1970); John and Carol Garrard, *Inside the Soviet Writers' Union* (London, 1990); M. Dewhirst and J. Farrell, *The Soviet Censorship* (Metuchen, NJ, 1973); *Pervyi s"ezd sovetskikh pisatelei: stenograficheskii otchet* (Moscow, 1934); N[ina] P[erlina], 'Censorship', in Victor Terras (ed.), *A Handbook of Russian Literature* (New Haven, Conn., 1985), 74–5. For an extended discussion of the incoherences in Socialist Realism as an aesthetic doctrine in an abstract sense, see Régine Robin, *Le Réalisme socialiste: un esthétique impossible* (Paris, 1986).

[9] The importance of 'informal' publications before 1925 is made clear by A. M. Vitman, *Vosem' let russkoi khudozhestvennoi literatury (1917–1925)* (Moscow-Leningrad, 1926); cf. also the important anthology of I. S. Ezhov and E. I. Shamurin, *Russkaya poeziya XX veka* (Moscow, 1925). On Union representation, see the details given in *Pervyi s"ezd sovetskikh pisatelei*, 700–1. Though according to her own account Anna Karavaeva had an editorial say at *Molodaya gvardiya*, no major Soviet literary journal was (or is) edited by a woman.

As we shall see, the decline in publishing outlets for women's writing was to make internal emigration, which is to say withdrawal from the official literary scene and producing work 'for one's desk drawer', a particularly important phenomenon amongst women writers, many of whom were to endure official neglect or disapprobation. Granted, women were rarely subjected to political persecution in a direct sense: one advantage of their relatively insignificant status in the world of cultural politics was that they were to succumb less frequently to purges than men. The women writers who were rounded up in the Terror were usually Party members who were arrested for some offence not directly connected with their literary activity: the poet Anna Barkova, for example, appears to have been denounced for a chance remark which she made at a party, rather than for the anti-Soviet character of her work. However, the 'invisibility' of women writers meant that they might remain in technical freedom, but that they often suffered terrible economic deprivation, many being forced into hack journalism or subjected to the relentless pressures of production-line translation in order to secure their daily crust, whilst the writers who did enjoy official favour were rewarded with sinecures almost as large as the print-runs of their books, and with all the other appurtenances of bourgeois comfort (flats, servants, dachas, holidays on the Black Sea, full wardrobes and larders) which the Party had at its disposal.[10]

But if the ideogical, social, and cultural pressures of official Soviet literature made women writers take a prominent place amongst the writers of the internal emigration, as well as amongst the writers of the actual emigration (which is to say, the huge Russian diaspora abroad), that does not mean that women were entirely unrepresented in the Soviet literary establishment. It would be a mistake to over-simplify the sheer variety of choices made by women. In conversation with Lidiya Chukovskaya in the 1940s, Anna Akhmatova looked forward with horror to the time when she, Lily Brik, Anna Radlova, Larisa Reisner, and Zinaida Gippius would be labelled by historians 'women of one generation'; and there was indeed little resemblance between the post-Revolutionary lives of these five women. Akhmatova was a writer of remarkable talent and a steadfast opponent of Bolshevism from the early days, yet she chose to remain in Russia; Gippius, who was just as talented a writer, and who was still more overtly hostile to Bolshevism, left Russia for good in 1918.

---

[10] On Barkova's arrest see Irina Ugrimova and Nadezhda Zvezdochetova's brief biography in S. S. Vilensky (ed.), *Dodnes' tyagoteet* (Moscow, 1989), 335–7. For the very different conditions experienced by two well-known writers during the 1930s and 1940s, Akhmatova and Panova, see Lidiya Chukovskaya's *Zapiski ob Anne Akhmatovoi* (Paris, 1976–80), and Vera Panova, *O moei zhizni, knigakh i chitatelyakh* (Leningrad, 1975).

None of the other three was anti-Soviet, but their biographies also diverged to a high degree from each other. Larisa Reisner was, as we have seen, a not terribly talented practitioner of 'committed Symbolism', but she played a significant role after the Revolution as a symbol of Bolshevik feminine heroism; Anna Radlova was a moderately able poet who became a prominent translator in the 1930s; and Lily Brik was one of the many Russian women to achieve prominence solely by virtue of her relationship with a famous man, since she spent many years as Mayakovsky's official mistress.[11]

There is no evidence that women were any less likely than men to share the beliefs that propelled writers into co-operation with the Bolshevik regime in the early days; in fact, class origins played probably a bigger role in identification with the Communist cause than gender did. The central class supporting Bolshevik cultural policy was one that could be termed (for want of a better name) the 'petty intelligentsia'. These were people of relatively humble origins (the children of provincial teachers, priests, factory workers, or peasants) who had been given new educational and professional opportunities—as teachers, Party workers, engineers, journalists—by Bolshevik rule. Understandably grateful to the new Soviet regime for the change in their lives, they were also enthusiastic supporters of Stalin, who in the late 1920s had explicitly stated the importance of the intelligentsia in giving guidance to the working classes, and had stepped up the official onslaught on the 'cultural bohemia', the reconstituted new arts groups, who were now branded as parasitic subversives. The so-called 'politics of envy' may have played some role in making the 'petty intelligentsia' prepared to endorse such policies; but of far greater importance were the rather literal-minded views of literary value prevalent amongst Russian auto-didacts, and their messianic attitude to 'culture' in the broad sense of education, right-thinking morality, hard work, and personal commitment. If the central members of the 'petty intelligentsia' were those in the mainstream professions of engineers and teachers, as well as middle-ranking Party officials, there were many writers who shared their background and values. Examples of women writers who did were the prose writers Anna Karavaeva and Lidiya Seifullina, both of whom began their literary activities in provincial creative writing groups in the early 1920s before getting a foothold in the capitals, and the poet Elizaveta Polonskaya. Youthful idealism was another obvious factor prompting women to identify with Soviet ideology; the first generation of women to be educated under Soviet rule supplied numbers of notable cultural activists,

---

[11] Chukovskaya, *Zapiski*, i. 62 (8 Feb. 1940).

including the poet Olga Berggolts and the writer Vera Panova, both born in 1910.[12]

Once allied with the Soviet literary establishment, women writers were just as subject as their male colleagues, too, to the insidious pressures of fear and self-interest which kept successful Soviet citizens in line. A typical instance was the poet Vera Inber, who complied partly because she felt under constant threat, being a first cousin of Lev Trotsky, and partly because she knew that literary conformity would secure her the trips abroad which were her one source of unalloyed pleasure. For similar reasons, Aleksandra Kollontai, the only Bolshevik theorist who made any serious attempt to incorporate feminist ideas into her writings and political policies, recanted on many of her early works after 1930.[13]

But if age and class meant that gender was not a once-and-for-all determining factor, these qualities did not necessarily play definitive roles in themselves. Reisner, Akhmatova, and Gippius were not only more or less 'of a generation'; they were also from much the same sort of comfortable, privileged gentry background; so, too, was Olga Forsh, who was soon to become perhaps the most celebrated Soviet woman writer. Finally, the motivation of individuals is beyond slick generalizations or categorizations. What one can safely say, though, is that, slippery as the role of gender may have been in dictating political positions in a broad sense, its role once those political positions were adopted was a good deal more definite. Gender had quite clear-cut effects on women writers' lives once they had opted for or against emigration. As we shall see, there was a high degree of coherence in women's writing within the official tradition, and some degree of coherence in women's writing outside it. And it was women's writing outside the official tradition which was most productively to consolidate and extend the radical developments in the 'feminine' tradition which had come about before the Revolution.

That is not to say that no good work was produced by women who wrote for official Soviet outlets, or that women in emigration wrote under

[12] Class identity in the early Soviet years is a vexed issue, and not all commentators would approve this thumbnail sketch of value changes. For a recent exchange of views on the subject, see Sheila Fitzpatrick and others in *Slavic Review*, 47/4 (Winter 1988), 599–626. 'On workers' identification with the Bolshevik emphasis on Bolshevik privileging of economic over civil rights, see also S. A. Smith, 'Workers and Civil Rights, 1899–1917' in Olga Crisp and Linda Edmondson (eds.), *Civil Rights in Imperial Russia* (Oxford, 1989), 168–9. For Stalin's views on the leadership of the intelligentsia, see his speech of 18 Apr. 1929, quoted in 'Stalin o kul'ture', *KN* (1939), 12: 11. An early attack on the literary intelligentsia is M. Reisner, 'Bogema i kul'turnaya revolyutsiya', *Pechat' i revolyutsiya* (1928), 5: 81–96. On Karavaeva's background, see her 'Iz vospominanii starogo "ognelyuba" ', *Po dorogam zhizni* (Moscow, 1957), 697–719; Lidiya Nikolaeva, 'Avtobiografiya', *O literature* (Moscow, 1958), 27–34; on Polonskaya's, see her introduction to *Izbrannoe* (Moscow, 1966), 7–14; on Berggol'ts, see her *Dnevnye zvezdy* (Moscow, 1972).

[13] On Vera Inber, see L. Gendlin, *Perebiraya starye bloknoty* (Amsterdam, 1986), 188–97; on Kollontai, Farnsworth, *Aleksandra Kollontai*, 378–404.

no kind of constraints. The separation into 'insider' and 'outsider' traditions made here has analytical convenience; like the notional categorizations which I have used elsewhere, it helps to establish similarities as well as differences. Both Socialist Realism and anti-Soviet traditions could, as we shall see, exercise an inflexible attitude towards 'the feminine' that was most inconvenient to women as actual historical subjects, despite, or perhaps more accurately because of, the importance of *Woman* as a metaphor for certain permutations of national identity within each separate tradition.

Insiders

For the most part, the ideologists of Bolshevism displayed impatience with abstract speculation on gender issues, considering this a 'bourgeois' concern. Even before the Revolution, Lenin had dismissed the argument expressed by Tolstoy in *The Kreutzer Sonata*—that women would not be free in politics until they were free in the bedroom—as 'absurd'. With the famous exception of Aleksandra Kollontai, the leaders of the Soviet government remained little interested in the study of gender identities after the Revolution too. Quite logically, the left thinkers of the 1920s and the 1930s (here including Kollontai as well) produced no theories of women's writing as such. Prior to 1930, however, the idea of 'women's writing' in a crude sense was in common currency as a ritual term of abuse. In Lev Trotsky's *Literature and Revolution*, for example, women's poetry is associated, predictably enough, with 'backward' religious beliefs: women poets, Trotsky asserts, exemplify the Russian proverb 'nowhere without a prayer'. In Bryusov's essay of 1922, 'Yesterday, Today, and Tomorrow in Russian Poetry', women poets are relegated to the 'yesterday' of Russian poetry; the 'tomorrow', it is suggested, will belong to male poets of proletarian orientation, with their hymns to the male factory worker.[14]

In texts of the 1920s, even formalist arguments often carry an ideological load. Women's language is never visualized apart from women's culture, and hence it too is backward: feeble, uneducated, incompetent. (In 'Yesterday, Today, and Tomorrow', Bryusov had, for example, asserted that even the average member of a proletarian writing studio would have been ashamed to turn out versification as substandard as Akhmatova's.) Here, as in political ideology, vital energy is mascu-

[14] V. *Lenin o Tolstom* (Moscow, 1928), 81; the inadequacies of Bolshevik gender theory are noted in Buckley, *Women*, chs. 1–2; see also Elizabeth Wood, 'Prostitution Unbound: Representations of Sexual and Political Anxieties in Post-Revolutionary Russia', in Costlow, Sandler, and Vowles (eds.), *Sexuality*; Lev Trotsky, *Literatura i revolyutsiya*, i. 34–5; Bryusov, 'Vchera, segodnya i zavtra v russkoi poezii' (1922), *Sobranie sochinenii*, vi. 493–543.

line, historical redundancy feminine. Unlike notions of women's political backwardness, ideas about women's literary backwardness do not, however, seem to have been accompanied by any drive to re-educate women. The 'proletarianization' of literature was dominated, in ideology and in practice, by men. At the 1934 Congress of Writers, one delegate did call for the institution of women's proletarian writer groups; but by then the 'worker writing' movement was all but dead.[15]

It was not only women's negative class associations as a gender that coloured views on women's writing. In *Literature and Revolution*, again, Trotsky used the term 'gynaecological' to describe the work of the poet Mariya Shkapskaya. The description is inaccurate (Shkapskaya's work does indeed refer to the state of maternity, but in symbolic rather than physiological terms). But it is most indicative: like Russian Romanticism, and like the post-Symbolist groups of pre-Revolutionary days, the left arts movements of the 1920s derived their views of creative energy from essentialist notions of gender characteristics. If Trotsky praises Shkapskaya (rather patronizingly) for her expression of feminine biology, this was an anomaly: by and large 1920s thinking elevated the masculine at the expense of the feminine. So Mayakovsky's self-assertion in the narrative poem *About That* partly depends on invective directed at feminine addressees, who replace 'love by the darning of socks', whilst some of Mandelstam's later poems take a Weiningerian view of women's language, associating it with childish prattle, and representing a world in which women are silenced by the language of men.[16]

The essentialist elements in conceptualization of the creative process were in turn to affect the constructs which predominated in experimental writing. There were very few women writers who were associated with the avant-garde literary world in the 1920s. No more than before the Revolution did women poets make excursions into the poetry of *zaum*, or transrational language, interest in which continued to preoccupy left poets of the 1920s.[17] Nor were they much represented amongst the

[15] On women's language, cf. Bryusov and Trotsky above; Mandel'shtam, 'Zametki'; on the neglect of women in 'proletarian art' projects, cf. Lynn Mally, *Culture of the Future: The Proletkult Movement in Revolutionary Russia* (Berkeley, Calif., 1990), 178–81; on the belated call for recognition of women proletarian writers, see *Pervyi s"ezd sovetskikh pisatelei*, 209–11.

[16] V. Mayakovsky, *Pro eto, Sochineniya v 3-kh tomakh* (Moscow, 1978), iii. 160; Mandel'shtam, 'Masteritsa vinovatykh vzorov', *Stikhotvoreniya* (Leningrad, 1979), 173–4. Idealized craftsmen appear in numerous prose tales written between 1920 and 1940, including V. Kaverin's collection *Mastera i podmaster'ya* (Moscow-Petersburg, 1923); a distant connection with the tradition can be seen also in Bulgakov's use of a guild name for his writer cypher in *The Master and Margarita*.

[17] The two exceptions to this generalization on women's involvement in the avant-garde are the painters Varvara Stepanova and Ol'ga Rozanova, both of whom produced transrational work on the border between visual arts and poetry. (See M. A. Yablonskaya, *Women Artists of Russia's New*

practitioners of metafiction, the literary direction which shapes the text as a commentary upon itself and its own fabrication, which was one of the most significant and original tendencies in prose writing of the 1920s. Two women writers who did practise metafiction, Marietta Shaginyan and Olga Forsh, unconsciously illustrated the obstacles to women's endeavours in this supposedly neutral and abstract direction: both of them, like their male contemporaries, used masculine figures as representations of authorship. The instigator of the literary contest which leads to the composition of the texts which make up Shaginyan's *Kik* is a man, and three out of the four authors who produce these texts are also men. The only woman author contributes a stylistically conventional text on a topic appropriate to her gender: the tale of a nun who has collaborated with the White forces in the Civil War.[18] In Olga Forsh's *The Crazy Ship* (1933), an obliquely narrated and technically brilliant fiction concerning the Petrograd House of Writers in the 1920s, the central figure/narrator is referred to throughout as 'the author', and a masculine pronoun is always employed.[19] Forsh's play *The Substitute Lecturer* (1930) made her one of the few Russian women writers to venture into the avant-garde theatre; this was an eccentric play-within-a-play whose technique to some extent prefigures Brecht's. But here, too, adventurousness was applied to 'masculine' material: the only female characters, apart from a servant, are a chorus of the mothers and wives of Copernicus's pupils, who urge him to comply with the church's demands.[20]

As in the pre-Revolutionary period, alternative representations of identity were to be associated with the memoir rather than with the novel. In the early 1930s Vera Gedroits, who wrote (as she had before the Revolution) using the male first name Sergei, published a substantial three-volume fictionalized autobiography: *The Little Caftan* (1930), *The Polack* (1931), and *The Break* (1931).[21] The first section is made up of fractured and lyrical reminiscences of childhood, criss-crossed by symbolic motifs, among them the 'caftan' of the title, which becomes both the

Age (London, 1990), 141–2.) When unable to exhibit in the 1930s, the painter Antonina Sofronova began writing poetry rather than in the Surrealist manner: ibid. 179.

[18] Marietta Shaginyan, *KiK, Sobranie sochinenii v 9 tomakh* (Moscow, 1971–5), ii. 494–613. On Shaginyan, see David Shepherd, 'Canon Fodder? Problems in the Reading of a Soviet Production Novel', in Catriona Kelly, Michael Makin, and David Shepherd (eds.), *Discontinuous Discourses in Modern Russian Literature* (London, 1989), 39–59; David Shepherd, *Beyond Metafiction: Self-Consciousness in Soviet Literature* (Oxford, 1992), 64–89.

[19] Ol'ga Forsh, *Sumasshedshii korabl'* (Leningrad, 1988).

[20] Forsh, *Lektor-zamestitel'*, *Sobranie sochinenii v 8 tomakh*, vii (Moscow, 1962), 331–51. (See also *The Substitute Lecturer* in Anthology.)

[21] Sergei Gedroits, *Kaftanchik* (Leningrad, 1930); *Lyakh* (Leningrad, 1931); *Otryv* (Leningrad, 1931).

metaphor for, and the fetish of, the narrator, Vera's, determination to change herself into a boy. Vera's problems of gender identification become more evident later on. 'Does being a girl disgust you?' a doctor asks her, and she replies that it does (*The Polack*, 116). Her relationships with women develop a homo-erotic character; eventually, when her brother dies, she takes his name and identity. Yet this is no simple and unproblematic realignment. Vera's change to 'Sergei' appears to furnish her with an easy new identity, but the shift depends on an asymmetrical polarization. Had her brother been her exact opposite, he would also have been a transsexual: instead, he has had an ostentatious affair with a peasant woman. Yet he is no paragon of machismo either, having been forced out of cadet school by his disgust at the brutal treatment he received there, and so Gedroits is not able to assimilate to a caricature of resolute masculinity. The instability of this gender understanding is reflected in the generic instability of Gedroits's memoirs, which shift from bleakly documentary observation (of Vera's mother's alcoholism, for example) to rich lyricism, and from the linear progression of the provincial tale (as Vera goes through her medical and political education) to a modernist emphasis on memory as an anti-linear, cyclic mode of narrative.

Gedroits's trilogy was praised in the highest terms by the writer Konstantin Fedin, who read it for the Leningrad State Publishing House. He compared it with Pasternak's *The Childhood of Luvers*, and suggested that it would enjoy an equal success. But the literary climate of the day was increasingly hostile to 'impressionism', or non-realist narrative modes, and Gedroits's text in fact had the distinction of being the last substantial piece of stylistically ambitious prose fiction to be published by a woman between 1932 and Stalin's death.[22]

Even before Socialist Realism was officially imposed on writers, the emphasis on originality as necessarily masculine had tended to push women prose writers in the direction of realist fiction. And since realist fiction was even more tightly connected with progressive ideology than it had been before the Revolution, this meant that they were exposed to the full pressures of Bolshevik thinking on women's liberation. Like their male counterparts, the women writers of the 1920s saw women's

---

[22] K. A. Fedin, 'Otzyv o predstavlennoi v Izd-vo Pisatelei povesti Gedroitsa Sergeya "Kaftanchik"', 22 Aug. 1929, Saltykov-Shchedrin State Public Library Manuscript Section f. 709 Sobr. avt. sovetskikh pisatelei i kritikov op. 1 N.56. An indication of changing attitudes is a review of a first-person narrative published not long after Gedroits's text, which criticizes 'unhealthy moods', 'impressionist tendencies', and 'elements of the literary tendency known as decadence' (T. Nikolaeva, 'T. Velednitskaya, *Povest' moei zhizni*', *KN* (1931), 5–6: 241–2). The use of first-person 'impressionism' continued, however, to be permissible in 'minor genres' such as the lyric poem and even the short story—see e.g. A. Krachkovskaya, 'Lavanda', *Molodaya gvardiya* (1939), 9: 90–5.

liberation in terms of encouraging members of backward classes to take a full part in the new society; and their representations hinged round similar positive and negative stereotypes. The 'positive' heroine of women's realist writing is normally a young woman worker, equal to her male contemporaries in self-confidence and determination; the 'negative' characters are peasant and bourgeois women, who are represented as being unable to adjust to the new social and cultural realities.[23] Occasionally peasant women or women with frivolous tendencies may prove reformable: in N. Chertova's 'The New Galoshes', for example, a woman white-collar worker who buys new footwear on the black market undergoes a Damascene conversion when she hears of Lenin's death.[24] But often women seem beyond hope. In texts such as Anna Karavaeva's novel *The Sawmill* or Lidiya Seifullina's novella *Mulch*, the peasant women are shown to be benighted repositories of folklore and popular medical belief, or else vessels of blindly bestial sexual feeling.[25] A typical such woman is Zinoveika, a village girl in *The Sawmill*, who, repulsed by the man on whom she has staked her affections, 'howls like a hungry, wounded she-animal'.

No less hostile were the 1920s representations of bourgeois women. Sometimes these 'ladies' can be seen driving good honest workers to distraction with their snobbish and uppity ways (as in N. Karatygina's short story 'Over the Furrows').[26] Frequently, though, we see them getting their come-uppance at the hands of sturdy representatives of proletarian machismo. In texts of the 1920s the rape or murder of a bourgeois or petit bourgeois woman is used with dispiriting regularity as a metaphor for class subjugation. One famous example of this tendency is Blok's narrative poem *The Twelve*, whose climax is the murder of a prostitute.[27] A still more shocking scene occurs in Khlebnikov's poem *The Night Search*, in which a White Russian officer's female relative is humiliated by a group of Red soldiers, in an act of verbal rape:

---

[23] 1920s texts which celebrate the working-class woman and denigrate the bourgeoise or peasant woman include, besides those cited below, L. Seifullina, 'V budnii den'', *KN* (1928), 7: 23–36; Tat'yana Igumnova, 'Ledokhod', *Pereval*, 3 (1925), 90–101; V. Gerasimova, 'Nedorogie kovry', *Pereval*, 1 (1925), 168–84; M. Chistyakova, 'Chetyre dnya', *KN* (1923), 7; 73–88; cf. the following text by a man: Nikolai Aseev, 'Tri Anny', *Sobranie sochinenii v 5 tomakh* (Moscow, 1963), ii. 155–8.

[24] N. Chertova, 'Novye galoshi', *Pereval*, 3 (1925), 176–87.

[25] Anna Karavaeva, *Lesozavod* (1927): citations to Moscow, 1935 edn.; Lidiya Seifullina, 'Peregnoi' (1922), citations to *Pravonarushiteli. Peregnoi* (Moscow, 1929). Xenia Gasiorowska, *Women in Soviet Literature 1917–1964* (Madison, Wis., 1968), expresses an approbatory view of 'Peregnoi', but in doing so also adopts a total identification with the masculine viewpoint, glossing the plot thus: 'The hero's utter dedication to the Soviet cause . . . is overcome by his tragic, lustful infatuation with a foolish little schoolteacher' (p. 18).

[26] N. Karatygina, 'Cherez borozdy', *Pereval*, 1 (1925), 83–114.

[27] Blok, *Dvenadtsat'*, *SS* iii. 347–59.

—А ну-ка,
Милая барышня в белом,
К стенке!
—Этой? Той?
Какой?
Я го-то-ва!
—А ну, к чертям ее!
—Стой!
Довольно крови!
Поворачивайся, кукла!
—Крови? Сегодня крови нет!
Есть жижа, жижа и жижа.
От скотного двора людей,
Видишь, темнеет лужа?
Это ейного брата
Или мужа.[28]

Dear young lady in white,
Back to the wall!
'This one? That one?
Which?
I-am- rea-dy.'
'To hell with her!'
'Stop!'
'Enough blood!
Turn round, doll!'
'Blood? There's no blood today!
Only slime, slime, slime.
See the puddle run dark
Where they butchered those people?
That's 'er brother, you know,
Or 'er husband.'

What Ronald Hingley has described as 'the characteristic atmosphere of the 1920s, compounded of pornography and sadism'[29] pervades the work of many authors who enjoy a high reputation in Russia and outside it; it is by no means something unique to the efforts of forgotten incompetents. Other texts in which violence against women is represented with equally prurient intensity are Bulgakov's *The White Guard*, and Babel's *Red Cavalry*.[30]

[28] Khlebnikov, 'Nochnoi obysk', *Tvoreniya* (Moscow, 1988), 321.
[29] Ronald Hingley, *Russian Writers in Soviet Society* (London, 1979), 175.
[30] Bulgakov, *Belaya gvardiya* (1924), in *Belaya gvardiya. Teatral'nyi roman. Master i Margarita* (Moscow, 1973), 13–271; see esp. the scene in the morgue, p. 247; Isaak Babel', *Konarmiya* (Moscow, 1928); see also Joe Andrew, ' "Spoil the Purest of Ladies": Male and Female in Isaak Babel's *Konarmiya*', EP 14/2 (1989), 1–27.

Women writers of the left were just as ready to include such scenes. In Seifullina's *Mulch*, for example, the village elder hero, one of the few Bolshevik sympathizers in an outpost of rural primitivism, is driven to fury by seeing a man emerge from the living quarters of the local schoolmistress, to whom he is himself attracted. His response is to rush in and rape the woman. The scene is depicted entirely through the perception of the man concerned; as the woman responds to him in a sexual sense, and then abases herself, she becomes an object of contempt both for him and for the reader:

He flung her to the ground by the door, and, stopping her mouth with his knee, closed the latch. 'You try squealing, you bitch, and I'll smash your head in! [. . .] You were flirting with me, but you gave it to someone else, eh! Here, show me! Still wet, are you? Eh, you filth, you w[hore]!' [. . .]

The squalor and cruelty of that act of possession, that worst insult to human nature, brought feeling with it; out of habit her body answered: 'A-ah!'

He got up, spat in her face, booted her away and turned to the door. Thin white hands grasped at him. She got up and pressed her body to his—once so passionately, so sacredly desired, now it was loathsome. [. . .]

'Sofron, don't tell anyone . . . I love you . . . I'll be yours . . . for a long time . . . for ever . . . Don't tell anyone . . . Don't shame me . . .'

Sucking up to him now, was she! All she cared about was that folks shouldn't turn their noses up . . . Revulsion and torment in his eyes, legs shaking from his coarse act of possession, but whispering, 'I'll be yours!' (pp. 90–1)

At the end of the story, an act of violence against a woman again becomes the occasion of the protagonist's suffering, and a metaphor for his internal conflicts: his wife is bayoneted by White soldiers as they attack the village. In contrast, another story by Seifullina, *Virineya*, depicts a heroine who is a model of monolithic resolution, rather than a wilting punch-ball for masculine aggression. But there is an important difference: Virineya, the eponymous protagonist, is from the working classes—though, unusually, she is a rural factory worker rather than a member of the urban proletariat.[31]

Occasionally, woman writers do make adjustments to the 'class war' stereotypes. One interesting and unusual treatment of the revolutionary heroine is Anna Barkova's play *Nastasya Bonfire* (1923).[32] The play is set in early seventeenth-century Russia; the distance between fictional time and the time of the play's composition may have facilitated the ambivalence with which it portrays revolutionary endeavour. Nastasya, the bandit-rebel heroine, is the match for any man in her sexual rapacity

[31] Seifullina, *Virineya*, in her *Sobranie sochinenii*, iii (Moscow, 1926).
[32] Anna Barkova, *Nastas'ya Koster: dramaticheskie stseny* (Moscow-Petrograd, 1923).

and lust for blood, but she is also a tragic figure, who is forced to recognize the limitations which the way of violence brings with it. As she puts it herself, in a moment of insight, 'Yes, I am strong. I'm dead strong. My strength will be the death of me' (p. 72). Expressing love solely by aggression herself, she also expects to be assaulted by her lovers; her end, quite logically, is to be betrayed by an associate, but to go down fighting. The play reworks motifs which had also been developed in Barkova's collection of poetry, *Woman*, published in 1922, but its language, interweaving popular songs, folkloric motifs, and demotic speech, is far richer than that of Barkova's early lyric.[33]

Until the crack-down on unofficial groups began in 1925, women writers generally could use poetry in order to express more diverse notions of the self than could find their way into prose. As we have seen, Anna Akhmatova's published poetry of the early 1920s such as 'Fear turns objects over', included work which not only evoked the victimization of women in the Red Terror, but also used historical and literary references to give this a particular grandeur. Poets were aided by the fact that in the 1920s, as in the 1840s, it was prose rather than poetry which carried prestige; as a peripheral literary medium, poetry was subject to less overt regulation. Affiliations in poetry were also more unpredictable than in prose, leading, for instance, to the publication of selected lyrics by one extremely conventional 'feminine' poet in a provincial anthology of proletarian poetry.[34]

Despite the peculiar restrictions of their medium, however, some prose writers of the 1920s were also able to loosen the straightjacket of the class-war vignette. Ekaterina Strogova's story-cycle 'Peasant Women' (1927), for example, begins with a predictable enough narrative relating how a housemaid turned baroness inspires the peculiar loathing of her own servants, and then is rejected for Party membership by her work-mates, who include her own former housemaid, after the Revolution.[35] However, the stories that follow are much more complex and subtle. We see women factory workers who are politically active and able to determine their own concerns, yet who can also regard 'the feminine' as a source of pride; in a pleasantly ironic passage, Strogova shows how the working women are always concerned to wear the best clothes that they can afford, and that they feel a slight sense of contempt for the intellectual Party activists playing at workers in their leather jackets.

[33] Barkova, *Zhenshchina* (Petrograd, 1922).

[34] See e.g. the work of N. Kugusheva, published in *Golgofa strof: stikhi* (Ryazan, 1920).

[35] Ek[aterina] Strogova, 'Baby: fabrichnye ocherki', *Pereval*, 5 (1927), 175–97. See also 'Women-folk' in *Anthology*.

Whilst not in any sense idealizing the women workers (she depicts an unsavoury incident in which one woman is ostracized by her workmates because they suspect that she is a lesbian), Strogova sees the conflict of values between them and Party ideology in rather less jejune terms than most of her contemporaries. For her, 'backwardness' is a rational and functional system of behaviour, with its own codes and beliefs; it is not perceived simply as a pathetic tangle of rudimentary and inadequate perceptions, which can easily be weeded out and replanted with the coherent and complex growths of advanced thinking.

Most other women writers contemplated official ideology less thoughtfully than Strogova, though, and their laudatory representations of Bolshevik policy often throw up unconscious ironies. In Karavaeva's *The Saw Mill*, for example, the women's section activist heroine is struck by the repetitive and tedious work to which women are consigned in the village. Her solution is to recruit them to routine, unskilled, ancillary tasks in the saw mill—progress indeed. Often, in literature as in ideology, there is a direct link between assimilation to the public life and assimilation to masculinity. The hero of Seifullina's 'The Delinquents' (1922), for example, is a youth leader in a Soviet orphanage, whose strategies of social engineering—which is to say treating the girls like boys—effect positive changes in the lives of the children in his care: the girls are now able to take a full part in society.[36] The emphasis (as in radical writings of the nineteenth century) is on subordination of 'feminine' desires to the Cause: the heroine of *The Saw Mill*, for example, takes her baby along to political meetings; there is never any suggestion that the child could be left with her partner, and in fact an important strand in the narrative is that she learns to adjust her emotional and sexual demands on him in accordance with his work and Party duties. A similar rationalization of work and personal life in favour of the former is advocated in a much better-known text, Kollontai's trio of short stories *The Love of Worker Bees* (1923). The central character in the collection's most famous component, its first story 'The Love of Three Generations', is a young woman who has learnt not to waste any time on the soul-searching and emotional dependency of her mother and grandmother, nor on her own biology: her final gesture of independence is an abortion. And in the last of the three stories, a woman worker whose husband has gone off with the usual caricature bourgeois floosy is able to sublimate emotional upheaval in work. Just to press the point home, the collection ends with a paean to the 'worker bees' of the title,

---

[36] Seifullina, *Pravonarushiteli*, in *Peregnoi, Pravonarusheteli* (Moscow, 1929). (Trans. as 'The Lawbreakers' in G. Reavey and M. Slonim (eds.), *Soviet Literature* (New York, 1934).)

appropriate metaphors of a sterile, obedient, and diligent femininity, who are exhorted to 'live and love life' as they labour away.[37]

All this was utterly in tune with official policy on equality, as well as with the traditional resolution of the provincial tale; but Kollontai did also absorb from nineteenth-century women's social criticism its emphasis on the need for men to reform their behaviour, and to take on some of the 'feminine' attributes of affective frankness and sympathy for others. She has, too, a positive view of gender solidarity, delineating relations between women in favourable terms; in 'Sisters', the second story of *Worker Bees*, she illustrates how a prostitute is persuaded to reform herself by meeting the wife of the man who has accosted her. Similar material is also incorporated by Anna Karavaeva, who gives an idyllic view of a women's section at work in *The Saw Mill*, and who shows the hero as well as the heroine being re-educated: if she learns to be less demanding, he also learns to be more responsive. In such tales we can see how the didactic fable of sensibility again reworks itself in a new context, one incorporating both the celebration of work now requisite and the late nineteenth-century orthodoxy attributing women's emotional satisfaction primarily to their sexual satisfaction.

But if occasional writers did place some emphasis on the specificity of women's inner life (however schematically depicted), the real concern of 1920s fiction was to show women as men's equals in the sense of being competent workers in the factory and the Party. This concern was to be made explicit at, and perpetuated by, the 1934 Congress of Writers, but with a new shift of emphasis, as group after group of factory and collective farmers was sent on to the platform to demand literary representations appropriate to the leading roles in industry and agriculture which, they declared, Soviet rule had now given women.[38] These carefully orchestrated speeches were signals that literature should now take on board Stalin's suspension of the 'woman question' in 1930; they indicated that women must now be represented as necessarily equal, rather than as necessarily (except in extraordinary class circumstances) unequal.

The declaration of equality for women in fiction was to have a variety of effects. It meant that attacks on women writers on the grounds of their sex were now to become much less frequent; but on the other hand, it was now no longer possible to confront the problem of discrimination against women. All writers, men and women alike, were to produce plain tales, simply told, which celebrated the participation of women in

[37] Aleksandra Kollontai, *Lyubov' trudovykh pchel* (Moscow-Petrograd, 1923). (Available with other writings by Kollontai in *Selected Writings*, ed. and trans. Alix Holt (London, 1977).)

[38] *Pervyi s"ezd sovetskikh pisatelei*, 62, 73, 395.

industry and agriculture. There was to be an end to tales of desperation and deprivation in the villages and factories, and fables of conscious-ness-raising amongst women. At the same time, a ban on 'naturalism', or expression of the 'physiological', signalled a new puritanism about sex; rape, for example, had become unmentionable not only as a punishment for those born in the wrong class, but in any context whatever. Rather than succumbing to sex or violence, negative characters might now be subjected to verbal invective, and represented satirically, satire having been given canonical status at the 1934 Congress as a counter-pole to Socialist Realism, an ancillary force which was to support the mythic puissance of Socialist Realism by routing its enemies through laughter.

The impact of satire's new significance on the representation of women was to be registered by Lidiya Seifullina in an article written three years after the Congress, in 1937. Underlining the importance of equal treatment for both sexes in fiction, she called for an end to the idealization of women, and suggested that the negative qualities of vanity and sexual jealousy should appear more frequently in delineations of women characters.[39] Women writers in particular were to make sure that Seifullina's wishes came true: the satirical portraits of a petty-minded and materialistic cosmetician in Karavaeva's obese trilogy *The Motherland* (1951) or of a young woman's disastrous and humiliating attempt to pluck her eyebrows in Panova's *The Troop Train* (1947) are typical examples of how female foolishness was mocked.[40]

The persistence in satire of traditional 'feminine' stereotypes makes all too evident the hollowness of the declaration that inequality for women was at an end. Even in fiction (let alone in real life), women had by no means achieved parity. Successful women engineers and brigade leaders may people the pages of Soviet novels and stories of the 1930s and 1940s, but in fact these fictions are more concerned with the lives and deeds of men than with the lives and deeds of women. In her stimulating analysis of the Socialist Realist novel, the critic Katerina Clark has identified what she terms a 'master plot', a narrative stereotype in which the hero is subjected to various trials and rites of passage in his path to enlighten-ment.[41] 'Master plot' is in fact exactly the right term, for this narrative of masculine heroic progress has no feminine equivalent. Heroines are generally represented as Athenas who spring into life fully armed in ideological rectitude. This is true, at any rate, of the intelligentsia women

[39] Seifullina, 'O zhenskom obraze', *O literature*, 27–34.

[40] Karavaeva, *Rodina* (Moscow, 1951): a trilogy consisting of three novels earlier published separately, *Ogni* (Moscow, 1944), *Razbeg* (Moscow, 1947), *Rodnoi dom* (Moscow, 1950); Panova, *Sputniki* (Moscow, 1947) (trans. as *The Train* (Moscow, 1977)).

[41] Katerina Clark, *The Soviet Novel: History as Ritual* (Chicago, 1981).

on whom women writers concentrate, such as Nina, the engineer heroine of Panova's *Kruzhilikha*, or Olga in *The Motherland*, the engineer's daughter and would-be pianist who has gone on to the factory floor in the national interest.[42] These women have their occasional bursts of self-criticism (a vaunted virtue in Stalinist ideology)—Olga, for example, realizes that she should be allowing more time for a brigade-leader to breast-feed her child—but such twinges of doubt occupy an insignificant place by comparison with the weighty deliberations of the men. Equally, though negative female characters may occasionally prove reformable, and there is some emphasis on the importance of education to women collective farmers, these, too, are peripheral narrative elements.[43] The Socialist Realist novel depicts the ideal society of the socialist future; yet it invariably represents a world in which the leaders (factory and Party chiefs, ideologues) are all men. The quintessence of the Socialist Realist heroine is the female partisan of war literature, who fights at the front along with the men, but who is subordinated to higher male authority in the form of her military commanders.[44]

The Socialist Realist ethic did not simply underline male power through its representation of work hierarchies, but also through its representation of the family. The model most frequently advocated for writers at the 1934 Congress was Gorky's *Mother*, the tale of a simple working woman who turns out to be capable of having her consciousness raised, but also the portrait of a rapt and adulatory mother–son relation.[45] And from the mid-1930s, maternity in that restricted sense, the breeding and training of active new male citizens, was to become an increasingly important element in Soviet fiction, including fiction by women. In 1935, the year before abortion was made illegal, and at a stage when restrictions on its availability had already been introduced, Tatyana Tess published a story in one of the most prestigious Soviet literary journals, *Krasnaya nov*, which depicted a woman's agonies of guilt as she went to the abortion clinic, a place full of women 'screaming

[42] Panova, *Kruzhilikha* (Moscow, 1948).

[43] Both Karavaeva's *The Motherland* and Galina Nikolaeva's novel *Zhatva* (Moscow, 1950), represent minor female characters who manage to better themselves: in both cases the transition is achieved without problems so far as these women themselves are concerned. In the case of Nikolaeva's novel, the difficulties of men in adjusting to the change provide more narrative interest.

[44] Tales of Soviet war heroines, whether those fighting on the front line or those keeping the furnaces of the munitions factory going, are collected e.g. in *Soviet Women in the War against Hitlerism* (Moscow, 1942); *Soviet War Stories* (London, 1944); *Zhenshchiny goroda Lenina: ocherki o zhenshchinakh Leningrada v dni blokady* (Leningrad, 1944); see also Aliger's celebration of the partisan heroine Zoya Kosmodemyanskaya, 'Zoya' (1942), *Sobranie sochinenii v 3 tomakh* (Moscow, 1984), i. 277–321.

[45] For particular commendations of Gorky's *Mother* see *Pervyi s"ezd sovetskikh pisatelei*, 62, 366.

and writhing in pain'. The reader is shown how this woman's sufferings continue afterwards as she contemplates the duty of motherhood which she has neglected, and sees 'other people's children [. . .] other people's future already achieved'.[46]

The year 1935, which also saw the production of *To Dine with the Mothers*, an enormous icon painted by Gaponenko which represented women breast-feeding their plump pink offspring during a break from the harvest, was a turning-point in Soviet representations of women. As late as 1933 or 1934, official literature had still harked back to the traditions of the 1920s: early poems by Margarita Aliger, for example, showed a young working woman expressing pity for a contemporary stuck in the mire of domesticity ('Wife', 1934), or poked fun at a young woman jealous of her beloved's female colleagues at work ('The Tempest', 1933).[47] But from 1935, there is an insistence that women may at one and the same time contribute to the cause of industrialization *and* perform their duties as brood mares by state appointment. In a story published in 1940, 'Rose, My Rose', Anna Karavaeva showed how a young woman, first discovered breast-feeding her baby in appropriate Madonna and Child style, is persuaded by an older woman friend to leave home and child and go out to work; she and her husband are anxious at first, but soon find that their relationship is working still better than before.[48] Sometimes motherhood is even celebrated independently of any work duties. For example, a poem by Tatyana Volgina, published in 1941, both apotheosized burgeoning maternity, and asserted adult woman as servant to infant man:

> О себе он криком зычным
> Громко станет заявлять:
> Все соседи с непривычки
> Будут уши закрывать.
> И от криков этих маме
> Уж не спать тогда ночами,
> До зари качать его . . .
> Только зто ничего.
> Пой, жужжи, моя машина!
> Рупашонки шей для сына,
> Чтоб не складок, не морщин,
> Чтобы был доволен сын![49]

[46] Tat'yana Tess, 'Materinstvo', *KN* (1935), 8: 156–60.
[47] For a reproduction of the Gaponenko picture, see Igor Golomstock, *Totalitarian Art* (London, 1990), 192. Margarita Aliger, 'Zhena', 'Burya', *Sobranie sochinenii v 3-kh tomakh*, i. 29–31, 22–4.
[48] Karavaeva, 'Rozan moi, rozan', *KN* (1940), 7–8: 27–43.
[49] Tat'yana Volgina, 'Pridanoe', *KN* (1941), 3: 89.

His noisy yells
Will ring like bells,
And our neighbours all around
Will shut their ears against the sound.
No sleep for his mum
In nights to come,
She'll rock him for hours at a time,
But that's no matter, she'll be fine.
Sewing-machine, rattle and hum!
Making rompers for my son!
Not a wrinkle let there be,
So my son is pleased with me!

When the Second World War began, the need for womanpower again became paramount, and the insistence that women should place duty to State above duty to family again became the main theme of official literature. Typical war stories dealt with women who refused to betray their partisan comrades even when their babies were cut in two before their very eyes, or who left a comfortable life at home to work sixteen-hour shifts in munitions factories.[50] But in the late 1940s, as the exigencies of population replacement after the war made themselves felt, the representation of motherhood was to become a near-obligatory part of Soviet literature (and of painting too, for that matter).[51] However, the continuing needs of the factory floor also dictated that fictional women should still be shown displaying an unabated commitment to work. To production and reproduction were added the duties of appropriate conjugality: though in practice unmarried liaisons were tolerated as an alternative method of insemination, and single women were granted maternity incentives, the conventional nuclear family was perceived as the fulcrum of social stability, and so its symbolic role became still further entrenched. In ideology and literature, babies are always born to, and brought up by, two legally wedded parents; even single mothers in the sense of war widows are a rarity.[52]

The heroines of late 1940s magazine articles, stories, and novels are treated as equals by their work and Party colleagues; they weld and lay bricks as expertly as anyone; but once their overalls are off and they have crossed the thresholds of their model flats, they don their aprons and fall

[50] See O. Kurganov, 'Motherhood', *Soviet Women in the War Against Hitlerism*, 42.

[51] On motherhood in painting and statuary, see Golomstock, *Totalitarian Art*; Alison Hilton, 'Women in Soviet Art', in Liljeström, Mäntysaari, and Rosenholm (eds.), *Gender Restructuring*.

[52] A war-widow mother in Karavaeva's *Rodina* e.g. is restored to proper status when her husband is rediscovered. Nikolaeva's sketch 'Zhivye golosa', *Sobranie sochinenii v 3 tomakh* (Moscow, 1973), iii. 308–26, which refers to an unmarried mother, is based on material collected in the late 1940s and early 1950s, but was not published until 1957.

with enthusiasm to their household tasks. As an article by a professional woman which was published in the magazine *Soviet Woman* during 1947 put it:

Many people believe to this day that a woman who chooses a scientific career ceases to be feminine, neglects her looks, and doesn't care about her home. I must say I have never felt that in my own case. I have always enjoyed taking care of my appearance. I still like to dance, I adore my home, and love to make it cosy.[53]

Like other women's magazines in the 1940s, *Soviet Woman* carried endless portraits, both photographic and verbal, of such superwomen—female heroes of labour, record-breaking milkmaids, and Stalin-prize-winning professionals, often shown with their beaming, well-fed broods arranged around them in their 'cosy homes'. Such hymns to successful femininity, Soviet style, are sandwiched between educational material for aspiring all-round women: fashion photographs, recipes, tips on housekeeping and child care, and cheering poems on such subjects as 'Our Soviet Mothers', crafted with all the imagination and originality of greetings-card verse.[54]

The heroines of 1940s novels display an equal ability to harmonize their lives. Having worked on the production line until the last possible minute, women brigade members go off and produce bouncing sons for the motherland, and the fusion of state and private interests may be symbolically crowned by a marriage between the engineer heroine and the Party organizer hero.[55] The day-to-day demands of work and home are juggled by women characters with eye-stretching competence and efficiency. Just occasionally there are hints that even superwomen may not always cope entirely on their own. One woman may help another look after the children for a while, or a heroic husband put himself out to help his wife. In Galina Nikolaeva's novel *The Harvest* (1947), for example, there is a scene in which Valya, an agronomist, is late back from a meeting, and so keeps her husband waiting for supper. But he, we learn, treats this disruption of his rights remarkably tolerantly, and has 'even set the table' by the time that she returns.[56] A different kind of co-operation is sketched in Karavaeva's *Motherland*: here domestic arrange-

---

[53] See *Soviet Woman* (the English version of *Sovetskaya zhenshchina*) (1947), 3: 31.

[54] Apart from *Soviet Woman/Sovetskaya zhenshchina*, such material also appeared in *Rabotnitsa* and *Krest'yanka*.

[55] Among characters who produce sons more or less inside the factory is Tanya in Karavaeva's *The Motherland*; symbolic marriages include that between Ol'ga and the party organizer Plastunov in this novel, and between Nonna the engineer and Listopad the manager in Panova's *Kruzhilikha*.

[56] Nikolaeva, *Zhatva* (for publication details see n. 43 above).

ments at the house of the heroine's parents are in the hands of a devoted elderly nanny, who has also (as it happens) protected the piano and the furniture from the atrocities to which they might otherwise have been subjected by German barbarians after the evacuation of the city.

For all the preposterousness of such scenes, they do indicate, if only remotely and obliquely, that Soviet women in the 1940s were often thrown on non-State resources in order to cope at all. In particular, help from other women and domestic servants was of great importance in enabling working women to overcome the exigencies of the 'double burden', women's simultaneous subjection to work and to domestic commitments; for, as a Soviet manual for prospective mothers, *Mother and Baby*, firmly informed its readers in 1951, child care outside work hours was considered to be the responsibility of parents, not of the State.[57] Writings of the 1940s and early 1950s also throw out hints that maternity was in practice often accompanied by physical discomfort and difficulty. The stress in fiction on the devotion of women who work practically to the moment of parturition can be seen as a dim reflection of the still not terribly generous provisions for maternity leave; mothers who have to breast-feed during shifts are illustrations of the inadequacies of postnatal leave. The unconsciously enlightening lapses here are similar to those in other propaganda sources. For example, the following passage from *Mother and Baby* indirectly indicates, for all its military rhetoric, something of the grim realities of maternity care: 'Like a soldier in the heat of battle, who is borne up by the thought of moving ever onward, so a woman dreaming of a child feels no pain when giving birth.' Proper women, in other words, need no pain-killers.[58]

But if 1940s and 1950s texts do afford insights through their occasional oversights, all the same, the gap between the happy fictional families of the 1940s, and the actual conditions of the day, was nothing less than immense. Soviet literature, like Soviet ideology, silently ignored the families atomized by war; the fresh rounds of political persecutions; the ubiquity of squalor and overcrowding in bomb-blasted cities; the constant food and goods shortages; the utterly deprived conditions of work and life in the countryside that had been brought by the devastation of agriculture during collectivization; and the struggles of women to bring up children without male partners in a society where concrete help for mothers, as opposed to their decoration with the trumpery medals of

---

[57] B. A. Arkhangel'sky and G. N. Speransky, *Mat' i ditya: shkola molodykh materei* (Moscow, 1951), 12.

[58] Ibid. 33. Though the authors go on to state that 'pain-killers are available', they give no details, and the battlefield analogy is hardly confidence-inspiring on this point.

'Hero Mothers of the Soviet Union', remained inadequate, and where labour-saving devices were non-existent.[59]

Read in the comfort of a modern Western country, Socialist Realist fictions come across as harmless kitsch: banally reassuring fantasies laced with occasional dollops of unconscious humour (such as the scene in *The Motherland* in which a character alleges that he forgets the pain caused by his industrial accident as soon as he thinks of Stalin). The intellectual and technical level of these fictions approximates to that of some Western popular genres, such as the hospital romance—save that the importance of work and of emotional attachments is exactly reversed. Like hospital romances, women's Socialist Realist novels deal with manly men and womanly women: resolute, craggy-browed Party organizers, shapely women in high heels, sheer stockings, and discreetly-applied lipstick, and slender but energetic young girls whose delicacy of mind is such that they rinse their mouths out (as a young woman in Panova's *The Troop Train* actually does) when first kissed by a man.

To apply the analytical tools of literary criticism to such material would be sophistical; it is not the discovery of untold profundities in such fictions which is important, but the discrepancy between their comical literary naïvety and the eminently serious campaigns of terror waged in order to ensure their unchallenged place as the central expressions of Soviet literary culture. For official Soviet literary consciousness, this writing was anything but harmless trash. It was literature intended to lay the foundations of a new integrated national-popular and socialist culture, to form a breakwater against, and provide an uplifting alternative to, the tide of decadence which had overwhelmed the countries of the bourgeois West. Karavaeva's work was published in magazines for a worker and peasant audience, yes, but it also appeared regularly in the most prestigious literary journals, and *The Motherland* trilogy gained its author a Stalin Prize (third class).

But what of the readers? To an even greater extent than with nineteenth-century literature, one wonders who was reading these novels, and what people's private reactions to them were. The question will probably never be answered definitively. Soviet culture of the 1930s and 1940s required no reader surveys or market research: its ideology was both dogmatic and self-reinforcing. Critical reception was simply another branch of official ideology; it expressed views identical, or nearly identical, with those evident in the texts in any case. It is fair enough to suppose, however, that these texts seemed an irritating and even

---

[59] It is probably memoir literature which gives the best view of 1940s realities: see e.g. Evgeniya Kiseleva's memoirs, 'Kishmareva, Kiseleva, Tyuricheva', *NM* (1991), 2: 9–27.

disgusting irrelevance to some readers who had an idea of the realities of the Terror. But for many others they probably functioned as an uplifting or consoling vision of a socialist utopia just round the corner, or as a wish-fulfilling fantasy of a normal, decent life without stress or hardship, a vital counterbalance to the exigencies of actuality.[60]

And whilst historical accuracy requires that we have an adequate sense of the coercive processes which propelled the Socialist Realist novel to centre stage, it equally demands that we should also not overlook Socialist Realism's links with the traditions of women's writing. In terms of these traditions, much 1920s women's fiction had been in some senses aberrant. Though the 'class war' narratives did draw on traditions worked out in the 1890s and 1900s, many of them had overtones of an misogyny more overt and extreme than any evident in women's writing of earlier generations. Given that many texts by male writers of the day expressed a similar, or greater, hostility to women, the obsequious gallantries of the 1930s and 1940s may well have come as something of a relief to women writers and readers. As Vera Panova writes in her memoirs, the resurrection of 'bourgeois' family relations had been welcomed by some women, now tired of the tyranny of the silly young men who had branded, say, terms of endearment as ideologically unsound.[61] And in her memoirs, Olga Berggolts recorded the inevitable slow erosion of the orderly communes set up in the early Soviet years by the consequences of human nesting:

We were a group of young (very young!) engineers and workers who'd set up [our commune] at the very beginning of the 1930s, pooling our state rations as supplies. It was all part of an all-out fight against the 'old domestic order' (i.e. cooking and nappies). So not one single flat had anywhere you could prepare food, let alone a kitchen. There weren't even lobbies where you could hang clothes—the cloakroom was communal too, and on the same floor, as you came in, was a communal nursery and a communal playroom; we'd decided that all our time should be spent communally. There was to be no individualism. . . . But not very much later, a couple of years at most, when rationing had come to an end and we had grown up a bit, we discovered that we had rushed into things and made our domestic life so communal that there was no retreat, except for the window-sills. And it was there that the first backsliders started cooking their own private meals.[62]

Whilst the Socialist Realist novel hardly reflected the slow creeping of

[60] On the wish-fulfilling character of 1940s literature, see particularly Vera Dunham, *In Stalin's Time: Middle-Class Values in Soviet Fiction* (Cambridge, 1976); the bourgeois values of the time are also given a balanced analysis in Zernova's story 'Elizabet Arden' (see Ch. 13 n. 63).

[61] Panova, *O moei zhizni*, 129.

[62] Berggol'ts, *Dnevnye zvezdy*, 67.

human disorder that Berggolts describes, its roots may have lain in a similar nostalgia for old-fashioned domesticity. The mid-1930s saw a myth of a woman who was either entirely committed to public life, or else the rightful victim of a proletarian hero, replaced by a sentimentally coloured vision of a woman 'self-confident in the manner of a woman revolutionary and yet full of feminine gentleness', as a prophetic phrase from Karavaeva's *The Saw Mill* had put it (p. 326). There were certainly more people who celebrated the arrival of the latter than who mourned the departure of the former.

But if some of Socialist Realism's roots lay in a response to the repressive habits of thought prevalent in the 1920s, that did not make it less repressive itself. The only stage at which a brief breathing-space from compulsory celebration of static female heroism was allowed was the Second World War. Then, the authors of the 'home front', such as the women poets of the Leningrad Blockade, Olga Berggolts and Vera Inber, could write of a world where 'exceeding one's norm' meant simply spending the next few days alive:

> Был день как день
> Ко мне пришла подруга.
> Не плача, рассказала, что вчера
> единственного схоронила друга,
> и мы молчали с нею до утра.
>
> Какие ж я могла найти слова,
> я тоже—ленинградская вдова.
>
> Мы съели хлеб
>   что был положен
>   на день,
> в один платок закутались вдвоем,
> и тихо-тихо стало в Ленинграде.
> Один, стуча, трудился метроном.[63]

> A day like any other,
> A friend of mine came round.
> She said to me, dry-eyed,
> Her only love was buried yesterday.
> And she and I sat silent till first light.
>
> What words could I say.
> I am a Leningrad widow too.
>
> We ate the bread,
>   our ration for the day,

---

[63] Berggol'ts, *Izbrannye proizvedeniya* (Leningrad, 1983), 225. On the war poetry of Berggol'ts and other women poets, see Katharine Hodgson, 'Russian Soviet War Poetry 1941–45', Ph.D. thesis (Cambridge University, 1991), 216–68.

Sat wrapped together in one scarf.
Silent, silent was the town,
The only sound a labouring metronome.

The wartime relaxation of the Party line was not the only unpredictable ideological softening that occurred from time to time, even in the high days of Stalinism; but it was the most notable of these.[64] Such respites aside, women writers hostile to Socialist Realism could only keep writing without the slightest hope of being published in the foreseeable future, if they did not cease writing altogether. But such cases belong in the second part of this survey.

Outsiders

As well as the writers domiciled in the Soviet Union who shunned what might be termed 'totalitarian literature', the group that I term 'outsider writers' includes the many writers who actually lived in emigration, outside the borders of Russia. Though political exile was nothing new for Russian writers, including women writers (Zinaida Volkonskaya having been one notable pre-Revolutionary example), the Bolshevik Revolution initiated a diaspora whose scale, accelerated by the final defeat of the White Russian forces in 1921, and the end of the Russian Civil War, rapidly exceeded anything seen before in Russian history. Amongst such *émigrés* proper, as amongst the 'internal *émigrés*' of Soviet life, women were well represented. Those who took up residence outside their homeland included some of the best-known women writers of pre-Revolutionary Russia, such as Marina Tsvetaeva, Zinaida Gippius, Lyubov Stolitsa, Nadezhda Teffi, and Elizaveta Kuzmina-Karavaeva (who was now known as Elizaveta Skobtsova, the surname of her second husband, and who was to adopt the religious name Mother Mariya when she became an Orthodox nun in 1932). All these writers continued to produce work after leaving Russia, a good deal of which was of a quality to belie the received opinion (subscribed to by many Soviet Russians) that writers cannot create when separated from their native land. After 1930 these writers were joined by a new, younger, generation, none of whom had published in Russia itself: notable female members of this included Anna Prismanova, Vera Bulich, Raisa Blokh, Ekaterina Bakunina, Nadezhda Gorodetskaya, and Alla Golovina. Within the Soviet Union, the poets and writers of the other, internal,

---

[64] Another period of relative relaxation was 1940, during which Anna Akhmatova was wooed by two official publishing houses at once for the rights to her new collection. (See Chukhovskaya, records for 1940 in *Zapiski*, vol. i.)

emigration included established figures such as Anna Akhmatova, Adelaida Gertsyk, Anna Barkova, and Sofiya Parnok, besides younger or less prominent writers such as Mariya Shkapskaya, Vera Merkureva, and Lidiya Chukovskaya.[65]

Both internal and external *émigrés* had put themselves beyond the bounds of the explicit constraints suffered by those who wrote for official publication in the Soviet Union, at any rate after 1925, when attitudes began to harden, and the Soviet establishment, having previously taken a line that might be summed up as 'whoever is not against us is with us' began increasingly to work according to the principle, 'whoever is not with us is against us'. Outside the Soviet Union, the mechanics of publication were not subject to overt legal control. In every city where *émigrés* settled (Paris, Berlin, London, Prague, Belgrade, Warsaw, Riga, Tallinn, Helsinki, Harbin, and even Buenos Aires) there was a range of publishing houses, and of journals publishing and reviewing poetry and fiction. All gave space to large numbers of women writers (not to speak of the occasional man writing under a female pseudonym). Economic constraints (the Russian readership for serious literature was not enormous) meant that placing collections might be more difficult, but there was always the possibility of publishing and distributing these privately. This was a method adopted by several women poets, as well as some men. In the 1920s some internal *émigrés*, too, placed their work abroad; thereafter, opportunities to publish were limited to the circulation of material in manuscript, or through the oral rather than the written medium (which were methods that were so dangerous as to be a rarity). Examples of texts that were circulated in this way, by being read aloud or recited, include the stories of Lidiya Chukovskaya, Akhmatova's poems on the Terror (later to be grouped in the cycle *Requiem*), and certain of the poems which Olga Berggolts wrote following her arrest in 1937.[66]

---

[65] The fullest survey of general cultural aspects of the Russian diaspora is Marc Raeff, *Russia Abroad: A Cultural History of the Russian Emigration, 1919–1939* (Oxford, 1990); Gleb Struve's *Russkaya literatura v izgnanii* (2nd edn.; Paris, 1984) is still the most informative general study of literary matters. See also L. Fleishman, R. Khyuz [Hughes], O. Raevskaya-Khyuz, *Russkii Berlin* (Paris, 1983); Georges Nivat (ed.), *Odna ili dve russkikh literatury* (Geneva, 1981). The memoirs of *émigré* writers, whilst not invariably accurate in a factual sense, are valuable guides to the mentality of the emigration: see e.g. Vladimir Nabokov, *Speak, Memory* (1951; London, 1986); Nina Berberova, *Kursiv moi* (Munich, 1972) (trans. Philippe Radley as *The Italics are Mine* (London, 1969)); Irina Odoevtseva, *Na beregu Seny* (Paris, 1983). There is still no general history of the 'internal emigration'; materials of relevance are cited under individual authors below.

[66] Summaries of *émigré* publishing history are given in Raeff, *Russia Abroad*, 75–94; see also T[emira] P[achmuss], 'Émigré Literature', in Terras, *Handbook*, 119–24. One man who published in *émigré* journals under a female disguise was Konstantin Bal'mont, who used the pseudonym Aglaya Gamayun for poems published in the Riga journal *Perezvony*. On the circulation of Akhmatova and Chukovskaya, see Chukovskaya, *Zapiski*; on the circulation of Berggol'ts, Efim Etkind's introduction to Berggol'ts, 'Bezumstvo predannosti', *Vremya i my*, 57 (1980), 271.

Literary Russians abroad were acutely sensitive to cultural events in their homeland; a certain, if necessarily limited, awareness of life in the emigration was also evident amongst at least some writers at home. But at least as important as direct contact in connecting the two groups was their shared alienation from Bolshevik, and later from Stalinist, cultural policy. Both in and outside the Soviet Union, reactions inspired by this alienation might take two directions. On the one hand, the apparent disintegration of pre-Revolutionary Russian cultural tradition provoked the development of new and more genuinely modernist literary ideologies; but Russian *émigrés'* sense of loss also provoked, on the other hand, attempts to recover or salvage the threatened past via a consolidation of pre-Revolutionary nationalist values, and a further entrenchment of a neo-Romantic emphasis on the sacred function of art and the hieratic role of the writer.

The second of these two directions, whilst apparently conservative, was in fact quite innovative, since it required the construction of an alternative, non-Bolshevik, myth of national identity, a myth which very often had religio-mystical overtones.[67] Like Soviet ideology, this anti-Soviet ideology was based on a centre-periphery dichotomy, with the centre dominated by myths that were invariably gendered as masculine. Governing constructs for the poet as the true voice of Russia and the people were the prophet and the martyr, in the latter case often with allusions to the Passion of Christ. The support and legitimation for this new national-populist ideology was a literary canon of great writers: Blok, Tyutchev, Dostoevsky, and above all Pushkin. Women were not ignored within the national-populist trend in the non-Soviet literary tradition. But they were subordinated within it: as the male worker hero had a female worker consort, so the male martyr or Messiah was paired with or accompanied by persistent metaphors or female mourners or suffering mothers, who stood both for the collective identity of Russian women, and for the Russian motherland as a whole.

Where women's writing was considered the vehicle of individual, rather than collective, insights, another set of equally restrictive assumptions came into play, which were the more powerful for never being questioned or analysed. No doubt because the central vehicle of *émigré* criticism was a literary essay whose aesthetic perspective had been heavily influenced by Acmeism, 'feminine writing' was understood to be

---

[67] On the importance of 'Messianic' motifs in writing by men after the Revolution, see e.g. Gregory Freidin, *A Coat of Many Colors: Osip Mandelstam's Mythologies of Self-Transformation* (Berkeley, Calif., 1988); on the prehistory of such motifs, see George Ivask, 'Russian Modernist Poets and the Mystic Sectarians', in George Gibian and H. W. Tjalsma (eds.), *Russian Modernism: Culture and the Avant-Garde 1900–1930* (Ithaca, NY, 1976), 85–106.

characterized by subtlety in the presentation of suitably restrained feeling, by verbal fastidiousness and elegance. In other words, it was a tradition which compensated for narrowness of view and stylistic resource by a perfection equally microscopic. Glorification of this traditional 'femininity' increased in proportion to what was seen as its denigration in the Soviet Union; typical was a review of a Soviet art exhibition deriding the portraits of women workers as the representations of 'sexless robots'.[68]

These circumstances suggest that the assertion of one recent critic, who has declared that Russian women *émigré* writers enjoyed conditions of 'absolute freedom', might well be a mite naïve.[69] And in fact the restrictive character of *émigré* national-populism was enhanced by its cultural dominance. It is true that *émigré* writers living in the West were naturally brought into contact with the international modernist movement, and this had profound effects on certain individuals, notably Vladimir Nabokov and Ilya Zdanevich amongst prose writers, Anatoly Shteiger and Boris Poplavsky amongst poets. But by and large the central characteristics of the international modernist movement (among which one might name cultural eclecticism, questioning of what is signified by identity, and interrogation of the notion that literary texts have a single definite and definable meaning) did not develop amongst either *émigré* writers or amongst *émigré* poets.[70]

How were these various possibilities represented amongst women writers? Perhaps surprisingly, given the proscriptions just mentioned, the most characteristic directions were 'feminine prose' and 'feminine poetry' in the rather traditional sense in which *émigré* critics understood those terms: the celebration of reticence, modesty, beauty, and frailty. So far as large numbers of women writers were concerned, this tradition was in fact coloured by, and on occasion even fused with, national populism; the most important way in which women writers attempted to rival the

---

[68] The remark about 'sexless robots' comes from an exhibition note published in *Zhurnal sodruzhestva* (1934), 2: 35. Indicative reviews of 'feminine' poetry and prose are: Vladislav Khodasevich, '"Zhenskie" stikhi' (1935), *Koleblemyi treugol'nik* (Moscow, 1991), 577–80, which contrasts the 'human' and 'the feminine'; P. Bitsilli, 'Galina Kuznetsova. *Prolog: Roman*', *SOZ* 53 (1933), 453–4, which describes the 'feminine principle' as that of unanalytical zest and joy in life; Georgy Adamovich, 'Literaturnye zametki', *PN*, 24 Jan. 1935, 2, which describes Akhmatova as having brought the 'feminine as an essential, natural force' into Russian poetry, and praises the 'childishness' of Golovina's verse.

[69] See Marina Ledkovsky(-Astman)'s otherwise balanced and informative article, 'Russian Women Writers: An Overview. Post-Revolutionary Dispersal and Adjustment', in Linda Edmondson (ed.), *Women and Society in Russia* (cf. 376 n. 76.) (Cambridge, 1992), 145–59.

[70] See e.g. Il'ya Zdanevich ['Iliazd'], *Pis'mo/La Lettre*, illus. Picasso (1948; repr. Paris, 1990); *idem, Prigovor bez molvy/Sentence sans paroles*, illus. Braque and Giacometti (1961; repr. Paris, 1990); Vladimir Nabokov, *Priglashenie na kazn'* (Paris, 1938); Boris Poplavsky, *Sobranie sochinenii* (3 vols.; Berkeley, Calif., 1980–1); Anatoly Shteiger, $2 \times 2 = 4$: *Stikhi* (New York, 1982).

myth of the martyred male poet was by associating themselves with the traditionally 'feminine' role of suffering motherhood, and hence stressing their connection with, and intimate understanding of, the sorrows of Russia. Modernism as such was no commoner amongst women writers than amongst men: though a post-Symbolist multiplicity of different poetic doubles was often in evidence, the majority of women poets and writers were chary of investigating identity in the sense of openly questioning preconceived notions about gender. A more characteristic direction amongst women poets is one which might be described as 'accidental modernism'. In some cases, the attempt to use an alternative national-populist mask for the poet, and speak in the feminine voice, could set up a hiatus between what was expected of women writers as women on the one hand, what was expected from writers aspiring to the national-populist tradition on the other. This hiatus, though not always fully recognized, could make certain religious and mystical works subversive in effect, if not in intention: the attempt to speak as a feminine figure of authority satisfied the expectation that biological women should write in the feminine voice, yet it also marked a departure from what convention deemed acceptable for that feminine voice.

I intend to survey these various directions and possibilities in turn, and shall begin by looking in detail at 'feminine poetry and prose', since this is by far the best represented, and most popular, strand in 'outsider' tradition.

Much 'feminine verse' written by 'outsiders' was characterized by imitation of the paradigms set up in Akhmatova's early collections, *Evening* and *The Rosary*. A similarly *distraite* heroine finds herself in a similar urban setting; the tone is, with depressing regularity, submissively haughty or haughtily submissive. Few such women poets would have taken issue with Berberova's jingle in declaration of female emotional power:

> Call her Laura, call her Juliet,
> Or call her Helen: what's in a name?
> There's no life without love. We all dream,
> Love never skipped a person yet.[71]

Another standard motif, again in the Akhmatovian tradition, was that of

---

[71] Nina Berberova, *Stikhi* (New York, 1984), 85. Apart from Berberova, other conventional love poets are Irina Odoevtseva (see e.g. 'Proshchan'e na vokzale', *SOZ* 57 (1935), 235; Mariya Karamzina, *Kovcheg* (Tallin, 1939); Lidiya Chervinskaya, *Rassvety* (Paris, 1937); poets who wrote conventional love poems, though not limited to such a repertoire, included Natal'ya Krandievskaya: see e.g. 'Lift, podnimayas' . . .', *Doroga: stikhotvoreniya* (Moscow, 1985), 100; Ekaterina Tauber, 'Prostaya radost' bytiya', *SOZ* 67 (1938), 156; Raisa Blokh, 'Pust' nebo chernoe', *Chisla*, 2/3; 13; and Tat'yana Klimenko-Rapgauz: see many of the poems in *Vsya moya zhizn': stikhotvoreniya i vospominaniya ob otse* (Riga, 1987).

religious repentance for erotic misdemeanour; poems of this kind place the woman speaker or protagonist in a more or less sharply defined ecclesiastical setting, and examine her sensibilities as the ritual unfolds. However, if the manner of *émigré* women poets is Akhmatovian, their declared literary references are less frequently to this female predecessor than to the heroines celebrated by male poets, and most especially to Pushkin's Tatiana. Even more than before the Revolution, the celebration of heterosexual involvement as a governing theme entailed the representation of other women only as sexual rivals, and the association of the lyric heroine with a restricted range of subject positions. Motherhood in the individual sense is, for example, an acceptable subject only where it, too, may be integrated with (or subordinated to) the sentiments felt by woman for man. One topos is the heroine who laments the fact that she is a 'bad mother' because some illegitimate erotic entanglement is distracting her from her child.[72]

Like the 'feminine' tradition of poetry, the 'feminine' tradition of realist prose attracted large numbers of women. There are large numbers of texts dealing with the psychological dilemmas of ordinary lives, especially women's lives. These in many senses perpetuate the traditions of the 1890s and 1900s; the escape plot has vanished, leaving as the central narrative form a melancholy tale of failure, in which domestic *minutiae* symbolize not only the entrapment of women as women, but also the distress and alienation suffered by Russians come down in the world since their departure from home. One exponent of this genre was the prolific and widely-published author of short stories, Aleksandra Damanskaya.[73] Another, more interesting, moulder of such material was Teffi, whose witty and ironic pre-Revolutionary sketches continued to be published in many editions, but who was now, in her new work, taking as her heroes the distressed gentlefolk of *émigré* life, and giving a greater emphasis to her role as moralist in her depiction of their desperate predicament.[74]

---

[72] The motif of repentance occurs e.g. in the work of Ekaterina Bakunina, *Stikhi* (Paris, 1931); Natal'ya Krandievskaya, 'Takoe yabloko', *Doroga: stikhotvorenii* (Moscow, 1985), 81; and Vera Bulich (see Ch. 12 below); Tatiana and Onegin references are made e.g. by Chervinskaya, *Rassvety*, 39; Vera Bulich; Anna Prismanova's *Pis'mo* clings to the stereotype although denying its value: 'I am not Tatiana, and I know that you are not Onegin', see *Sobranie sochinenii*, ed. Petra Couve'e (The Hague, 1990), 61–2; the motif of sexual rivalry occurs e.g. in Alla Golovina's 'Net sil usnut'', *Gorodskoi angel* (Brussels, 1989), 83; the 'bad mother' motif is extensively developed by Ekaterina Bakunina, *Stikhi*; on the child as reflection of the father, see e.g. Emiliya Chegrintseva, 'Nasledstvo', *SOZ* 69 (1939), 213; conversely, the lover is seen as a reflection of the child in Raisa Blokh's 'Ya tebya lyublyu, kak babushka vnuchenka': see Blokh and Mikhail Gorlin, *Izbrannye stikhi* (Paris, 1959), 38.

[73] See e.g. A. Damanskaya, 'Plonzher', *Perezvony*, 1 (1925), 76–81.

[74] Teffi, *Gorodok* (Paris, 1927); on Teffi's later prose, see also the observations in Ch. 7 above.

It was not only Russians abroad who practised the genre of 'feminine prose'. Perhaps the most impressive examples of this tradition are Lidiya Chukovskaya's two short novels *Sofya Petrovna* (1937) and *Going Under* (1949).[75] Both are narrated from the viewpoint of a woman; both are linear narratives dealing not with 'a day in the life of', but with a few months in the lives of, their heroines. The heroine of the first story is presented to us in third-person indirect narrative; she is an ordinary Soviet woman, whose comfortable, conformist life is shattered when her model Young Communist son is arrested on a charge of industrial sabotage. The reader versed in Russian nineteenth-century literature recognizes this woman immediately as a representative of the complacent *meshchanstvo* and *poshlost'* (petit bourgeois, philistine vulgarity) so often satirized there. The achievement of Chukovskaya's minutely detailed narrative is to turn this unpromising character into a figure of near tragedy, as she finds her own fiction to counteract the monstrous fictions of the system.

Chukovskaya's second novel, *Going Under*, deals with the second wave of purges, those of the late 1940s, and with their aftermath, but here in terms of intelligentsia life. Once again a woman is the central character. But she is presented more directly, by means of a first-person narrative, and as a woman with an informed intellectual outlook she can be identified more immediately with Chukovskaya than can Sofya Petrovna. The story is Tolstoyan in its concern for truth and sincerity, opposing the plainly expressed views of this decent, morally upright woman to the labyrinthine sophistries and linguistic contortions set up by official cliché.

To achieve its assigned task and lay bare the reality behind Stalinist rhetoric, Chukovskaya's narrative must be absolutely unambiguous. Like the Socialist Realist dogmaticians (though with quite different results), she sets herself the task of 'reflecting Soviet reality'. This task is to be achieved by means of plain language and the description of one special area of actual Soviet life: the suffering of women whose menfolk have been taken away. Only one alternative form of literary discourse is recognized: official myth; and this appears only in order that it may be debunked. *Going Under* contains the following vicious, and accurate, parody of a 1940s novel's identikit plot:

Victory over the Fascists has led to an upsurge of unprecedented zeal for work. Peter the coal-face-worker is back from the front to join his wife Fedosya. Fedosya used to work the pit lift, but during the war she, like the millions of

---

[75] Both Chukovskaya's stories are now available in a convenient recent edition, *Dve povesti* (Moscow, 1988). English edns. are available as *Sofia Petrovna*, trans. David Floyd (London, 1989) and *Going Under*, trans. Peter Weston (New York, 1972).

other Soviet women on whom the economy depended, has developed both professionally and ideologically. [. . .] Whilst Peter was away at the war she went out to work, cared for the children and studied to be an engineer. Now she is battling to get advanced technology installed . . . (p. 209)

So far, so like Nikolaeva's *Harvest* or Karavaeva's *The Motherland*. And the rest of Chukovskaya's parody novel proceeds exactly like its real prototypes: naturally, the marital conflict precipitated by female en-lightenment and male backwardness is resolved on the initiative of the Party representative and all live happily ever after.

Building on her original dualism, that between 'myth' and 'reality', Chukovskaya predicates a secondary and absolute division between the world of official language and lies, controlled by men, and the world of private language and truth, controlled by women. This binary opposition is etched in a number of memorable scenes in both stories. In *Sofya Petrovna*, monstrously ugly men sit behind desks receiving the female victims of the purges; in *Going Under* the narrator lies in her therapeutic pine-scented bath, listening to two complacent male authors discussing the success which their conformity has brought them. If the positive female characters, like their Socialist Realist counterparts, are observers and moral regulators, their negative counterparts are venial sinners: petty informers, self-deceiving conformists, and painted wives. Women are numbered neither amongst the executives of the purges, nor amongst the major beneficiaries of Stalinist largesse, which is fair enough, but the exact degree of their complicity with the system is never made clear.

The schematism of Chukovskaya's novel is as marked as is that of official writing: for both, women necessarily take a secondary place, passive before male authority. But the anti-heroic character of Chukov-skaya's stories allows her more flexibility of representation than Socialist Realists had at their disposal. She presents a detailed counter-image to the official celebrations of women's lives: here we see women struggling to combine wide-ranging family responsibilities with full-time employ-ment, and to maintain their dignity despite the daily humiliations of life in a communal flat. Her purpose is to delineate the effects of Soviet power structures on women, rather than to analyse the degree of their involvement in the system as a sex; but the delineation is sharply and vividly achieved, and Chukovskaya's prose style has a honed laconicism rather than the lumpish, building-brick simplicity of the Socialist Realist giants.

How insidious conventional notions of the feminine were can be appreciated not only from this overview of texts intended for the public eye, but also from private statements such as letters and journals. An example is Olga Berggolts's recently published private diaries, kept during the Blockade.[76] On the one hand these are powerfully atmospheric accounts, not only of the physical privations of civilian life during wartime, but of its psychological deprivations, above all the overwhelming boredom of waiting for something to happen. On the other hand they are documents which present a person whose obsession with her own saccharine femininity grates on the reader. Consider, for example, the following account of Berggolts's flirtation with Georgy Makogonenko, who was later to become her lover:

He's very attentive, but it's precisely that attentiveness which is getting me down. It seems he feels no attraction for me as a woman, but he can see what I feel about him and he thinks he can do what he likes, he has only to stretch out a hand and I'll fall to pieces like a nonentity. Incidentally, he's quite right, but I want to show him that I don't depend on him, that I'm totally indifferent to him in a certain regard.... The future reader of my diaries will feel disgust at this point: the heroic defence of Leningrad is in full swing and all she can find to think and write about is how soon a man will make a declaration of love to her or something like that.[77]

Elsewhere Berggolts wears a mask of sexual coyness which is rather different. In a passage whose bathos is monumental in the most literal sense of the word, she recollects the moment when she said farewell to her husband before his departure for the army:

He was naked and I kissed him, kneeling before him, his feet, his knees, his thighs, all over his glorious, cool body, which might even tomorrow be mutilated or cut to pieces. But now it was beautiful, young and full of strength.

I kissed his thighs, his belly, his shoulders, raising my lips gradually from his knees, and he stood immobile, without embarrassment, because he understood that these were not the kisses of a wife and lover, but the kisses of a woman sending her man into battle (as all women kiss all men going into battle).

I got up and we kissed each other on the lips long and deep. No, we did not desire each other, neither I him nor he me. For this was not the farewell of lovers; it was the farewell of those going into War.[78]

One does not need to know that in actual fact Berggolts's husband was a middle-aged intellectual, and also seriously ill, to find his transformation into a neo-classical statue of Mars for this patriotic effusion absurd and even distasteful. Even in private, war could not be represented as something that might lead to disillusion with the idea of manly men and womanly women, or to a sense of internal division in individuals; no Russian woman prose writer, either during or after the war, was to

[76] Berggol'ts, 'Bezumstvo predannosti'; 'Dnevnye zvezdy', *Ogonek*, 5 May 1990, 15–16.
[77] Berggol'ts, 'Bezumstvo predannosti', 296.
[78] Berggol'ts, 'Dnevnye zvezdy', 15.

produce anything remotely comparable to Elizabeth Bowen's novel of wartime paranoia and betrayal, *The Heat of the Day* (1948).[79]

The traditions of 'feminine writing' as just described were so potent that they often infused themselves into national-populist writing too. The frail victim, the principled non-combatant and the nineteenth-century ideal beloved are all masks which women adopted in order to confer the right upon themselves to speak for the nation or the collective. The way in which women spoke for the collective was intimately connected with the ways in which they might speak as individuals. Olga Berggolts's lyrics written from prison, for example, draw on the tradition of the popular love-song: the incarcerated heroine is both tormented and sustained by the thought of her 'beloved' outside the gaol, and dreams of communicating with him. The motif of worship as a comfort in anguish is also evoked (though here without erotic links): the Mother of God's own 'way to Cavalry' is a model for that of Berggolts's speaker.[80]

Very similar patterns are woven into the most famous commemoration of 'outsider' national populism, Akhmatova's *Requiem*.[81] But Akhmatova's approach is in various ways more complex than Berggolts's. This complexity is evident compositionally, to begin with: the series of episodes in *Requiem* is ordered into a narrative which, though not sequential, displays a high degree of symmetrical internal organization.[82] In terms of its frame of reference, too, *Requiem* is more sophisticated than Berggolts's work: like the latter, it draws on the love-song of post-eighteenth-century Westernized folk tradition. But it also directly refers to Western religious culture (as the title suggests), thus creating a nationalism of more than national roots, a populism above the narrow patriotism of Stalinism, with its triumphalist hymns to a heroic Motherland decked in pseudo-folkloric habiliments. However, Akhmatova's text itself distances and mystifies maternity. The text is apophatic: maternity is termed 'indescribable', rather than described, its importance conveyed by silence:

> Но туда, где молча Мать стояла . . .
> Так никто взглянуть и не посмел.   (p. 78)

---

[79] Elizabeth Bowen, *The Heat of the Day* (1948; London, 1986).

[80] The fullest selection of Berggol'ts's prison poetry is that in 'Bezumstvo predannosti'.

[81] Akhmatova, 'Rekviem', *Neva* (1987), 6: 74–9. The version printed in Akhmatova, *Sochineniya*, i (Munich, 1965), 361–70 is slightly inferior in a textological sense.

[82] On the problematics of *Rekviem*, see Michael Basker, 'Dislocation and Relocation in Akhmatova's *Requiem*', in Rosslyn (ed.), *The Speech of Unknown Eyes*, i. 5–25; on its structure, see Anna Lise Crone; 'Antimetabole in *Rekviem*: the Structural Disparity of Themes and Motifs', ibid. 27–43. Most interesting analyses of *Requiem* and *Poem Without a Hero* also appear in Susan Amert, *In a Shattered Mirror: The Later Poetry of Anna Akhmatova* (Stanford, Calif., 1992).

> No one dared look
> At the Mother, standing silent . . .

A visual act of turning away parallels a verbal act of turning away: what cannot be seen is also in a quite fundamental sense what is unsayable.

Akhmatova's representation of the maternal recalls 'feminine' conventions both in terms of its abstraction, and because the relation between mother and grown son, as here invoked, in a sense replicates, rather than intruding on, the preferred relation between male and female lovers. By contrast, the poet Mariya Shkapskaya drew on the Russian popular tradition of filial veneration for the earth ('mother damp earth') in order to achieve representations of maternity which were both intenser and more physical. In the penultimate poem of her 1921 collection, *Mater Dolorosa*, the relation between earth and living beings parallels that between infant children and the mother's body. The earth appears as the object of everyone's tactile desire:

> О, древняя, твоих живых касаний
> Повсюду ждут иссохшие уста.[83]

> O, how parched lips everywhere
> Long for the life you give, ancient one.

The earth 'feeds one and all with one life-giving | Dew'; and finally, in death, will take them into its 'silent lap'.

Shkapskaya's poetry also breaks down any simplistic opposition between 'individual' and 'collective' voices; her work draws on maternity as cultural totem, but at the same time shows how women's voices can speak of maternity in quite diverse ways: as mothers and of their own mothers, as those who nurture and those who seek protection. A remarkable example of her ability to interweave the symbolic and the everyday aspects of motherhood is the long poem 'No Dream'. The piece is a dramatic narrative depicting an atrocity of the Civil War, but for once this is an atrocity which men perpetrate on a man, not a woman (an officer is hanged in public). The man's wife stands with his two children and watches in the classic mourner pose; but this embodiment of maternity is not easily attractive and reassuring:

> Вот и встала в сторонке под старую акацию,
> Стоит,
> Молчит,

---

[83] Mariya Shkapskaya, *Stikhi* (London, 1971), 68. (References to this edn. henceforth in text.) On Shkapskaya and maternity see also Barbara Heldt, 'Motherhood in a Cold Climate: The Poetry and Career of Mariia Shkapskaia', *Russian Review*, 51/2 (1992), 160–71.

Только губы белые,
Помертвелые,
И маленький грудь не теребит—пустая.[84]   (p. 89)

So there she stood under the old acacia,
Still,
Silent.
But her lips were white,
Bloodless,
And the babe didn't pull at the empty breast.

And this woman, like Hecuba or Clytemnaestra, is not simply a victim: although all she can do is stand and watch, she calls on her children to take vengeance, and utters a challenge to God:

Да запомни,
Слышишь,—запомни.
На всю свою жизнь, и память
Положи как камень,
Отцовские страсти.—

.   .   .   .   .

Тихонечко, на ухо говорила,
И глядела, глаз не отрывая.
Божеских сил не хватило бы,—
Человеческих хватает.
Человечья страшная сила:
        И те, и эти,
        И какие-нибудь третьи—
        Никого не милуем,
        Только—запоминаем.   (p. 91)

'Remember it all,
You hear me—remember.
Let this, your father's Passion,
be laid on your life, your memory,
heavy as a stone slab.'

.   .   .   .   .

She whispered, soft in his ear,
her eyes staring out.
God's powers may not do it,
Human powers can do it,
The terrible powers of man.

[84] Shkapskaya, 'Yav'', *Stikhi*, 88–93. See also 'No Dream' in *Anthology*.

> See those, and those,
> And those yet again—
> We shall not forgive them,
> We shall not forget them.

Shkapskaya's poem, like *Requiem*, sets up parallels between this political execution and the Crucifixion (the hanged man is suspended for 'three days', and the 'slab' standing for the children's duty of revenge recalls the stone laid on the sarcophagus in the Gospel accounts of Christ's entombment). But at the end of the piece, the rule of religion, like the 'terrible powers of man' is challenged: the most precious icons of Russia come out of the church and lie in the grass at the feet of the gallows, and the crosses on the church fall to the ground, as the woman has commanded that they should; the miracle inspired by vengeance has subordinated the power of the 'miraculous' itself.

The collage-like structure of Shkapskaya's poem, with its snatches of popular song, fragments of demotic speech, and political slogans, recalls the compositional pattern of Blok's *The Twelve*. As in Blok's poem, stretches of dialogue alternate with sections of third-person descriptive narrative; the narrative is more or less undifferentiated, in stylistic terms, from the dialogue, and perspective shifts constantly. As in Blok's text, too, populist material is used, not to support a monolithic alternative myth of nationalism, but to subvert ordinary perceptions of the 'people' and of 'Russia', replacing these with ambivalent and uncertain entities. 'No Dream' has taken us from national populism towards modernism. But Shkapskaya's poem differs from Blok's in its overtly choric and dramatic qualities. Rather than following a protagonist or a central group, she examines the relationship between the actors in the tragedy and the onlookers, showing how events and the perception of events are created collectively, and not only by men, but also by women.

Shkapskaya's elision of any controlling voice of individual authorship evades the tricky question of how that voice should be gendered. A rather similar process can be observed in her *Tsa tsa tsa* (1923), a collection of seven tiny pieces in rhythmic prose.[85] These cover a variety of subjects: some are stories of love, some philosophical reflections which draw moral conclusions from observations of detail. The title refers to the third piece: here the typical 1920s view of art as product is untypically presented through a portrait of a female producer. The tale describes a woman spinning silk, whose work of art, once finished, will be worn by a rich woman, who has never seen the garment's weaver, as the garment's weaver will never see her.

The narratives are preceded by a foreword which gives them an

---

[85] Shkapskaya, 'Tsa-tsa-tsa', *Stikhi*, 125–34.

invented history. Linguistic and cultural blurring are equated with gender blurring, and various types of possession (of artefacts, of tradition, and sexual possession) are blended:

She was Russian, he Chinese.

They both lived in Paris, and their Russo-Chinese relations were carried on in French dialect.

He knew about Russian snow and polar bears, she drank China tea and collected buddhas.

Neither of them could return home, and so, grieving, she told him Russian fairy-tales; he recited Chinese poetry.

If you want to know what he remembers from those Russian fairy-stories, ask him yourself; but what she remembers of Chinese poetry is recorded here. (p. 125)

Another poet who composed innovative prose texts, but to quite different effect, was Anna Prismanova, who lived and worked in Paris. Her short story 'On Guard and on Town Gardens', which probably dates from the mid-1930s, introduces the reader to the comically prosaic life of Amalia Sontag, a German music-teacher living in a small Baltic city.[86] Then follows a disclaimer of authorial responsibility:

When heroes fall into the hands of an author with a vivid imagination, he leads them by the nose and arranges a complicated fate for them, full of love-affairs and other things of that kind. But woe betide the heroine who finds herself in the hands of an author with no imagination at all. Instead of leading her in a direction where something interesting might happen, he passively follows her, only describing what really does happen.   (p. 192)

Thus the reader is led to believe that Amalia will dictate circumstances, and indeed she at first seems to. The tale follows her through the 'modest decency' of her life: visiting the sick (a nephew in the insane asylum), a brief encounter with the piano tuner who is too shy to confess his admiration. This chronicle of tedious uprightness is summed up in the penultimate sentence, in which we are told that no one in the town could 'cast a stone into her garden' (i.e. cast aspersions on her virtue). But this triumphantly bathetic conclusion reached, the final sentence switches direction completely. Author and heroine, it transpires, have been in league to deceive the reader about Amalia's activities: 'However, the stocky market-gardener who lived next door to Fräulein Sontag would often throw a few stones into her garden, as a signal for one of their not infrequent assignations. And at such times one could certainly not have

---

[86] Prismanova, 'O gorode i ogorode', *Sobranie sochinenii*, 192–3. See also 'On Guard and on Town Gardens' in *Anthology*.

said that Fräulein Sontag was on her guard.' The narrator's sincerity proves to be as double-edged as the heroine's virtue.

But the only way in which Prismanova can execute these subtle manœuvres is to fade the authorial function into the background, making it seem simply a device; and the only manner in which she can do this is to use the 'neutral' (i.e. masculine) form of the noun and pronoun ('*he* leads them by the nose . . . *he* follows them'). The use of a masculine author figure to indicate that an abstract debate on literariness is to be initiated was general practice in the Russian emigration, as it had been in official Soviet writing of the 1920s and 1930s. Where feminine narrators are used, the effect is to mark the text in rather a different way: to suggest a fallibility which has more to do with conventional views of female irrationality than with an assault on the omniscient narrator of high realism.

In this respect, there is an instructive contrast between two stories in Nina Berberova's 1948 collection, *Making Things Easier*, 'The Accompanist' and 'Roccanvale'.[87] The first story is narrated by two women, and is a 'frame' narrative in the manner of the 1830s: the manuscript which makes up the bulk of the story has been discovered in a second-hand shop in Paris along with a 'lamp which was still in fairly good working order' and other trivia, 'everything that is left behind when a woman dies'. The narrator of this manuscript, the story proper, is the 'Accompanist' of the title, a naïve young woman perpetually in the shadow of her employer, a singer whose seductive egotism makes the reader think of Chekhov's Madame Arkadina in *The Seagull*. The story hinges on a melodramatic peripeteia. The singer's perfect marriage proves unexpectedly vulnerable: her husband learns that his wife's ex-lover has returned to Paris, and shoots himself. All ambiguity in the story rests on the 'untrustworthy' narrator's simplistic misreading of her employer's marriage, and the fact that she undervalues this plain man's feeling for his wife. Though the frame narrative structure gives this story some connections with the manner of Zhukova or Gan, Berberova does not exploit these: there is no sense of parody, nor even overt intertextuality, in this well-crafted, but plain and conventional narrative of shipwrecked lives.

'Roccanvale', by contrast, has a male narrator, and is more adventurous in precisely the senses of parody and intertextuality. The narrator dabbles in poetry and is an active reader. He is a summer visitor to a French château; he himself recognizes that his experiences of living at

[87] Berberova, 'Akkompanersha', 'Rokkanval'', *Oblegchenie uchasti: 6 povestei* (Paris, 1948). (See also *The Accompanist*, trans. Marian Schwartz (London, 1987); *Three Novels*, trans. *eadem* (London, 1990).)

Roccanvale, and of its gallery of eccentrics, are filtered by reading. Though he has no direct memories of Russia, he 'remembers' this place:

All the same, one day, reading Tolstoy or Turgenev—or maybe even Chekhov, because it was Russian books above all that my mother taught me to love—reading the description of some fairy-tale country house, I suddenly imagined—at first only in the most general outlines—that drive going up to the house, to the Empire style balcony, to the low jasmines. (p. 126)

The literary nature of his perceptions is the source of anxiety, too: the parasitic flavour of his observations and reminiscences is repeatedly stressed. His emotional attachment to Kira, the granddaughter of the house, proves illusory: when she is called away by her father, her departure leaves both parties indifferent. At the end of the story all the other characters have left, and the narrator is alone. But then another daughter of the house arrives, pregnant and in distress. Her appearance, however, excites idle curiosity rather than fellow-feeling in the narrator, and he remains an impassive recorder of her suffering.

'Rocanvalle', the most intelligently constructed and least melodramatic of Berberova's major stories, deals directly with the problem of who controls reminiscence, and of what that reminiscence may be worth when its controller is so obviously fallible. Unlike 'The Accompanist', this is no character study, but a neutral debate on textuality and ethics; as such it requires a 'neutral' narrator: that is, a male one.

Like their Soviet counterparts, women prose writers of the emigration in any case generally passed over self-consciousness in the form of literary introspection, and favoured other modes of introspection. Here, too, discourses of interiority now acquired a much greater significance. But the dominance of an easy and simplistic polarization between 'there' (which is to say, Russia) and 'here' (in the West) led to a certain standardization. The classic impressionistic *émigré* prose narrative is one in which a female drifter recalls her helpless progress through different stages of the historical cataclysm in terms of separation from a man (or men) with whom she has been involved; her only sense of stability is in her exact recollection of physical sensations.[88] No *émigré* writer was to produce anything as imaginative, in gender terms, as the fictional trilogy by Sergei Gedroits which was analysed in detail above.

Nor was the fact that a far greater degree of sexual explicitness was possible in *émigré* writing much reflected in women's prose, with the notable exceptions of two novels published in the mid-1930s by the Paris

[88] See e.g. Nadezhda Gorodetskaya, *Neskvoznaya nit'* (Paris, 1929); *eadem*, 'Belye kryl'ya', *Volya Rossii* (1929), 3: 3–24; Galina Kuznetsova, *Utro: rasskazy* (Paris, 1934); Alla Golovina, 'Dva rasskaza', *SOZ* 68 (1939), 114–24.

writer and poet Ekaterina Bakunina, *The Body* (1933) and *Love for Six* (1934).[89] The relish with which these two texts, both narrated by women, dwelt on anatomical details was to cause something of a scandal in the *émigré* press. Zinaida Gippius, reviewing *Love for Six*, asserted that these were particular instances which demonstrated a general rule. 'The feminine', she censoriously observed, 'can only remain the feminine so long as it keeps silent; as soon as it begins to speak, it becomes the prattle of a strumpet.'[90] Little as one would wish to endorse Gippius's comment as a generally applicable philosophical truth, her disapproval does illuminate the problems faced by Russian women in finding an appropriate language to describe sexual matters. And Bakunina's books, though they certainly are unusually frank pieces of writing, are also exceptionally silly ones. Of the two novels, much the stronger is *The Body*, which is so short and intense that it has something of the flavour of a spoken monologue, and which conveys quite powerfully the frustrations of the narrator's failed marriage, and the pleasures of her later adultery. But the central male character, an Englishman with whom the heroine eventually achieves a two-page orgasm in a rowing boat, is the sort of faceless male inflatable doll or walking dildo that peoples the pages of Anaïs Nin, equipped with a mighty organ, but little else. If *The Body* is at least a true piece of erotica in its overheated banality, *Love for Six* is both more pretentious and more vacuous. This much longer novel purports to be a letter addressed by the heroine to her lover describing a day spent whilst her family (the other 'five' making up the 'six' of the title) are absent in the country. In a device which panders to the expected voyeurism of a male reader, rather than ensuring verisimilitude, Bakunina requires us to believe that a woman who sees her lover almost every day would bother to set down a complete record of their relationship in flashback, and to remind him of how often, and in what position, they have engaged in sexual intercourse. We are also expected to derive enlightenment from the narrator's endless details of what she does minute by minute, right down to her morning session of onanism and her defecation according to the Kellogg system. This revelatory logorrhea is occasionally interrupted by painfully funny and embarrassing excursions into a sub-Rozanovian sexual mysticism ('for monks and nuns, Jesus and Mary are the equivalent of the penis and the clitoris', and so on and on).

All in all, the 'alternative' Russian prose tradition in fact all too often proved to offer women no real alternative at all. The result was that a

---

[89] Ekaterina Bakunina, *Telo* (Paris, 1933); *Lyubov' k shesterym* (Paris, 1934).
[90] Zinaida Gippius, 'E. Bakunina, *Lyubov' k shesterym*', *SOZ* 58 (1936), 478–9.

number of *émigré* women writers made their way into French literature, which offered them rather more expansive and congenial conditions. Nadezhda Gorodetskaya and Elsa Triolet were two writers who made this transition, and who produced more original and more substantial work in their new language. In a series of striking and often bizarre episodes, Gorodetskaya's novel *The Children in Exile* (1936) narrates the intersecting lives of young second-generation *émigrés*, for whom Russia is identified either with the abstract ideals of socialism, or else the curious and eccentric preoccupations of their elders.[91] Triolet, a much better-known and more prolific writer, was to become a central figure in French literary culture. Among her many successful later writings were four stories collected as *A Fine of Two Hundred Francs* (1945), two of which, 'The Lovers of Avignon' and 'The Notebooks' display her capacity for a sharp observation of incidental detail and for a luminous depiction of eddying thought which go well beyond those evident in the thematically rather similar traditions of Russian *émigré* prose.[92]

In general, then, *émigré* women writers did not succeed in establishing narrative patterns which at once allowed the representation of femininity at first hand, and were explicitly modernist in form. Their strategies were, rather, to oppose a conventional femininity to an unconventional masculinity, or to sideline the dispute between masculine and feminine, either by adopting a 'neutral' narrative voice (and 'neutral' in practice, as I have noted, meant 'masculine'), or by eliding the concept of individual authorship.

Even in the traditionally more personal genre of the lyric, those women poets who gravitated to modernism often adopted an ungendered voice, as if sensing an incompatibility between analytic self-consciousness and the feminine gender. Galina Kuznetsova, Sofiya Pregel, and Raisa Blokh are examples of women poets who adopt a feminine voice in the portrayal of an alienated speaker in a concrete urban or suburban setting, but who express philosophical speculation on identity itself without alluding to gender, often using the present rather than the past tense, or employing impersonal constructions so as to displace the subject.[93] Each

---

[91] Gorodetskaya, *L'Exil des enfants* (Paris, 1936).

[92] Elsa Triolet, *Le premier accroc coûte deux cents francs* (1945; repr. Paris, 1983; trans. anon. as *A Fine of Two Hundred Francs*: 2nd edn.; London, 1986). On Triolet see also Elizabeth Klosty Beaujour, *Alien Voices: Bilingual Russian Writers of the 'First' Emigration* (Ithaca, NY, 1989); Lachlan Mackinnon, *The Lives of Elsa Triolet* (London, 1992).

[93] Where Raisa Blokh uses a gendered first person, this is linked with an erotic motif: see e.g. 'Pust' nebo chernoe' (see above, n. 70) and contrast 'Naletaet veter', *Chisla*, 6 (1932), 8; see also 'Zaidi syuda' and other poems, *Roshcha: vtoroi sbornik berlinskikh poetov* (Berlin, 1932), 10–14; *Moi gorod* (Paris, 1928); Galina Kuznetsova, 'Kogda dlya dnya', *Perezvony*, 43 (1927), 1150; *Olivkovyi sad: stikhi 1923–1929* (Paris, 1933); Sofiya Pregel', *Razgovor s pamyat'yu* (Paris, 1935); *Solnechnyi proizvol* (Paris, 1937); *Polden': tret'ya kniga stikhov* (Paris, 1939).

of these poets had her own, distinctive voice: Blokh was a melancholic, neo-classical 'Petersburg' poet, whilst Kuznetsova employed innovative stanza forms to depict stereotypically picturesque Mediterranean scenes; Pregel was concerned, especially in her early work, with the perceivable and tangible characteristics of the external world (which unusually here include charcuterie and butchers' meat, as well as flowers and dresses) rather than with shifting interior sensibilities. Collectively, however, their work represents an identifiably 'feminine' direction within *émigré* poetry.

One way in which the conflict between 'the feminine' and 'the analytical' might be avoided, and questions of identity synthesized with questions of gender, was through the post-Symbolist method of representation according to which an obviously mythical persona was appropriated to the discussion of artistic practice and status. Amongst poets who chose to appropriate such personae, there was a preference for figures already familiar from pre-Revolutionary Russian Symbolist poetry by men. Masks drawn from the classical tradition, or evoking the street entertainers of cities, now began to make their way into women's writing. Following Vyacheslav Ivanov, women poets wrote of the Sibyls; following Blok, Khodasevich, and Sologub, they decorated their work with gypsies, cabaret singers, street musicians, and circus artistes. If they did not use explicitly feminine personae, women poets might select some traditional masculine construct for the poet, such as Orpheus, and examine it from an explicitly feminine perspective, or else place it alongside an externalized representation of 'the feminine' *per se*.[94]

Urban popular tradition was preferred by many of the women poets uprooted to the West; mythic treatments of peripatetic and marginal entertainer figures were attractive vehicles for depicting the psychological dislocations and transformations wrought by life abroad. These well-worn poetic constructs were given an explicit gender by allusion to certain key details. Clothing had symbolic importance, for example, since it could suggest an identity adopted, rather than given. Anna Prismanova's 'soul in heavenly tulle, dancing for too long in tight shoes' is one striking example of this kind of persona.[95] A more sophisticated chain of associations is made in Alla Golovina's collection *Swan Roundabout* (1935), which uses circus and fairground motifs both as the material of representation and as parallels to the process of representa-

---

[94] References to Orpheus occur e.g. in the work of Marina Tsvetaeva (see Ch. 11 below) and Anna Prismanova, 'Yad', *SS* 56; to classical heroines in Vera Merkur'eva: see Vera Merkur'eva, 'Iz literaturnogo naslediya', ed. M. L. Gasparov, *Oktyabr'* (1989), 5: 149–59; to street musicians in Tsvetaeva, Prismanova ('Sharmanka', 'Tsyganka', *SS* 15, 17); a variant here is Tatiana Klimenko-Rapgauz's use of the cabaret singer as *alter ego* (see 'Mona Liza', *Vsya moya zhizn': stikhotvoreniya i vospominaniya ob otse* (Riga, 1987)).

[95] Prismanova, 'Dusha v nebesnom tyule', *SS* 10.

tion: such motifs are both actual recollections of childhood made manifest in the present, and a metaphor for the selective, aestheticizing manner in which poetry may capture such recollections.[96]

Often, too, women writers appropriated figures from folklore or popular legend. Alla Golovina, again, reworked the Cinderella motif to suggest a woman's life shipwrecked:

> В зтом зале, где музыка—сверху,
> Словно роспись, поет с потолка,
> Лишь пожатью, браслету и меху
> Доверяет нагая рука.
> В этом зале, где сводные сестры
> Незаметно поблекли у стен,
> Наконец обьясняется просто,
> Одиночество, ужас и плен.
> В коридорах поет перестарок.
> За решетку схватилась рука.
> —Нежный принц, оставляю подарок:
> Два ковровых своих башмака.—
> И под топот настойчивый крысий,
> И под тыквенный стук гробовой,
> Кто услышит смятенье и выстрел
> Над чудесной твоею судьбой?[97]

> In that hall, where sounds sing from the ceiling,
> Ringing loud as the fresco's paint,
> Only a bracelet and furs and a necklace
> Are trusted by the skin of your hand.
> In that hall, where the silent stepsisters
> Go invisibly pale by the walls,
> Solitude, horror, imprisonment,
> Are clearly explained at last.
> A senile voice sings in the corridor,
> A hand has snatched at the bars.
> 'Dear prince, I leave a gift for you,
> My two carpet slippers are yours.'
> The rats' feet scamper so loudly,
> The pumpkin hearse thuds along,
> Who will hear the sorrow, the shot fired
> Where your grandiose fate belongs?

In Golovina's poem, unaesthetic details such as a 'senile voice', the 'skin of your hand' undermine the conventional equation between femininity and grace, an equation which is also disrupted by the hideously

---

[96] Alla Golovina, *Lebedinaya karusel'* (Paris, 1935).
[97] Alla Golovina, *Gorodskoi angel*, 97.

flirtatious tone adopted by the madwoman. But the danger that such decorative motifs might become as tawdry as worn-out theatre costumes, or as twee as china figurines, is not always avoided. They are, perhaps, less successful in lyric poetry than in genres where historical pastiche is an expected element of stylization, and visual spectacle is emphasized. For example, they work well in pieces for the theatre, such as Marina Tsvetaeva's mystery/masque/pantomime *The Stone Angel* (1919), Sofiya Parnok's opera libretto *Gulnara* (1929), and the ballet libretti of Vera Bulich.[98]

Another form of self-consciousness which was much in evidence amongst 'outsider' women (a tribute, this time, to the *women* poets of pre-Revolutionary post-Symbolist tradition rather than to the men) was the use of multiple viewpoint across a collection or cycle. Such diversity of perspective might be constructed in various different ways: by layering literary references, or by using the lyric cycle structure to emphasize the artificialities of composition. If the latter device (used, for example, in Vera Bulich's poetry, to be considered in detail later) often recalls the 'frame narratives' of the Romantic era, the former technique is taken to levels of sophistication far beyond those attained in Russian Romanticism. A most striking example is Akhmatova's *Poem Without a Hero*. As the title suggests, this is not a *poema*, long poem, in the sense of an epic, or even of a linear narrative. Instead, like Blok's unfinished late poem *Retribution, Poem Without a Hero* is an exploration of history, biography, and of the lyric biography as genre, through a montage of motifs drawn from the facts of Akhmatova's biography, and from her own lyric poetry. Alongside these motifs are set references to the 'future', that is, to the richly detailed perspective offered by hindsight, and to the 'past', in other words, to a huge range of literary and cultural parallels collected from Russian and Western tradition; these references are at once parodied, and given a transcendent historical significance. The familiar masks of Symbolist and post-Symbolist poetry veil allusions to friends of Akhmatova's who had died or been removed abroad before the poem was written; but they are also metonyms of a vanished culture, that of the St Petersburg new arts bohemia. Though protesting to Chukovskaya (in the passage cited at the beginning of this chapter) that she was no representative of a historical era, Akhmatova was at the same moment,

---

[98] Tsvetaeva, *Kamennyi angel, Neizdannoe: stikhi, teatr, proza* (Paris, 1976), 135–201; Bulich's ballet libretti 'Solnechnyi prints' (The Sun Prince, 1934) and 'Son poeta' (The Poet's Dream, *c.*1934–5), are pieces about living statues and natural forces personified: the influences are, evidently, the work of the Ballets Russes and of the painter Konstantin Somov. (These libretti are held in the Bulich Archive: see introductory note to Ch. 12 below.) Cf. also Sofiya Parnok's opera libretto, *Almast, SS* 261–87.

in 1940, composing the drafts of *Poem Without a Hero*, a text which would turn her into precisely that. The hostility to writing by and for women to which Akhmatova frequently gave vent in her later years here leads her not to ignore convention, but to exploit and undermine it.[99]

The manipulation of widely accepted and easily recognizable stereotypes or constructs was the preferred means by which *émigré* women poets addressed the problems of writing poetry as women. Much more unusual was direct confrontation of the implications of modernism in themselves. Few women writers seemed to sense, for example, that the modernist assault on notions of the unified personality might strengthen women's writing by breaking down the sense of emotional division inherent in nineteenth-century views of the 'feminine', and especially by assaulting the dichotomy of sensibility and intellect enforced on women since the late eighteenth century. An exception, however, was Anna Prismanova. Many poems in her collection *Twins* (1946) simply reiterate conventional binary oppositions between emotion and intellect, whose effect is seen to be devastating to their female victim ('two trees pull me to pieces').[100] But in 'Granite', a more unconventional progression takes place: the split between mind and reason creates energy, which itself leads to a further split, from which, in turn, the aestheticizing impulse arises. The poem moves from an idea of the poet as instrument to an idea of the poet as craftsman, from a submissive to a controlling subject. The poet's inner self is repeatedly identified with the stone, but at the same time it is clear that this is no automatic or inevitable identification. In fact, Prismanova's iteration of a connection already established begins to call this connection into question retrospectively. Thus the reader is prepared for the complete change in tone, and the shift in grammatical structure (passive to active), which mark the final stanza, with its sarcastic compliment to an anonymous lover:

> Едва-ли мне удастся Вас забыть—
> Не потому, что так я Вас любила,
> а потому, что удалось Вам быть
> огнем, которым душу я рубила.   (*SS* 65)

> One might suppose that I shall not forget you,
> but that won't be because I loved you so,

---

[99] It is impossible to do justice to *Poema bez geroya* in a survey of the present scope. Interpretative material on the text is now extensive, but there is no one definitive study. However, good introductory guidance is given by Elizabeth von Erdmann-Pandzic's variorum edition, *Poema bez geroja von Anna A. Achmatova: Variatenedition und Interpretation von Symbolstrukturen* (Vienna, 1987); see also the relevant contributions in Rosslyn, *The Speech of Unknown Eyes* and the bibliography to Amert, *In a Shattered Mirror*, for hints on further reading.

[100] Anna Prismanova, *Bliznetsy* (Paris, 1946): repr. in *SS* 38–96.

rather because you chanced to be the fire
which I myself employed to hew my soul.

In 'Liberation' Prismanova moves in a similar way from a conventional
dualism to a relation at once more problematic and more energetic. She
sets up an opposition between 'spiritual' and 'physical' language, and,
inevitably, places women on the latter side of that dichotomy. But, rather
than simply observe this dichotomy, she uses it to achieve the 'liberation'
of her title: the freeing of women to speech by feeling, and so *through*
self, rather than *from* self:

> Жена построит щаткие устои,
> извилины ума в себе любя.
> Ей нужно чувство—самое простое—
> освобожденье от самой себя.
>
> Такая сила ей необходима,
> чтоб о земных препятствиях забыть,
> чтоб быть тропой в тайге непроходимой,
> чтоб быть в ударе ... чтобы просто быть!   (*SS* 101–2)

> A woman will put up her frail defences,
> admiring her own twists of intellect,
> but she needs feeling—that is, something simple—
> to liberate her from herself.
>
> The power of feeling is essential for her,
> that she may forget the impediments of earth,
> that she may be a path through primal forest,
> be brought to strength—that she may be, in short!

Prismanova was also one of the very few Russian poets who explicitly
acknowledged her affiliation to women's writing in a historical sense.
She was directly inspired by the work of Karolina Pavlova, a quotation
from whose poetry is used as an epigraph to one of her collections. And
in a lyric of 1946, 'The Brontë Sisters', she uses Emily and Charlotte (who
come out in Russian as 'Emiliya and Sharlotta') to symbolize the
physical and spiritual dimensions of the feminine. Here again the binary
opposition is dissolved, for the third sister, Anne ('Anna'), is replaced by
Prismanova herself. The process of doubling takes the poem in another
direction altogether, from philosophical and historical abstraction into
real and imaginary autobiography. The elusive figure of the vanished
Anne suggests Prismanova's own precarious state, and yet the possibility
of that state's resolution:

> Скрыв страсти под непрочной оболочкой,
> держу и я чернильный край крыла.

> Дочь лекаря, я пасторскою дочкой—
> одной из Бронтэ—некогда была.
>
> Увы, для нас, в конце как и в начале,
> преграда счастью—внутренний наш суд.
> Но вдохновенье, знание печали,
> и время—неудачников спасут.   (*SS* 42)

> Hiding my passions under a frail cover,
> I too cling to the feather's inky edge;
> A doctor's daughter, I was once a pastor's,
> another Brontë sister I once was.
>
> Alas for us, our end is our beginning,
> our joys are bounded by an inner judge;
> but inspiration, and the taste of suffering,
> and time will save those whom success eludes.

Through elaborating the myth of the Brontës, Prismanova is able to create her own version of Horace's 'Exegi monumentum', a poem which, in Pushkin's imitation, is one of the key texts of Russian poetry.

For other poets working in the generations after the Revolution, contact with modernism could allow questioning of conventional notions of sexuality. We shall see later how the poems of Sofiya Parnok, for example, manipulated tradition in order to liberate depictions of love between women, and forge a genre independent of Romantic stereotypes. But the way in which cultural change might enforce, rather than erode, conservatism is underlined by the fact that, on the whole, interrogation of heterosexuality is less important for the post-Revolutionary generation of poets than it had been in the years just before the Revolution. With the exception of Parnok's lyrics, texts which refer to erotic feeling between women are rare; of those which do exist, a number cast their material in the stereotypes of heterosexual love familiar from the tradition of 'feminine' poetry and prose. This is the case, for example, with Marina Tsvetaeva's late story *The Tale of Sonechka*, detailed commentary on which will follow.[101]

Because of a general hostility to analysis and self-conscious speculation in the cultural tradition on the one hand, and the tyranny of 'feminine writing' on the other, modernism in the Western manner is a relatively insignificant direction in non-Soviet women's writing. But not all non-modernist texts are straightforward or conventional. As mentioned earlier, texts generated in the conflict between two orthodoxies,

---

[101] On *The Tale of Sonechka*, see Ch. 11 below. Compare Tsvetaeva's later French text, addressed to Nathalie Barney, *Mon frère féminin: lettre à L'Amazone* (1939; Paris, 1979) which not only represents lesbian sexuality as proto-masculine, but also argues that women's psychological need to produce sons (*sic*) dooms lesbian relationships from the beginning.

national and feminine, could become modernist by accident. As women strove to find themselves equivalents to the Messianic personae adopted by their male colleagues, they were confronted by the scarcity of such equivalents within Russian tradition, and specifically within Orthodox Christian tradition. Russian Orthodoxy did not have an extensive or well-developed tradition of female spiritual leadership; national models of female heroic sainthood were in rather short supply (the Western warrior saint Joan of Arc has, for example, no Orthodox equivalent), and there was no named tradition of theological or religious writing by women in the Eastern church. As in the Western church, moreover, theological recognition that women were as likely to enjoy salvation as men had not hindered the development of an ecclesiastical hierarchy exclusively composed of men. And so women who wished to allude to an Orthodox heritage of spirituality could only draw either on figures of popular religious authority such as the female holy fool, or on the Virgin Mary in her role as *Pokrov*, which is to the embodiment of Protection as abstract quality, and wearer of the Protecting Veil as symbol and attribute of her protective powers. Allusions to both these kinds of female authority had adverse reverberations, however. The female holy fool had, historically, inspired as much revulsion as devotion amongst educated believers; the problem with the Protection was, rather, that the more elevated Mary's status was, the less appropriate aspirations to that status on the part of the ordinary Christian were likely to seem.[102]

Poems by two poets of the post-Revolutionary generation which allude to these religious models indicate the confusions and uncertainties suffered by women poets wishing to write in a literary tradition shaped by Slavophilism and Orthodoxy. Vera Merkureva's poem, 'The Grandmother of Russian Poetry' (1918) recognizes the ambiguity of the female holy fool in a series of oxymora; the 'unnaturalness' of this role is emphasized by references to 'barrenness', and so threatening is the 'grandmother' that she must be referred to obliquely in the third person, rather than directly in the first:

> Свой бубен переладив на псалмодии,
> Она пешком на богомолье ходит
> И Зубовскую пустынь посещает.
> Но если церковь цирком называет,
> То это бес ее на грех наводит.
>
> . . . .

---

[102] For more detailed analysis of the background to religious poetry by Russian women after 1917, see Catriona Kelly, 'Writing an Orthodox Text: Religious Poetry by Russian Women, 1917–1939', in Joe Andrew (ed.), *Poetics of the Text* (Amsterdam, 1992), 153–70.

Ей весело цезуры сбросить пояс,
Ей—вольного стиха по санкам полоз,
Она легко рифмует *плюс* и *полюс*,
Но—все ее *не, нет* и *без,* и *полу—*
Ненужная бесплодная бесполость.[103]

Fitting her clashing bells to the psalm's sounds
She goes on foot to hear the service sung,
And wanders to the Zubovo hermitage.
But if she says a church is like a circus
Then that's the Devil tempting her to sin.

.   .   .   .   .   .

She'll gladly put off strict caesura's girdle,
And free verse cuts the track of her toboggan,
She'll often rhyme you *have* and *halfwit*,
But since she has no sex or gender,
Her *no*, her *not*, and *half*, are barren.

The struggle between contradictory cultural pressures has a resolution that has a strong flavour of self-hatred. Merkureva internalizes intellectual hostility to popular religious tradition, and sees her 'unsexing' as an admission of powerlessness, rather than an appropriation of power.

A less emotionally charged, but equally problematic, attempt to confront these pressures is evident in a poem by Elizaveta Skobtsova. Here, adoption of female spiritual authority in imitation of the succouring powers of the Mother of God leads to a conflict with the submission required by male authority; this can only be resolved when forgiveness is requested of that authority:

Господи, Господи, я высоту—
Даже Твою—полюбить не умею.
Что мне добавить еще в полноту?
Как Всеблаженного я пожалею?

Там лишь, где можно себя отдавать,
Там моя радость—и в скорбе, и в плаче.
Господи, Боже, прости мне,—я мать,—
И полюбить не умею иначе.[104]

My Lord, my Lord, I am not able
To love what is high, even when it is Yours;
How can I make what is filled up fuller,
How can I pity the blessed beyond words?

[103] Vera Merkur'eva, 'Babushka russkoi poezii', Gasparov (ed.), 'Vera Merkur'eva', 153; see also 'The Grandmother of Russian Poetry' in *Anthology*.

[104] Elizaveta Skobtsova, 'V lyudyakh lyubit'; see ['Neizdannye stikhi Materi Marii'], ed. B. Plyukhanov, *Vestnik russkogo khrist'yanskogo dvizheniya*, 161 (1991), 155; Kelly, 'Writing an Orthodox Text', 163.

> Only where I can surrender myself
> Can I find joy—though in sorrow and pain.
> Forgive me, o Lord—for I am a mother
> And I can love in no other way.

A rather different form of 'accidental modernism' is practised in two lyrics which Anna Barkova produced during her incarceration in a Soviet labour camp, 'In the Barracks' and 'Tatar Anguish'. In both pieces, Barkova adopts the persona of a Tatar (or Mongol) princess, as Elizaveta Skobtsova (then Kuzmina-Karavaeva) had in her first collection, *Scythian Sherds*. But the mask that in Kuzmina-Karavaeva's poem had conveyed a 'decadent' transgression of accepted boundaries has here been given a new and tragic significance by the motifs of imprisonment which creep into both poems; at the same time, the association of the protagonist in each text with the enemy of Russian national identity gives her a complex role; she is the perpetrator of oppression, as well as its victim.[105]

This survey of the non-Soviet literary tradition has already illustrated that 'conformity' is not simply a question of whether to write within official literary tradition or not; it is a phenomenon with many different aspects. That the problems of women's writing after 1920 were far from straightforward is suggested also by the history of those women writers who stopped being able to publish. The silence which many women writers imposed on themselves went well beyond the normal use of the word 'self-censorship'—that is, excision by the author of material which would not be passed by the political censor. By no means all the writers in the USSR who found themselves 'ideologically unacceptable' turned to writing for the drawer. Mariya Shkapskaya's grasp of the regulations censoring religious material led her not only to hesitate about republishing her poems, but to cease writing poetry altogether. 'I have only a dozen or so new poems [i.e. written since 1925], as well as a fragment of a narrative poem, which will never be finished, as I have no intention of going back to poetry,' she wrote to A. G. Lebedenko in late 1928.[106] Her resolution did not waver, and she turned herself into a writer of *ocherki*, or 'sketches'; the same course was adopted by other writers, not only poets, but also the prose writers Marietta Shaginyan and Lidiya Seifullina.[107]

---

[105] Barkova, 'V barake', 'Toska tatarskaya', Vilensky, *Dodnes'*, 341, 344.

[106] Shkapskaya, letter to A. G. Lebedenko, 3 Nov. 1920: Saltykov-Shchedrin State Public Library, Manuscript Section, f. 1077, arkh. A. G. Lebedenko, ed. khr. 652.

[107] Shkapskaya, *Sama po sebe: ocherki* (Leningrad, 1940); Marietta Shaginyan, *Po dorogam pyatiletki* (Moscow, 1947). Lack of space precludes detailed consideration of sketches, or of another

There were cases where women not so much could not publish, as did not. For example, when Elizaveta Skobtsova (as Mother Mariya) published her religious diary in verse in 1937, she excluded many of the poems which she had written in the late 1920s and early 1930s.[108] The exclusions do not seem to have been made at the direction of any publisher. Scruples about writing might spring from many causes, among them a sense that life was too insignificant for commemoration. This was to stop Shkapskaya, again, from writing a journal. As she wrote to A. G. Gornfeld in 1940:

[Fedin's] memoirs are extremely interesting, anyway. I've always been breathless with admiration at the ability to write memoirs like *that*. I've begun writing, not a diary exactly, but sort of memoirs like those, several times, but what I wrote always came out very long-winded and anything of significance was lost in a mass of details.[109]

Besides these conceptual problems, practical matters might intervene. The extreme poverty in which many internal and external *émigrés* lived was especially disadvantageous to women, since it was they who had to provide food and keep house (and these were matters in which well-bred women born in the 1900s were not necessarily more capable than their male contemporaries). If some fortunate women (Akhmatova, for example) were kept afloat by a support system made up of other women, others, such as Adelaida Gertsyk, who were not, could sink into a condition of such exhaustion and demoralization that writing, and in the end living, became impossible.[110]

In the last three years, the effective disappearance of publishing censorship in Russia has led to the rediscovery, or in some cases the discovery, of important women writers, as well as to the recovery, for a Russian audience, of material by established authors. With access to archival holdings becoming less difficult, other examples may well come to light. But the social and psychological obstacles which I have outlined here suggest that their number is unlikely to be infinite.

The 1920s, 1930s, and 1940s were years of diversity and experiment, during which Russian women produced some most adventurous and artistically successful texts. Yet these years also saw the institution

genre to which women writers of post-Revolutionary Russia had recourse, children's writing. Both deserve extensive specialized treatment.

[108] See Mat' Mariya [Kuz'mina-Karavaeva-Skobtsova], *Stikhi* (Berlin, 1937).

[109] Shkapskaya, letter to A. G. Gornfel'd, 15 Mar. 1940, Saltykov-Shchedrin State Public Library, f. 211, arkh. A. G. Gornfel'da, no. 1104.

[110] On Akhmatova's support network, see particularly Chukovskaya, *Zapiski*; on Tsvetaeva's, the most illuminating source is Véronique Lossky, *Marina Tsvetaeva v zhizni: neizdannye vospominaniya sovremennikov* (Tenafly, NJ, 1989). Cf. the observations on Anna Prismanova by Petra Couvée in her introduction to *SS* p. xiv.

within the Soviet Union of Socialist Realism, an idiom peculiarly hostile to women's writing of quality, and the further entrenchment of some of the more proscriptive nineteenth-century literary traditions outside it. The difficulties which this overview of post-Revolutionary poetry and prose has outlined will be confirmed in detail by the studies of three poets, two of whom emigrated and one of whom stayed, that follow this chapter. But at the same time, these individual studies will give greater weight than the general survey has to the particular advantages which modernism could offer women writers, whether as 'innovators' or 'archaists', those who broke away from traditional patterns, or those who recast them.

10

Sofiya Parnok (1885–1933)

SOFIYA PARNOK was a poet whose gifts stood out even in the unusual circumstances of Russian literary life during the 1920s. She combined a sharp and multi-faceted intelligence with a formidable independence of mind; both these qualities were given forceful and pointed expression in her poetry. In 1923, for example, she wrote a poem addressed to Valery Bryusov, who was by now one of the chief figures in the Soviet literary administration. In it she made an incisive and memorable statement of her right to artistic independence:

> Ради рифмы резвой не солгу,
> уж не обессудь, маститый мастер—
> мы от колыбели разной масти:
> я умею только то, что я могу.
>
> Строгой благодарна я судьбе,
> что дала мне Музу недотрогу;
> узкой, но своей идем дорогой,
> обе не попутчицы тебе.[1]

> I shall not lie to find a lurid rhyme,
> Honoured master, no harsh words from you:
> Since the cot your choice has not been mine,
> I can only do what I can do.
>
> How heartily I thank relentless Fate
> For the prickly Muse that I've been given.
> The path we walk is ours, though it be strait,
> She and I aren't fellow-travelling women.

This declaration makes clear Parnok's literary autonomy in several

---

[1] Sofiya Parnok, *Sobranie sochinenii*, ed. S. Polyakova (Ann Arbor, Mich., 1979), 222. References to this edition henceforth in text as *SS*. Parnok's 'Through a Window-Light', 'I shall not lie', and 'A childhood memory' appear in *Anthology*.

different ways. She rejects the call for new forms which Bryusov had made in his important article, 'Yesterday, Today and Tomorrow in Russian Poetry'; at the same time, she refuses to ally herself with the male poets whom he had commended. Parnok's recognition of the gender bias behind Bryusov's call is made clear both in her formulation of autonomy as 'walking with the Muse', and in the feminine form in which she gives the word *poputchik*, 'fellow-traveller', a familiar jargon term of the 1920s, which is ordinarily used in the masculine. But, in opposing a 'feminine' autonomy to a 'masculine' slavishness, Parnok falls into no alternative conformity based on the celebration of conventional ideals of womanly virtue. She represents the Muse as another woman, certainly, but she does not adopt the Akhmatovian pattern according to which the Muse-double reflects and adorns the heroine's beauty and grace. The 'prickliness' of Parnok's Muse offers no prospect of easy aestheticization or assimilation.

In another short poem, this time of 1927, Parnok shaped similar material rather differently. 'From terminal solitude', like 'I shall not lie', juxtaposes political and aesthetic conformity with a non-conformity that avoids the stereotypes of dissidence. Parnok speaks, in time-honoured Russian tradition, from a 'solitude' that has overtones of idiorrhythmic monasticism (being associated with 'prayer'); yet at the same time she rejects the easy authority of 'prophecy'. However, this time the metaphor of autonomy is not explicitly feminized: instead, the gender-neutral term 'humanity' is invoked. Parnok emphasizes the opposition between assimilation and autonomy through a pun on the terms 'bit' chelom veku' (to petition, or literally 'to bow the head) and 'byt' chelovekom' ('to be a human being').

> Из последнего одиночества
> прощальной мольбой—не пророчеством
> окликаю вас, отроки-други:
> одна лишь для поэта заповедь
> на востоке и на западе,
> на севере и на юге—
> не бить
> > челом
> > > веку своему,
> но быть
> > челом века
> > > своего,—
> быть человеком. (SS 214)

> From terminal solitude
> I call you, not with prophecy

but with a farewell prayer, young friends:
there is only one commandment
for poets East and West,
and South and North—
not to bow
      the head
           to your times,
but to be
      the head
           of your times,—
a human being.

The contrast between the two poems is instructive: when Parnok chooses, she emphasizes gender as an important part of her rejection of society; but emphasis on gender is not an inevitable part of her disputatious strategy, and when she chooses, she speaks without alluding to it.

Parnok's ability to comprehend gender as a facet of her identity at will, rather than to accept its dictates passively, makes her outstanding amongst Russian women poets of her generation. Her mature poetry expresses a fluidity of identity which eschews gender stereotypes in the ordinary sense, or any androgynous combination of these. Without ever writing of herself as a man, she escapes from essentialist notions of how women should speak. When locating herself within literary tradition, she is able to affiliate herself both with male poets and with women poets, to speak in gender-neutral and in gender-specific terms. 'To Khodasevich', for example, is a moving tribute to a male contemporary and fellow spirit, in which Khodasevich is invoked both as object and as addressee. The sensations of reading his verse are compared to a reminiscence from childhood, which Khodasevich, and through him the reader, is invited to share:

ХОДАСЕВИЧУ

С детства помню: груши есть такие—
сморщенные, мелкие, тугие,
И такая терпкость скрыта в них,
что едва укусишь,—сводит челюсть:
так вот для меня и эта прелесть
злых, оскомистых стихов твоих.   (SS 225)

TO KHODASEVICH

A childhood memory: those pears,
wrinkled, little, tight,
and hidden inside
tart flesh that puckered the mouth;

exactly so my delight
in the bitter shards of your verse.

This poem invokes an experience from childhood that transcends gender; by contrast, a number of the poems which Parnok wrote during the early 1920s, when she was living in the Crimea in very difficult circumstances, are moving commentaries on the female friendships and literary friendships which sustained her at the time. In one poem, the pale, transparent, and emaciated body of Vera Grinevich, a woman who had lost her son during the Civil War, is evoked through the beautiful image of a flame shining through blue glass:

Как пламень в голубом стекле лампады,
в обворожительном плену прохлады,
преображенной жизнью дыша,
задумчиво горит твоя душа.   (SS 178)

The flame in a lamp's blue globe,
Bewitched, trapped by cold,
breathing life transformed,
thoughtful, your soul burns.

In the sense that it is an enclosing space, Grinevich's body is 'maternal', but its 'transfiguration' through want is not gender-specific.

Parnok's refusal to separate the 'masculine' and 'feminine' absolutely is often connected with a refusal to distinguish the physical and the metaphysical. In another poem written in the Crimea, 'The Vegetable Garden', Parnok writes of her struggles to force the hard ground into giving up its fruits. Suggestions of the nightmare fertility of Gogol's pastoral scenes are woven into a text that avoids the obvious equation between the feminine speaker and 'mother earth', showing one pitted against the other. But the very irritation and frustration of the struggle, the sense of incompatibility, leads to a peculiar rapprochement: the earth's resistance provokes strong sexual feeling in the speaker, a feeling which she names with the provocative word 'possession':

Здесь резвый закурчавится горох,
взойдут стволы крутые кукурузы,
распустит, как Горгона, змеи-косы
брюхатая, чудовищная тыква.
Ах, ни подснежники, ни крокусы не пахнут
весной так убедительно весною,
как пахнет первый с грядки огурец!

        .   .   .   .   .

и никогда блаженство обладанья
такой неомраченной полнотой
и острой гордостью меня не прожигало   (SS 169)

The pea will burst out in impetuous curls,
the massive stalks of maize will tower up,
the monstrous pumpkin, big with child,
will shake her hideous Gorgon locks.
A crocus or a snowdrop does not smell,
so strongly of the spring, in spring,
as a first hot-bed cucumber!

.   .   .   .

Never did the pleasure of possession
burn into me with such a bitter pride,
with such unclouded fullness

Here, the fracturing of dominant notions of femininity occurs less through the adoption of gender-marked personae or masks, than through an adept manipulation of perspective and lexicon. The process is typical of Parnok's mature poetry. Analytical in its sense of language's powers of inscription and identification, this poetry is, though, also remarkably concrete. The pears of the tribute to Khodasevich, the warm first cucumber in 'The Vegetable Garden', the blue lamp-glass of Grinevich's body, appeal to the senses in themselves; and the verse in which they are evoked, though not easily melodious, has a dense and satisfying phonetic patterning.

In a more substantial late poem, 'Through a Window-Light' (1928), Parnok uses exact observation not only in order to counterpoint an underlying sense of vacuity, but also in order to avoid any easy polarization between 'here' and 'there', 'imprisonment' and 'escape', 'male' and 'female'. The speaker kneels on a window-sill and looks out through a 'light', the top flap of a Russian double window which may be kept open for air all through the year. She meditates on the possibility of escape. Gradually, however, not only the practical possibility, but the abstract idea of escape is undermined: the speaker can only imagine crawling 'on her knees', as she is, in order to get away, a position whose physical difficulty conveys an overwhelming sense that the physical world cannot be overcome. The speaker's vision of Hell on earth as a bath-house, with a 'miasma' of evil rising from it like dirt from a sweaty skin, recalls an observation made by Dostoevsky's Svidrigailov in *Crime and Punishment*. However, no Dostoevskian spiritual transcendence derives from the reference; it is subverted by a second reference to Dostoevskian material. An ironic allusion to Father Zosima, the *starets* (spiritual elder) in *Brothers Karamazov*, whose physical degeneration after death causes a crisis in the hero, Alyosha, is used in order to question once more the existence of any metaphysical world:

В какой-нибудь дремучий скит забытый,
чтобы молить прощенья и защиты—.
и выплакать, и вымолить . . . Когда б
я знала, где они,—заступники, Зосимы,
и не угас ли свет неугасимый?   (*SS* 231)

Perhaps to a hermitage somewhere,
repent my sins in tears and prayer—
But where is Zosima, faith's defender,
or is the world without end ended?

In the final part of the poem, the speaker reveals that her skewed perspective of Moscow includes the 'glint' of a dome. The dome's colour and shape might in other circumstances have made it seem an obvious symbolic contrast to the 'greyish sack' of air mentioned in the opening lines of the poem; but in the context of the poem it emerges as a visual parallel to the 'sack', the vital breathing apparatus for a TB sufferer that also keeps that sufferer trapped in the bedroom, and hence reinforces the sense of imprisonment.

The claustrophobic sense of suffering is, however, broken down, at the end of the poem, by an allusion to the possibility of intellectual progress beyond the window-light, as the speaker recognizes that imprisonment is a condition endured by others too:

И где-нибудь на западе, в Париже,
в Турине, в Гамбурге—не все ль равно?
Вот так же высунувшись в душное окно,
дыша такой же ядовитой жижей,
и, силясь из последних сил вздохнуть,
стоит, и думает, и плачет кто-нибудь
не белый, и не красный, и не черный,
не гражданин, а просто человек,
как я, быть может, слишком непроворно
и грустно доживающий свой век.   (*SS* 232)

And somewhere in the West, in Paris,
Turin or Hamburg—who cares where?
Pressing against the pane for air,
forcing its sour slops past the larynx,
breathing with last reserves of strength,
another stands and weeps and thinks.
Not Red, White, Black; a woman or a man,
a human being and not a citizen,
like me, perhaps: someone whose life now ebbs
in stagnancy, and not in happiness.

No individual affliction, this *malaise* is also not traceable simply to humanity's oppression by totalitarian politics (Moscow and Turin may make a pair, but Paris and Hamburg do not complete a neat quartet). Parnok's speaker refuses to be defined in the terms of fanaticism or nationalism, as she has refused to identify with patriarchal religion; she also declares herself capable of a general identification with others who refuse to be so defined (no matter how useless the gesture of solidarity might be). As in 'From terminal solitude', the gender-neutral notion of 'humanity' is introduced. But Parnok herself has spoken not as 'a woman or a man', but as a woman. The entire poem uses feminine verbal and adjectival forms (e.g. *popolzla by*, I would crawl), systematically linking these with the 'unfeminine' activity of intellectual speculation. As the speaker struggles for air, and also struggles to speak, she is 'bullied' by 'the magic syllable', the power of the word; but the utterance to which she gives voice is not the usual 'feminine' magic discourse of prophecy, but a speculation on existence itself. Or, as the poem has it, 'I'm still | Stubborn. I think.' —an ambiguous formulation which means both, 'I think (and therefore I must exist)' and 'I assume that I am still stubborn, and so I must exist'. 'Through a Window-Light' illustrates Parnok's capacity to confront, rather than avoid, the suggestion that philosophical poetry is an inappropriate feminine genre.

The paradoxes of internal debate are underlined by the poem's clashing registers. Rhetorical questions are used in two quite different ways: to suggest the expansive manner of an eighteenth-century elegy (as in 'or is the world?'), and also to evoke the colloquial hesitancies of stream-of-consciousness, as here:

> Не странно ли? Мы все болезни лечим,
> саркому, и склероз и старость ...   (*SS* 231)

> Strange, don't you think? Ills of all kinds
> are treatable; sarcoma, age's slow decline ...

Parnok's invention of a way of speaking which did not polarize 'the human' and 'the feminine', but which moved between them flexibly, harnessing layers of parody and irony to its purpose, also had profound effects on her late love poetry. All of this is addressed to other women, and is written from a perspective that is feminine in the grammatical sense, but the stereotypes of love poetry addressed by women to men, or, conversely, those of the love poetry addressed by men to women, are interrogated and transformed.

Some of Parnok's poems are amongst the most frankly hedonistic Russian love lyrics of the twentieth century. Discarding the metaphysical sophistries with which Russian eroticism has often had to legitimate itself, they yet do not pander to an unthinking voyeur. 'You are young, you have long legs' (1929), is a celebration of sensuality addressed to a young woman, Marina Baranovich, who is portrayed in terms of tactile pleasure. Parnok refers through her to the 'beating of warmth', 'silkiness', 'mother-of-pearl face', and 'snaky coldness' of her namesake, Marina Tsvetaeva (*SS* 234).

If this poem evokes a femininity which would conventionally be understood as attractive, Parnok's last poems, addressed to her late love Vedeneeva, and collected in the two cycles 'Ursa Major' (1932) and 'Needless Bounty' (1932–3), chose a more original object. These cycles concern a passionate attachment between two women, neither of whom has the youthful beauty conventionally demanded from objects of desire. Many poems allude to the physical frailty of the poet as well as her lover, and Parnok mercilessly conveys the sense that late love is absurd, painful to both parties, and that exhaustion increasingly mingles with passion. The essentially tragic realization of impending mortality is invoked in a spirit of analytic detachment, even amusement. Parnok compares herself, for example, to 'some idiot in a gallery seat' clapping on when a theatrical performance is long over (*SS* 244). The peculiar nature of this late love is conveyed by means of a transformation of the clichés of love poetry: the addressee is a 'grey rose', rather than a dewy one, she is Dante's Virgil, not his Beatrice. And in one short humorous lyric, Parnok takes the common saying, 'I could eat you up', and turns it into a statement which is both self-deprecating and ardent: a cannibal might 'crack his teeth' on Vedeneeva, she is so bony, but Parnok will solve that problem by munching with her lips alone (*SS* 247).

Parodistic allusions to literary love are also used by Parnok in order to achieve an idiosyncratic fusion of eroticism and self-mockery. In 'At the Beginning Chapter Five' (*SS* 243), we hear that this is a textbook 'romance' (meaning both a copy-book love-affair, and a stereotypical narrative). Every appropriate scene takes place in it, but in the wrong order:

> Опять о том, как пили чай,
> как чинно восседали рядом,
> как обменялись невзначай
> каким-то сумасшедим взглядом ...
> Давайте же читать вдвоем
> роман «отменно длинный-длинный».
> Хотите вместе мы начнем?
> Но только прямо с середины!   (*SS* 243–4)

And on and on: they drank their tea
and sat about, most properly.

But now and then their eyes would meet
in a crazy look, hard to predict.
So let us read now, both at once,
a 'really, really long romance.'
I'd like to start at once; would you?
All right; but only, half-way through.

The plot of the poem imitates that of a society tale (no doubt Parnok had read Karolina Pavlova's *At the Tea-Table*, republished in 1915): decent social occasions are disrupted by the 'madness' of love. However, the line 'a really, really long romance' comes from Pushkin's *Count Nulin*, where a visitor to a country house attempts a heartily physical affair with his hostess. The evocation of the farcical plot of *Count Nulin* counterpoints the tragic irony of the society tale, though it does not efface this irony entirely; in alluding to a case where sturdy sexual passion has ended in failure, Parnok can also allude to her erotic feelings for Vedeneeva in a manner that is at once self-deprecating and assertive.

Parnok's concern with how emotional satisfaction and physical pleasure can be united works against the canons of the post-Romantic love lyric, where the two qualities are always assumed to be contradictory. Her emphasis on love's physicality also means that, rather than stress that romantic attachments escape limits of space and time, she writes of a love which, even when it creates imaginary worlds, is conscious of boundaries not to be escaped, and knows the absurdity of its own constructions. As in 'Through a Window-Light', the possibility of escape is extended only to be withdrawn. In 'She is still carefree' (*SS* 255), for example, Parnok refers to an ideal locus of secret love, 'a village lost in its gardens', but warns that it 'cannot be found on a map', and then describes a place that is an obvious counterfeit, a fiction:

Где домик с жасмином и гостеприимная ночь,
и хмеля над нами кудрявые арки,
и жажда, которой уж нечем помочь,
и небо, и небо страстней, чем небо Петрарки.

With hospitable night and a jasmine-twined cottage,
and tendrils of hop knotting over our heads,
and thirst—though it's got far too late now to slake it,
and a sky of more passion than Petrarch described.

In a further revision of tradition, the addressee of this poem constantly escapes her role as heroine, and the formal compliments with which she is lavished. She becomes an independent companion, not a coy mistress:

Она беззаботна еще, она молода,
еще не прорезались зубы у Страсти,—

не водка, не спирт, но уже не вода,
а пенистое, озорное, певучее Асти.
Еще не умеешь бледнеть, когда я подхожу,
еще во весь глаз твой зрачок не расширен,
но знаю: я в мыслях твоих ворожу
сильнее, чем в ласковом Кашине или Кашире.   (*SS* 255)

She is still carefree, she is still youthful,
for the time being Passion's cut none of her teeth;
not vodka, not spirit, but not water either,
like Asti, she's melody, bubbles and fizz.

Your eyes are still very much smaller than saucers,
you haven't yet learnt to go pale when I'm close;
things have changed though since tender Kashin and Kashir,
for now I have stolen into your thoughts.

Self-aware and witty in its handling of literary tradition, Parnok's late love poetry is also resourceful in terms of its metrics. In some poems, such as 'She is still carefree', shifts in register are facilitated by the use of mixed 'logaoedic' forms, which allow Parnok to move between lines of strict metre, and lines whose looser rhythmic structure may be adapted to colloquial syntax; in other poems, accentual verse, and approximate rhyme, convey an impression of relaxation and spontaneity.

The confidence and apparent effortlessness of this poetry should not, however, conceal from us the very considerable difficulties that lay behind its composition. Parnok's increasing sense of personal and literary isolation was not simply the product of personal conviction or of intellectual speculation. After 1925 it had become very difficult for her to publish; her last collection, *In an Undertone*, appeared in a print-run of only 200 copies, with the stipulation 'copyright as manuscript' (a form of limited circulation normally reserved for the abstracts of dissertations). Official censorship instigated cuts in what she did manage to publish, and dictated changes in her opera libretto, *Almast*, which was produced by the Bolshoi in 1930.

Like many other marginalized writers of the Soviet period, Parnok was forced to take up translation as a means of physical survival. Already in poor health from tuberculosis, she did not survive the demands of this work for long.[2] Condemned to 'writing for the drawer', without possibility of publication, she began to dwell on the 'uselessness' of writing. 'Every pine rustles in its forest | but who will hear my news?' she asks in a poem of 1929 (*SS* 233). In another piece, written two years later, she

---

[2] On Parnok's biography, see Polyakova's excellent introduction to *SS* 7–106, which is also an indispensable critical guide to the poetry. The best introduction in English to her poetry is Diana Burgin, 'Sophia [*sic*] Parnok and the Writing of a Lesbian Poet's Life', *SR* 51/2 (1992), 214–31.

speaks of her poetry as a fire lit for herself alone, and as 'needless bounty' which will be bequeathed to no one (*SS* 236). In some of her last poems, language seems almost on the point of breaking down. Some pieces in the cycle 'Grey Rose', for example, give the impression of mnemonic jottings, or indecipherable private jokes, being composed of obsessively repeated half-phrases. As Mirsky wrote of Khodasevich, this work sometimes 'reaches the boundaries where poetry ends and sophistry [*umnoe delanie*] begins'. Parnok's last poem, described by Polyakova as 'a fragment', is hardly more incomplete than many 'finished' late poems:

> На голову седую
> Не   глаз
> Это я   целую
> Последний раз.[3]

> On your grey head
> Not   eye
> It is I kiss
> Last   time.

And yet the withdrawal into self which was forced on Parnok was not simply a distortion of what had gone before. Her career cannot be divided into a period before 1925 when she could say what she wished, and a period after 1925 when she could not. On the contrary, even the early part of her life was marked by difficulties and conflicts, both of a personal and of an aesthetic kind. She lost her mother as a small child, and did not get on well with her father's second wife; in her teens she left Taganrog on the Black Sea, her birthplace, and was thereafter to lose contact with the family. Born into a Jewish family, she, like Mandelstam, converted to Christianity at some stage in early adulthood; she was also to adopt the surname 'Parnok' in preference to her parental surname, 'Parnokh'.[4]

In her poetry Parnok refers to her Jewish descent only obliquely, and in a context of repudiation. In a poem of 1915, for example, she begins with an assertion and a question:

> Я не знаю своих предков.—Кто они?   (*SS* 125)

> I do not know my ancestors. Who are they?

She then reinvents her family history, speaking of the 'quickened heart-

---

[3] 'Na golovu seduyu' is quoted by Polyakova, *SS* 35; the remark by Mirsky on Khodasevich is taken from *Uncollected Writings*, 106. One undecipherable private joke is the reference to 'Violgolosa', *SS* 242—unless this is a mistranscription for 'Vpolgolosa', 'in an undertone', the title of Parnok's last collection.

[4] See Polyakova, *SS* 8–10. In Ezhov and Shamurin, *Russkaya poeziya*, Parnok describes herself as of 'Russian' rather than 'Jewish' nationality—contrast, say, Elizaveta Polonskaya.

beat' which she feels when Madrid is mentioned, and wondering whether a 'pallid descendant' of hers will feel a similar thrill on seeing a guitar or a red carnation. With its perfunctory references to Spanish culture, then the height of fashion all over Europe, this piece has a flavour of the cardboard cut-out settings used by turn-of-the-century photographers; anyone can become anything by putting their head through a backdrop with the right emblems on it. Parnok's imaginary trip into genealogy mythologizes her family origins into something distant and exotic; in answering the question, 'who were her ancestors', she could avoid the question of who her parents were.

Alienation from her father undoubtedly played some part in this rejection by Parnok of her early biography, but there were larger cultural factors involved too. Though Parnok did assimilate to Russian society's sexual norms for a while—she was briefly married, from 1907 until 1909, to the writer and literary journalist V. M. Volkenstein—she made an absolute break with heterosexuality after her separation from her husband. Given the proscriptive pressures of turn-of-the-century Russian culture, to write as a lesbian *and* a Jew would have been appallingly difficult. In a poem from *The Vine* (1922), she makes a glancing reference to this point. Speaking of being 'cast out' by God because of her erotic preferences, she links her fate with the fate of the Jews, expelled by divine anger to Egypt:

> И люди пьют мои уста,
> а жар последний все не выпить.
> Как мед столетний, кровь густа,—
> о, плен мой знойный! Мой Египет! (*SS* 161)

> People are drinking from my lips;
> yet they could not drain my heat.
> Thick as age-old honey runs my blood,
> O burning prison! O my Egypt!

But if Parnok is an Old Testament prophet here, she is a false one (the phrase 'drinking from my lips' plays on the saying *tvoimi by ustami med pit'*, 'I wish you were right'). And in the end she sets the Hebraic motif aside, stating that she 'dreams' of a resolution in which she would rise to God's presence, and stand 'face to face'. This allusion to the afterlife, like the image of hell-fire in the first stanza, and the reference to God as 'Gospod' (Lord), indicate that the God whose judgement is accepted is a Christian God.

Both lesbianism and Jewishness made Parnok an outcast from Russian cultural tradition; her response was to elide Jewishness as part of her poetic subjectivity through the metaphors in which she referred to her ancestry. In referring to Jewish culture by evoking modish Hispanophilia, or by alluding to the Old Testament, her early work stated its affiliation with a cultural heritage from mainstream Russian tradition, rather than suggesting the fate of a marginalized group outside that mainstream. Her early lesbian poetry does not, however, represent a 'frankness' which may be contrasted with her mythologization of her family origins. On the contrary, her 'ancestry' poems shed light on her problems in finding an appropriate language for her lesbian poetry.

In her famous essay, 'Notes on "Camp"', Susan Sontag has described the appeal which the self-consciously artificial strands in the Symbolist and post-Symbolist aesthetic have held for homosexual writers working in prohibitive cultures.[5] The cultural circumstances in which Parnok lived were as repressive of the written expression of lesbianism as the Anglo-American tradition of which Sontag writes; it is hardly surprising that they should have fostered similar strategies of evasion through theatrical self-assertion. Parnok's dream of being related to flamenco-dancer blood-lines is a classic piece of 'camp' writing. Though entirely lacking the naïvety which Sontag sees as essential to real 'campness', she was to experiment with many forms of 'dressing up' in her early love poetry too.

Sometimes the costumes which Parnok borrowed came from contemporary heterosexual love poetry. In one poem, for example, she visualizes the addressee as an Akhmatovian innocent not yet touched by the deceiving 'bridegroom' (*SS* 124–5). She also made use of the conventional link between 'Sapphic' stanzaic forms and homo-erotic themes, and borrowed from Sappho suggestive figures of speech: the phrase 'you laid your head on my breast' is used, for example, to suggest sexual contact. There is a certain defensiveness in such neo-classical ornamentalism, whose traditional, 'Anacreontic', flavour was recognized in Parnok's own subtitle of 'Anthology poems' for *Roses of Piraeus*, a collection of 1922. Similarly defensive is Parnok's borrowing of religious imagery to pay the beloved hyperbolic compliments. Parnok concludes one declaration of love, for example, with an assurance that the Deity himself is charmed:

> А там, над нами, Самый Строгий
> старается не хмурить бровь,
> но сам он и меньшие броги,—
> все в нашу влюблены любовь.   (*SS* 168)

and there above us the Most Stern
tries to suppress an angry frown:

---

[5] Susan Sontag, 'Notes on "Camp"', *Against Interpretation and Other Essays* (2nd edn.; London, 1987), 275–92.

but he, like all the minor gods
is quite besotted with our love.

'When you mutter in sleep', another poem of 1919, radiates a more
powerful and threatening eroticism; perhaps for that reason, it was not
published during Parnok's lifetime. Here Parnok discards her 'camp'
trappings, and displaces the feminine voice through a strategy similar to
that in 'The Vegetable Garden': a network of grammatically feminine
nouns subliminally suggests the gender of the actors in the poem. The
second stanza moves through *dver'* (door), *stvorka* (flap), *skorogovorka*
(gabble), *bol'* (pain), and *dusha* (soul). The use of grammatical manipulation to conceal an explosive sub-text is paralleled in the plot of the
poem, which concerns an unconscious revelation of what cannot be
spoken openly:

Когда забормочешь во сне,
и станет твой голос запальчив,
я возьму тебя тихо за пальчик
и шепну: «Расскажи обо мне,—
как меня ты, любовь моя, любишь?
Как меня ты, мой голубь, голубишь?»

И двери, закрытой дотоль,
распахнутся страшные створки.
Сумасшедшей скороговоркой
затаенная вырвется боль,—
и душа твоя, плача, увидит,
как безумно она ненавидит.   (*SS* 190)

When you start to talk in your sleep,
and your voice becomes fretful,
I shall take your finger gently,
and whisper, 'Speak to me, speak—
tell me, my love, how you love me,
how dear, my dear one, you hold me.'

And the hideous flaps of the door,
shut till now, will swing wide.
In a torrent of maddened words
hidden pain will burst out—
and weeping, your soul will see
the crazed hatred you feel for me.

Most of Parnok's pre-1925 love poems show signs of unease; few have
the energy and passion of 'The Woman Friend', the cycle addressed to
her in 1915 by Tsvetaeva. 'How could I not remember' one of Tsvetaeva's poems from this cycle, eschews neo-classical generalities; through a
progression of exact detail, erotic feeling rises in crescendo:

Могу ли не вспомнить я
Тот запах White Rose и чая,
И севрские фигурки
Над пылающим камельком . . .

Мы были: я—в пышном платье
Из чуть золотого фая,
Вы—в вязаной черной куртке
С крылатым воротником.

Я помню, с каким вошли Вы
Лицом, без малейшей краски,
Как встали, кусая пальчик,
Чуть голову наклоня.[6]

How could I not remember
The scent of White Rose and tea,
And the Sèvres porcelain figurines
Over the flaring fire . . .

And our clothes—I had a foaming dress
Of faille, with a flicker of gold,
You wore a black knitted jacket
With a stand-up collar, like wings.

I remember your face as you entered:
Pale, without any colour;
How you rose and chewed at your finger,
Head upright, thrown slightly back.

By contrast, even Parnok's more successful love poems addressed to
Tsvetaeva, such as 'Like a slim coltish girl I saw you before me' (*SS* 141),
are inhibited by the customary decencies of 'Sapphic verse'; here, the
charming detail of the girl delighted by new love, as she might be by a
coloured slipper or a handful of beads, vanishes under a tattered cloak of
poeticisms—emotion like 'an arrow-shot', 'maternal tenderness replacing passion', and so on.

Some of the frustrations of Parnok's search for the appropriate
expression of subjectivity, for an individual voice to suit her far from
ordinary experience, can be sensed in the series of reviews which she
wrote as 'Andrei Polyanin' in 1913–16. These are filled with tart,
judicious, but often rather repressive comments about contemporary
poets and prose writers. Parnok makes rather pedantic objections to
linguistic improprieties in Klyuev and Severyanin, for example, and
expresses a deep hostility to Andrei Bely's modernist novel *Petersburg*;

---

[6] Tsvetaeva, 'Mogu li ne vspomnit'', Parnok, *SS* 297; see also Diana Burgin, 'Silver Age
Perceptions', and *eadem*, 'Signs of a Response: Two Possible Parnok Replies to Her *Podruga*', *SEEJ*
35/2 (1991), 214–28.

she finds herself in sympathy only with the early poems of Mandelstam, which lead her, however, to praise the 'sculptural quality of language' in his work, and its verbal 'music'.[7] This bland formulation is in striking contrast to the flamboyant disgust which Parnok lavished on Akhmatova's verse; reading this, she asserted, recalled the experience of being trapped 'in someone else's uncomfortably intimate bedroom', one tricked out with bric-à-brac and meretricious ornaments.[8] Parnok's violent rejection of this overly 'feminine' material on the one hand, and her lukewarm acceptance of Mandelstam on the other, make her dilemma clear: here was a poet whose aesthetic judgements were individual from the beginning of her career, but who could so far shape the practical implications of that individuality only through assaults on others' beliefs, rather than through an authoritative statement of her own opinions.

Like Karolina Pavlova (a poet for whom Parnok, like another independent-minded poet of the 1920s and 1930s, Anna Prismanova, declared her admiration), Parnok was remade as a writer by her 'terminal solitude'.[9] Sofya Polyakova, the Russian literary historian who has been responsible for recovering Parnok's work for posterity, has spoken of her late work as expressing a sense of 'inner freedom'.[10] Terrible as it was to work with the fear that only close friends would ever see what she had written, Parnok could, at least, in her solitude, utter what she could never have printed, and give voice, for the first time in Russian culture, to a lesbian sensibility. In this she was ahead, not only of her own time, but also of future generations. No full edition of Parnok's work has yet been published in Russia, and even now, the quality of her work is hardly recognized there. The modernism of her late poetry remains as incomprehensible, in terms of the full-blooded Romanticism expected by many Russian readers, as its explicit lesbianism is for them indefensible.

---

[7] Parnok [as 'Andrei Polyanin'], 'Otmechennye imena'; 'V poiskakh puti iskusstva', *SZ* (1913), 5–6: 227–32; 'Peterburg', *SZ* (1914), 6: 134–42; 'M. Kuzmin, *Plavayushchie-puteshestvuyushchie*', *SZ* (1915), 4: 108–11; 'Osip Mandel'shtam: *Kamen''*, *SZ* (1916), 4–5: 242–3. In the same number, Parnok describes the work of another favoured poet, A. Lipskerov, just as blandly, speaking of 'harmony of content and form': ibid. 241.

[8] Parnok, 'Otmechennye imena'.

[9] See the early poem, 'Karoline Pavlovoi', *SS* 118; still more striking is 'Otryvok', *SS* 195, in which Parnok sees Pavlova as 'rightless in her own time', and yet 'the great-grandmother of Russian poetry'.

[10] Polyakova in *SS* 91.

II

Marina Tsvetaeva (1892–1941)

IF Akhmatova is the only woman writer who is regularly admitted to the company of the greats in Russia itself, Tsvetaeva now occupies a similarly unassailable position in the West, her reputation eclipsing that of any other Russian woman writer. Before the publication of Simon Karlinsky's path-breaking study of her life and work in 1965, her name was hardly known to non-Russians; since then, however, academic articles, popular and scholarly biographies, and above all translations, have acquainted a broad public with the major events of her life, and given it a taste of her work. Her defiantly anti-Soviet stance in the early years after the Revolution, her emigration to Berlin in 1921, and thence to Prague in 1922, before finally moving to Paris in 1925, her increasing isolation in the *émigré* literary world, her return to the Soviet Union in 1939, and suicide in the Crimean town of Elabuga in 1941, just after the outbreak of the Second World War—these occurrences are now as familiar in the West as the history of Pasternak's persecution after he was awarded the Nobel Prize, or the marital vicissitudes of the Tolstoy household, and a good deal more familiar than the story of Pushkin's duel with d'Anthès.[1]

---

[1] Simon Karlinsky's pioneering study, *Marina Cvetaeva* (Berkeley, Calif., 1965), was followed by a flood of Western monographs, both scholarly and popular, and translations. The introduction to Karlinsky's rev. 2nd edn. of his 1965 study, *Marina Tsvetaeva: The Woman, her World and her Poetry* (Cambridge, 1985), surveys this material; a well-annotated recent article is Michael Makin, 'Text and Violence in Tsvetaeva's *Molodets*', in Catriona Kelly, Michael Makin, and David Shepherd (eds.), *Discontinuous Discourses in Modern Russian Literature* (London, 1989), 115–35. The biographical parts of Karlinsky (though not his critical commentaries) have now been superseded by Viktoriya Schweitzer [Shveitser], *The Life and Work of Marina Tsvetaeva*, trans. Harry Willetts and Robert Chandler (London, 1992). On the work, see also Joseph Brodsky's two articles, 'A Poet and Prose' and 'Footnote to a Poem', *Less than One* (London, 1987), 176–94, 195–267; Jane Taubman, *Marina Tsvetaeva: A Life Through Poetry: Marina Tsvetaeva's Lyric Diary* (Columbus, Ohio, 1988). A recent popular biography is Elaine Feinstein's *A Captive Lion: The Life of Marina Tsvetaeva* (London, 1987); cf. the same author's *Marina Tsvetayeva* (London, 1989); Feinstein is also the translator of Tsvetaeva's *Selected Poems* (London, 1986). Other translations

Like Akhmatova, Tsvetaeva has become a symbol of the artist tormented by political repression. True, the myths encrusting her life and poetry are of a less hagiographical kind. She did not live long enough to organize her own heritage industry, and though her daughter Ariadna Efron made assiduous efforts to ensure her mother's posthumous reputation, the very difficult relationship between mother and daughter did not make for the construction of a monolithic myth of virtue. (On one occasion, Efron even referred to her mother as 'a policeman of the human soul', which must be one of the more devastatingly hostile comments ever made by one blood relation about another.)[2] Besides, Tsvetaeva's life was patently unsuited to domestication or aestheticization. One cannot imagine Akhmatova recalled, as Tsvetaeva has been, by an anecdote recording how she insisted to a superficial male acquaintance in Moscow that they should eat at a worker's canteen, not in a grand hotel, then afterwards demanded where she might find 'a bog'.[3] Nor has any reminiscence of Akhmatova's living quarters suggested that 'a milk can serving as a chamber pot' occupied a prominent position there, as it did in the flat which Tsvetaeva occupied after the Revolution.[4]

Such details illustrate how inimical the Tsvetaeva icon is to the anxious gentility which is prevalent in Russian intellectual culture, but at the same time they enhance her reputation as the quintessential Romantic genius. The frequent comparisons between her and Beethoven are not fortuitous; the two shared not only a carelessness about chamber-pots, but also a capacity to affront patrons and well-wishers with their arrogant behaviour. But since Tsvetaeva's material was words, rather than the more obviously abstract medium of music, her work has been seen not simply as the expression of intensity, of pain and conflict, but as the expression of stress which can be traced to particular biographical experiences—which for Tsvetaeva's biographers has meant above all her love-affairs with various men. (Her love-affairs with women, most

include *Selected Poems*, trans. David McDuff (Newcastle, 1987). A translation of *Staircase* appears in *Anthology*. Recently, material of value has also begun to emerge from the (former) Soviet Union: see e.g. Mariya Belkina's unusually full memoir of Tsvetaeva's last years, *Skreshchenie sudeb: popytka Tsvetaevoi, drukh poslednikh let ee zhizni* ... (Moscow, 1988). On bibliography and translations, see also Robin Kemball (ed.), *Marina Tsvetaeva: trudy 1-go mezhdunarodnogo simpoziuma (Lozanna 30 VI–3 VII 1982)* (Bern, 1991).

[2] Efron's remark is quoted in Véronique Lossky's useful recent anthology of memoirs, *Marina Tsvetaeva v zhizni: neizdannye vospominaniya sovremennikov* (Tenafly, NJ, 1989), 167. A similar attitude on occasion breaks through in Efron's own memoirs, *Marina Tsvetaeva: vospominaniya docheri* (Paris, 1987).

[3] Lossky, *Marina Tsvetaeva v zhizni*, 252–3.

[4] Ibid. 59.

particularly Sofiya Parnok, have received significantly less attention, though they were at least as important.)[5]

Concentration on Tsvetaeva's biography for its own sake is understandable. There is still a need to clarify details and establish facts, and to go beyond the excessively judgemental approach, alternating praise and blame, which has been adopted by most chroniclers of the life.[6] There is considerable interest also (as in the case of Akhmatova) in tracing the process by which Tsvetaeva, who at the beginning of her career had been considered just one among many 'poetesses', gradually attained an overwhelming stature and authority.[7] But the use of biographical material as a definitive commentary upon the poetry is an obstacle to appreciation of both life and work. Tsvetaeva's life was not simply the inert material of poetry; it was a life lived in order to supply that material. Encouraged by her mother from early childhood to think of herself as outstandingly able, she exemplified the Russian term *zhiznetvorchestvo*, the fashioning of one's own biography as art. Self-martyrdom was a fundamental part of this fashioning process; Tsvetaeva enjoyed significantly better living conditions in the emigration than many other writers, yet she engined herself on the belief that she languished in particular neglect and privation.[8] Similarly, always being in love with the wrong man (or woman) was not only a source of suffering, but also a source of productive conflict and a goad to composition.

If experience was partly the expression of poetry, poetry was far from being simply the vehicle of experience. Certainly, biographical material

---

[5] On Tsvetaeva's love-affairs with men, see especially Feinstein, *A Captive Lion*; Shveitser, *Life and Work*, and Karlinsky, *Marina Tsvetaeva*, give far more honest treatments of her affairs with women, but the fullest account of Tsvetaeva and Parnok's relations is Polyakova's *V zakatnye oni dni*.

[6] Both Feinstein, *A Captive Lion* and (though to a far lesser extent, given her vastly superior level of factual documentation) Shveitser, *Life and Work*, alternately praise and chide Tsvetaeva; Karlinsky's *Marina Tsvetaeva* offers a much less moralistic treatment. For an interesting recent study of the 'Tsvetaeva mythology', see Svetlana Boym, *Death in Quotation Marks: Cultural Myths of the Modern Poet* (Cambridge, Mass., 1991), 192–240.

[7] For analysis of Tsvetaeva's change of attitude to writing between 1912 and 1916 see Irina Shevelenko, 'Marina Tsvetaeva v 1911–1913 godakh: formirovanie avtorskogo samosoznaniya', *Blokovskii sbornik*, 11 (Tartu, 1990), 50–66. As with Akhmatova, however, external factors played a huge role in Tsvetaeva's elevation; a full treatment of this subject would have to pay particular attention to *émigré* criticism between 1922 and 1939, a bibliography of which is now available in L. A. Mnukhin, *Marina Tsvetaeva: bibliograficheskii ukazatel' literatury o zhizni i deyatel'nosti 1910–1941 gg. i 1942–1962 gg.* (Wiener Slawistischer Almanach Sonderband, 23; Vienna, 1989.)

[8] On Tsvetaeva's living conditions, see e.g. Vladimir Nabokov, *Selected Letters 1940–1977*, ed. Dmitri Nabokov and Matthew J. Bruccoli (London, 1989), 430; cf. Lossky, *Marina Tsvetaeva v zhizni*, 126–32, and Belkina, *Skreshchenie, passim*. Belkina reveals, *inter alia*, that one of the confidantes on whom Tsvetaeva unloaded her complaints was Vera Merkur'eva, whose circumstances were at least as bad as her own: see p. 146.

(in however transmogrified a form) does dominate the texts that have become canonical in the West: the grandiloquent rebuff to a rival, 'Attempt at Jealousy' and the powerfully intense narrative poems *Poem of the Mountain* and *Poem of the End* were all directly inspired by Tsvetaeva's affair with the third-rate playboy Konstantin Rodzevich.[9] But Tsvetaeva is a much richer poet than any narrowly biographical interpretation would suggest. Erotic love is central to her work, but so is the meditation on female identity and the contemplation of prophecy and writing; her associative range encompassed Russian folklore, Greek myth, historical and political *realia*, and a defiantly independent selection of favourite writers, including Casanova and Rostand, Mariya Bashkirtseva, and Pearl Buck, as well as the more obviously 'good taste' choices of Rilke, Akhmatova, and Pasternak.[10] Her output was both outstandingly prolific and remarkably varied, encompassing verse plays, memoirs, literary essays, short stories, and narrative poems as well as lyrics. To the innate gifts of an exact verbal memory and a capacity for infinite linguistic improvisation she added an extraordinary commitment and an unstinting dedication; she is in many ways the embodiment of Dorothy Cowan's assertion that 'a capacity for indefatigable work has always been the distinguishing characteristic of a genius'.[11]

In any case, when confronted with the dense allusiveness of, say, the narrative poem *Attempt at a Room*, the reader is little aided by knowing that the poem's supposed occasion was Tsvetaeva's friendship with Pasternak and Rilke.[12] The problem with reading the poem is not naming the anonymous male addressee, but working out that addressee's semantic and spatial situation in a narrative which is at once fragmentary and oblique. The redundancy of biographical readings in such cases makes it understandable that some critics have turned to formalism, to a

[9] Tsvetaeva, 'Popytka revnosti', *Stikhotvoreniya i poemy v 5 tomakh* (New York, 1979–), iii. 111; (references to this edn. henceforth in text as *SP*).

[10] On Tsvetaeva's reading, see especially Michael Makin, 'The Rewriting of the Inherited Text in the Poetic Works of Marina Tsvetaeva', D.Phil. thesis (Oxford University, 1985). Two recent published studies dealing with Tsvetaeva and classical mythology from a (rather unfocused) mythographical viewpoint are Alexandra Smith, 'The Cnidus Myth: Tsvetaeva's Interpretation of Pushkin's Love for Natalya Goncharova', *EP* 14/2 (1989), 83–102; Laura D. Weeks, ' "I named her Ariadne . . .": The Demeter-Persephone Myth in Tsvetaeva's Poems for her Daughter', *SR* 49/4 (1990), 568–84.

[11] Quoted in Dido Davies, *William Gerhardie: A Biography* (Oxford, 1990), 208.

[12] On Tsvetaeva's friendship with Rilke as the occasion of *Popytka komnaty*, see the note to *SP* iv. 377. A recent study of such material is Alexandra Smith, 'Tsvetaeva and Pasternak: Depicting People in Poetry', *EP* 15/2 (Sept. 1990), 94–101. The Rilke–Tsvetaeva–Pasternak correspondence is published as *Rainer Maria Rilke, Marina Zwetajewa, Boris Pasternak: Briefwechsel*, ed. Jewgenij Pasternak, Jelena Pasternak, and Konstantin M. Asadowskij (Frankfurt am Main, 1983).

study of Tsvetaeva's use of word-play, folk etymology, and metrics.[13] But here again there are problems. Without some basic appreciation of formal considerations, it is impossible to understand Tsvetaeva's work: one needs to comprehend the process by which a sound similarity— sometimes suggested by a wilful miscomprehension or mis-stress—will set off a chain of associations or oppositions, often reinforced by processes of stress and subordination which work within, or against, the metre. However, formal study in itself can provide us with only a phrase-book to Tsvetaeva's work, and phrase-books are not a means to sophisticated linguistic understanding. As Tsvetaeva herself asserted, the 'formal problem' was never significant in her poetry for its own sake.[14] Her language was not abstract or transrational; it was a material expression of materiality.

In *Attempt at a Room*, for example, there is an absolutely direct relation between sound congruences and the text's meaning. A series of punning associations links the topography of the room in the title, described in terms of its six surfaces, with the physical borders of a woman's body, that of the female speaker in the poem. This speaker can perceive and record only three surfaces herself (front and sides). A fourth surface, the 'back', can be glimpsed in a mirror, where it, however, resolves as an image which by definition has no containing end wall, a 'corridor'. In order to resolve the anxieties generated by her uncertainty about the extent of her own body, the speaker conjures another individual, the male addressee of the poem, into her presence. This male individual and addressee enters the room in a manner which neatly reverses the Judaeo-Christian birth myth: rather than woman emerging from the rib of man, man emerges from the 'back' of woman, that is, from the fourth wall of the room. Repudiating patriarchy's generative origins, the poem also refuses any sense of violent incursion or penetration in its description of the addressee's arrival (his presence is protective, closing off the 'draught', *dulo*, a word which also signifies the barrel of a gun). A shift in metrics, from quatrains to couplets, now marks the construction of a further set of associations, between physicality and creativity: the arrival of the male addressee has enabled 'the journey of verse' to 'Psyche's palace'. Again, banal expectations are confounded,

[13] Recent studies dealing with Tsvetaeva's work from a formalist viewpoint include Bettina Ebersprächer, *Realität und Transzendenz: Marina Cvetaevas poetische Synthese* (Munich, 1987); L. V. Zubova, *Poeziya Mariny Tsvetaevoi: lingvisticheskii aspekt* (Moscow, 1989); M. L. Gasparov, 'Slovo mezhdu melodiei i ritmom', *Russkaya rech'* (1989), 4: 3–10; G. S. Smith, 'Logaoedic Metres in the Lyric Poetry of Marina Tsvetaeva', *SEER* 53/132 (1975), 330–54; *idem*, 'Marina Tsvetaeva's "Poema gory"': An Analysis', *Russian Literature*, 6 (1978), 365–88.

[14] Tsvetaeva, 'Poet o kritike', *Izbrannaya proza v 2 tomakh* (New York, 1978), i. 121–41.

for the rendezvous of the two sexes has not introduced, but destroyed, the notions of 'sex' and 'gender' (*pol*—a word that also signifies 'floor', which is to say, the room's fifth surface, and so, metaphorically, the feet). By registering, and then dismissing, sexuality, the poem has been able to move to an ideal vision, in which sexuality is transcended and gender overcome; at the end, the two bodies are left reduced to 'nothing', whilst the ceiling (that is, the sixth surface, the head) sings 'like all the angels'. This sophisticated and complex text responds less readily to either a biographical or purely formal interpretation than to a feminist reading concerned with issues of sexuality and language. The poem illustrates the threat of the 'male gaze': the ability to see a female body from outside is perceived as a manifestation of power.[15] Hence, a process of conjuration and naming is invoked, in order to surround and restrict the male addressee as he is invited in: 'I know the name', the speaker says. And it is she who through her own 'head' and 'feet' establishes the poem's hierarchy, its polarization of spiritual and physical love.

A similar attempt to circumscribe the 'masculine' is made in 'Orpheus', a poem written a little earlier, in 1921 (*SP* ii. 137). Tsvetaeva turns the familiar legend of Orpheus' dismemberment by the Maenads into a poem which evokes the 'head' and 'lyre' of the poet hero transported by the sea. The poem averts the power of the male body by reducing it from a (threatening) whole to vulnerable, feminized pieces (both *lira* and *golova* are grammatically feminine). It also places a passive man at the disposal of active women: destroyed by the Maenads' act of violence before the poem opens, Orpheus is reconstituted at its end by a woman of Lesbos, who catches his 'remnants' in her net. And the allusions in the poem transform the adult male into a dependent child, floating in the 'crib' of the billows and swaddled in the 'bedclothes' of the water.

The indirect processes of synecdoche and metonymy by which the male body is perceived here, the assimilation by demystification, are characteristic of Tsvetaeva's poetry in general. If *Attempt at a Room* demonstrates patterns of representing the female body seen from within which have been recorded in many recent critical studies of women's writing, the strategies of 'Orpheus' anticipate the dynamic of female

---

[15] On the 'male gaze', see e.g. John Berger, *Ways of Seeing* (London, 1972). A recent study of Tsvetaeva informed by feminist theory is Irina Kuzminsky, 'The "Language of Women?" A Study of Three Women Writers: Marina Tsvetaeva, Ingeborg Bachmann and Monique Wittig', D.Phil. thesis (Oxford University, 1989); see also Barbara Heldt, *Terrible Perfection: Women and Russian Literature* (Bloomington, Ind., 1987), 130–43; Sibelan Forrester, 'Bells and Cupolas: The Formative Role of the Female Body in Marina Tsvetaeva's Poetry', *SR* 51/2 (1992), 232–46.

subject looking at male object which has been set out in recent work by Roszika Parker and Sarah Kent.[16]

Attempt at a Room displaces female physicality by using the 'room' as a metaphor, but there are many poems by Tsvetaeva in which, by contrast, the body is referred to directly. 'I opened my veins', for example, connects blood-letting and the writing of verses; in 'A woman's breast!' the breast appears as a marker of feminine identity (*SP* ii. 133). With Tsvetaeva, one has come very far from the tortuous *inoskazanie* (saying otherwise, euphemism) which constitutes the sexual language of other women writers. In its astonishing disruption of expected standards of decorum, her poetry resembles a *sheila na gig* on the outside of an Irish church.[17] Here, too, frankness of expression and marginality of site are directly connected. Even sophisticated and liberal Russian readers have been shocked by Tsvetaeva's work. Sofiya Parnok, for example, described *Poem of the End* as 'very talented, but quite unbridled'.[18] In turn, material related to the female body has, for Russian woman poets, acquired 'Tsvetaevan' connotations, allowing a protective mythology to develop: she said all that is the idea, and hence there is no need for other women poets to say it; since the taboo has once been disrupted, it can by definition no longer exist. It would not be too much to say that Tsvetaeva plays the role of Russian culture's national 'madwoman in the attic', its embodiment of the repressed feminine. And so, though her technical devices have been parroted, she has rarely been imitated; the appeal of formal and lexical allusions is that these can suggest her unusual daring without the danger that would come from reproducing this directly.[19]

But if Tsvetaeva seems in some ways a poet divorced from her time and culture, to overstress her specificity would be to misrepresent her. She may have occasionally arrived at the same point as modern feminist writing, but the point from which she started off was quite different. The fundament of her work is not a celebration of creativity deriving from the

[16] Women's representations of men are analysed, e.g. in Roszika Parker, 'Images of Men', and Sarah Kent, 'The Erotic Male Nude', in Sarah Kent and Jacqueline Morreau (eds.), *Women's Images of Men* (London, 1985), 44–54, 75–105.

[17] The sheila-na-gig is an early medieval sculptured figure representing a woman holding her labiae open: a well-known example is fixed to the outside of the church in Kilpeck, Herefordshire. The purpose of such figures is unknown, and my analogy is meant to suggest their effects on a contemporary observer, rather than hypothesize their possible function in their own culture.

[18] Parnok is quoted by Polyakova in Parnok, *SS* 355. Cf. D. S. Mirsky's description of Tsvetaeva as 'a talented, but rather wild [*raspushchennaya*] Muscovite woman', *Uncollected Writings*, ed. G. S. Smith (Berkeley, Calif., 1989), 101–2.

[19] The term 'madwoman in the attic' is borrowed from Gilbert and Gubar's study of that name; here I mean to suggest that Tsvetaeva has functioned in her own culture as a metaphor for the repressed aspects of femininity. Of recent poets, perhaps only Bella Akhmadulina and Elena Shvarts have inherited more than stylistic affinities with Tsvetaeva, and neither has anything like her range.

female body, but a celebration of creativity achieved *in spite* of the female body. Her important narrative poem *On a Red Horse* refuses 'feminine' friendship with the Muse, and expresses allegiance with a *Sturm-und-Drang*-like vision of an energetically masculine genius (*SP* iv. 155–60). In 'The Sibyl', prophecy is represented as the information and insemination of an inarticulate embodiment of the feminine by a masculine god (*SP* iii. 24–5). In such texts, Tsvetaeva shows herself to be as subject as any other writer to the understanding of androgyny current in turn-of-the-century Russia, according to which the rational/active was always masculine, the irrational/passive feminine.

Still greater constraints were placed on Tsvetaeva by the received understanding of what constituted 'femininity' in a positive sense. Her assimilation of this understanding was evident not only in the 'girlish' intonations of some early poems, but also in some of her mature work. One memoirist has recalled that she would respond to public demand by reading her early poems at public readings in Paris, though by then the contrast between dewy lyric heroine and gaunt middle-aged poet had become painfully sharp.[20] Tsvetaeva was, likewise, unable to liberate herself completely from general beliefs about the sanctity of motherhood. A lyric which she wrote in April 1920, to commemorate the death of her younger daughter, Irina, who had starved to death in a Soviet orphanage, shows her first withstanding, and then succumbing to, a conventional metaphorization of maternity. In the first stanza, motherhood is glossed as fierceness. The speaker has 'snatched the elder [daughter] out of Hell'. Medea-like, she declares her right to dispose over the lives of the two daughters: their heads are her 'hands', an image which establishes their instrumentality. One hand has 'turned out to be enough' (lit.: one hand is superfluous)—a line which suggests not only that there is now no need to stroke one of the heads, but also that the important hand, the writing hand which produced the poem, has been saved. But, whilst asserting maternity in the unacceptable sense of domination, the poem at the same time averts the ghastly vision: rather than say that she did not save her daughter, the speaker switches to the passive, 'was not saved'. And the poem concludes with the rather banal metaphor of the children's heads as dandelions, an ending which jangles uneasily with the vision of God-given power projected earlier:

> Две руки, легко опущенные
> На младенческую голову!
> Были—по одной на каждую—
> Две головки мне дарованы.

---

[20] T. P. Milyutina, 'Tri goda v russkom Parizhe', *Blokovskii sbornik*, 10 (Tartu, 1991), 146.

Но обеими—зажатыми—
Яростными—как могла!—
Старшую у тьмы выхватывая—
Младшей не уберегла.

Две руки—ласкать-разглаживать
Нежные головки пышные.
Две руки—и вот одна из них
Зá ночь оказалась лишняя.

Светлая—на шейке тоненькой—
Одуванчик на стебле!
Мной еще совсем не понято,
Что дитя мое в земле.   (*SP* ii. 235)

Two hands, resting lightly on
The infant head!
I was given—one for one—
Two hands, two heads.

But with both hands pressed together,
Fiercely—as best I could—
I snatched the elder out of Hell,
The younger was not saved.

Two hands—to caress, to stroke
Two soft heads of fluff.
Two hands—but now just one
Turns out to be enough.

Bright girl—like a dandelion's
Stalk your little neck!
I cannot grasp, cannot imagine
That my child is dead.

Tsvetaeva's indifference to her second daughter was much remarked on amongst her acquaintance when news of Irina's death reached them. 'I feel such pity for the child—two years on earth and nothing but cold, hunger, and beatings,' Vera Efron, Tsvetaeva's sister-in-law, wrote in a letter to a friend.[21] A certain amount of rationalization after the fact must be taken into account here; still more, of course, the classic pattern of mother blame in such cases. The point I wish to make is less concerned with the apparent contradiction between indifference in life and the rhetoric of lament, than with the disturbing contradiction, in the poem itself, between indifference and the attempt to smooth over indifference. The conventional proprieties are restored in what can only be described as a failure of poetic nerve.

---

[21] Shveitser, *Life and Work*, 190–1; on Tsvetaeva's younger daughter generally see pp. 186–93.

A text which manifests a similar triumph of conventionality is the long prose story, *The Tale of Sonechka* (1937), a chronicle of Tsvetaeva's infatuation with the young actress Sonechka Holliday.[22] Reasonably innovative in a formal sense (the temporal perspective frequently shifts from the Moscow of 1919 to the Paris of the mid-1930s where the tale was written), the piece is yet apparently devoid of self-consciousness in the sense of irony and self-parody. This deficiency is the more significant in that the heroine appears as the perfect stereotype *ingénue* of Russian nineteenth-century literature, with long plaits and big dark eyes. Yet there are hints that Sonechka's innocence might be only a seeming innocence; though the narrator compares her at one point to the heroines of early Dostoevsky, a confession by Sonechka that she has 'often been kissed' seems to approximate later Dostoevsky: Liza in *Brothers Karamazov*, Stavrogin's juvenile seducer in *The Devils*, and the pre-pubescent temptress of Svidrigailov in *Crime and Punishment*. And, like Dostoevsky's narrators, Tsvetaeva acts as voyeur and manipulator. Sonechka's vulgar tastes in songs and poetry are the subject of her amused condescension. An anecdote turns on a charming malapropism that reveals Sonechka's gaucherie (she thinks that the term 'haemorrhoids' refers to a disease of the liver). Though linguistically impoverished, she can, however, inspire poetry in others by the odd unselfconsciously felicitous turn of phrase. Not offering the intellectual stimulation which is the contribution of her male rival, she shows herself an excellent companion to the children, and generally complements the 'female' part of Tsvetaeva's life. So she herself recognizes in a quarrel with Volodya:

'Volodechka, so you've never ever been in Marina's kitchen then?'

'No, Sofya Evgenevna. Well, I have once, actually, at Easter.'

'Good Lord, poor you! And you've never ever seen Irina?'

'No, Sofya Evgenevna. Well, I have once, that same Easter—but she was asleep.'

'Good Lord, imagine being friends with a woman and not knowing how many teeth her child has! You don't know how many teeth Irina has, do you?'

'I don't, Sofya Evgenevna.'

'So it's all clever stuff with you. You're only friends with Marina's head.'

(N 298)

When Sonechka finally tires of the role of human pet or speaking doll, she escapes, like a Chekhovian actress, to a life in the provinces. The narrator assures the reader that she was not 'angry' with this betrayal of

---

[22] Tsvetaeva, *Povest' o Sonechke, Neizdannoe: stikhi, teatr, proza* (Paris, 1976), 203–61 (references henceforth in text as *N*).

trust. And careful to distance herself, lest the reader take this sentimental crush too seriously, she adds as envoi an apology for this expression of love between women:

Her leaving of me was an act of simple and honest obedience to the Apostle's word: 'Man is to leave his father and mother . . .' I was more than a father and mother to her, certainly more than a beloved, but there is no doubt that it was essential for her to prefer him. For that is the law God made when He made the world. (N 347)

This *sententia* on God's law is ironic enough in itself, for the reader knows from a coy confession made by Sonechka earlier that she is infertile, so that it is rather questionable what God-given natural law is fulfilled by the dissolution of the affair. Still greater is the irony for any modern reader aware that this text, whose love object is represented as the mouthpiece of abject and unreciprocated devotion, and who is herself submerged beneath a litter of conventional sentiments, was Tsvetaeva's only public voicing of homo-erotic feeling in the Russian language, since she had suppressed publication of her cycle 'The Woman Friend', addressed to Sofiya Parnok.[23]

'Two hands' and *The Tale of Sonechka* indicate how directly Tsvetaeva's work is related to the traditions of women's writing as practised in Russia. However, the relation was not simply expressed in terms of inhibition. Much more frequently than she paid lip-service to the traditional prescriptions on what could be said in a feminine voice, Tsvetaeva dealt with the accepted material of 'women's writing' in a radically new manner, taking the tradition to its limits. Where other women poets, for example, had used masks drawn from the circus or the menagerie in order to suggest a delicate melancholy occasionally verging on the precious, Tsvetaeva made these masks seem fierce and threatening. Alla Golovina had spoken of a 'crippled lioness' musing on her former life; Tsvetaeva refers to a caged lion which gathers itself for the attack (*SP* iii. 174–5). In another poem she reworks the traditional motif of internal division to suggest anger, rather than anguish:

> Жив, а не умер
> Демон во мне!
> В теле как в трюме,
> В себе как в тюрьме. (*SP* iii. 122)

> Alive, not expired
> Is the demon in me!

---

[23] On 'Podruga' see Ch. 10; on Tsvetaeva's other 'public' lesbian text, *Mon frère féminin*, see Ch. 9, n. 101.

In body as in ship's hold,
In self as in gaol chamber.

Still more significant than Tsvetaeva's redirection of affectivity was her ability to find a new language for the familiar elements of nineteenth- and early twentieth-century women's writing. In the passage which I have just quoted, for example, the words *tyurma* and *tryum* are at once near-homonyms and representations of opposites: if a ship's hold suggests what is submerged below the water-line, the Russian word *tyurma*, prison, which folk etymology derives from the German *Turm*, a tower, suggests an association with what is raised above the ground. The process of parallelism and contrast here points to the larger and more surprising paradox of life as imprisonment, a situation whose expected resolution is ambiguous (it may be that death will let the demon out). The linguistic complexity of the poem draws on, yet alters, the emphasis on escape which had been so important in nineteenth-century women's prose, both by turning the idea of flight inwards upon itself, and by clothing a simple skeleton in the meat of imagery and word-play.

Russian critics have tended to organize their readings of Tsvetaeva by emphasizing her polarization of *byt* (ordinary life) and *bytie* (spiritual life).[24] The division is essential to her poetry, certainly, but it is not here where the distinction between her work and that of other women writers lies. On the contrary: the contempt for domesticity felt by an exceptional heroine, the assertion of autonomy in love through a simultaneous exaltation of emotional intensity and denigration of its object are, as we have seen, the canonical themes of Russian women's fiction in the nineteenth century. The point is that Tsvetaeva, rather than simply enumerating such themes as sufficient in themselves, *names* them, finding appropriate expression at last for what had been mechanical oppositions, and at the same time using the process of linguistic pairing and differentiation in order to make these oppositions dissolve or explode.

A most significant and dramatic instance of how the conventional material of nineteenth-century fiction is at once triumphantly asserted and radically transformed is the narrative poem, *Staircase* (1926), which Simon Karlinsky has rightly described as being 'at the pinnacle of Tsvetaeva's lyric-narrative achievement'.[25] At one level, *Staircase* deals with the liberation of material from itself: a tenement staircase cluttered with objects is burnt to the ground in a conflagration, so that the earthbound attains to the spiritual elements of air and fire. But the poem

---

[24] The Russian title of Shveitser's *Life and Work*, for example, is *Byt i bytie Mariny Tsvetaevoi*, and the book examines this dichotomy at length; so, too, does Zubova's structural analysis, *Poeziya*.
[25] Karlinsky, *Marina Tsvetaeva*, 170.

represents much more than an elemental or elementary conflict between material existence and spiritual existence. It is a magnificent portrait of the material domain. In the opening section of the poem, the physical presence of the staircase emerges unforgettably, with cinematic glimpses of it and its inhabitants—worn carpets, briefcases, rushing feet—and evocations of its stinks and its dins: gurgling pipes, creaks, shouts, hawking coughs, assorted food smells, garlic, perfume, piss.

Even at the symbolic level, the staircase is much more than a metaphor for materiality: it is divided within itself, standing for the polarization of society in a social sense. It has its *nizy*, meaning 'bottom' in a physical sense, but also 'lower classes' or 'groundlings'; it also has its *verkhi*, 'top', or 'upper classes'. But Tsvetaeva's delineation of the divisive hierarchy has an ironic quality: the inhabitants are levelled by poverty: spatial positioning is not reflected by social positioning. The *verkhi* and *nizy* oppress each other with smells—the stenches of cooking, and with sounds—the grotesque cadenzas of their coughs. Yet the intrusive presence of poverty is also an absence, a point made clear in a passage commenting on the oxymoron 'paupers' things':

> Вещи бедных. Разве рогожа—
> Вещь? И вещь—эта доска?
> Вещи бедных—кости да кожа,
> Вовсе—мяса, только тоска.
>
> Где их брали? Вид—издалека,
> Изглубока. Глаз не труди!
> Вещи бедных—точно из бока:
> Взял да вырезал из груди!   (*SP* iv. 268)

> Paupers' things. So is that sacking
> A thing? And is that board a thing?
> Pauper's things are bone and skin,
> Lack of meat, whatever is lacking.
>
> Where did they get them? You can see far away.
> You can see from the depths—don't strain your eyes!
> Paupers' things may come from their sides,
> Hewn on a sudden from their chests!

It is the contradictory inner qualities of 'paupers' things' that are at the centre of the poem. Tsvetaeva uses the feminine grammatical gender of the Russian word *veshch'*—thing or object—to suggest a link between things and women:

> Вещь как женщина нам поверила!
> Видно, мало нам было дерева
> И железа—отвесь! отбей!—
> Захотелось досок, гвоздей,—

Щепь! удобоваримой мелочи!
Что мы сделали, первый сделавши
Шаг? Планету, где все о Нем—
На предметов бездарный лом?   (*SP* iv. 266–7)

The thing was confiding as a woman—
It wasn't enough to grab the wood
And iron—size it up! weigh it out!
No, we had to have planks and screws—

Chip! small stuff that we could swallow!
What have we done, we who first walked,
Done with this planet which speaks of Him—
Made it a heap of dull spayed things?

The thing is at once an aberration, a sign of how 'Man' has mangled the 'most animate world of any ever', and itself a sign of that 'animate world': pauper's things are three-quarters part of the spiritual world, yet are human flesh, 'hewn from the side', as Eve was sliced from Adam. By extension, the poem associates the rebellion of things, which soon take horrible revenge on man, with the rebellion of women. But the poem is not simply a call to free femininity from the domestic sphere, though female addressees are exhorted to leave their accustomed tasks:

В вечной юбке сборчатой—
Не скреби, уборщица!

Пережиток сельскости—
Не мети, метельница!   (*SP* iv. 270)

In your gathered working skirt,
Charwoman, don't scrub the dirt!
Relic of the rural past—
Cleaner, put the broom down fast!

A thing herself, woman cannot easily escape from the thing. Therefore, *Staircase* is not a portrait of revolution in the conventional sense; indeed, it satirizes the very idea of political revolution. The destruction of the staircase puts paid to a structure which was ubiquitous in early Soviet writing and ideology as a metaphor for historical progress, and for the new post-Revolutionary hierarchy, being used in the visual arts, in film, in avant-garde theatre. The Social Darwinist overtones which the image had are perhaps most evident in Mandelstam's beautiful poem on the construction of the Moscow metro, in which Soviet society is portrayed as a glowing chain of being, rising from the tiniest organisms to the greatest.[26] Tsvetaeva attacks such associations directly, by parodying the

---

[26] Mandel'shtam, 'Lamark', *Stikhotvoreniya*, 163.

evolutionary slogans of the Revolution: in describing the woman sweeper as a 'relic', she adopts one of the standard terms associated with 'backwardness' in Soviet rhetoric. And, rather than seeing technological progress as a phenomenon arising from and analogous to the processes of nature, she sees it as a phenomenon imposed on nature.

As in Virginia Woolf's early story 'The Mark on the Wall', Tsvetaeva turns from the contemplation of objects as fashioned by man to the contemplation of 'real' objects. For both writers, too, it is trees which are the central 'real' objects. Woolf ceases meditating on objects' function in a man-made historical hierarchy (the dusty pots of Troy), and in a man-made social hierarchy (the socially indispensable, but perfectly useless table-cloth) to think about the trees which have played at the fringes of her consciousness earlier, as they 'tapped on the pane':

> Thus, waking from a midnight dream of horror, one hastily turns on the light and lies quiescent, worshipping the chest of drawers, worshipping solidity, worshipping reality, worshipping the impersonal world which is proof of some existence other than ours. That is what one wants to be sure of . . . Wood is a pleasant thing to think about. It comes from a tree, and trees grow, and we don't know how they grow. For years and years they grow, without paying any attention to us, in meadows, in forests, and by the sides of rivers—all things one likes to think about.[27]

For Tsvetaeva, it is the return of furniture to the wood from which it was constructed that is the central illustration of how slavery will be thrown off:

> Просвещенная сим приемом
> Вещь на лом отвечает—ломом.
> Стол всегда утверждал, что—ствол.
> Стул сломался? Нет, стук подвел.   (*SP* iv. 266)

> The thing has learnt by experience,
> And now it gives as good as it gets.
> The table has always said it's a trunk.
> Did the chair break? No, it was the branch.

There are, of course, fundamental differences between the two writers as well: where Woolf's perspective is contemplative and aesthetic, drawing attention to 'what one likes to think about', Tsvetaeva's is militant and involved: she represents what one *has* to think about, and represents the liberation of things as lying not in the sliding consciousness of the observer, but in the internal revolution of the thing. The association of *veshch'* here, as in 'The Sibyl', is both its proper adjective *veshchnyi*

---

[27] Virginia Woolf, 'The Mark on the Wall', *The Complete Shorter Fiction* (London, 1985), 39.

(thing-y) and the unrelated, but similar-sounding *veshchii* (prophetic). As the Sibyl's reduction to a desiccated skin hanging in a bottle has made her the vessel of prophecy, so the imprisonment of the things in *Staircase* leads to their rebellion and to their freedom. The restrictions of femininity are the subject of invective, but the energizing potential of restriction and deprivation is recognized.

It has been argued that what we know now as *Staircase* is in fact a fragment, part of a poem originally projected on a much larger scale.[28] But as it stands the text has its own completeness; in just over ten pages, it achieves a far greater complexity and density than many novellas or novels. Tsvetaeva managed to effect a combination between the two historically incompatible topics of gender and class, to create a flexible notion of female identity, denominated neither by affiliation with the domestic nor with the need to escape domesticity. This difficult, demanding, and extraordinary piece is in no sense a feminist fable in an ordinary sense, but it is also untouched by anti-feminist cliché: no attempt is made to elude the implications of femininity in an imagined 'masculine freedom'.

Tsvetaeva was not a writer who could ever have accepted that 'the feminine' might be a linguistic construct or a metaphysical abstract. The modernist questioning of identity, the proliferation of possible personae, was in a quite fundamental sense foreign to her. So, too, were the shifts of stylistic register typical of international modernism. Her 'Sibyl' takes a reference to the prophetess as a 'tree' from a poem by Rilke on the Sibyl, but where Rilke moves from a splendid neo-classical opening to an offhand colloquial second line, Tsvetaeva's language is all of a piece.[29] Whether archaic, folkloric, liturgical, or colloquial, Tsvetaeva's language was always 'other' from the point of view of the ordinary literary language. Magnificently uncompromising, her position had its limitations. In her last years, she was to reject the easy categorizations of identity, such as nationality, and write poems which expressed a cynicism towards the myths of patriotism as deep as that expressed by Anna Barkova.[30] But there was a difference: where Barkova was sustained by cynicism, Tsvetaeva was destroyed by it. With the death of belief, she could not take refuge in analytical distance; instead, she gradually stopped being able to write poetry at all.

---

[28] See note to *SP* iv. 379.

[29] Rilke, 'Eine Sibylle', *Sämtliche Werke*, i (Frankfurt am Main, 1955), 568.

[30] On Barkova's civic verse, see Ch. 13. On Tsvetaeva's poetic crisis, cf. her observation in the note 'My fate—as a poet' (7 July 1931) that she was experiencing a drought 'not at the level of keeping my notebooks full, but in a deep creative sense': 'Zapisi iz rabochikh tetradei', *Znamya* (1992), 9: 180–9.

Elaine Feinstein has observed that 'there is nothing like Tsvetaeva in English'.[31] There is nothing like her in Russian either. The result of a fusion between elements drawn from the nineteenth-century realist tradition, both in its 'incentive' and in its 'empirical' strands, and the Symbolist cult of women's 'irrational' creative powers, she appears to transcend her time, yet she was absolutely rooted in it as well. And so, though her emphatic manner may be (and is) caricatured or parodied, she remains in a final sense, indeed in most senses, inimitable.

[31] Feinstein, *Marina Tsvetayeva*, 12.

12

Vera Bulich (1898–1954)

The point is not that culture is being destroyed—but that culture
itself leads to a dead end and destroys.

(Vera Bulich, diary entry for 17 Mar. 1938)[1]

VERA BULICH came from a well-off haut bourgeois St Petersburg family
of strong intellectual leanings; her father, Sergei Bulich, was a distinguished historian and musicologist, and several other male members
of the family were also academics. Vera herself was well educated: she
had attended a good girls' school in St Petersburg, and had gone on to
study at the city's university; but her degree course was interrupted by the
Revolution. In 1918 the family took refuge at their dacha in Finland; a
year or two later they moved to Helsinki, and here Vera was to remain for
the rest of her life. In adulthood she was to gravitate to her family's
scholarly interests, rather than its musical ones, although she had a
knowledgeable appreciation of music, and was an able amateur pianist.
A second Bulich daughter, Sofya, became a professional singer; Vera, by
contrast, spent most of her adult life working as a librarian, and she was
to publish all her four collections of verse whilst so employed.[2]

Citations to 'the Bulich archive' refer to the six boxes of Bulich's papers held in the Slavonic
Library of the University of Helsinki. The papers comprise personal documents, correspondence,
variants of poems ranging from first draft to final typescript, drafts and typescripts of Bulich's
esssays, radio talks, and ballet libretti, diaries, albums of cuttings, photographs, and commonplace-
books of quotations. The items are not catalogued individually, and sorting is haphazard. Citations
appear by kind permission of the Slavonic Librarian.

[1] Taken from a diary held in the Bulich Archive (see n. 6 below).

[2] Bulich's internal passport, held in the Bulich Archive, indicates that she was born on 17 (29)
Feb. 1898, that she belonged to the class of the hereditary nobility, and that she was in 1917 a
student of the History and Philology Faculty of St Petersburg University. 19th-c. reference sources
(e.g. ES, NES, and N. P. Zagoskin (ed.), Biograficheskii slovar' professorov i prepodavatelei Imp.
Kazanskogo universiteta 1804–1904 (2 vols.; Kazan, 1904), vol. i) indicate that, apart from Bulich's
father, members of the family who were academics included her grandfather and two of her uncles.
(On Sergei Bulich see MERSL; on Bulich's life in emigration, the fullest source is Temira Pachmuss,

This humdrum biography, or sketch for a biography, immediately associates Bulich with several famous Western European modernist writers, such as Stephane Mallarmé, T. S. Eliot, Franz Kafka, or Philip Larkin, whilst putting her at a distance from the neo-romantic practice of *zhiznetvorchestvo*, or making one's life into a work of art, which characterized several of her more famous Russian contemporaries, such as Marina Tsvetaeva. In an untitled poem of 1949 from her last collection, *The Branches* (1954), Bulich recognizes this biographical pattern in a characteristically modernist way, by drawing a series of contrasts between internal and external space, memory and heritage, literary and non-literary life. The poem is at once an abstract meditation and a precise evocation of a scene glimpsed through the library window; meditation and evocation are linked in the motif of plant growth. Bulich appropriates to herself the 'masculine' motif of conception as the act of insemination, 'spilling seed on the ground':

> Нет у меня детей. Мой взгляд и голос
> Ни в ком не оживут. Не передам
> Зерна земле, как полный спелый колос,
> Не завещаю ничего годам.   (*V* 19)

> I have no children, so my voice, my stare
> will live in no one. I shall not pass on
> seed to the earth, as does the full ripe ear.
> I shall leave nothing to the years that pass.

But the identification with a 'masculine' role is incomplete. Rather than suggest that books, or texts, are her children (a strategem in such classic modernist texts by men as Mallarmé's 'Le Don d'un Poème'), Bulich leaves the tension unresolved. Books may be pregnant in a metaphorical sense, hiding the 'stirrings' of life between their bindings, but they are not children, and a life dedicated to them remains barren:

> Весна. Цветут в садах чужие вишни,
> Играют дети солнечным песком,
> И солнце светит всем. Никто не лишний
> Под всеобьемлющим его лучом.

> Живая жизнь в окно кивает мне.
> А день мой отдан тщательным заботам
> В библиотечной пыльной тишине
> О жизни, спрятанной под переплетом.

Russian Literature in the Baltic Between the Two World Wars (Columbus, Ohio, 1988), 394–422.) Bulich's four collections are *Mayatnik* (Helsinki, 1934) (henceforth in text as *M*), *Plennyi veter* (Tallinn, 1938) (henceforth in text as *PV*), *Burelom* (Helsinki, 1947), and *Vetvi* (Paris, 1954) (henceforth in text as *V*). She also published a collection of prose tales for children, *Skazki* (2 vols.; Belgrade, 1932). Translations of 'From my Diary: III' and 'The Omnibus' appear in *Anthology*.

In gardens others' cherries bloom for spring:
the children play in sand the sun makes gold.
The sun shines on each one, its light enough,
not leaving any out, to bathe them all.

Vitality nods at me through the glass.
My task's to tend the life that's here inside,
spending my days in library quiet and dust
amongst the stirrings that these bindings hide.

In 'I have no children', Bulich accepts the cultural imperative of reproduction for women, but her acceptance is troubled rather than quiescent. Recognizing herself as 'unwomanly' because she has not bred, she at the same time refuses to accept the male motif of writing as a substitute for pregnancy, and so achieves her own variant of the fragmented modernist text that questions its own validity.

A similar uncertainty about the value of literary activity is expressed in another late poem, in which Bulich reflects on the fate of her manuscripts after her death. By a coincidence, the language of this poem is strikingly similar to that used by Akhmatova in her late cycle 'Craft Secrets', but parallel motifs are employed to utterly different effect.[3] Akhmatova's playfully self-deprecating tone litotically augments, rather than undermining, the self-confidence of her autobiographical declarations; Bulich displays a genuine lack of confidence in the possibility of inheritance, which is exemplified in her rhymes: at one time, once (*s nekikh por*) rhymes with rubbish (*sor*), and *vazhno* (important) with *bumazhnyi* (paper). In the opening poem to *Branches*, Bulich had repeated the traditional invocation to the Muse as a symbol for poetic inspiration: here she suggests a much more tenuous link between writing and the Muse:

Живешь и копишь всякий сор,
Воспоминаний сор бумажный,
Всё то, что сердцу с неких пор
Казалось дорого и важно.
Стихи, наброски, дневники,
Программы, вырезки и снимки …
Как выбросить черновики
Вот эти, в карандашной дымке?
Концом легчайшего крыла
Их, может быть, коснулась Муза …

---

[3] Akhmatova, 'Tainy remesla', *SP* 201–6. It is possible that Bulich's reference to 'rubbish' is taken from the second poem of this cycle, first published in 1940, but the rhyme 'muza/obuza', which is also used by Akhmatova, cannot be a borrowing on Bulich's part, since this poem was written five years after she died, in 1959.

Но всё, чем я сама жила,
Моим наследникам обуза.   (V 26)

The paper rubbish which one hoards,
Discarded scraps of memory,
All that once seemed of such great worth,
So dear and so worth cherishing,
The poems, notes, abandoned drafts,
The programmes, cuttings, photographs . . .
How to throw out those notes in rough,
Those there, in smoky pencil script?
Suppose the Muse in passing touched
The pages with one feathery wing?

But all the things by which I lived
Will be a burden to my relatives.

Again, writing and family roles are perceived to be incompatible, an incompatibility which is not resolved; the 'archive' will become just so much detritus.

Some of Bulich's late poems side-step the conflict of biographical *realia* and artistic expression by substituting the sense of a divided exterior world for the sense of a divided self, and taking refuge in a neo-platonic meditation on the greater reality lying beyond the visible world. In 'The mirrored evening lies on the flood', for example, the reflection of a train provokes speculation on the essence and substance of things. Rather than ally herself with the tangible actuality of the 'rattling train', Bulich chooses to enter the insubstantial, shadowy world of its reflected double, the metaphor of the spiritual world:

А поезд-призрак бесшумен и пуст,
В нём воспоминаний невидимый груз.
Идет он в потерянную страну,
За черту, в мечту, в глубину.

Мне с шумным поездом не по пути,
Того, что мне дорого, в нем не найти.
Но тихо войду я, как входят в сон,
В отраженный последний вагон.   (V 34)

But the phantom train is empty and quiet,
It carries memory's invisible load,
Making its way to the land that is gone,
To dreams, to the depths, beyond the bounds.

I shall not ride on the rattling train;
For there I shall never find what I want.
Instead I shall slip, as we slip into sleep,
Through the last mirrored door on the deep.

Other poems from *Branches* of this kind include 'The transparent lilac branches' (p. 6) and 'Branches' (p. 16). In them, Bulich escapes the dilemma of expressing a gendered modernism by means of a dualism typical of the post-Symbolists: art is understood as properly dealing with a domain beyond and above the body, and hence beyond gender.

In escaping the problems set up by writing poetry as 'a woman' and 'a modernist', Bulich's purely philosophical poems however also substituted an emphasis on the results of abstract enquiry for an emphasis on its processes, and hence sacrificed the dramatism and originality of her best late work. 'Branches' or 'The mirrored evening' could have been written by any other competent poet of the Russian emigration, male or female; Bulich's particular and individual contribution, by contrast, was that she, like Sofiya Parnok, wrote work expressing involved contemplation rather than detached speculation, and confronting, rather than evading, the problems of writing philosophical poetry as a 'feminine' subject. 'The paper rubbish' or 'I have no children' explore the restrictions on expression of the self inherent in conventional, biological expectations of women; other poems take a contradictory and fluid view of the automatic association between women and belief. 'In Memory of My Sister' (1950), for example, shows the lyric heroine engaging in the customary religious rituals of 'feminine' belief. But rather than automatically placating a higher spiritual authority, these rituals have now become outward forms, like the radio recordings and photographs of Bulich's dead sister that encode her physical existence without evoking it. And the poem ends with a bleak recognition of oblivion, rather than with reconciliation:

> И неужели не будет,
> Не будет и тени блаженства,
> Ни проблеска света во мгле
>
> За эту мольбу о чуде,
> За муку несовершенства
> На черной слепой земле!   (V 29)

> Can we not expect
> Even a shadow of joy,
> Nor a shaft of light in the dark
>
> In answer to our prayer for a miracle,
> In answer to the torment we endure
> Living imperfect lives on the blind black earth?

In 'The Omnibus' (1938–51) the classic 'feminine' dream of escape is negated by a text which refuses any peripeteia: the lyric speaker remains trapped where she is, not only because she is subordinated to outward fate, but also because the making of a work of art demands that time be frozen. Glimpsing a man raising a gun to fire as the bus goes past, the speaker anticipates the shot which would release the 'heavy body'. Yet this event would also destroy the 'picture', the aesthetic image itself, and hence the possibility of creation:

Сейчас раздастся громкий, резкий выстрел,
как разрешенье страшной немоты,
и распадется на куски картина,
и все придет в движенье. Автобус,
качнув на повороте, мчится дальше,
мелькают палисадники, дома . . .
Напрасно напрягаю слух, не слышно
ни выстрела, ни эха. Странной мукой
все так же сковано все тело. Пыль,
с дороги поднятая, бьется в окна . . .
 . . . И кажется, что мы летим в тумане,
вращаются колеса в пустоте,
и никогда мы не достигнем цели,
обречены на вечное скитанье
в самих себе, в плены и в немоте,
с беззвучным голосом в тяжелом теле.   (V 38)

Now I shall hear the gun's loud snap,
the fruitful silence will collapse,
the picture will be smashed to pieces,
a *perpetuum mobile* begin.
The bus pauses, turns a corner, then speeds on,
fences and walls go past and past;
I strain my eyes, but cannot hear
a shot, not even an echo. My body's trapped,
held stiff and chained. A fog of dust
flies off the road, and beats the glass;
the wheels are spinning in vacancy.
We'll never reach our destination,
Like nomads, we're condemned to stray
within ourselves, captive and mute,
with silent voices in our heavy bodies.

The formal beauty of Bulich's last poems, and their emphasis on an alienated, but analytical subject, place this work in the best *émigré* traditions; but Bulich's writing also has an urgency and pathos which takes it beyond the mere good manners of Galina Kuznetsova or the later Pregel, or of such male poets as Yury Mandelstam. This emotional force was partly derived from immediate biographical circumstance—Bulich was dying of lung cancer when she wrote the poems in *Branches*, and barely lived to see the collection published. But her last volume was not only the product of biography; it was also the culmination of concerns long evident in her work, which had always been marked by conflict between, on the one hand, Bulich's drive to self-conscious analysis, and on the other, her acceptance of rather conventional possibilities of constructing possible feminine behaviour.

A philosophizing and analytical tendency was evident quite early in Bulich's writings; several poems written in the 1920s reflect, for example, on the metaphysical significance of natural phenomena.[4] But where a feminine persona does appear, it is presented in a manner owing a great deal to the early poetry of Anna Akhmatova. Deference to Akhmatova is evident even in the relatively mature selection printed in Bulich's first collection, *The Pendulum* (1934), which contains the best of her poems written in the 1920s as well as a good deal of work from the early 1930s. As with Akhmatova, the lyric heroine is portrayed most frequently at moments of parting and rejection, which are accepted fatalistically. Her alert mind, at one level unblunted by feeling, continues to record the appearance of physical objects, but blame is not apportioned, and the causes of her unhappiness not sought:

> ... И тихо подошел последний вечер.
> Старинные часы пробили шесть,
> Взметнули трепетное пламя свечи,
> И звезды в окна кинули мне весть.
>
> .   .   .   .
>
> Часы стучат, как сердце, неуемно,
> И гулкий маятник все близит срок.
> А в глубине пустых вечерних комнат
> Разлуки тень ложится на порог.   (M 21)

> And quietly the last evening approached,
> The antique clock struck six.
> The candles' trembling flames shone out,
> And stars brought the news to my window.
>
> .   .   .   .
>
> The clock is sounding, boundless as my heartbeat,
> The hollow pendulum brings in the hour,
> Deep in these empty evening rooms
> The shade of parting creeps up to the door.

Occasionally, however, Bulich's heroine achieves a hedonistic sensuality which is unusual not only in Akhmatova, but amongst her female

---

[4] Bulich's earliest published poems, 'Stansy' (Stanzas) and 'Severnoe siyanie' (Northern Lights), *Novaya russkaya zhizn'*, Apr. 1920, are examples of this type of analytical nature poem; see also 'Zemlya' (Earth), ibid., 25 Dec. 1921.

imitators. This is so, for example, in 'To watch, propped on the lover's knees', where the literary parallels are Fet, or Mandelstam's *Tristia*, rather than Akhmatova:

> Облокотясь о милые колена,
> Следить, как всходит, медля, чуть смутна,
> За стогом хрусткого сухого сена
> Тяжелая медовая луна.
>
> Насыщен воздух сочным ароматом
> Нескошенного клевера полей.
> С деревни тянет дымом горьковатым.
> Во ржи тягучий скрип коростелей.
>
> ... Мы сено теплое с тобой рассыпем,
> Чтоб лечь среди прожженных солнцем трав,
> И, лунный мед с росой мешая, выпьем
> Слачайшую из всех земных отрав.   (M 27)

> To watch, propped on my lover's knees
> The heavy copper risen moon
> Crawling through the hazy skies
> Above a stook of crunchy corn:
>
> The clover meadows, still unmown,
> Infuse their scent into the air;
> From the village acrid smoke is blown,
> The corncrake's voice grates in the rye.
>
> I'll scatter the warm hay with you
> So we can lie on sun-scorched grass
> Mix honey from the moon with dew:
> The sweetest poison on the earth.

On the whole, though, *The Pendulum* is a collection where gentle, self-preoccupied melancholy is more prevalent than energetic involvement with the outer world, and where observation tends to be rather vague and abstract: the 'trembling' candle flames of 'And quietly the last evening' are more characteristic of the volume than the 'crawling' moon or the 'crunchy' corn of 'To watch'.

The struggle to escape conventional emotional rhetoric became acute in Bulich's next collection, *The Captive Wind* (1938), which centres on a group of poems describing a parting after an unhappy love-affair. Like Akhmatova's hero, Bulich's is given to acts of thoughtless cruelty; he is also a self-regarding philanderer, who appears in the masks of Don Juan (in the cycle of that name), and Eugene Onegin (in the poem 'The Letter', in which the lyric heroine herself speaks in imitation of Tatiana, writing after a long absence). Bulich's hero and heroine are locked in a relation of 'power' on the masculine side and 'submission' on the feminine. The only possibility of escape for the female voice is in recognizing the man's victimization: he is himself subordinate to the blind power of fate. As in Akhmatova's case, too, readers assumed that the collection was autobiographical. 'Reading good poems is always like looking through the key-hole,' Zinaida Shakhovskaya wrote in a letter of congratulation to Bulich in April 1938.[5]

Bulich's diaries of 1934–8 (the only significant run preserved after her adolescent diaries, kept during 1917 and 1918, end) do indeed reveal that the genesis of these poems was an extremely unhappy love-affair with a man whose name has been carefully censored out of the preserved manuscript with an ink rubber, and replaced with a pencilled asterisk.[6] But I am less concerned with the diaries as evidence for this biographical coincidence, than with the evidence they give for Bulich's systematic search for the appropriate literary interpretation of biographical *realia*. Two contradictory impulses underlay this search. Bulich, like a lot of other women poets, did strive for transparency in her poetic compositions; in a diary entry for 29 September 1937 she argued that the purpose of writing was 'to express my experience sincerely and as clearly and strikingly as possible'. But an equally important impulse was her consciousness of style's primacy, her conviction that 'artistic truth lies for an artist above all in "given" lines, melodies, images, which by his own will he cleanses of everything unnecessary'.[7] The sense of 'the given', of things said before, is manifested also in Bulich's commonplace-books of quotations from poetry and essays, the bulk of which, judging by the dates of the texts cited in them, were also put together in this key period, the mid-1930s.

Bulich's diaries for certain years are a literary record which complements her poetic accounts; the diaries contain material outside the scope of her poetry. In 1947, for example, she kept a pencil notebook with the title 'How I spend my time', which is mostly concerned with practical domestic details. '9 January: A whole hour spent on the damn darning.' '10 January. Did the washing' are two typical entries. Neither the fabric of this domestic existence, nor the fear of being consumed by it which Bulich had voiced to her diary in April 1944, ever forms any part of her poetry's material. Similarly, the mastectomy which she underwent in 1943 as a consequence of breast cancer, and which, understandably, provoked traumatic fears of 'mutilation', is a subject on which her diary

[5] Letter from Shakhovskaya to Bulich of 4 Apr. 1938: held in the Bulich Archive.

[6] Bulich's diaries for 1917–18, 1934–8, and 1950 are all held in the Bulich Archive. Citations henceforth in text as 'Diary 3 Mar. 1938', etc.

[7] From part of a draft for a talk entitled 'Love for the Muse' given to the Helsinki Russian literary society 'Svetlitsa' (The Chamber). The extract appears in a commonplace-book of Bulich's labelled

is eloquent, and her verses silent. The diaries from the early 1940s, in other words, lay bare a process of self-censorship: the purpose of poetry is not so much the record of experience as the record of *suitable* experience.

The diaries from 1936–8 give different insights; they overlap with the poetry rather than adding to it. They illustrate both how deep-rooted Bulich's attachment to sentimental rhetoric was, and how hard she worked to overcome this attachment. Bulich as diary writer can record moments of high melodrama without trace of irony. When her lover observes that she looks lifeless, she responds that it is his fault: he is draining her life away (entry for 9 May 1938). But at other moments the expression of feeling is put through filters, which most commonly include literary precedent, memory, narrative, and a sense of the physical space of the text (the need to end a narrative, and the amount of room on a page).

The entry for 3 March 1936 is especially revealing. The diary tells us how the man concealed by a pencilled asterisk, 'like the soft-spoken executioner from [Nabokov's] *Invitation to a Beheading*', takes his leave. This scene of parting provokes the appropriate Romantic response; like Marianne in Jane Austen's *Sense and Sensibility*, Bulich would have thought herself most hard-hearted if she had been able to sleep a wink. However, the reflections which are inspired by this insomnia are laid out with dispassionate detachment and a concern for accurate depiction of physical detail; they are brought to a close by a reference which makes clear the literariness of the diary record:

A kiss on the head, stroking my hair, my hands. 'Look, Verun, this must stop.'
    We said goodbye on the square.
    'All the best then.' 'All the best.'
    He kissed my hand. Went back feeling empty, weightless.
    Couldn't sleep. Took sleeping draught at 2 a.m., woke at 6, dawn was breaking. An odd thing: whenever I wake like that, I hear the rumble of the Srednii prospekt [on the Vasilievsky Island in St Petersburg]: the traffic going down to the sea, the noise from the Orphanage opposite, the din and hoots floating over from the centre. The phantom Petersburg of my youth waits to show itself outside my window.
    There's no more room in the notebook. The chapter's finished.

In *The Captive Wind* some of the same imagery appears: for example, in the third poem from a cycle entitled 'Partings', a draft of which is dated 3 March 1936. But here the minute detail is employed to different

---

'Poetika' (Poetics), Bulich Archive. Bulich was working on this piece in 1938, according to her diaries.

effect: emphasis has moved from the particular to the general, and no definite biographical parallel can be drawn:

> Одно и то же расписанье:
> Сдвиг незаметный, роковой
> Колючей стрелки часовой,
> И в безнадежность—до свиданья! ...
>
> Рука выскальзывает из руки,
> Шаги последние быстры, легки,
> Шаги последние и тишина.
> Ладонь опущенная холодна.   (*PV* 52)

> The familiar timetable is posted:
> The pointed clock-hands slink by,
> Crawl, fateful, unnoticed,
> To despair and goodbye.
>
> Hand from hand is slipped,
> Last steps come quick and light,
> Last steps, then silence.
> The dropped palm goes cold.

Detachment is also ensured by the organization of the collection, which exposes the careful reader to a number of poems dealing with the nature of representation, before the third section, in which 'Partings' appears, is reached. The opening poem of the whole collection, for example, deals with what is left unsaid, the 'paradisical delirium of unborn stanzas', and introduces the 'captive wind' as a metaphor for words unuttered (*PV* 5). In 'Old Film' (*PV* 13) this theme is elaborated by the idea of memory: the 'old film' shows a procession in 'the land beyond the grave' disrupted by gusts of wind in the trees. Memory becomes a more explicit concern in the next section, in which poems are dedicated to the St Petersburg of Bulich's childhood ('Palm Week' (*PV* 21)) describes the seasonal sale of pussy willows traditional on Palm Sundays in Russia before the Revolution, and to memories of summer visits to the family house at Kuolemaari ('Departure' (*PV* 31)).

The final section, in which the most explicitly 'autobiographical' poems are placed, begins, like the first, with a warning that all experience unrolls according to a set of textual relations. 'Fate' (*PV* 41) represents life as no more than the power relations into which a hero and an author are locked. Bulich borrows Nabokov's famous image of the lessening pile of book pages from *Invitation to a Beheading* to suggest the author's control over the hero's life:

> Страниц все меньше. Уж близка расплата.
> Борьба напрасна. Автор будет прав.

> The pages dwindle. The reckoning's at hand.
> Authors will have their way, though heroes fight.

At the end of the poem, however, the motif of the author, intertwining life and art, is replaced by another metaphor: the typesetter whose letters are made out of stars. No longer an assertion of the text as ultimate reality, the poem now refers to 'writing' in its Symbolist associations, as a vehicle for spirituality:

> И знаю, нет ни счастья, ни свободы
> В пределах нам отмеренных страниц.
> Нам суждено томиться годы, годы
> Завидуя веселым крыльям птиц,
>
> Пока рукой наборщика суровой
> Из звездных букв не сложится венец,
> Последнее, сияющее слово
>
> К о н е ц.

> I know that happiness and freedom won't be ours
> Within the pages measured out to us:
> We are condemned to suffer year on year
> And envy the birds with their glad flight,
>
> Until the evening's glowing stardust type
> Is laid out by the setter with stern hand:
> To make those final, shining words
>
> THE END.

The 'Don Juan' poems follow immediately on this ambiguous statement about the meaning of an artistic utterance; and they are also grounded in an ambivalent appreciation of the text's status. Sometimes we are encouraged to see this history of a love-affair as a confession, sometimes as a reflection on masculine and feminine psychological archetypes, which transcend context or history, and sometimes as a dissection of love as it is customarily represented in literature. The events of the text, from encounter to parting to fits of erotic guilt, are surveyed from a perspective that sometimes belongs to an external narrator surveying a third person 'Donna Anna' and third person 'Don Juan', and sometimes to 'Donna Anna' herself, as she addresses 'Don Juan' in the second person. Further nuances are introduced by the use of different types of citation. This may be direct speech within the first-person narrative ('Everyone has his own Commendatore. | Look!' the speaker cries in poem 7); it may be indirect speech: ('But whether he is to blame | If he is doomed'—so poem 3 debates Don Juan's departure from Donna Anna). Using Blok's famous poem 'The Commendatore's Footsteps' as a sub-text, and accepting its vision of Don Juan as a symbol for predatory male sexuality, Bulich revises the poem by concentrating on the effects of male sexuality on its female victim. Though identified with the 'innocent' Donna Anna, this 'female victim' has several, contradictory identities; she is both a passive and an active voice, a narrator and a character narrated. Control exercised by the narrator over the narrative also varies, for she has both 'dreamt' the narrative, that is, invented it (in poem 1), and seen it presented on stage, that is, been a spectator who realizes that this performance is a reflection of her own experience (in poem 8, the final poem).

None of the other poems in this section of *The Captive Wind* uses masks so overtly; they generally deal, as we have seen, with scenes also represented in the diary, but here they are abstract, where there they are portrayed in a direct and personal manner. So, where the diary records the physical actuality of meetings as they happen, the poetry speculates on the pointlessness of any such real meeting ('We shall meet. | But parting has made a river between us' (*PV* 54)).

Both *The Captive Wind* and Bulich's diary of the 1930s reveal a process by which a traditional rhetoric of emotional conformity is undermined by layers of cultural reference, and multiplicity of viewpoint. Concern with emotional 'truth' was combined in Bulich with increasing uncertainty about exactly what such a concept might signify. 'If anyone read through these notes of mine, he would have a completely false impression of me': this disclaimer of 6 March 1941 could equally well be attached to any of her poetry or diary records of the years immediately preceding. The difficulty was that this tension stifled Bulich, rather than stimulating her. In 1938 she reinterpreted the conventional wisdom about twentieth-century cultural crisis in the words quoted at the head of this chapter. 'The point is not that culture is being destroyed, but that culture itself leads to a dead end and destroys.' She had, indeed, herself met a dead end. Reading and reflection had destroyed the illusion of a transparent and integral personality, but the cultural stereotype of womanly good behaviour was too potent to be abandoned: it could only be placed off-centre, and understood as *one* possibility amongst many.

Bulich's initial response to this unresolvable conflict of values was a move to greater conventionality, a search for truth outside her own subjectivity. The final poems in *The Captive Wind* express the resolution to jettison romantic experience in favour of spiritual values:

> Отрекайся, душа, понемногу
> От любви осязанья слепой
> И готовься в большую дорогу,
> Где лишь звезды и ветер пустой.   (*PV* 59)

> Renounce, O soul, little by little
> The grip of love, which is blind,
> And prepare for your great journey,
> To the stars and the empty wind.

The poem '1837', a commemoration of Pushkin's death, and the three poems collected as the cycle 'From my Diary' also reflect the new mood of renunciation. In place of the personal and erotic, Bulich nominates as her themes the celebration of literature in a specifically nationalist sense, of patriotism (Pushkin's 'hand' will make 'the centuries bless Russia'), of music, and of religious feeling.

The final poem of the book, the third poem of the minicycle 'From my Diary', restates the shift of Bulich's concerns in narrative, rather than programmatic, form. Attending the Orthodox service for Good Friday, the heroine at once repents her erotic misdemeanours, and reconciles herself with the national church, which is described as 'that truth, the same for everyone'. The importance of this psychological turning-point is emphasized by *realia* which pick up the central motifs of the collection: trees coming into leaf outside the church not only supply a traditional image of resurrection, but also foreground Bulich's own association between trees and spirituality; the music of the choir and bells is at once a symbol of collective creativity, and a sacred substitute for the secular music of *Don Giovanni*, to which Bulich has obliquely alluded earlier in the collection.

The end of *The Captive Wind* sees Bulich's lyric heroine back in the fold again; a similar restoration of cultural values was to be evident in Bulich's own biography. At Easter of the year following the publication of *The Captive Wind*, on 25 March 1939, Bulich noted in her diary that she had taken communion, for the first time in many months, and felt a sense of relief that her guilt might now be forgiven. In Bulich's artistic biography, too, assimilation to a collective rather than an individual sense of identity seemed at first to offer some respite from the pressures of representing a biography at once tame and aberrant. In her correspondence, Bulich had claimed that the tradition of 'civic verse' was one peculiar to Russia; objectively speaking, this claim is, of course, ridiculous, but it does indicate a defensive need to identify with a greater cause.[8] And it was precisely civic verse which was to make up the core of Bulich's next collection, *Wind-Fallen Wood* (1947), which was written in response to two wars, the Russo-Finnish War of 1939–40, and the Second World War. For Bulich, as for many other Russian *émigrés*, Soviet Russia became ideologically acceptable once it seemed to come

---

[8] Letter to V. Rittenberg of Mar. 1950, quoted in Bulich's diary for that year, Bulich Archive.

under threat from outside, and many poems in *Wind-Fallen Wood* reflect a Great Russian patriotism idealized from beyond. Indeed, the poem commemorating a *politruk* (military political activist) fallen in battle against the Finns, with his packet of White Sea Canal cigarettes, is perfectly in tune with the tone of official Soviet war poetry, and it is no surprise to learn that the collection was praised in the Soviet press.[9] A further mark of Soviet approval was the fact that, in 1947, the year in which *Wind-Fallen Wood* was published, Bulich became the director of the Finno-Soviet Institute Library, a position which she retained until her death.

For all that, there are indications that Bulich's nationalism was not without ambivalence. She referred indirectly to the sense of being caught between two parties in a profile of the Finnish woman poet Katri Vala, dwelling on her subject's refusal to observe conventional party lines, and on the unpopularity which this had brought her.[10] And *Wind-Fallen Wood* was her only excursion into civic verse; in *Branches*, as we have seen, her scrutiny of identity reasserted itself, but was now realized in a markedly different manner to that adopted in *The Captive Wind*.

In *The Captive Wind* Bulich adopts a typically post-Symbolist approach, alternating different masks of identity. Taken out of context, such poems as 'Letter', with its heroine comparing herself to Tatiana, or 'From my Diary: III', with its repentant woman speaker, appear, for all that their choice of language is unusually sophisticated, and their technical accomplishment outstanding, little different from many poems published by *émigrées* during the 1930s. In order to appreciate the collection, it is essential to read it as a whole. As Yury Mandelstam wrote in a review on its first publication, the order of the poems is also vital.[11] Only over the collection as a whole does Bulich achieve the effect which is captured in smaller space by some of her late poems.

It is doubtful whether the intricate construction of Bulich's second collection was clear to the majority of her readers. *Branches* was the only book of poetry which she was able to place with an *émigré* publishing house. The circulation of all the earlier collections, which were published privately, depended on her own energy; it amounted, in each case, to no more than a few hundred copies.[12] Most readers, therefore, would have

[9] On the reception of *Burelom*, see Pachmuss, *Russian Literature*, 405.

[10] The typescript of Bulich's talk on Vala is held in the Bulich archive. One source of Bulich's uneasiness with her new-found Soviet patriotism was her distaste for atheism: see Pachmuss, *Russian Literature*, 398.

[11] Yury Mandel'shtam, 'Vera Bulich: *Plennyi veter*', *Zhurnal Sodruzhestva* (1938), 4: 22.

[12] *Branches* was published by the *Rifma* press of Paris, run by Aleksandr Ginger and Sergei Makovsky. A rather high-handed letter from Makovsky to Bulich about the collection is held in the

been familiar only with the individual poems which she had printed in periodicals. Even her late poetry suffered through this method of dissemination, since the choice of editors invariably fell on her least adventurous work: 'The mirrored evening' and 'Branches' were printed in periodicals and anthologies, whilst 'I have no children' was not. The result was that Bulich acquired the reputation of being a more conventional poet than she actually was, attracting the reproach traditionally levelled at 'feminine' poetry, that of 'intellectual poverty'.[13] In fact, as this brief survey of her work has shown, the rebuke was singularly unfair, since Bulich was one of the few women poets in her generation who not only made a serious attempt to engage with intellectual issues, but also, on occasion, to speak of them in a feminine voice. Muted and introspective, her work is less immediately striking than that of, say, Tsvetaeva, Merkureva, Shkapskaya, or Barkova; but it has in fact far more to offer than the mere linguistic facility, or 'elegance', for which Bulich is customarily, and patronizingly, commended.

Bulich Archive. Accounts for sales of the earlier books are preserved in exercise books, also stored there.

[13] See e.g. Adamovich, cited in Pachmuss, *Russian Literature*, 394; cf. the recent remarks of V. Blinov, writing in Victor Terras's *Handbook of Russian Literature* (New Haven, Conn., 1985), 64.

PART IV

13

Who Wants to be a Man?
De-Stalinizing Gender, 1954–1992

Feminism? But you don't want to be a man, do you?

(Russian woman academic, to me in August 1991)

ONE of the greatest triumphs of the 'cult of personality', which is to say the Soviet State's propagandizing of Stalin as genius, was to impress his omnipotence on Soviet citizens, yet ensure that he remained elusive: that he was blamed for nothing, and credited with everything. The process of demystification and disillusion after his death reversed the terms of the equation, but left its central premiss in place: the tendency now was to credit Stalin with nothing, and blame him for everything. The central myth of his all-powerful tyranny was convenient to his successors, many of whom had held office under the dictator, and wished to avoid confronting the issue of their own complicity in his policies; but it also suited their opponents, who could present themselves as successors to a tradition of dissident probity, uncorrupted by any compromise with 'the system'.[1]

The emphasis on 'Stalinism' as personal dictatorship pure and simple has had the effect of diverting attention from the actual mechanisms of social and political authority. But it is only by comprehending the nexus of interests vested in Soviet institutions that it is possible to grasp their success, and understand why it should be so difficult to change them (a

---

[1] On fluctuating official attitudes to Stalin, see Robert Conquest, *The Great Terror: A Reassessment* (London, 1990), 63–6, 447, 476–83. Conquest points out that Brezhnev's leadership saw a partial rehabilitation of the Stalin years; in the Gorbachev period, though, the *ad hominem* assault on Stalin began again. Examples of biography-centred history by individual critics of the Stalin period include Lev Razgon, *Nevydumannoe* (Moscow, 1988); Khava Volovich, 'O proshlom', in S. Vilensky, *Dodnes' tyagoteet* (Moscow, 1989), 461–94; an example of how dissident self-righteousness could elide the actual pressures of Soviet society in the 1930s is Gendin's assault on the 'cringing' Vera Inber (see above, Ch. 9, n. 13).

difficulty which is all too obvious at the moment). This applies not only to the self-evidently subordinate organs of government, but also to the apparently more 'independent' institutions of culture: educational establishments, state theatres, unions of cultural workers, and specialist academic institutions. These have rewarded conformity to the State's various ideological needs both in material terms, and in terms of prestige. Even Russians who are hostile to the Soviet State in an abstract sense have often been prepared to enjoy the benefits of the Soviet establishment; at the very least, they have unquestioningly accepted that the State would and should continue to pay huge subsidies to support culture, education, and the arts. The bitter contradictions in the oppositional position made themselves blatant, for instance, at a Writers' Union meeting held in Moscow after the failure of the August 1991 *putsch*, at which speaker after speaker called for the abolition of the Union and its replacement by a grant-awarding body, the Literary Fund, which, it was simple-mindedly argued, would be 'non-political' in character. No anxieties were expressed about whether a post-coup government was likely to continue making massive grants to cultural institutions, and the meeting ended with the election of a dozen or so young writers to the Writers' Union itself, though by far the majority of those who attended were in favour of abolishing the institution.[2]

Yet, conversely, the rational terms of historical analysis can themselves obscure the very large part which irrational matters have played in Soviet history. Soviet rule has depended at least as much on symbolic power as on economic or political power. Symbolism has not simply deflected attention from the workings of institutions; it has also been a force in its own right; the role of the leader has been both a crucial underpinning of symbolic rule, and an instrument allowing it to function effectively.[3] If we should not interpret 'the cult of personality' so that we naïvely overvalue Stalin's actual power, it would, on the other hand, be equally naïve to underestimate the extent of 'the leader' or 'the boss's' *perceived* authority. Beliefs and myths attributing characteristic features of the Soviet cultural system to his personal preferences are both multiplicitous and ubiquitous. It is widely held that the Hotel Moscow was built with asymmetrical wings because Stalin signed two plans which the architect had presented as alternatives; another very popular

[2] On cultural institutions, see esp. John and Carol Garrard, *Inside the Soviet Writers' Union* (London, 1990); Igor Golomstock, *Totalitarian Art* (London, 1990); Riitta Pittman, 'The Writers and the Coup', *Rusistika*, 4 (1991), 22–5; the account of the 26 Aug. 1991 meeting is based on my personal impressions.

[3] Two extant studies of symbolic power in the Soviet system are Christel Lane, *The Rites of Rulers: Ritual in Industrial Society: The Soviet Case* (Cambridge, 1981); Nina Tumarkin, *Lenin Lives! The Lenin Cult in Soviet Russia* (Cambridge, Mass., 1983).

story is that a live radio performance which had pleased the leader was recorded overnight when he asked how he might acquire a copy of 'that nice record'. The quasi-folkloric character of such anecdotes immediately points to their apocryphal nature, but apparently more authoritative statements often mask remarkably similar beliefs. Among such one could mention the writer Elena Vorontsova's insistence that the reintroduction of single-sex schooling in the 1930s came about because 'Stalin had a penchant for patriarchy'.[4] And even intelligent and well-informed Russians will often assert that the doctrine of Socialist Realism was no more than a reflection of Stalin's personal tastes.

Such views are, of course, not so much simplistic as downright misleading in objective terms. As was explained in Chapter 9, the resurrection of patriarchal structures in the 1930s reflected much more than a 'penchant' of Stalin's; similarly, wooden-headed servants of the official cultural establishment have been by no means the only commentators to support the continuing dominance, in Russia during recent years, of narrow and proscriptive aesthetic doctrines, whether or not these are termed 'Socialist Realism'.[5] However, there is absolutely no doubt that the extent of the powers popularly attributed to Stalin made his death an event of cataclysmic significance everywhere in Soviet society, and not least in the literary world. Certainly, there had been rumblings of dissatisfaction with the products of high Socialist Realism even during the early 1950s, in which a conflict of interests between fidelity to party interests, and what was seen to be 'literary merit', had made itself evident. However, after Stalin's death such rumblings rapidly began to gain in number and audibility. The years under Khrushchev in no sense represented a steady progress towards the weakening of literary censorship and the broadening of political discussion, and such gains as were made were partly reversed during Brezhnev's leadership, the so-called 'period of stagnation'. But unquestionably, there was a marked qualitative distinction between political and cultural repression before Stalin's death, and afterwards. The consequence was that the years after 1953 saw the Russian intelligentsia regain at least part of its pre-Revolutionary oppositional role, both in politics and in cultural politics. Under

[4] Elena Vorontsova, 'Women Writers in Russia', *Index on Censorship* (1989), 3: 26. Cf. Tatyana Tolstaya's comments on Stalin 'the tyrant' in Peter I. Barta, 'The Author, the Cultural Tradition and glasnost': An Interview with Tat'yana Tolstaya', *Russian Literature Journal*, 44/147–9 (1990), 279–80.

[5] For a stimulating and wide-ranging critique of post-Thaw literary ideology's limitations, see David Shepherd, *Beyond Metafiction: Self-Consciousness in Soviet Literature* (Oxford, 1992), esp. 31–7. An example of a far from simple-minded study which, however, derives from simplistic notions of realism's aesthetic superiority is Lidiya Ginzburg's *O psikhologicheskoi proze* (Leningrad, 1977), which attacks e.g. Joyce and the *nouveau roman*.

Khrushchev, and especially between 1956 and 1964, a huge burst of energy made itself felt throughout the cultural sphere. And though the Brezhnev years saw this energy gradually vanish from official culture, they also saw a significant waning of official culture's coercive powers. The Brezhnev era has recently been described as *seryi terror* (the grey terror); the adjective, with its associations of ignorance, prejudice, and intellectual stultification, eloquently evokes the flabbiness of official cultural ideology at the time.[6]

An early sign of change in the literary world after Stalin's death was the publication, in 1954, of an article by Mikhail Lifshits, entitled 'Marietta Shaginyan's *Diary of a Writer*'.[7] Lifshits's piece was an acidly sarcastic attack on the self-important maunderings of a writer who had enjoyed unchallenged prestige in the 1930s and 1940s; it enumerates some of the many ludicrous errors into which Shaginyan's attempt to pose as a polymath had led her, and is abundantly illustrated with examples of her pronouncements, whose threadbare inanity is only matched by their pomposity. Lifshits creates a bitterly funny picture of the writer rushing from train to plane to factory, discoursing malapropistically on blast furnaces and mine-shafts, and advising everyone, from school cleaners to factory managers, how they should do their own jobs. In fact, as the critic harpoons the wretched Shaginyan, the informed reader senses a much bigger fish in the background: the 'coryphaeus of all experts', Stalin himself, who had exercised a similar ignorant authority to far more devastating effect.[8]

Lifshits's article—which would probably have got its author sued for libel if it had been published in the West—created uproar when it

---

[6] One sign of disquiet over the effects of high Socialist Realism was Lev Levin's review of Karavaeva's *The Motherland*, which took the author to task for sentimentality and formulaic writing: 'Sila kollektivnogo truda', *LG*, 7 Dec. 1950, 3. See also the final chapters of Katerina Clark, *The Soviet Novel: History as Ritual* (New York, 1981). On the Thaw, see Helen Segall, 'The Thaw', in Victor Terras, *A Handbook of Russian Literature* (New Haven, Conn., 1985), 469–70; V. Lakshin, *Novyi mir vo vremya Khrushcheva* (Moscow, 1989); Geoffrey Hosking, *Beyond Socialist Realism: Soviet Fiction Since 'Ivan Denisovich'* (London, 1980); Edith Rogovin Frankel, *Novyi mir* (Cambridge, 1981); Lidiya Chukovskaya, *Protsess isklucheniya: ocherk literaturnykh nravov* (Paris, 1979). The term 'grey terror' seems to have been coined by the poet Olga Sedakova, whose important essay 'O pogibshem literaturnom pokolenii' is discussed in detail in Ch. 16. Political institutions witnessed something of the same progress through revivification to ideological disillusion and opportunism, though more slowly: for a recent synopsis of change, see R. Hill, 'The CPSU: Decline and Collapse', *ISS* 12 (1991), 97–111.

[7] M. Lifshits, 'Dnevnik Marietty Shaginyan', *NM* (1954), 2: 206–15. The writer herself preferred to be known as 'M. Shaginyan', eliding her emphatically feminine forename; Lifshits's use of the full name may be another indication of underlying gender bias.

[8] Stalin's best-known personal intervention was in the field of linguistics, in which he published a volume in 1950 refuting the doctrines of Marx, which he had earlier supported (*Marksizm i voprosy yazykoznaniya* (Moscow, 1950); see also Elliott Mossman (ed.), *The Correspondence of Boris Pasternak and Olga Freidenberg*, trans. *idem.* and Margaret Wettlin (London, 1982), 302–3).

appeared in *Novy mir*: it was one of the key early texts of post-Stalinist literary commentary.[9] It is therefore worth pausing a moment to consider an aspect of this article which, though less immediately striking than its annihilating exposé of the Stalinist literary establishment's vacuities, is just as significant. This text is not simply a piece attacking a successful Stalinist writer; it is a piece attacking a successful Stalinist woman writer. Though Lifshits never states directly that Shaginyan's gender is of relevance to his criticisms, there are moments when his description of her activities reveals a definite gender bias. Early in the article, for example, he evokes a confrontation between Shaginyan and the chairman of a collective farm:

Here she is, visiting a collective farm in Areni, noting down its production statistics, and then upbraiding the chairman for his poor results, before rushing off again. The chairman (a fat man with a dicky heart) feels winded by the onslaught; he may even mutter a rather naughty word (with a flavour of Bandello, shall we say), in his visitor's wake. But by now Marietta Shaginyan is somewhere way off, noting the names of the local breeds of sheep, and recording the fat content of their milk ... (p. 207)

Lifshits's allusion to the hostility which the director voices the moment he is freed from constraint (and voices in the 'masculine' language of swear-words at that) is an early instance of a shift in attitude towards prominent women which was to become increasingly evident during and after the Thaw, as writers (most especially male writers) began to emphasize that professional women's public success was bought at the price of social isolation.[10] But an even more important element in Lifshits's depiction is the contrast between the director, who does know what he is doing, and Shaginyan, who does not. The point is that she has no right to comment on matters of which she has no experience. Though Shaginyan's ignorance of Marxist theory, and the shoddiness of her preparatory research, also come in for criticism, it is this first objection, that she has no experience of the institutions and conditions on which she pontificates, that Lifshits repeats most frequently. Elsewhere, he approvingly cites another adverse reaction to Shaginyan's royal progress—this time of a cleaner who said, when Shaginyan waxed lyrical

---

[9] On reactions to Lifshits, see Lakshin, *Novyi mir*, 15; Shepherd, *Beyond Metafiction*, 65.

[10] On changing attitudes to Soviet career women, see for example Elena Uspenskaya, 'Zhena shagayushchego', *NM* (1958), 1: 25–46, which sets the problems of an ill-prepared and vulnerable woman teacher against the insecurities of a construction director's wife. See also the general observations in Xenia Gasiorowska, *Women in Soviet Literature 1917–1964* (Madison, Wis., 1968); Adele Barker, 'Are Women Writing "Women's Writing" in the Soviet Union Today?' *Studies in Comparative Communism*, 21/3–4 (Autumn/Winter 1988); Mary Seton-Watson, 'Women in Soviet Society', *Scenes from Soviet Life through Official Literature* (London, 1986), 13–36.

about the conditions on another collective farm, 'Well, you don't have to live here, do you?'

Lifshits's article at one and the same time championed the old values of critical realism, and pointed to the indirect effects which the resurrection of the critical realist ethic would have on women's writing. He asserted that writers should no longer have the impersonal role of myth-makers; instead, they should be accurate and involved observers. They should record what they did see, not plunge into 'epic' flights of fancy about what they *ought* to have seen. In fact, the 'epic' is now intrinsically untrustworthy: Lifshits polarizes Shaginyan's celebration of a new town miraculously sprung from the earth, and the description of the struggles to build it that she had given a few pages earlier, and argues that the description necessarily invalidates the celebration. So far, debate is gender-neutral. However, in arguing his case, Lifshits again and again shows confrontations between knowledgeable men and an ignorant woman, and so encodes an interpretation of the writer as observer which gives the woman writer a marginal status in the new critical-realist ethic.

'Marietta Shaginyan's Diary of a Writer' was an early and lucid statement of the Russian literary world's changing priorities, and an accurate prediction of likely developments within that world. Though block-busting novels about factories and collective farms continued to be published in Russia long after Stalin's death, they were no longer to be the staples of the prestigious literary journals.[11] As in the 1880s, 1890s, and 1900s, so in the 1960s, 1970s, and 1980s the most productive and influential genre in Russian literature was to be a self-declaredly mimetic, technically more or less unadventurous, medium-length prose narrative of more or less socially critical standpoint. Within this critical realist tradition, women's writing was to be an important, but also for various reasons a marginal, strand. Under Socialist Realism women had been expected to write production and collective-farm novels along with the men; now doubts were to be raised about whether such 'masculine' topics were suitable to their talents.[12]

The next important point to consider is what 'women's experience' was deemed to be in the context of post-Stalinist Soviet culture, since in

[11] As Natal'ya I'lina's satirical article 'Literatura i massovyi tirazh: o nekotorykh vypuskakh "Roman-gazety"', *Belogorskaya krepost'* (Moscow, 1989), 270–308, indicates, substantial 'work, home and love' pieces in the classic Socialist Realist style went on being published in popular journals during the 1960s and 1970s. However, the prestigious literary journals no longer concentrated on such material; as early as 1955, articles in *NM* indicated the new direction: cf. I. Lezhnev, 'Kratkost'—sestra talanta', *NM* (1955), 5: 218–30, and I. Kozlov, 'O szhatosti v proze', *NM* (1955), 6: 263–78.

[12] Irina Grekova was attacked for the publication of her story 'Na ispytaniyakh' (see n. 31 below) on the grounds that its military material was not suited to a woman writer: see Barker, 'Are Women Writing "Women's Writing"'.

recent years, just as much as in the late nineteenth and early twentieth century, treatment of 'the woman question' in prose has been shaped and fostered by developments outside the cultural arena as well as by literary ideology itself.

At the famous de-Stalinizing Twentieth Party Congress in 1956, Khrushchev in passing announced a very important change in Soviet policy for women. In a reversal of the position which the Soviet State had held since the early 1930s, he stated that discrimination against women was a continuing problem, and thus reopened the discussion of their position in Soviet society. Particular stress was placed by Khrushchev on women's exclusion from public life. The method of dealing with discrimination which he put forward constituted a partial reversion to the early days of Soviet rule. Women were once again to be classified as a special interest group; their needs were once more to be served by official women's organizations, (termed 'women's soviets' instead of the earlier 'women's sections').[13]

As Khrushchev's emphasis on public life suggests, his announcement left two central tenets of Soviet ideology in place. First, women were still assumed to be servants of the State, and were held to be a group with special needs in that context first and foremost. Secondly, the dichotomy between productive and unproductive labour was left unexamined: domestic labour was a matter of official significance solely where it could be perceived to detract from women's participation in the official labour market. Because of these assumptions, the policies of Khrushchev and his successors offered only partial solutions to the problems faced by women. Whilst important legal measures (the relegalization of abortion in 1955, and the liberalization of divorce in 1968) to some extent mitigated the pro-natalist policies of the 1940s, the old incentives to philoprogenitive mothers were left in place. The effect was that child-bearing was still impressed on women as a duty to the State. But no more than in the 1940s was emphasis on women's reproductive capacities offset by any attempt to play down their importance in the sphere of production. On the contrary, during the Khrushchev and Brezhnev years new industrialization drives brought huge numbers of country women into factory jobs, forming a new urban and suburban proletariat on the one hand, and stripping villages of their able-bodied female population on the other. The elderly women who were now the only inhabitants of some villages might find themselves abruptly and callously relocated to concrete blocks in regional centres, as 'villages with no future' were

---

[13] For a detailed survey of Khrushchev's policy on women, see Mary Buckley, *Women and Ideology in the Soviet Union* (Hemel Hempstead, 1989), 139–60.

closed down; but the migrants' route to prosperity was by no means a smooth one. Like the factory workers of former days, members of new industrial communities often lived in conditions of squalor and deprivation. Food shortages were less significant than in the 1940s (though still persistent), and consumer goods, whilst of low quality, were now more widely available. But the level of state support for women still remained far from adequate. Child care was available only during working hours; provisions for the sick and elderly were unsatisfactory; the service and food supply infrastructure was poorly organized. And, if more families were now allocated separate flats, rather than having to live in communal flats or in nineteenth-century style hostel accommodation, this could bring its own disadvantages, since it sometimes deprived women of the support which some rural or urban-proletarian communities had been able to offer them, so subjecting already over-taxed nuclear family units to still greater stress.[14]

But if post-Stalinist changes in official policy for women did not necessarily mean that women's lot showed consistent improvements in a practical sense, they did effect important changes at the level of ideology, propaganda, and public discussion. Though the terms of debate continued to be set in place by Party decisions, it was now possible for political activists, journalists, and above all women writers, to address women's problems, and probe the causes of their dissatisfaction. And there was every reason why precisely women writers should have rushed to take up the opportunity. If Soviet working-class women were, all in all, probably rather better-off in the 1960s and 1970s than they had been in the 1940s and 1950s, the most privileged layers of the Soviet intelligentsia were in some ways worse off in the post-Stalin years than they had been under Stalin. From the early 1960s, well-off Soviet women could no longer automatically rely on the private domestic help which many of them had enjoyed throughout the 1940s and 1950s. The peasant girls who had formerly lived illegally in cities and worked as servants could now obtain passports officially, and could then find more lucrative and attractive employment in factories. A live-in servant became a luxury affordable by few families; even part-time help was beyond the means of many. A Soviet middle-class woman might find herself, for the first time, trying to balance professional commitments with domestic duties and

---

[14] There is now an extensive literature on women under Khrushchev, Brezhnev, and Gorbachev. See e.g. Gail Lapidus, *Women in Soviet Society: Equality, Development and Social Change* (Berkeley, Calif., 1978); Barbara Holland, *Soviet Sisterhood* (Bloomington, Ind., 1985); Alistair McAuley, *Women's Work and Wages in the Soviet Union* (London, 1981); Susan Bridger, *Women in the Soviet Countryside: Women's Roles in Rural Development in the Soviet Union* (Cambridge, 1987); Mary Buckley (ed.), *Perestroika and Soviet Women* (Cambridge, 1992).

with child care. The increased availability of consumer goods did little to aid such women, since labour-saving devices remained scarce, unreliable, and expensive. Increased contact with the outside world brought by the slow process of *détente* also brought a heightened awareness of conditions in Western countries; these affected the metropolitan intelligentsia more than other sectors of Soviet society, sharpening their expectations of what Soviet society ought to be providing, and hence their resentment at the deficiencies of what it actually was providing. It is from this class of women, some of whom were now doubly emburdened for the first time, and bitterly hated their additional burdens, that Soviet women writers have been drawn. It is therefore not surprising that for many of them 'critical realism' has meant especially the representation of *byt* (daily life), the domestic difficulties suffered by women. It is also the case that the domestic background has been far more prominent in the work of recent women writers than in that of almost any of their female predecessors.[15]

We need now to engage again with the question of why this emphasis on women's experience should be constraining. At first sight it seems odd: in the period since 1954, male writers, such as Yury Trifonov or Vladimir Makanin, have also been noted chroniclers of *byt*; indeed, the focus of recent Soviet literature has in general been private, rather than public.[16] Nor is public life now, as it was in the nineteenth century, understood to be something which women are by reason of gender unlikely to know at first hand. Numerous fictions by women have dealt with women working as the 'responsible officials' who make up the backbone of the Soviet administration. Women writers have not represented the highest levels of the political hierarchy; no ministers or General Secretaries caper through their books; but then, these vertiginous heights have been off-limits to Soviet literature as a whole.[17] The problem does not lie with the representation of politics in an institutional sense; the point is that 'politics' in the looser sense of analysis of individual experience according to general political-philosophical categories has eluded many women writers.

This is not to say that women have been excluded from involvement

---

[15] These observations are based on personal conversations with Russian women in the age range 30–50, since the topic of Soviet domestic service and its effects on the quality of life for middle-class women has yet to be researched.

[16] See e.g. Yury Trifonov, *Obmen* (Moscow, 1976); Vladimir Makanin, *Portrety vokrug: Odin i odna, romany* (Moscow, 1991).

[17] Female 'responsible officials' appear e.g. in Panova's *The Seasons* and in the stories of Grekova (see below), and also in the films of Kira Muratova: see esp. *Brief Encounters*, 1969. The doings of ministers have, so far as I know, been depicted only by such (male) *émigré* satirists as Sasha Sokolov (in *Palisandria*) and Zinoviev (in *The Yawning Heights*).

in Soviet political developments. On the contrary: women's voices began to be audible at an early and important occasion of the de-Stalinization process: the Second Writers' Union Congress of 1954. The women writers and functionaries who spoke included some of the most striking representatives of the congress's polarization between Stalinist reactionaries and those pressing for change.[18] Amongst the latter, Olga Berggolts was perhaps the speaker to give most forceful expression to the wearily cynical irony which has been an increasingly powerful emotion in post-Stalinist Russia. She made an extraordinarily bold attack on the monstrous, monolithic character of Soviet literature, comparing the huge towns which it was impossible to live in with the massive books that no one wanted to read, and making a most cogent case for the immediate suspension of high Socialist Realist norms.[19]

Since 1954, and most particularly since Khrushchev's de-Stalinizing speech at the Twentieth Party Congress in 1956, Soviet women have continued to be involved on all sides of the post-Stalinist intellectual debate. True, amongst conservatives women's position has been, to some extent, eroded since the 1950s. Within the Writers' Union, for example, the most prominent defenders of the status quo during and after the Thaw were elderly war-horses such as Marietta Shaginyan and Anna Karavaeva. Both died during the Brezhnev years, and neither was replaced by a woman. Whilst women have certainly been supporters of cultural and political repression, they have tended to be supporters of a secondary importance: as censors, as publishers' editors, as critics, and as consumers of reactionary literature, but not as major functionaries in the Party or in cultural institutions. Nor have they been represented amongst the chief editors of publishing houses, or the controlling editors of journals (posts which in any case more or less signified the same as 'political functionaries' until the late 1980s). Their absence has also been noticeable amongst the ideologues of right-wing nationalism. The only prominent woman supporter of the August 1991 *putsch* was Nina Andreeva, the leader of 'Unity', a small group of reactionary Communists; the single right-wing all-women organization to be formed so far is the equally insignificant 'Women for the Future of Our Children'. Equally, women are under-represented amongst the supporters of 'patriotic' literature. There is no female equivalent of Valentin Rasputin or of

---

[18] The women delegates of the 1954 congress included, beside Berggol'ts, Ol'ga Forsh, who made an emollient and conservative opening speech; Aliger, who emphasized the 'leading role' of criticism; Karavaeva, who in proper Stalinist style dwelt on ideas over expression; Shaginyan, who hedged her bets between a demand for consensus and a plea for diversity; and Vera Ketlinskaya, who attacked bureaucratization and over-proscriptiveness in ideology. See *Vtoroi s"ezd sovetskikh pisatelei 15–26 dekabrya 1954 goda* (Moscow, 1956).

[19] Ibid. 343–6.

Vasily Belov, two writers who have become notorious advocates of Russian cultural reaction. Given the emphasis amongst many conservatives on women's duty to fulfil family and domestic roles, the under-representation of women in positions of power is only to be expected.[20]

However, women have certainly been active in the opposition to Soviet power adumbrated by Berggolts. Amongst the most prominent dissidents of the Brezhnev and post-Brezhnev years were two poets, Natalya Gorbanevskaya and Irina Ratushinskaya, both of whom received draconian sentences for their 'crimes against the Soviet State'. The legalization of 'informal' political and cultural organizations under the last Communist General Secretary, Mikhail Gorbachev, was in its turn to bring several women to prominence as organizers and activists. The most famous of these is the former ethnographer Galina Starovoitova, who acquired her reputation through her support of Armenian rights, but whose closeness to Boris Yeltsin made her, until November 1992, perhaps the most important woman politician in the post-coup Russia. Women active in informal cultural organizations include the poet Yunna Moritts, a founder-member of the 'April' group, a liberal caucus within the Writers' Union; the critic Natalya Ivanova has lately been playing a role of great significance in the debates about whether the Union should be reformed, or indeed dissolved.[21]

---

[20] Shaginyan and Karavaeva's non-replacement was part of a general decline in women's representation at the top levels of the Union of Writers since the 1930s, though their representation in the membership had risen significantly. In 1934, there were only 7.4 per cent women members, but 6 out of 101 women board members; in 1967 there were 880 women members in a membership of 5,687, but only 12 out of 253 RSFSR delegates were women; in 1986 there were 1,486 : 9,561 women members, but 9 : 143 and 8 : 127 women delegates in the Moscow and RSFSR contingents. See *Pervyi s"ezd sovetskikh pisatelei*; *Chetvertyi s"ezd sovetskikh pisatelei, 22–27 maya 1967 goda* (Moscow, 1969); *Vos'moi s"ezd sovetskikh pisatelei, 24–28 iyunya 1986* (Moscow, 1988). There are, so far as I am aware, no statistics on women's involvement in censorship and editorial work, but their ubiquity is suggested by the remarks by Soviet writers recorded in Martin Dewhirst and Robert Farrell, *The Soviet Censorship* (Metuchen, NJ, 1973); Marianna Tax Choldin and Maurice Friedberg, *The Red Pencil* (Boston, 1988). On Nina Andreeva's support for the *putsch*, see 'Khronika dnya', *Smena*, 20 Aug. 1991; I owe the information on 'Women for the Future of Our Children' to Mary Buckley. On Rasputin, Belov, *et al.*, see David Gillespie, 'Apocalypse Now: Village Prose and the Death of Russia', *The Modern Language Review*, 87/2 (Apr. 1992), 407–17. Belov's novel *Vse vperedi* (The Worst is Yet to Come; Moscow, 1987), was a particularly virulent intervention into the debate on women's roles; it contained vicious caricatures of Moscow professional women as bibulous, nymphomaniacal harridans.

[21] See Natal'ya Gorbanevskaya, *Red Square at Noon*, trans. A. Lieven (New York, 1972); Irina Ratushinskaya, *Seryi: tsvet nadezhdy* (London, 1989) (trans. Alyona Kojevnikov as *Grey is the Colour of Hope*, London, 1988). On Starovoitova and another prominent woman democrat, Marina Salei, see Geoffrey Hosking, Jonathan Aves, and Peter Duncan, *The Road to Post-Communism: Independent Political Movements in the Soviet Union 1985–1991* (London, 1992), per index. On Starovoitova's sacking, see *Guardian*, 6 Nov. 1992. The newsletter *Women East–West* carried eyewitness reports of women's participation in the defeat of the August coup: see the issues of Sept. and Dec. 1991. See also Buckley, 'Political Reform', in Buckley (ed.), *Perestroika and Soviet Women*, 54–71.

In the sense that women have been involved at every level in the new post-Gorbachev democratic parties, these parties are representative; but it should be noted that the participation of women in such organizations has never been associated with any commitment to women's rights as such. Like the token women of the official Soviet administration, or the revolutionary heroines of the nineteenth century, the token women of the new democratic movement function as 'women' only in the sense that they may be invoked by their male colleagues as feminized metaphors of heroism. The same was true of the dissident and oppositional anti-Communist movements from which such parties grew. For its part, whilst it existed the Soviet regime continued to disparage and misrepresent 'bourgeois' feminism, by which was meant both the pre-Revolutionary Russian tradition, and the modern Western feminist movement. But 'feminism' in both these senses was also an orientation which the anti-Communist political opposition perceived, and which its successors perceive, with considerable hostility.[22]

One reason behind this hostility is that Russian women and men who fought against Soviet power, and now strive to combat its legacies, believe—reasonably, up to a point—that a country whose record on human rights in the broadest sense is as undistinguished as their homeland's can hardly afford to give the rights of women priority over the rights of any of the many other oppressed groups. Another factor is that it is difficult, in the context of recent Russian history, to visualize such a thing as a women's group which might actually achieve anything positive for women. Perhaps to an even greater extent than the women's sections of the 1920s, the women's groups which were sanctioned by officialdom under Khrushchev and later, acted as the passive mouthpieces of official policy. Members of the women's soviets were assigned ancillary roles in the administration of social policy above all; the Soviet Women's Group was designed as a globe-trotting propaganda organization, rather than as a domestic lobby group; for its part, the Women's Peace Movement expressed the hypocritical commitment to 'peace' of a nuclear state. Though the women's soviets were successful in organizing grass-roots philanthropy and self-help, in political terms they were on the whole less radical than the Women's Institutes of British rural and suburban life. Neither they nor the other groups campaigned effectively

---

[22] On official Soviet hostility to feminism, see Linda Edmondson, *Feminism in Russia 1900–1917* (London, 1984), 171–3; on unofficial hostility, see John Cunningham, 'Freedom is Feminine' (interview with Nella Bielski), *Guardian*, 23 Mar. 1988; Jonathan Steele, 'Sister Russia' (interview with Ol'ga Lipovskaya), *Guardian*, 4 Apr. 1991; Rosalind Marsh, 'Olga Lipovskaya and Women's Issues in Russia', *Rusistika*, 5 (1992), 16–21; Vorontsova, 'Women Writers'; Tolstaya, 'Notes from Underground', *New York Review of Books*, 31 May 1990, 3–7.

for the improvement of women's political or legal rights, or for the amelioration of social deprivation.[23]

Besides the failures of recent Soviet official policy, the complexity and confusion of *idées reçues* about gender in Russia are also causative factors in the rejection of feminism. It is arguable that Bolshevik policy was from the beginning informed by hidden assumptions about gender divisions—indeed, I argued as much myself in a previous section of this book. But there is no doubt that there has been an increasingly overt and increasingly shrill insistence, in recent Soviet thought, that such divisions not only exist, but should be fostered and enhanced in the process of socialization. A recent Soviet manual dealing with sexual relations and with the role of parents in ensuring the normal sexual behaviour of their children puts the point like this:

A boy should be made to feel that he is a boy, and that boys do not cry. It is necessary to get a little girl interested in women's tasks (sewing, preparing food, etc.) and to dwell on the fact that scarves, hair-ribbons, and skirts suit her ('Only girls wear that, it looks really nice, it suits you!').[24]

The immediate cause for the dissemination of such material was the so-called 'demographic crisis'. In the late 1960s the Soviet administration was presented with evidence that the birth-rate in European Russia had declined to the extent that the population was no longer reproducing itself. The solution was to bombard this recalcitrant population with material stressing the joys of child-bearing and family life, and the importance of rigidly demarcated and complementary sex roles.[25]

Extreme as it may sound, such pro-natal propaganda was in a sense tautologous; it reflected views already widely present in Soviet society. Many (even most) Russian women would agree, quite independently of exposure to recent state indoctrination, that child-bearing is one of life's major joys; the problem is, they would argue, that social conditions do not allow this joy to enough women. They would also agree that a major reason for the ills of Soviet society is the 'feminization' of Soviet men (and, by extension, the 'masculinization' of Soviet women). A nostalgia for what are perceived to be traditional gender values is much in

---

[23] For a sardonic assessment of the official Soviet women's organizations, see Ol'ga Lipovskaya in Buckley (ed.), *Perestroika and Soviet Women*, 73–4; on the women's soviets, see Genia Browning, 'The Zhensovety Revisited', ibid. 87–117.

[24] A. M. Svyadosh, *Zhenskaya seksopatologiya* (3rd edn.; Moscow, 1988), 161. Cf. V. I. Zdravomyslov, Z. E. Anisimova, and S. S. Libikh, 'Funktsional'naya zhenskaya seksopatologiya' (Alma Ata, 1985), 30–1; a more popular source with the same attitudes is V. Vladin and D. Kapustin, *Garmoniya seksual'nykh otnoshenii* (Moscow, 1991), 82–107.

[25] For a full study of this subject, see Lynne Attwood, *The New Soviet Man and Woman: Sex Role Socialisation in the USSR* (London, 1990).

evidence; it has provoked the totally erroneous and unhistorical opinion that Soviet rule has been solely concerned with trying to turn women into men. (The pro-natalist policies of the 1940s, and the resurrection of traditionally 'feminine' stereotypes at that stage, go unconsidered when such views are voiced, perhaps because the most vocal generation of Soviet women, that born in the 1940s, encountered such pro-natalist material at a pre-analytical stage of their mental development.) On the other hand, some Russian women are also disturbed by the 'vulgarity' of traditionally 'feminine' stereotypes (not surprisingly, when one bears in mind texts such as the one on bringing up children which I have just quoted). But in such cases the solution is to brand the discussion of gender as 'vulgar' in itself, and to attempt escape into a transcendent or alternative reality, rather than to interrogate the actual shortcomings of the stereotypes themselves.[26]

These factors (the hostility to separatist organizations; the misrepresentation of the pre-Revolutionary Russian feminist tradition and the contemporary Western feminist tradition; the misunderstanding of history after the Revolution; and the feeling that women should be 'real women', or, conversely, that the concept 'real women' makes any discussion of women as a group a faintly disgusting notion) have combined to make political expression for women as women extremely rare. Generally speaking, Russian women believe that feminism depends on an assertion of women's right to equality irrespective of gender, rather than their right to autonomy as a gender; that is, they believe that the feminist goal is to erode women's identity and turn them into men. Western feminists, in the shocked minds of many Russians, are women who affect cropped hair, dungarees, and hobnailed boots, and campaign for women to be allowed to work down mines. Yet Russian women, whilst eager to retain a rather rigidly defined femininity, are equally reluctant to be defined in terms of their sex, since they associate that with the sort of patronizing condescension towards females which is all too common in mixed Russian society; and so radical separatist feminism is out of the question as well.

Despite all these obstacles, some small groups of a self-declaredly feminist direction have been set up from time to time in Russia. But all have encountered significant difficulties. In 1979 dissatisfaction with the opposition's record, as well as that of Soviet official culture, led to the formation of a small women's group in Leningrad. Its founders were Tatyana Mamonova, Yuliya Voznesenskaya, Tatyana Goricheva, and Natalya Malakhovskaya. The group was able to publish only a small

---

[26] For a non-official source pontificating on the feminization and masculinization of Soviet men and women, see e.g. Tolstaya, 'Notes from Underground'.

amount of material before the State cracked down on it, deporting its leaders, and putting an end to internal pressure for women's rights during the next decade.[27]

Only in the late 1980s, when Mikhail Gorbachev's policies allowed greater tolerance to 'informal' groups, were women's groups again to appear on the scene. At the moment there are perhaps twenty or thirty such groups in different parts of Russia, some publishing their own journals or newsheets and organizing meetings. The most prominent groups are in Moscow and Leningrad/St Petersburg, but even these are still very small and not particularly influential; they probably have at least as many supporters in America or Western Europe as they have in Russia itself. To date, the embryonic feminist groups have also remained separate from the mainstream of discussions in the opposition, where women's rights are simply not considered as a separate issue, and are given no prominence in manifestos or policy formulations. The one exception to this generalization is perhaps the gay rights group 'Tema', which has campaigned on behalf of both gays and lesbians during the last three years; but even here the legal situation (like pre-Revolutionary Russian law, Soviet law bans male homosexuality, but leaves female homosexuality unregulated) means that lobbying has tended to concentrate on the interests of men.[28]

Women writers, like other women, are affected by all these ideological and cultural pressures. Writers are no more likely than any other women to become involved in women's groups, sharing the reservations of other intelligentsia women about them. The hostility to women's groups in general has also made women writers reluctant to identify with each other in an institutional sense. A recent attempt, initiated by the poet Larisa Vasileva, to form a women's caucus within the Writers' Union, and to press for the admission and publication of young women writers in greater numbers, attracted support from no established names; in private at least, many women expressed their contempt for the venture.[29]

---

[27] On the late 1970s feminist groups, see Alix Holt, 'The First Soviet Feminists', in Holland, *Soviet Sisterhood*, 242–51; *Women and Russia: First Feminist Samizdat* (London, 1980).

[28] The embryonic feminist groups include an academic institution, the 'Centre for Gender Studies' at the Academy of Sciences, as well as various lobby groups in Moscow, St Petersburg, and provincial cities. The most prominent newsletter is perhaps Ol'ga Lipovskaya's *Zhenskie chteniya*, published out of St Petersburg. See Lipovskaya, 'New Women's Organisations', in Buckley (ed.), *Perestroika and Soviet Women*, 72–81. See also Ruth Steele, 'A National Network for Women', *Guardian*, 4 Apr. 1991; on the *Tema* organization and women, the observations of the lesbian activist Ol'ga Zhuk, *Guardian*, 31 Mar. 1992. The best source of up-to-date information on feminist groups is the *Women East–West* newsletter, which carries regular coverage.

[29] On Vasil'eva's group, see her article, 'Zhenshchina. Zhizn'. Literatura', *LG*, 20 Dec. 1989, 7. Vasil'eva's lack of success in attracting the better-known writers is partly attributable to her prominence in the pre-*glasnost* Writers' Union; cf. the indifference with which women writers

Discussions of women's writing in the abstract have also been hindered by the cultural background which I have outlined. 'Women's writing' has become a taboo term, which the vast majority of Russian women writers recognize only as an appropriate denomination for a category to which other, by definition inferior, writers may be assigned. In an article first published in 1981, for example, the critic Alla Latynina described 'women's writing' as what one would expect to find in the slush pile of the average publishing house, to whit, naïve, garrulous, and sentimental novels about love and the family. (She conceded that 'women's writing' of this kind is often produced by men as well, but implied that the big question was whether women in general were capable of composing anything else.) Occasionally the term 'women's writing' *is* assumed to have positive value, but the definitions then assigned to it are such as to set the teeth on edge. As popular sociology advocates the conditioning of 'real men' and 'real women', so literary commentaries praise 'real women's writing'. This means writing that celebrates women for their physical attractiveness, intuition, sympathy for others, love of the home and family, and self-sacrifice. Writing of this kind was assembled, for example, in an anthology entitled *Always a Woman*, published in 1987, a volume that was every bit as conservative as its title; there is a similar resonance to the titles of other, in fact more adventurous, selections of Soviet women's prose, such as *Feminine Logic* (1989) or *A Very Pure Life* (1989). It is not surprising that most of the more self-conscious writers wince at the idea of allowing their work to be placed in such anthologies (although financial considerations may prompt them to do it all the same). It is also understandable, though unfortunate, that they should extend their suspicions to any enterprise dealing with women's writing—including subject-dedicated conferences and specialist publishing houses in the West.[30]

But the bitter fact is this: even those women writers who are in terms of their own subjectivity not 'women writers' are, in terms of their own culture's general values, exactly that. This was brought home to me in

responded to Maiya Ganina's stirring call at the 1986 Writers' Congress for women's publishing houses and representational groups (*Vos'moi s"ezd*, 377–9), which to a Westerner sounds like a feminist war-cry, but to a Soviet citizen was placed in quite a different context by the speaker's conservative emphasis, earlier in her speech, on the need for writers to reflect 'the life of the people' and go on study trips to factories.

[30] Alla Latynina, 'Lyubov', sem'ya i kar'era', in her *Znaki vremeni: zametki o literaturnom protsesse* (Moscow, 1987), 287–95; *Always a Woman: Stories by Soviet Women Writers* (Moscow, 1987); *Chisten'kaya zhizn'*, ed. A. V. Shavkut (Moscow, 1990); *Zhenskaya logika*, ed. L. V. Stepanenko, A. V. Fomenko (Moscow, 1989); of a higher calibre are *Ne pomnyashchaya zla*, ed. Larisa Vaneeva (Moscow, 1990); *Novye amazonki: sbornik zhenskoi proze* (Moscow, 1991) and *Glas* 3 (1992). For views on 'real women's writing', see e.g. the editor's preface to *Chisten'kaya zhizn'*, and Irina Grekova's introduction to *Soviet Women Writing* (London, 1990); cf. also Voronkova, 'Soviet Women'.

1989, when I was discussing one well-known Soviet writer (a woman) with another well-known writer (a man). The woman in question has vociferously, and repeatedly, condemned the notion of 'women's writing' as a vulgarism; in conversation with me on an earlier occasion she had equated it with 'writing for homosexuals', and then, when I asked her what might be wrong with that, had said, 'well, then, cats and dogs'. 'Well, it's no wonder that it was a disaster when X was translated into English,' the male author observed; 'she's the sort of writer who really has to be translated by a woman.'

That there is such a thing as 'women's writing' is indicated not only by the prejudices of men, but by the actual character of the writing which Russian women have produced in recent years. This is not to say that one need lament the decline of the supposedly egalitarian traditions of the 1930s and 1940s. As I have illustrated, the writing that followed on the 'solving of the woman question', in so far as it had anything to do with 'women's writing' at all, represented a reversion to the crude incentive models of the first half of the nineteenth century, according to which women's participation in public life—a participation whose restrictions were never scrutinized—was the glorious end-point of the plot. The point is, though, that the pseudo-parity which women writers were munificently granted by Socialist Realism has been replaced, in recent years, by an overt assymetry between men and women authors, one evident both in terms of their status, and in terms of their concerns. In the 1930s and the 1940s women could write what then passed for committed fiction; since 1954 few of them have participated in the resurgence of political commentary. If the women critical realist chron-iclers of *byt* have their male equivalents, there is no female equivalent of Solzhenitsyn or of Vasily Grossman, of Voinovich, or of Zinoviev. Panoramic war novels or huge historical chronicles have been eschewed; even magisterial examinations of central social issues have on the whole been avoided.

Where women writers have essayed such examinations, they have centred them around male characters. Irina Grekova's story 'At the Testing Station' (1967) is one illustration of this pattern. The story is an account of corruption and low morale in the Soviet armed forces, narrated from the point of view of an officer in the Air Force. Its core is a series of man-to-man scenes which convincingly represent the conversa-tion of Soviet men when no woman is present, especially concentrating on the patronizing and disparaging manner in which they talk about women.[31] Another far less well-known, and if anything more interesting,

[31] Irina Grekova, 'Na ispytaniyakh', *Na ispytaniyakh* (Moscow, 1989), 241–384; cf. Lyubov' Kabo's quite lively and interesting story 'V trudnom pokhode', *NM* (1956), 11: 105–206; 12: 82–189,

fiction by a woman in similar vein is Tatyana Esenina's hilarious satire
'Zhenya, the Wonder of the Twentieth Century', first published in
1962.[32] Like Grekova's text, this story deals with all-male occasions
(conferences between hard-bitten journalists, drinking bouts, and gambling sessions); however, it is much more than an anthropological record
of behaviour in single-sex circles. Set in a provincial town, and narrated
by a young male journalist who, for all his boasts of toughness, has in
fact a Candide-like limpidity of perception, it records the chaos that
arises after a local veterinary surgeon asserts that he can manufacture a
'new Soviet man' in his laboratory. The chaos grows still greater when
this 'new man' actually turns up. His various adventures allow Esenina
to poke fun at more or less every official institution in the town,
exploring the bureaucratic idiocies of the local police, the laxities of
educational establishments, and the tolerance of objects falling off lorries
in the construction industry and in the food distribution networks.

And there is a further, purely literary, level to Esenina's satire too. The
blue-eyed, blond-haired, muscular, and upstanding Zhenya, made in a
test-tube, is an outrageous parody of the equally perfect and equally
artificial Socialist Realist hero. The humour lies both in transporting this
product of cerebration to a real setting, which soon corrupts him, and in
illustrating that the 'heroism' of the Socialist Realist protagonist derives
from the fact that he is actually too stupid to understand the impossibility of his various quests, and hence may occasionally achieve the end in
view. A more remote literary association lies in the hero's first name. Like
Pushkin's Onegin, he is a Evgeny; but the use of his name only in its
diminutive form suggests how far the twentieth-century literary tradition
has belittled and domesticated what it inherited from the nineteenth-
century classics.

Esenina's story juxtaposes various literary constructions of masculinity
in a way that is both comic and thought-provoking. She does not,
however, explore the Socialist Realist hero's feminine counterpart. The
test-tube Adam has no test-tube Eve as consort; instead, he falls in love
with a young woman doctor, who is portrayed with only traces of the
irony which Esenina exercises towards her hero, and who occupies a
peripheral place in the narrative. The story illustrates a central and
important point: whilst de-Stalinizing the hero, women writers have
failed to de-Stalinize the heroine. There is no major work of fiction by a
Russian woman writer resembling Doris Lessing's *The Golden Note-*

which deals with changing educational and cultural ideology through the observations of a largely
male cast of characters.

[32] Tat'yana Esenina, 'Zhenya—chudo XX-go veka', *NM* (1962), 1: 82–164. An extract from
'Zhenya' (entitled 'Male Bonding Sessions') appears in *Anthology*.

book, in which a woman who has been a Western Communist during the Stalin years lives through the political and personal crises that follow de-Stalinization.[33]

Here we can see how the modern critical-realist tradition's concentration on 'daily life' displaces difficult questions: in its scrutiny of women's political powerlessness, it does not ask why women are powerless, and in avoiding that question, it avoids confronting the issue of how far they might be responsible for their own fates. The result is that women writers can both bewail their own victimization and lay claim to the moral high ground. In this sense, Soviet prose continues the traditions of the 'internal emigration' fictions of Lidiya Chukovskaya. Much post-Thaw political poetry by women also avoids such questions, modulating between an 'abstract' tradition which suppresses gender, and a gender-marked tradition which suppresses abstract questions of responsibility. But some women poets have managed to construct a more multi-faceted and ambiguous sense of identity than their colleagues in prose. Notably, Inna Lisnyanskaya has written several lyrics registering the conflicts and frailties of a female member of the political opposition.[34] Lisnyanskaya rarely touches on the field of sexual politics, but the recent work of Yunna Moritts, again, includes some superbly pugnacious pieces on the condition of the woman writer. In one lyric she contemplates how she might behave if she were a male poet, swearing, drinking, and arrogantly swaggering; in another, she turns the archetypal Soviet woman, worn down by carrying loads of potatoes, into a portrait of a hag with hidden gifts. 'Between Scylla and Charybdis' begins with the memorable epigraph, 'The unit of women's poetry | In Russia, is one akhmatsvet'; it then goes on to attack the artificial position in which women poets write, forever suspended between their two canonical predecessors, Akhmatova and Tsvetaeva.[35] Lucid, pointed, and witty, these poems are amongst the very few pieces of recent work by women poets to acknowledge that the jaundiced view generally taken of women's writing might affect the way in which one may define oneself as a writer, as well as the way in which other female writers are defined.

If the post-Stalinist Russian intelligentsia has in some senses regained its pre-Revolutionary role of opposition to the State, it has also inherited internal divisions which recall those in operation before the Revolution.

---

[33] Doris Lessing, *The Golden Notebook* (London, 1962).

[34] Inna Lisnyanskaya, 'Krug', *Znamya* (1988), 9: 186–90; Elena Aksel'rod, 'Vozvrashchenie', *NM* (1989), 5: 156–9; cf. Elena Ushakova, 'Skvoz' sneg', *NM* (1992), 1: 3; and Galina Serebryakova's trilogy devoted to the life of Marx, *Prometei: romanticheskaya trilogiya* (4 vols.; Moscow, 1963).

[35] Yunna Moritts, 'Ya s geniyami vodku ne pila', 'Blagodarnost'', 'Mezhdu Stsilloi i Kharibdoi', in her *Na etom berege vysokom* (Moscow, 1987), 7, 79, 154.

The post-Stalin years have seen a strong revival of religious philosophy and of metaphysics; and in cultural politics, a politically and socially committed, rationalist, and formally conservative realist tradition is opposed by a strong anti-realist lobby, whose very diverse preoccupations range from mysticism to occultism to all shades of avant-garde aestheticism and libertarian eroticism. For women writers now as then, restrictions in the 'feminine' realist tradition and especially in its representation of doubt and fluidity, have led to the resurgence of forms of writing that lie outside the critical-realist tradition. However, one factor that distinguishes the current literary scene from its turn-of-the-century precedent is the hostility of most women *realist* writers, as well as non-realist writers, to feminism. Current women prose writers lack the analytical sophistication evident in the work of their most talented predecessors, a failing which has aesthetic as well as ideological results. Women writers are as ready as their male colleagues to attribute social problems to the 'masculinization' of women. And so, by a painful irony, even anti-Stalinist texts may represent women according to patterns which closely resemble those current in the high Socialist Realist novel of the 1940s.

These general limitations in the Russian women's realist tradition will be discussed in more detail below (though due attention will also be paid to the achievements of this tradition, which at its best has a lively intensity). But I shall show that we should not regard the insistence on 'transcendence' of reality too uncritically either: as I shall demonstrate, the attempt to escape Soviet received opinions about gender has in some cases meant that 'alternative' Russian women's writing has simply perpetuated a different, but just as pernicious, kind of gender asymmetry, one depending on a facile and all too often sentimental eulogization of 'feminine' creative powers. On the other hand, some such 'transcendental' writing, notably the poetry of Elena Shvarts and Olga Sedakova, ranks amongst the best work ever produced by Russian women.

The division between realism and anti-realism is the most important polarization in post-Thaw Soviet literature; but that does not mean that it is the only defining factor, or that its effects are always clear-cut. The distinction between 'critical realism' and 'transcendence' is beginning to be subjected to various pressures. One of these is a shift in the thick journals' political allegiances. Since Aleksandr Tvardovsky's editorship in the 1950s and 1960s, *Novy mir* has been considered to be the flagship of liberalism. It still is so considered. But certain other thick journals, such as *Nash sovremennik* and *Moskva*, have recently become much more overtly reactionary; reflecting important currents in mainstream politics, these journals give the 'transcendent' direction a new edge, as the revival of 'Holy Rus' is asserted to be a practically feasible project.[36] If the fiction and poetry published by such journals has generally been of low quality, other new writing is beginning to place my dichotomy under threat from an aesthetic, rather than a political, position. As a new generation of women writers, among whom one might name Lyudmila Petrushevskaya, in some of her various incarnations, as well as such less experienced and (on current showing) less diverse talents as Tatyana Tolstaya, Nina Sadur, Svetlana Vasilenko, Larisa Vaneeva, and Valeriya Narbikova, comes to public attention, and techniques such as free internal monologue are increasingly employed, my division becomes progressively more redundant. These prose writers are heirs to several women poets, among them Natalya Gorbanevskaya and Bella Akhmadulina, whose work can be labelled neither 'realist' nor 'anti-realist', but which occupies a position discursively located between those two tendencies. Both in the general survey which follows, and in the shorter chapters at the end of this Part, due consideration will be given to writers of this kind, who stand outside the general division of allegiances, and whose texts I have labelled as 'fusions'.

The New Critical Realism: Prose after 1954

In 1954 the writer Vera Panova published a substantial new piece of work, a novel entitled *The Seasons*—and was promptly attacked by many critics on the grounds of 'excessive pessimism and naturalism'.[37] Outwardly, Panova was dealing with much the same material as she had in her earlier novels: the life of a Soviet industrial town, and her characterization also departed little from accepted stereotypes. A greater emphasis was given to negative qualities in some of the male characters than had been the case in her 1940s novels—indeed, some of the 'heels' now included Party organizers, a matter that did not go unnoticed in hostile appraisals. But the women were all as tirelessly virtuous and competent as their high-Socialist-Realist predecessors. A much more significant novelty was the intrusion of detail into Panova's narrative, an aspect which can be observed even in the first chapter of the novel. After a prologue portraying the preparations in the town of Ensk for the New

---

[36] Reflections of, or parallels to, the nationalist ideas propagandized by these journals in daily life have included, besides the increasing prominence of right-wing groups of all shades, the ceremonial interment of Grand Duke Vladimir Kirillovich, the pretender to the Romanov throne, in the Peter and Paul Fortress church.

[37] *Vremena goda* was, for example, the subject of intensive debate at the Second Congress of the Union of Writers the same year that it was published. (See *Vtoroi s"ezd*, esp. 92–3. See also V. Nazarenko, 'Ideinost' i masterstvo', *Zvezda* (1954), 11: 181–91.)

Year, Panova launches into a portrait of some women factory workers getting ready for a party:

At ten the girls began to arrive, all of them friends of Larisa and Yulka. They laid the table and decorated it, making it look a real picture, then they got to work on themselves. Every girl had brought a smart pair of shoes with her, all wrapped up in newspaper; someone needed an iron to press her clothes, someone else asked for a needle. The house was full of the sound of girlish voices, and the ceiling shook as they ran about.[38]

The cheerful, bustling women could be taken from the opening scene of any Socialist Realist novel; it is the 'shoes wrapped in newspaper' which stand out. They are important both in themselves (as an anti-heroic, down-to-earth detail), and because they are given such a prominent position in the narrative. Throughout Panova's novel, domesticity dominates over public life, and this domesticity is often portrayed as the territory of women who work to overcome stress and mess, rather than as a sphere of harmonious relaxation effortlessly and unnoticeably created by women for the enjoyment of their menfolk. The neo-classical bas-relief has been replaced by the genre painting, the Stalinist superwoman by the Dutch housewife.

As the Khrushchev years progressed, women writers began to expand on the beginnings made by Panova. The changes came slowly. In the 1950s a good deal of published work by women portrayed the heroic past, narrating, say, stirring tales of work in Krupskaya's office, or thrilling stories of partisan campaigns during the Second World War.[39] But with the beginning of the 1960s, genuinely innovative pieces of realist prose began to be published. For example, the early writings of Irina Grekova, such as 'The Far Courtyard' (1961), 'Under The Street-light' (1962), and 'The Ladies' Hairdresser' (1963), showed women characters who did not soar above the tensions of home and work, as Stalinist heroines had done, but who were subject to incessant irritations and distractions. Professionally successful, they still had to deal with patronizing male colleagues in their places of work; at home, rather than being supported by ever-understanding husbands, they were pestered by their idle male dependants. Grekova's work prefigured much writing of the 1960s and 1970s in its thematic reorchestration of pre-Revolutionary women's writing. Her protagonists, like the heroines of the first Russian woman realists, are almost invariably women of above average standing,

    [38] Panova, Vremena goda (Moscow, 1954), 12.
    [39] See e.g. E. Drabkina, 'Povest' o nenapisannoi knige', NM (1961), 6: 135–70; 7: 191–230; idem, 'Moskva 1918', NM (1958), 9: 147–88.

who know and understand social conditions better than their fellows. But, unlike pre-Revolutionary heroines, whether those of the 'escape plot' or of the later, empirical realist tradition, Grekova's heroines do not invariably triumph over or sink under adversity. Their mistakes are as frequent as their insights, but the mistakes lead to new psychological perceptions, rather than prompting self-destruction and despair. Like her turn-of-the-century predecessors, though, Grekova is sensitive to class as well as to gender resonances. In 'The Ladies' Hairdresser' the narrator's idealization of the 'creativity' of the man who does her hair is brought to an abrupt conclusion when the man becomes intolerant of the inflexible regime at work and finds a factory job. 'The Rothschild Violin' ironically depicts how a Soviet woman teacher's idealistic (and clichéd) view that contact with great literature is certain to transform lives is thrown into question by her materialistic neighbour's dramatic, but short-lived, response to a Chekhov story.[40]

Though women critical realists have followed quite diverse paths, Grekova's prose is the prototype in one important way. The central character in women's prose since the 1960s has been an ambivalently handled female member of the intelligentsia. Unlike their turn-of-the-century predecessors, recent Soviet critical realists have been little concerned with peasant women. The tradition of 'village prose', an important alternative official direction of the 1960s and 1970s, had almost no female adherents. The hindrance to women's participation probably stemmed less from village prose's actual characteristics, such as its reinvention of the traditional peasant family as harmonious nuclear unit, or from the genre's reactionary political associations, than from the fact that most contemporary women writers work in the two Russian capitals, whilst 'village prose' is very much a provincial, indeed a regional, movement. The rare woman writers who have set stories in Russian villages have portrayed peasant women not in the terms of 'village prose', but much in the manner of, say, Dmitrieva in the 1890s. The central characters of Yunna Moritts's 'New Potatoes' and Galina Volodina's 'Arisha' are apparently put-upon figures, but manage somehow to survive, in the first case through deliberate trickery, and in the second through a passivity so complete that active malice founders

[40] Grekova, 'Damskii master', *Na ispytaniyakh* (Moscow, 1989), 554–602; 'Pod fonarem', *Na ispytaniyakh*, 533–53; 'Khozyaika gostinitsy', *Kafedra* (Moscow, 1980), 221–386; 'Skripka Rotshil'da', *Na ispytaniyakh*, 387–99; on Grekova see Adele Barker, 'Are Women Writing "Women's Writing"'; 'Women without Men in the Writings of Contemporary Soviet Women Writers', in Daniel Rancour-Laferrière (ed.), *Russian Literature and Psychoanalysis: Linguistic and Literary Studies in Eastern Europe*, 31 (1989), 431–49; Sigrid McLaughlin, *Images of Women in Soviet Fiction* (London, 1989), 18–20.

before it.[41] These women are very different from the wise old peasant grandmothers, the tirelessly stoical bastions of a dying folkloric tradition, who populate most 'village prose' stories written by men. As in the adaptation of 'escape plots' to the lives of working women in the 1890s, we see a process by which representations which have become traditional amongst women writers can be radical and vital when transferred to a new literary context.

The metropolitan bias of Soviet critical realism might lead one to expect that working-class women would figure more prominently in Soviet women's writing than peasants; but in fact their presence is of only slightly greater significance. On the whole they are introduced merely in order to counterpoint an intellectual woman who is the central character; and Socialist Realist stereotypes of idealized 'workers' and satirized 'petit bourgeois' remain in force. In Maiya Ganina's 'Marie-Antoinette', for example, a male geologist falls for the plain-faced Margarita when he sees her washing sheets in grey suds, feeling that the activity lends her a dignity far beyond beauty. Not just any work can be celebrated in this way, however. In another story by Ganina, 'Mariya', the central character is a circus artiste, a much more dodgy occupation that has overtones of vagrancy and parasitism in official Soviet post-Revolutionary ideology (as, indeed, in pre-Revolutionary realist writing too). Ganina dwells on the degrading nature of Mariya's work (bleeding feet, abusive trainers, drunken partners) and the story of this 'empty life' ends, predictably enough, in suicide. In 'On Tour', which also deals with a woman of obviously 'petit-bourgeois' tastes, Ganina at least credits this woman, Galya, with some tenacity in her adverse circumstances. But her narrative again makes a great show of distancing itself. After a reference to Galya's 'dyed hair', the reader is informed, with heavy-handed irony, that, astonishingly enough, Galya supposed that she had rather a good dress sense; then, in consideration of any dullards who may still have failed to grasp the point, the narrator adds that in fact her taste was appalling.[42] In other texts by realist writers whose resources are rather less limited than Ganina's, a similar assault on inappropriate values is effected by means of schematic character juxtapositions which recall those of the provincial tale. For example, Grekova's novella *Ship of Widows* contrasts a gallery of staunch but ignorant or at any rate limited

---

[41] Yunna Moritts, 'Molodaya kartoshka', *Vremya i my*, 105 (1989), 89–99; Galina Volodina, 'Arisha', in *Ne pomnyashchaya zla*, 125–30. The originator of the 'village prose' old woman is Matrena in Solzhenitsyn's *Matrenin dvor* (1962); for some trenchant remarks on the tradition, see Barbara Heldt, 'The Burden of Caring', *Nation*, 13 June 1987, 820–4.

[42] Maiya Ganina, 'Margarita', *Poka zhivu—nadeyus'* (Moscow, 1987), 325–32; 'Mariya', ibid. 445–60; 'Na gastrolyakh', ibid. 426–45.

working women, and self-serving *petites-bourgeoises*, to an upstanding intellectual heroine, the pianist Olga Flerova.[43] The representation of acceptable and unacceptable non-intellectual female behaviour, in much 1960s and 1970s women's writing, indicated the persistence of the moral purviews of the Socialist Realist classic. In the last three years, however, there have been signs that things are beginning to change. Galina Volodina's 'He Spoilt My Whole Life' and 'The Elections' (1989) portray the struggles of working-class women with appalling living conditions and irrational bureaucratic processes from the inside, rather than from the outside.[44] And Marina Palei's 'Kabiriya from the Obvodny Canal' (1991), has a heroine, Monka, whom Soviet *idées reçues* would consign to the 'dregs' of society, but who is shown to have a low-life energy, vitality, and capacity for pleasure which provoke the introverted middle-class narrator to self-doubt, rather than to homily. The reprehensible but indestructible Monka is described in a prose as lively as herself; the reader's enjoyment is only impaired by one passage discoursing on Monka's sexual feelings, which has all the rapt and unsmiling phallo-centrism of Lawrence's *Aaron's Rod*.[45]

If recent critical realism has maintained pre-Revolutionary realism's interest in aspirant middle-class heroines, the characteristics of those heroines have also shown a capacity for long-term survival. Sexuality is still as much of a problem area as it was in the 1890s. The notorious prudery of the Soviet censorship has been one, but by no means the only, cause for this; just as important has been the continuing tendency of women writers to see sex as a matter imposed on them from outside. In 'Mute Phone Calls' (1974), for example, a story by Ruf Zernova, the narrator is grateful to be spared 'the loveless sex of the single woman'.[46] This bald generalization has wide acceptance in Russian women's writing; one needs to add to it only that 'the loveless sex of the married woman' is also a preoccupation in many stories. As in the nineteenth century, so in the late twentieth, celibacy is frequently presented as a guarantee of independence, and the incompatibility of physical and

---

[43] Grekova, *Vdovii parokhod*, *Porogi* (Moscow, 1986), 270–401; cf. Catriona Kelly, 'Soviet Women's Writing and De-Stalinisation: I. Grekova and N. Baranskaya', *Rusistika*, 5 (1992), 39–43; 6 (1992), 14–18. For a more appreciative view, see however Barker (in 'Women without Men'), and Cathy Porter, 'Introduction' to Grekova, *A Ship of Widows*, trans. Cathy Porter (London, 1989).

[44] Volodina, 'Vsyu zhizn' isportil', *Ne pomnyashchaya zla*, 131–40; 'Vybory', ibid. 140–9.

[45] Marina Palei, 'Kabiriya s Obvodnogo kanala', *NM* (1991), 3: 47–81. It is possible that populist themes of this kind are about to go through a revival, judging by the many Russians who have suggested to me that the best piece of women's writing in 1991 was the memoirs of a peasant woman, Evgeniya Kiseleva: 'Kishmareva. Kiseleva. Tyuricheva', *NM* (1991), 2: 9–27.

[46] Zernova, 'Mute Phone Calls', trans. Helen Reeve in *Mute Phone Calls* (New Brunswick, NJ, 1991), 163–214.

intellectual matters asserted. Nor have other expressions of the internal life become less vexed. It is only fair to say that Grekova and her successors give greater space to discourses of interiority than the turn-of-the-century woman realists: first-person narrators are used more frequently. But interior monologue in third-person narrators is still employed infrequently; and, as in the 1890s and 1900s, it mainly occurs in texts representing men. Nina Katerli, perhaps Tsekhovskaya's closest successor, is the author of clever stories which, though often including striking cameos of women characters (see especially her long tale 'The Farewell Light', 1982), are composed of the fragmentary and vacillating recollections of nondescript middle-aged men, who yet display a serendipitous capacity for wayward and fantastical observation.[47]

If women remain as shut off from scrutiny as they did, Grekova and her successors, following Panova, have, however, contributed something new to the realist tradition by allowing objects and customs to figure in the delineation of middle-class heroines as well as of class outsiders. This is not to say that such material has been easily or readily absorbed: recognition of the fact that problems of *byt*, and of sexuality, might affect 'us' as well as 'them' was to come relatively slowly. In Grekova's 'The Lady's Hairdresser', for example, information such as where to acquire a pair of tights or a sexual partner is the prerogative of the heroine's secretary. Inhibitions arising from the traditional Russian intelligentsia view that domesticity is inimical to literary culture have been augmented by censorship prohibitions, which meant that food shortages and other hardships have been most frequently represented in stories (and films) set during the Second World War, since they could appear safely neutral when placed in this ideologically unexceptionable setting.[48] Another way of dealing with 'forbidden' practical problems was to transfer them to the context of Western capitalism; the appearance of a prostitute in Ganina's 'On Tour' was possible because this particular 'tour' had taken a Russian circus company to Paris.

An outstanding exception to the euphemistic treatment of social setting, though, was Natalya Baranskaya's famous story 'A Week Like Any Other', which caused a tremendous stir when it was first published

[47] Nina Katerli, 'Proshchal'nyi svet', *Tsvetnye otkrytki* (Leningrad, 1987), 4–26; see also Helena Goscilo, *Balancing Acts: Recent Writing by Soviet Women* (Bloomington, Ind., 1989), 143–64. Cf. Katerli, 'Zhara na severe', *Zvezda* (1988), 4: 3–73; 'The Monster', trans. Bernard Meares, in *Soviet Women Writing*, 107–16; 'The Barsukov Triangle', trans. David Lapeza, in Carl and Ellendea Proffer (eds.), *The Barsukov Triangle, the Two-Toned Blonde and Other Stories* (Ann Arbor, Mich., 1984), 3–71. Katerli's other collections include *Okno* (Leningrad, 1981) and *Kurzal* (Leningrad, 1990).

[48] For instance, Ganina, 'Bestoloch'', *Poka zhivu*, 270–89, is a wartime narrative which is much starker in its depiction of privation than this author's other stories.

in 1969.[49] A classic piece of documentary realism, the story is narrated in diary form, the device being motivated by the assumption that this is material gathered by the narrator as she attempts to collect her thoughts and fill in a questionnaire. Almost every event in Olga, the narrator's, day is recorded; nothing is too trivial. We see Olga queueing for food, chaotically organizing her children's departure for school, swapping anecdotes with her workmates, and struggling to keep up with her unrealistic work schedules. We learn that she has considered having an abortion when pregnant with her second child, and that she and her husband seldom have time for sex (not surprisingly, as they are lucky to manage six hours' sleep a night).

The shock value of 'A Week Like Any Other' lay in the fact that it put into print material which, though the subject of quotidian oral discourse, had rarely made its way into written culture so completely and directly. In fact, the freshness of the text in that sense has not worn off; though sex crimes or murders are now the staple fare of critical realism, the practical day-to-day difficulties of women are not. Though her early critics fretted because Baranskaya placed so little emphasis on 'spiritual values', the boldness of her text lay precisely in its confrontation of the fact that, in extreme social conditions, values might prove expendable.[50] And, unlike many pieces of Soviet critical realism, 'A Week Like Any Other' is also a neatly constructed and technically adept piece of writing. The narrator's own naïvely confiding tone by reciprocity justifies her role as confidante to the other women in the office, and makes her seem, at one level, a reliable informant to the reader. But it also allows for much unconscious irony: Olga's insistence that her husband, Dima, is a great support to her at home is undermined by her narration of anecdotes demonstrating that he in fact does very little when not under constant supervision.

'A Week Like Any Other' is also one of the few Soviet texts which, in its uncensored version, confronts the issue of women's alienation from politics. In a scene not published until 1989, Baranskaya portrays one of the political and social indoctrination sessions compulsory in all Russian places of work until a decree made by Boris Yeltsin in August 1991 officially separated politics and employment. The narrator disgraces herself by an outburst against the sheer waste of time represented by these meetings. Fortunately for her, the chairman of the meeting is a humane elderly man who handles the situation tactfully and without

---

[49] Natal'ya Baranskaya, 'Nedelya kak nedelya', *Den' pominoveniya* (Moscow, 1989), 263–317.
[50] The fuller version of 'A Week' is the 1989 one cited in n. 49 above. On Baranskaya's other work, see Ch. 14.

authoritarianism; but Baranskaya makes it clear that such flexibility is a matter of individual choice, rather than of institutional dictate. Baranskaya's later publications were not all so outspoken, but they all vividly reflected her hostility to bureaucratic processes and to authoritarian mentalities, as the chapter devoted to her will make clear.

If Baranskaya is perhaps the most capable woman writer in a traditionally critical realist mode, the early work of another writer, Lyudmila Petrushevskaya, who began publishing in 1972, and whose output includes plays as well as short stories, started to initiate a shift to genuinely new forms of writerly practice. Petrushevskaya is a writer of great talent, whose achievements have been widely acknowledged— sometimes reluctantly, since her work is both far less transparent, and far more unsettling, than that of either Grekova or Baranskaya. Her plays were not performed in mainstream theatre companies until the late 1980s, a date which also saw the publication of some stories formerly held back by censorship. Both in these and in her fiction, she was an early forerunner of the current trend of hyper-realism, which is popularly (and rather dismissively) known as *chernukha* (black stuff/verismo, cf. *pornukha*, porno). Unlike some other contemporary practitioners of this genre, however, Petrushevskaya is more than a sensationalist, though she concentrates on extreme anguish and conflict. Her work has the moral commitment of critical realism, but does not display the comfortable class prejudices of its Soviet variant, nor its banal assumptions about gender roles. If men are often absent from the narratives of Grekova or Ganina, in Petrushevskaya's work it is the problems of their presence which are in the centre of attention. In some texts, such as the play *Cinzano* (1973), which delineates a squalid all-male drinking party, men appear as pathetic automatons; a different approach is taken in 'Viewing Platform' (1982), which is narrated from the perspective of a man of chilling self-interest and detachment. What is still more unusual is Petrushevskaya's lack of sentiment about women's behaviour. Perhaps her best early story is 'Our Crowd' (published in 1988, but written significantly earlier), another story in the first person, but this time with a woman narrator. As this narrator, a woman in the last stages of terminal illness, struggles to ensure that her child will not be destroyed by her egocentric relatives and friends, the problems of a doubtful good achieved by morally dubious machinations are handled with a subtlety worthy of Brecht's *The Caucasian Chalk Circle*. And, unlike many women writers, Petrushevskaya strips away illusion by means of fictional devices, not in spite of these. Her narrators are always indwelling, involved, no better than those they observe. In 'Medea', for example, the woman narrator who listens to a 'terrible' story of revenge murder is left, after the story has been told, as incapable of action as the man who has told it to her.[51] As we shall see, Petrushevskaya's inventiveness is demonstrated also by her work in modes outside the boundaries of strict critical realism; but her critical-realist texts already reveal an unusual imaginativeness.

The 'feminine' tradition of critical realism has been practised by a very large number of other Soviet authors, not all of whom operate at the level of sophistication attained by Grekova or Baranskaya, let alone Petrushevskaya. The anthology *Always a Woman*, which has already been mentioned in the introduction to this survey, assembles a number of stories in which women's aspirations are presented in terms of keeping children and husband happy by running a nice home, wearing pretty clothes, and applying make-up at regular intervals.[52] Indeed, 'niceness' is the central value recognized in these stories: their heroines are always attractive, and whilst they may experience problems, these are never such as to confound their equanimity, let alone provoke them into anger or bitterness. Neither in technique nor in world-view are these stories distinguished from the sort of material which gets published in the lower-brow women's magazines of Western Europe; in them, too, the 1940s values of 'work, home, and family superwomen' to some extent live on, though the real ambition of heroines is generally now to be shock homemakers, rather than shock workers.

If its emphasis on 'niceness' as the ultimate aim of human existence has been one bane of the Soviet critical realist tradition, another has been the tendency to give unreflective and servile consideration to issues which official ideology has decreed to be of burning current interest. The late 1980s attempt to impress upon Soviet women the evils of abortion, for example, inspired stories of approximately the literary quality of those which were published on the subject in Stalin's time. Perhaps the most bizarre effort, Natalya Sukhanova's 'Delos', showed a hospital ward of pregnant women under the benign care of a male gynaecologist, into whose hands they happily resigned their decisions about childbirth and abortion. The story emerged not only as a condemnation of

[51] Petrushevskaya, *Cinzano* and *Den' rozhdeniya Smirnovoi, Tri devushki v golubom* (Moscow, 1989), 107–23, 125–40; 'Smotrovaya ploshchadka', *Druzhba narodov* (1982), 1: 56–70; 'Svoi krug', *NM* (1988), 1: 116–38; trans. Helena Goscilo in *eadem* (ed.), *Glasnost' Prose* (Ann Arbor, Mich., 1989); 'Medeya', *Aprel'*, 2 (1990), 110–15; trans. Brian Oles in *Anthology*. On Petrushevskaya see McLaughlin, *Images of Women*, 98–100; Barker, 'Women without Men'.

[52] See e.g. L. Uvarova, 'Small Part Star', Ekaterina Markova, 'A Stranger at the Door', and Irina Strelkova, 'Vera Ivanovna', *Always a Woman*, 383–98, 249–88, 309–28; Lyubov' Yunina, *Zhenshchina v odnokomnatnoi kvartire* (Moscow, 1985); Lyudmila Uvarova, 'Be Still, Torments of Passion', and Nadezhda Kozhevnikova, 'Home', in Helena Goscilo (ed.), *Balancing Acts: Recent Writing by Soviet Women* (Bloomington, Ind., 1989), 173–90, 191–8.

abortion, but also as an argument for keeping men in charge of women's fertility.[53]

Sukhanova's story was typical in that the alienation of women from their own bodies has become one of the canonical themes of realist writing during the last three years. In Mariam Yuzefskaya's 'Oktyabrina', for example, the heroine comes to after a period of catatonic depression only to be revolted by her own physical presence:

Suddenly she sensed an acrid animal smell, and stood still for a few minutes sniffing warily at the air. It smelt of sweat and urine, it smelt of unwashed human body. Abruptly she realized that the smell came from her, from her armpits, her hair, her crotch.[54]

It is scarcely surprising that it often seems preferable to consign the body's disturbing existence into the care of others. The clinical anonymity of the hospital makes it a convenient place for this surrender of responsibility; for this and other reasons, it has become a favourite locus of Soviet women's writing. If the hospital functions for some writers as a convenient metaphor of women's subordination at the hands of men, a subordination which may be either celebrated or denounced, for others it functions as a conveniently partial form of social allegory, because it allows the displacement of indignation from the remote men who form the top layers of the medical (i.e. political) hierarchy on to the more visible and accessible perpetrators of oppression, the women who make up its bottom layers. If in the former case gender issues are reduced to a simplistic polarization of male and female interests, in the latter such issues are recognized only from a misogynistic point of view (women are seen to suffer most at the hands of other women). And whether in the one case or the other, the hospital narrative finally attributes the subordination of women to a cause which is organic, and hence insuperable or inevitable.[55]

If all these elements make the hospital narrative a quiescent genre of containment, it does, though, have one potentially radical feature. The maternity ward is the one place in which Soviet women from the

[53] Natal'ya Sukhanova, 'Delos', NM (1988), 3: 69–84; reprinted almost immediately in Chisten'-kaya zhizn'. The story is analysed in some detail by Barbara Heldt in 'Gynoglasnost', Buckley (ed.), Perestroika and Soviet Women, 168–9.

[54] Mariam Yuzefskaya, 'Oktyabrina', Druzhba narodov (1992), 8: 33.

[55] Examples of narratives set in hospitals or other 'total institutions' such as orphanages or homes include Zernova, 'Ved'my', Zhenskie rasskazy (New York, 1981), 153–60 (trans. Ann Harleman as 'Witches' in Mute Phone Calls (New Brunswick, NJ, 1991)); Marina Palei, 'Den' topolinogo pukha', in Novye Amazonki; Nataliya Bianki, 'Surgeon Fyodorov', Soviet Literature (1981), 1: 85–90; Inna Goff, 'Infirmary at the Station', in Soviet Women Writing, 301–16; cf. Vaneeva's 'Venetian Mirrors' and Zhuravleva's 'Black Hole', mentioned below. The point about hospital fiction is also made in a slightly different context by Goscilo in Balancing Acts, p. xxii.

intelligentsia can normally expect to have extensive contact with women from the working classes. This fact is reflected in Yuliya Voznesenskaya's *The Women's Decameron*, which is amongst the few pieces of recent Russian women's writing to express any sense of cross-class gender solidarity, or any sense of sympathy for the difficulties of proletarian women.[56]

Shaped on the one hand by unreflective attitudes to 'the feminine' (and for that matter to 'the masculine'), and on the other by notions of what constitutes 'literary quality' that are at once inflexible and hesitant, it is scarcely surprising that much women's critical realism seems to have lost its way. Many of the stories in this tradition would certainly be of interest to sociologists attempting to index the margins of women's dissatisfaction or tolerance, but a literary historian can only be estranged by their lack of diversity and their conceptual simplicity.

By contrast, another form of documentary prose, the autobiography, though it shares the techniques of critical realism, has a quite different perspective, and has offered an altogether bleaker and less naïvely reassuring view of women's place in society than has been offered by most critical realists (Petrushevskaya excepted). This is explained by the fact that until very recently, documentary autobiography was an almost entirely underground direction, since its central genre was the memoir depicting life in the prison camps, institutions whose very existence could not be named in print during much of the post-Stalin period. No important text by a woman writer having sneaked into print during the short period of openness in the early 1960s which saw the publication of Solzhenitsyn's *One Day in the Life of Ivan Denisovich*, most women's prison memoirs have only begun appearing in Russia since 1989, though a number had appeared abroad well before that.[57]

One of the earliest, and one of the best, pieces of documentary prose to be published was Evgeniya Ginzburg's long memoir *Into the Whirlwind*, the two volumes of which came out in Italy in 1967 and 1979.[58] Ginzburg's narrative, like that of critical-realist fiction, gave a considerable emphasis to *realia*, which here were those of the prison and the camp; she carefully enumerated the overcrowding in cells, the indignities

---

[56] Yuliya Voznesenskaya, *Zhenskii dekameron* (Tel Aviv, 1987); trans. W. B. Linton as *The Women's Decameron* (London, 1986).

[57] 'Tonechka', a story by Zernova set in a prison camp, was written in the late 1950s, but its publication at the time was suppressed, and the text appeared many years later in the USA: see the remarks by Helen Reeve in *Mute Phone Calls*, p. xiii. Besides this story, work appearing abroad includes Raisa Orlova, *Memoirs*, trans. Sam D. Cioran (New York, 1983), and the memoirs of Ginzburg, Ratushinskaya, Gagen-Torn, and Zernova cited below.

[58] Evgeniya Ginzburg, *Krutoi marshrut* (Milan, 1967); trans. Paul Stevenson and Manya Harari as *Into the Whirlwind* (London, 1967); Evgeniya Ginzburg, *Krutoi marshrut*, ii (Milan, 1979); trans. Ian Boland as *Within the Whirlwind* (London, 1981).

of being subjected to body-searches, the mind-bending routines of interrogation, the humiliations of having essential items of clothing removed, the degradations of 'slopping out'. But the book is not only a record of external experience: it also depicts the prison camp as the site for a psychological transformation like that described in the *Bildungs-roman*: the neophyte attains political understanding, as well as a broader social experience, in the crucible of relations between women who share a prison cell or camp barracks. Social divisions are not overcome—the demarcation line between the mostly working-class criminals and the mostly middle-class political prisoners remains rigid. But Ginzburg's book is for all that a direct, albeit non-participant, account of Soviet popular life; the same can be said of several other memoirs of camp life.[59]

Many other features that were initiated by Ginzburg are evident in later memoirs, too, though by no means all later memoirists wrote so ably as she; her account has an exceptional clarity and urgency. Nor do they all record such dramatic changes in world-view as those which she chronicled: where Ginzburg unflinchingly portrays her younger self, a Party activist who submitted without question to the Party's authority, other memoirists often give accounts of their early biographies which are either more equivocal, or more self-righteous.[60] Sometimes, too, there is an intrusive emphasis on the absolute incorruptibility of moral convic-tion; few writers suggest that survival in the camps might have dictated any compromise with principle. Generally, too, memoirists give little emphasis to moments of despair and demoralization, though authors' monolithic representations of themselves may sometimes be softened by the insistence that co-operation between women was more crucial than individual heroism.[61] However, at least some of the memoirs are equal to Ginzburg's in raw power, whilst at the same time allowing due weight to the diversity of individual perception and voice. Amongst outstanding examples are Khava Volovich's harrowing account of the Ukrainian famine and of her own imprisonment, which braves such unmentionable topics as the sexual frenzy that could overcome zeks, and the appalling guilt of women who became pregnant as a result; Nadezhda Frankina's

[59]   The most representative collection of memoirs written by former women prisoners is Vilensky, *Dodnes'*, which assembles the reminiscences of more than twenty women, most previously unpublished. See also Nina Gagen-Torn, 'From my Memoirs', trans. M. Molnar, *Index on Censorship* (1991), 8: 12–16. Another remarkable document is Efrosinya Kersnovskaya's 'Life' ('Zhitie'), which is semi-folkloric in character and illustrated with the author's own naïve paintings: see *Ogonek*, 13 Jan. 1990; 20 Jan. 1990.

[60]   A particularly self-righteous tone is adopted by Ratushinskaya in *Seryi: tsvet nadezhdy*; whilst the memoirs collected by Vilensky generally avoid self-righteousness, most also avoid much in the way of reflection.

[61]   See particularly Zoya Marchenko, 'Tak bylo', Vilensky, *Dodnes'*, 309–25.

short and particularly bleak account of the physical privations of prison; or Mira Linkevich's magnificently sarcastic memoir of her trainee interrogator's grotesque attempts to frighten her, 'How the Cadres Were Tempered'.[62]

For all its links with critical realism, women's documentary prose is a direction not so much of non-fiction as of anti-fiction (hence, no doubt, the stylistic clumsiness of some accounts). However, an original twist of interpretation is evident in Ruf Zernova's 'Elizabeth Arden' (1978), a first-person narrative which locates itself between memoir and short story.[63] And 'Elizabeth Arden' is original in other ways too. It alters the accepted procedure of the camp memoir: though the narrator's arrest is a peripeteia here as there, the importance of 'before' and 'after' is reversed. Here it is not the camp which is the focus of Zernova's detailed delineation of a world shared by women, with its *realia* held in common, and its specific emotional relations, but the beauty salon which the narrator has attended before her arrest. The result is that solidarity between women emerges as a quality disrupted by political repressions, rather than as something hammered out in their wake. In other words, the structural hierarchy of Zernova's text makes it the mirror-image of the camp memoir. And 'Elizabeth Arden's' status as fiction has also facilitated more radical departures from the memoir mode: the narrative is fragmentary rather than linear, depending on diverse layers of memory: the narrator moves from memories of life before the camps, to memories of the camps themselves, to reminiscences of life before the camps as she has recalled it whilst in the camps.

Though women have made important contributions to other genres of memoir besides the memoir of life in the camps, they have rarely made women's subjectivity and psychology the centre of analysis here. Authors who have chronicled the literary world, for example, have tended to follow Panaeva in seeing the woman memoirist as a reticent and self-effacing chronicler of others' opinions and witticisms. Olga Ivinskaya's memoirs of Boris Pasternak, whose mistress she was for many years, venture literary opinions only when asserting that various of the poems composed for *Doctor Zhivago* are addressed to Ivinskaya herself.[64] Given

---

[62] Khava Volovich, 'O proshlom'; Nadezhda Frankina, 'Zapiski vashei sovremennitsy', in Vilensky, *Dodnes'*. The memoir of Bukharin's second wife Anna Larina, 'Nezabyvaemoe' (*Znamya* (1988), 10–12; trans. Gary Kern as *This I Cannot Forget: Memoirs of Bukharin's Widow* (New York, 1993)) is, as one would expect, much more politically aware than most others, but adopts the perspective of an observer, rather than a participant.

[63] Zernova, 'Elizabet Arden', *Zhenskie rasskazy*, 9–53; see also *Mute Phone Calls*, 101–40.

[64] Ol'ga Ivinskaya, *V plenu vremeni* (Paris, 1978); see also *A Captive of Time*, trans. Max Hayward (London, 1980).

the rather silly and novelettish tone of Ivinskaya's writing, her self-effacement is perhaps fortunate. But three memoirs of incomparably higher intellectual calibre, Lidiya Chukovskaya's recollections of Akhmatova, Nadezhda Mandelstam's account of her life with her husband, and Lidiya Ginzburg's autobiographical recollections *The Writer at His Desk*, have also, in their different ways, followed Panaeva.[65] Chukovskaya's account adopts a Boswellesque deference; the right to hold opinions is displaced on to Akhmatova herself, whose conversation is aphoristic and acerbic to an unforgettable degree. An entirely different approach is adopted by Nadezhda Mandelstam, who emphasizes her own distance from literary matters rather as Panaeva did (referring to herself as an 'ordinary mortal' by comparison with Tsvetaeva, for example, and stressing her silence during literary discussions). But if Mandelstam lays claim to reticence in the conversations of her youth, the written narrative of her old age has amply compensated for that: this is an argumentative, cantankerous, and at times a studiedly unfair document. Though Mandelstam's bravery and capacity for self-sacrifice were not in question, she never attempts to force an appreciation of these qualities on the reader. And 'reticence' becomes here not simply the appropriate quality of a female outsider in literary life, but also a characteristic deriving from Mandelstam's philosophical concern with the difficulty of constructing an appropriate expression of identity in a culture which, as she frequently argued, could conceive selfhood only as self-interest of the lowest kind. Lidiya Ginzburg's text is yet a further variation on the literary memoir. It has a tone of literary authority which does not at all accord with the ordinary ethic of modest withdrawal; however, modesty is not the only 'feminine' characteristic which has been excised. The account is carefully impersonal; Ginzburg's memoir of the Leningrad siege, 'Notes of a Blockade Survivor', for example, has none of the lapses into dubious sentimentality which are evident in Berggolts's private diaries, but it has none of their immediacy or their sense of place either. Only in the earliest and least polished (but also liveliest) part of this heterogeneous collection of essays and memoirs is

---

[65] Lidiya Chukovskaya, *Zapiski ob Anne Akhmatovoi* (2 vols.; Paris, 1978–80); cf. her *Pamyati detstva* (New York, 1983), which is really a memoir of her father; Lidiya Ginzburg, *Chelovek za pis'mennym stolom* (Leningrad, 1988); Nadezhda Mandel'shtam, *Vospominaniya* (New York, 1970); trans. Max Hayward as *Hope Against Hope* (London, 1971); *Vtoraya kniga* (Paris, 1972); trans. Max Hayward as *Hope Abandoned* (London, 1974). On Ginzburg's memoirs see Sarah Pratt, 'Lydia Ginzburg and the Fluidity of Genre', in Jane Gary Harris (ed.), *Autobiographical Statements in Twentieth-Century Russian Literature* (Princeton, NJ, 1990), 207–16; on Chukovskaya's, Stephanie Sandler, 'Reading Loyalty in Chukovskaya's *Zapiski ob Anne Akhmatovoi*', in Wendy Rosslyn (ed.), *The Speech of Unknown Eyes: Akhmatova's Readers on her Poetry* (Nottingham, 1989), ii. 267–84.

Ginzburg's reflection on abstract questions of culture and ethics interrupted by the sense of the world beyond the study.[66]

Of these three writers, it is only Nadezhda Mandelstam who ventures
anything approaching political analysis or even political comment in any
broad sense; such analysis and commentary are generally missing from
prison-camp memoirs as well.[67] In autobiography, as in other domains,
poetry has filled the gap. The post-1953 poetic autobiographies of Anna
Barkova, who was incarcerated for more than twenty years between 1935
and 1965, express not only a prickly sense of autonomy, but also a
nihilistic anti-patriotism which is fiercer than anything else in Russian
women's writing. Barkova's fierceness, as in her 1930s poems, derived in
part from self-disgust; in applying the imagery of blood-letting to the
society in which she lived, she also proclaimed herself an executioner.
Whilst expressing a desire that vengeance should be as ruthless as the
punishment inflicted upon her, her lyric speaker acknowledges that the
cruelty which she suffers is the responsibility of her own generation. In
'The Heroes of Our Time', for example, she both pays tribute to the
gallantry of her generation, and portrays its monstrous qualities of self-
delusion:

> Мы герои, веку ровесницы,
> Совпадают у нас шаги.
> Мы и жертвы, и провозвестники,
> И союзники, и враги.[68]

> We're the heroes, born with the century,
> Walking in step with the years;
> We are victims, we're prophets and heralds,
> Staunch allies, fierce enemies.

Barkova expresses an allegiance to 'the feminine' through the gender-
marked voice of every poem, as well as through declarations that she is
both 'a woman' and 'a poet'; but she refuses the accustomed strategies of
'feminine' oppositional writing, depicting herself as both more forceful
and more ordinary than other chroniclers of the camps. In 'A Few
Autobiographical Facts', for example, a poem of 1954, she makes the
ringing declaration, 'all my life ... | I was a *she*', and speaks with a

---

[66] Ginzburg kept a private diary which recorded details of her emotional attachments to women,
but the material remained unpublished at her death; I have been informed that it is now in her
archive in St Petersburg.

[67] Political commentaries are ventured by Ginzburg and Volovich in passing, but there is nothing
by a woman writer which attempts the general historical analysis of Razgon's *Nevydumannoe*, let
alone Solzhenitsyn's *The Gulag Archipelago*.

[68] Barkova, 'Geroi nashego vremeni', in Vilensky, *Dodnes'*, 352. Cf. 'Rossiiskaya toska', in
Barkova, *Geroi nashego vremeni* (Moscow, 1992), 32.

causticity exceptional for a Russian woman writer: imagining a pompous academic banally mythologizing her life after her death, she
describes herself as 'fit to vomit'. Yet at the same time, Barkova refuses to
eulogize her own suffering or her own virtue, stressing that her 1930s
ordeals were 'ludicrous', and that her body is only one amongst many
that have 'rotted' in the Terror.[69] Exploding both the myth of universal
female victimization, and the myth of necessary feminine superiority,
Barkova asserts that corrupt societies corrupt those who suffer as well as
those in power. This conviction, and also her readiness to pair the sacred
word 'motherland' with such adjectives as 'embittered' and 'degraded',
make her one of the most remarkable Russian writers of recent years.

The Anti-Realists: Poetry after 1954, Prose after 1980

As my survey of women's realist writing has illustrated, there are
significant resemblances between the prose tradition after 1880 and the
prose tradition after 1954; a further similarity is that the rise of a mimetic
and *realia*-centred prose has led, in this era as in that, to the assertion of a
self-declaredly apolitical aestheticism as an alternative tradition. But, if
the turn-of-the-century realists and anti-realists did not exactly esteem
one another, their relations were a good deal less overtly antagonistic
than those of the realist and anti-realist lobbies of recent years. This
antagonism is explained by the Soviet political context. Official Tsarist
culture had better things to do than to pursue every instance of decadent
épatage; Mayakovsky and his friends could wear wooden spoons in their
button-holes with impunity. In a country as obsessed with political and
social deviance as the Soviet Union, however, writers' adoption of a
standpoint that attempts to transcend reality has inevitably been perceived as a significant act of symbolic defiance, a declaration of
dangerously counter-cultural values. Conversely, self-conscious aestheticism is seen by its advocates as a perspective which is, if not revolutionary, at least bravely oppositional. A Soviet friend of mine who studied at
a musical institute in the early 1950s passed on a reminiscence which
neatly encapsulates the congruence of aestheticism and political alienation. On the day of Stalin's death she met an acquaintance whom she
found sympathetic, but whom she did not know very well. 'You've
heard who's died?' he asked. 'Yes?' she answered uncertainly; there was
no knowing, in the atmosphere of those times, whether this might not be
a question designed to ensnare. But his answer both surprised and
reassured her. 'Sergei Sergeevich Prokofiev,' he said.

---

[69] Barkova, 'Nechto avtobiograficheskoe', in *eadem*, 'Stikhi raznykh let', *Lazur'* (1989), 1: 343–5.
(See also 'A Few Autobiographical Facts' in *Anthology*.)

If active intervention in politics seems futile, active non-intervention is an attractive alternative; if events may not be altered, they may at least be pointedly ignored; if a critique of the exterior world would seem an indirect acknowledgement of that world's right to exist, an imaginative interior world may be created to shut it out. Such has been the decision of many Russian writers during the last four decades, a decision which was most particularly evident between the late 1960s and the late 1980s.

Given the appalling primitivism of the poetry which women were generally able to publish under Stalin, and the strength of the women's 'outsider' tradition at that time, it is scarcely surprising that the voices of women poets were amongst the first to speak for the dignity of non-participation, and declare for the virtues of withdrawal into an interior world. One early manifesto for this shift in direction was Olga Berggolts's spirited defence, in an article of 1954, of 'lyric poetry' in its traditional sense as the voice of the individual subject, speaking a personal language; another was a two-part article, published in the same year, in which Vera Inber attacked the civic values of Stalinist lyric. Like other events of the Thaw, the publication of these documents did not signal a complete reversal of official policy. The 1954 Congress was to see the expression of views on poetry directly opposed to those of Inber or Berggolts; if factory poetry went into a decline after 1954, civic poetry in a broader sense was to retain its importance. There was to be no once-and-for-all abandonment of Socialist Realist values, no blanket endorsement of individualism in poetry. But, shifts in the Party line notwithstanding, it is safe to state that in general post-1954 Soviet literary journals and publishing houses have tolerated a far greater degree of deviation from the positive values of *partiinost* (Party commitment) or 'reflection of reality' than before; they have also manifested a more marked orientation to the negative values of 'formalism' and technical adventurousness than would have been tolerated between 1930 and 1953.[70]

A further sign of growing pluralism was the rehabilitation, or partial rehabilitation, of work produced in internal or external emigration. Important literary texts of the 1930s and 1940s were published or republished, and their emergence acknowledged by critics and historians. Besides, though penalties for circulating material published unofficially (*samizdat*), or Russian-language material published in the West (*tamizdat*), were still heavy, they were no longer so draconian as in the late

---

[70] See Berggol'ts, 'Protiv likvidatsii liriki' (first published in *LG*), in K. Ozerova (ed.), *Razgovor pered s"ezdom: sbornik stat'ei, opublikovannyi pered Vsesoyuznym s"ezdom pisatelei* (Moscow, 1954), 279–83; Inber, 'Vdokhnovenie i masterstvo', *Znamya* (1956), 9: 157–69; (1957), 8: 168–78. A collection which makes clear that 'socialist construction' poems continued being written well after 1954 is *Budni velikikh stroek: stikhi russkikh poetov o trude*, ed. V. Zheleznov (Moscow, 1988).

1930s or the 1940s.[71] In consequence, a reasonably extensive intellectual public, at any rate in the major cities, was able to familiarize itself, legally or illegally, with non-Soviet Russian literature: at first with the classic works of the 'first and second waves' of emigration (i.e. those who had left after the Revolution and during the Second World War), and later with the fiction and poetry published by the increasing numbers of Soviet writers who chose to leave the country in the 1970s, when emigration restrictions were relaxed for a while. Through the channels of *samizdat* and *tamizdat*, material which was officially inadmissible could find its way into the literary mainstream. The consequence was a growing congruence between 'Soviet' and '*émigré*' work.[72]

Women's writing was also affected by this process, but rather idiosyncratically. For Soviet writers in general, it was prose authors who were the most important discoveries (or rediscoveries) of the 1950s, 1960s, and 1970s. The official publication of hitherto unknown work by the internal *émigrés* Andrei Platonov and Mikhail Bulgakov, and increasing covert familiarity with the novels of Vladimir Nabokov, had huge effects on young Soviet writers.[73] The rehabilitation of women's writing, by contrast, centred on poetry—logically enough, since poetry had indeed made up the bulk of women's work outside the official tradition. And this was not the only difference between the recovery of men's and of women's work. Publication of previously inadmissible material by women was more selective than was publication of material by men. From the late 1950s, the Symbolists, villified from the mid-1930s as 'idealists' and 'decadents', began to be quietly reabsorbed into literary history, and there were important and prestigious editions of such central figures as Annensky, Blok, Bryusov, Bely; but even the work of the best-

---

[71] Article 58 of the 1926 Criminal Code dictated penalties up to and including execution for activities hostile to the State; under Article 70 of the 1960 Criminal Code the maximum penalty was ten years. See Zhak Rossi, *Spravochnik po GULAGU* (London, 1987), 496, 501; Rossi also prints a graph of average sentence length on p. 483.

[72] Important publications of *samizdat* abroad include Konstantin K. Kuzminsky and Gregory L. Kovalev (eds.), *The Blue Lagoon Anthology of Modern Russian Poetry* (5 vols. in 9; Newtonville, Mass., 1980–6). In the late 1970s and early 1980s, Russians with Western friends could gain access to *tamizdat* materials, since Russian customs officers would at their discretion allow Western visitors to import single copies of Western-published Russian materials. Overlap between Soviet and Western Russian traditions is evident, for instance, in the similarity between the work of Andrei Bitov (Soviet resident, publishing at home and abroad), Vasily Aksenov (publishing at home and abroad before he was expelled from the USSR in 1981), Fazil Iskander (Soviet resident, publishing at home and abroad), Sasha Sokolov, and Zinovy Zinik (who began to publish in emigration). See also Georges Nivat (ed.), *Odna ili dve russkikh literatury* (Geneva, 1981), Arnold McMillin (ed.), *Under Western Eyes: The West as Reflected in Recent Russian Writing* (London, 1991).

[73] Andrei Platonov, *Izbrannye rasskazy* (Moscow, 1958); Bulgakov's *Master i Margarita* was first published in full in 1973 (a censored edn. had appeared in 1966), and his *Teatral'nyi roman* in 1967. On Nabokov cf. the writer's letter to Lauren G. Leighton of 14 Mar. 1968: Nabokov, *Selected Letters*, 431–2.

known women Symbolists was not reissued in book form. (The indiffer-ence of the Symbolist women to political directions that could be labelled 'democratic' in the narrow Soviet sense of that term, and the religious flavour of their work, of course played some role here, but that does not explain why, say, Gertsyk and Lokhvitskaya could not have been selectively republished, as, say, Vyacheslav Ivanov was.) The early work of Akhmatova was the only poetry by a woman writer from the post-Symbolist tradition which was to be published or studied systemati-cally after 1960, although the years between 1910 and 1917 were soon to become the single most significant field in literary scholarship, and hence, by extension, the most influential material to which young poets were exposed through formal training, or their own reading.[74]

Among *émigré* poets, only Tsvetaeva was to re-emerge after the 1960s, and for a variety of reasons, the reverence which her work excited in the abstract was not often to be translated into concrete poetic practice by other women writers. Of the many female internal *émigrés*, it was to be only Akhmatova who was to be rehabilitated in anything like a full sense before the late 1980s. As the literary establishment made belated reparation for its former neglect, she was to become next thing to a cult figure for many young poets, not only those amongst her immediate acquaintance, but those from a far wider circle.[75]

The importance of Akhmatova's work is one factor which explains the striking similarity, evident in perspective and lexicon as well as thematics, between post-1954 Soviet poetry and the poetry of the various women poets belonging to the pre- and post-war emigration. Like their *émigré* predecessors, Soviet women poets of the 1960s and 1970s, and *émigré* women poets of the 1950s, 1960s, and 1970s, specialized in sensitive representations of an alienated subject in an urban landscape, in which, by a binary metonymic process, the setting is dissected down to its microscopic components, and a broad psychological time-span is captured through evocation of a significant moment. Occasionally a very abstract version of the natural world, composed usually of such obviously picturesque objects as trees or flowers, acts as a different kind of setting for such work. The ubiquity of such themes and technique means that the work of Lidiya Alekseeva, or the late poems of Sofiya

---

[74] Major editions of Blok and Bryusov appeared in 1960–3 and 1973–5; editions of the poetry of Annensky and Bely in 1959 and 1966; the work of Gippius began to be republished *in extenso* only in the late 1980s. Adelaida Gertsyk, Elena Guro, Poliksena Solov'eva, Sofiya Parnok, Anna Prismanova, and Mirra Lokhvitskaya are only the most important of the Symbolist and post-Symbolist poets whose work has not been extensively recovered for a Russian readership.

[75] The anomalous publication of Tsvetaeva was attributable to the fact that she had returned to the 'motherland': cf. the publication of work by another returnee, Natal'ya Krandievskaya (in *Doroga*); but contrast Irina Knorring, *Novye stikhi* (Alma Ata, 1967).

Pregel, offer no identifiably '*émigré*' alternative to the late work of Olga Berggolts or Vera Zvyagintseva, or to the early work of, say, Yunna Moritts, or to the lyric of such more recent poets as Natalya Vankhanen or Larisa Miller.[76]

Apart from such generic similarities, interesting material from the forgotten past may spontaneously resurface through individual similarities of vision. Like Vera Bulich, for example, Alekseeva represents poetry in some of her work as a painful and inappropriate substitute for child-bearing; and a similar motif is also explored by Bella Akhmadulina in her 1974 poem, 'I envy the well-known custom'.[77] However, Akhmadulina, who is one of the few poets to challenge the polished good manners of much post-1954 women's poetry, is dangerously exact in a physical sense, recording the displacement of maternal feeling not only by guilt but by vengefulness and fear: poisoned itself, the instinct to motherhood also dispenses poison to others. Yet as the woman poet avoids its imperative, attempting to assert herself through talent and physical beauty, she becomes more useless and more hollow. As the paroxical aphorism at the end of the poem has it:

> Все более я пред людьми безгрешна,
> все более я пред детьми виновна.
>
> Each day more sinless in the eyes of men,
> each day more guilty in the eyes of children.

If memory for the poetic emigration is partial, forgetfulness of the women's prose tradition outside Socialist Realism is all but complete (Lidiya Chukovskaya being the single exception). True, certain early Soviet women writers were republished in the 1960s and 1970s, among them Lidiya Seifullina, Marietta Shaginyan, and Olga Forsh, but the presentation of these writers as 'Soviet literary classics' effectively smothered any possibility that anyone might find them interesting.[78] Nor

[76] Pregel', *Berega* (Paris, 1953); *eadem, Vstrecha* (Paris, 1958); *eadem, Vesna v Parizhe* (Paris, 1966); Lidiya Alekseeva, *Lesnoe solntse: stikhi* (Frankfurt am Main, 1954); *eadem, V puti: stikhi* (New York, 1962); Aliger, *Neskol'ko shagov* (Moscow, 1964); Berggol'ts, *Izbrannye proizvedeniya* (369–64); Vera Zvyagintseva, *Izbrannye stikhi* (Moscow, 1968); Moritts, *Razgovor o schast'e* (Moscow, 1957); Mariya Petrovykh, *Prednaznachen'e* (Moscow, 1983); cf. Nataliya Vankhanen, *Dnevnoi mesyats* (Moscow, 1991); Tat'yana Bek, 'Vosem' stikhotvorenii', *Znamya* (1988), 8: 44–7. On women's poetry after 1954, see also Marina Ledkovsky-(Astman), 'Russian Women Writers: An Overview. Post-Revolutionary Dispersion and Adjustment', in Linda Edmondson (ed.), *Women and Society in Russia* (Cambridge, 1992).

[77] On Bulich, see the analysis of 'I have no children' in Ch. 12 above; Alekseeva, 'Ne zhena i ne lyubovnitsa', *V puti*, 4; Bella Akhmadulina, 'Zavidna mne izvestnaya privychka', *Izbrannoe* (Moscow, 1988), 197.

[78] Forsh, *Sobranie sochinenii v 8 tomakh*; Shaginyan, *Sobranie sochinenii v 6 tomakh* (Moscow, 1956–8); *eadem, Sobranie sochinenii v 9 tomakh* (Moscow, 1971–5); Seifullina, *O literature* (Moscow, 1958).

has women writers' want of 'grandmothers' been filled by any affiliation to prose as practised by famous male writers. Russian women writers have produced no Bulgakovian magic fables, nor post-Platonovian dislocations of the accepted literary language by means of non-standard speech. New 1960s and 1970s genres, such as 'beat prose', evolved without their participation, and they made no individual contribution to science fiction, perhaps the most important semi-legitimate genre of adventurous prose which was practised in the 1960s and 1970s. Women science fiction writers, as Diana Greene has argued, people their new planets with all too recognizable Soviet men and women. On the other hand, the impossibility of imagining coherent other worlds has been turned into a strength in Lyudmila Petrushevskaya's futuristic short story 'The New Family Robinson'.[79] Petrushevskaya explores a post-nuclear-holocaust Russia whose horror comes not from the degeneration of moral norms or the growth of strange and alien social relations, but from the entire and exact preservation of claustrophobically recognizable Soviet behaviour despite the event that should have ensured its terminal crisis.

As for metafiction, women writers' avoidance of that has generally been more marked even than in the 1920s and 1930s, though in some of her recent work, the young Leningrad writer Bella Ulanovskaya has been producing meditative accounts of village life, fictionalized travelogues which intersperse recollection and allusion, subjective and objective experience, so as to interrogate the notions of 'women's writing' and of the 'woman writer'.[80] On the whole, though, women narrators are still associated with psychological case-studies rather than with discussions of writing as such. Lyudmila Petrushevskaya's powerful recent story, 'Time Night' (1992), for example, purports to be a 'found document' of paper fragments and jottings.[81] Though composed by a woman poet, these jottings function as evidence of psychological decline, not as an exemplar of women's writing as such.

Excursions into fictional experimentalism of other kinds have been made from time to time. A notable example was Bella Akhmadulina's fanciful anti-narrative' 'Many Dogs and One Dog', published in the almanac *Metropole* (1979), a literary sensation of the late Brezhnev

---

[79] On women and science fiction, see Diana Greene, 'An Asteroid of One's Own: Women Soviet Science Fiction Writers', *ISS* 8 (1987), 127–40; Petrushevskaya, 'Novye Robinzony', *NM* (1989), 8: 166–72; trans. George Bird in Oleg Chukhontsev (ed.), *Dissonant Voices: The New Soviet Fiction* (London, 1991), 414–24.

[80] Bella Ulanovskaya, 'Puteshestvie v Kashgar', *Neva* (1991), 2: 69–81 (translated as 'Journey to Kashgar' in *Anthology*); *eadem*, 'Voluntary Seclusion: The Life of an Old Woman in a Deserted Village', *Russian Review*, 51/2 (1992), 198–203; *eadem*, 'Volchii len' (publication in preparation).

[81] Petrushevskaya, 'Vremya noch'', *NM* (1992), 2: 65–110.

days.[82] More recently, several young women writers, such as Larisa Vaneeva and Valeriya Narbikova, have been moving towards total narrative fragmentation. But such experiments have been rare, and it must be acknowledged that they have also been rather unsuccessful. The most extended and accomplished exercise in unconventional ways of telling, the second two-thirds of Narbikova's short novel *Equilibrium of Day and Night Stars* (1989), is, all the same, a rather laboured exercise in sub-Gertrude Steinian rambling whimsy whose occasional pieces of wit and aphorism appear like small pieces of mixed peel suspended in a bulky and indigestible dough.[83] It is to be hoped that the appearance of work by Nathalie Sarraute may give women writers of the next few generations an inspiration to produce work with a harder intellectual edge and a more exact appreciation both of syntactical improvisation and of language as the subject of philosophical debate.

So far, at any rate, experimental work by women poets, a wholly new development of the last few years, appears rather more promising; perhaps the most talented poet working in this direction is Nina Iskrenko, whose witty verses sift through a variety of clichéd situations and expressions to comic and magical effect, and whose situational and chronological eccentricities suggest a teasing multiplicity of meaning, rather than simply a jejune desire to perplex the reader at all costs.[84]

Avant-garde techniques have remained an occasional enthusiasm only. On the whole, the central means of suggesting transcendence for women writers of the post-Stalin years, as for women writers of the Stalin years, has been references to mysticism and religion. One factor here has been the rediscovery by the post-Thaw Russian intelligentsia of the religious and artistic philosophy of the Symbolist era, which has led, in its turn, to a revival of the association between women and spirituality.[85] But still more important has been the continuing sense of support which women derive from the traditions and rituals of Russian Orthodoxy.

---

[82] Akhmadulina, 'Mnogo sobak i sobaka', *Metropol'* (Moscow, 1979), 21–47.

[83] Valeriya Narbikova, *Ravnovesie sveta dnevnykh i nochnykh zvezd* (Paris, 1989). On Narbikova see also Riitta Pittman, 'Valeriya Narbikova's Iconoclastic Prose', *Forum for Modern Language Studies* (Autumn 1992). Two recent pieces of experimental work by Vaneeva are 'Mezhdu Saturnom i Uranom', *Ne pomnyashchaya zla*, 251–314 and 'Parade of the Planets' in *Soviet Women Writing*, 317–32.

[84] Nina Iskrenko, *Ili: stikhi i teksty* (Moscow, 1991). A recent publication with reasonable representation of avant-garde women poets (about 80 out of 360) is Karen Dzhanginov (ed.), *Antologiya russkogo verlibra* (Moscow, 1991).

[85] Solovyov's poetry was republished in the 1960s, and though other religious philosophers and mystics, such as Berdyaev and Shestov, have been rehabilitated more slowly, many Soviet Russian intellectuals are familiar with their work through pre-Revolutionary and Western editions. On admiration for Berdyaev, see for example Leonid Borodin's novel of the fashionable Moscow intelligentsia, *Partings*, trans. David Floyd (London, 1989).

Here, as in the poetry of emigration, it has been woman as worshipper who has figured most frequently; the majority of modern women writers have manifested the traditional tendency to associate active spirituality with the masculine. Vera Panova's collection of four novellas, *Faces at Dawn* (1969), was the subject of a great deal of fuss when first completed because of its overt, and far from hostile, portrayal of religion in Old Russia; it took the best part of two years to get through the censorship.[86] However, if Panova's emphasis on spirituality was new in a Soviet context, her treatment of spirituality itself was far from radical. She depicts a society in which all the spiritual leaders are men, both inside and outside the hierarchy. In Volkonskaya's 1820s version of the Olga story, Olga's conversion is shown to be achieved by a woman believer; in Panova's 1960s text, it is a priest who is responsible.

As a piece treating religion in prose, rather than in poetry, Panova's *Faces at Dawn* is relatively unusual; but her version of a dependent 'feminine' religious subject is typical. Most of the writers of the post-1953 period have adopted the worshipper stereotype long prevalent in women's writing. Olesya Nikolaeva's recent poem 'Chorister', for example, is spoken by a woman from the Moscow intelligentsia who attempts to forget sorrow at a village church. The speaker's acute sense of being out of place is sharply conveyed, but when she alludes to 'cauterizing passion' in worship, we know that we are back with the 'repentant sinner' motif familiar from Akhmatova, Vera Bulich, and many other of their contemporaries.[87] More interesting is the juxtaposition, in some poems by Inna Lisnyanskaya, of a strong sense of religious belief and a hostility to or an alienation from religion; Lisnyanskaya conveys the anxieties and the resentment which the religious ethic of self-abnegation demands.[88] And in the 'Laviniya' cycle of Elena Shvarts, whose work will be considered in detail in Chapter 15, the portrait of an inconsistently straying and unpredictably repentant female believer (here a nun, not simply a worshipper) is set at a distance by layers of parody and sometimes of self-parody.

Elsewhere, there has occasionally been a departure into metaphysical speculation for its own sake, rather than as arising out of an erotic context. But here, traditionally again, a masculine voice tends to be used. This is so, for example, in Olesya Nikolaeva's moving poem 'The Rich Young Man', an adaptation of motifs from the St Luke's Gospel (among

---

[86] Panova, *Liki na zare* (Leningrad, 1969).
[87] Oles'ya Nikolaeva, 'Pevchaya', *Zdes'* (Moscow, 1991), 29–30.
[88] Lisnyanskaya, 'Sluchai', 'Lampada', 'Vidish', *sama ya sebe zapadnya*, *Stikhotvoreniya* (Moscow, 1991), 50, 51, 63.

them the tale of the man who would not give up his riches to follow Christ in chapter 18, and the parable of the rich man and Lazarus in chapter 16). Nikolaeva's speaker begins with a sonorous list of personal accoutrements, but then goes on to belittle these; and the poem ends with a devastating confession of spiritual paltriness, which transforms not only the story told here, but also its Gospel precedents:

Я богатый юноша, и мне жалко
расставаться с сабелькой из Эфеса,
и с камзолом бархатным с алой лентой,
и с пером на шляпе, и с крепким перстнем,

.   .   .   .   .   .

И отдам я сабельку с портупеей,
и камзол, и перстень, и пруд с аллеей,
и рожок охотничих, и дорогу,
неизвестному молодому Богу.

Юный взор отдам ему, сердце, голос,
каждый вьющийся своевольем волос,
это пенье тайное в каждой фразе—
я, богатый юноша, весь в проказе.[89]

I am a rich young man; it is painful
to part with my honed Ephesian sword,
my velvet cloak with its scarlet piping,
my feather-plumed hat, and my thick gold ring,

.   .   .   .   .   .

I shall give my sword with its braided strap,
my ring and my cloak, my pond and my shady walk,
and my hunting-horn, and my gravelled lanes
to this new young God, to this stranger.

I shall give him a young man's sight, heart, voice,
every wilfully waving hair on my head,
the silent music of all I utter—
for I, the rich young man, am a leper.

Immediately striking in its own right, but also drawing on the exoticism which the Bible, and all religious matters, hold for a culture where they were until recently taboo material, Nikolaeva's poetry has been given particularly wide publicity in the last two or three years. As journals expressing right-wing reaction begin publishing slavishly pro-clerical pieces, amongst them peculiarly dreadful stories and poems by women, Nikolaeva's work serves as an acceptable alternative for Russian liberals,

---

[89] Nikolaeva, 'Bogatyi yunosha', *Zdes'*, 28.

many of whom remain resolutely secular and agnostic in their world-view.[90]

The persistence of the passive feminine—active masculine dichotomy in the delineation of spirituality means that, like their predecessors, contemporary Russian women poets are inclined to escape the dominance of male spirituality by moving outside the Christian tradition to a larger world of myth. The young Leningrad poet Elena Chizhova, for example, has prefaced her cycle of poems devoted to the Trojan War, 'Helen: a Game of Seers and the Blind' (1984) by a piece in which Cassandra speaks of her prophetic gift in metaphors representing a femininity at once stifling and threatening. Cassandra must 'bury her voice in the maw of this steed | Of wood'—that is, of the Trojan Horse which will bring about her own destruction as well as that of her city.[91] Still richer is the poetic canvas of Elena Shvarts, whose range of reference, as we shall see, incorporates material from Russian and Western European history and literature, and from international mythology as well as from Slavonic folklore, in a way that owes something to Jung's theories of the collective unconscious, but also to her own iconoclastic and idiosyncratic talent for montage. Mythic syncretism is also of importance in the introverted, as well as intellectually sophisticated, religious and meditative poetry of Olga Sedakova, whose complexity likewise demands analysis at length.

Experimental prose rarely seems to offer women writers a promising future; religious or spiritual material often (but not always) seems simply to revive the past. And so it is not surprising that the most stimulating and diverse writing of post-Thaw women writers has had a re-examination of the binary opposition between 'realism' and 'anti-realism' at its base. This re-examination has, on the one hand, allowed women writers to illustrate the supposedly infinite possibilities of literary subjectivity, the 'inner freedom' of the writer, in conflict with critical realism's sense of claustrophobia and imprisonment, and so given their work a productive sense of aggression or irony; on the other hand, it has enabled some of

---

[90] Recently Nikolaeva has been published in such liberal journals as *NM* and *Znamya*. Another text dealing with religious material in a way acceptable to Russian liberals is Elena Rzhevskaya's affectionate prose evocation of a Bible-basher: 'Na asfal'te', *Znaki prepinaniya* (Moscow, 1989), 383–5; trans. Catriona Kelly as 'On the Tarmac' in Chukhontsev, *Dissonant Voices*, 386–8. Cf. Lyudmila Razumovskaya's emotional statement of the need for spirituality in Russia, 'I koni ustali, i vsadnikov net', *Leningradskii literator*, 21 Oct. 1989. An example of the awful religious writing now being paraded by the Russian right was Valeriya Alfeeva, 'Prizvannye, izbrannye i vernye', *Moskva* (1991), 4: 3–60; such material is attacked by Ol'ga Gazizova in 'Damy i monakhi', *LG*, 10 Apr. 1991, though she unfortunately does not distinguish swooning pro-clericalism from serious religious writing, and trots out 1920s-style clichés about backwardness.

[91] Elena Chizhova, 'Kassandra', from 'Elena: igry zryachikh i slepykh' (unpublished typescript: archive of G. S. Smith, Oxford). See 'Cassandra' in *Anthology*.

them to adopt a detached, rather than engaged, position, from which they, like post-Romantics or post-Symbolists, have been able to explore clashes of genre and of narrative orientation.

Fusions

Whilst the construction of completely impossible worlds has on the whole not appealed to recent women writers, the incursion of fantastical or lyrical elements into the domestic concerns of critical realism has been a notable aspect of the literary process over the past decade or so. As long ago as 1959, in fact, Ruf Zernova's striking story 'Scorpion Berries' had gone some way towards initiating this process: it represented the ideologically correct material of wartime history in a way that foregrounded issues of individual, rather than national, identity. A young girl living in a village learns that the 'scorpion' of the title, her witch-like neighbour, who is shunned by the girl's entire family, is in fact her own aunt, who has been ostracized for betraying a relative to the Nazi occupiers. The gradual dawning of enlightenment is set against the girl's increasing sensitivity to her surroundings, and most particularly her awareness of mysterious changes in the appearance of an ancient tree in the neighbour's garden, whose astonishing flowering, so late in life as to be ridiculous, occurs at the precise moment when the 'scorpion' is unmasked, thus at once providing an element of narrative surprise, and undermining any possibility of crude pathetic fallacy since the unmasking leads to painful, not lyrical, insight.[92]

Though the *émigré* writer Alla Ktorova was to produce a number of whimsical accounts of Moscow life during the 1970s, notably *Firebird* (1984; began in the early 1970s), Zernova's story was to remain exceptional in terms of Soviet publications until the early 1980s, when fantastical and lyrical elements began to come to the surface again. A pioneer in such matters was Viktoriya Tokareva, whose appealingly unpretentious stories of urban life, many of which were markedly folkloric in tone, concentrated on improbable and preposterous occurrences.[93] It is, no doubt, this flavour of folklore, added to the fact that Tokareva's gallery of characters was drawn from the Soviet working class as well as the middle class, which helped her get her work through the censors, since on a hasty judgement she could appear congenial to the tastes of official populism. However, the folkloric nuances of Tokareva's

[92] Zernova, 'Scorpion Berries' (1959), trans. Ann Harleman in *Mute Phone Calls*, 55–74.
[93] Alla Ktorova [Viktoriya Shandor], *Litso Zhar-ptitsy* (New York, 1984); Viktoriya Tokareva, *Letayushchie kacheli. Nichego osobennogo* (Moscow, 1987). On Tokareva see also McLaughlin, *Images*, 159–83.

plots and narratives also gave her narrative manner a matter-of-fact confidence in dealing with the bizarre, which means that she, unlike some later woman writers, has avoided any obvious and bathetic polarization between 'real' and 'fantasy'.

In the late 1980s fantastical elements started becoming more and more popular; now they are almost ubiquitous. A particularly prevalent trend is the depiction of stylized acts of violence, often directed against men, which are narrated in a half-ironic, half-hyperbolic tone. Such eccentric treatments of unmentionable topics include Larisa Vaneeva's 'Lame Pigeons'.[94] This begins with an account of two small girls who coldly submit a bird to suffering in order to satisfy their curiosity. It ends with a bald, brutal portrait of a male suicide seen through their eyes:

Towards evening, Valera hanged himself in the lavatory. Without finding anything suitable, without having washed himself or prepared himself the way a person should. Valera just hanged himself on his imitation leather belt. ... Valera was slumped on the lavatory seat, his trousers down without the belt to hold them up, and the blood had drained from his body and gathered in the pillar of flesh between his pale, hairy thighs, which had swollen in a most disgusting manner and turned the colour of a headmistress's nose, its size exceeding all known norms. (p. 233)

In Valeriya Narbikova's story 'First Person. And Second Person', one of the two shadowy male characters is cooked and eaten by the other as a 'hedgehog stew', after a series of displays of rivalry and exchanges fraught with danger has taken place.[95] But perhaps the most talented exponent of such material is Nina Sadur, whose plays and stories cannot be interpreted (unlike those of many of her contemporaries) in terms of a simple role reversal, in which women have taken on 'masculine' qualities.[96] Though the 'eternal feminine' in a mystical sense does play some part in Sadur's narratives, it is a most ambiguous force; and in her plays and stories, as we shall see in due course, men and women are locked into bizarre and complex struggles for dominance.

The dead-pan treatment of violence and cruelty in the work of 'new

[94] Larisa Vaneeva, 'Khromye golubi', *Iz kubika* (Moscow, 1990); trans. Rosamund Bartlett as 'Lame Pigeons' in Chukhontsev, *Dissonant Voices*, 215–34; the quotation below is taken from this translation.

[95] Narbikova, 'Plan pervogo litsa. I vtorogo', *Vstrechnyi khod: povesti i rasskazy molodykh pisatelei*, ed. I. V. Del'sal (Moscow, 1989), 119–56.

[96] Examples of recent work which depends on masculinity/femininity reversals include many stories by Lyudmila Petrushevskaya, as well as Kira Muratova's impressive film, *The Asthenic Syndrome* (1990), which consists of a main narrative dealing with an 'asthenic' male schoolteacher who is incapable of action, and a subsidiary narrative portraying a woman whom bereavement has made brutal and violent. (The work of Muratova and Petrushevskaya is to be the subject of a study in progress by Jane Taubman, who kindly allowed me to see an unpublished paper of hers on the subject.)

wave' women writers has obvious affinities with time-honoured and well-established practices in the work of the Western avant-garde (most particularly, perhaps, the 1950s 'theatre of cruelty'). But the violent crime rate in Russia now is (and outside the tourist centres always was) so appallingly high that fictional violence can hardly compete in terms of shock effect. No doubt for this reason, this fictional violence has generally not attracted comment. In the case of Narbikova, for example, disquiet has been expressed on account of the supposed 'eroticism' of her prose, not on account of its representation of aggression.[97] Western readers, by contrast, are more likely to be disturbed by scenes of cannibalism and beating than by Narbikova's oracularly euphemistic references to heterosexual intercourse and masturbation. Take this sex scene (if that is the appropriate term) from 'First Person. And Second Person':

On the bed she kissed him so that he shouldn't have any idea that she might love him, so he would think she was just doing it. But all the same she forgot what she was doing once and said, 'Even if it's not true, say you love me.' And he paused and said 'I love you'. And after that she said boldly, 'I don't love you either, we're just doing it.' She was turned on by his coldness, and she asked him to repeat a caress several times which had pleased her. (p. 135)

It hardly seems worth while working out what the couple are up to, let alone extending to them either sympathy or indignation.

One matter that is said to have inspired disgust in Narbikova's home country is the fact that her heroines often have two lovers on the go at once—though both *Equilibrium* and 'First Person. And Second Person' are so fanciful as to leave it unclear whether the idea of 'two lovers' is meant to be understood in a metaphysical or a physical sense: the central woman character, for all we know, may simply be in love with two different facets of the same man. Apart from this possible affront to male machismo, Narbikova's main offence seems to be that she is the first Soviet woman to become notorious for publishing erotic material. As it happens, far more explicit handling of sexual relations can be found in the work not only (surprise, surprise) of Narbikova's male contemporaries, such as Viktor Erofeev, but also in material produced by some women writers of the 'third wave' emigration.[98] One such is Natalya Medvedeva, a model, performance artist, and *soi-disant* poet. Medvedeva's activities, besides the decoration of her own naked body with paint,

[97] See for example A. Vasil'evsky, 'Bez predel', *LG*, 12 Dec. 1990, 4; Dmitry Urnov, 'Plokhaya proza', *LG*, 8 Feb. 1989, 4–5; cf. the indignant letter of reader A. Prokof'eva, *LG*, 8 Feb. 1989. (I would like to thank Riitta Pittman for these references.)

[98] Viktor Erofeev, *Russkaya krasavitsa* (Moscow, 1990); see also *idem*, 'Sex and Perestroika', *Liber*, 2/1 (1990), 17.

include the composition of lyrics commemorating her own sexual adventures and proclaiming her desire to shock through display:

> хоть бы верить кому-то
> какое счастье
> как они все мне претят
> я б не пожалела задницы
> и выколола бы
> имена всех преданных ребят.[99]

> I wish I could believe someone
> what joy
> they make me sick yes they do
> I wouldn't spare my bum
> I'd make a place for tattoos
> With the names of the boys who love me.

This is perhaps enough to indicate that the relative obscurity in which Medvedeva languishes may be fortunate. Compositionally and conceptually her poetry conforms to the type of girlie magazine 'true confessions' and other erotica produced for the male gaze; it is scarcely surprising that she is given quite disproportionate space in *The Blue Lagoon Anthology of Modern Russian Poetry*, a collection which as a rule underrepresents the work of women poets, and whose co-editor has himself contributed an article pouring vitriol on most women poets and all feminists.[100]

For my money, Medvedeva's work is 'pornographic', whilst that of Narbikova is not, in that Medvedeva's poems are so vacuous that they can have no other function than to excite lust (and to suppose that they can even achieve that end is to give them the benefit of the doubt). In fact, so far from being 'pornographic', Narbikova's writing is not really even erotic. Despite the rather pretentious linguistic experimentation which she practises, she has not managed to create an effective new literary rhetoric for the depiction of previously unsayable experience: her sexual language is made up of banal euphemisms and of nursery terms. Though it is possible that the closeness of this writing to real bedroom chat could be another matter explaining its shock effect in Russia, in a different cultural context such writing seems cloying and tedious. Narbikova finds her greatest strength when she avoids such schoolgirlish

---

[99] Medvedeva, 'Opyat' opozdala na zaryu', in Kuzminsky and Kovalev (eds.), *Blue Lagoon Anthology*, ii B. 751.

[100] Around six women poets appear in *The Blue Lagoon Anthology*, apart from those whose lines, taken out of context, are quoted in Kuzminsky's scurrilous article (prefixed with diagram of the female genitals) 'Zachem ya eto sdelala', iv A. 600–9; cf. also his comments on Elena Shvarts, quoted below.

gush, and instead uses her anacoluthic sentences to create strange visual perspectives in words, evoking a sense of alienated human beings in indifferent landscapes that recalls the stick-figures in shattered grey fields of her own (rather interesting) paintings.[101]

Another problem is that the anti-narrative character of Narbikova's work automatically reduces its audience. It is likely that the more mundane project of finding an appropriate erotic lexicon *within* conventional narrative forms will prove more productive. The invention of such language is currently seen by many Soviet women, not simply writers, as an urgent and central task. There is no vocabulary of sexual relations intermediate between obscene language and clinical terminology. Soviet women can mostly not bring themselves to use the former, and are unfamiliar with, or alienated by, the latter. On the other hand, the common lexicon of love has been devalued by its use in very second-rate official literature.[102] One younger writer who has, however, on occasion contrived to avoid both bald studies in the anatomical and sugary sentimentality is Larisa Vaneeva. Her story 'Venetian Mirrors' is in many ways a stylistically uneven and technically uncertain production, introducing several of the clichés of transcendence (at the end of it the magnified image of a dead child is transported to the sky before the protagonist's eyes).[103] But the story's peripeteia is an elegantly paradoxical scene in which the heroine and her estranged husband are brought back together by force of circumstance, as the hairs of their (artificial) fur coats freeze together in the snow. The sense of mingled heat, chill, reluctance, and pleasure is exquisitely conveyed in a portrayal more genuinely 'erotic' than Narbikova's tangles of naked, but physically and psychologically anonymous, bodies in beds. Another writer in whose work eroticism plays an equally important part is Svetlana Vasilenko, whose story, 'The Saigak Hunt' is an extraordinarily energetic, but also subtly contrived, account of the sexual attraction between two anonymous young people.[104]

If the search for appropriate discourses of sexuality has led to the publication of much that is puerile, banal, and vulgar, it has also fostered one or two worthwhile pieces of writing. Besides, the very fact of such a search has itself helped push back the boundaries of prose writing. The

---

[101] A comparison of Narbikova's work with the diminutive-free erotic writing of Erofeev (in his short stories) or Eduard Limonov would also suggest that Narbikova's sexual discourse is shocking because it is 'feminine'.

[102] The point about the difficulties of articulating sexual experience was made to me by a Russian psychotherapist friend who had worked as a counsellor for patients with sexual problems, and said that her patients had huge problems in finding an acceptable language in which to communicate.

[103] Vaneeva, 'Venetsianskie zerkala', *Chisten'kaya zhizn'*, 159–70.

[104] Svetlana Vasilenko, 'Za saigakami', *Zhenskaya logika*, 101–31.

depiction of sexual relations is quite clearly a matter of symbolic importance, and one, moreover, that has eluded representation in terms of the *realia*-bound world of critical realism. And, as in earlier decades, there is a crucial association of the discourses of sexuality with other discourses of interiority. If the critical-realist tradition has tended to leave authorial control in place, and has allowed only a limited space to the investigation of characters' own discourse, newer women writers, by contrast, are beginning to employ interior monologue quite widely in their psychological portraits. Tatyana Zhuravleva's story 'Black Hole', for example, is a first-person narrative which bravely attempts to represent madness as a linguistic situation, as well as a theme, representing the confused thoughts and feelings of a young woman who reflects on her relationship with her alcoholic mother, and whose reminiscences veer between the apparently authentic and the blatantly improbable.[105]

In poetry, too, uncertainty and self-questioning have become much more prevalent in recent years; the clash between assertion of subjective experience, and a sense of the limitations of that experience, has been a central topic. The Romantic sense of an infinite striving for self-transcendence has been replaced by a modernist association between self-questioning and the desire to scrutinize questions of representation. Inna Lisnyanskaya's poem 'Break Between Courses' opens with an assertion by a woman speaker that culinary activities are an obstacle to her writing, even a threat to her life:

> Не чувствую давно, не мыслю, не рифмую
> Ни местных новостей, ни тамошних вестей.
> Я перестала быть, я рыбу ФАРШИРУЮ,
> Я перестала быть, я созвала гостей.[106]

> I cannot think or feel, I long ago stopped rhyming
> The news that comes my way, over- or underground.
> I've ceased to be, I'm filling fish with stuffing,
> I've ceased to be, and so I've called my friends around.

The reference to the preparation of fish then acts as a running metaphor around which crystallize various paradoxes and ironies to do with the woman speaker's role as poet. On the one hand she becomes a 'netted fish', doubly reinforcing the incompatibility of cooking and creativity for women; on the other, she uses a metaphor drawn from cooking to refer to the poetry of a male guest, who 'stews his vulgar theme in elevated verse'. The two negatives become a positive; through suggesting that kitchen activities are abject both for women *and* for men, the poem

[105] Tat'yana Zhuravleva, 'Chernaya dyra', *Yunost'* (1989), 1: 11–14.
[106] Lisnyanskaya, 'Dolgii pereryv', *Stikhotvoreniya*, 36.

makes for itself a mode of composition neither traditionally 'feminine' nor traditionally 'masculine'; at the same time, by a familiar modernist paradox, the denial that poetry is possible has also become the occasion of a poem.

A similar standpoint is adopted (though with less histrionic intonations) in some poems which Natalya Gorbanevskaya has written since her emigration to Paris. In 'The day of washing and verses', domesticity does not inhibit composition, but itself forms a space in which different and autonomous modes of composition can be explored; in 'I am— maybe no sort of a woman—but I am', the moral imperative of nurturing is ironically appropriated to the writing of poetry: ('So wrap | my verses round your chest, like a scarf').[107]

The hugely popular young guitar poet Veronika Dolina reworks conventional Soviet views of the 'woman's role' in a quite different way in her song 'The Puppeteer', which shows a sinister puppeteer figure manipulating a female puppet and her 'puppet husband'. The poem represents the process of the puppet wife's oppression, recording how she 'can't keep abreast of the washing and cooking', and also how she 'doesn't dare to look' (at the puppeteer? the audience?), though she herself is a spectacle for others. Yet at the end of the poem, Dolina shifts position; the reader is invited to withdraw the sympathy which has previously been solicited, leaving 'the puppet wife' on her own:

Только ей и страшны злодеянья твои,
Только ей и важно покаянье.[108]

Only she is frightened by the things you do,
Only she values your repentance.

Dolina is one of the few Russian women poets who has ever appeared in the pin-up sections which are published by the mass-circulation women's monthlies; if any current woman poet could be described as a star, it is she. Some of her work is as ephemeral and facile as that background might suggest, playing on immature and conventional ideas of femininity. But in 'The Puppeteer' she has written a piece which has some of the strangeness and threat of the popular stage tradition towards which she gestures, frightening both in its evocation of brutality and in

[107] Gorbanevskaya, 'Vremya stirki i stikhov', *Poberezh'e* (Ann Arbor, Mich., 1973), 66; 'Kakaya-nikakaya—a ya', *Gde i kogda: stikhi iyun' 1983–mart 1985* (Paris, 1985), 7; cf. also 'Komu-to podarila ispisannyi listok', ibid. 44. Gorbanevskaya is also the author of some splendidly dry love lyrics: see e.g. 'I'm visiting the lover I wrote about | Twice in my poems already', *Gde i kogda*, 16.
[108] Veronika Dolina, 'Kukol'nik', *Stikhi* (Paris, 1987), 50. See also the same author's *Vozdukhoplavatel'* (Moscow, 1989), which also contains dozens of snapshots of Dolina posing in different costumes and attitudes.

its refusal to resolve the dilemma in which such brutality places 'feminine' passivity.

The last three or four years have seen the first publication of work by several other younger poets who explore similar conflicts between different possibilities of identity. Mariya Avvakumova, for example, interweaves references to manual labour and evocations of art as spiritual activity, in poems such as 'Salted Honey' (1988). Speaking as one who has 'fought as hard as three' amongst the *sans-culotte* women of factories', she talks of how she has 'snatched salted honey', which stands for both soul and speech.[109] And, though in general Russian women poets remain more inclined to Romantic self-mythologization than their Western counterparts, the 'self' which they declare is nevertheless often broader and more complex than the authorial identity which may be fashioned by those of their contemporaries who work in prose; and their work also analyses the relation between 'I' and 'Other' more subtly.

The continuing restrictions on the prose tradition's treatment of interiority are evident, for example, in the work of the Russian 'new wave' prose writer who has become best known in the West, Tatyana Tolstaya. Tolstaya's writing has a *fin de siècle* ornamentalism, but it is certainly not 'modernist' in that it functions by suggesting the frailty of a writerly utterance; nor is Tolstaya a writer of much ambiguity in any other sense. Her narratives maintain a satirist's omniscient distance from the characters, most particularly the female characters. Several of her stories, such as 'Sonya', 'The Most Loved', and 'Hunting the Woolly Mammoth', are withering denunciations of female folly; in particular, Tolstaya mocks the idiocies into which women are led by their determination to play the burnt offering even if the god to whom sacrifices may be made is dead. Tolstaya's attitude is refreshing, given the continuing Russian emphasis on self-denial as a proper end in life for women; but her characterizations sometimes edge towards superficiality, even triteness. 'Sonya' has a certain subtlety because the central character, who appears a perfect fool throughout, executes an act of such disinterested heroism that the idea of 'self-sacrifice' is transfigured. And 'The Most Loved' is at once judicious and hilarious in its representation of a stiflingly well-meaning childless woman who adopts a family, and of that family's vacillations between guilt and sheer boredom when they outgrow their attachment to her. On the other hand, the magical female figures who flit through such stories as 'The Phoenix' remain faintly

---

[109] Mariya Avvakumova, 'Solenyi med', *Znamya* (1988), 5: 177; see also *eadem*, 'O sebe. Stikhi', *Poeziya*, 55 (1990), 44–8; Bronislava Taroshchina, 'Tam zreet svet: s poetessoi Mariei Avvakumovoi beseduet korrespondent LG Bronislava Taroschina', *LG*, 25 June 1990, 5.

tiresome cyphers; and 'Hunting the Woolly Mammoth' is just one of the many stories by Russian writers which, in lampooning the vulgar materialism of the petit bourgeois, achieves only an obviousness which is at once intellectually lazy and itself not free from vulgarity.[110]

The limitations of Tolstaya's capacity to represent psychological profundity have become evident in a recent narrative attempting stream-of-consciousness, 'Sleepwalker in a Fog', which is both over-long and over-worked.[111] In fact, her depictions of adult men and women tend to manifest a shallowness of perception regarding the human psyche, and she escapes a predictable set of stereotypes only where (as in 'Peters', for example), she portrays children.[112] Denying empathy to human beings, Tolstaya displaces sensibility on to her own descriptive prose, and most particularly on to the depiction of objects. It is details, not plots or characters, which stay in the mind. We remember the laundry numbers which the philandering hero of 'The Circle' uses to engineer his liaisons long after we have forgotten the tiresome affairs themselves; the gramophone of 'The River Okkervil', with its horn like a 'scalloped orchid', and the incombustible dove of 'Sonya', are described with a lyrical sympathy, an exact eye, and a verbal richness rarely extended to Tolstaya's human objects.[113] The prose-poetry style that Tolstaya favours has rightly been compared to that of Bunin (comparisons with Nabokov are to my mind less apt, though the thought of how much Nabokov himself would have hated them is entertaining). Tolstaya's narrative techniques also recall those adopted by some turn-of-the-century 'decadent' women writers, such as Zinovieva-Annibal; the difference is that Tolstaya's scrutiny is turned on the external, rather than the internal world. She is a writer not without puritanism, in that the adult female body and sexuality are the occasions of suspicion, and the authorial gaze rests with enjoyment only on women's attire. But the effect of the stories is not puritanical, because inanimate objects are

---

[110] Tolstaya, 'Sonya', 'Okhota na mamontov', *Na zolotom kryl'tse sideli* (Moscow, 1987), 136–47, 49–60; trans. Antonina Bouis as 'Sonya' and 'Hunting the Woolly Mammoth', *On the Golden Porch* (London, 1988); 'Samaya lyubimaya', *Chisten'kaya zhizn'*, 272–83; trans. Jamey Gambrell as 'The Most Loved', in Tolstaya, *Sleepwalker in a Fog* (London, 1992). The view that Tolstaya's representations are essentially ironic is advanced by Helena Goscilo, 'Tatyana Tolstaya's "Dome of Many-Coloured Glass": The World Refracted through Multiple Perspectives', *SR* 47/2 (1988), 280–90.

[111] Tolstaya, 'Sonambula v tumane', *NM* (1988), 7: 8–27; see also *Sleepwalker*.

[112] Tolstaya, 'Peters', 'Na zolotom kryl'tse', *Na zolotom kryl'tse*, 169–86, 40–8; see also *On the Golden Porch*. In a further story, 'Noch'', Tolstaya deals with a retarded adult whose perceptions are those of a child: *Oktyabr'* (1987), 4: 95–9: see also *Sleepwalker*.

[113] Tolstaya, 'Krug', 'Reka Okkervil', *Na zolotom kryl'tse*, 61–73, 16–28. For a judicious appraisal of Tolstaya's qualities as a writer, see Lucy Hughes-Hallett, 'Tatyana Tolstaya: *Sleepwalker in a Fog*', *Literary Review* (1992), 4.

made into flesh of a kind. The inwardness of objects is also, as we shall see, a preoccupation of the poet Olga Sedakova; in Sedakova's work, though, objects are more than simply vehicles for their depictor's untiring coruscation; they tell their own stories rather than being forced into well-defined niches in others' stories.

Both Tolstaya and Sedakova are writers who are profoundly indebted to early twentieth-century literary tradition (in Sedakova's case, Western tradition; in Tolstaya's, Russian), but these are writers who have internalized this tradition, subordinating it to their own objectives. Some other recent writing, by contrast, has worked precisely and deliberately in order to mark its indebtedness to literary tradition, achieving its effects by the use of different kinds of parody and re-configuration. Lyudmila Petrushevskaya's brilliant short play *Columbina's Flat* reworks Blok's famous tragedy *The Puppet Booth*: the love triangle is here placed in an absurdly humdrum modern context, the flat of 'Columbina' the actress, and the grandiose narcissism of Blok's original is parodied as the petty vanities of a fading beauty.[114] As already mentioned, Petrushevskaya's 'A Modern Family Robinson' is a literary parody in that it is an anti-science-fiction story; the hectic pace and crammed detail of Petrushevskaya's narrative also suggest a post-modern emphasis on placing things out of scale, so that the material for a many-paged novel becomes the matter for a short story. A similar effect of parody by reduction is achieved also in Irina Povolotskaya's story 'The Rosy-Fingered Dawn', which juxtaposes the aspirant heroine and patronizing older man of many a nineteenth-century Russian novel, but reduces the scale so that the subject appears more trivial, yet paradoxically also more touching.[115]

All these new directions have gone some way towards breaking down the opposition between realism and non-realism, and establishing the basis for a properly independent late Soviet or post-Soviet women's writing. But there are grounds for asserting that there is (in the case of prose writers at least) still some distance to go before true independence is achieved. As one Soviet critic, Alla Latynina, has acutely observed, many young Soviet prose writers seem to be visitors to, rather than inhabitants of, the literary world.[116] And, whilst women writers are neither more dilettantish nor more self-indulgent than their male colleagues, there are some grounds for suggesting that their dilettantism and

---

[114] Petrushevskaya, 'Kvartira Kolumbiny', *Tri devushki v golubom*, 201–54. On the 'metatheatrical' aspects of Petrushevskaya's plays, see also the note by Roman Timenchik, ibid. 394–8.

[115] Irina Povolotskaya, 'The Rosy-Fingered Dawn', trans. Kelly in Chukhontsev, *Dissonant Voices*, 144–67. A version of this story appeared in 'Uncle Sasha and Anechka', *Oktyabr'* (1986), 12: 188–205.

[116] Latynina, 'Vzglyad na literaturu', *Moskovskii vestnik* (1989), 1: 286.

self-indulgence can have different results. One problem is hinted at in an observation from an unexpected source, a conversation of the early 1960s between the poet Aleksandr Tvardovsky, then editor of *Novy mir*, and a literary censor of the day:

The censor told Tvardovsky that he had been unhappy with one passage in a satirical story by Tatyana Esenina (daughter of the poet Esenin) which had just been published in *Novy mir*. There was a scene in one chapter where a Soviet homunculus is created in a retort.

'Well, you know these women writers,' Tvardovsky agreed. 'What can you do?'

'Women writers. That's it, women writers,' the old man parroted delightedly.[117]

Here we are dealing with a misreading (deliberate on Tvardovsky's part) of a text which, as we have seen, *did* have political implications. But however crass the misreading, it indicates the prevalence of the view that flights of charming, if slightly irrational, fancy are characteristic of women's writing. Women writers themselves have not been entirely free of guilt in the matter. A certain tendency to sugary whimsy in the deployment of the fantastic can be observed; the only writers who convey a genuine sense of threat (and that only occasionally) are Nina Sadur and Larisa Vaneeva. A distinct laziness of imagination can also be in evidence. The motif of flying, as an impossible but banally imaginable event, occurs *passim*; it is, indeed, the single most important signal of the fantastic for Russian women writers. Apart from these faults, one could mention a certain lack of self-criticism, manifested in the inordinate length and repetitiveness of many stories, and a prevalent insecurity of tone: the mixture of declaratory melodrama with facetiae, or of high rhetoric with poetry, can be challenging, but it can also be simply paltry or ridiculous. Here again, the poets often display more sophistication; the work of Akhmadulina or Gorbanevskaya never seems uncertain in its shifts of direction, since these poets also have a sophisticated command of intonation; the energy of Elena Shvarts seldom flags, and Olga Sedakova displays consistent skill in her choices of lexicon and register.

It is widely believed that Russian women writers were until recently a group whose achievements were negligible, and that they have come into their own in the last few years. The post-Thaw period of women's writing is far better documented than any other in terms of subject-dedicated anthologies and critical studies; a reasonable sample of women writers of recent generations has also routinely been included in

---

[117] Lakshin, *Novyi mir*, 51.

general anthologies and histories of Russian literature.[118] The implication is that some writers, such as Grekova, Akhmadulina, Petrushevskaya, or Tolstaya, are of higher quality than their predecessors (Tsvetaeva and Akhmatova always excepted), and that they deserve closer
attention than writers of other eras. In my survey, by contrast, it has been
argued that the writers of the last thirty years have faced very similar
problems to those faced by women writers in earlier generations; and that
they, like their predecessors, have overcome these problems with various
degrees of success, in the sense that some of them have spoken
individually, whilst others have not. I have not found evidence from the
last few decades to make me rethink my sceptical view of the notion of
cultural progress; I definitely do not think that Irina Grekova is a better
writer than Olga Shapir, or Bella Akhmadulina than Anna Prismanova,
or Tatyana Tolstaya than Lidiya Zinoveva-Annibal, and I would insist
that any representative historical, or even critical, interpretation of
women's writing ought not to privilege recent writing at the expense of
the past.

I do not argue in this way out of studied perversity or a desire to excite
controversiality for its own sake, still less out of a desire to belittle
contemporary women's writing. What I wish to emphasize is the need for
an informed understanding of the past in its relation to the present. This
understanding is especially vital in Russia, a country which, like Ireland,
is both bedevilled by historical myth, and forgetful of all aspects of the
past that happen to be inconvenient. It is not until the past has been
confronted that separation from it is possible; to date Russian women
have not made such a confrontation, so that they are still umbilically
attached to past convention. Without a proper understanding of why
'Socialist Realism' attracted women as writers and (especially) as readers,
Socialist Realism will continue to function as an insidious undercurrent
in realist prose. Without some comprehension of the dead-end to which
an emphasis on 'prophecy' or 'religion' can lead, the recent 'transcendent'
directions will continue to share the limitations of turn-of-the-century
poetry. If Russian women continue to believe that it is meaningful to
say, 'I'm not a woman writer, just a good writer', or 'I'm not interested in

---

[118] Standard literary histories list a greater number of women writers for the period since 1953 than
they do for the whole two hundred years before that. See for example Vera Aleksandrova, *A History
of Soviet Literature 1917–1964: From Gorky to Solzhenitsyn* (New York, 1964); Edward J. Brown,
Russian Literature Since the Revolution (Cambridge, Mass., 1982); Evelyn Bristol, *A History of
Russian Poetry* (New York, 1991); Charles Moser (ed.), *The Cambridge History of Russian
Literature* (Cambridge, 1990); Victor Terras, *A History of Russian Literature* (New Haven, Conn.,
1991). An exception is a recent literary history in French, *Histoire de la littérature russe: le XX siècle*,
ed. E. Etkind, G. Nivat, I. Serman, and E. Strada (3 vols.; Paris 1980–7), whose coverage of women
writers is just as bad for the late 20th c. as it is for earlier eras.

women's writing, just good writing', then they will never come within reach of the achievements of self-consciously 'feminine' writers outside the Russian tradition, such as Doris Lessing, Angela Carter, Monique Wittig, or Adrienne Rich, or be able to sense the huge energy which now informs women's writing internationally.

Even so, we should not deny Russian women's writing its own constitution and constituency. The last three decades have certainly been richer in experiments and in beginnings than in works of true conviction and unquestionable importance, but some stories and plays by Lyudmila Petrushevskaya, some poems by Elena Shvarts, Bella Akhmadulina, Natalya Gorbanevskaya, and Olga Sedakova, can stand comparison with the best of women's writing anywhere. In the context of recent Russian writing in general (by men as well as women), the achievements not only of these writers, but also Tolstaya, Sadur, Vaneeva, and of the older generation, Grekova and Baranskaya, amongst prose writers, and Avvakumova, Iskrenko, Lisnyanskaya, and Dolina amongst poets, must be recognized as outstanding. My relative neglect of the critical-realist direction in its more traditional manifestations, and of post-Akhmato-vian poetry, in these evaluations may seem contrary; however, there has been a tendency amongst Western critics, as amongst their Soviet colleagues, to display a certain timidity towards demanding work by women, and it is high time that tendency was overcome.

There are some signs that Russian women's writing may be on the point of a change of direction comparable with that which occurred in women's poetry during the 1840s or in women's writing in general around 1900. In the last two or three years, there has been a strong sense of despondency and lack of direction in the Soviet—or now the post-Soviet—literary establishment. But women writers—at any rate younger women writers—do not seem to have suffered a loss of conviction. The question, 'What shall we criticize now?', has not been heard from women critical realists as much as it has from men. There is quite a lot of evidence that economic change is likely to worsen women's position, rather than ameliorate it, since they are especially threatened by unem-ployment; and, as support for reactionary movements grows, so too will pressure on women to return to their 'true' domestic and child-bearing duties, pressure which is likely to cause resentment amongst the most vocal sectors of the female population, including writers. It may well be that this background will contribute to the development of a full-scale Russian feminist movement, and thence to a revivification of feminist realist writing. The anti-realists, for their part, are quite likely to have more and more pressing reasons to seek freedom and autonomy in literature rather than anywhere else.

If Russian women writers can build on the new confidence which has begun to be evident over the last few years, and develop a sense of writing as self-analysis rather as an explosion of molten talent on to the blank page of a notebook, there is every chance that the beginning of the next century, like the beginning of this century, will see women's writing not only change direction, but also create new perspectives and realize new opportunities. Even now, the landscape of women's writing looks more interesting than it did ten years ago; in another ten years it may require quite different maps.

14

Natalya Baranskaya (1908–)

THOUGH a good part of Natalya Baranskaya's professional life has been devoted to literature, writing as such is an activity to which she came very late. After studying philology and ethnology at Moscow University, from which she graduated in 1929, she spent some time working in publishing. After the War, she obtained a postgraduate qualification by part-time study, before finding herself employment as a museum worker. For the last eight years of her working life (1958–66), she held a post at the Pushkin Museum in the Moscow Arbat, at first helping to set up the displays in the museum, and then participating in its academic programme. In the course of her work there, she also collaborated on several academic editions, including a major bibliography of early nineteenth-century literary journals. Unlike some Soviet museum workers, Baranskaya did not, however, produce any substantial independent publications whilst in tenure of her research post, perhaps because she was a single mother (she had been left to raise her two children alone after her second husband was killed in 1943) and therefore lacked the requisite leisure. It was only after her retirement that she began to write, launching straight into the composition of fiction; as she herself has recorded, the publication of her early stories, notably 'A Week Like Any Other' (1969) then gave her the confidence to exploit the specialist knowledge gained in the course of her museum work, and to produce a series of semi-factual, semi-belletristic articles and sketches devoted to Pushkin.[1]

---

[1] See Baranskaya's comment in *Portret, podarennyi drugu: ocherki i rasskazy o Pushkine. Povest'* (Leningrad, 1982), 3 (references to this edn. henceforth in text as *PPD*). 'U Nikitskikh i na Plyushchikhe' and 'Provody' were first published in *NM* (1968), issue 5, 'Nedelya kak nedelya' in *NM* (1969), 11. 'U Nikitskikh' also appeared in Baranskaya's first collection, *Otritsatel'naya Zhizel'* (Moscow, 1977) (references to this edn. henceforth in text as *OG*), 'Provody' in her second collection, *Zhenshchina s zontikom: povest' i rasskazy* (Moscow, 1981) (references to this edn. henceforth in text as *ZZ*). 'Nedelya kak nedelya' was reprinted in *ZZ*; a longer text appears in *Den' pominoven'ya: roman, povest'* (Moscow, 1989) (references to this edn. henceforth in text as *DP*). The following stories by Baranskaya have appeared in English translation: 'A Week Like Any

In itself all this might seem scarcely worthy of remark. In the context of any Western country, it is perfectly normal for a woman whose professional life has ceased to absorb her completely to begin developing a second career, and the choice of authorship as a second career is not in the least eccentric. Simone de Beauvoir, Anita Brookner, and George Eliot are only three examples of late-beginning women writers who have made their way to artistic esteem and to large-scale success. For all the tenacity of the post-Romantic cult of youth and inexperience in Russia, there have been comparable instances there too: Vera Merkureva, an outstanding poet who began to write when she was in her forties, is one example; Nadezhda Durova, whose memoirs and fiction were composed when she had reached a similar age, another; similar, but more recent, case-histories include those of Nadezhda Mandelstam and Evgeniya Ginzburg. What does make Baranskaya's case unusual is the so-called 'professionalization' of the Soviet literary establishment. The hegemony of the Writers' Union, and the belief that all creative writers require a period of formal training before entering the profession, have combined to dictate that the majority of new writers since the mid-1930s have been graduates of a creative writing institute, particularly of the prestigious Gorky Institute of Literature in Moscow. The creative writing institutes have themselves in turn exercised a preference for young people more or less straight out of school (and in the case of the metropolitan institutes, a school in Moscow or Leningrad). The privileged position of the writing schools' graduates is enhanced by the huge importance of 'connections' in the far from purely meritocratic conditions of (post-)Soviet life generally, and (post-)Soviet literary life particularly. Any young writers of outstanding talent who train at the Literary Institutes will almost certainly have been spotted long before they leave by one of the well-known writers who teach courses at the schools. Whilst the extension of patronage by such a writer by no means guarantees success in placing work, it most certainly facilitates it. To give one concrete instance: a

Other', 'Lyubka', 'The Purse', 'The Petin Affair', 'The Woman With the Umbrella', and 'At Her Father's Place and at Her Mother's' [i.e. 'U Nikitskikh . . .'], in Baranskaya, *A Week Like Any Other and Other Stories*, trans. Pieta Monks (London, 1989); 'The Retirement Party', in Proffer (ed.), *The Barsukov Triangle: The Two-Toned Blonde and Other Stories* (Ann Arbor, Mich., 1984); 'The Spell' in Sigrid McLaughlin (ed.), *Images of Women in Soviet Fiction* (London, 1989); 'Laine's House' in *Soviet Women Writing* (London, 1990). The best biographical source on Baranskaya is the account of her life in Peter Doyle's annotated edition of *Nedelya kak nedelya* (London, 1993). See also Sigrid McLaughlin, *Images of Women*; Wolfgang Kasack, *Lexicon der russischen Literatur des Zosten Jahrhundert* (2nd edn.; Munich, 1992); Pieta Monks, 'An Interview with Natal'ya Baranskaya', in Mary Chamberlain (ed.), *Writing Lives* (London, 1988); Helena Goscilo, *Balancing Acts: Recent Writing by Soviet Women* (Bloomington, Ind., 1989).

recent autobiography by Galina Volodina, whose 1970s work remained unpublished until the late 1980s, attributes her difficulties in ensuring publication of her early stories to the death of her famous patron, Yury Trifonov.[2]

Given this background, Baranskaya's début, aged 60, in the most prestigious literary journal in the Soviet Union, *Novy mir*, might well be termed a peculiar event. Like the emergence of her near coeval and immediate precedent on to the Soviet literary scene, Irina Grekova, Baranskaya's arrival indicated just how important a place was now given to women's issues, and to 'the woman's view', in Soviet official discourse. And in fact both Baranskaya's first stories, 'By the Nikitsky Gates and on the Plyushchikha' and 'The Retirement Party' dealt with the canonical theme of post-Stalinist women's writing, the stress suffered by women in their attempt to balance their professional and their personal life. If the first story was, as we shall see later, rather unusual, not only in its historical setting (the 1920s), but also in its anti-heroic treatment of the Soviet past, 'The Retirement Party', a study of the tribulations of a fit and energetic elderly woman eased out of her work by an insensitive new superior, conformed to the tradition which had been initiated by Irina Grekova. Baranskaya's next story, 'A Week Like Any Other', however, as was made clear in my survey of the 1960s, broke new ground in the frankness with which it handled the difficulties of Soviet women's lives.

That the promptings for the publication of 'A Week Like Any Other' were as much socio-political as aesthetic was suggested by critical response to the text, which treated it as a factual document, rather than as a piece of fictional writing. For example, a full-page article by a woman critic, published in *Literaturnaya gazeta* a few months after the appearance of 'A Week Like Any Other', used Baranskaya's story, in tandem with a popular-sociological article by Elena Polyakova, as the occasion for an agonized meditation on the position of women in Soviet society.[3] Since then Baranskaya has generally been classified, by Soviet commentators, as a writer whose sociological acuity and sensitivity to topical issues vastly outstrip her technical abilities as a writer. And, whilst Western commentators are less inclined to dismiss Baranskaya as a candidate for literary merit on the grounds that she concentrates too

[2] On Volodina see *Ne pomnyashchaya zla*, ed. Larisa Vaneeva (Moscow, 1990), 124.

[3] T. Rezvova, 'U kogo—shchi ne gusty, a u kogo—zhemchug melok', *Literaturnaya Rossiya*, 26 June 1970, 11; the sociological article is E. Polyakova, 'I nastupaet vremya otdykha', *NM* (1969), 12: 192–207. Soviet articles on Baranskaya also include N. Vladimirova, 'Ne tol'ko byt', *Neva* (1981), 8: 181–2; N. Denisova, 'Otritsatel'naya Zhizel'', *Literaturnoe obozrenie* (1977), 1: 25.

much on *byt*, for most people Baranskaya remains associated exclusively with 'A Week Like Any Other', though she has produced numerous other works of fiction.[4]

By advocating that a broader view of Baranskaya's work is taken, I do not wish to suggest that one should underestimate the significance of the 'documentary' aspects of her fiction in the Soviet and post-Soviet context. There are few Soviet fictional texts that confront women's material deprivation and social exploitation as directly as 'A Week Like Any Other'; as I pointed out in the survey, the fact that no contemporary woman writer has yet produced a sequel to the text dealing with the post-Soviet period speaks for itself. Similarly, Baranskaya's most substantial text, *Remembrance Day* (DP 7–262), which interweaves the fates of six women during and after the War, is one of the few fictional studies to give any hint of how appalling conditions on the 'home front' often were. Baranskaya's accounts of Marya Nikolaevna, forced to transport her children hundreds of miles on overcrowded trains from Saratov in order that they may have enough to eat, or Nonna Romanovna, whose children disappear during the evacuation, and are found again in a traumatized condition, bring material into literary tradition which had until its publication been available only in non-Soviet publications, or in oral history. *Remembrance Day* is also one of the few fictional texts by Russian women writers to place the hardships of the war in a broader context: for all these women, evacuation or wartime bombardment is just one of many trials which they have endured. In sum these women's life histories add up to a reasonably full account of ordinary women's experience in the Stalin years. Marya Nikolaevna has spent the last years of the 1930s terrified by the arrests going on in Moscow; Nonna Romanovna has struggled to survive in the provincial town of Uralsk during the famines induced by collectivization; Lora Yakovlevna's father has been arrested during the Purges, but her ultimate crisis comes when Stalin, whom she, like many Soviet citizens, has considered her spiritual father, is denounced by Khrushchev. Held up from publication by the censors for several years, Baranskaya's novel first appeared in 1989. Since then much material which is more overtly iconoclastic has appeared (for example, attacks on the heroic status of the military command); but as a study of the less glamorous subject of

---

[4] On 'Nedelya kak nedelya' see for example McLaughlin, *Images of Women*; Susan Kay, 'A Woman's Work', *ISS* 8 (1987), 115–26; Edward Brown, *Russian Literature since the Revolution* (Cambridge, Mass., 1982), 319–21; Mary Seton-Watson, 'Women in Soviet Society', *Scenes from Soviet Life through Official Literature* (London, 1986), 15–18.

ordinary 'feminine' experience in wartime, Baranskaya's novel can still stand on its merits.[5]

By suggesting that Baranskaya has generally been underrated in surveys of recent Russian writing, I, equally, do not mean to suggest that her fiction is outstandingly adventurous, whether in conceptual or formal terms. On the contrary, she has generally practised the kind of competent neo-realism which is the mainstay of most Northern European literary cultures, and certainly of recent Russian literary culture. The point which I wish to make is this. Baranskaya was subject to the constraints under which Russian official women's writing had to operate between the late 1960s and early 1980s, and hence can be considered a 'typical' Soviet woman writer; but she also achieved more, in a quiet way, than most of her contemporaries. Compared with her limpid and frequently ironic manner, her deft handling of narrative structure and her capacity for stylistic diversity, Grekova can seem laboured and pompous, and Zernova (in her weaker stories) flat-footed and diffuse.[6]

There are occasions when Baranskaya's writing, particularly in her stories for young people, seems simplistic rather than simple, and when her emphasis on the possibility of reconciliation in unpropitious circumstances seems sentimental rather than startling or enlightening. 'The Thief' (*OG* 19–45), for example, deals with a series of thefts in an office; the charmless newcomer who has originally been suspected proves innocent, and the culprit emerges as the established office favourite. The denouement is neither unexpected nor psychologically interesting. There are occasions, too, when Baranskaya's sentimentality inclines to the Soviet cliché: *Remembrance Day*, for example, contains eulogies to 'Mariya, the symbol of motherhood' (pp. 49–50) and the virtuous stoicism of the Russian peasant woman (p. 237), which are hackneyed to the point of embarrassing the reader, whilst the book's emphasis on 'harmony between nations' occasionally smacks of the propagandizing of the official Women's Peace Group.[7] When on form, though, Baranskaya writes both fluently and laconically, yet with a hidden intricacy and depth that elude many of her more earnest and costive colleagues; apparently harmonious endings, and safe conclusions, are almost always more complicated, if read carefully, than they seem.

---

[5] The Moscow weekly magazine *Stolitsa* was, for example, carrying material on the realities of front-line fighting during most of the first half of 1991.

[6] The nearest post-Stalinist writer to Baranskaya in tone is probably Nina Katerli, who shares her humorous and benevolent view of ordinary Soviet life, but who, however, often chooses to concentrate on the perceptions of men. (See Ch. 13 above.)

[7] This judgement may be unfair, since the views which Baranskaya reflects here are, as in 'Nedelya kak nedelya', precisely those of the average Soviet woman of the given generation; but artistically speaking her lack of distance is still a problem.

'Borya's Bicycle' (*OG* 76–92), for instance, a story about an adolescent who finds a cache of money on the street in one of the deprived post-war years, does not point an easy moral contrasting honesty and self-serving rapacity; instead, it shows how Borya's crisis over what to do with the money brings two generations and their values into conflict. The story ends with the boy and his mother neither separated, nor reconciled, by the decision to take the money to the police, as they walk down the street 'silently, not in step, yet together in a way all the same' (p. 92). The formulation conveys less a unity beyond words, than an uneasy and fragile truce. The most 'Chekhovian' of post-Stalinist women writers, Baranskaya combines an absolute sense of moral values (the boy should, we know without a shadow of doubt, *not* have kept the money) with a sense that those who maintain moral values are seldom attractive, and that the actual costs of the imposition of values are seldom met by them.

The narrow-minded hypocrisy of those who dictate how others should behave, or 'the righteous', as one story has it ('The Sinful Woman and the Righteous Woman', *ZZ* 82–92) is a recurrent theme in Baranskaya's writing. Although she is in no sense (as will already be clear) an anti-Soviet writer, whether overtly or at a deeper level, her work is informed by an awareness of what a dangerous symbiosis could link the meddlesome-ness of private individuals and the dictatorial proselytizing of official-dom within that system. The long story 'Lyubochka' (*OG* 124–84), for example, depicts a young girl who openly enjoys all the activities associated with early 1970s youth culture, dressing extravagantly and holding parties with loud music. Her adult neighbours object in the same way that members of their generation might in any overcrowded European city; however, their objections are more threatening, in that, by denouncing the girl to the authorities, they can call on the structures which Soviet society has at its disposal for the control of dissidence. Lyubochka is then subjected to what is to all intents and purposes a public trial of her morals, rather than of the practical nuisance which she has caused, at a court of arbitration. In 'A Negative Giselle' (*OG* 45–56), a young girl is transported to a new world of the imagination by her first visit to the ballet; but her mother, who finds the whole spectacle most disedifying, is able to find words for her outrage in the rhetoric of classificatory and castigatory Soviet official puritanism, damning *Giselle* as 'negative' and 'pessimistic'. Even in this storehouse of *sententiae*, however, she cannot find quite the right phrase in which to describe just what the hero of the ballet has been up to with the heroine, and contents herself with saying, 'Of course, they don't actually show you what's been going on, but you can easily work it all out' (p. 56). Her poverty of thought and vocabulary could not be more clearly exposed.

In line with the perceptions common to post-Stalinist Soviet culture, Baranskaya emphasizes the important role which is played by women in setting and maintaining moral standards. But her interrogation of the valuers' behaviour, and sometimes also their values, means that her representation of women is more multi-faceted than that which characterizes the work of Grekova or Ganina. Rather than standing aside from or looking down on the power struggles of men, many of Baranskaya's women are deeply involved in these power struggles, and often not only as victims, but as executioners. Among the characters in 'A Week Like Any Other', for example, is a woman who, during her heroic record of service in Party organizations, has manifested a dedication so extreme that it extended even to the repudiation of her own children (placed in an orphanage so that they should not distract her from her work). Baranskaya shows how this seasoned 'class warrior' is quite unable to understand the more mundane, but in some senses equally taxing, struggles of women from another generation, those who are forty years her junior. But if female superiors often prove incapable of the empathy that is banally supposed to be a natural attribute of femininity, male superiors, who are often more sympathetic in human terms, do little in a concrete sense to better the lot of their employees. The limitations of male support are entertainingly conveyed in one story, 'Blackie' (OG 107–22), that describes the celebrations for International Women's Day, an annual festival at which, until its suspension in 1992, overworked Soviet women were bought chocolates and flowers by their partners and colleagues as a palliative for the other 364 days in the year. Unable to depend on real help from above, the women in Baranskaya's stories are thrown back on a network of their peers, a rough-and-ready support system characterized by bickering and suspicion as much as by sisterly solidarity.

Baranskaya's hostility to facile didacticism, and to hypocritical, rather than real, gestures of support, is also conveyed in the frequent and ironic references, in her stories, to such mindlessly hortatory authorities as behaviour manuals and etiquette books. Uncertain what to wear for her visit to the theatre, Slava in 'A Negative Giselle' is scarcely reassured by her mother's copies of *How to Have Good Taste* and *The Art of Dressing Well*, both of which dictate that she affect items of dress which, even if Soviet shops could supply them, would not suit her own wishes or her pocket (OG 45–6). In 'First Fruits' (ZZ 103–11), the editor of a Soviet journal commissions a formulaic filler story from a young writer; when a piece of disturbingly imaginative and emotional fiction results, he remoulds it into the proper shape himself. Dictatorial voices of this kind chime into the chorus of conflicting imperatives and statements that resonates in Baranskaya's stories, almost drowning out the words of individual women, who struggle to find words to say what they mean. Sometimes Baranskaya conveys the struggles of these women directly, either through dialogue or first-person narrative, sometimes indirectly, refracting an individual perspective through a third-person narrative. Avoiding avant-garde techniques such as stream-of-consciousness or dream discourse, Baranskaya handles free indirect speech as deftly as the best turn-of-the-century realists.

Baranskaya's structuring of her narratives also reveals both her orientation to traditional realism, and her competence in its strategies. As we have seen, she prefers its favourite concluding device, the ambiguous closed ending, the resolution that does not quite seem a resolution; and this accords with her emphasis on the inconsequential, the inexplicable, in human behaviour generally. Many of her narratives introduce us to individuals who float through experience, rather than learning from it or engaging with it, who are cushioned in their own self-absorption. 'A Lively Young Fox-Terrier', for example, deals with a middle-aged man, the sterility of whose marriage is fleetingly, but tellingly, reflected in a Pavlovian cry to his wife of 'Woof, woof' as he enters the kitchen. Against his own will this man becomes obsessed with a private advertisement for a dog wanting a new home which he has seen posted in the street. Through this notice he meets a woman who attracts him; she turns out to have a violent husband, but the protagonist fails to rescue her, or indeed to decide on any possible course of action, and finally forgets her number as easily as he has learnt it ('it had vanished as completely as if he had dropped it in the river', ZZ 69). Two other stories in *Woman with an Umbrella* deal with similar individuals, both women this time. The title story (pp. 176–91) narrates how a woman wearing white, with an umbrella, appears each day to walk in a park where a collection of Muscovites are spending time during their holiday. A symbol to those who watch her, at first of the mysterious and other-worldly, later of the sinisterly aberrant, she emerges through flashback as a survivor of the Terror, a woman whose life is outwardly entirely meaningless, but who has somehow found her own rationale for existence, and a way to preserve her own memories, despite the disapproval of others. 'Laine's House' (pp. 164–75), describes a Lithuanian woman whose wartime traumas have been sublimated in the careful routines of domesticity, in servicing a house that has now become far more important than family, friends, or visitors.

These narratives may be interpreted as studies in psychopathology, portraits of the morbidly marginal; but they are also celebrations of those who stubbornly refuse to conform, to act and think in the way that is expected of them. Baranskaya's tolerance of diversity and ambiguity is a feature that marks her out from many other Soviet women writers, and makes her in some senses a predecessor of Tatyana Tolstaya—though she is more concerned with women than Tolstaya, as well as considerably less virtuosic. Even in her more conventional stories, Baranskaya reveals some tolerance and understanding for different modes of existence, dealing as she does with women's behaviour in a wide variety of contexts. The Soviet office is one favourite situation, allowing Baranskaya to illustrate the fluid and dynamic relationships between women working in groups; but schools, shops, family, and street life all figure in her work as well. Sharing her contemporaries' marked pro-urban (and more narrowly, pro-Moscow) bias, Baranskaya handles a much larger social range than many of them. She extends an unusually ready sympathy to the struggles which working-class girls live through in trying to define themselves, suggesting that they suffer at least as much from official interference as their middle-class contemporaries. In 'Lyushka's Job' (*OG* 4–18), for example, the central character is a young girl who leaves school to take a job in a shop. Rather than illustrate how much the outlook and opinions of this girl diverge from those of her intelligentsia companions, Baranskaya dwells instead on the awkwardness she is made to feel by her teachers' emphasis on university or college education as the norm of aspiration, and how, when she does succeed in finding a job, authoritarian managerial structures nearly destroy any pride that she is able to feel in her work.

Besides her sensitivity in this respect, Baranskaya also stands out as one of the first post-Stalinist Soviet writers to manifest any empathy towards working-class culture's customs and traditions. In the novel *Remembrance Day*, two of the chief characters, Marya Nikolaevna and Lora Yakovlevna, are members of the intelligentsia, but the other four come from working-class or peasant backgrounds; most memorable amongst them is Lizaveta Timofeevna, who herself narrates her life history, recalling that her unusually deep religious belief was used by her mother to force her into marriage to a man for whom her strongest feeling was dislike. The sense that custom may both sustain and ensnare is illustrated also in the story 'Panteilemon, Panteleimone' (*ZZ* 79–102). A working-class marriage nearly falls apart when the husband first begins drinking heavily, and then starts to be suspected by his wife of infidelity. The code of self-sacrifice to which Marusya has been brought up is effective, but it has its limits: she has been taught 'never to complain of a man who arrives home tipsy—just be glad that he has come back home at all' (p. 80); but the result is that when he does once stay out all night, the marriage immediately begins to crack. In showing how the couple survives, Baranskaya makes no reference at all to the conventional Soviet idea of marriage as the corner-stone of social stability; instead she shows the centrality of private and collective custom to the institution's own survival. Sustained by memories of the shared rituals of courtship, Marusya and Vitya are also supported by the rituals of gender solidarity, and by traditional belief. She is advised by a wise-woman, he by a chance male acquaintance; the fact that the latter's name, Panteilemon, belongs to a doctor-saint, is what finally convinces Marusya that her husband really is 'cured' of his straying.

Another aspect of Baranskaya's fiction which demonstrates her ability to understand the diversity of women's experience is the fact that she, unlike Irina Grekova or Maiya Ganina, very seldom chooses a central character whose life reflects her own—the exceptions being Marya Nikolaevna in *Remembrance Day*, who is exactly the same age as Baranskaya, who is widowed in the same year, and whose professional life follows similar paths. But the woman in 'A Week Like Any Other' who is nearest Baranskaya in age is the inhuman Stalinist Marya Sergeevna, not Olga or any of her friends. The narrative reverses the pattern of another remarkable fictional autobiography, Sofya Soboleva's story of 1863, 'Pros and Cons', where a woman writer in her twenties had selected a woman twenty years older as her first-person narrator. As in the case of Soboleva's story, too, the sympathy with which Baranskaya draws her protagonist is not untinged with irony. If the joke in Soboleva is that the narrator propagandizes a women's liberation which is already hers by virtue of her enviable economic circumstances, the joke in Baranskaya, by contrast, is that the narrator, all sympathy for the difficult circumstances in which her friends live, does not always register the inequalities on which her own marriage rests.

Baranskaya's sense of diversity has also made her one of the few Soviet women writers who has produced outstanding historical fiction. 'By the Nikitsky Gates and on the Plyushchikha' (OG 56–68) is a partly autobiographical tale of a girl growing up in Moscow during the 1920s as the daughter of divorced parents. She is torn between the material comforts offered to her by her father, which ease part of her nostalgia for the vanished family home, and her pride in her mother, a Party Women's Section activist who has no time for domestic matters, and precious little more for her daughter. Showing events through the eyes of the girl herself, Baranskaya neither celebrates the mother's professional existence as liberation from traditional femininity (in the manner of 1920s or 1930s fiction), nor laments her involvement in work as the abdication of femininity in a positive sense (according to the neo-conservative ortho-doxy which became increasingly evident in the 1960s and 1970s).

Instead, she produces one of her most atmospheric evocations of the conflict between ordinary human decencies, and the demands of institutional imperatives, the point being here that the latter also embody the former, so that no comfortable conclusions may be drawn.

If 'By the Nikitsky Gates' draws partly on the circumstances of Baranskaya's own childhood, one of her longest stories, 'The Colour of Dark Honey' (*PPD* 163–223), achieves a similar imaginative empathy in the case of much more remote historical material. The story portrays Natalya Nikolaevna Pushkina, wife of the poet, in the months after her husband's death. Baranskaya's standpoint is much more ambivalent than that of former fictional portraitists of Pushkina, who have tended to see her as a woman of almost demonic frivolity, in large part responsible for the death of her husband, a beauty empty not only of intelligence, but also of human warmth.[8] Baranskaya's Pushkina, by contrast, is a woman who struggles to realize her own morality in a world that constantly slips out of her grasp, who is reduced to almost complete silence by the verbal aggression of those around her, who is confused and perplexed, rather than delighted, by her own physical attraction and by her own body. Unlike other society beauties, she is not prepared to undergo abortions, and so goes to full term every year 'like some woman of the lower orders', as a vitriolic acquaintance, Idaliya Poletika, puts it (*PPD* 172). But for all this, Baranskaya's Natalya Nikolaevna is no shining-eyed brood mare; she fears and dreads the physical upheavals of pregnancy, and worries anxiously over the care of her children after birth. Her hatred of pregnancy and remoteness from the reproductive processes, but desperate contrary sense that her fecundity props up her insecure sense of identity, are exemplified in the phantom pregnancy which occurs after her husband's death. Proud of the social success to which her beauty has given her access, but knowing its ephemerality, so lacking in self-confidence that she seizes with alacrity on the fashionable notion of magnetism as an explanation for the pull between her and Pushkin's rival d'Anthès, Natalya Nikolaevna emerges as a pathetic innocent, surrounded by a manipulative and half-mad gang of relatives, whose persecution of her is dictated by jealousy rather than by esteem for Pushkin. (*His* status amongst them is captured in an aside by one lady: 'Writing poems? What sort of occupation is that for a grown man?' (*PPD* 205).)

---

[8] On 'The Colour of Dark Honey' see also Stephanie Sandler's intriguing essay 'Pushkin's last love: the myth of Natalya Nikolaevna in Russian culture', in Marianne Liljeström, Eila Mäntysaari, and Arja Rosenholm (eds.), *Gender Restructuring* (Helsinki, 1993), which places Baranskaya's story in the context of other representations from fiction, poetry, and memoir.

With the portrayal of these relatives Baranskaya, whose ordinary tone is that of Barbara Pym or E. M. Delafield, edges close to the hysterical world of Jean Rhys. Natalya Nikolaevna's father-in-law fantasizes lubriciously about a second marriage to her sister Aleksandrina, who, however, herself nurtures a private obsession for Pushkin the son, and vents her sexual frustration after his death on her own saddle-mare, whom she keeps barren; the Goncharov heir struggles desperately to keep up appearances on his wretched income, whilst his sisters eye each other with dislike, and his mother tipples on ratafias. All these joyless manœuvres are observed, from within, by a collection of beady-eyed and vengeful servants, and, from without, by the Goncharovs' sententious and envious 'betters', the ladies of high society. The swirling eddies of suspicion and recrimination are captured in a text which is a montage of fragmentary and diverse materials: letters; society gossip; prayers; private reveries; letters planned, but never written, let alone dispatched. And the narrative shows how objects, particularly clothes, acquire not so much a symbolic, as a fetishistic, significance. Idaliya Poletika hates Pushkina because of an undignified squabble over the bolt of honey-coloured silk to which the story's title refers; a trunk of ball-dresses stands both for the Goncharova sisters' memories, and for the shaky honour of the family, as shallow-rooted as its material position, and under constant assault. Many of the dresses have been gifts, an indication of Pushkina's financially dependent status; a maid amuses herself by vengefully riffling through the store. The story's effect is of a society tale rewritten, in part, by the narrator of Gogol's 'Diary of A Madman'.

Baranskaya's other bits of Pushkiniana, also collected in *A Portrait Given to a Friend* are far less original, though they do at least avoid the freezing reverence with which 'the father of Russian literature' is sometimes treated. Some are essays which recount, detective-story style, how points of Pushkin's biography were clarified, others are workmanlike fictionalized accounts of passages from the poet's biography. 'The Colour of Dark Honey' is outstanding not only in terms of this collection, but in terms of Baranskaya's work as a whole. Bleakly desperate and vehement in tone, rather than translucently enlightened and moderate, it could not be more different from the well-mannered realism of 'A Week Like Any Other'. Showing Baranskaya's characteristic virtues (skilled handling of narrative perspective, stylistic variety, sensitivity to cultural pressures) to greatest advantage, 'The Colour of Dark Honey' also takes her into the territory of dreams and subconscious desires, which for her is a new one. By returning to the early nineteenth century, which is usually nostalgically regarded by Russians as the paradisical dwelling-place of cultivation and enlightenment, an escape from the oppressions of the present, and representing this instead as a sphere of nightmare and paranoia, Baranskaya has, at last and in her last major story, entered the modern world.

15

Elena Shvarts (1948–)

THOUGH Elena Shvarts had not published a collection in Russia until 1990, poetry readings and Western publications had established her reputation long before that as one of the most boldly imaginative and accomplished young Russian poets. Born in Leningrad, she had an education there which, by comparison with the well-marked paths usually trodden by Soviet citizens, could only be called bizarre. She was never at a writers' school; she dropped out of university, finding it 'just as boring as school', and then attended a drama school with no greater enthusiasm, though she did complete the course this time. This series of false starts made Shvarts an unlikely candidate for official hand-outs (to put it mildly); but she has all the same contrived to work full-time as a poet since the early 1970s.[1]

Shvarts's unusual talent was evident from the beginning; her early output included not only short lyrics, but also large-scale works (cycles or segmented narrative poems) such as 'Gypsy Songs', 'Black Easter', 'Sale of a Historian's Library'. Both these substantial pieces and her miniatures displayed a confident independence of mind and of craftsmanship; Shvarts showed great originality in terms of imagery, and also in terms of metrics, her use of approximate rhyme being especially novel and ingenious.[2]

Shvarts's early achievement was such that it would be futile to subject her work to conventional linear analysis and attempt to trace 'develop-

---

[1] On Shvarts's reputation and biography, see Barbara Heldt, 'The Poetry of Elena Shvarts', *World Literature Today* (Spring 1989), 381–3. The article is followed by a good translation of 'Two Poems Ending in the Word "Blind"', by Michael Molnar.

[2] The Soviet edition of Shvarts is *Stikhi* (Leningrad, 1990); the Western edns. are *Tantsuyushchii David: Stikhi raznikh let* (New York, 1985) (cited henceforth in text as *TD*); *Stikhi* (Paris, 1987) (cited henceforth in text as *S* 1987: NB this vol. lacks page numbers); *Trudy i dni Lavinii, monakhini ordena Obrezaniya serdtsa (ot Rozhdestva do Paskhi)* (Ann Arbor, Mich., 1987) (cited in text as *TDL*).

ment', steady progress to greater intellectual independence, and technical accomplishment. But that is not to suggest that her work is monotone. Certainly, there are persistent concerns, but these are diverse and varied. If on the one hand she has exploited her generation's drive to transcendence with particular success, attaining its desire of inhabiting a mythic domain, on the other she has been able to enjoy a close, affectionate, and matter-of-fact contemplation of the physical world, including the human body.

To some extent, these two directions cannot be separated, since the core of Shvarts's mythology is the myth of birth; conversely, the study of physicality can often lead her to mythologize or aestheticize the body. In Shvarts's poetry, as in Ariel's song, eyes may become pearls, bones coral. For example, in the large-scale piece 'The Virgin Rides on Venice, and I on Her Back' (*TD* 81–3), rhyme chains suggest links between mythical figures and parts of the body—the 'triton' (*triton*) as attribute of the city is linked to the 'palm' (*ladon*) on which the virgin carries the city, the ceremonially Baroque enclosed in the domestic and miniature. In another substantial work, the remarkable poem, 'Sale of a Historian's Library' (*TD* 34–7), physical and mythical worlds are still more closely intertwined.[3] Here the heroic uselessness of the male protagonist's attempt to escape his own time by contemplating the past is captured in two sets of opposing, but interconnected, images, which suggest that his flight from his immediate world is both a rejection and a recreation of the body. The historian rushes from the 'cloth caps' of the present to eighteenth-century Russia, a domain of 'golden stirrups' and 'mantuasoys', where bodies are kept pickled in jars ('cheek-bones sprinkled in spirit'), and translucent chickens, hatched from hard-boiled eggs, 'have a headless shine' (these latter being references to exhibits in Peter the Great's *Kunstkamera*, cabinet of grisly curiosities). Don Quixote-like, the historian flails his sword at 'hearts that are fleshless'. Yet his apparently life-denying gestures also confer on him the power to create life, to 'give the world an odalisque's shine'; and, like another of his historical 'doubles', Marat, whose 'slipper runs with blood' as he dances, but who is also 'a king', the historian can craft magnificence from absurdity and from physical suffering.

But if Shvarts does not separate the physical from the metaphysical in any final sense, there is nevertheless a distinction of structure and of manner between, say, the poems grouped in *The Days and Labours of Lavinia, Nun of the Order of Circumcision of the Heart* (which purport

[3] For a translation of 'Rasprodazha biblioteki istorika' (as 'Sale of a Historian's Library'), see *Anthology*.

to be the naïve *pensées* of a lively and occasionally rebellious young nun) or the big mythic ode 'The Virgin Rides', and such poems of private self-contemplation as 'I was born with an unlined palm'. If mythical material makes up the fabric of the first group of texts, it is introduced by way of digression in the second, and the degree to which lyric speakers or personae are characterized also varies: the nun of *Lavinia* or the self-confessed sinner of 'The Virgin Rides' are far more obviously theatrical alternative identities than the speakers in 'I was born with an unlined palm' (*TD* 84) or 'Remembering a Strange Treat' (*TD* 13). If the latter poems are not biographical in the ordinary sense, they do depend on the shock effect of inserting impossible or extraordinary elements into what at first appearances seems a confession or a confidence to the reader; rather than making the extraordinary tangible, they make the apparently ordinary intangible.

Shvarts has described herself as 'an autodidact', and she certainly has an autodidact's compulsive and eclectic acquisitiveness for ideas and for cultural material (though, as we shall see, her work is quite without the earnest pedantry that sometimes also characterizes the self-taught).[4] Her mythical poems are many-layered, and constructed from head-spinning mosaics of citations from literature, painting, architecture, from folklore and from popular belief (especially popular religious belief). This overwhelming array is not hierarchically ordered in terms of either values or perspective; it is patchwork, rather than appliqué. As in post-Symbolist poetry, disparity of material may be used to suggest diversity of identity. 'The Virgin Rides', for example, depends on a triad of female individuals (the 'sinner' and speaker, the Virgin, the city) each of which is herself mutable: the Virgin not only moves between her various functions of intervention and intercession, but becomes by turns a 'hag', then a woman 'naked in black lace', and then a 'giantess'. The city exists as a series of Proteanly shifting objects and mythic beasts—tritons, dragons, sea-horses, brocades. Most of these objects and beasts act as metonyms for the city, or as emblems of it, but in time Venice is also given a human identity, as a bather who plunges into the sea: 'You have got so chilled | that it is warm for you in the waves' (*TD* 83). The 'sinner' and speaker has an equally contradictory nature, having 'murdered, lied, fornicated', yet clinging to the Virgin's shoulders as a child rides on its mother (*TD* 82).

Occasionally, as in 'Orpheus and Eurydice' (*S* 1987), in which a horrified Orpheus sees his beloved transformed into a snake, Shvarts's representations of the feminine have a degree of resemblance to Gippius's

---

[4] Shvarts's remark is cited by Heldt, 'The Poetry', 381.

menacing and predatory feminine figures. Or Shvarts may organize her glimpses of feminine beings in a manner that absorbs the traditional positive/negative dualism within the feminine. In 'Earth, earth, you feed on people' (*S* 1987), for example, the earth is said to be a snake who 'rubs rot' into the heels of those who walk on her, a reference that recalls the Christian iconographic tradition in which the Virgin Mary is represented treading on the head of the metamorphosed Satan, and so evokes the customary split between madonna and temptress. But the imagery which Shvarts uses is so energetic and unsettling that it dispels any thought of Gippius, or anyone else. In 'Earth, earth', for example, the earth is said 'to exude black milk like venom'. Similarly, in Shvarts's work the erosion of gender boundaries usually comes about through a much more startling and dynamic process than is familiar from the post-Symbolist tradition of androgyny. Only occasionally, as in 'Animus' (*S* 1987), a trite poem revealing the ill-digested influence of Jung, does Shvarts treat androgyny in terms merely of spiritual conflict. Usually the liminality of sex is represented in terms of the transformation of the body itself. In one of the poems from the cycle 'Horror Eroticus', for example, the female lyric speaker takes the part of Adam, and instructs God to make a new being from her rib:

> Я бы вынула ребро свое тонкое,
> из живого вырезала бы тела я.
> Сотвори из него мне только Ты
> друга верного, мелкого, белого.
> Ни мужа, ни жену, ни среднего,
> а скорлупою одетого ангела . . .   (*TD* 53)

> I would pull out my slender rib,
> would tear it from my living body,
> if You would only make from it
> a faithful friend for me, small, gleaming white.
> Not a man, not a woman, not something in between,
> but an angel dressed in mother-of-pearl . . .

In 'Leviathan', a poem from *Lavinia*, Shvarts contrives a still more extraordinary birth myth: the speaker, like Jonah, is swallowed by a ferocious and razor-toothed whale. But rather than spitting her out, as biblical precedent would dictate, he begins to 'writhe in the pangs of labour', before ejecting her in a 'spurt of blood' (*TDL* 22).[5]

Perhaps the most extraordinary instance of Shvarts's border crossings, however, occurs in 'Sale of a Historian's Library'. The culminating

---

[5] A trans. of 'Leviathan' by Kelly is available in *Nimrod*, 33/2, p. 39. For other work by Shvarts, see Robert Reid's translations in *EP* (1992), 17/1 and 17/2.

stanza of the poem represents identities as entirely incidental before the anonymity that prevails in the 'other', metaphysical, world:

> У входа, впрочем, душ един клубится вал.
> А имена, как жребии мы тянем.   (*TD* 37)

> A tide of souls eddies where we come in,
> and we pull our names from a hat, like straws.

But if this concluding insight is serenely abstract, the explorations of history which have taken the protagonist to it are vivid and violent. As he identifies now with the victims and now with the aggressors of the past, the historian also goes floating from man to woman and back again. In two stanzas which are central both structurally (being placed ninth and tenth out of nineteen) and thematically, he becomes in turn Marie Antoinette, Charlotte Corday, and then Marat. From female victim, he becomes female aggressor, and then male aggressor as victim:

> Идет, острижена, на плаху королева,
> но чтоб замкнулся зтот круг—
> вперед затылком мчится дева
> и смотрит пристально на юг.

> Когда она подходит ближе,
> из-под корсета вынимая нож,
> хоть плещешься в ботинке с красной жижей,
> Марат, ты в этот миг на короля похож.   (*TD* 35)

> The crop-haired Queen mounts the steps to the scaffold,
> but the ends of the circle must be joined,
> so the nape of a girl's neck shines in the distance
> as she stands and fixes her gaze on the south.

> Nearer and nearer she comes: from her corset
> she draws out a knife, and closes in;
> you look like a king for a moment, Marat,
> though your slipper is running in blood as you dance.

The next stanza further complicates matters by using the slippage between passive and active as a general principle of historical philosophy; the organizing instinct is seen as passive and contemplative ('the glint in my finger'), but is also visualized in terms of action and violence ('the ruptured maw of a slaughtered soldier') (*TD* 35–6). The following stanzas then introduce a line of historical figures who are as vividly ambiguous as Marat or Corday, culminating in Peter the Great, whose androgynous status is suggested in two opposing images: he has 'split Russia in two with his new-whetted knife', and yet, in a strangely domestic gesture, has 'spread his serfs on the streets like dark jam [lit.: caviare]' (*TD* 36).

If the above quotations convey the raw power of much of Shvarts's work, they have also made it clear that her poetry would be likely to inspire strong feelings. And indeed Shvarts has been the subject of some particularly vicious public and private attacks by other poets, who have described her as a 'Wunderkind' on the one hand, a 'graphomaniac' (an evocative Russian term suggesting pretentious logorrhea) on the other.[6] A note of petulant jealousy can often be heard in such accusations, and if taken to apply to all Shvarts's work they are patently absurd; but they cannot be entirely discounted. Shvarts is not the most consistent of poets, and her less successful poetry can seem lurid and excessive. 'The Forgotten Pram' (*TD* 11–12), for example, consists of a string of more or less improbable metaphors which lack either representational conviction or conceptual consistency. Night 'has arrived on the edge of dusk | dragging her basket of bloody berries'; 'they' [the child's parents?] 'cry like birds over the ice | as he falls in a fishing-hole as he circles'; the ice then 'rustles a newspaper', whilst 'reason has not gone out | though its holy oil is used up'. Conversely, such poems as 'Aphrodite Goes Away for Saturday Night' (*TD* 85–6) promise more than they deliver: here a wonderfully evocative title is attached to a rather dull piece of fantasizing about a garden landscape. Very occasionally, Shvarts seems pretentious: 'Kostroma—Dionysus' (*TD* 89–91) is an identification of the Greek god with his Slavonic counterpart which lacks any of her usual facility in assembling image clusters, and so emerges as a wearisome exercise in comparative anthropology.

Shvarts does not altogether escape transcendental Russian writing (and painting)'s dangerous predilection for fictions that are hyperbolical and technicolor, but at the same time curiously sketchy and schematic. However, even her weaker work is often redeemed by an edge of humour; her mythic fantasies are never solemn, or pregnant with weighty judgements. 'The Elder Nun' from *Lavinia*, for example, is a naïve and fanciful account of how the heroine swallows a needle in her soup, and then has to ask for advice from the resident wise woman in her monastery; when she spits the needle out as directed, the heroine finds that it has been transformed into a sting (*TDL* 76). The mundane details of 'spitting' and 'soup', and the rattling pace of the verse, transform what could have seemed sheer silliness into a living piece of fantasy. And Shvarts's better writing has an acrobatic vigour that is positively Baroque.

---

[6] The description of Shvarts as an 'alcoholic and a Wunderkind' is taken from Konstantin Kuzminsky and Gregory Kovalev, *The Blue Lagoon Anthology of Modern Russian Poetry* (5 vols., in 9; Newtonville, Mass., 1980–6), ii B. 444. It was another woman poet who used the term 'graphomaniac' about her, in conversation with me in August 1991: her remarks were, it was clear, partly prompted by jealousy of Shvarts's supposedly inflated reputation in the West.

Figures fly through the air, plunge through water, and trample cities under their feet, rocketing backwards and forwards through time as well as space. But however mutable and mobile people and objects may be, some geometrical and textural continuity is maintained. In 'The Virgin Rides', for example, references to 'scales' are picked up and reworked: the Virgin rides on hard, curved, and overlapping 'pantiles | that are heaped like somebody's splayed-out brain'; Venice is a 'dragon with golden scales', whose patterns then suggest the figuring on 'gold brocade'. The sound congruence between *cherepitsy* (pantiles) and *cherepakha* (turtle) is also used to initiate another, and parallel, chain of association: the implied 'turtle' becomes the 'pointed mollusc' on which the speaker dives, its shape in turn suggesting a further progression to the 'crust of bread' pecked by birds, which the speaker makes a metaphor for herself, assaulted by sins.

At the end of the poem, an image of dirt in veined marble is used to suggest both the quality of human life itself, and the final dissolution and fusion of the three female creatures with their load of sins in the hereafter:

И когда мы вживили в этот мир лиловый
Потемневший в дыхании долгих веков
Кровь живую и жилы натужно-багровы
И нечистоты общих грехов

Там—высоко—в космической штольне
            (пролетев через шар насквозь)
Там—Творец пожалеет очерненные камень и кость,
Мрамор с грязью так срощены, слиты любовно—
Разодрать их и Богу бы было греховно,
Может быть и спасется все тем—что срослось.

And when we infused into that lilac world,
Darkened by the breath of the past,
The living blood, the swollen crimson veins
And the impurities of shared sins

There—high above—in a cosmic mineshaft
            (having flown from pole to pole),
There—the Creator will pity the blackened stone and the bone,
The marble and dirt are so fused, grown together in love—
Even God may not sinlessly put them asunder,
Perhaps the growing together's enough.

All the qualities of Shvarts's mythic writing—vigour, but also buoyancy, humour, and inventiveness—are evident in the writing where she evokes the physical world as well. 'Remembering a Strange Treat', for example, begins with a shocking revelation:

> Я отведала отнажды
> Молоко моей подруги . . .   (*TD* 13)

> One day I tasted
> My girlfriend's milk . . .

But the poem does not dwell self-importantly on the breaching of taboo: instead it deflects taboo. Shvarts supplies concrete detail of the process, rather than of its result: we learn that the girlfriend has 'squeezed milk from her left | Breast into a cup', and hear about the sound the milk made as it 'tinkled' into the china. By a contrary set of manœuvres, however, the expected and repellent references to other sensations, smell and taste, are not made; instead, Shvarts switches into the mythic, observing that the milk 'had a taste of bird about it' ('bird's milk' being the Russian term for something so rare as to be non-existent). She then goes on to mention a decently classical literary precedent: that of the daughter who fed her father milk in prison (here recast as 'in the desert wastes'). At the end of the poem, we do finally reach an exclamation of genteel horror, but by now most readers might consider this so belated as to be superfluous. The incongruity of the exclamation is still further underlined by the fact that it refers with loathing to vampirism—a far more acceptable activity, in terms of literary tradition, than the degustation of another woman's breast milk:

> Из протока возле сердца
> напоила ты меня,
> не вампир я—ой ли ужас—

> From the deluge near your heart
> you gave me to drink,
> I'm not a vampire—yeuch! the thought of it!

Shvarts's standpoint here suggests that physical activities are unproblematic for the writer; they are controllable at two levels, when beheld as they happen, and when they are intepreted in poetry. In some other poems Shvarts underlines this point by writing of the process of composition as a capacity to dispose over physical resources with impunity. 'I was born with an unlined palm' (*TD* 84), for example, uses a reference to the technique of palmistry in order to suggest how the speaker has escaped having fate mapped out for her; instead, she is visited at night by a spirit who confers her destiny on her. If this visitation recalls the Romantic tradition according to which a personified 'insomnia' visited poets and granted them poetic inspiration, the 'unlined palm' itself suggests a much more novel idea of the body as *tabula rasa*, waiting to have the results of poetic inspiration inscribed upon it.

For all that, Shvarts's work does express ambivalence towards the physical aspects of femininity. In a particularly fine poem, 'The Unseen Hunter' (*TD* 16), she links the capacity of work to live after its creator's death with the skin of a wild animal cured after its 'brain has rotted, its soul flown'. The birthmarks on human skin, the spots on animal's fur are associated with punctuation marks and letters, and with musical notes; the skin after death becomes a 'palimpsest', something whose original identity will vanish in the curing or interpretive process. A sense of threat is conveyed not only through references to the figure of the 'unseen hunter' who spies out and hastens the end of his quarry, but also by a series of insinuations that the poet's 'skin' is not her own possession even in life. She does not inhabit her skin easily—the marks on it resembling constellations can only be named in language that alienates and even 'frightens' her—yet others have free access to it: some scrawlings may have been 'made by a flautist as an aide-memoire'.

'Elegy on an X-Ray of My Skull' (*TD* 17) is in a sense a companion piece to 'The Unseen Hunter', since in it Shvarts alludes to the myth of Marsyas, the poet flayed by Apollo as a punishment for his excessive pride in his craft. And here again the standpoint fluctuates between identification with the body and alienation from the body. The X-ray image of the speaker's skull becomes a double for her, and this doubling process at first inspires distrust and embarrassment:

Боже, что мне с ним делать?
В глазницы ли плюнуть?
Вино ли налить?
Или снова на шею надеть и носить?   (*TD* 18)

My God, what should I do with it?
Spit in its eye-holes?
Pour it a glass of wine?
Or put it back round my neck and wear it?

But later, the skull picture becomes an interlocutor, announcing itself as the 'brother' of a skull which the speaker has kept for ornament, which had led 'the deathlife of a wilting plant', and had served as a collecting box for drink money at parties. The shift from the revulsion which the skull at first inspires to the sense of odd companionship is paralleled by a similar dynamic of affectivity with regard to the body as a whole: the speaker cannot sense 'skeleton | skull, meat, bones,' in herself, and feels only a fog; yet her contemplation of a life beyond the body is made

melancholy by the realization that no one will 'fill you [the skull] up |
with old soft curds'.

In the occasional poems in which Shvarts deals with erotic material,
her ambivalence towards the body becomes particularly evident, the
addressee being placed in the position either of sympathizer or antagonist. 'Horror Eroticus' abounds in startling images for the violence of
coupling, which is repeatedly compared to murder or to vicious assault.
In the first poem of the cycle, for example, male predatory sexuality is
represented first as a diner stuffing himself at table, and then as the
uncontrollable autonomic reflex of a venomous creature:

> Верно, хочется тебе
> деву разломать, как жареную курицу,
> как спелый красный апельсин
> и разорвать, и раздрать,
> и соком смерти напитать
> до самых жизни до глубин.
> Разве ты виноват?
> Против воли—тупое жало
> вздымается из брюха кинжалом
> и несет томительную смерть.   (*TD* 48)

> I expect that you want
> to take a woman apart like a roast chicken,
> like a round ripe blood orange,
> tearing her, slashing, ripping.
> You want to siphon the juice of death
> steeping your life to its depths.
> But are you to blame?
> Against your own will the blunt sting
> rises up from your belly, a dagger,
> bringing a death that lingers.

In later stanzas, images of violence are reiterated, alternating with
expressions of religious guilt. But in the fourth stanza there is a shift of
mood; the two partners are united by exhaustion and by a sense of
desperate closeness:

> Как ссадина, синяк, любовь пройдет,
> Но вот она болит, еле цветет.
> Казалось, жизнь идет наоборот—
> увял мой мозг, расцвел живот.
> Как пена она, как воздух легким стал,
> живот расцвел, а мозг увял.
> Но он вернется, станет он
> гнездом для двух кочующих ворон.
> Начнется половодье ли, содом,

но он всплывет—вороний крепкий дом.
Войди же в кровь мою, как в новую тюрьму,
а я войду в твою,
и превратимся в тьму.

Like a bruise, a scratch, love's bound to go:
but it still hurts, but it still glows.
My life was running back to front:
my belly in bloom, my brain dried up.
It was as light as air, as foam:
my brain dried up, my belly in bloom.
But my brain's not gone for good, just look:
it's a nest with a pair of wandering rooks.
This may be Sodom, or Noah's flood,
but the rookery is left sticking up:
come here, into my blood, your gaol,
and I'll creep into your blood as well,
we'll turn ourselves as dark as coal.

However, in the following stanzas, there is a resurgence of guilt and disgust, which culminates in the penultimate stanza. Here Shvarts asserts that the impossibility of achieving joy by crude means is inscribed on the body itself, by the 'sneer, etched | low on the abdomen' (*TD* 53).

A miniature which handles erotic material in much the same way as 'Horror Eroticus' is 'And then you said the words' (*S* 1987) which also represents physicality as both a necessity and a distraction. Absorbed in their involvement with each other like two cats—a comparison which Shvarts handles with every sensitivity to the roughness of feline mating and its lack of potential for sentimentalization—the lovers cannot contemplate emotion in an abstract sense, and 'love' stands ignored like an uninvited guest or voyeur.

The matter that distinguishes these poems from 'The Strange Treat' or 'I was born with an unlined palm' is the presence in them of a male spectator or actor, whose intrusive gaze or aggressive predation prevents the woman speaker from pleasurably contemplating the female body in general, or from inhabiting her own body in particular. For Shvarts, androgyny is a metaphysical ideal which may occasionally choose to give itself physical substance, rather than a possibility attainable within the ordinary physical world, and the masculine can be a positive 'other' only in the context of myth. Indeed, outside myth there can be no positive 'other' at all, not even a feminine one, but only a proliferation of different variants of one self (or oneself). And so, despite its physicality, this poetry ignores the topic of maternity, which would raise the ultimate issue of difference within the feminine, and so might ruffle the sense of an ideal, solipsistic contemplation of the feminine body by the feminine eye.

The most sexually explicit woman poet since Marina Tsvetaeva, Shvarts also shares some of Tsvetaeva's powerful laconicism. However, Shvarts is less stylistically monolithic than her predecessor: some of her treatments of the body are quite without the aggression and self-hatred which marked Tsvetaeva's work, and her work often mixes melodrama with humour and self-irony. The folkloric tradition to which she allies herself is not the high-serious lyric song or formal lament, but the various genres of carnival joke and comedy, whose visual and verbal puns and dismembered bodies people her poems. True, Shvarts's relentless sense of comedy occasionally leads to a loss of conviction: the second stanza of 'Horror Eroticus', which shows the woman speaker pursued by a man across a church to a bell-tower, and then shot in the groin, is neither chilling nor amusing; it is simply jejune. But on the whole her poetry uses the ridiculous, rather than being used by it, and has the liveliness and spontaneity of naïve art without being in any way simple-minded. If Olga Sedakova is an exceptional instance of a Russian poet who is a modernist in the Western sense, then, by contrast, Shvarts's eclecticism, humour, and vitality make her perhaps the Russian woman poet who would be best fitted by the label 'post-modernist', assuming that these denominations are taken to refer to distinct but coexisting and complementary types of sensibility in twentieth-century tradition, rather than to successive phases in literary history's linear progression.

16

Olga Sedakova (1949–)

APART from Elena Shvarts, Olga Sedakova is probably the most important woman poet in the post-Stalinist tradition of 'internal emigration'. She began publishing her work in Russia only recently: individual poems started to appear in literary periodicals in the late 1980s, and in 1990 these were followed by a first collection, composed of three separate short books of verse, *The Chinese Journey. Steles and Epigraphs. Old Songs*. Sedakova's earliest collection had in fact appeared four years earlier, in Paris, under the title *Gateways, Windows, Arches*. Until 1990 the Soviet publications had mostly reprinted work already available in this volume, but since *The Chinese Journey* Sedakova has published all her new work in Russia. Some pieces, such as 'The Journey of the Magi' (published 1991) and 'Fifth Stanzas' (published 1992) have made evident Sedakova's increasing preference for long rather than short forms, and her attainment of both intellectual and artistic maturity.[1] They have a conceptual and technical complexity which places them with the hermeneutic traditions of Western high modernism, rather than with Russian poetry's continuing preference for flamboyant exercises in Romantic self-declaration.

Sedakova's lack of official Soviet profile makes her, as she has pointed out in a dignified and resolute statement of her position originally written in 1984, though not published until 1989, one of a 'lost generation'.[2] This generation is made up of those who refused any compromise with the

[1] Ol'ga Sedakova, *Vrata, okna, arki* (Paris, 1986); *eadem*, 'Solovei, filomela, sud'ba', *Druzhba narodov* (1988), 10: 121–3; *eadem*, 'Elegiya osennei vody', *Den' poezii* (Moscow, 1989), 144; *eadem*, *Kitaiskoe puteshestvie. Stely i nadpisi. Starye pesni* (Moscow, 1990), hereafter referred to as *KP*; *eadem*, 'Puteshestvie volkhvov', *Znamya* (1991), 6: 139–40; 'Pyatye stansy', *Nezavisimaya gazeta*, 15 Feb. 1992. The fullest published source of biographical information on Sedakova is Katya Young (ed.), *New Writing from the Soviet Union* (Glasgow, 1989) (programme for the 'New Beginnings' arts festival), 23. A translation of 'Fifth Stanzas' appears in *Anthology*.

[2] Sedakova, 'O pogibshem literaturnom pokolenii: pamyati Leni Gubanova', *Volga* (1990), 6: 138.

'grey terror' of the Brezhnev days, and whose youthful rebellion was
expressed less in a rejection of the attitudes and beliefs of their own
parents, than in a repudiation of the attitudes and beliefs of intervening
generations, which is to say, the successful, privileged Soviet writers,
film-makers, and theatre directors who lapped up fame at home and
abroad during the 1960s, 1970s, and early 1980s. What makes Sedakova's
position remarkable is not her fastidious refusal to condone such
behaviour (which, as she points out herself, was made by many other
intellectuals of roughly her age), but her sense of detachment from her
own position. Her article not only criticizes the servility of those who
benefited from the system; it also ironizes the self-righteousness of their
critics—and Sedakova's own self-righteousness in particular:

'It's all right for some'—that phrase exactly expresses the attitude that's
ingrained in my consciousness, though I might not put things quite so crudely.
'It's all right for some'—the phrase is so characteristic of the indignation that
you get in cases of *less than extreme* hardship. That's the way bitter and greedy
beggars, spoilt and ungrateful servants, talk about their betters. (p. 138: her
emphasis)

If successful official poets and their admirers are Philistines, the puritanical self-congratulation of their opponents allies them, it is clear, to a
scarcely more positive biblical stereotype, that of the Pharisees. Sedakova
does not introduce this term herself. But at the end of her essay, she
confronts its implications indirectly, suggesting that the self-inflicted
penury and humility of an anti-hierarchical Christian mystic and Gospel
fundamentalist, St Francis, should be the model for those who wish to
effectively realize a contemplative self in the world.

   Not surprisingly, a strongly religio-mystical strand also runs through
Sedakova's poetry. 'Fifth Stanzas' hinges on the recurrent image of a
monastery in both its contemplative and its public functions: the
monastery is both a *skit* (a desert hermitage) and a hospitable Serbian
institution greeting pilgrims with fruit and honey. But if Sedakova's
mysticism can draw on Orthodoxy as a convenient and domestic
repository of the spiritual, she is equally at home with Western spirituality (as the reference to St Francis suggests), or Oriental traditions
(which are, as one would expect, worked into 'A Chinese Journey'). In
fact the general character of Sedakova's contemplative poetry is neither
Orthodox nor orthodox Christian, but syncretic. This is evident, for
example, in her 'Journey of the Magi', which both resembles, and does
not resemble, the poem of the same name by T. S. Eliot.[3] References to
aspects of the setting (snow, 'running stream'), and to the difficult

---

[3] T. S. Eliot, 'Journey of the Magi', *Selected Poems* (London, 1961), 97.

progress of the journey itself, appear in both poems, but in a quite different order. Like Eliot, Sedakova sets in to her poem a fragment of unattributed monologue, but places hers at the end of the poem, rather than at its beginning; and the perspective of her poem is in total contrast to Eliot's. His 'Journey of the Magi' is a straightforward anecdote in which a readily identifiable speaker's account of his journey works according to dramatic irony: any reader furnished with the elementary experiences of Western culture is able not only to construe which 'birth' is being referred to, but also to appreciate that the birth which seemed like death *is* a death: the death of the old world. In Sedakova's poem, on the other hand, we have a philosophical meditation on the nature of journeys and new beginnings, whose speculative rather than anecdotal character is marked immediately by the third-person generalization in the first line: 'He who goes so long and so far . . .'. Further, the simple binary opposition of time and place in Eliot (according to which Oriental luxury stands for the old world, the stern winter's voyage for the hard asceticism of post-Christian spirituality) has been replaced, in Sedakova's poem, by a complex orchestration of motifs. This voyager's progress across the steppe returns him to childhood impressions (the sick-bed) and to the familiar, secure ritual of his study at night. But it also brings him into contact with the strangeness of sacred books and cultic objects: 'sight [. . .] runs over the ancient script | as it does over the festival candles on the bushy tree.' Whilst having a particular resonance for Christian believers, these references at the same time point to patterns and objects universal in historic and prehistoric cult, sacred trees and sacred scripts standing for the overwhelming world of myth and religion. Representing a huge extra-textual unity, Sedakova's poems are themselves unified by what she herself has called, in 'Fifth Stanzas', the 'pull of images aslant with silvery gleams': the repetition of certain key tropes, which are often derived from the natural world. In 'Journey of the Magi' such images are strung around the ideas of sight and light; in 'Fifth Stanzas' it is the idea of water, and vessels containing water or other liquids, which links the stanzas: a fish-pond, a scoop of honey, a well, a cup, a cistern, appear one after the other.

'Journey of the Magi' and 'Fifth Stanzas' can be read as companion pieces: both deal with a search for spirituality whose syncretic manner of representation suggests its universality, but which turns out to be limited in gender terms: in both texts a male figure, a magus or a monk, emerges as the central image of self-discovery and the mystical inner life. As a properly philosophical or even theological poet, Sedakova could not be at a greater distance from the deferential confessional pieties of Russian 'feminine' religious poetry as it was and is most widely practised; but the 'women's tradition' in any sense is something which she in many poems represents in abstract historical or anthropological terms, rather than in an empathetic or in-dwelling manner. For example, in a series of moving poems dedicated to her grandmother, which are grouped as the third book of 'Old Songs', a woman speaker, 'the grandmother', appears as the teller of tales, the keeper of tradition, especially religious tradition. Her voice is counterpointed, however, by the voice of an alienated outsider, who speaks about 'the feminine' from the outside, and places it at a distance:

> Женская доля—зто прялка,
> как на старых надгробьях.

> A woman's lot is the spindle
> as on the gravestones of old.

At the end of the poem the voice shifts from this evocation of 'the lot of women' to the contemplation of 'larger' analytical questions:

> Что в груди так вьюга воет?

> Крикнуть бы—нечем крикнуть,
> как жалко прекрасную землю!   (*KP* 71)

> Why does the storm so howl in one's chest?

> If one could cry—but there's nothing to cry with,
> cry pity for the beautiful earth.

Eschewing direct identification with the 'feminine', Sedakova's poetry also effaces all reference to the imputed facts of the poet's own biography, avoiding both familiar confessional genres such as the love lyric, and the accustomed diary-like personae of women poets. She is a poet directly concerned with 'the beautiful earth', or more specifically, as her ode 'The Grasshopper and the Cricket' (*Vrata, okna, arki*, 64) suggests, with the fabrication of beauty out of earth.

Sedakova's use of the 'grasshopper and the cricket' as metaphors for the poetic process carries a heavy associative freight. Her epigraph here is a quotation from Keats's sonnet 'On the Grasshopper and the Cricket'. But where Keats's poem suggests the tangible pleasures of poetry made in direct contact with the natural world, compounded of the sensations of a summer meadow recollected in winter tranquillity, Sedakova is concerned, rather, to represent poetry as an activity of the inner mind, the voice of those who are 'blind' and 'pale-eyed', yet who 'forge oceans | on the anvils of mysterious sound'. Not concerned, as Keats is, with memory in an everyday and accessible sense, the recollection of personal experience, Sedakova nuances it as a universal mythic domain, where the cricket and grasshopper appear as vehicles for the topos of poetry as flight (they however 'above the golden manes | of young and alien horses'). And, for all her overt citation of Keats, Sedakova plays urgently on the most immediate and pressing associations which the word 'cricket' (or 'cicada') has for a Russian reader: these derive from the word's use in the poetry of Osip Mandelstam and Innokenty Annensky. For both these two poets, the cricket or cicada's voice suggests the composition of poetry as a descent to the underworld. And, as in their verse, so in Sedakova's poem, the reunion with earth is no unproblematic fusion, but a hard transition demanding physical death, the loss of identity, a journey 'floating with open eyes | to the deep, as the wounded Tristan went'. The Wagnerian motifs that are borrowed include not only motifs taken from *Tristan and Isolde*, but also from the *Ring* cycle, whose craftsmen-gnomes appear metonymically, through the 'anvils' of the cicadas. These enslaved craftsmen reinforce the essentially tragic view of poetic composition which Sedakova mythologizes here; suffering in life is to be concluded by death and anonymity, the ubiquity of the death motif suggesting death's ineluctability.

The mythic heroes (Tristan, the poet Demodocus) cited by Sedakova in this important ode are men; but it would be a gross over-simplification to see her work as dominated by, and organized through, a suppression of, or escape from, the 'feminine'. As her quotation from Keats suggests, poetry in the abstract is *of* the earth, not just escape from the earth. The artistic identity is masculine, but it is only by loss of this identity through contact with the enveloping 'feminine' medium of the earth that the immortal 'poetry of earth' can be beaten out. Moreover, for all the complexity of this poem's associative structure, its lexicon and intonations are not mandarinic or classically rhetorical: on the contrary, the linguistic medium in which Sedakova's fragments from the past is embedded is unpretentiously colloquial, that of Annensky or Mandelstam's 'domestic Hellenism'.[4]

If 'The Grasshopper and the Cricket' depends on a polarization of 'masculine' and 'feminine' (though one in which the feminine is by no means merely inert), elsewhere, Sedakova scrutinizes the complexity of femininity itself. In a piece from *Steles and Epigraphs*, she writes of 'feminine' phenomena in a manner which is at once remote and intimate, analytical and emotional. The two women in 'Mistress and Maid-servant' are locked into a world whose distance from the viewer is suggested by the technical world 'stele', and by the cycle's acknowledgement to an academic friend of the writer, Nina Braginskaya, 'who has studied this subject in such great depth' (that is, the subject of classical

---

[4] Osip Mandel'shtam, 'O prirode slova', *Sobranie sochinenii* (Washington, DC, 1967–81), ii. 254.

gravestones). The poems in the cycle both represent, and imitate, 'steles', which is to say, upright tombstones, normally prominently placed on the approaches to great cities; on them 'were carved the names of the dead, often accompanied by sculptured reliefs recalling their manner of life or the circumstances of their death'.[5] Each of Sedakova's 'steles' evokes such a tiny scene from sculpture; in 'Mistress and Maidservant', the small portrait portrayed is that of a maid holding a mirror out to her bas-relief mistress, who looks at her decorated self. No personal names or histories are given in these representations of 'sculptured reliefs'; for these names is substituted a different kind of 'epigraph', interpreting the scenes represented by the steles themselves.

The contrast between 'portrait' and 'inscription' might lead one to expect a distanced representation of the 'feminine' like that in 'The lot of women is a spindle . . .' And 'Mistress and Maid' begins by adopting a position of self-declared objectivity, asking what this woman can possibly see in her mirror:

> Женщина в зеркало смотрит: что она видит—не видно;
> вряд ли там что-нибудь есть.   (*KP* 30)

A woman looks in a mirror: but we cannot see what she sees there, one might hardly suppose there is something.

But the poem in fact breaks down the opposition between contemplator and contemplated. First, the commentator turns the dispassionate observation of this woman's self-centredness into an enquiry centred on the nature of selfhood in general:

> Впрочем, зачем же тогда
> любоваться одним и гадать, как поправить другое
> той или этой уловкой? зачем себя изучать?
> Видно, что-то там есть. Что-то требует пасковой мази,
> бус и повесок.

> But if so, then why
> should one marvel at one thing, or think how to handle another,
> in such or such manner; why, then, do we study ourselves?
> You see, then there *is* something in it. Something prompting those
>   pampering unguents,
> those beads and those pendants.

The perspective of the poem then broadens out to take in the servant who stands at her mistress's side, waiting for 'a request she will never fulfil'. At the end of the poem, the mistress's unspoken 'request' to her

---

[5] Howard Colvin, *Architecture and the After-Life* (New Haven, Conn., 1991), 16.

servant is used to make a philosophical point: human life is always a search (though of what kind is tantalizingly unclear):

Просьба одна у нас всех;
                    ничего-то и нет кроме зтой
просьбы.

We all have but one request
                    we have nothing at all but that
one request.

What at first appeared to be simply an antiquarian excursion has become a reflection on human communication; the poem moves from a historical to an empathetic view, and then back to a generalization informed by empathy. This conceptual dynamic is reflected in the poem's metrical patterning. It begins with three near-perfect elegiac couplets, the appropriate metre for contemplation of such scenes in late eighteenth- or early nineteenth-century German literature.[6] But the *sententiae* which follow are cast in fragmentary lines of accentual verse: where the moral should be pointed, the structure of the verse precludes a rounding off. The expected movement away from the scene (to a sententious conclusion) has become a movement towards it, in an incoherent meditation, the first line of which answers an unheard speaker—'Yes, we did not understand each other ...'—so that an imperfect spoken dialogue replaces the perfect mute dialogue of mistress and maidservant.

Metrical and intonational shifts of this kind add to the complexity of Sedakova's work; like such classic Western modernist texts as Rilke's *Duino Elegies*, her poetry fractures the structure of *sententiae* so as to suggest the process of thought. Changes in register may also accompany shifts in intonation; so, in 'Mistress and Maidservant', the impression of a definitive commentary is unsettled by the use of the colloquial particle 'to' 'nichego-to' (nothing much) and the interjection 'eshche by' (I'd say so!). Through these devices, Sedakova can give cerebral material an unexpected flavour of the spoken voice, and so make her poems read as dramatic soliloquies.

The dramatism of her language means that Sedakova, whilst she is certainly an erudite poet of ideas, is not really a *poeta doctus*, or 'learned poet' in the conventional sense, still less a poet merely of the learned. It is in the tension between intellectual and emotional elements that we can see a potential for feminist readings. Like other Russian women writers, Sedakova has little interest in the idea of 'women's writing', an idea

[6] Amongst the most famous German neo-classical poems using the elegaic couplet are Goethe's 'Die Metamorphose der Pflanzen' (1798) and 'Euphrosyne' (1797–8): see *Werke* (10th edn.; Stuttgart, 1981), i. 199–203, 190–2.

which she in fact finds baffling. Her writings about poetry (she is an able literary critic as well as a poet and essayist), such as her article on box symbolism in Akhmatova's *Poem Without a Hero*, have employed the 'neutral' discourses of formalism and cultural history, and have eschewed any reference to gender.[7] She has been evolving a theory of vowel tonality in poetry based on musical notation which has allowed her to make the interesting observation that the insistency of Tsvetaeva's verse depends on her relentless exploitation of front vowels (especially 'ee')—but she also describes Tsvetaeva's insistency as 'hysterical'.[8] But, though feeling no special kinship on gender grounds with any literary 'ancestresses' (in fact, rather the reverse), Sedakova has said that she does sense an affinity with the painting of Olga Florenskaya, sister of the theologian and cultural theorist Pavel Florensky, who, in despite of her brother's directions to the contrary, decorated her canvasses with the oblique lines which he had decreed were 'satanic'.[9] Here, as in the case of Karolina Pavlova, we can see how acceptance of 'feminine' identity is possible once that identity is associated with transgression or marginality. She is a writer of whom one might say (as Julia Kristeva said of herself) 'Perhaps one needs to be a woman to think like this', but not one of whom one could say 'She thinks like this because she is a woman'; the connection between gender and linguistic expression is elusive.[10] And so, if we are to read Sedakova's work properly, we must abandon the thematically-based interpretation according to 'personae' which has sufficed in the analysis of post-Symbolist Russian women poets, and address the question of 'femininity' at the level of impersonal symbolism and language.

One poem that illustrates how illuminating it might be to scrutinize 'femininity' at this level is the large-scale, and at first sight baffling, ode, 'Fifth Stanzas'. The series of vessels round which the poem groups itself have symbolic connections with an enclosed 'feminine' world, and this is in turn reflected in the grammatical gender of the most important such vessel, the 'great thing' (*bol'shaya veshch'*), which is repeatedly referred to in the poem's leitmotiv, 'a great thing is a refuge for itself'. As in Tsvetaeva's *Staircase*, this 'thing' suggests chains of imagery that are not only referentially linked, but also sound-linked: the adjective *veshnii*,

---

[7] Sedakova, 'Shkatulka s zerkalom: ob odnom glubinnom motive A. A. Akhmatovoi', *Struktura dialoga kak printsip raboty semioticheskogo mekhanizma: Trudy po znakovym sistemam*, 17 (1984), 93–108.

[8] Sedakova's theory of vowel tonality was expounded by her to me during a conversation in 1990.

[9] This observation was also made to me by Sedakova in conversation.

[10] Julia Kristeva, *Desire in Language: A Semiotic Approach to Literature and Art*, ed. Leon S. Roudiez, trans. *idem*, Thomas Gora, and Alice Jardine (Oxford, 1981), x.

'vernal', is fancifully derived from it, and *vetkhii* (frail) and *vek* (age, eternity) are also sound-chimes. Like Tsvetaeva, Sedakova makes the 'thing' to which she refers at once obey, and transcend, the dictates of materiality and time: it is associated with eternity and with frailty/transience, and with 'spring', the season at once of death and of renewal. The thing's visual associations are also binary: it is both a 'trap', and a 'secret cistern', a storage-place for what gives life when a city is beleaguered. The place and the medium for contemplation (the 'desert hermitage' or 'cell'), this 'thing' is simultaneously the material that inspires contemplation, and a metaphor for the withdrawal into self that accompanies the act of contemplation.

'Fifth Stanzas' represents a femininity that is at once self-contained and overflowing, like the pregnancy that is insidiously, but powerfully, suggested by the enclosing images of the poem. The poem represents this femininity in terms of a linguistic space produced through assertion of the feminine self. If one (grammatically masculine) speaker laments the insufficiency of the isolated intellect (in a monologue beginning 'O, that is all; I knew that I was doomed | And that my reason died for lack of food'), another (grammatically feminine) appropriates to herself an active existence amidst the world's pleasures, rather than in retreat from the world:

> Минуту, жизнь, зачем тебе спешить?
> Еще успеешь ты мне рот зашить
> Железной ниткой.
>
> Why hurry, life, why chivvy on the hour?
> You'll soon have time to sew my mouth right up,
> stitching with iron threads.

This determination not to subordinate the self to time defies Horace's instruction to 'seize the hour'; but, more importantly, it takes issue with another famous 'masculine' text, Mandelstam's 'Mistress of guilty glances',[11] in which another progression of water and fish images culminates in the silencing of the woman addressee for ever as she is sewn with the poet into a sack:

> Мы не рыбы красно-золотые,
> Нащ обычай сестринский таков:
> В теплом теле ребрышки худые
> И напрасный влажный блеск зрачков.
>
> .   .   .   .   .   .
>
> Не серчай, турчанка дорогая,
> Я с тобой в глухой мешок зашьюсь,

---

[11] On Mandel'shtam, 'Masteritsa vinovatykh vzorov', see Ch. 9 above.

Твои речи темные глотая,
За тебя кривой воды напьюсь.

We have no red-gold scales,
But we are sisters to the fish:
Thin spines curl our warm bodies
And our moist eyes vainly glitter.

.   .   .   .   .

Turkish lady, do not grumble:
I shall be sewn in a sealed sack with you
And swallow your foggy speeches
Drinking the poisoned water for your sake.

Here, as in the case of the Eliot parallel, Sedakova seems to be taking the constituent elements of a sub-text, and arranging them to profoundly different conceptual and ideological effect. An explicitly sexual love lyric becomes a meditation on metaphysics, yet one mediated through a representation of the physical world, where a feminized voice can speak through a displacement of the feminine body. An intellectual contemplation of the physical, 'Fifth Stanzas' is at the same time a reflection on the necessarily real existence of the intellectual world. A central image, the 'nut trees' that grow along the walls of Serbian monasteries, is used to stand for an intellectual and religious poetry which is at the same time pleasurable and of collective benefit. Of all Sedakova's poems, 'Fifth Stanzas' perhaps most achieves that end; and in its combination of philosophical complexity with exact physical presence, this elegy is also outstanding in the context of Russian women's writing as a whole.

17

Nina Sadur (1950–)

THE variously attributed statement that 'we [i.e. the Russian realists] have all came out from under Gogol's overcoat' is probably the most familiar aphorism in Russian literary history. It might with equal justice be asserted that most current young Russian women prose writers of standing have come out from under the overskirt of Lyudmila Petrushevskaya, who is without any doubt the most influential Russian woman writer of the last twenty years. Many of the governing concerns and practices in recent women's writing first appeared in her work: the bleakly explicit treatment of sexuality and family relations, the contempt, ranging from angry silence to insults to outright violence, with which women characters treat their ineffectual or brutish menfolk, the absorption of surrealist or absurdist techniques to shape material long considered the stuff of mainstream critical realism. But in the seven or eight years since the younger generation, most of whom were born around 1950, have come to prominence, the more talented of them have begun to develop their own identities and to move in new directions.[1]

The three writers who currently seem to have most successfully established their own ground, and secured their own identities, are Svetlana Vasilenko, Larisa Vaneeva, and Nina Sadur. Of the three, Sadur, a dramatist who has recently turned to prose, is the only one who shares Petrushevskaya's generic diversity, producing stories ranging in length from miniature anecdote to novella, and one-act plays as well as full-length dramas. She is perhaps the writer who most clearly exemplifies both the new generation's imitativeness, and its autonomous

---

[1] The remark about Gogol's overcoat is also cited, to rather different effect, in the introduction to *Novye amazonki: sbornik zhenskoi prozy*, ed. Svetlana Vasilenko (Moscow, 1991). Not all young women writers are so directly linked to Petrushevskaya: Tolstaya and Narbikova, whose affiliations are to *fin de siècle* ornamentalism and the Paris avant-garde of the 1930s respectively, are two obvious exceptions.

vitality; she is also the outstanding member of the first group of women writers in Russian theatre history to have properly established themselves in the performing arts.[2]

Sadur, who is partly of Tatar descent, was born in Siberia, but left for Moscow after finishing school to study at the Gorky Institute of Literature; after graduating from the Institute, she remained in the capital, and has gone on living there ever since. She began publishing only in her late thirties, and her first work to appear in print, two plays, *New Acquaintance* (1986) and *If They're Spared* (1987), was, in fact, 'published' only in a very restricted sense of the word. The two texts were brought out in mimeographed editions, with tiny print-runs, by VAAP, the publicity and rights-handling organization for Soviet writers, in order to make them available to drama groups for performance.[3] The appearance of the plays, so far from being an exceptional promotion of Sadur's work, in fact bowed to the inevitable: many Moscow theatre-goers were already familiar with Sadur's work, which had begun to be staged a few years previously by the so-called 'studio theatres', fringe drama groups whose official registration as 'amateur' institutions gave them some freedom from the extremely rigid censorship applied to the repertoire of the mainstream Soviet theatre. By the late 1980s Sadur was generally considered the most talented of the 'new wave' dramatists, and her work continues to enjoy a high repute, despite the now rather depressed condition of the Russian theatre.[4]

The plays selected for publication by VAAP in 1986 and 1987 were both relatively conventional, more or less straight critical-realist in themes and techniques. *New Acquaintance* is set in a provincial town, and deals with a new police officer who is trying to impose his official

---

[2] Other notable young women dramatists include Ol'ga Pavlova-Kuchkina, Lyudmila Razumovskaya, Elena Gremina, and Marina Arbatova. See *Teatr* (1988), 2: 28–31, and Melissa T. Smith's survey, 'Women Writing and Re-writing Women's Roles: Universalizing Women's Experience', presented at the AAASS panel 'Women Writers Transcending Reality Today', Nov. 1991. On some women dramatists (though not Sadur) see Phyllis Johnson Kaye, *American/Soviet Playwrights' Directory* (Waterford, Conn., 1988). In contrast to earlier writers who produced occasional dramas (e.g. Shapir, Panova), Sadur *et al.* are committed to the theatre, and aware of its technical specificities.

[3] Nina Sadur, *Novoe znakomstvo: p'esa v dvukh deistviyakh*, VAAP-Inform (Moscow, 1986). Mimeographed edn. of 75 copies, marked 'Sent for distribution by the Theatre Directive'; *eadem, Poka zhivye: p'esa v 7 kartinkakh*, VAAP-Inform (Moscow, 1987). Mimeographed edn. of 250 copies, as above. On Sadur's early career, cf. also: T. Khoroshilova, 'Zagadka Niny Sadur', *Komsomol'skaya pravda*, 1 June 1989; Anon., 'Dramaturg iz kommunalki', *Sobesednik* (1990), 4: 14; O. Volozova, 'Vo sne glaza dushi sverkayut', *Teatr* (1991), 10: 76; Aleksandr Denisenko, 'I rozy, i ved'miny slezki', *Sudarynya*, 28 May 1991, 8; Vladimir Tuchkov, 'Cherti, suki, kommunal'nye kozly', *Paritet* (1992), 4: 8.

[4] See e.g. N. Ovchinnikov, 'Davaite sporit'!', *Vechernyaya Moskva*, 6 Jan. 1988; Anon., 'Mir v drugom izmerenii', *Sovetskaya Sibir'*, 17 Nov. 1990, 1; L. Sumnikova, 'Prem'era', *Novosibirskaya stsena* (1991), 3: 10; Alyona Solntseva, 'Transition: The Theatre Studio', *Theater*, 3 (1989), 21–7.

authority on a block of flats where he is already known to most of the inhabitants as an amiable and harmless young man, and the admirer of Larisa, one of the girls living on the block. The action of the play moves towards a violent climax, distinctly 'Petrushevskian' in tone, in which Misha, a young lad who is jealous of Larisa's feelings, makes a verbal outburst against her mother, and is answered by a direct physical retaliation on the part of Larisa. The other play, *If They're Spared*, is equally conventional in a technical sense, being both mimetic and discursive, but is rather more original in plot and setting: it concerns two elderly village women whose successful urban relatives want to annexe them as cheap child-minders. Though the handling was far more abstract than that in the plays which Sadur was able to publish two years later, this piece pointed forward to some of the concerns which would be evident in her later work, especially in its representation of power relations as unstable and mutable, with violence eddying from different and unpredictable directions (the old women are threatened by their predatory and sophisticated relatives, and yet they also threaten these relatives in their turn, since one of them has strange gifts of healing and magic). And *If They're Spared*'s view of women's culture as located between the mundane and the other-worldly was also, as we shall see, to be extensively developed in other plays by Sadur. Moreover, though the linear plot of *If They're Spared*, proceeding through development to denouement, was again safely conventional, the play gave a foretaste of one of Sadur's characteristic theatrical techniques, in which the dialogue is exact in its use of linguistic idiom, and saturated with references to *realia*, but is offset by a staging whose abstraction suggests less other-worldliness than limbo, the quality of being nowhere.

Two years later, in 1989, a much wider selection of Sadur's work became available to the reading public, when a substantial volume, *The Weird Peasant Woman*, was brought out in Moscow, having taken the best part of a year to get through the censorship body.[5] In line with its clever *trompe-l'œil* cover, representing a newspaper jacket with two tram tickets tucked on the inside flap, this edition provided further examples of Sadur's hyper-realist 'Petrushevskian' style. 'Gah on' (Ekhai, *CB* 44–73) for example, is a numbingly inconsequential, rambling dialogue between two working-class men, an engine-driver who has stopped somewhere on a suburban railway line, and a peasant. The only narrative shift is provided by the arrival of an old woman from a nearby village, who proves to be well on into her dotage.

---

[5] Sadur, *Chudnaya baba* (Moscow, 1989) (henceforth in text as *CB*). Sadur's story-cycle 'Pronikshee', in *Ne pomnyashchaya zla*, ed. Vaneeva, 217–48, is cited in text as *P*.

But the new publication also made it clear that hyper-realism was only one direction in Sadur's work. Absurdism for its own sake was evident in some of the short plays. 'The Strength of Hairs' (*CB* 295–313), for example, is a short lyrical drama in which 'a million hairs' speak either singly or *en masse*, rather like a Greek chorus as interpreted by some turn-of-the-century post-Maeterlinckian Russian dramatist. More a play for the study than for the stage, the drama would be as difficult to perform as Konstantin Treplev's play-within-a-play in *The Seagull*; as this compari-son suggests, it moves dangerously close to the borderline between absurdism and absurdity.[6] Far more successful are other plays in the collection in which the impossible jostles the possible. An indicative instance is Sadur's adaptation of Gogol's Ukrainian story 'Vii' for the stage ('Pannochka', *CB* 230–94). The play's relation to the plot of the original is distant, but it follows Gogol in constructing a montage of everyday and extraordinary: the extraordinary is not integrated into the everyday, does not arise out of it, but exists alongside and intrudes into the everyday at unpredictable intervals. The Romantic view of woman as mediator between supernatural and natural worlds is also appropriated by Sadur in the first part of 'The Weird Peasant Woman', in which the peasant healer and sorceress, a subsidiary character in *If They're Spared*, is translated to centre stage, appearing apparition-like in the middle of potato fields to a woman who has been sent from the city for compulsory manual work. The peasant woman's speeches are laconically everyday and matter-of-fact, yet every so often she slips into myth, drawing out strange riddling narratives that defy her interlocutor's banal attempts to classify her milieu. A question about soil erosion, for example, provokes a discourse on the 'three whales' who, according to Russian folk cosmogony, hold the world on their backs:

PEASANT WOMAN. Give that wellie here! [*Snatches the boot and puts it on.*]
LIDIYA PETROVNA. I know who you are. You're something elemental.
PEASANT WOMAN. So why do you call me auntie?
LIDIYA PETROVNA. I can't say. But you're not a real person. You're . . . Why is the earth like that?
PEASANT WOMAN. The top's washed off.
LIDIYA PETROVNA. Washed off? What do you mean.
PEASANT WOMAN. It's gone in the sea.
LIDIYA PETROVNA. What sea?
PEASANT WOMAN. Don't you know anything? What does the earth float in?
LIDIYA PETROVNA. In the cosmos, I suppose.

---

[6] Another play in the same vein is 'Krasnyi paradiz', *Novye amazonki*, 255–74, whose denouement consists of a man slicing himself in half. In Sadur's better plays the violence is more plausible, and hence more threatening.

PEASANT WOMAN. That's right, in the cosmos, the cosmos. Look, my heel's come off, it's all your fault.
LIDIYA PETROVNA. The cosmos? Bloody woman!
PEASANT WOMAN. The earth floats in the sea, Lida. On the backs of three whales. The earth's skin all split up and peeled off, now she's all fresh and smooth again, fresh as a pickled apple, smooth as a fish's skin. (*CB* 19)

By so mythologizing the world, the 'weird peasant woman' puts an end to the existence of the ordinary world for Lidiya Petrovna. But if Sadur is arguing here that language creates reality, she is equally concerned with the limitations of language. In the second part of 'The Weird Peasant Woman', Lidiya Petrovna returns to her ordinary office life, where she entirely fails to persuade her colleagues of the momentous cosmic change that has taken place. 'You're talking poetry, and I can't understand you, but I like listening anyway,' says one man (*CB* 30).

Sadur herself is often 'talking poetry'; her plays, whilst not sharing the metrical patterns of 'verse', frequently incorporate 'poetic' techniques. 'The Nose' (*CB* 161–87) begins with a musical setting of an absurdist poem by Olga Kovalevskaya, whose linguistic oddities reverberate through the play, as the mundane conversations and inept gestures of friendship amongst a group of Moscow students suddenly become self-examination or confession. Such changes of tone are underlined in Sadur's plays by sudden alterations in dramatic technique: 'The Weird Peasant Woman', for example, ends with a 'dumb scene', turning verbal drama into visual drama.

In the best of Sadur's plays, shifting linguistic strategies are tied to a complex examination of identity and of power relations. In 'Mongrel', the bleak and grim opener to a diptych of short plays, 'The Dawn Rises', for example, a married couple's sickly expressions of affection for each other turn out to conceal depths of aggression and hatred; rather than being the catalyst for their conflict, a young adolescent, Egor, whom they have adopted, is drawn into their orgy of self-destruction against his will. Both the other-worldly associations of marginal feminine roles, and the qualities of 'poetic language' are treated ambivalently, as Zoya, the wife, tries to persuade Egor to murder her, saying that she 'dreams of a cloak covered in stars' (*CB* 213). In 'Frozen' (*CB* 141–59; see also *Anthology*), a short four-hander set in a Soviet theatre, where a group of women is cleaning the front lobby, women's conventional role as culture-bearer and muse is ironized as conversation floats unpredictably between the banal and the elevated, or blends the two inextricably. Most impressive of all is the full-length play 'The Trapped Swallow', a powerful and threatening study of how a married couple's relationship is gradually destroyed by a psychotherapist, Darya, who is attempting to cure the wife, Alla, of memory loss. The counsellor affects a neutral and disinterested standpoint whilst in fact manipulating the insecurities of her patients; her therapy, so far from reassuring them of their 'real' identities, actually strips them of any identity whatever. In an early scene, for example, Darya persuades Alla that the man whom she thinks of as her husband is in fact a chance acquaintance:

DARYA. [. . .] Since you managed to speak to him as though you'd known him for ten years at least, they let you out. They were sure you really were you.
ALLOCHKA. But I'm not me.
DARYA. Of course you're not. But all they know in the clinic is that you're not completely sane yet, they know that you've no memory of the events that must have provoked your reactive psychosis, so you'll have to see the doctor again in a week or so. Something has to be done.
ALLOCHKA. You have an odd way of putting things. Worrying, really. Am I in some sort of danger?
DARYA. I can't say. I don't know you, do I? [*Drops the broken bits of the ashtray on the floor, then wraps them in paper and puts them down the waste disposal chute.*]
ALLOCHKA. You threw them away.
DARYA. You don't remember anything about them.
ALLOCHKA. You're angry with me, aren't you?
DARYA. No.
ALLOCHKA. I have this feeling that you're waiting for something.
DARYA. All I'm waiting for is for you to get your memory back, and then . . .
ALLOCHKA. What then?
DARYA. Then you and I can get to know each other.   (CB 86)

Having stripped her patients of any independent sense of reality, Darya then writes them in to her own narrative, persuading Andrei, the husband, that he is in fact involved with another woman, Liza, and assuring the couple that a crime perpetrated against her nephew gives her connections with them that are far more than professional. Woman as confidante and nurturer is transformed into woman as aggressor; 'I can't talk woman's talk,' protests a man produced by Darya as witness to Allochka's supposed earlier self, and baffled by Darya's manipulations (CB 115).

In composing roles for others, this female bully, however, also loses her own sense of self. Convinced by Darya's arguments that life is useless, Allochka jumps out of the window of her flat. Yet in this apparent success also lies Darya's greatest failure: she loses control, blaming Allochka's 'silence' for what has happened, and abdicating power through the abdication of responsibility. The end of the play finds her 'sitting on Allochka's chair, copying her pose exactly'. In finding her authority through her victim, the aggressor has become her victim, the violator the object of violation.

The articulation from one kind of subjectivity to another through shifting power relations is a theme that is also extensively developed in Sadur's narrative fiction. Though Sadur herself has praised her 'literary mentors' for the fact that 'they never lied in what they wrote', her own group of anecdotes, 'Things that Came Up', which was published in the innovative anthology *She Who Recalls No Evil*, is in fact a whole collection of lies. It is preceded by a health warning, suggesting that the composition of deceptive and 'unstable' pictures such as these might threaten the sanity:

It's like the summer air—at first everything looks ordinary and clear, but then it seems to be stretched and jolted out of shape, as though this weren't an image of reality, but a picture taken from reality, as though the warm air were trembling, eddying, and oozing in all directions.

But humanity should avoid all this; our age, the most just, the most humane of all ages, has closed its eyes to all this, so that man may not be frightened by anything foggy, anything which doesn't fit in to life as we usually understand it.

Anyone who is so stubborn that he still wants to investigate *this* is doomed. He will certainly go mad, or die, or take to the bottle. (P 217)

The stories do indeed follow the pattern suggested by this introduction, distorting the apparently familiar and recognizable in unexpected, and disturbing, ways, which make 'the truth' far from readily appreciable.

Many of Sadur's themes here are those common to the new generation of Russian women writers as a whole. The modish interest in magical and strange occurrences is evident in, for example, 'The Witch's Tears' (P 244–9), which relates how a young girl who consults a wise woman in order to avenge herself on her boyfriend finds that the spell in fact rebounds on her, condemning her to spend eternity as an impotently furious water spirit. Violence figures in several of the stories, and a particular prominence is given (yet again) to violence against men. 'The Two Fiancées' (P 229–31), deals with the mysterious suicide of an Afghan veteran after one of the two women to whom he was engaged rejects him. 'The Worm-Ridden Lad' (P 234–5) is a diatribe against the 'sham' of masculinity, which is seen as a 'mask' covering a skull crawling with maggots. The female narrator, typical of the current feminine sensibility in her despairing cynicism, advises her readers to do as they would not be done by, to use violence to pre-empt violence: 'Treat him like you should—kick him right in the head, or else he'll come over and eat and drink up all you have' (p. 235).

But the stories also give weight to another fashion of the moment: the representation of counter-cultural, 'decadent' activities by women. The central character of 'The Blue Hand' (*P* 238–40), for example, is a young woman who 'liked a drop now and again, and she had male company quite a lot' (*P* 238). But in contradistinction to many other writers, Sadur does not employ such themes for their own shock value; she weaves them into a complicated formal and linguistic framework. The point is not the what, but the how: the oddest of these stories are not those which deal in the supernatural, or the self-evidently peculiar, but those in which ordinariness is so transformed as to seem uncannier than magic.

This transformation is often traceable to narrative structure (the 'wrong' parts of the story are emphasized) or to an incongruity between the events which are described and the tone in which they are depicted. 'The Little Red-Haired Man' (*P* 220–4), which tells how a young college student ends up sharing a flat with a sorceress, may deal with the improbable, but its narrative manner is consistent, and its function as entertaining fairy-tale, or tall story, is readily appreciable. On the other hand, 'A Flash of Light' (*P* 217–20), the perfectly plausible history of how a girl eventually gave in and married a man whom she found boring and unattractive, is narrated so that these banal events seem both odd and sinister. The story begins in a reassuringly anecdotal manner ('Something happened to this girl I knew at college') which begins to grate more and more as the narrative proceeds. Finally, the oddest events in the text are squeezed into a short concluding paragraph. Olga did get married, we learn, but she said, 'He'll be crippled very soon in any case', and this disablement did indeed come about. The narrator then reports, with no preamble of any kind, that 'Olga was perfectly happy after the divorce', before concluding, 'And that was the end of it, really' (*P* 219). The end of quite what is not clear. Similarly, 'The Two Fiancées' breaks off half-way through the perfectly transparent story of how the Afghan veteran killed himself, despite the 'double indemnity' of being engaged to two women at once, and moves to a digression on the oddness of veterans in general. This digression, for all its authoritative tone, proves to be entirely inconsequential and irrelevant: the narrator's friend's brother, we learn, has gone mad 'because they all catch some fungus from all that dirt in the army'. And in any event, this digression does not help explain the central case, because, as the narrator herself ineptly concludes, 'There was still something mysterious about Kolya and his two brides' (*P* 231). Though the jocular tone of the piece is remarkably tasteless when applied to material as tragic and explosive as the Afghan War, 'The Two Fiancées' is not merely or even mainly an off-key joke: the neat resolution anticipated by anecdotal form (in which everything has to be resolved to a humorous *pointe*) is withheld: nothing can be explained, after all, and nothing interpreted, and so there is nothing to laugh at (except in bewilderment).

Generally, any message that one might hope to derive from one strand in these stories is refused or undermined by another element. As in her plays, Sadur constructs patterns of bullying and exploitation whose apparent obviousness is disrupted by unexpected peripeteiai of plot, or by shifts in generic convention or in style. In 'The Bad Girls' (*P* 235–8) the narrator, who has been the rival of her friend Emka for the affections of a thug named Garri, is able, through a ruse, to transfer Garri's feelings to herself. The shock effect of the story lies less in this alteration of circumstances than in the narrator's attitude: recognizing that Garri has ill-treated her friend, she is yet determined to inflict Emka's fate on herself:

Anyway, he beats her. Emka gets wound up easily, once she got pissed and she started yelling. He says to her, 'Shut up, the neighbours'll hear.' But she just goes on shouting and stamping. So he tells her again, 'Shut up. The neighbours can hear you.' But she just went right on yelling. So then he rushed at her and started beating her. Emka went arse over tip, she stopped yelling right away, but he starts kicking her and howling at her in German. Beat her till the blood ran, the pig. They've been together a year, and he's beat her three times already. She told me, 'He's got white blood, like water. He cut himself shaving, I saw it.' She thinks they can stick it out together. She says to me, 'He won't beat me no more. We can stick it out.' But I says to her, 'I know you better than that, girl!' (p. 236)

In 'Silky Hair' (*P* 231–4), a relationship between exploiter and exploited also takes on strange twists. A woman suspects her best friend of witchcraft against her son, and goes to try to force the friend's hand. The story concludes with violence against an innocent, the accused friend's son; the moral levelling of the antagonists has been prepared for by Sadur's asymmetrical naming of her characters (we know the 'wronged' character only as 'the woman', whilst her friend is identified as 'Elena', and thus turned into an individual). A rather similar conflict of plot and linguistic strategies is evident in 'The Blue Hand' (*P* 229–31), in which the young woman protagonist is bullied by her neighbour in a communal flat, Marya Ivanovna, a vindictive lower-class woman with criminal connections. The central character suffers so much from Marya Ivanovna's bullying that she becomes disfigured by huge warts; eventually the bully is found dead 'with the marks of a blue hand on her neck', the young woman having vanished. The apparently simple revenge narrative is transformed by its dedication: 'To Marya Ivanovna', a device which not only pretends the authenticity of these preposterous events, but also plays with the reader's sympathies.

Sadur is not an out-and-out experimentalist; she rarely exploits avant-garde techniques for their own sake. Her best work is not self-consciously apolitical so much as it is anti-political: the moralities of realism or of the fable are suggested in order that they may be undermined. While apparently more accessible than the work of, say, Narbikova, Sadur's writing proves more elusive in a philosophical sense. Her work is a radical departure from the moralistic traditions which have so often obtained in women's writing; its closest parallel is perhaps found in the Russian avant-garde writing of the 1930s, in the dead-pan absurdism, for example, of Daniil Kharms, whose incongruously flat narration of horrible or astonishing events prefigures that in Sadur's short stories, and whose plays represent characters caught up in spirals of unpredictable violence.[7] But Sadur has 'feminized' the absurdist genre as practised by Kharms, not only in the obvious sense of questioning whether women always have to be victims, but also by linking her alternative view of language with representations of extraordinary, and unpredictable, 'feminine' behaviour. The world she creates is no feminist utopia, nor is her critique of it feminist in an institutional sense; but her particular view of moral decay and social atomization gives effective voice to the preoccupations of intellectual metropolitan women writers in Russia today, and is likely to play a significant part in any future campaign to alter the lot of Russian women.

[7] A representative selection of Kharms's work is Daniil Kharms, *Polet v nebesa: stikhi, proza, dramy, pis'ma* (Leningrad, 1988); Neil Cornwell (ed.), *Daniil Kharms and the Poetics of the Absurd* (London, 1991) includes documents and secondary material; on Kharms's representation of women, see Graham Roberts, 'The Vanishing Old Women: Sexual/Textual Politics in the Work of Daniil Kharms' (unpublished paper; Oxford, 1991).

18

Instead of an Afterword: Some Concluding Points

IT is not customary to append formal conclusions to literary histories, no doubt because to do so would convey an artificial sense that the process of history has itself been terminated. This is more particularly the case with general surveys, such as this one, whose final date is close to the time of their composition. Besides, as I argued in Chapter 13 of this history, Russian women's writing has, like the rest of Russian culture, recently been in a condition of such fluidity and uncertainty as to defy any kind of final analysis. However, the material that I have covered in reaching the present day has been so scattered and disparate, and in many cases so unfamiliar, that some attempt to restate the underlying themes of the history would seem to be in order.

Between its origins in the late eighteenth century and the present day, we have seen Russian women's writing existing in the interstices of patriarchal Russian culture. The writing of women has at some times been more or less benignly neglected by male writers and critics; however, at other times there have been concerted efforts to define and classify the phenomenon in the abstract, and to prescribe what women should write in the concrete. Women writers have also been affected, like other women, by generally accepted beliefs about the nature of women on the one hand, and by ideals of feminine behaviour on the other. The result of this has sometimes been to make women writers follow traditions and practices that are evident in the work of their male contemporaries, but selectively. They ignore some apparently attractive techniques (such as, say, internal monologue in the case of early twentieth-century fiction), and fasten on others that are superficially no more preferable (or sometimes superficially less preferable)—such as the fossilized mythologies of Socialist Realism. This selection process can make women writers appear out of step with literary fashion. In nineteenth-century poetry, for example, the topoi of neo-classical poetry remain in circulation amongst women poets for rather longer than they do amongst men; the stereotypes of the didactic novel predominate for longer in women's prose than they do in the work of at least some Russian men. However, these persistences have their own logic: the language of neo-classicism is more permissive to women's identification with the role of poet than are the gender-marked conventions of 1820s Romanticism, and the utopian coloration of the didactic novel, its emphasis on perfectability, is ideally suited to the expression of the concerns of the early women's liberationists. And Russian women's writing has not simply existed on crumbs dropped from the table of men. Women writers have shown a considerable degree of independence in their writing, an independence that is partly traceable to their conscious or unconscious sense of the work of other women. Whether striving for difference or (more rarely) emphasizing affiliation, women have always felt the presence of a 'women's tradition'. The associations between Akhmatova and Rostopchina or Gertsyk, Parnok and Pavlova, or Tsvetaeva and Gan, to name only three prominent instances, have been no less important than the more familiar and overt links between Akhmatova and Pushkin or Dante, Parnok and Khodasevich, and Tsvetaeva and Pasternak or Rilke. Another significant factor has been awareness of women's writing in the West, which was especially evident in the nineteenth century—in the early years of which women's prose was more of an international than a national phenomenon—but which has on occasion played an unexpected and idiosyncratic role in the twentieth (as in the cases of Tsvetaeva and Bettina Brentano, or Prismanova and the Brontë sisters).

This history has set down some general points in women writers' relation with these two traditions: the supposedly universal, but in fact male-dominated, 'great tradition' of Russian literary history, as constantly reinvented by writers and critics, and the private, invisible, particular history of women's own tradition, which has been subject to just as many shifts of direction. It has also explored a number of case-histories, illustrating particular choices and dilemmas. For me personally, too, working on this book has been a most enjoyable, if taxing, exercise. It has introduced me to many writers of whom I had not heard before beginning my research, and has given me a new interest in areas of Russian literary history (such as women's late nineteenth-century prose, or the writing of the 'first wave' emigration) of which I formerly knew very little.

In the future, other studies are certain to revise and expand many, even most, aspects of the analysis that is given here. Other writers are sure to come to light, and areas that I have scarcely touched on (such as the relationship between women's writing and the visual arts, or music, or the cinema; the writing of women before 1820; the reception of women's writing by ordinary readers) will receive a properly full appraisal. Other chroniclers will also, no doubt, give fuller weight to the theoretical advances that have been made by feminist criticism, and to the insights afforded by such new approaches as cultural studies, than I, constrained by the need to establish basic facts and introduce fundamental issues of discussion or contention, have been able to allow. If my analytical hints can act as a stepping-stone to such efforts, and my enthusiasm be some sort of stimulus for them, and indeed offer guidance and stimulus to all readers with any interest in Russian women's writing, I shall consider my efforts well rewarded.

Bibliography

Note: this is a bibliography of sources actually cited in the *History*, rather than a bibliography of Russian women's writing in general: for a wider spread of material, see the sources listed under Section 1 below. The bibliography is divided into three sections:

1. *Bibliographies and Reference Sources with Material Relating to Russian Women Writers*

2. *Publications by Russian Women Writers; Studies on Individual Women Writers and on Women's Writing; Collections and Anthologies of Russian Women's Writing*

3. *Women's History in Russia; General Russian History; Publications by Russian Male Writers; Non-Russian Women's Writing; Feminist Theory and Criticism; Miscellaneous*

1. *Bibliographies and Reference Sources with Material Relating to Russian Women Writers*

Bol'shoi entsiklopedicheskii slovar' obshchedostupnykh svedenii po vsem otraslyam znanii (22 vols.; St Petersburg, 1900–9).
BRAININA, B. YA, NIKITINA, E. F., and DMITRIEVA, A. N. (comps.), *Sovetskie pisateli: avtobiografii* (4 vols. in 5; Moscow, 1959–72).
BUCK, CLAIRE (ed.), *The Bloomsbury Guide to Women's Literature* (London, 1992).
BUCKMAN, W. W., and ZEPPER, J. T., *Russian and Soviet Education 1731–1989: A Multilingual Annotated Bibliography* (New York, 1992).
Entsiklopedicheskii slovar' izd. Brokgauza i Efrona, ed. I. Andreevsky (38 vols. and 4 supp. vols.; St Petersburg, 1887–1907).
FOSTER, LYUDMILA, *Bibliografiya russkoi zarubezhnoi literatury 1918–1968* (2 vols.; Boston, 1970).

448   *Bibliography*

GENNADI, GRIGORY, and SOIKO, NIKOLAI (eds.), *Spravochnyi slovar' o russkikh pisatelyakh i uchenykh, umershikh v XVIII i XIX stoletiyakh: spisok russkikh knig 1725–1825* (Berlin, 1880).

GOLITSYN, N. N., *Bibliograficheskii slovar' russkikh pisatel'nits* (St Petersburg, 1889).

IGNASHEV, DIANE NEMEC, and KRIVE, SARAH (comps.), *Women and Writing in Russia and the USSR: A Bibliography of English-Language Sources* (New York, 1992).

KASACK, WOLFGANG, *Lexikon der russischen Literatur des 20sten Jahrhundert* (2nd edn.; Munich, 1992; 1st edn. also available in English and Russian).

KAYE, PHYLLIS JOHNSON (ed.), *American/Soviet Playwrights' Directory* (Waterford, Conn., 1988).

KOZ'MIN, B. P. (ed.), *Pisateli sovetskoi epokhi: bio-bibliograficheskii slovar' russkikh pisatelei XX veka* (Moscow, 1928).

Kratkaya literaturnaya entsiklopediya (9 vols.; Moscow, 1962–75).

LEDKOVSKY, MARINA, ROSENTHAL, CHARLOTTE, and ZIRIN, MARY, *A Bio-Bibliographical Guide to Russian Women Writers* (2 vols.; Westport, Conn., 1994).

MASANOV, I. F., *Slovar' psevdonimov russkikh pisatelei, uchenykh i obshchestvennykh deyatelei* (4 vols.; Moscow, 1958).

MEZIER, AVGUSTA, *Russkaya slovesnost' s XI po XIX stoletii vklyuchitel'no* ... (2 vols.; St Petersburg, 1899).

The Modern Encyclopedia of Russian and Soviet Literature, ed. Harry B. Weber (Gulf Breeze, Fla., 1977–).

MURATOVA, K. D. (ed.), *Istoriya russkoi literatury XIX v.: bibliograficheskii ukazatel'* (Moscow-Leningrad, 1962).

—— (ed.), *Istoriya russkoi literatury kontsa XIX–nachala XX vv. Bibliograficheskii ukazatel'* (Moscow-Leningrad, 1963).

Novyi entsiklopedicheskii slovar' izd. Brokgauza i Efrona, ed. K. K. Arsen'ev (29 vols. only published; St Petersburg/Petrograd, 1911–16).

Russkie pisateli 1800–1917: bio-bibliograficheskii slovar' (vol. 1 and continuing; Moscow, 1989–).

Russkie sovetskie pisateli-prozaiki: bibliograficheskii slovar' (7 vols. in 9; Leningrad, 1959–71).

RUSSOV, S. V., *Bibliograficheskii slovar' rossiiskim pisatel'nitsam* (St Petersburg, 1826).

Svodnyi katalog russkikh knig XVIII veka (1725–1800) (5 vols.; Moscow, 1962–65).

TERRAS, VICTOR (ed.), *A Handbook of Russian Literature* (New Haven, Conn., 1985).

VITMAN, A. M., *Vosem' let russkoi khudozhestvennoi literatury (1917–1925)* (Moscow-Leningrad, 1926).

WILSON, KATHARINA M. (ed.), *An Encyclopedia of Continental Women's Writing* (2 vols.; New York, 1991).

YAZYKOV, D. D., 'Obzor zhizni i trudov russkikh pisatalei i pisatel'nits, umershikh v 1881–1893 gg.' (13 pts.), *Sbornik otdeleniya russkogo yazyka i slovesnosti Imperatorskoi Akademii Nauk*, 1903–13.

2. *Publications by Russian Women Writers; Studies on Individual Women Writers and on Women's Writing; Collections and Anthologies of Russian Women's Writing*

ADAMOVICH, GEORGY, 'Literaturnye zametki', *PN* 24 Jan. 1935, p. 2.
AKHMADULINA, BELLA, *Uroki muzyki* (Moscow, 1969).
—— 'Mnogo sobak i sobaka', *Metropol'* (Moscow, 1979), 21–47.
—— *Izbrannoe* (Moscow, 1988).
AKHMATOVA, ANNA, *Vecher* (St Petersburg, 1912).
—— 'N. L'vova, *Staraya skazka*', *RM* (1914), 1, sect. 2, 127–8.
—— *Stikhotvoreniya i poemy* (Leningrad, 1976).
—— *Sochineniya* (3 vols.; Munich, 1967–78).
—— *Sochineniya* (2 vols.; Moscow, 1986).
—— 'Rekviem', *Neva* (1987), 6: 74–9.
—— *Poema bez geroja von A. Achmatova: Variatenedition und Interpretation von Symbolstrukturen* (Vienna, 1987).
—— *Selected Poems*, trans. Richard McKane (Newcastle upon Tyne, 1989).
—— *Sobranie stikhotvorenii* (Moscow, 1989).
—— *Complete Poems*, trans. Judith Hemschemeyer, ed. Roberta Reeder (2 vols.; Somerville, Mass., 1990).
—— *My Half Century: Selected Prose*, ed. Ronald Meyer (Ann Arbor, Mich., 1992).
Akhmatovskii sbornik, i (Paris, 1989).
AKSEL'ROD, ELENA, 'Vozvrashchenie', *NM* (1989), 5: 156–9.
ALEKSEEVA, LIDIYA, *Lesnoe solntse: stikhi* (Frankfurt am Main, 1954).
—— *V puti: stikhi* (New York, 1962).
ALFEEVA, VALERIYA, 'Prizvannye, izbrannye i vernye', *Moskva* (1991), 4: 3–60.
ALIGER, MARGARITA, *Neskol'ko shagov* (Moscow, 1964).
—— *Sobranie sochinenii v 3 tomakh* (Moscow, 1984).
Always a Woman: Stories by Soviet Women Writers (Moscow, 1987).
AMERT, SUSAN, *In a Shattered Mirror: The Later Poetry of Anna Akhmatova* (Stanford, Calif., 1992).
ANDREW, JOE, *Narrative and Desire in Russian Literature, 1822–1849: Feminine and Masculine* (London, 1993).
—— (ed.), *An Anthology of Russian Women's Writing, 1830–1855* (forthcoming).
ANNENSKY, INNOKENTY, 'O sovremennom lirizme: One', *Apollon* (1909), 3: 5–29.
Anon., 'Dramaturg iz kommunalki', *Sobesednik* (1990), 4: 14.
Anon. [as 'A. Pushkin'], 'K zhenshchine-poetu', *Sovremennik*, 10 (1838), 177.

Anon., 'Mir v drugom izmerenii', *Sovetskaya Sibir'*, 17 Nov. 1990.

ANTALOVSKY, TATJANA, *Der russische Frauenroman: exemplarische Untersuchungen* (Munich, 1987).

APLIN, HUGH ANTHONY, 'Mariya Zhukova and Elena Gan: Women Writers and Female Protagonists, 1837–1843', Ph.D. thesis (University of East Anglia, 1989).

AVILOVA, LIDIYA, 'Pervoe gore', *RB* (1900), 8: 240–50.

—— 'Obman', *VE* (1901), 7: 53–93.

—— 'Po sovesti', *VE* (1901), 12: 532–645.

—— *Rasskazy, vospominaniya* (Moscow, 1984).

AVVAKUMOVA, MARIYA, 'Stikhotvoreniya', *Znamya* (1988), 5: 174–7.

—— ['O sebe. Stikhi'], *Poeziya*, 55 (1990), 44–8.

BAKUNINA, EKATERINA, *Stikhi* (Paris, 1931).

—— *Telo* (Paris, 1933).

—— *Lyubov' k shesterym* (Paris, 1934).

BAL'MONT, KONSTANTIN, 'Sibilla', *ZR* (1909), 10: 29.

BANNIKOV, N. V. (ed.), *Russkie poetessy XIX veka* (Moscow, 1979).

BARANSKAYA, NATAL'YA, 'Nedelya kak nedelya', *NM* (1969), 11: 23–55.

—— *Otritsatel'naya Zhizel': rasskazy, povest'* (Moscow, 1977).

—— *Zhenshchina s zontikom: povest' i rasskazy* (Moscow, 1981).

—— *Portret, podarennyi drugu: ocherki i rasskazy o Pushkine. Povest'* (Leningrad, 1982).

—— *Den' pominoveniya: roman, povest'* (Moscow, 1989).

—— *A Week Like Any Other and Other Stories*, trans. Pieta Monks (London, 1989).

—— *Nedelya kak nedelya*, ed. Peter Doyle (London, 1983).

BARKER, ADELE, 'Are Women Writing "Women's Writing" in the Soviet Union Today? Tolstaya and Grekova', *Studies in Comparative Communism*, 21/3–4 (Autumn/Winter 1988), 357–64.

—— 'Women without Men in the Writings of Contemporary Soviet Women Writers', in Daniel Rancour-Laferrière (ed.), *Russian Literature and Psychoanalysis: Linguistic and Literary Studies in Eastern Europe*, 31 (1989), 431–49.

BARKOVA, ANNA, *Zhenshchina* (Petrograd, 1922).

—— *Nastas'ya Koster: dramaticheskie stseny* (Moscow-Petrograd, 1923).

—— 'Stikhi raznykh let', *Lazur'* (1989), 1: 343–5.

—— *Geroi nashego vremeni* (Moscow, 1992).

BARTA, PETER I., 'The Author, the Cultural Tradition and glasnost': An Interview with Tatyana Tol'staya', *Russian Literature Journal*, 44/147–9 (1990), 265–81.

BASHKEVICH, NADEZHDA, 'Mashkina dolya', *Drug zhenshchin* (1883), 2: 43–54.

BASHKIRTSEVA, MARIYA, 'Dnevnik', *SV* (1892), 1–12.

BASKER, MICHAEL, 'Recent Akhmatoviana: Some Post-Centennial Publications and Prospects', *Scottish Slavonic Review*, 17 (1991), 168–72.

BEK, TAT'YANA, 'Vosem' stikhotvorenii', *Znamya* (1988), 8: 44–7.

—— 'Predvaritel'nye itogi: stikhi', *NM* (1992), 3: 3–5.

BELETSKY, A. I., 'Turgenev i russkie pisatel'nitsy 30-kh–6okh godov', in N. L. Brodsky (ed.), *Tvorcheskii put' Turgeneva* (Petrograd, 1923), 135–66.

BELKINA, MARIYA, *Skreshchenie sudeb: popytka Tsvetaevoi, dvukh poslednikh let ee zhizni* . . . (Moscow, 1988).

BERBEROVA, NINA, *Oblegchenie uchasti: 6 povestei* (Paris, 1948).

—— *The Italics are Mine*, trans. Philippe Radley (London, 1969). (A translation of *Kursiv moi* (Munich, 1972).)

—— *Stikhi* (New York, 1984).

—— *The Accompanist*, trans. Marian Schwartz (London, 1987).

—— *Three Novels*, trans. Marian Schwartz (London, 1990).

—— *The Tattered Coat and Other Stories*, trans. Marian Schwartz (New York, 1991).

BERGGOL'TS, OL'GA, 'Protiv likvidatsii liriki', in K. Ozerova (ed.), *Razgovor pered s"ezdom: sbornik stat'ei, opublikovannyi pered Vsesoyuznym s"ezdom pisatelei* (Moscow, 1954), 279–83.

—— *Dnevnye zvezdy* (Moscow, 1972).

—— *Izbrannye proizvedeniya* (Leningrad, 1983).

—— 'Bezumstvo predannosti', *Vremya i my*, 57 (1980), 270–302.

—— 'Dnevnye zvezdy', *Ogonek*, 5 May 1990, 15–16.

BEZRODNAYA, YULIYA, 'S ulitsy: rasskazy', *VE* (1894), 5: 255–81.

—— 'Pyatyi akt', *RB* (1909), 4: 1–41; 5: 3–36.

BLOKH, RAISA, *Moi gorod* (Paris, 1928).

—— 'Pust' nebo chernoe' and other poems, *Chisla*, 2/3 (1930), 12–13.

—— 'Zaidi syuda' and other poems, *Roshcha: vtoroi sbornik berlinskikh poetov* (Berlin, 1932), 10–14.

—— 'Naletaet veter' and other poems, *Chisla*, 6 (1932), 8–9.

—— *Tishina: stikhi 1928–1934* (Berlin, 1934).

—— and GORLIN, MIKHAIL, *Izbrannye stikhi* (Paris, 1959).

BRODSKY, JOSEPH, 'A Poet and Prose', in his *Less than One* (London, 1987), 176–94; 'Footnote to a Poem', ibid. 195–267.

BRYUSOV, VALERY, 'Zhenshchiny-poety', *Sobranie sochinenii v 7 tomakh*, vi (Moscow, 1974), 318–21.

BULICH, VERA, *Skazki* (2 vols.; Belgrade, 1932).

—— *Mayatnik* (Helsinki, 1934).

—— *Plennyi veter* (Tallinn, 1938).

—— *Burelom* (Helsinki, 1947).

—— *Vetvi* (Paris, 1954).

BUNINA, ANNA, *Pravila poezii, sokrashchenno-perevedennye iz abbata Blatë, s prisovokupleniem rossiiskogo stikhoslozheniya* (St Petersburg, 1808).

—— *Sobranie sochinenii* (3 vols.; St Petersburg, 1819–21).

BURGIN, DIANA, 'Signs of a Response: Two Possible Parnok Replies to her *podruga*', *SEEJ* 35/2 (1991), 214–28.

—— 'Tatiana Larina's Letter to Onegin and *la plume criminelle*', *EP* 16/1 (Sept. 1991), 12–23.

BURGIN, DIANA, 'Silver Age Perceptions of Lesbian Sexuality and Sofiya Parnok's Poems', in Jane Costlow, Stephanie Sandler, and Judith Vowles (eds.), *Sexuality in Russian Culture* (Stanford, Calif., 1993).

—— 'Sophia Parnok and the Writing of a Lesbian Poet's Life', *SR* 51/2 (1992), 214–31.

CATHERINE II. See EKATERINA II

CHEBYSHEVA-DMITRIEVA, E., 'Ol'ga Andreevna Shapir: ee zhizn' i deyatel'nost'', *VE* (1916), 10: 375–95.

CHEGRINTSEVA, EMILIYA, 'Nasledstvo', *SOZ* 69 (1939), 213.

CHERTOVA, N., 'Novye galoshi', *Pereval*, 3 (1925), 176–87.

CHERVINSKAYA, LIDIYA, *Rassvety* (Paris, 1937).

Chisten'kaya zhizn', ed. A. V. Shavkut (Moscow, 1990).

CHISTYAKOVA, M., 'Chetyre dnya', *KN* (1923), 7: 73–88.

CHIZHOVA, ELENA, 'Igry zryachikh i slepykh', narrative poem of 1984. Unpublished typescript, archive of G. S. Smith, Oxford.

CHUKOVSKAYA, LIDIYA, *Going Under*, trans. Peter M. Weston (New York, 1972).

—— *Zapiski ob Anne Akhmatovoi*, i (Paris, 1976; rev. edn., Moscow, 1989); ii (Paris, 1980).

—— *Protsess isklyucheniya: ocherki literaturnykh nravov* (Paris, 1979).

—— *Pamyati detstva* (New York, 1983).

—— *Dve povesti* (Moscow, 1988).

—— *Sofia Petrovna*, trans. David Floyd (London, 1989).

CHULKOV, G., 'Anna Akhmatova, *Vecher*', *Zhatva* (1912), 3: 275–7.

CHYUMINA, OL'GA, 'Pamyati Bashkirtsevoi', *RB* (1888), 7: 115.

CLEMENTS, BARBARA EVANS, *Bol'shevik Feminist: The Life of Aleksandra Kollontai* (Bloomington, Ind., 1979).

COSTLOW, JANE, 'Speaking the Sorrow of Women: Turgenev's "Neschastnaia" and Evgeniia Tur's "Antonina"', *SR* 50/2 (1991), 328–35.

CUNNINGHAM, JOHN, 'Freedom is Feminine' (interview with Nella Bielski), *Guardian*, 23 Mar. 1988.

DAMANSKAYA, A., 'Plonzher', *Perezvony*, 1 (1925), 76–81.

DAVIDSON, PAMELA, and TLUSTY, ISABELLA (eds.), *Posvyashchaetsya Akhmatovoi* (Tenafly, NJ, 1991).

DAVYDOVA, MARIYA, *Stikhotvoreniya* (St Petersburg, 1899).

DENISENKO, ALEKSANDR, 'I rozy, i ved'miny slezki', *Sudarynya*, 28 May 1991, 8.

DENISOVA, N., '*Otritsatel'naya Zhizel'* [N. Baranskoi]', *Literaturnoe obozrenie* (1977), 1: 25.

DMITRIEVA, VALENTINA, 'Akhmetkina zhena', *RB* (1881), 1: 1–59.

—— 'Tyur'ma', *VE* (1887), 8: 543–96; 9: 5–67; 10: 502–63.

—— 'Progulka', *RB* (1892), 9: 1–64.

—— 'Gomochka', *SV* (1894), 8: 260–80; 9: 1–44; 10: 65–98.

—— 'Po derevnyam', *VE* (1896), 10: 521–65.

—— *Povesti i rasskazy* (3 vols.; St Petersburg, 1916).

—— *Povesti. Rasskazy* (Voronezh, 1983).

DOLGORUKOVA, NATAL'YA, *The Memoirs of Princess Natal'ja Borisovna Dolgorukaja*, ed. Charles Townsend (Columbus, Ohio, 1977).

DOLINA, VERONIKA, *Stikhi* (Paris, 1987).

—— *Vozdukhoplavatel'* (Moscow, 1989).

DRABKINA, E., 'Moskva 1918', *NM* (1958), 9: 147–88.

—— 'Povest' o nenapisannoi knige', *NM* (1961), 6: 135–70 : 191–230.

DUROVA, NADEZHDA, *Povesti i rasskazy* (4 vols.; St Petersburg, 1839).

—— *Izbrannoe* (Moscow, 1984).

—— *Devushka-kavalerist: proisshestvie v Rossii* (Leningrad, 1985).

—— *The Cavalry Maiden*, trans. and ed. Mary Fleming Zirin (London, 1990).

D'YAKONOVA, ELIZAVETA, *Dnevnik na vysshikh zhenskikh kursakh (1895–1899)* (St Petersburg, 1904).

—— *Dnevnik russkoi zhenshchiny (Parizh 1900–1902)* (St Petersburg, 1905).

DZHONSTON, VERA, 'V irlandskoi glushi: iz dnevnika peterburgskoi baryshni', *VE* (1892), 8: 571–627.

EBERSPRÄCHER, BETTINA, *Realität und Transzendenz: Marina Cvetaevas poetische Synthese* (Munich, 1987).

EFRON, ARIADNA, *Marina Tsvetaeva: vospominaniya docheri* (Paris, 1987).

EKATERINA II [Catherine II], *Zapiski*, ed. A. Gertsen (London, 1859).

—— *Dramaticheskie sochineniya*, ed. A. N. Pypin (4 vols.; St Petersburg, 1901).

—— *Zapiski* (St Petersburg, 1907).

—— *Mémoires de Cathérine II, écrits par elle-même*, ed. Dom. Maroger (Paris, 1953).

—— *Memoirs of Catherine the Great*, ed. D. Maroger, trans. Moura Budberg (London, 1955).

ESENINA, TAT'YANA, 'Zhenya—chudo XX-go veka', *NM* (1962), 1: 82–164.

FAINSHTEIN, M., *Pisatel'nitsy Pushkinskoi pory* (Leningrad, 1989).

FARNSWORTH, BEATRICE, *Aleksandra Kollontai: Socialism, Feminism and the Bolshevik Revolution* (Stanford, Calif., 1980).

FEDIN, K. A., 'Otzyv o predstavlennoi v Izd-vo Pisatelei povesti Gedroitsa Sergeya "Kaftanchik"', dated 22 Aug. 1929, Saltykov-Shchedrin Library Manuscript f. 709, Sobr. avt. sovetskikh pisatelei i kritikov, op. 1 no. 56.

FEINSTEIN, ELAINE, *A Captive Lion: The Life of Marina Tsvetaeva* (London, 1987).

—— *Marina Tsvetayeva* (London, 1989).

FIGNER, VERA, 'Moya nyanya', *Sbornik Znanie*, 14 (1906), 199–212.

—— *Zapechatlennyi trud* (2 vols.; Moscow, 1920).

FORRESTER, SIBELAN, 'Bells and Cupolas: The Formative Role of the Female Body in Marina Tsvetaeva's Poetry', *SR* 51/2 (1992), 232–46.

FORSH, OL'GA, *Sobranie sochinenii* (7 vols.; Leningrad, 1928–30).

—— *Sobranie sochinenii v 8 tomakh* (Moscow, 1962).

—— *Sumasshedshii korabl'* (Leningrad, 1988).

'GABRIAK, CHERUBINA DE' (Elizaveta Dmitrieva), 'Stikhi', *Apollon* (1909), 2: 3–10.

—— 'Stikhi', *Apollon* (1910), 10: 3–14.

GAGEN-TORN, NINA, 'From my Memoirs', trans. M. Molnar, *Index on Censorship* (1991), 8: 12–16.

'GALINA, GLAFIRA' [Rinks, Glafira], *Stikhotvoreniya* (St Petersburg, 1902).

GAN, ELENA, *Polnoe sobranie sochinenii* (St Petersburg, 1909).

GANINA, MAIYA, *Poka zhivu—nadeyus'* (Moscow, 1987).

GANZBURG, G. I., 'K istorii izdaniya i vospriyatiya sochinenii El. Kul'man', *Russkaya literatura*, 1 (1990), 148–55.

GASIOROWSKA, XENIA, *Women in Soviet Literature 1917–1964* (Madison, Wis., 1968).

GASPAROV, M. L., 'Slovo mezhdu melodiei i ritmom', *Russkaya rech'* (1989), 4: 3–10.

GAZIZOVA, OL'GA, 'Damy i monakhi', *LG*, 10 Apr. 1991, 11.

GEDROITS, VERA ('Sergei Gedroits'), *Stikhi i skazki* (St Petersburg, 1910).

—— *Veg* (St Petersburg, 1913).

—— *Kaftanchik* (Leningrad, 1930).

—— *Lyakh* (Leningrad, 1931).

—— *Otryv* (Leningrad, 1931).

GERASIMOVA, V., 'Nedorogie kovry', *Pereval*, 1 (1925), 168–84.

GERTSYK, ADELAIDA, 'O mire detskikh igr', *Russkaya shkola* (1902), 3: 31–45.

—— *Stikhotvoreniya* (St Petersburg, 1910).

—— 'O tom, chego ne bylo', *RM* (1911), 5: 130–46.

—— 'Moi romany', *SZ* (1913), 2: 77–89; 4: 47–53.

—— 'Iz detskogo mira', *SZ* (1915), 9: 6–13.

—— 'Moi bluzhdaniya', *SZ* (1915), 10: 22–38; 11–12: 52–68.

—— 'Zharok byl tsvet dushi', *Nashe nasledie* (1991), 3: 123–9.

GERTSYK, EVGENIYA, 'Vyacheslav Ivanov, *Eros*', *ZR* (1907), 1: 90–1.

—— *Vospominaniya* (Paris, 1973).

GINZBURG, EVGENIYA, *Krutoi marshrut* (Milan, 1967).

—— *Into the Whirlwind*, trans. Paul Stevenson and Manya Harari (London, 1967).

—— *Krutoi marshrut*, ii (Milan, 1979).

—— *Within the Whirlwind*, trans. Ian Boland (London, 1981).

GINZBURG, LIDIYA, *Chelovek za pis'mennym stolom* (Leningrad, 1988).

GIPPIUS, ZINAIDA, 'V gostinoi i v lyudskoi', *VE* (1895), 3: 91–139.

—— *Zerkala* (St Petersburg, 1898; repr. Munich, 1977).

—— *Tret'ya kniga rasskazov* (St Petersburg, 1902; repr. Munich, 1977).

—— *Literaturnyi dnevnik 1899–1907* (St Petersburg, 1908).

—— *Sobranie stikhov* (2 vols.; Moscow, 1904–10).

—— 'E. Bakunina, *Lyubov' k shesterym*', *SOZ* 58 (1936), 478–9.

—— *P'esy*, ed. Temira Pachmuss (Munich, 1972).

—— *Stikhotvoreniya i poemy* (2 vols.; Munich, 1972).

—— *Selected Works*, trans. and ed. Temira Pachmuss (Urbana, Ill., 1972).

—— *Peterburgskie dnevniki* (New York, 1982).

GLADKOVA, TAT'YANA, and MNUKHIN, LEV, *Bibliographie des œuvres de Marina Tsvetaeva* (Paris, 1982).

Glas, 3 (1992). (A women's writing issue.)

Golgofa strof: stikhi (Ryazan, 1920).

GOLOVINA, ALLA, *Lebedinaya karusel'* (Paris, 1935).

—— *Gorodskoi angel* (Brussels, 1989).

GOLOVKINA, NATAL'YA, *Elisabeth de S., ou l'histoire d'une russe, écrite par une de ses compatriotes* (Paris, 1802).

—— *Elisaveta S., ili istoriya Rossiyanki, napisannaya odnoyu iz ee sootechest-vennits* (St Petersburg, 1803).

GÖPFERT, FRANK, *Dichterinnen und Schriftstellerinnen in Russland von der Mitte des 18. bis zum Beginn des 20. Jahrhunderts: eine Problemskizze*, Slavistische Beiträge, 289 (Munich, 1992).

GORBANEVSKAYA, NATAL'YA, *Red Square at Noon*, trans. A. Lieven (New York, 1972).

—— *Poberezh'e* (Ann Arbor, Mich., 1973).

—— *Gde i kogda: stikhi iyun' 1983—mart 1985* (Paris, 1985).

GORODETSKAYA, NADEZHDA, *Neskvoznaya nit'* (Paris, 1929).

—— 'Belye kryl'ya', *Volya Rossii* (1929), 3: 3–24.

—— *L'Exil des enfants* (Paris, 1936).

—— 'Princess Zinaida Volkonsky', *OSP* 5 (1954), 93–105.

—— 'Zinaida Volkonsky as a Catholic', *SEER* 39/92 (Dec. 1960), 31–43.

—— 'Princess Zinaida Volkonskaya: An Approach'. Unpublished typescript, held in Taylor Institution Slavonic Annexe, Oxford.

GOSCILO, HELENA (trans. and ed.), *Russian and Polish Women's Fiction* (Knoxville, Tenn., 1985).

—— 'Tatyana Tolstaya's "Dome of Many-Coloured Glass"': The World Refracted through Multiple Perspectives', *SR* 47/2 (1988), 280–90.

—— *Balancing Acts: Recent Writing by Soviet Women* (Bloomington, Ind., 1989).

—— 'Inscribing the Body in Recent Russian Women's Writing: Cross-Dressing à la Holbein', in Marianne Liljeström, Eila Mäntysaari, and Arja Rosenholm (eds.), *Gender Restructuring in Russian Studies* (Slavica Tamperensia, 11; Helsinki, 1993).

GREENE, DIANA, 'Karolina Pavlova's "Tri dushi"': The Transfiguration of Biography', *Proceedings of the Kentucky Foreign Language Conference: Slavic Section* (Lexington, Ky., 1984), 15–24.

—— 'An Asteroid of One's Own: Women Soviet Science Fiction Writers', *ISS* 8 (1987), 127–40.

'GREKOVA, IRINA' [Elena Venttsel'], *Kafedra* (Moscow, 1980).

—— *Vdovii parokhod. Porogi* (Moscow, 1986).

—— *Na ispytaniyakh* (Moscow, 1989).

—— *A Ship of Widows*, trans. Cathy Porter (London, 1989).

GUMILEV, N., 'Gorodetsky, Akhmatova i drugie', *Apollon* (1914), 5: 34–42.

GUREVICH, LYUBOV', 'M. K. Bashkirtseva: biografichesko-psikhologicheskii etyud', *RB* (1888), 2: 73–122.

—— *Ploskogor'e* (St Petersburg, 1897).

GUREVICH, LYUBOV', *Sedok i drugie rasskazy* (St Petersburg, 1904).

—— *Literatura i estetika: kriticheskie ocherki i etyudy* (St Petersburg, 1912).

—— *Pochemu nado dat' zhenshchinam takie zhe prava, kak muzhchinam* (Petrograd, 1917).

'GURO, ELENA' [Elena von Notenburg], *Sharmanka* (St Petersburg, 1909).

—— *Nebesnye verblyuzhata* (St Petersburg, 1914).

—— *Selected Prose and Poetry*, ed. Anna Ljungren and Nils Ake Nilsson (Stockholm, 1988).

HACKEL, SERGEI, *One of Great Price: The Life of Mother Mariya Skobtsova* (London, 1965).

HAIGHT, AMANDA, *Anna Akhmatova: A Poetic Pilgrimage* (Oxford, 1976).

HARUSSI, YAEL, 'Women's Social Roles as Depicted by Women Writers in Early Nineteenth-Century Russian Fiction', in J. Douglas Clayton (ed.), *Issues in Russian Literature Before 1917* (Columbus, Ohio, 1989), 35–48.

HELDT, BARBARA, *Terrible Perfection: Women and Russian Literature* (Bloomington, Ind., 1987).

—— 'The Burden of Caring', *Nation*, 13 June 1987.

—— 'The Poetry of Elena Shvarts', *World Literature Today* (Spring 1989), 381–3.

—— 'Motherhood in a Cold Climate: The Life and Poetry of Mariia Shkapskaia', *Russian Review*, 51/2 (1992), 160–71.

—— 'Gynoglasnost'', in Mary Buckley (ed.), *Perestroika and Soviet Women* (Cambridge, 1992), 160–72.

IGUMNOVA, TAT'YANA, 'Ledokhod', *Pereval*, 3 (1925), 90–101.

INBER, VERA, *O Leningrade: poema i stikhi* (Leningrad, 1943).

—— 'Vdokhnovenie i masterstvo', *Znamya* (1956), 9: 157–69; (1957), 8: 168–78.

—— *Sobranie sochinenii v 4 tomakh* (Moscow, 1965–6).

ISKRENKO, NINA, *Ili: stikhi i teksty* (Moscow, 1991).

IVANOV, VYACHESLAV, '*Stikhotvoreniya* Adelaidy Gertsyk', *Apollon* (1910), 7: khronika, 41.

IVANOVA, LIDIYA, *Vospominaniya* (Paris, 1990).

IVINSKAYA, OL'GA, *V plenu vremeni* (Paris, 1978).

—— *A Captive of Time*, trans. Max Hayward (London, 1980).

JENSEN, KJELD BJORNAGER, *Russian Futurism, Urbanism, and Elena Guro* (Arhus, 1977).

KABO, LYUBOV', 'V trudnom pokhode', *NM* (1956), 11: 105–206; 12: 82–189.

KALINA-LEVINA, VERA, 'Through the Eyes of the Child: The Artistic Vision of Elena Guro', *SEEJ* 25 (1981), 30–43.

KARAMZINA, MARIYA, *Kovcheg* (Tallinn, 1939).

KARATYGINA, N., 'Cherez borozdy', *Pereval*, 1 (1925), 83–114.

KARAVAEVA, ANNA, *Lesozavod* (Moscow, 1935).

—— 'Rozan moi, rozan', *KN* (1940), 7–8: 27–43.

—— *Ogni* (Moscow, 1944).

—— *Razbeg* (Moscow, 1947).

—— *Rodnoi dom* (Moscow, 1950).

—— *Rodina* (Moscow, 1951).

—— *Po dorogam zhizni* (Moscow, 1957).

KARLINSKY, SIMON, *Marina Cvetaeva* (Berkeley, Calif., 1965).

—— *Marina Tsvetaeva: The Woman, her World and her Poetry* (Cambridge, 1985).

KATERLI, NINA, *Okno* (Leningrad, 1981).

—— *Tsvetnye otkrytki: povesti i rasskazy* (Leningrad, 1987).

—— 'Zhara na severe: povest'', *Zvezda* (1988), 4: 3–73.

—— *Kurzal: povesti* (Leningrad, 1990).

KAY, SUSAN, 'A Woman's Work', *ISS* 8 (1987), 115–26.

KELLY, CATRIONA, 'Writing an Orthodox Text: Religious Poetry by Russian Women, 1917–1939', in Joe Andrew (ed.), *Poetics of the Text* (Amsterdam, 1992), 153–70.

—— 'Soviet Women's Writing and De-Stalinisation: I. Grekova and N. Baranskaya', *Rusistika*, 5 (1992), 39–43; 6 (1992), 14–18.

—— 'Missing Links: Russian Women Writers as Critics of Women Writers', in Faith Wigzell (ed.), *Russian Writers on Russian Writers* (forthcoming).

—— 'Life at the Margins: Women, Culture and *narodnost'* 1890–1920', in Marianne Liljeström, Eila Mäntysaari, and Arja Rosenholm (eds.), *Gender Restructuring in Russian Studies* (Slavica Tamperensia, 11; Helsinki, 1993).

KEMBALL, ROBIN (ed.), *Marina Tsvetaeva: trudy I-go mezhdunarodnogo simpoziuma (Lozanna, 30 VI–3 VII 1982* (Bern, 1991).

KERN, ANNA, *Vospominaniya* (Leningrad, 1929).

KERSNOVSKAYA, EFROSIN'YA, 'Zhitie', *Ogonek*, 13 Jan. 1990; 20 Jan. 1990.

KHODASEVICH, VLADISLAV, 'Grafinya E. P. Rostopchina', in his *Stat'i o russkoi poezii* (Petrograd, 1922), 7–42.

—— 'Odna iz zabytykh', in his *Sobranie sochinenii*, ii (Ann Arbor, Mich., 1990), 218–19.

—— '"Zhenskie" stikhi', in his *Koleblemyi treugol'nik* (Moscow, 1991), 577–80.

KHOROSHILOVA, T., 'Zagadka Niny Sadur', *Komsomol'skaya pravda*, 1 June 1989.

KHVOSCHINSKAYA, ELENA (Golitsyna), 'Vospominaniya', *Russkaya starina*, 89–91 (1897), 93–5 (1898).

KHVOSHCHINSKAYA, NADEZHDA, *Sobranie sochinenii* (5 vols.; St Petersburg, 1892).

—— *Povesti i rasskazy* (Moscow, 1963).

KHVOSHCHINSKAYA, SOF'YA, 'Prostye smertnye', *OZ* 120 (1858), 1–39.

KIREEVSKY, I., 'Russkie pisatel'nitsy', *Polnoe sobranie sochinenii v 2 tomakh* (Moscow, 1911), ii. 65–75.

KISELEVA, EVGENIYA, 'Kishmareva. Kiseleva. Tyuricheva', *NM* (1991), 2: 9–27.

KLIMENKO-RAPGAUZ, TAT'YANA, *Vsya moya zhizn': stikhotvoreniya i vospominaniya ob otse* (Riga, 1987).

KNORRING, IRINA, *Novye stikhi* (Alma Ata, 1967).

KOLLONTAI, ALEKSANDRA, *Rabotnitsa-mat'* (St Petersburg, 1914).

—— *Novaya moral' i rabochii klass* (Moscow, 1918).

KOLLONTAI, ALEKSANDRA, *Lyubov' trudovykh pchel* (Moscow-Petrograd, 1923).

—— *Selected Writings*, ed. and trans. Alix Holt (London, 1977).

KOLTONOVSKAYA, E. A., *Zhenskie siluety* (St Petersburg, 1912).

KRACHKOVSKAYA, A., 'Lavanda', *Molodaya gvardiya* (1939), 9: 90–5.

KRANDIEVSKAYA, ANASTASIYA, 'Doch' naroda', *RM* (1904), 4: 98–111.

KRANDIEVSKAYA, NATAL'YA, *Doroga: stikhotvoreniya* (Moscow, 1985).

KRESTOVSKAYA, MARIYA, 'Artistka', *VE* (1891), 4: 615–57; 5: 38–111; 6: 631–90; 7: 5–76; 8: 445–85; 9: 5–54; 10: 509–67; 11: 5–59; 12: 434–84.

—— 'Syn: povest'', *VE* (1893), 11: 47–78; 12: 453–505.

KRÜDENER (or KRIDENER), JULIA, *Valérie*, ed. Michel Mercier (Paris, 1974).

'KTOROVA, ALLA' [Viktoriya Shandor], *Litso Zhar-ptitsy* (New York, 1984).

KUL'MAN, ELISAVETA, *Piiticheskie opyty* (3 vols.; St Petersburg, 1833).

—— [as ELISABETH KULLMANN], *Sämmtliche Gedichte*, ed. K. F. von Grossheinrich (Leipzig, 1841).

KUSKOVA, EKATERINA, 'Pestrye kartinki', *SOZ* 12 (1922), 138–63.

KUZMIN, MIKHAIL, 'Zametki o russkoi belletristike', *Apollon* (1910) 4: *khronika*, 65–7.

KUZ'MINA-KARAVAEVA, later Skobtsova, Elizaveta, *Skifskie cherepki* (St Petersburg, 1912).

—— *Ruf'* (St Petersburg, 1916).

—— [as MAT' MARIYA], *Stikhi* (Berlin, 1937).

—— [as MAT' MARIYA], *Stikhi i poemy, misterii. Vospominaniya ob areste i lagere v Ravensbryuke* (Paris, 1947).

—— [as MAT' MARIYA], ['Neizdannye stikhi'], ed. B. Plyukhanov, *Vestnik russkogo studencheskogo khristianskogo dvizheniya*, 161 (1991), 140–57.

KUZMINSKY, IRINA, 'The "Language of Women"? A Study of Three Women Writers: Marina Tsvetaeva, Ingeborg Bachmann and Monique Wittig', D.Phil. thesis (Oxford University, 1989).

KUZNETSOVA, GALINA, 'Kogda dlya dnya', *Perezvony*, 43 (1927), 1150.

—— *Olivkovyi sad: stikhi 1923–1929* (Paris, 1933).

—— *Utro: rasskazy* (Paris, 1934).

LARINA, ANNA, *This I Cannot Forget: The Memoirs of Bukharin's Widow*, trans. Gary Kern (New York, 1993).

LASUNSKY, O. G., *Tvorchestvo pisatel'nitsy V. I. Dmitrievoi i literaturnoe dvizhenie kontsa XIX–nachala XX vv. Avtoreferat dissertatsii* (Voronezh, 1967).

LATYNINA, ALLA, 'Lyubov', sem' ya i kar'era', in her *Znaki vremeni: zametki o literaturnom protsesse* (Moscow, 1987), 287–95.

—— 'Vzglyad na literaturu', *Moskovskii vestnik* (1989), 1: 285–6.

LEDKOVSKY (Astman), MARINA, 'Russian Women Writers: An Overview. Post-Revolutionary Dispersion and Adjustment', in Linda Edmondson (ed.), *Women and Society in Russia* (Cambridge, 1992), 145–59.

LEITER, SHARON, *Akhmatova's Petersburg* (Cambridge, 1983).

LETKOVA, EKATERINA, 'Lishnyaya', *RM* (1893), 7: 77–109.

—— 'Lushka', *SV* (1894), 3: 87–97.

—— 'Otdykh', *RM* (1896), 1: 180–96.

—— 'Bab'i slezy', *MB* (1898), 5: 26–40.

LEVIN, L., 'Sila kollektivnogo truda', *LG*, 7 Dec. 1950, 3.

LIFSHITS, M. 'Dnevnik Marietty Shaginyan', *NM* (1954), 2: 206–15.

LISNYANSKAYA, INNA, 'Krug', *Znamya* (1988), 9: 186–90.

—— *Stikhotvoreniya* (Moscow, 1991).

LOKHVITSKAYA, MIRRA, *Stikhotvoreniya* (5 vols.; St Petersburg, 1903–14).

—— *Pered zakatom* (St Petersburg, 1908).

LOSSKY, VÉRONIQUE, *Marina Tsvetaeva v zhizni: neizdannye vospominaniya sovremennikov* (Tenafly, NJ, 1989).

LUNACHARSKAYA-ROZENEL', N., *Pamyat' serdtsa* (2nd edn.; Moscow, 1965).

L'VOVA, NADEZHDA, 'Ya odenus' nevestoi v atlasnoe beloe plat'e', *RM* (1911), 11: 250–6.

—— *Staraya skazka* (St Petersburg, 1913).

—— 'Kholod utra: o novom zhenskom tvorchestve', *Zhatva* (1914), 5: 250–6.

MACKINNON, LACHLAN, *The Lives of Elsa Triolet* (London, 1992).

MCLAUGHLIN, SIGRID (ed.), *Images of Women in Soviet Fiction* (London, 1989).

MAKIN, MICHAEL, 'The Rewriting of the Inherited Text in the Poetic Works of Marina Tsvetaeva', D.Phil. thesis (Oxford University, 1985).

—— 'Text and Violence in Tsvetaeva's *Molodets*', in Catriona Kelly, Michael Makin, and David Shepherd (eds.), *Discontinuous Discourses in Modern Russian Literature* (London, 1989), 115–35.

MANDEL'SHTAM, NADEZHDA, *Vospominaniya* (New York, 1970).

—— *Hope Against Hope* (London, 1971).

—— *Vtoraya kniga* (Paris, 1972).

—— *Hope Abandoned* (London, 1974).

MANDEL'SHTAM, YURY, 'Vera Bulich, *Plennyi veter*', *Zhurnal Sodruzhestva* (1938), 4: 22.

MARSH, ROSALIND, 'Olga Lipovskaya and Women's Issues in Russia', *Rusistika*, 5 (1992), 16–21.

MERKUR'EVA, VERA, 'Iz literaturnogo naslediya', ed. M. L. Gasparov, *Oktyabr'* (1989), 5: 149–59.

MIKHAILOVSKY, N. M., 'Literatura i zhizn'', *RB* (1899), 8, sect. 2, 157–66.

MILYUTINA, T. P., 'Tri goda v russkom Parizhe', *Blokovskii sbornik*, 10, *Uchenye zapiski Tartuskogo gosudarstvennogo universiteta*, 881 (Tartu, 1991), 141–67.

MIROVICH, ANASTASIYA, 'Yashcheritsy' and 'El'za', *Severnye tsvety na 1902 god* (Moscow, 1902), 80–1.

MNUKHIN, L. A., *Marina Tsvetaeva: bibliograficheskii ukazatel' literatury o zhizni i deyatel'nosti 1910–1941 gg. i 1942–1962 gg.* (Wiener Slawistischer Almanach Sonderband, 23; Vienna, 1989).

MOGILYANSKY, A. N., 'Novye dannye o M. K. Tsebrikovoi', *Russkaya literatura* (1871), 1: 102–11.

MOISEEVA, G. N. (ed.), *Zapiski i vospominaniya russkikh zhenshchin XVIII–pervoi poloviny XIX veka* (Moscow, 1990).

MONKS, PIETA, 'Interview with Natal'ya Baranskaya', in Mary Chamberlain (ed.), *Writing Lives* (London, 1988).

MORITTS, YUNNA, *Razgovor o schast'e* (Moscow, 1957).

—— *Na etom berege vysokom* (Moscow, 1987).

—— 'Molodaya kartoshka', *Vremya i my*, 105 (1989), 89–99.

MURAV'EV, V. (ed.), *V tsarstve muz* (Moscow, 1987).

NAGRODSKAYA, EVDOKIYA, *Gnev Dionisa* (6th edn.; St Petersburg, 1911).

NAIMAN, ANATOLY, *Rasskazy o Anne Akhmatovoi* (Leningrad, 1989).

—— *Remembering Anna Akhmatova*, trans. Wendy Rosslyn (London, 1991).

NARBIKOVA, VALERIYA, *Ravnovesiesveta dnevnykh i nochnykh zvezd* (Paris, 1989).

—— 'Plan pervogo litsa. I vtorogo', *Vstrechnyi khod: povesti i rasskazy molodykh pisatelei*, ed. I. V. Del'sal' (Moscow, 1989), 119–56.

NAUMOVA, ANNA, *Uedinennaya muza zakamskikh beregov* (Moscow, 1819).

NAZAREVA, KAPITOLINA ['K. Nikulina'], 'Spetsialist', *VE* (1879), 1: 63–94.

NEATROUR, ELIZABETH, 'Miniatures of Russian Life at Home and in Emigration: The Life and Works of N. A. Teffi', Ph.D. thesis (University of Indiana, 1972).

NEELOVA, ANNA ('Devitsa N. N.'), *Leinard i Termilia, ili pokhozhdeniya dvukh lyubovnikov* (St Petersburg, 1784).

Ne pomnyashchaya zla, ed. Larisa Vaneeva (Moscow, 1990).

NIKIFOROVA, L., 'Dve lestnitsy', *Sbornik Znanie* 30 (1910), 1–118.

NIKOLAEVA, GALINA, *Zhatva* (Moscow, 1950).

—— *Sobranie sochinenii v 3 tomakh* (Moscow, 1973).

NIKOLAEVA, LIDIYA, 'Avtobiografiya', *O literature* (Moscow, 1958).

NIKOLAEVA, M. N., 'Prevysprennye geroini', *RB* (1891), 12: 101–64.

NIKOLAEVA, OLES'YA, *Zdes'* (Moscow, 1991).

NIKOLAEVA, T., 'T. Velednitskaya, *Povest' moei zhizni*', *KN* (1931), 5–6: 241–2.

NIKOL'SKAYA, T. L., 'The "Contemporary Woman" in Early Twentieth Century Russian Literature', *ISS* 8 (1987), 107–14.

—— 'Tvorcheskii put' L. D. Zinov'evoi-Annibal', *Blokovskii sbornik*, 8, *Uchenye zapiski Tartuskogo gosudarstvennogo universiteta*, 813 (Tartu, 1988), 123–38.

—— 'Tema misticheskogo sektanstva v russkoi poezii 20-kh godov', *Uchenye zapiski Tartuskogo gosudarstvennogo universiteta*, 833 (1990), 157–69.

NOVIKOVA, OL'GA, *The M.P. for Russia: Reminiscences and Correspondence of Madame Olga Novikoff*, ed. W. T. Stead (2 vols.; London, 1909).

Novye amazonki: sbornik zhenskoi prozy, ed. Svetlana Vasilenko (Moscow, 1991).

ODOEVTSEVA, IRINA, *Na beregu Seny* (Paris, 1983).

OVCHINNIKOV, N., 'Davaite sporit'!', *Vechernyaya Moskva*, 6 Jan. 1988.

PACHMUSS, TEMIRA, *Zinaida Hippius: An Intellectual Profile* (Carbondale, Ill., 1971).

—— (trans. and ed.), *Women Writers in Russian Modernism* (Urbana, Ill., 1978).

PALEI, MARINA, 'Kabiriya s Obvodnogo kanala', *NM* (1991), 3: 47–81.

PANAEVA, AVDOT'YA, 'Semeistvo Tal'nikovykh', *Illyustrirovannyi al'manakh* (St Petersburg, 1848; delayed for censorship reasons until 1866), 1–115.

—— *Zhenskaya dolya*, *S* (1862), 3: 40–176; 4: 503–61; 5: 207–50.

—— 'Fantazerka', *S* 104 (1864), 169–219.

—— *Vospominaniya* (Moscow, 1956).

PANOVA, VERA, *Sputniki* (Moscow, 1947).

—— *Kruzhilikha* (Moscow, 1948).

—— *Vremena goda* (Moscow, 1954).

—— *Liki na zare* (Leningrad, 1969).

—— *O moei zhizni, knigakh i chitatelyakh* (Leningrad, 1975).

—— *The Train* (Moscow, 1977).

PARNOK, SOFIYA (as 'ANDREI POLYANIN'), 'Otmechennye imena', *SZ* (1913), 4: 111–15.

—— 'V poiskakh puti iskusstva', *SZ* (1913), 5–6: 227–32.

—— 'Peterburg', *SZ* (1914), 6: 134–42.

—— 'M. Kuzmin, *Plavayushchie-puteshestvuyushchie*', *SZ* (1915), 4: 108–11.

—— 'Osip Mandel'shtam: *Kamen''*, *SZ* (1916), 4–5: 242–3.

—— *Sobranie sochinenii*, ed. S. Polyakova (Ann Arbor, Mich., 1979).

PAVLOVA, ANNA, 'Machikha', *Russkii vestnik*, 33 (1861), 307–74, 637–743.

PAVLOVA, KAROLINA, *Das Nordlicht* (Dresden, 1833).

—— *Les Préludes* (Paris, 1839).

—— *Stikhotvoreniya* (Moscow, 1863).

—— *Sobranie sochinenii* (2 vols.; Moscow, 1915).

—— *Polnoe sobranie stikhotvorenii* (Moscow-Leningrad, 1964).

—— *A Double Life*, trans. and ed. Barbara Heldt (2nd edn., Oakland, Calif., 1986).

PETROVYKH, MARIYA, *Prednazanachen'e: stikhi raznykh let* (Moscow, 1983).

—— *Cherta gorizonta* (Erevan, 1986).

—— *Koster v nochi: stikhi i perevody* (Yaroslavl, 1991).

PETRUSHEVSKAYA, LYUDMILA, 'Smotrovaya ploshchadka', *Druzhba narodov* (1982), 1: 56–70.

—— *Bessmertnaya lyubov'* (Moscow, 1988).

—— 'Svoi krug', *NM* (1988), 1: 116–38.

—— *Tri devushki v golubom* (Moscow, 1989).

—— 'Novye Robinzony', *NM* (1989), 8: 166–72.

—— 'Vremya noch'', *NM* (1992), 2: 65–110.

PITTMAN, RIITTA, 'Valeriya Narbikova's iconoclastic prose', *Forum for Modern Language Studies*, Autumn 1992.

PLATONOV, ANDREI, *Izbrannye rasskazy* (Moscow, 1958).

POLONSKAYA, ELIZAVETA, *Izbrannoe* (Moscow, 1966).

POLYAKOVA, SOF'YA, *V zakatnye oni dni: Tsvetaeva i Parnok* (Ann Arbor, Mich., 1983).

POVOLOTSKAYA, IRINA, 'Dyadya Sasha i Anechka', *Oktyabr'* (1986), 12: 47–60.
—— 'Sem' avangardov', *Zerkala*, 1 (Moscow, 1989), 188–205.
PRATT, SARAH, 'Lydia Ginzburg and the Fluidity of Genre', in Jane Gary Harris (ed.), *Autobiographical Statements in Twentieth-Century Russian Literature* (Princeton, NJ, 1990), 207–16.
PREGEL', SOFIYA, *Razgovor s pamyat'yu* (Paris, 1935).
—— *Solnechnyi proizvol* (Paris, 1937).
—— *Polden': tret'ya kniga stikhov* (Paris, 1939).
—— *Berega* (Paris, 1953).
—— *Vstrecha* (Paris, 1958).
—— *Vesna' v Parizhe* (Paris, 1966).
PRISMANOVA, ANNA, *Sobranie sochinenii*, ed. Petra Couvée (The Hague, 1990).
PROTOPOPOV, M., 'Yarmarka zhenskogo tshcheslaviya', *RM* (1882), 4, sect. 2, 178–203.
—— 'Zhenskoe tvorchestvo', *RM* (1891), 1, sect. 2, 98–112; 2, sect. 2, 161–81; 4, sect. 2, 123–41.
RAPGOF, BORIS, *Karolina Pavlova: materialy dlya izucheniya zhizni i tvorchestva* (Petrograd, 1916).
RATUSHINSKAYA, IRINA, *Grey is the Colour of Hope*, trans. Alyona Kojevnikov (London, 1988). (The English version of *Seryi: svet nadezhdy* (London, 1989).)
RAZUMOVSKAYA, LYUDMILA, 'I koni ustali, i vsadnikov net', *Leningradskii literator*, 21 Oct. 1989.
REISNER, LARISA, 'Atlantida: pésa v 5 deisviyakh', *Shipovnik*, 21 (Moscow, 1913), 143–219.
REZVOVA, TAMARA, 'U kogo—shchi ne gusty, a u kogo—zhemchug melok', *Literaturnaya Rossiya*, 26 June 1970, 11.
RILKE, R. M., *Rainer Maria Rilke, Marina Zwetajewa, Boris Pasternak: Briefwechsel*, ed. Jewgenij Pasternak, Jelena Pasternak, and Konstantin M. Asadowskij, trans. Heddly Pross-Werth (Frankfurt am Main, 1983).
ROSENHOLM, ARJA, 'Auf den Spuren des Vergessens: zur Rezeptionsgeschichte der russischen Schriftstellerin N. D. Chvoščinskaja', *Studia Slavica Finlandensia*, 6 (1990), 61–91.
ROSENTHAL, CHARLOTTE, 'Zinaida Vengerova: Modernism and Women's Liberation', *ISS* 8 (1987), 97–106.
—— 'The Silver Age: High Point for Women?', in Linda Edmondson (ed.), *Women and Society in Russia* (Cambridge, 1992), 32–47.
ROSSLYN, WENDY, *The Prince, the Fool and the Nunnery: The Religious Theme in the Early Poetry of Anna Akhmatova* (Avebury, 1984).
—— (ed.), *The Speech of Unknown Eyes: Akhmatova's Readers on her Poetry* (2 vols.; Nottingham, 1990).
ROSTOPCHINA, EVDOKIYA, *Stikhotvoreniya, proza, pis'ma* (Moscow, 1986).
—— 'Poedinok', in *Russkaya romanticheskaya novella* (Moscow, 1989), 239–95.

RUNOVA, OL'GA, 'Bez zaveta: rasskaz', *SM* (1913), 10: 29–69.

'A Russian Lady', *Raznye povestvovaniya, sochinennye odnoyu Rossiyankoyu* (St Petersburg, 1779).

RZHEVSKAYA, ELENA, *Znaki prepinaniya* (Moscow, 1989).

SABASHNIKOVA, MARGARITA, 'Lesnaya svirel'', *Tsvetnik or*, 203–13.

SADUR, NINA, *Novoe znakomstvo: p'esa v 2 deistviyakh* (mimeographed edn.; VAAP-Inform, Moscow, 1986).

—— *Poka zhivye: p'esa v 7 kartinkakh* (mimeographed edn.; VAAP-Inform, Moscow, 1987).

—— *Chudnaya baba* (Moscow, 1989).

—— *Povesti i rasskazy* (Moscow, 1992).

Sbornik na pomoshch' uchashchimsya zhenshchinam (St Petersburg, 1901).

SEDAKOVA, OL'GA, 'Shkatulka s zerkalom: ob odnom glubinnom motive u A. Akhmatovoi', *Trudy po znakovym sistemam*, 17 (1984), 93–108.

—— *Vrata, okna, arki* (Paris, 1986).

—— 'Solovei, filomela, sud'ba', *Druzhba narodov* (1988), 10: 121–3.

—— 'Elegiya osennei vody', *Den' poezii* (Moscow, 1989), 144.

—— 'O pogibshem literaturnom pokolenii: pamyati Leni Gubanova', *Volga* (1990), 6: 135–46.

—— *Kitaiskoe puteshestvie. Stely i nadpisi. Starye pesni* (Moscow, 1990).

—— 'Puteshestvie volkhvov', *Znamya* (1991), 6: 139–40.

—— 'Pyatye stansy', *Nezavisimaya gazeta*, 15 Feb. 1992.

SEIFULLINA, LIDIYA, *Virineya*, in her *Sobranie sochinenii*, iii (Moscow, 1926).

—— 'V budnii den'', *KN* (1928), 7: 23–36.

—— *Peregnoi. Pravonarushiteli* (Moscow, 1929).

—— *O literature* (Moscow, 1958).

SEREBRYAKOVA, GALINA, *Prometei: romanticheskaya trilogiya* (4 vols.; Moscow, 1963).

SETON-WATSON, MARY, 'Women in Soviet Society', *Scenes from Soviet Life through Official Literature* (London, 1986), 13–36.

SHAGINYAN, MARIETTA, *Po dorogam pyatiletki* (Moscow, 1947).

—— *Sobranie sochinenii v 6 tomakh* (Moscow, 1956–8).

—— *Sobranie sochinenii v 9 tomakh* (Moscow, 1971–5).

SHAKHOVA, ELIZAVETA, *Sobranie sochinenii v stikhakh*, ed. N. N. Shakhov, (3 vols.; St Petersburg, 1911).

SHAPIR, OL'GA, *Povesti i rasskazy* (St Petersburg, 1889).

—— *V burnye gody*, *RM* (1906), 1: 1–55; 2: 49–82; 3: 67–108; 4: 57–106; 5: 96–156; 6: 87–116; 7: 1–44; 8: 70–109; 9: 108–49.

—— *Sobranie sochinenii* (10 vols.; St Petersburg, 1910).

SHCHEPKINA, ALEKSANDRA, *Vospominaniya* (Sergiev Posad, 1915).

SHEPHERD, DAVID, 'Canon Fodder? Problems in the Reading of a Soviet Production Novel', in Catriona Kelly, Michael Makin, and David Shepherd (eds.), *Discontinuous Discourses in Modern Russian Literature* (London, 1989), 39–59.

SHEVELENKO, I. D., 'Marina Tsvetaeva v 1911–1913 godakh: formirovanie avtorskogo samosoznaniya', *Blokovskii sbornik*, 11, *Uchenye zapiski Tartuskogo gosudarstvennogo universiteta*, 917 (Tartu, 1990), 50–66.

SHEVYREV, S. P., 'Bolezn' knyagini', Saltykov-Shchedrin State Public Library, Manuscript Section, f. 850, Shevyrev, S. P., no. 16, 11. 22–3; 'Otchet o bolezni', ibid. 11. 24–32.

SHISHKOV, A. S. 'Pis'mo Anne Buninoi', 6 May 1813, Saltykov-Shchedrin State Public Library, Manuscript Section, f. no. 862, Shishkov, A. S., no. 7, 1. 7.

SHKAPSKAYA, MARIYA, 'Pis'mo A. G. Lebedenko', 3 Nov. 1928, Saltykov-Shchedrin State Public Library, Manuscript Section, f. 1077, arkh. Lebedenko, A. G., ed. khr. 652.

—— 'Pis'mo A. G. Gornfel'du', Saltykov-Shchedrin State Public Library, Manuscript Section, f. 211, arkh. Gornfel'da, A. G., no. 1104.

—— *Sama po sebe: ocherki* (Leningrad, 1940).

—— *Stikhi* (London, 1971).

SHUSTOV, L., 'Doch' Rossii', *Belye nochi* (Leningrad, 1985), 198–227.

SHVARTS, ELENA, *Tantsuyushchii David: stikhi raznykh let* (New York, 1985).

—— *Stikhi* (Paris, 1987).

—— *Trudy i dni Lavinii, monakhini ordena Obrezaniya serdtsa (ot Rozhdestva do Paskhi)* (Ann Arbor, Mich., 1987).

—— *Stikhi* (Leningrad, 1990).

SHVEITSER, VIKTORIYA, *The Life and Work of Marina Tsvetaeva*, trans. Harry Willetts and Robert Chandler (London, 1992).

SKABICHEVSKY, A. M., 'Pesnya o zhenskoi nevole', in his *Sochineniya*, ii (St Petersburg, 1903), 230–47.

SKAVRONSKAYA, MARIYA, 'Stradan'ya, muchen'ya i grazhdanskaya smert'', *Drug zhenshchin* (1883), 1.

SLAVSKAYA, SVETLANA, '"Everyone Knew Her, and No-One Noticed Her": The Fate of the *Vospitannitsa* (Female Ward) in Nineteenth-Century Russian Literature', Ph.D. thesis (Columbia University, New York, 1991).

SLYUSAREVA, IRINA, 'Opravdanie zhiteiskogo: Irina Slyusareva predstavlyaet "novuyu zhenskuyu prozu"', *Znamya* (1991), 11: 238–40.

SMIRNOVA, SOF'YA, 'Khimera', *SV* (1897), 1: 1–39; 2: 3–27; 3: 1–24.

—— *Povesti i rasskazy* (St Petersburg, 1897).

SMITH, ALEXANDRA, 'The Cnidus Myth: Tsvetaeva's Interpretation of Pushkin's Love for Natalya Goncharova', *EP* 14/2 (Sept. 1989), 83–102.

—— 'Tsvetaeva and Pasternak: Depicting People in Poetry', *EP* 15/2 (Sept. 1990), 94–101.

SMITH, G. S., 'Logaoedic Metres in the Lyric Poetry of Marina Tsvetaeva', *SEER* 53/132 (1975), 330–54.

—— 'Marina Tsvetaeva's "Poema gory": An Analysis', *Russian Literature*, 6 (1978), 365–88.

SMITH, MELISSA T., 'Women Writing and Re-writing Women's Roles: Universalising Women's Experience', unpublished paper presented at the AAASS panel 'Women Writers Transcending Reality Today' (Nov. 1991).

SMITH, T. STRATTON, *The Rebel Nun: The Moving Story of Mother Maria of Paris* (London, 1965).

SOBOLEVA, SOF'YA, 'Eshche razbitoe serdtse', *Biblioteka dlya chteniya* (1862), 10: 223–312; 11: 101–93.

—— 'I pro i contra', *OZ* 158 (1863), 395–448.

—— 'Bezvykhodnoe polozhenie', *Russkoe slovo* (1864), 3: 117–58; 4: 29–79.

—— 'Dobroe staroe vremya', *Russkoe slovo* (1865), 4: 38–72; 5: 1–40.

SOKHANSKAYA, NADEZHDA ('N. Kokhanovskaya'), 'Sosedi', *S* (1850), 12: 161–244.

—— 'Posle obeda v gostyakh', *RV* 16 (1858), 641–96.

—— 'Lyubila', *Biblioteka dlya chteniya* (1858), 7: 1–86.

—— 'Iz provintsial'noi galerei portretov', *RV* 20 (1859), 61–157.

SOLNTSEVA, ALYONA, 'Transition: The Theatre Studio', *Theater*, 3 (1989), 21–7.

SOLOV'EVA, POLIKSENA ('Allegro'), *Stikhotvoreniya* (St Petersburg, 1899).

—— *Inei: risunki i stikhi* (St Petersburg, 1905).

—— *Plakun-trava* (St Petersburg, 1906).

—— 'Ya tekh slov, chto ty mne prosheptala', *RM* (1911), 3: 184.

—— *Perekrestok: povest' v stikakh* (St Petersburg, 1913).

—— *Poslednie stikhi* (Moscow, 1923).

Soviet Women Writing (London, 1990).

STARCHEVSKY, A. V., 'Roman odnoi zabytoi romanistki', *IV* 25/8 (1886), 203–34, 509–31.

STARYNKEVICH, EKATERINA ['Elena Sal'yanova'], 'Ne oni vinovaty', *VE* (1871), 1: 133–66; 2: 667–704.

STOLITSA, LYUBOV', 'Na kachelyakh', and other poems, *ZR* (1906), 10: 33–4.

—— 'O krasnom plyushche', and 'V nemuyu noch'', *ZR* (1907), 2: 23.

—— 'Vesennyaya girlanda' and 'Levkoi', *ZR* (1907), 4: 30–1.

—— 'Moya muza' and 'Zhrebii', *SZ* (1916), 7–8: 41–2.

Sto zhemchuzhin: lirika russkikh zhenshchin XX veka (Omsk, 1989).

STROGOVA, EKATERINA, 'Baby: fabrichnye ocherki', *Pereval*, 5 (1927), 175–97.

SUKHANOVA, NATAL'YA, 'Delos', *NM* (1988), 3: 69–84.

SUMNIKOVA, L., 'Prem'era', *Novosibirskaya stsena* (1991), 3: 10.

TAROSHCHINA, BRONISLAVA, 'Tam zreet svet' [interview with Mariya Avvakumova], *LG*, 25 June 1990, 5.

TAUBER, EKATERINA, 'Prostaya radost' bytiya', *SOZ* 67 (1938), 156.

TAUBMAN, JANE, *A Life Through Poetry: Marina Tsvetaeva's Lyric Diary* (Columbus, Ohio, 1988).

TEFFI, NADEZHDA, *Vosem' miniatyur* (St Petersburg, 1913).

—— *Sem' ognei* (St Petersburg, 1910).

—— *Gorodok* (Paris, 1927).

—— *Nostal'giya: rasskazy, vospominaniya* (Leningrad, 1989).

—— *Yumoristicheskie rasskazy* (Moscow, 1990).

TERRY, GARTH, *Anna Akhmatova in English: A Bibliography 1889–1966–1989* (Nottingham, 1989).

TESS, TAT'YANA, 'Materinstvo', *KN* (1935), 8: 156–60.

TIMENCHIK, ROMAN, *Akhmatova i muzyka: issledovatel'skie ocherki* (Leningrad, 1989).

TOKAREVA, VIKTORIYA, *Letayushchie kacheli. Nichego osobennogo* (Moscow, 1987).

TOLSTAYA, TAT'YANA, *Na zolotom kryl'tse sideli* (Moscow, 1987).

—— 'Noch'', *Oktyabr'* (1987), 4: 95–9.

—— 'Sonambula v tumane', *NM* (1988), 7: 8–27.

—— *On the Golden Porch*, trans. Antonina Bouis (London, 1988).

—— *Sleepwalker in a Fog*, trans. Jamey Gambrell (London, 1992).

TOPOROV, V. N., *Akhmatova i Blok: k probleme postroeniya poeticheskogo dialoga* (Berkeley, Calif., 1981).

—— 'Aptekarskaya ostrov kak gorodskoe urochishche (obshchii vzglyad)', in *Noosfera i khudozhestvennoe tvorchestvo*, ed. N. V. Zlydneeva, V. V. Ivanov, V. N. Toporov, and T. V. Tsiv'yan (Moscow, 1991), 200–73.

TRIOLET, ELSA (as El'za Triole), *Zemlyanichka* (Moscow, 1926).

—— *Le premier accroc coûte deux cents francs* (1945; repr. Paris, 1983).

—— *A Fine of Two Hundred Francs* (2nd edn.; London, 1986).

TSEBRIKOVA, MARIYA, 'Anglichanki-romanistki', *OZ* 197 (1871), 403–60; 198 (1871), 121–72; 199 (1871), 175–205.

TSEKHOVSKAYA, VARVARA ['Ol'nem'], 'Pred rassvetom: kartinki provintsial'noi zhizni', *RB* (1905), 6: 3–44; 7: 4–43; 8: 33–72.

—— 'U teplogo morya', *RB* (1909), 7: 6–35; 8: 189–207.

TSIV'YAN, TAT'YANA, 'Antichnye geroini—zerkala Akhmatovoi', *Russian Literature*, 7–8 (1974), 103–19.

TSVETAEVA, MARINA, *Vechernii al'bom* (Moscow, 1910).

—— *Izbrannye proizvedeniya* (Moscow, 1965; 2nd edn.; Moscow, 1991).

—— *Neizdannoe: stikhi, teatr, proza* (Paris, 1976).

—— *Izbrannaya proza v 2 tomakh* (New York, 1978).

—— *Stikhotvoreniya i poemy v 5 tomakh* (New York, 1979–).

—— *Mon frère féminin: lettre à l'Amazone* (1939; Paris, 1979).

—— (as M. TSVETAYEVA), *Selected Poems*, trans. E. Feinstein (2nd edn.; London, 1986).

—— *Selected Poems*, trans. D. McDuff (Newcastle upon Tyne, 1987).

—— *Teatr* (Moscow, 1988).

—— 'Zapisi iz rabochikh tetradei', ed. E. Korkina, *Znamya* (1992), 9: 180–9.

TUCHKOV, VLADIMIR, 'Cherti, suki, kommunal'nye kozly', *Paritet* (1992), 4: 8.

'TUR, EVGENIYA' [E. Sailhas de Tournemire], 'Oshibka', *S* (1849), 10: 137–284.

—— 'Dolg', *S* (1850), 11: 4–60.

—— *Plemyannitsa* (St Petersburg, 1851).

—— 'Zhenshchina i lyubov' po ponyatiyam g. Mishle', *RV* (1859), 6, pt. 1, 461–500.

—— *Sem'ya Shalonskikh* (St Petersburg, 1880).

UCHENOVA, V. V. (ed.), *Dacha na Petergofskoi doroge: proza russkikh pisatel'nits pervoi poloviny XIX veka* (Moscow, 1986).

—— (ed.), *Svidanie: proza russkikh pisatel'nits 60–80 gg. XIX veka* (Moscow, 1987).

—— *Tol'ko chas: proza russkikh pisatel'nits kontsa XIX–nachala XX veka* (Moscow, 1988).

—— *Tsaritsy muz: russkie poetessy XIX–nachala XX vekov* (Moscow, 1989).

ULANOVSKAYA, BELLA, 'Puteshestvie v Kashgar', *Neva* (1991), 2: 69–81.

—— 'Voluntary Seclusion: The Life of an Old Woman in a Deserted Village', *Russian Review*, 51/2 (1992), 198–203.

URNOV, DMITRY, 'Plokhaya proza', *LG*, 8 Feb. 1989, 4–5.

URUSOVA, EKATERINA, *Pollion* (St Petersburg, 1774).

—— *Iroidy: muzam posvyashchennye* (St Petersburg, 1777).

—— 'Ee velichestvu Gosudaryne Imperatritse Marii Feodorovne', *Syn otechestva*, 24 (1815), 56.

—— 'Moi semidesyatyi god', *Syn otechestva*, 31 (1816), 160–1.

USPENSKAYA, ELENA, 'Zhena shagayushchego', *NM* (1958), 1: 25–46.

VANEEVA, LARISA, *Iz kubika* (Moscow, 1990).

VANKHANEN, NATALIYA, *Dnevnoi mesyats* (Moscow, 1991).

VASIL'EVA, E., 'Desyat' mesyatsev v zemskoi psikhiatricheskoi kolonii', *RB* (1900) 11: 187–215; 12: 167–84.

VASILEVSKY, A., 'Bez predel', *LG*, 12 Dec. 1990, 4.

VERBITSKAYA, ANASTASIYA, *Istoriya odnoi zhizni* (Moscow, 1905).

—— *Schast'e: novye rasskazy* (Moscow, 1905).

—— *Moim chitatelyam: Avtobiograficheskie ocherki s dvumya portretami* (Moscow, 1908).

—— *Klyuchi schastya* (6 vols.; Moscow, 1909–13).

VESEL'KOVA-KIL'SHTET, MARIYA, *Pesni zabytoi usad'by* (St Petersburg, 1912).

VILENSKY, S. S. (ed.), *Dodnes' tyagoteet* (Moscow, 1989).

VIL'KINA, L., 'Protivorechie', *ZR* (1906), 3: 46.

VOLGINA, TAT'YANA, 'Pridanoe' and other poems, *KN* (1941), 3: 89.

VOLKONSKAYA, MARIYA, *Zapiski*, ed. M. S. Volkonsky (St Petersburg, 1904).

VOLKONSKAYA, ZINAIDA [as Zenaïde Volkonsky], *Quatre nouvelles* (Moscow, 1820).

—— 'Snovidenie: pis'mo', *Galateya* (1829), 5: 21–31.

—— *Oeuvres choisies de la princesse Zenaïde Volkonsky* (Paris and Karlsruhe, 1865).

—— *Sochineniya* (Paris and Karlsruhe, 1865).

—— 'A Madame de Staël', in M. Azadovsky, 'Iz materialov "Stroganovskoi akademii" ', *Literaturnoe nasledstvo*, 33–4 (1939), 210.

VOLKOVA, ANNA ALEKSANDROVNA, *Stikhotvoreniya devitsy Volkovoi* (St Petersburg, 1807).

VOLKOVA, ANNA IVANOVNA, *Vospominaniya* (Moscow, 1913).

VOLOZOVA, O., 'Vo sne glaza dushi sverkayut', *Teatr* (1991), 10: 76.

VORONTSOVA, ELENA, 'Women Writers in Russia', *Index on Censorship* (1989), 3: 26.

VOZNESENSKAYA, YULIYA, *The Women's Decameron*, trans. W. B. Linton (London, 1986). (Russian text published as *Zhenskii dekameron* (Tel Aviv, 1987).)

WEEKS, LAURA D., ' "I named her Ariadna": The Demeter-Persephone Myth in Tsvetaeva's Poems for her Daughter', *SR* 49/4 (1990), 568–84.

YAN'KOVA, E. YA., *Rasskazy babushki: iz vospominaii pyati pokolenii, zapisannye ee vnukom D. Blagovo* (1877), ed. T. I. Oriatskaya (Leningrad, 1989).

YUNINA, LYUBOV', *Zhenshchina v odnokomnatnoi kvartire: rasskazy* (Moscow, 1985).

ZEIDE, ALLA, 'Larisa Reisner: Myth as Justification for Life', *Russian Review*, 5/2 (1992), 172–87.

ZERNOVA, RUF', *Zhenskie rasskazy* (New York, 1981).

—— *Mute Phone Calls*, ed. Helen Reeve (New Brunswick, NJ, 1991).

ZHADOVSKAYA, YULIYA, *Stikhotvoreniya* (St Petersburg, 1858).

ZHELIKHOVSKAYA, V. I., FADEEVA, N. A., and AKHMATOVA, E. N., 'Po povodu stat'i "Roman odnoi zabytoi romanistki" ', *Istoricheskii vestnik*, 26/11 (1886), 456–64.

Zhenskaya logika, ed. L. V. Stepanenko and A. V. Fomenko (Moscow, 1989).

ZHUKOVA, MARIYA (as 'M. Zh——va'), *Vechera na Karpovke* (2 vols.; St Petersburg, 1837–8).

—— (as 'M. Zh——va'), *Povesti* (2 vols.; St Petersburg, 1840).

—— *Ocherki Yuzhnoi Frantsii i Nittsy* (2 vols.; St Petersburg, 1844).

—— 'Dacha na Petergofskoi doroge', *OZ* 39 (1845), 225–326.

—— 'Epizod iz zhizni derevenskoi damy', *OZ* 52 (1847), 1–116.

—— 'Naden'ka', *S* 40 (1853), 137–82.

—— 'Dve svad'by', *OZ* 112 (1857), 591–663; 113 (1857), 51–138.

—— *Vechera na Karpovke* (Moscow, 1986).

ZHURAVLEVA, TAT'YANA, 'Chernaya dyra', *Yunost'* (1989), 1: 11–14.

ZINOV'EVA-ANNIBAL, LIDIYA, 'Pevuchii osel. Trilogii pervaya chast': altsvet', *Tsvetnik or: Koshnitsa pervaya: Stikhotvoreniya* (St Petersburg, 1907), 121–69.

—— *Tragicheskii zverinets* (St Petersburg, 1907).

—— *Tridtsat' tri uroda* (St Petersburg, 1907).

—— 'Teni sna', *Severnye tsvety: assiiriiskii al'manakh*, 4 (Moscow, 1915), 134–46.

—— *Net!* (St Petersburg, 1918).

—— 'Thirty-Three Abominations', trans. Sam Cioran, *Russian Literature Tri-Quarterly*, 9 (1974), 94–116.

ZUBOVA, L. V., *Poeziya Mariny Tsvetaevoi: lingvisticheskii aspekt* (Moscow, 1989).

ZVYAGINTSEVA, VERA, *Izbrannye stikhi* (Moscow, 1968).

3. Women's History in Russia; General Russian History; Publications by Russian Male Writers; Non-Russian Women's Writing; Feminist Theory and Criticism; Miscellaneous

ABRAMOVICH, N. YA., *Istoriya russkoi poezii ot Pushkina do nashikh dnei* (Moscow, 1915).

AGAFONOV, V., 'Polovoi vopros', *MB* (1908), 3, sect. 2, 1–38; 4, sect. 2, 1–28.

ALEKSANDROVA, VERA, *A History of Soviet Literature 1917–1964: From Gorky to Solzhenitsyn* (New York, 1964).

ALEKSEEV, V., 'Yazyk svetskikh dam i razvitie yazykovoi normy v XVIII veke', *Funktsional'nye i sotsial'nye razvitiya russkogo literaturnogo yazyka XVIII veka: sbornik nauchnykh trudov* (Leningrad, 1984), 82–95.

ANDERSON, BONNIE S., and ZINSSER, JUDITH P., *A History of Their Own: Women in Europe from Prehistory to the Present* (2 vols.; London, 1990).

ANDREW, JOE, *Women in Russian Literature* (London, 1988).

—— ' "Spoil the Purest of Ladies": Male and Female in Isaak Babel's *Konarmiya*', *EP* 14/2 (1989), 1–27.

—— (ed.), *Poetics of the Text: Essays to Celebrate Twenty Years of the Neo-Formalist Circle* (Amsterdam, 1992).

—— *Narrative and Desire: Masculine and Feminine in Russian Literature, 1822–1849* (London, 1993).

ANNENSKY, INNOKENTY, *Melanippa-filosof* (St Petersburg, 1901).

—— 'Laodamiya: liricheskaya tragediya', *Al'manakh Severnaya rech'* (St Petersburg, 1906), 137–208.

Anon., *An Englishwoman in Russia, by a Lady Ten Years Resident in that Country* (London, 1855).

Anon., *Russian Chit-Chat* (London, 1845).

Antaeus Jubilee Edition: Fiction, Poetry, Documents (London, 1990).

ANUSHKIN, N. S., *Ushedshaya Moskva: vospominaniya sovremennikov o Moskve vtoroi poloviny XIX veka* (Moscow, 1964).

APUSHKIN, N. (ed.), *Valery Bryusov v avtobiograficheskikh zapisyakh, pis'makh, vospominaniyakh sovremennikov i otzyvakh kritiki* (Moscow, 1929).

ARKHANGEL'SKY, B. A., and SPERANSKY, G. N., *Mat' i ditya: shkola molodykh materei* (Moscow, 1951).

ASEEV, NIKOLAI, *Sobranie sochinenie v 5 tomakh* (Moscow, 1963).

ATTWOOD, LYNNE, *The New Soviet Man and Woman: Sex-Role Socialisation in the USSR* (London, 1990).

BABEL', ISAAK, *Konarmiya* (Moscow, 1928).

BARATYNSKY, EVGENY, 'Istoriya koketstva', *Polnoe sobranie sochinenii* (2 vols.; Petrograd, 1915), ii. 204–7.

—— *Polnoe sobranie stikhotvorenii* (Leningrad, 1957).

—— *Selected Letters*, ed. G. Barratt (The Hague, 1973).

BARSOV, E. V. (ed.), *Prichitaniya severnogo kraya: antologiya* (2 vols.; Moscow, 1872–82).

BARTHES, ROLAND, *Image—Music—Text*, trans. Stephen Heath (London, 1977).

BARTLETT, R. (ed.), *Russia and the World of the Eighteenth Century: Proceedings of the Third International Conference Organised by the Study Group on Eighteenth-Century Russia* (Columbus, Ohio, 1988).

—— and HARTLEY, JANET M. (eds.), *Russia in the Age of the Enlightenment: Essays for Isabel de Madariaga* (London, 1990).

BEAJOUR, ELIZABETH KLOSTY, *Alien Voices: Bilingual Russian Writers of the 'First' Emigration* (Ithaca, NY, 1989).

BELINSKY, V., *Polnoe sobranie sochinenii* (13 vols.; Moscow, 1953–9).

BELOV, VASILY, *Vse vperedi* (Moscow, 1987).

BELYAEVA, L. N., ZINOV'EVA, M. K., and NIKIFOROV, M. M., *Bibliografiya periodicheskikh izdanii Rossii 1901–1916* (3 vols.; Moscow, 1958–60).

BERGER, JOHN, *Ways of Seeing* (London, 1972).

BERNSHTEIN, A. N., 'Voprosy polovoi zhizni v programme semeinogo i shkol'nogo vospitaniya', *RM* (1908), 3, sect. 2, 51–71.

BESTUZHEV-MARLINSKY, A., *Sochineniya v 2 tomakh* (Moscow, 1988).

BILIBIN, I., 'Narodnoe tvorchestvo Severa', *Mir iskusstva* (1904), 11: 303–18.

BINYON, T. J., 'Valery Bryusov: Life, Literary Theory, Poetry', D.Phil. thesis (Oxford University, 1969).

BLACK, J. L., 'Educating Women', in his *Citizens for the Fatherland: Education, Educators and Pedagogical Ideals in Eighteenth-Century Russia* (New York, 1979), 152–72.

BLOK, ALEKSANDR, *Sobranie sochinenii v 8 tomakh* (Moscow, 1960–3).

BOBORYKIN, P., 'Goluboi lif', in his *Sobranie romanov, povestei i rasskazov*, iii (St Petersburg, 1897), 146–80.

BOGDANOVICH, TAT'YANA, 'Zhenskoe dvizhenie za poslednie pyat'desyat let', *MB* (1903), 9: 204–37.

—— 'Povest' moei zhizni: vospominaniya 1880–1909'. Typescript of *c.*1940. Publication in preparation, ed. A. Konechny and K. Kumpan.

BORODIN, LEONID, *Partings*, trans. David Floyd (London, 1989).

BOWEN, ELIZABETH, *The Heat of the Day* (1948; London, 1976).

BOYM, SVETLANA, *Death in Quotation Marks: Cultural Myths of the Modern Poet* (Cambridge, Mass., 1991).

BRIDGER, SUSAN, *Women in the Soviet Countryside: Women's Roles in Rural Development in the Soviet Union* (Cambridge, 1987).

BRISTOL, EVELYN, *A History of Russian Poetry* (New York, 1991).

BRITTAIN, VERA, *The Testament of Youth* (London, 1979).

BROOKS, JEFFREY, *When Russia Learned to Read* (Princeton, NJ, 1984).

BROWER, DANIEL, *The Russian City: From Tradition to Modernity* (Berkeley, Calif., 1990).

BROWN, EDWARD J., *Russian Literature since the Revolution* (Cambridge, Mass., 1982).

BRYUSOV, VALERY, 'Segodnyashnii den' russkoi poezii', *RM* (1912), 7, sect. 3, 17–28.

—— *Sobranie sochinenii v 7 tomakh* (Moscow, 1973–5).

BUCHWALD, EVA A. J., 'Ideals of Womanhood in the Literature of Finland and Russia 1894–1914', Ph.D. thesis (London University, 1990).

BUCKLEY, MARY, *Women and Ideology in the Soviet Union* (Hemel Hempstead, 1989).

—— (ed.), *Perestroika and Soviet Women* (Cambridge, 1992).

BUDDE, E. F., *Polozhenie russkoi zhenshchiny po bytovym pesnyam* (Voronezh, 1883).

Budni velikikh stroek: stikhi russkikh poetov o trude, ed. V. Zheleznov (Moscow, 1988).

BUKHSTAB, B. YA. (ed.), *Poety 1840–1850 gg.* (Leningrad, 1972).

BUKOV, M. (ed.), *Okhrana zhenskogo truda: sbornik deistvuyushchego zakonodatel'stva i rukovodyashchikh ukazanii VTsSPS po prorabote sredi zhenshchin* (Moscow, 1926).

BULGAKOV, MIKHAIL, *Belaya gvardiya. Teatral'nyi roman. Master i Margarita* (Moscow, 1973).

BUNIN, I., *Sobranie sochinenii v 9 tomakh* (Moscow, 1965–7).

BUTLER, MARILYN, *Jane Austen and the War of Ideas* (2nd edn.; Oxford, 1987).

BYNUM, CAROLINE WALKER, *Jesus as Mother: Studies in the Spirituality of the High Middle Ages* (Berkeley, Calif., 1982).

CAROCCI, RENATA, *Les Héroides dans la seconde moitié du XVIII siècle* (Paris, 1988).

CHERNYSHEVSKY, N. G., *Polnoe sobranie sochinenii* (15 vols. and 1 supp. vol.; Moscow, 1939–53).

—— *Izbrannye proizvedeniya v 3 tomakh* (Leningrad, 1978).

Chetvertyi s"ezd sovetskikh pisatelei, 22–27 maya 1967 goda (Moscow, 1969).

CHOLDIN, MARIANNA TAX, and FRIEDBERG, MAURICE (eds.), *The Red Pencil* (Boston, 1988).

CHUKHONTSEV, OLEG (ed.), *Dissonant Voices: The New Soviet Fiction* (London, 1991).

CHULKOV, M. D., *Peresmeshnik* (Leningrad, 1987).

CLARK, KATERINA, *The Soviet Novel: History as Ritual* (Chicago, 1981).

CLEMENTS, BARBARA EVANS, ENGEL, BARBARA ALPERN, and WOROBEC, CHRISTINE (eds.), *Russia's Women: Accommodation, Resistance, Transformation* (Berkeley, Calif., 1991).

COLVIN, HOWARD, *Architecture and the After-Life* (New Haven, Conn., 1991).

CONQUEST, ROBERT, *The Great Terror: A Reassessment* (London, 1990).

COPLESTONE, FREDERICK C., *Russian Religious Philosophy: Selected Aspects* (Tunbridge Wells, 1988).

CORNWELL, NEIL (ed.), *Daniil Kharms and the Poetics of the Absurd: Essays and Materials* (London, 1991).

COSTLOW, JANE, SANDLER, STEPHANIE, and VOWLES, JUDITH (eds.), *Sexuality in Russian Culture* (Stanford, Calif., 1993).

CRISP, OLGA, and EDMONDSON, LINDA (eds.), *Civil Rights in Imperial Russia* (Oxford, 1989).

DAL', V., *Tolkovyi slovar' velikorusskogo yazyka* (4 vols.; Moscow, 1882).

DAVIDSON, PAMELA, *The Poetic Imagination of Vyacheslav Ivanov: A Russian Symbolist's Perception of Dante* (Cambridge, 1989).

DAVIES, DIDO, *William Gerhardie: A Biography* (Oxford, 1990).

DAVYDOV, D., *Stikhotvoreniya* (Leningrad, 1984).

DAVYDOV, N. V., *Iz proshlogo* (Moscow, 1913).

DEANE, SEAMUS (ed.), *The Field Day Anthology of Irish Writing* (3 vols.; Derry, 1991).

Dekrety sovetskoi vlasti (13 vols. and continuing; Moscow, 1957–).

DE LA SUZE, HENRIETTE, and PELISSON, P., *Recueil des pièces galantes en prose et en vers* (1663; 2 vols.; Paris, 1748).

DEL'VIG, ANTON, *Sochineniya* (Leningrad, 1986).

DEWHIRST, M., and FARRELL, J., *The Soviet Censorship* (Metuchen, NJ, 1973).

DOBROLYUBOV, N. A., *Sobranie sochinenii v 9 tomakh* (Moscow-Leningrad, 1961–4).

Docheri Rossii, ed. I. Chernyaeva (Moscow, 1975).

DOHERTY, JUSTIN, 'Culture of the Word: Aspects of Acmeist Poetic Theory and Fiction', D.Phil. thesis (Oxford University, 1989).

DONCHIN, GEORGETTE, *The Influence of French Symbolism on Russian Poetry* (The Hague, 1958).

DOSTOEVSKY, F. M., *Polnoe sobranie sochinenii v 30 tomakh* (Leningrad, 1972–90).

Drammaticheskii slovar' (Moscow, 1787; repr. St Petersburg, 1880).

DUNHAM, VERA, *In Stalin's Time: Middle-Class Values in Soviet Fiction* (Cambridge, 1976).

DURYLIN, S., 'G-zha de Stal' i ee russkie otnosheniya', *Literaturnoe nasledstvo*, 32–4 (1939), 215–30.

DZHANGINOV, KAREN (ed.), *Antologiya russkogo verlibra* (Moscow, 1991).

EDMONDSON, LINDA HARRIET, *Feminism in Russia 1900–1917* (London, 1984).

—— (ed.), *Women and Society in Russia* (Cambridge, 1992).

—— 'Women's Emancipation and Theories of Sexual Difference (1850–1917)', in Marianne Liljeström, Eila Mäntysaari, and Arja Rosenholm (eds.), *Gender Restructuring* (Helsinki, 1993).

EFIMENKO, ALEKSANDRA, *Issledovaniya narodnoi zhizni* (Moscow, 1884).

ELEONSKAYA, M., *Russkaya chastushka* (Moscow, 1910).

ELIOT, T. S., *Selected Poems* (London, 1961).

ENGEL, BARBARA ALPERN, *Mothers and Daughters: Women of the Intelligentsia in Nineteenth-Century Russia* (Cambridge, 1983).

—— 'The Woman's Side: Male Outmigration and the Family Economy in Kostroma Province', *SR* 45/2 (1986), 257–71.

—— 'St. Petersburg Prostitutes in the Late Nineteenth Century: A Personal and Social Profile', *Russian Review*, 48 (1989), 21–44.

—— 'Engendering Russia's History: Women in Post-Emancipation Russia and the Soviet Union', *SR* 51/2 (1992), 309–21.

ENGELSTEIN, LAURA, 'Morality and the Wooden Spoon: Russian Doctors View

Syphilis, Social Class and Sexual Behavior, 1890–1905', *Representations*, 14 (1986), 169–208.

EROFEEV, VIKTOR, *Russkaya krasavitsa* (Moscow, 1990).

—— 'Sex and Perestroika', *Liber* 2/1 (1990), 17.

EZHOV, I. S. and SHAMURIN, E. I., *Russkaya poeziya XX veka* (Moscow, 1925).

FIDLER, F. (ed.), *Pervye literaturnye shagi* (Moscow, 1911).

FIESELER, BEATE, ' "Ein Huhn ist kein Vogel—ein Weib ist kein Mensch." Russische Frauen (1860–1930) im Spiegel historischer Forschung', in Beate Fieseler and Birgit Schulze (eds.), *Frauengeschichte: gesucht, gefunden? Auskünfte zum Stand der historischen Frauenforschung* (Cologne, 1991), 214–35.

FILTZER, DONALD, *Soviet Workers and Stalinist Industrialisation: The Formation of Modern Soviet Production Relations* (New York, 1986).

FLEISHMAN, L., KHYUZ [Hughes] R., and RAEVSKAYA-KHYUZ, O. (eds.), *Russkii Berlin* (Paris, 1983).

FRANKEL, EDITH ROGOVIN, *Novyi mir* (Cambridge, 1981).

FREIDIN, GREGORY, *A Coat of Many Colors: Osip Mandelstam's Mythologies of Self-Transformation* (Berkeley, Calif., 1988).

G. SH., 'Filosofiya polov Otto Veiningera', *RM* (1908), 6, pt. 2, 147–59.

GARRARD, JOHN, and GARRARD, CAROL, *Inside the Soviet Writers' Union* (London, 1990).

GASPAROV, M. L., *Ocherki istorii russkogo stikha* (Moscow, 1984).

GAY, PETER, *The Bourgeois Experience: from Victoria to Freud* (2 vols.; New York, 1984–6).

GENDLIN, L., *Perebiraya starye bloknoty* (Amsterdam, 1986).

GENLIS, MADAME DE, *Les veillées du château* (Paris, 1784).

—— *L'Épouse impertinente par air, suivie du Mari corrupteur et de la femme philosophe* (Paris, 1804).

—— *Sainclair, ou la victime des sciences et des arts* (Paris and St Petersburg, 1808).

—— *Hortense, ou la victime des romans et des voyages, pour faire suite à Sainclair* (Paris and St Petersburg, 1808).

—— *Histoire des femmes françaises les plus célèbres et de leur influence sur la littérature française* (2 vols.; Paris and London, 1811).

GERTSEN [HERZEN], A., *Sochineniya v 9 tomakh* (Moscow 1955–8).

GILBERT, SANDRA M., and GUBAR, SUSAN, *The Madwoman in the Attic: the Woman Writer and the Nineteenth-Century Literary Imagination* (2nd edn.; New Haven, Conn., 1984).

—— *No Man's Land: The Place of the Woman Writer in the Twentieth Century* (2 vols. and continuing; New Haven, Conn., 1988–).

GILLESPIE, DAVID, 'Apocalypse Now: Village Prose and the Death of Russia', *The Modern Language Review*, 87/2 (Apr. 1992), 407–17.

GINZBURG, LIDIYA, *O psikhologicheskoi proze* (Leningrad, 1977) (trans. Judson Rosengrant as *On Psychological Prose* (Princeton, NJ, 1991).

GINZBURG, LIDIYA, and VATSURO, V. E. (eds.), *Poety 1820–1830 godov* (2 vols.; Leningrad, 1971).

GIPPEL'SON, M. I., and KUMPAN, K. A. (eds.), *Russkaya epigramma* (Leningrad, 1988).

GIPPIUS, Z. N., *Vosem'desyat vosem' sovremennykh stikhotvorenii, izbrannykh Z. N. Gippius* (Petrograd, 1917).

GLICKMAN, ROSE, *Russian Factory Women: Workplace and Society, 1880–1914* (Berkeley, Calif., 1984).

GLINKA, SERGEI, *Novoe detskoe chtenie, izdannoe Sergeem Glinkoyu* (Moscow, 1822).

—— *Moskovskii al'manakh dlya prekrasnogo pola: izdanyi [sic] na 1826–i god Sergeem Glinkoyu* (Moscow, 1825).

GOETHE, J. W. VON, *Werke: Hamburger Ausgabe in 14 Bänden* (10th edn.; Stuttgart, 1981).

GOLOMSTOCK, IGOR, *Totalitarian Art* (London, 1990).

GORBUNOVA, MINNA, 'Zhenskie promysly v Moskovskoi gubernii', *Sbornik statisticheskikh svedenii po Moskovskoi gubernii*, 7/4 (1882).

GORODETSKY, SERGEI, 'Nekotorye techeniya v sovremennoi russkoi poezii', *Apollon* (1913), 1: 46–50.

GRIBOEDOV, ALEKSANDR, *Polnoe sobranie sochinenii v stikhakh* (Leningrad, 1988).

GROMOV, PAVEL, *A. Blok, ego predshestvenniki i sovremenniki* (Moscow-Leningrad, 1966).

GROSSMAN, JOAN DELANEY, *Valery Bryusov and the Riddle of Russian Decadence* (Stanford, Calif., 1985).

GUMILEV, NIKOLAI, 'Zavety simvolizma i akmeizm', *Apollon* (1913), 1: 42–5.
—— *Neizdannoe i nesobrannoe*, ed. Michael Barber and Sheelagh Graham (Paris, 1986).

HAMMARBERG, GITTA, *From the Idyll to the Novel: Karamzin's Sentimentalist Prose* (Cambridge, 1991).

HANSEN-LÖVE, A. A., *Der russische Symbolismus: System und Entfaltung der poetischen Motive* (1 vol. and continuing; Vienna, 1989–).

HERMANN, LESLEY SINGER, 'George Sand and the Nineteenth-Century Russian Novel: The Quest for a Heroine', Ph.D. thesis (Columbia University, New York, 1979).

HEYM, G., *Novyi rossiisko-frantsuzskii-nemetskii slovar'* (Moscow, 1799).

HILL, R., 'The CPSU: Decline and Collapse', *ISS* 12 (1991), 97–111.

HINGLEY, RONALD, *Russian Writers and Soviet Society* (London, 1979).

Histoire de la littérature russe: le XX siècle, ed. E. Etkind, G. Nivat, I. Serman, and E. Strada (3 vols.; Paris, 1980–7).

HOBSBAWM, ERIC, and RANGER, TERENCE, *The Invention of Tradition* (Cambridge, 1986).

HODGSON, KATHARINE, 'Russian Soviet War Poetry 1941–45', Ph.D. thesis (Cambridge University, 1991).

HOFMANNSTHAL, HUGO VON, *Sämtliche Werke: Gedichte 1* (Frankfurt am Main, 1984).

HOLLAND, BARBARA (ed.), *Soviet Sisterhood* (Bloomington, Ind., 1985).

HOSKING, GEOFFREY, *Beyond Socialist Realism: Soviet Fiction Since 'Ivan Denisovich'* (London, 1980).

—— AVES, JONATHAN, and DUNCAN, PETER, *The Road to Post-Communism: Independent Political Movements in the Soviet Union 1985–1991* (London, 1992).

HOWELLS, D. L. L., 'The Origins of *Frantsel' Ventsian* and *Parizh i Vena*', *OSP* 19 (1986), 29–45.

HUGHES, LINDSEY, *Sophia, Regent of Russia* (London, 1990).

ILIC, MELANIE, 'Soviet Protective Labour Legislation and Female Workers in the 1920s and 1930s', in Marianne Liljeström, Eila Mäntysaari, and Arja Rosenholm (eds.), *Gender Restructuring in Russian Studies* (Slavica Tamperensia, 11; Helsinki, 1993).

IL'INA, NATAL'YA, *Belogorskaya krepost'* (Moscow, 1989).

IVANOV, VYACHESLAV, 'Ellinskaya religiya stradayushchego boga', *Novyi put'* (1904) 1: 110–34; 2: 48–78; 3: 38–61; 5: 28–40; 8: 17–26; 9: 4–70.

—— *Sobranie sochinenii* (4 vols. and continuing; Brussels, 1974–).

IVASK, GEORGE, 'Russian Modernist Poets and the Mystic Sectarians', in George Gibian and H. W. Tjalsma (eds.), *Russian Modernism: Culture and the Avant-Garde 1900–1930* (Ithaca, NY, 1976).

IZGOEV, A. S., 'Po st. 1001', *RM* (1908), 9, sect. 2, 187–93.

IZMAILOV, ALEKSANDR, *Polnoe sobranie sochinenii* (3 vols.; Moscow, 1890).

JOHANSON, CHRISTINE, *Women's Struggle for Higher Education in Russia, 1855–1900* (Kingston, Ontario, 1987).

JONES, MALCOLM, *Dostoevsky after Bakhtin* (Cambridge, 1990).

KARAMZIN, N. M., *Bednaya Liza* (Moscow, 1796).

—— *Sochineniya* (8 vols.; Moscow, 1803–4).

KARP, CAROLE, 'Sand and the Russians', *The George Sand Papers: Conference Proceedings 1976* (Hofstra, 1980), 151–61.

—— 'George Sand in the Estimate of the Russian "Men of the Forties"', *The George Sand Papers: Conference Proceedings 1978* (Hofstra, 1982).

KAVERIN, VENIAMIN, *Mastera i podmaster'ya: rasskazy* (Moscow-St. Petersburg, 1923).

KELLY, CATRIONA, 'Bacchic Revels: Innokentii Annenskii's *Famira-kifared* and the Satyrs', *Essays in Poetics*, 10/2 (1985), 76–92.

—— 'Innokenty Annensky and the Classical Ideal: Poetry, Translations, Drama and Literary Theory', D.Phil. thesis (Oxford University, 1985).

—— MAKIN, MICHAEL, and SHEPHERD, DAVID (eds.), *Discontinuous Discourses in Modern Russian Literature* (London, 1989).

—— *Petrushka, the Russian Carnival Puppet Theatre* (Cambridge, 1990).

KENT, SARAH, and JACQUELINE MORREAU (eds.), *Women's Images of Men* (London, 1985).

KHARMS, DANIIL, *Polet v nebesa: stikhi, proza, dramy, pis'ma* (Leningrad, 1988).

KHLEBNIKOV, VELIMIR, *Tvoreniya* (Moscow, 1988).

KNYAZHNIN, YAKOV, *Izbrannye proizvedeniya* (Leningrad, 1984).

KOENKER, DIANE, *Moscow Workers and the 1917 Revolution* (Princeton, NJ, 1981).

KOONZ, CLAUDIA, *Mothers in the Fatherland: Women, the Family and Nazi Politics* (New York, 1987).

KOZLOV, I., 'O szhatosti v proze', *NM* (1955), 6: 263–78.

KRECHETOV, SERGEI, 'Arnol'd Ariel', *Doloi zhenshchin*, Moscow, 1905 [. . .] Georg Groddek, *Problema zhenshchiny*, St Petersburg, 1905' (review-article), *Vesy* (1905), 3: 68–71.

KRISTEVA, JULIA, *Desire in Language: A Semiotic Approach to Literature and Art*, ed. Leon S. Roudiez, trans. *idem*, Thomas Gora and Alice Jardine (Oxford, 1981).

KURGANOV, N. G., *Pis'movnik, soderzhashchii v sebe nauku russkogo yazyka [. . .]* (5th edn.; St Petersburg, 1793).

KUZMINSKY, KONSTANTIN K., and KOVALEV, GREGORY L. (eds.), *The Blue Lagoon Anthology of Modern Russian Poetry* (5 vols. in 9; Newtonville, Mass., 1980–6).

LAKSHIN, V., *Novyi mir vo vremya Khrushcheva* (Moscow, 1989).

LANE, CHRISTEL, The Rites of Rulers: Ritual in Industrial Society: The Soviet Case (Cambridge, 1981).

LAPIDUS, GAIL, *Women in Soviet Society: Equality, Development and Social Change* (Berkeley, Calif., 1978).

LEIKINA-SVIRSKAYA, V. R., *Intelligentsiya v Rossii vtoroi poloviny XIX-go veka* (Moscow, 1971).

—— *Russkaya intelligentsiya v 1900–1917 godakh* (Moscow, 1981).

V. Lenin o Tolstom (Moscow, 1928).

LERMONTOV, MIKHAIL, *Sobranie sochinenii v 4 tomakh* (Leningrad, 1980).

LESSING, DORIS, *The Golden Notebook* (London, 1962).

LEZHNEV, I., 'Kratkost'—sestra talanta', *NM* (1955), 5: 218–30.

LIEVEN, DOMINIC, *Russia's Rulers under the Old Regime* (London, 1989).

LILJESTRÖM, MARIANNE, MÄNTYSAARI, EILA, and ROSENHOLM, ARJA (eds.), *Gender Restructuring in Russian Studies* (Slavica Tamperensia, 11; Helsinki, 1993).

L.L.F., 'Materinstvo i umstvennyi trud', *MB* (1902), 9, sect. 2, 7–20.

LOMONOSOV, MIKHAILO, *Izbrannye filosofskie proizvedeniya* (Moscow, 1950).

LOTMAN, YU. M., *Aleksandr Sergeevich Pushkin: biografiya pisatelya* (Leningrad, 1982).

—— and AL'TSHULLER, M. G. (eds.), *Poety 1790–1810 godov* (Leningrad, 1971).

—— and USPENSKY, B. A., *The Semiotics of Russian Culture*, ed. Ann Shukman (Ann Arbor, Mich., 1984).

LUDMER, YA., 'Bab'i stony', *Yuridicheskii vestnik* (1884), 11: 446–87; 14: 658–75.

L'VOV, PAVEL, *Rossiiskaya Pamela, ili istoriya Marii, dobrodetel'noi posel-yanki* (2 vols.; St Petersburg, 1789).

L'VOVA, NADEZHDA, 'Ya odenus' nevestoi v atlasnoe beloe plat'e', *RM* (1911), 11: 71.

LYALL, ROBERT, *The Character of the Russians, and a Detailed History of Moscow* (London, 1823).

M. and O., 'Tsifry i fakty iz perepisi Sankt Peterburga v 1900 godu', *RM* (1902), 11, sect. 2, 72–92.

MCAULEY, ALISTAIR, *Women's Work and Wages in the Soviet Union* (London, 1981).

MCMILLIN, ARNOLD (ed.), *Under Western Eyes: The West as Reflected in Recent Russian Writing* (London, 1991).

MADARIAGA, ISABEL DE, *Russia in the Age of Catherine the Great* (London, 1981).

MAKANIN, VLADIMIR, *Portrety vokrug; Odin i odna, romany* (Moscow, 1991).

MALLY, LYNN, *Culture of the Future: The Proletkult Movement in Revolution-ary Russia* (Berkeley, Calif., 1990).

MANDEL'SHTAM, OSIP, *Sobranie sochinenii* (4 vols.; Washington, DC, 1967–81).

—— *Stikhotvoreniya* (Leningrad, 1979).

MANNING, R., *The Crisis of the Old Order in Russia: Gentry and Government* (Princeton, NJ, 1981).

MANSFIELD, KATHERINE, *Selected Stories* (Oxford, 1981).

MARKOV, VLADIMIR, *Russian Futurism* (London, 1969).

—— (ed.), *Manifesty i programmy russkikh futuristov* (Munich, 1967).

MARTINDALE, CHARLES (ed.), *Ovid Renewed: Ovidian Influences on Literature and Art from the Middle Ages to the Twentieth Century* (Cambridge, 1988).

MAXWELL, MARGARET, *Narodniki Women* (Oxford, 1981).

MAYAKOVSKY, VLADIMIR, *Sochineniya v 3-kh tomakh* (Moscow, 1978).

MEEHAN-WATERS, BRENDA, 'From Contemplative Practice to Charitable Ac-tivity: Russian Women's Religious Communities and the Development of Charitable Work, 1861–1917', in Kathleen McCarthy (ed.), *Lady Bountiful Revisited: Women, Philanthropy and Power* (New Brunswick, NJ, 1990).

MEL'GUNOV, S. P., and SIDOROV, N. P. (eds.), *Masonstvo v ego proshlom i nastoyashchem* (2 vols.; Moscow, 1914–15).

MICHAUD, GUY, *Message poétique du symbolisme* (Paris, 1961).

MICHIE, HELENA, *The Flesh Made Word: Female Figures and Women's Bodies* (New York, 1989).

MIKHNOV, S., *Zhenshchina s biologicheskoi tochki zreniya* (Yurev [Tartu], 1904).

MINTS, Z. G., 'O nekotorykh "neomifologicheskikh" tekstakh v tvorchestve russkikh simvolistov', *Blokovskii sbornik*, 3, *Uchenye zapiski Tartuskogo gosudarstvennogo universiteta*, 459 (Tartu, 1979), 76–120.

MIRSKY, D. S., *Contemporary Russian Literature 1881–1925* (London, 1926).

—— *A History of Russian Literature from its Earliest Times to the Death of Dostoevsky* (London, 1927).

MIRSKY, D. S., *A History of Russian Literature* (London, 1949).
—— *Uncollected Writings*, ed. G. S. Smith (Berkeley, Calif., 1989).
MOI, TORIL, *Sexual/Textual Politics* (London, 1985).
MØLLER, PETER ULF, *Postlude to the Kreutzer Sonata: Tolstoy and the Debate on Sexual Morality in Russian Literature in the 1890s*, trans. John Kendal (Amsterdam, 1989).
MOSER, CHARLES (ed.), *The Cambridge History of Russian Literature* (1990; rev. edn.; Cambridge, 1992).
MOSSMAN, ELLIOTT (ed.), *The Correspondence of Boris Pasternak and Olga Freidenberg*, trans. Elliot Mossman and Margaret Wettlin (London, 1982).
NABOKOV, VLADIMIR, *Priglashenie na kazn'* (Paris, 1938).
—— *Speak, Memory* (London, 1986).
—— *Selected Letters 1940–1977*, ed. Dmitri Nabokov and Matthew J. Bruccoli (London, 1989).
NEKRASOV, N. A., *Polnoe sobranie sochinenii i pisem v 15 tomakh* (Moscow, 1981–).
NIVAT, GEORGES (ed.), *Odna ili dve russkikh literatury* (Geneva, 1981).
Noveishii vseobshchii pesennik ili sobranie otbornykh i vsekh dosele izvestnykh pesen (4 vols.; Moscow, 1822).
OSTENC, MICHEL, 'La Conception de la femme fasciste dans l'Italie mussolinienne', *Risorgimento* (1983), 3: 155–74.
OVID, *Heroides and Amores* (London, 1914).
OVTSYN, V., 'K istorii i statistiki gorodskogo proletariata v Rossii', *RM* (1891), 5, sect. 2, 60–85.
PACHMUSS, TEMIRA (ed.), *Russian Literature in the Baltic between the Two World Wars* (Columbus, Ohio, 1988).
PAPERNO, IRINA, *Chernyshevsky and the Age of Realism: A Study in the Semiotics of Behavior* (Stanford, Calif., 1988).
PERRIE, MAUREEN, *The Agrarian Policy of the Russian Socialist–Revolutionary Party from its Origins through the Revolution of 1905–7* (Cambridge, 1976).
Pervyi s"ezd sovetskikh pisatelei: stenograficheskii otchet (Moscow, 1934).
PETINA, L. N., *Khudozhestvennaya priroda literaturnogo al'boma 1-i poloviny XIX veka. Avtoreferat dissertatsii* (Tartu, 1988).
PISAREV, D. I., *Sochineniya v 4 tomakh* (Moscow, 1955–6).
PITTMAN, RIITTA, 'The Writers and the Coup', *Rusistika*, 4 (1991), 22–5.
Poety revolyutsionnogo narodnichestva, ed. A. Bikhter (Leningrad, 1967).
POKROVSKAYA, M. I., 'O zhilishchakh peterburgskikh rabochikh', *RB* (1897), 6: 19–38.
—— *Po podvalam, cherdakam i uglovym kvartiram Peterburga* (St Petersburg, 1903).
POKROVSKY, V., *Damskoi zhurnal 1806–1906* (Moscow, 1906).
POLEVOI, N., 'E. Baratynsky, *Nalozhnitsa*', *Moskovskii telegraf*, 38 (1831), 235–43.
POLONSKY, GRAF, 'Filosof pola i kharaktera', *MB* (1908), 9: 111–48.
POLYAKOVA, ELENA, 'I nastupaet vremya otdykha', *NM* (1969), 12: 192–207.

POPLAVSKY, BORIS, *Sobranie sochinenii* (3 vols.; Berkeley, Calif., 1980–1).
POPOV, T., *Russkaya narodno-bytovaya meditsina* (St Petersburg, 1903).
PORTER, CATHY, *Fathers and Daughters: Russian Women in Revolution* (London, 1976).
Poshchechina obshchestvennomu vkusu (Moscow, 1912).
PRAWER, SIEGBERT (ed.), *The Romantic Period in Germany* (London, 1970).
Prichitaniya, ed. K. V. Chistov and B. E. Chistova (Moscow, 1960).
PROFFER, CARL, and PROFFER, ELLENDEA, *The Barsukov Triangle: The Two-Toned Blonde and Other Stories* (Ann Arbor, Mich., 1984).
PUSHKAREVA, N. L., *Zhenshchiny drevnei Rusi* (Moscow, 1989).
PUSHKIN, A. S., *Polnoe sobranie sochinenii v 10 tomakh* (4th edn., Leningrad, 1977).
—— *Eugene Onegin*, trans. from the Russian with a commentary by Vladimir Nabokov (rev. edn.; 4 vols.; Princeton, NJ, 1975).
PYLYAEV, M. I., *Staryi Peterburg* (St Petersburg, 1887).
—— *Staroe zhit'e* (St Petersburg, 1892).
PYMAN, AVRIL, *The Life of Aleksandr Blok* (2 vols.; Oxford 1978–80).
PYPIN, A. N., *Obshchestvennoe dvizhenie v Rossii pri Aleksandre I: istoricheskie ocherki* (St Petersburg, 1900).
RAEFF, MARC, *Russia Abroad: A Cultural History of the Russian Emigration, 1919–1939* (Oxford, 1990).
RANGER, TERENCE, 'The Invention of Tradition Revisited: The African Case', in T. O. Ranger and O. Vaughan (eds.), *Legitimation and the State in Twentieth-Century Africa* (London, 1993).
RAZGON, LEV, *Nevydumannoe* (Moscow, 1988).
REISNER, M., 'Bogema i kul'turnaya revolyutsiya', *Pechat' i revolyutsiya* (1928), 5: 81–96.
REITBLAT, A. (ed.), *Lubochnaya kniga* (Moscow, 1990).
RENDALL, JANE, *The Origins of Modern Feminism: Women in Britain, France and the United States 1780–1860* (Chicago, 1985).
RILKE, RAINER MARIA, *Sämtliche Werke* (6 vols.; Frankfurt am Main, 1955–66).
ROBERTS, GRAHAM, 'The Vanishing Old Woman: Sexual/Textual Politics in the Work of Daniil Kharms' (unpublished paper; Oxford, 1991).
ROBIN, RÉGINE, *Le Réalisme socialiste: Un ésthetique impossible* (Paris, 1986).
ROSENTHAL, BEATRICE GLATZER, *D. S. Merezhkovsky and the Silver Age* (The Hague, 1976).
—— *Nietzsche in Russia* (Princeton, NJ, 1986).
ROSSETTI, CHRISTINA, *Selected Poems*, ed. C. H. Sisson (Manchester, 1984).
ROSSI, ZHAK [Jacques], *Spravochnik po GULAGU* (London, 1987).
ROZANOV, V. V., 'Afrodita-Diana', *Mir iskusstva* (1899), 2: 85–8.
—— *Kogda nachal'stvo ushlo* (St Petersburg, 1910).
—— *Lyudi lunnogo sveta* (St Petersburg, 1913).
RUDNINSKY, NIKOLAI, 'Znakharstvo v skopinskom i dankovskom uezdakh ryazanskoi gubernii', *Zhivaya starina* (1886).
Rukonog: al'manakh Centrifuga (Moscow, 1914).

RYBAKOV, B. A. (ed.), *Ocherki russkoi kul'tury vosemnadtsatogo veka* (2 vols., Moscow, 1985–7).

Sadok sudei, i (St Petersburg, 1913); ii (St Petersburg, 1913).

SAND, GEORGE, *Lélia*, ed. P. Reboul (Paris, 1960).

—— *Indiana*, ed. Pierre Salomon (Paris, 1983).

SANDLER, STEPHANIE, *Distant Pleasures: Aleksandr Pushkin and the Writing of Exile* (Stanford, Calif., 1989).

SCHERRER, JUTTA, *Die Petersburger Religiös-Philosophischen Vereinigungen: die Entwicklung des religiösischen Selbstverständnisses ihrer Intelligencija-Mitglieder (1901–1917): Forschungen zur Ost-Europäischen Geschichte*, 19 (Berlin, 1973).

SCHULZE, ERNST, *Cäcilie: ein romantisches Gedicht in zwanzig Gesängen* (3 vols.; Leipzig, 1818–19).

SEMENOVA-TYAN-SHANSKAYA, OL'GA, *Zhizn' Ivana: ocherki iz byta krest'yan odnoi iz chernozemnykh gubernii* (St Petersburg, 1914).

SETON-WATSON, HUGH, *The Russian Empire 1801–1917* (Oxford, 1967).

SHELGUNOV, N. V., *Sochineniya* (3 vols.; St Petersburg, 1892).

SHEPARD, ELIZABETH C., 'The Society Tale and the Innovative Argument in Russian Prose Fiction of the 1830s', *Russian Literature*, 10 (1981), 111–61.

SHEPHERD, DAVID, *Beyond Metafiction: Self-Consciousness in Soviet Literature* (Oxford, 1992).

SHISHKOV, A. S. ('Pis'mo Anne Buninoi', 6 May 1816), Saltykov-Shchedrin State Public Library Manuscript Section f. N. 862, Shishkov A. S. N. 7, l. 7.

SHOWALTER, ELAINE, *A Literature of Their Own* (London, 1977).

—— *Sister's Choice* (Oxford, 1991).

SHTEIGER, ANATOLY, *2 × 2: Stikhi* (New York, 1982).

SIPOVSKY, V. V., *Ocherki istorii russkogo romana* (2 vols.; St Petersburg, 1909).

Sistematicheskii sbornik uzakonenii i rasporyazhenii Rabochego i Krest'yanskogo pravitel'stva (Moscow, 1919).

SONTAG, SUSAN, *Against Interpretation and Other Essays* (2nd edn.; London, 1987).

Soviet War Stories (London, 1944).

Soviet Women in the War against Hitlerism (Moscow, 1942).

STAËL, GERMAINE DE, *Delphine* (Paris, 1802).

—— *Corinne* (Paris, 1804).

—— *De la littérature considerée dans ses rapports avec les institutions sociales*, ed. Paul Van Tieghem (2 vols.; Geneva, 1959).

STALIN, I. V., 'Stalin o kul'ture', *KN* (1939), 12: 11.

—— *Marksizm i voprosy yazykoznaniya* (Moscow, 1950).

STALLYBRASS, PETER, and WHITE, ALLON, *The Politics and Poetics of Transgression* (London, 1987).

STAMBOLIAN, GEORGE, and MARKS, ELAINE, *Homosexualities and French Culture* (Ithaca, NY, 1977).

STEELE, JONATHAN, 'Sister Russia' (Interview with Ol'ga Lipovskaya), *Guardian*, 4 Apr. 1991.

STEIN, GERTRUDE, *Useful Knowledge* (New York, 1988).

STITES, RICHARD, *The Women's Liberation Movement in Russia: Feminism, Nihilism and Bolshevism 1860–1930* (Princeton, NJ, 1978).

STRIZHENOVA, TATIANA, *Soviet Costumes and Textiles 1917–1945* (Paris, 1991).

STRUVE, GLEB, *Russkaya literatura v izgnanii* (2nd edn.; Paris, 1984).

SUMAROKOV, ALEKSANDR, *Trudolyubivaya pchela* (St Petersburg, 1759).

—— *Elegii lyubovnye* (St Petersburg, 1774).

SUTTON, JONATHAN, *The Religious Philosophy of Vladimir Solovyov: Towards a Reassessment* (London, 1988).

Svod zakonov Rossiiskoi Imperii, ed. I. D. Mordukhai-Boltovsky (16 vols. and index; St Petersburg, 1912).

SVYADOSH, A. M., *Zhenskaya seksopatologiya* (3rd edn.; Moscow, 1988).

TERRAS, VICTOR, *A History of Russian Literature* (New Haven, Conn., 1991).

Teutsch-Lateinisch- und Russisches Lexicon (publ. anon.; comp. E. Weismann) (St Petersburg, 1731).

THACKERAY, W. M., 'The Sorrows of Werther', in J. M. Cohen (ed.), *A Choice of Comic and Curious Verse* (London, 1975), 45.

THOMSON, BORIS, *The Premature Revolution* (London, 1970).

TIMENCHIK, ROMAN, 'Zametki ob akmeizme', *Russkaya literatura*, 7–8 (1974), 23–46; 5/3 (1977), 280–300; 9 (1981), 179–89.

TISHKIN, G. A., *Zhenskii vopros v Rossii: 50-e i 60-e gody XIX veka* (Leningrad, 1984).

TODD, JANET, *Sensibility: An Introduction* (London, 1986).

TOLSTAYA, TAT'YANA, 'Notes from Underground', *New York Review of Books*, 31 May 1990, 3–7.

TOLSTOY, L. N., *Polnoe sobranie sochinenii: yubileinoe izdanie* (90 vols. and index; Moscow-Leningrad, 1928–64).

TREDIAKOVSKY, V. K., *Sochineniya* (3 vols.; St Petersburg, 1849).

TRIFONOV, YURY, *Obmen* (Moscow, 1976).

TROTSKY, LEV, *Literatura i revolyutsiya* (2 vols.; Moscow, 1925).

Tsvetnik or: koshnitsa pervaya; stikhotvoreniya [almanac] (St Petersburg, 1907).

TURZHE-TURMANSKAYA, E., *Belye nevol'nitsy: domashnyaya prisluga v Rossii* (Smolensk, 1906).

The Twilight of the Tsars: Russian Art at the Turn of the Century (London, 1991). (Catalogue of exhibition of turn-of-the-century Russian art held at the Hayward Art Gallery, London, Apr.–May 1991.)

TYNYANOV, YURY, *Arkhaisty i novatory* (Leningrad, 1929).

TYRKOVA, ARIADNA, 'Zhenskii trud i prostitutsiya', *RM* (1910), 4, sect. 2, 124–37.

USPENSKY, B. A., *Iz istorii russkogo literaturnogo yazyka XVIII-nachala XIX veka: yazykovaya programma Karamzina i ee istoricheskie korni* (Moscow, 1985).

VASIL'EVA, LARISA, 'Zhenshchina. Zhizn'. Literatura', *LG*, 20 Dec. 1989, 7.

VATSURO, V. E., *SDP: iz istorii literaturnogo byta Pushkinskoi pory* (Moscow, 1989).

VENGEROV, S., *Russkaya poeziya: sobranie proizvedenii russkikh poetov* (7 parts; St Petersburg, 1897–1901).

VENTURI, FRANCO, *Roots of Revolution: A History of the Populist and Socialist Movements in Nineteenth-Century Russia*, trans. F. Haskell (London, 1960).

VEREVKIN, N. N. ['Rakhmannyi'], 'Zhenshchina-pisatel'nitsa', *Biblioteka dlya chteniya*, 23/1 (1837), 19–134.

VIGEL', F., *Zapiski* (2 vols.; Leningrad, 1929).

VLADIN, V., and KAPUSTIN, D., *Garmoniya seksual'nykh otnoshenii* (Moscow, 1991).

VOLOSHINOV, N./BAKHTIN, M., *Freidizm* (Moscow, 1928).

Vos'moi s"ezd sovetskikh pisatelei, 24–28 iyunya 1986 (Moscow, 1988).

Vtoroi s"ezd sovetskikh pisatelei, 15–26 dekabrya 1954 goda (Moscow, 1956).

VYAZEMSKY, P. D., *Staraya zapisnaya kniga* (Leningrad, 1929).

—— *Stikhotvoreniya* (Leningrad, 1986).

WARD, MARGARET, *Unmanageable Revolutionaries: Women and Irish Nationalism* (2nd edn.; London, 1989).

WEININGER, OTTO, *Geschlecht und Charakter* (Vienna, 1903).

—— *Über die letzten Dinge* (Vienna, 1921).

—— *Gedanken über Geschlechtsprobleme* (Vienna, 1922).

WES, MARINUS, *Classics in Russia 1700–1855: Between Two Bronze Horsemen* (Leiden, 1992).

WESTWOOD, J. N., *Endurance and Endeavour: Russian History 1812–1980* (4th edn.; Oxford, 1992).

WHITE, ANNE, *De-Stalinization and the House of Culture: Declining State Control over Leisure in the USSR, Poland and Hungary* (London, 1990).

WILKINSON, L. P., *Ovid Recalled* (Cambridge, 1955).

WOLFF, JANET, *Feminine Sentences* (Oxford, 1991).

Women and Russia: First Feminist Samizdat (London, 1980).

WOOLF, VIRGINIA, *The Complete Shorter Fiction* (London, 1985).

—— *A Woman's Essays* (London, 1992).

WORONZOFF-DASHKOFF, A., 'Disguise and Gender in Princess Dashkova's Memoirs', *Canadian Slavonic Papers*, 33/1 (Mar. 1991), 62–74.

YABLONSKAYA, M. A., *Women Artists of Russia's New Age* (London, 1990).

YAKUB, ALEKSANDR, 'Sovremennye narodnye pesenniki', *Izvestiya otdeleniya russkogo yazyka i slovesnosti Imperatorskoi Akademii Nauk* (1914), 1: 47–92.

YOUNG, KATYA (ed.), *New Writing from the Soviet Union* (programme for the 'New Beginnings' arts festival, Nov. 1989) (Glasgow, 1989).

ZDANEVICH, IL'YA ['Iliazd'], *Pis'mo/La Lettre*, illus. Picasso (1948; repr. Paris, 1990).

—— *Prigovor bez molvy/Sentence sans paroles*, illus. Braque and Giacometti (1961; repr. Paris, 1990).

ZELINSKY, F. F., *Iz zhizni idei* (St Petersburg, 1904).

ZHBANKOV, A., 'Polovaya prestupnost'', *SM* (1909), 7: 54–91.

ZHDANOV, A., *The Central Committee's Resolution on the Journals Zvezda and Leningrad*, trans. F. Ashbee and I. Tidmarsh (Royal Oak, Mich., 1978).

ZHDANOV, P., *Slovar' anglo-rossiiskoi* (St Petersburg, 1784).

Zhenshchiny goroda Lenina: ocherki o zhenshchinakh Leningrada v dni blokady (Leningrad, 1944).

Zhenshchina v SSSR: statisticheskii sbornik (Moscow, 1937).

ZHUKOVSKY, V. A., *Sochineniya v 3 tomakh* (Moscow, 1980).

Index of Women Writers Cited

Where available, brief biographical details have been provided.

General Index

abortion 139, 227, 228, 244, 247, 366
Acmeism 170–1, 173–4, 214
album verse, *see* salon verse
Alexander II 19, 121
Andreeva, Nina 346
androgyny 48, 49–50, 168–9, 308
Annensky, Innokenty 173, 220, 374, 427
anti-realism 8, 13, 356–7, 372–81
　　see also mysticism
Artsybashev, M. 128n., 132
Aseev, Nikolai 240n.
aspirant myth, *see* escape plot
Austen, Jane 11, 78, 328
autobiography, *see* memoirs

Babel, Isaak 241
Baratynsky, Evgeny 37, 38n., 39n., 77,
　　99
Barthes, Roland 142n.
Beauvoir, Simone de 398
Belinsky, Vissarion 24–5, 41–2, 74, 84,
　　91, 95, 109, 113
Belov, Vasily 347
Bely, Andrei 163, 374
Berdyaev, Nikolai 378n.
Berger, John 306n.
Bestuzhev-Marlinsky, A. 58
bilingualism in women writers 53–6, 93,
　　268, 272
biologism, 75, 259, 314
Blok, Aleksandr 6, 163, 211, 240, 257,
　　273, 374
Borodin, Leonid 378n.
Bowen, Elizabeth 264
Brecht, Bertolt 238, 364
Brezhnev, Leonid 337n., 339–40, 343,
　　424
Brik, Lily 234
Brontë, Anne 73, 78

Brontë, Charlotte 48n., 73, 74
Brontë, Emily 73, 78
Brookner, Anita 398
Bryusov, Valery 155, 170, 236, 286, 374
Buck, Pearl 304
Bulgakov, Mikhail 241, 374, 377
Bulgarian, Faddei 57
Byron, George Gordon 3

Calvino, Italo 91
Carter, Angela 394
Casanova de Seingalt, Giacomo
　　Giolamo 304
Catherine II 1–2, 36
　　see also Index of Women Writers
　　Cited
censorship 127, 255–6, 282, 294, 328
Chartier, Roger 7
Chekhov, Anton 148, 200, 269, 359
Chernyshevsky, Nikolai 47, 231
　　What is to be Done 64–5, 67–8
Chulkov, Mikhail 51
Cixous, Hélène 7
Clark, Katerina 246
class 8, 19–20, 21–2, 28, 60, 82, 89, 135,
　　140–1, 235, 314, 343–5, 359–61
classical tradition 32, 160–1, 164, 273
class war 141, 242, 243
co-operation between women 32, 54, 65,
　　245, 282, 368
coquetry 38
Corinna 27, 32
Costlow, Jane 75
costume 231n., 273
critical realism 3, 8, 193, 342, 345,
　　357–72
　　see also empirical realism; escape plot;
　　provincial tale
cultural centralization 232